*Managerial
Economics*

# *Managerial Economics*

## *Robert F. Rooney*

*Department of Economics*
*California State University, Long Beach*

*Graduate School of Management*
*University of California, Irvine*

## Little, Brown and Company

*Boston   Toronto*

*To Armen A. Alchian*

**Library of Congress Cataloging in Publication Data**

Rooney, Robert F.
  Managerial economics.

  Includes index.
  1. Managerial economics.   I. Title.
HD30.22.R66 1985        338.5'024658        84-20155
ISBN 0-316-75596-6

Library of Congress Catalog Card No. 84-20155

ISBN 0-316-75596-6

9  8  7  6  5  4  3  2  1

BP

Published simultaneously in Canada
by Little, Brown & Company (Canada) Limited

Printed in the United States of America

# Preface

This text presents a complete treatment of microeconomic theory within the context of problem solving by business managers. It also offers a wide range of examples illustrating how microeconomic theory can be used to obtain the quantitative answers required in formulating business plans. These examples are presented on two levels. A large number of examples illustrate calculation of specific decision variables such as marginal cost, the profit maximizing output or price, the number of firms in an industry, and the level of risk associated with different outputs. Sixteen case studies combine one or more elements of economic theory with the appropriate calculation techniques to solve a decision problem. The result is a blending of economic theory with practical business planning that appeals to both the instructor and the business-oriented student.

The topics included in this book are those that the author has found most useful during twenty-five years of professional experience. During this period, I worked for six years in oil company departments of planning and market research; served four years on a government commission regulating coastal zone land use; was a consultant to several corporations, government agencies, and attorneys; and taught managerial economics at the undergraduate and MBA levels. Many of the applications of economic theory to managerial decision making in this book are based on these varied experiences.

Drafts of this text have been used in managerial economics courses at California State University, Long Beach (upper division students), and the University of California, Irvine (MBA students). Student comments on these courses and discussions with colleagues who teach courses closely following available texts strongly influenced the content design. The general lack of worked out examples in managerial economics texts often requires the instructor to spend considerable class time working out examples and discussing applications of the theory. Both professors and students wanted more time devoted to lectures on economic theory and model building, which is possible only if the text gives detailed examples of applications of the theory. Providing many examples in the text permits more classroom time to be spent on model building, a skill best learned through lectures on the analytical methods and assumptions used to construct models for solving practical decision problems. Less classroom time spent working out numerical examples is practical only if the textbook supplies detailed solutions to examples.

## *Philosophy*

One of the primary job assignments of managers is planning — determining how much output to produce, how many people to hire, which raw materials are lowest in cost, and how to price their products. The emphasis in this book is on assembling and analyzing the kinds of information required to make a broad range of planning decisions. Microeconomics provides a consistent set of theories for guiding managers in making decisions intended to maximize their firm's profits and market value. Statistics, accounting, computer science, algebra, differential calculus, and linear programming provide tools for converting economic theory into practical decision rules that managers can use in specific situations. Combining economic theory with techniques for developing numerical answers to business forecasting and planning problems makes managerial economics a unique course in the business and economics curriculum.

Managerial economics provides no pat formulas, saying that if event A occurs, then take action B and profits will rise. It is nonetheless a vital part of the prospective manager's education because it provides insights into the kinds of information that are relevant and into how abstract models facilitate organizing and utilizing that information to make better decisions. The decisions that managers make are diverse; no two problems are quite the same. Yet if the manager is to make consistently effective decisions, a framework is needed to draw together their diverse aspects so that the unity within them is captured and made apparent. Managerial economics provides techniques for constructing abstract analytical models, modifying them to reflect the specifics of the decision at hand, and utilizing the available data to guide the analyst toward a decision attaining the organization's goals.

This text includes numerous examples and cases to illustrate the many and varied applications of economic theory. A major problem facing the author of a managerial economics text is how to construct examples that are reasonably realistic and yet not so filled with real-world detail that the importance of economic theory in making the problem tractable is lost. Working managers and their staff analysts may spend weeks or months formulating models, gathering data, and working out the myriad details associated with a particular decision. The written material associated with a decision problem could fill several chapters or a whole book. Thus, the examples and cases in this text are necessarily simplified versions of real-world planning problems. Still, they are essential for illustrating the application of economic theory and statistics to managerial decisions.

## *Organization and Contents*

The chapter organization of this book generally parallels that of most existing managerial economics and microeconomics texts. There are, however, two notable exceptions: Risk management comes much later than in other texts so that it can be presented in the context of practical decision problems rather than as basically a theoretical topic. The other exception is the insertion after the chapter on competitive markets of a chapter on wealth maximization and decision making when more than one planning period is involved. A less extreme exception is that linear programming is placed after the chapter on costs rather than after the chapter on production, as is customary in managerial economics texts, because the applications illustrating its use are principally cost-minimization problems that include calculating average variable cost, marginal cost, and short-run average total cost.

Within the chapters, the general approach is to present first the standard economic theory using graphs, then examples of specific applications and associated computational methods, and finally additional topics extending the standard theory to a broader set of decision problems. The chapters conclude with a summary, a list of key terms, review questions, and problems and applications. Most of the chapters also include, after the summary, one or more cases emphasizing applications.

The emphasis on practical applications of economic theory to planning decisions has led to a number of major differences, beyond chapter organization, between this text and others presently on the market. The relationship between costs and factor productivity is made explicit throughout the book and is applied to a variety of decision problems. Numerical estimates of the firm's marginal and average cost curves are derived from a production function or total cost function, and statistical methods for estimating these functions are illustrated. Procedures for calculating prices, costs, profits, present values, and other numerical elements of the decision process are illustrated with examples. Multiple-period operations and investment planning based on the wealth maximization goal are discussed. Market structure is given more attention than in other managerial economics texts because the decisions made by managers often depend on assessing how their firm's rivals will react to its price, product quality, advertising, and other marketing-oriented policies. The treatments of transaction costs and how firms adapt to changing market conditions, for example, expose the student to the way that economic theory can be used to explain relatively simply market behaviors that appear to be highly diverse and unrelated.

This book differs substantially from other texts in its treatment of wealth maximization and risk management. These topics usually receive only superficial treatment in managerial economics texts in spite of the fact that they pose the most important analytical problems in many managerial decisions. In this text, both topics are introduced briefly in chapter 1 and then given in-depth treatment after demand, production, and cost theory have been fully developed. This structure permits development of wealth maximization and risk management models in greater detail and, most important, in the context of several of their more important applications. These applications include plant capacity, inventory, and maintenance-level decisions; output decisions when price is a random variable; and the use of insurance and hedging to transfer a portion of the firm's risks to others. Although these topics may appear to be relatively advanced, presenting them in the context of specific decision problems permits their treatment at the same level of difficulty as the more conventional chapters.

Two other topics are discussed that are not normally treated in managerial economics texts. One is use of public choice theory perspectives on the relationship between government and business. In this approach, government is viewed less as an adversary of business than as another aspect of the business environment that management can influence, and sometimes manipulate, to increase profit and the value of the firm. The other is an introduction to income and other taxes and how they can influence business decisions. These topics are principally discussed in chapter 14.

## Pedagogical Aids

Graphs are the primary pedagogical aid for explaining the fundamental theories of microeconomics. The standard demand, production, cost, and market response graphs are presented, and each graph includes a caption explaining its construction and interpretation. The emphasis in the examples and cases is oriented more toward calculating numerical answers to specific planning problems than toward graphical analysis. Illustrations of step-by-step computational procedures and tables summarizing the results of these computations are major pedagogical aids when microeconomic theory is applied to specific planning problems. The use of algebra and calculus is generally limited to calculating numerical values for outputs, costs, prices, profits, and present values.

Sixteen cases are spread throughout the book because the author feels that a managerial economics text should illustrate how several elements of a theory and brief examples can be combined and applied. Several of the early cases also illustrate the use of regression analysis for estimating demand, production, and cost functions. The applications in these cases are to somewhat more complex decision problems than are appropriate in the body of an intermediate text; hence, they are placed after the chapter summaries. The instructor who wishes to concentrate on presenting theory can assign these cases as supplemental reading or skip them altogether. Instructors wishing to emphasize applications, as is often the case at the MBA level, can utilize these cases for class discussions and as models for in-depth homework assignments.

The Review Questions at the end of each chapter are primarily intended for the student's use in testing his or her knowledge of the theory presented in the chapter. They range from questions on key definitions to analytical issues treated by the theory. The Problems and Applications section of chapters 3 through 14 provides an average of 12 to 15 problems that students can use to develop and test their analytical and computational skills. These problems range from being similar to the examples in the text to detailed and complex applications of the theory similar to that of a case. With the large number of computational examples in the text, which demonstrate most of the tricks needed to solve problems, and answers to the odd-numbered problems at the end of the book, most undergraduate students have been able to solve these problems with relatively little help from the instructor. This experience differs from that of instructors using other managerial economics texts, who find that assigning the more relevant end-of-chapter problems requires much classroom time working out examples or heavy use of their office hours.

Two other pedagogical aids can be of value. The Glossary has over 150 entries covering the principal technical terms used in this book. This glossary is particularly useful to students who are not economics majors or who have not taken an economics class recently. The other aid is the Supplemental Readings section provided in the back of the book. It contains the principal references used in writing the book. In addition to providing another discussion of the material covered in the chapter, a few of these references present alternative perspectives to those in the text. Specific references to the literature are not given in the text or footnotes but rather are available in the Supplemental Readings.

An instructor's manual is available that contains chapter outlines, teaching suggestions, examination questions with answers, answers to the even-numbered problems in the book, and an appendix that includes several computer programs used to calculate tables in the text.

## Prerequisites

The emphasis on understanding and using the most basic propositions of economic theory makes this book accessible to upper division business or engineering students with a course in microeconomic principles or MBA students who have never taken an economics course. If students have had a principles course emphasizing demand, supply, cost, and market equilibrium theory, the first couple of sections of chapters 3, 6, 8, and 10 can be assigned for review.

Differential calculus is used throughout to calculate numerical answers to planning problems. The functions to be differentiated are power functions. Any student with a reasonable background in algebra can learn the few calculus techniques used in this text. Except for the discussions of point-elasticity, marginal product, marginal rate of technical substitution, and marginal cost, calculus is not used to explain the theory, and those theories that are discussed using calculus are also developed using graphs. An algebra and calculus review is provided in section 2 of chapter 2.

Some knowledge of statistical techniques would be helpful but is not required if the course primarily emphasizes economic theory and its applications. The basic statistical tools for the material on risk management (standard deviation, coefficient of variation, and the normal probability distribution) are reviewed in section 3 of chapter 2. Instructors wishing to emphasize applications of the theory and the empirical aspects of managerial economics will find a review of regression analysis in section 4 of chapter 2.

## Acknowledgments

Professor Marshall Medoff provided comments, corrections, and much guidance in preparing the revisions of the first and second drafts. Advice and encouragement at various points in the preparation were provided by Professors Joseph Magaddino, Davender Singh, and Michael Tennenbaum. Professor Singh also used a draft of this book as the text for several of his managerial economics classes. In addition, assistance was given by the following reviewers: Bruce Allen (Michigan State University), Richard Eastin (University of Southern California), Ed Ericson (San Francisco State University), Herbert Eskot (Northeastern University), Donald Huffmire (University of Connecticut), Janet Rives (University of Northern Iowa), Peter Schwarz (University of North Carolina at Charlotte), and Charles Stokes (University of Bridgeport). The editorial staff of Little, Brown — especially William T. Ethridge, Elizabeth Schaaf, and Tim Baehr — went that extra mile many times to keep preparation of the manuscript on schedule and on target with respect to the goals set for the project.

Eleanor Rooney typed the entire manuscript and managed its preparation through the several drafts. Were it not for her cheerful cooperation and gentle prodding the project would have taken much longer to complete.

*Robert F. Rooney*
Rainbow, California

# Contents

# 1

# *Management Goals and Decisions*

Managers are rarely specialists. They are generalists who have a talent for looking at the broad dimensions and implications of problems and the necessary experience, training, and education to develop plans for solving them. Managers set goals for organizations, develop information and strategies for attaining goals, acquire the necessary resources, and then make the organization function.

Not everyone has the necessary gifts of intellect, temperament, self-discipline, and motivation to be a successful manager. Moreover, management is people-oriented; it is more an art than a science. The finest planning and budgeting procedures will not accomplish the organization's goals if the manager cannot lead the people who must implement the plans and budgets. However, the need for leadership ability should not overshadow the role of the ability to plan and budget in a successful managerial career. Excellent leadership without well-defined goals and the means necessary to attain them will not ensure success any more than great technique without leadership.

Managerial economics is a part of the education of managers. It provides a framework for assembling information and analyzing alternative decisions. The principal problems studied are those of optimization, prediction, and adaptation. Its principal tools are drawn from economic theory and statistics. Calculus and numerical calculations are used to develop and analyze the data that theory has demonstrated to be relevant. Studies utilizing the techniques of managerial economics provide the data that are assembled into budgets and pro forma accounting statements.

The principal goals for the firm are profit maximization and wealth maximization. (Actually, profit maximization is a special case of wealth maximization. Government agencies and nonprofit firms generally have as their goals maximizing the value of the services they provide or maximizing the prestige of the institution.) Attaining these goals is always subject to one or more constraints, such as the market price of a competitive industry's product, the debt and equity capital the firm can raise, or the government agency's budget. Competition for markets and resources is a constraint faced by all decision makers. Once the goals of the organization and the constraints on its choices have been specified, economic theory can be used to optimize its plans and budgets. Where uncertainty exists with respect to one or more of the decision variables, management is faced with multiple goals and must consider trade-offs between higher profits and greater risk.

The first section of this chapter, section 1.1, discusses the role of managerial economics in the planning and budgeting activities of the firm. Section 1.2 provides an introduction to the principal types of managerial activities for which managerial economics is most widely used — optimization, prediction, and adaptation. The role of economic theory in identifying relevant information and guiding management toward optimal decisions is discussed in section 1.3. Sections 1.4 and 1.5 describe the firm in terms of its decision-making centers and the goals of the decision makers who manage the firm. Section 1.6 provides an introduction to risk management. The last numbered section, as in all of the chapters, is a summary.

## 1.1  *Managerial Economics*

Managerial economics is primarily concerned with the planning and budgeting activities of business firms, government agencies, and nonprofit organizations. Planning involves determining the goals for the firm and the best strategies for attaining the goals during some specified period of time. Budgeting is the process of translating plans into resource requirements (for example, the number of workers required and the quantities of raw materials) and the amount of money that management expects to spend and receive during the planning period. The budget describes the financial implications of management's plans and provides a measure of control over how they will be implemented.

*Economic Theory As a Planning Tool.* Managerial economics differs from other administrative tools in that it uses economic theory to guide the development of optimal plans and budgets for attaining management's goals. Economic theory is used to predict the behavior of prices, costs, other firms, and government agencies. It provides a framework for determining the information required to analyze alternative decisions available to management. Since the future can never be predicted with certainty, economic theory can help management adapt its plans and budgets to unforeseen changes in the business environment. The resources required to attain management's goals are scarce, and economic theory is primarily concerned with the management of scarce resources. Thus, economic theory is an ideal source of information on the likely behavior of consumers, production activities, markets, and competitors.

The economic theories used in managerial economics have been empirically verified by many years of observations under a wide range of circumstances; hence, they are generally reliable guides for managerial decisions. When combined with other management disciplines (for example, accounting, finance, and marketing) or tools (for example, statistics and information sciences), managerial economics serves as a means for integrating the business curriculum around the theme of making optimal decisions.

*Relationship to Managerial Accounting.* Managerial economics and managerial accounting are closely related. Accounting provides a logical framework for reporting the financial results of operating a business. Its reports also provide an excellent framework for communicating the structure and projected results of managerial decisions and plans. Such reports are referred to as pro forma reports. Managerial economics bears directly on managerial accounting by providing the estimates of future prices, costs, and output to be entered into the pro forma accounting reports. Accounting takes the information about the firm's operations generated by managerial economics studies and presents them in a format that is widely understood by business managers.

*The Planning Period.* Since managerial economics focuses on planning problems, the concept of the planning period is an essential one. The term *current planning period* is frequently used in this book. The planning period is the period of time for which management is presently formulating its plans. If the planning period is one month and today is June 15, the current planning period is the month of July. Management will complete its planning for July by the end of June and adopt its plans and budget before July first. In July, the current planning period is August.

*The Operating Plan.* Operating plans are concerned with determining the optimal way to use the company's existing assets. Although most operating plans concentrate on only one period of time, such as next month or year, operating plans can span several planning periods when events planned for one period significantly influence management's options in the next or subsequent planning periods. Thus, the operating plan may involve consideration of events that will not occur for several months or years in the future. Operating plans that cover one year or less are referred to as short-term plans; long-term plans involve several years. The current operating plan starts at the expiration of the plan and budget guiding present operations. It ends at a time determined by management (for instance, after one month or one year).

*The Capital Plan.* Capital plans are concerned with the acquisition of new assets that will influence the level and nature of the company's operations for more than one year. Capital plans, by their very nature, are long-term plans involving several years. Their planning periods are normally one year long, although the first year or two may be subdivided into quarters or months to facilitate projections of the funds required to finance the projects. Embedded in the capital plan is a series of annual operating plans. The operating plans are generally presented as pro forma accounting statements, and they can be used as a basis for developing the initial operating budgets. However, unforeseen developments affecting prices, costs, or outputs generally occur between preparation of the capital plan and the first operating budget after the asset is put in service. These changes require modification of the initial operating plans and budgets.

*How Managerial Economics Differs from Courses in Economic Theory.* The empirically verified propositions of economic theory provide the framework for constructing abstract models of the behavior of prices, costs, and profits. Although managerial economics utilizes these models, it does not focus entirely on theory and the construction of theoretical frameworks for analyzing alternative decisions. Managerial economics also includes methods for calculating numerical estimates of labor and raw materials requirements, output, production and other costs, sales revenues, and profits, which are rarely covered in courses on economic theory. The ability to calculate numerical answers to decision problems is a highly prized managerial skill that is developed in the managerial economics course. Finally, managerial economics provides data that are consistent with the analytical models of economic theory and suitable for presentation using the techniques of managerial accounting. Thus, the emphasis in the managerial economics course is primarily on applying economic theory to arrive at numerical answers to decision problems. The development of theoretical models is generally emphasized in economic theory courses.

## 1.2 *Optimization, Prediction, and Adaptation*

For the purposes of studying managerial economics, the principal planning and decision-making activities of managers are optimization, prediction, and adaptation. These activities are discussed in this section.

*Optimum Use of the Firm's Resources.* Optimization is concerned with how the firm can best attain the goals of its management. One goal is profit maximization, in which, for example, management optimizes the firm's operations by setting its output rate and hiring the amount of labor to earn as great a profit as possible in the current planning period. However, maximizing profits in the current planning period may result in the firm's losing significant future profit opportunities, which will reduce the firm's value. Since most firms, especially large corporations, view themselves as ongoing entities with a virtually infinite life, their managements are more interested in the goal of maximizing the value (wealth) of the firm.

Where the firm's stockholders have little voice in its management, its managers may utilize a portion of the firm's profits to make themselves better off. They will conduct their manufacturing and marketing operations and make investments to maximize the firm's profits or wealth; however, these managers may use a portion of the resulting profits to provide themselves with elaborate offices and a large staff, and to make corporate contributions to charities and the arts that increase their personal prestige. These managers optimize the firm's operations, but they make decisions with respect to use of the resulting profits that may not be optimal from the point of view of the firm's stockholders.

Nonprofit firms or government agencies generally have as their basic managerial goal providing a specified level of services at the lowest feasible cost. Another goal, often pursued by universities, is maximizing the prestige of the institution. By optimizing the operations on the basis of one of these goals, management is best able to compete with other institutions for budgetary resources.

*Optimization Techniques.* The techniques of optimization can be applied to a wide range of decision-making institutions responsible for allocating a given set of resources to best attain a specified goal. They range from simple graphical and numerical techniques to linear programming. For the most part, optimization principles can be learned from graphs. Calculating several data points and interpolating between them can be used to arrive at numerical solutions. However, differential calculus is a more efficient method for solving relatively simple optimization problems. Calculus-based optimization techniques are stressed throughout this book. Linear programming is a widely used optimization technique for complex problems. Besides its ability to handle problems in which there are a number of constraints on management's choices, linear programming is ideal if the constraints are inequalities. Linear programming is discussed in chapter 7.

*Prediction As a Managerial Activity.* Prediction is primarily concerned with factors external to the firm, which it cannot directly control. The firm's management must base its operating and planning decisions on predictions relating to future prices and markets, the cost of labor and raw materials, the responses of competitors to its actions, the actions taken by government regulatory agencies, and many other economic, political, and social factors. These predictions are often based on determining the optimizing behavior of the entity whose behavior must be predicted. Thus, prediction and optimization are closely related branches of managerial decision making.

*Prediction and Uncertainty About the Future.* Predicting an uncertain future requires the firm to recognize that the outcomes of its actions are subject to probability distributions. In some cases, such as when controlling the quality of the output of a machining process is involved, the probability distribution can be based on past experience. Most business decisions are subject to "uncertainty," in which the probability distribution of the potential outcomes is unknown or difficult to estimate using past experience. When there is uncertainty, probability distributions are based on management's subjective evaluations of the future. This is why senior and middle-level managers are generally required to have considerable experience in a broad range of assignments. These experiences enhance their ability to make subjective probability judgments. Both an appropriate level of academic training and a variety of experiences that test their ability to make sound judgments under conditions of uncertainty are important parts of a manager's training.

*Adaptation As a Response to Decision Errors.* Managerial decision making is concerned with how firms adapt to changes in the business environment. The business firm is an adaptive social organization that responds to the profit opportunities provided by changes in prices, costs, technologies, taxes, and government regulations. Prior to the energy crisis of the early 1970s, adaptation primarily resulted from actions taken by competitors, particularly when they developed new technologies or marketing programs, or by government. With the generally unexpected rise in energy prices, virtually all business firms and public agencies were forced to adapt to the same event.

If consumer preferences for goods and services, technology, availability and price of supplies and factors of production, and government policies never or only rarely changed, the adaptive function of the business firm would lose its present importance. The adaptive responses of business firms permit the economy to respond to scarcity and take advantage of technological opportunities. Politicians may do no more than despair over the energy crisis or rising prices, but each business manager has the opportunity to work at developing ways to minimize their adverse impacts and turn them into profit opportunities. Solving the problems posed by unpredicted changes in the business environment can be a major source of profits; the rate at which a firm adapts to change is often a major determinant of its overall profitability. Moreover, decentralized decision making by many business firms, and experimentation with the wide range of different approaches to adapting to changes, generally yield the lowest-cost means for solving economic problems when there is uncertainty as to how they ought to be solved.

*Government Policy Changes As an Adaptive Response.* Large firms not only adapt to changes in the business environment, they, together with trade associations of smaller firms, can directly influence the business environment through their advertising, political lobbying, and research and development activities. In many cases, the tax and regulatory policy changes that influence managerial decisions are initiated within the business sector of the economy. Much of American regulatory policy and tax law began with the lobbying and political activities of business firms, trade associations, and labor unions. Purely government-initiated regulatory policies are primarily concentrated in the environmental protection and health and safety areas. Even these policies are often the result of political activities by environmental or consumer groups, rather than the initiatives of government officials.

## 1.3 *Role of Economic Theory*

Managerial economics makes extensive use of the widely observed, empirically verified propositions of economic theory. Economic theory is used to identify the information relevant to a particular decision and organize it so that optimal decisions can be made. It is also used in justifying management's political positions with respect to tax and regulatory law changes.

Managerial decision making is an art learned through training and experience. One of the objectives of this book is to show how the fundamental propositions of economic theory can be applied to optimization and prediction problems. The practice gained through study of the examples spread throughout this book, and through working the problems at the end of each chapter, provides an excellent way to learn how to apply economic theory to business management.

*General Applicability of Economic Theory.* The responses of different decision makers to the same change in the business environment can vary because they operate under different goal structures to guide their optimization decisions. Each decision maker normally has different technological and market information on which to base decisions, and each firm has a different set of resources under its control. Managers' responses differ because economic theory applies to small and large firms alike; size does not make a firm immune to economic forces. The decisions of General Motors or Exxon are just as subject to the fundamental propositions of economic theory as those of the corner drug store, the local electric utility, a city council, or an agency of the United States government. Different decisions under the same circumstances generally result from the decision makers' having different information on which to base predictions or analyzing it from their unique perspectives, rather than from economic theory's being inapplicable.

*Positive and Normative Economics.* The branch of economic theory based on empirically verified statements is generally referred to as positive economics. Managerial economics is a subfield within positive economics. Propositions of positive economics are used in optimizing the firm's activities and in developing predictions of the behavior of the businesses, consumers, and government agencies with which the firm deals. These propositions are equally applicable to the decision-making processes of public administrators and the managements of nonprofit firms.

The other major branch of economic theory is normative economics. It is the study of how to organize a society to best attain the political agenda of a majority of its citizens, a special interest group, or a ruling elite.

Business managers are primarily concerned with positive economics because they must make decisions based on the world as it actually exists. They become interested in the propositions of normative economics when attempting to justify changes in laws and regulations that will make their firm more profitable. That is, they use normative arguments to make their suggested changes appear to be in the public interest rather than only in their narrow private interest. By using the propositions of normative economics to argue that certain laws or regulations ought to be enacted, modified, or repealed, they hope to win the approval of politicians, bureaucrats, and the public. Normative economics is not covered in this book.

*Adapting Economic Theory to Specific Situations.* Since economic theory consists of relatively simple abstractions, it cannot always be applied without some adaptations. These adaptations are much like those that an engineer makes of the fundamental theories of physics to design a machine. For example, the law of falling bodies provides a value for the rate of acceleration due to the force of gravity of a body falling in a vacuum. This acceleration rate closely predicts the time required for a lead ball to fall from the top of the Empire State Building to the street below; however, it gives wildly inaccurate predictions of the time it would take a paper airplane to reach the street. To predict the flight time of a particular paper airplane design, the engineer would have to consider the laws of aerodynamics and determine the values of environmental factors, such as wind speed and air temperature. Even then the predictions are subject to a probability distribution because of measurement errors or additional factors not calculated by the engineer, such as the shape of a building one block away but to windward.

Managerial decision making is subject to the same kinds of problems when economic theory is applied to business decision problems. Where there is capital accumulation, technological change, or learning-curve effects, economic theory must be applied with great care and then only after gathering adequate background information relating to the decision. The resulting predictions of the firm's behavior are subject to probability distributions. Generally, the direction of the adaptation to a change in the firm's business environment is more likely to be correctly predicted than the rate or intensity of the adaptive response.

## 1.4   *The Firm*

The business firm is the principal subject of analysis in a managerial economics course. This section describes the nature of a firm relative to its role as a decision-making center.

*The Firm As a Decision Center.* The firm consists of one or more centers of decision-making authority controlling use of the firm's resources. One decision center is executive management — the board of directors, the president of the company, and the team of "home office" vice-presidents and their professional staffs. Delegating the authority to make decisions to the firm's operating departments creates additional decision centers. However, the range of decisions made by the managers of operating departments is limited, and their optimizing goals are specified, or at least approved, by executive management. In a small sole proprietorship, the decision-making authority may be exercised by one individual. In some enterprises, it may be a committee that takes actions on the basis of a majority voting rule or even unanimous agreement. It is these decision-making centers that are being referred to when the term *firm* is used.

*Who Is a Manager?* Decision-making centers are assigned a budget. Within the broad confines of the amount budgeted and its distribution among line items, the manager of the decision center has some discretion as to how the budget is spent to attain the goal or goals assigned by executive management. Individuals with the title "manager" but without discretionary authority over a budget are not managers. They are administrators of someone else's decisions. Managerial economics is principally concerned with decision techniques for managers and only minimally concerned with the efficient administration of decisions that have already been made.

*The Single-Product Firm Assumption.* Although many combinations of production and marketing activities may be undertaken by a firm, the basic principles of business decision making are best learned through the study of single-product firms. The managements of single-product firms make optimal decisions with respect to their pricing, output, and marketing policies; predict the behavior of their rivals and other firms likely to enter the industry; and make decisions with respect to cost-minimizing combinations of factors of production and whether to build a new plant. The managers of multiproduct or multiplant firms make these decisions plus additional decisions such as transfer prices between divisions of a vertically integrated firm or the allocation of joint costs among several products for pricing purposes. Although some of the unique problems faced by multiplant or multiproduct firms are briefly touched on, the emphasis in this book is on the single-product firm. The decision-making problems of multiproduct and multiplant firms are left to advanced courses in business management and economics.

## 1.5 *Goals of the Firm*

Optimizing requires that the firm have an articulated and well-understood goal that has been approved by executive management. Upon joining a new firm or department, a new manager or professional staff person must gain an understanding of its goals and the basic strategies used to attain them. In this book, the goal of the decision-making unit will be limited to profit or wealth maximization. The principles of managerial decision making are tough enough to learn even when a single goal is assumed. Moreover, the principles of decision making with a single goal must be learned before multiple goals can be tackled. Where trade-offs between goals are required, as occurs in risk management, a preference function specifying the acceptable trade-offs is provided.

The firm's goal depends on the circumstances in which management finds itself. These circumstances are primarily grouped under the heading of constraints on managerial discretion. Some of these constraints affect the selection by executive management of the basic goal for the firm. Others affect the ability of the firm or its departments to acquire budgetary resources. Still others are imposed by competition in the marketplace, collective bargaining with the firm's unionized workforce, or governmental (political) decisions regarding regulatory and tax policy.

### 1.5.1 *Maximize the Value of the Firm*

When management controls only a small percentage of a corporation's stock, the existence of competition for control of the corporation generally requires that management make decisions that will maximize the value of the firm. If management does not maximize the firm's value, its stock will be undervalued, making it an attractive candidate for acquisition. By replacing the firm's management with executives who will maximize the value of the firm, the acquiring firm can realize substantial stock market profits. The possibility of being acquired by another firm keeps managements efficient. It keeps them actively seeking new products and lower-cost methods of producing and distributing their products. Being forced to maximize the value of the firm reflects the existence of a constraint on the behavior of executive management resulting from competition for control of the firm. Firms owned or controlled by a single person may also use this goal. However, entrepreneur-controlled firms may also seek other goals, such as maximizing the overall well-being of the owner through various kinds of luxuries provided by the company.

*Short-Run Profit Maximization.* Short-run profit maximization takes place when managerial decisions for the current planning period will not affect profits in any subsequent period. Management assumes (1) that profits in subsequent planning periods do not depend on decisions made today or (2) that it cannot reliably predict the impact on profits in subsequent planning periods of decisions for the current planning period. Under either assumption, managerial decisions can be made one period at a time in response to the available opportunities. Very few companies with large investments in plant and equipment or consumer brand image development plan one period at a time. Small retail businesses, general-purpose job shops, and farms probably can, and do, make decisions using short-run profit maximization. However, the techniques used in short-run profit maximization are generally used in the first step of preparing the operating budgets of even the largest corporations.

*Wealth Maximization.* Large corporations generally make their operating and investment decisions using the goal of maximizing the present value of the firm's future profits. This goal is referred to as wealth maximization. It is used when decisions made today for the current planning period have predictable impacts on profits in subsequent planning periods. The most obvious example is investment in new plant and equipment. The new capacity will have a negative effect on the operating rates of the company's existing plant and equipment for a few years until a growing market absorbs the excess capacity inherent in the most profitable plant to construct. Advertising to build consumer brand image consciousness is likewise a long-term process spanning several years. Increased production from mining, oil field, or timber properties in the current planning period will reduce reserves and influence the cost and production rates attainable in future planning periods. Selling durable goods at a sharp discount today may increase sales in the current planning period at the expense of lower sales in the next couple of planning periods.

When profits vary from planning period to planning period, the relationship between decisions made for the current planning period and profits in subsequent planning periods must be predictable before decisions can be made with respect to the current planning period. The present value of future profits is calculated so that profits received in the several planning periods are comparable. That is, a dollar received in the next year is worth more than a dollar received five years hence, which would have a present value of only $\$1.00/(1 + 0.10)^5 = \$0.62$ at a 10 percent interest rate.[1] Although the calculations are more complicated when this goal is used, it is widely used in well-managed large companies.

*Constraints on Profit- or Wealth-Maximizing Decisions.* Whether the goal is short-run profit maximization or wealth maximization, management must always pursue its goal within the confines of one or more constraints. Some of these constraints are external to the firm. Examples are product prices, the behavior of competitors, government regulations such as environmental protection or worker safety regulations, and natural resource and skilled labor costs. Other constraints are internal to the firm, such as the rate at which costs increase as the firm grows or takes on additional product lines through internal expansion or merger. Another internal constraint is the ubiquitous budget constraint. A plant

---

[1]The techniques for calculating present values are covered in section 2.1.

manager is given a labor and raw materials budget and told to maximize output within the confines of that budget. Maximizing output without specifying the budget constraint does not make sense. The plant manager would hire labor and buy raw materials until they no longer added to the plant's output. The last units of labor are hired even though their productivity is very low. Low productivity means that cost is high, most certainly too high to be profitable. To prevent managers from hiring labor or buying raw materials that add little to productivity, they are given a sufficiently small budget so that the cost of the last units of output will be acceptable to executive management and contribute toward attaining the firm's short-run profit or wealth maximization goal.

*Interrelationships Among Several Departments of a Firm.* The existence of constraints on their discretionary actions forces managers to be efficient in their use of scarce resources. One of the major problems facing executive management is determination of the proper budget levels for the firm's several operating departments. The production department's budget cannot be set independently of the marketing department's budget, since what the production department produces must be sold by the marketing department. Setting the budgets for the various operating and staff services departments in an uncoordinated, haphazard manner will not maximize the value of the firm. This is why capital and operating budget proposals normally provide several budget levels and contain detailed analyses of the implications of each budget level. By carefully weighing the alternatives for each department and the interrelationships among the departments, executive management can develop budgets and plans that promise to maximize the value of the firm. Since the future is never known with certainty, a procedure must also exist through which coordinated changes in budgets and plans can be made in response to unforeseen changes in the market and overall environment of the firm.

## 1.5.2 *Maximize Sales or Assets Subject to a Minimum Profit Constraint*

The firm is able to pursue goals other than profit or wealth maximization when its management feels reasonably secure from loss of their jobs because of acquisition of the company. Firms in this situation are possibly, but not necessarily, very large firms. Other examples could be large firms in an industry subject to price regulation (e.g., electric utilities) or operating on the basis of cost-plus contracts (e.g., defense contractors).

An alternative to profit or wealth maximization is to maximize the sales or assets of the firm subject to a minimum profit constraint. Since obtaining capital for future growth from retained earnings, the bond market, and institutional lenders requires that the firm be profitable, management may set a minimum profit level for its operations. Management then plans its operations to maximize sales or its capital budgets to maximize assets. By setting its profit goal below the maximum profits attainable given the firm's production and marketing capabilities and market conditions, management is able to increase sales or acquire more assets. Corporations with larger sales or assets generally pay higher salaries to their top executives, which provides an incentive for these managers to adopt this goal.

### 1.5.3   *Maximize Services or Prestige*

Managerial economics can be utilized by the managers of government agencies and nonprofit firms. The principal difference in analyzing their decisions is that they do not have the same goals as profit-making firms. The two goals discussed in this section are to maximize the services provided and to maximize the institution's prestige.

*Maximize the Level of Service.* Nonprofit firms and government agencies generally maximize the level of services provided by the firm or agency given its budget constraints. This goal promotes the efficient use of resources through minimizing the unit cost of providing its services. A higher level of services attracts more private and public contributors in the case of a nonprofit firm or political support in the case of a government agency. Since nonprofit firms or agencies are in competition with other nonprofit firms or agencies for budget dollars, maximizing the services provided within a given budget provides at least some of the cost-minimizing discipline that is forced on profit-making firms when they compete for the consumer's dollar. Many of the approaches to managerial decision making discussed in this book are applicable to maximizing the services of nonprofit firms or public agencies.

*Maximize the Institution's Prestige.* Another managerial goal for a nonprofit firm or government agency is maximizing its prestige. The exceptional persons (e.g., a Nobel Prize–winning scientist or famous medical doctor) or great works of art that provide this kind of institutional prestige are scarce and expensive, with much of the expense arising from the support facilities, such as research assistants and equipment, that must be provided to attract them. Competition among institutions for the services of exceptional persons or other scarce prestige resources forces on these institutions cost-minimizing discipline. As with service-maximizing firms or agencies, the principle constraint is the level of the budget. Nonprofit firms and government agencies compete with each other for a greater budget. Competition in this case is for tax dollars, political support, and foundation support rather than for consumer dollars.

## 1.6 *Risk Management*

Uncertainty and risk are facts of life. Some business managements consciously seek risky situations, others abhor risks, and still others seek a middle ground. But no business manager can afford to ignore risk and act as if forecasts of the future will occur with certainty. The levels of risk and uncertainty faced by the firm are subject to a fair degree of managerial control, although it is not profitable for the firm to eliminate all risk. Decisions made with respect to the level of risk accepted by the firm are referred to as risk management.

*Institutions for Reducing Risk.* Several institutions have been created by specialized firms to assist business managers in reducing the level of risk they must accept. Fire insurance can reduce the risk of a large financial loss from a fire in a plant or warehouse. However, fire insurance is not free, and it may be more profitable for the firm to bear small risks. The firm may purchase a fire insurance policy with a $50,000 deductible from all losses at its $5 million plant because management believes that the lower premium will be more profitable than insuring against fire losses less than $50,000. Options and future contracts can protect against adverse future price movements for certain of the firm's products or assets, or for property that it wishes to acquire or sell. As with insurance, premiums are paid for options, and management can decide whether it is more profitable to reduce the risk than to bear it.

*Risks Borne by the Firm.* Some risks are traditionally borne by the firm. Finished product inventories are carried by the firm, even though inventories are costly, to protect against unexpected fluctuations in consumer demand that could result in lost sales if the firm did not maintain an adequate inventory. Investment risks are borne by the firm. Although the outlook for a new product is excellent and the company's investment is expected to yield a substantial profit, consumers may not buy the product in the projected amounts, costs may be higher than anticipated, competitors may enter the market, or a new technology may render the product or its production process obsolete. These risks are accepted by the firm when it commits its capital and managerial resources to that product.

*Financial Risks.* Some risks are basically financial. When the firm finances a portion of its investments by borrowing, it is increasing the risk of bankruptcy if its investments are not profitable. Interest and principal must be paid when due or the lender will take legal action to force payment. If the firm uses only its equity funds, this financial risk is eliminated. The stockholders may be unhappy if the project is unprofitable or yields only a small profit, and they may pressure the corporation's directors to fire the responsible top executives. But the firm does not risk going bankrupt and a total loss of the owners' investment. Yet, if management attempts to eliminate the risk of bankruptcy through reduced borrowing, it will not gain profits earned on assets financed with borrowed money. These risks are controlled through the mix of investments and limiting the use of debt.

*Investor and Managerial Risk Preferences.* Risk and uncertainty are among the constraints on the decisions of managers. Management's willingness to assume a higher level of risk is generally rewarded with greater profits if it is successful. The penalty for assuming greater risks and not being successful is greater losses. When assuming higher risks is accompanied by greater expected profits, there is a trade-off between risk and profit. Managements, like people generally, have differing preferences for risk. Most are averse to risk; a few will seek out risky situations. But within the constraint provided by the available trade-offs between risk and profit, managements can make choices between them.

This choice is not without a further constraint for publicly held corporations. If management assumes more risk than the owners of the firm's common stock and marketable debt are willing to accept, given the expected profits of the firm, they will sell their securities. Unless these securities are purchased at the existing market price by other investors who prefer the kinds of risks assumed by management, the result will be a decline in the value of the firm. This decline raises its cost of capital and makes the firm more vulnerable to being acquired by another firm. Thus, management must constantly be aware of the preferences of investors regarding its risk/profit decisions. The risk/profit trade-offs acceptable to existing or potential investors in its securities determine the level of risk that maximizes the firm's value.

## 1.7  *Summary*

Managerial economics is the study of decision making when there are constraints on the choices of the manager. Economic theory provides managers with a wide range of empirically verified observations of the behavior of consumers, competitors, the owners of resources, and government agencies to guide them in making decisions about resource use.

Managers make decisions about the use of resources owned by

their firm or provided to their institution through its budget. This characteristic of the manager's job is shared by the managers of business firms, nonprofit firms, and government agencies. In order to optimize the use of resources, the decision maker must have a goal, or possibly several goals with specific trade-offs among them. The goal of the organization depends on the circumstances within which management finds itself. Business firms generally have as their goal maximizing the value of the firm by short-run profit maximization or by wealth maximization. Profit-seeking business firms may have other goals, such as maximizing their sales or assets subject to a minimum profit constraint. The goals of nonprofit firms or government agencies may be to maximize the level of services provided or the prestige of the institution.

Managers make their decisions subject to one or more constraints. The possibility of losing control, for example, constrains the managers of most firms from spending a significant portion of the company's earnings on increasing their personal well-being and prestige. Competition for budgetary dollars or the consumer's dollar is a constraint faced by all managers. Other constraints are provided by government tax and regulatory policies.

The world is never certain; hence, all managers are concerned with risk management. There are a number of dimensions to the risk management problem, some of which are difficult or impossible to quantify. One of the primary responsibilities of managers is to develop predictions about the uncertain future. Another is to determine whether the firm should bear a risk or pay someone else to bear at least a portion of the risk through such techniques as insurance or options. The risk preferences of both the firm's managers and its investors must be evaluated when the firm engages in risk management.

The existence of risk and uncertainty means that the premises underlying the firm's operating and capital budgets will not always turn out to be correct. When they are incorrect, management must adapt to the world as it is. Adaptation is a major task of all managers. How successfully this adaptation is performed is a major determinant of the success of the firm in attaining its goals.

## Key Terms

| | | |
|---|---|---|
| adaptation | managerial economics | prediction |
| capital plan | minimum profit | profit maximization |
| current planning | constraint | risk management |
| period | normative economics | short-run profit |
| economic theory | operating plan | maximization |
| external constraints | optimization | uncertainty |
| internal constraints | positive economics | wealth maximization |

## Review Questions

1. Why does the firm need a goal if it is to optimize its operating and capital budgets?

2. Define the term *current planning period*. When is the planning for the current planning period done if it is the third quarter of the year?

3. When does short-run profit maximization attain the goal of maximizing the value of the firm?

4. Critique this statement: "You don't need managerial economics. All you need to take is managerial accounting."

5. Why does risk management involve trade-offs between risk and profits?

6. Describe some of the constraints on managers when they make decisions.

7. How does the term *short run* as used in managerial economics differ from the term *short term* as used in accounting?

228.5 ML9TM (Kearney Round) storage

658.15- H121 (Savage)

658 M319MB

Author: _____

Title: _____

LOCATION                    CALL NUMBER

_____            _____

_____            _____

_____            _____

Staff use:

# 2

# *Computational Methods*

This chapter provides a handy reference for a number of computational techniques that are widely used in managerial economics. The first section discusses calculating present values and the rate of return, along with some related concepts. These techniques are used whenever managerial decisions extend beyond more than one planning period. The second section contains a brief review of topics from algebra and differential calculus. The reader is expected to be proficient in the algebra of exponents and equations. The calculus review focuses on taking the derivative of a power function and using the derivative to find maximum and minimum points. The last three sections review the principal statistical techniques used in applications of economic theory to managerial decision making — statistical inference and regression analysis. Several sections of the book include calculations of probabilities using the normal distribution. Several of the cases require use of regression analysis to estimate demand or costs. Section 2.5 discusses several of the statistical problems that can be encountered when applying the regression technique to managerial problems.

## 2.1 *Present Value and Rate of Return*

Present values, rates of return, and the cost of capital are calculated whenever the decision involves two or more planning periods.

*Reasons for Calculating Present Values.* Decisions based on the wealth maximization goal require making profits received, say, 3 years hence comparable to profits received next year or 10 years in the future.

How is management to determine whether actions taken to increase profits next year will increase the wealth (value) of the firm if they reduce profits 2 or 3 years into the future? Computing present values makes the profits received in each period comparable. A dollar received in one year is worth less than a dollar received today because one may invest less than one dollar today to yield a dollar in one year. How much less than one dollar may be invested today depends on the rate of interest.

*Present Value of a Sum Received at One Point in Time.* The amount invested today to yield one dollar at some specified time, $t$, in the future is its present value, $V$. That is, $V$ dollars invested today at annual rate of interest $i$ will grow to one dollar at time $t$. In equation form, where $t = 1$ year (and thus does not figure in),

$$V + iV = \$1.00 \tag{2.1}$$

$V$ is the principal amount invested and $iV$ is the interest received in one year. Solving equation 2.1 for $V$ yields

$$V(1 + i) = \$1.00 \Rightarrow V = \$1.00/(1 + i)$$

If the interest rate is 12 percent, then $V = \$1.00/1.12 = \$0.89$. At interest rates higher than 12 percent, $V$ is less than $0.89, and at lower interest rates $V$ is greater. At an interest rate of 20 percent, $V$ for one dollar received in one year is $0.83. If $i = 7.4\%$, $V = \$0.93$.

If $1.00 is to be received after 2 years, equation 2.1 becomes

$$(V + iV) + i(V + iV) = \$1.00 \tag{2.2}$$

The first term is the principal amount plus the first year's interest, and $i(V + iV)$ is the interest on that amount received at the end of the second year. This equation can be solved for $V$ to yield

$$V + 2iV + i^2V = \$1.00$$
$$V(1 + 2i + i^2) = V(1 + i)^2 = \$1.00$$
$$V = \$1.00/(1 + i)^2$$

The present value of $1.00 received in 2 years is $\$1.00/(1.12)^2 = \$0.80$. At 12 percent interest, $0.80 is the present value of $1.00 received in 2 years. At a 20 percent interest rate, the present value of $1.00 in 2 years is $0.69.

To find the present value of $1.00 received in 1 year and again in 2 years, add together each of the individual present values. That is, at 12 percent interest, \$0.89 + \$0.80 = \$1.69. The general equation for calculating present values is

$$V = \sum_{t=1}^{m} F_t/(1 + i)^t \tag{2.3}$$

where $m$ is the last year of the profit series and $F_t$ is profit in the year $t$. The symbol $\Sigma$ means that all of the individual years' present values are summed to obtain $V$.

*Present Value of a Sum Received Continuously Over a Year.* Suppose that \$1.00 is received every day for one year, for a total of \$365. Its present value can be found by midyear centering the profit stream. The \$365 is treated as if it was received in the middle of the year ($t = 0.5$) so that $V = \$365/(1.15)^{0.5} = \$365/1.072 = \$340.49$ if $i = 15$ percent. One dollar received each day of the last quarter of the year is equivalent to receiving \$91.25 (a fourth of \$365) centered between $t = 0.75$ and $t = 1.00$, or at $t = (0.75 + 1.00)/2 = 0.875$. Thus $V = \$91.25/(1.15)^{0.875} = \$91.25/1.13 = \$80.75$. If the \$91.25 is received over the last quarter of the second year, $V = \$91.25/(1.15)^{1.875} = \$91.25/1.30 = \$70.19$.

*Using a Calculator to Find Present Values.* Although there are a number of different types of present value tables, the hand-held calculator has made them obsolete. Most practical situations involve fluctuating cash flow streams that are difficult to calculate using tables. For a calculator equipped with the $y^x$ key, the present value at 15 percent interest of \$1.00 received in 5 years is found by punching the following sequence of numbers and functions: 1 ÷ 1.15 $y^x$ 5 =. The result is 0.497. If the calculator has a memory, add the contents of the display register (the present value of one year's profits) to the memory using the SUM key to find the present value of a multiyear profit series. Learning how to use a calculator to perform present value calculations requires some practice. Try this example: Find the present value at a 15 percent interest rate of a profit of \$350 after one year, a profit of \$100 after 2 years, a loss of \$200 after 3 years, a profit of \$400 after 4 years, and then abandonment of the project. (The answer is \$477.16.)

*Calculating the Rate of Return.* The internal rate of return (or discounted cash flow, or DCF, rate of return) is the rate of interest that reduces to zero the present value of a time series of profits with positive and negative values. Unless the calculator is equipped with special programming, finding the internal rate of return is a trial-and-error process. This is done by calculating the present value of the profit stream using a trial value for the rate of interest. For example, examine the profit stream in the column of Table 2.1 headed "Undiscounted Profit." Since it has positive and negative entries, its internal rate of return can be calculated. To get started, calculate the present value of this profit stream at a 10 percent interest rate. The results are in the third column of Table 2.1. The total present value is $4.76; thus, the trial internal rate of return is too low since $V$, present value, is positive. The next trial interest rate is 13 percent, which yields a total present value of $-1.29$. Thirteen percent was too high because $V$ is negative. The next trial value is 12 percent and the total present value is $0.66. The last trial value is based on interpolating between the 12 percent and 13 percent results. The two present values differed by $0.66 − ($-1.29) = $1.95. Dividing $1.95 into $0.66 yields 0.338, yielding 12.3 as the next trial rate of interest. The rate of 12.3 percent yields a total present value of $0.06, which is sufficiently close to zero to be the internal rate of return. To test this, try 12.4 percent as the interest rate, which yields a total present value of $-0.12$.

*Problems with Using the Rate of Return.* The internal rate of return is not used in managerial decision making to the extent that present values are. A present value can be computed for any profit stream, not just for those streams with at least one negative value. Internal rates of return can also be ambiguous, since two or more positive internal rates of return may reduce the present value of a profit stream to zero. It can even be an imaginary number. Since the internal rate of return method assumes that profits are reinvested at that rate of interest, projects with different life spans may not be comparable. The present value method does not have these defects when the company's cost of capital is used as the interest rate; nonetheless, the rate of return is used in risk management and capital budgeting.

**Table 2.1   Calculating the Internal Rate of Return**

| Year | Undiscounted Profit | Present Value When the Interest Rate Is | | | | |
|---|---|---|---|---|---|---|
| | | 10% | 13% | 12% | 12.3% | 12.4% |
| 0 | $-100.00 | $-100.00 | $-100.00 | $-100.00 | $-100.00 | $-100.00 |
| 1 | 30.00 | 27.27 | 26.55 | 26.79 | 26.71 | 26.69 |
| 2 | 45.00 | 37.19 | 35.24 | 35.87 | 35.68 | 35.62 |
| 3 | 40.00 | 30.05 | 27.72 | 28.47 | 28.24 | 28.17 |
| 4 | 15.00 | 10.25 | 9.20 | 9.53 | 9.43 | 9.40 |
| Total | $ 30.00 | $ 4.76 | $- 1.29 | $ 0.66 | $ 0.06 | $ -0.12 |

*The Cost of Capital.* Before present value calculations can be made, the appropriate interest rate must be determined. Since firms are financed with a combination of debt and equity capital, the appropriate interest rate is a weighted average of the costs of debt and equity capital, called the cost of capital. The symbol used for the cost of capital is $k$, and $k$ replaces $i$ in equation 2.3 for calculation of present values.

The cost of capital depends on the market value of the company's debt and equity securities. Their market values depend on the nature and earning power of the firm's assets and a host of psychological, political, and economic factors. An expenditure (generally a capital investment) earns the cost of capital if the present value of the resulting profit series is zero, leaving the wealth of the firm unchanged.

The firm's wealth is measured by the market value of its debt and equity securities. If an expenditure of $1.0 million today yields a time series of profits that results in no change in the market value of the company's debt and equity securities, the rate of interest at which the present value of that profit series equals $1.0 million is the cost of capital. A profit series of $0.80 million in one year, $0.40 million in 2 years, and $0.11 million in 3 years has a present value of $1.0 million at a 20 percent interest rate. Thus, $k = 20$ percent is the cost of capital.

This cost of capital definition does not take into account the different risk levels for alternative managerial decisions. One decision may involve actions that are virtually risk free. Another may involve a risky course of action that has a relatively high probability of failure. The risk-adjusted cost of capital is the company's cost of capital plus the risk premium that management believes is adequate to compensate for the greater than average risk of the project. The present value of the project is calculated using the risk-adjusted cost of capital if the decisions vary with respect to risk. How to measure the relative riskiness of alternative actions and adjust the cost of capital for risk is covered in chapter 12.

*Net Present Value.* The net present value (*NPV*) of a project is the present value of the profit stream less the present value of the expenditures necessary to obtain the profit stream. Both present values are calculated using the cost of capital as the interest rate. For example, if the cost of capital is 20 percent, the initial expenditure on the project is $1.5 million, a second expenditure of $0.5 million is made at the end of the first year, profit in years two and three is $2.0 million, and profit is $0.5 million in year four, then the net present value (*NPV*) is

$$NPV = \$-1.5 - \$0.5/1.2 + \$2.0/(1.2)^2 + \$2.0/(1.2)^3 + \$0.5/(1.2)^4$$

$$NPV = \$0.87 \text{ million}$$

Since the project's *NPV* is positive, the project will increase the firm's wealth by \$0.87 million. If *NPV* is negative, the project reduces the wealth of the firm, and the wealth-maximizing decision is to reject the project.

The *NPV* calculation can be used when the time periods for the elements of the profit stream are not uniform. Assume that it takes 6 months to build a plant with the payments spread out evenly over the construction period. The total cost of the plant is \$0.5 million. The first 6 months of operations are expected to result in a loss of \$0.1 million. The next 3 years are expected to yield profits of \$0.8 million, \$1.4 million, and \$0.3 million respectively, after which time the plant is inoperable. If the cost of capital is 20 percent, the *NPV* equation, using the midyear centering method, is

$$NPV = \$-0.5/(1.2)^{0.25} - \$0.1/(1.2)^{0.75} + \$0.8/(1.2)^{1.5}$$
$$+ \$1.4/(1.2)^{2.5} + \$0.3/(1.2)^{3.5}$$
$$NPV = \$0.45 \text{ million}$$

This project adds \$0.45 million to the value of the firm.

## 2.2  *Math Review*

This review covers the principal mathematical tools used in this book. It is provided as a handy reference. The algebra review covers concepts from high school algebra that students often have forgotten. The calculus review is limited to those rules for taking derivatives that are used in this book.

### 2.2.1  *Algebra Review*

*Maintaining an Equation.* An operation performed on the left side of an equation must also be performed on the right side. If 5 is added to the left side, 5 must also be added to the right side. If the left side of an equation is squared, then the right side must be squared. That is, if $L^{0.5} = 5$, squaring both sides yields $L = 25$.

Equations are solved by performing the same operations on both sides until the variable being solved for is on one side, and the constants and other variables are on the other side. $2X + 7 = X - 11$ is solved by subtracting $X$ from both sides to obtain $X + 7 = -11$ and then subtracting 7 from both sides to yield the solution $X = -18$.

*Algebra of Exponents.* To multiply two terms with the same base $(X)$, add the exponents. That is, $X^{0.5}$ multiplied by $X^{0.3} = X^{0.5+0.3} =$

$X^{0.8}$. To divide two terms with the same base, subtract the exponents. $X^2/X^1 = X$; and $X^3/X^4 = X^{3-4} = X^{-1} = 1/X$. Also, note that $X^0 = 1$ and that the sign of an exponent changes when the variable goes from the numerator to the denominator, or vice versa, so that $X^{-1} = 1/X$ and $1/X^{-0.3} = X^{0.3}$.

To multiply two terms with the same exponent and different bases, multiply the bases and apply the exponent. That is, $X^{0.5}$ multiplied by $Y^{0.5} = (XY)^{0.5}$. To raise a term to a power, multiply the exponents. That is, $X^{0.5}$ squared is $(X^{0.5})^2 = X^{0.5\times2} = X^1 = X$.

*Factoring.* Factoring is used to simplify and solve equations. When two or more terms of an expression contain a common element, it may be factored out. For example, a common element in the expression $3X^3 + 9X$ is $3X$, and $3X^3 + 9X = 3X(X^2 + 3)$, which can be verified by multiplying the two terms on the right side of the equation. The expression $3X^2 - 16X + 20$ can be factored as $(X - 2)(3X - 10)$. This can be verified by multiplying the two factors together and simplifying the result to obtain the original expression. Factoring is something of an art best learned by rote practice.

*The Quadratic Formula.* The standard form of a quadratic equation is $aX^2 + bX + c = 0$. If the equation is $3X^2 - 10X + 2 = 0$, then $a = 3$, $b = -10$, and $c = 2$. To solve for $X$, use the formula

$$X = \frac{-b \pm \sqrt{b^2 - 4ac}}{2a} \tag{2.4}$$

If $b^2 - 4ac$ is negative, the solution values are imaginary numbers, which should not be encountered in business decision problems. To find the values of $X$ solving $3X^2 - 10X + 2 = 0$, calculate $b^2 - 4ac = (-10)^2 - (4 \times 3 \times 2) = 100 - 24 = 76$ and find the square root of 76, which equals 8.72. One value of $X$ solving the equation is $X = [-(-10) + 8.72]/(2 \times 3) = 18.72/6 = 3.12$ and the other is $X = [-(-10) - 8.72]/(2 \times 3) = 1.28/6 = 0.21$. To check the solution, write it as $(X - 3.12)(X - 0.21) = 0$ and multiply the two factors to obtain $X^2 - 3.33X + 0.6552 = 0$. Multiplying this equation by 3 yields the original equation.

*Cross Multiplication.* The first step in solving an equation where one or both sides contain fractions is to cross multiply, which means multiply the numerator of one side of the equation by the denominator of the other side. Do this for both sides and then solve the equation. If

$$2X^{0.5}/Y^{0.5} = 3Y^{0.5}/X^{0.5}$$

cross multiplication yields

$$(2X^{0.5})(X^{0.5}) = (3Y^{0.5})(Y^{0.5}) \text{ or } 2X = 3Y$$

Cross multiplication works because it is equivalent to multiplying both sides of the equation by

$$X^{0.5}Y^{0.5}$$

*Solving Two Equations for Two Unknowns.* The preferred method for the problems in this book, which include nonlinear equations, is to solve each equation for the same variable and then substitute one equation into the other. If the two equations are $X - 3Y = 7$ and $2X^{0.5}Y^{0.5} = 10$, rearrange the first equation to $X = 3Y + 7$ and square both sides of the second equation and solve it for $X$ to obtain $4XY = 100$ and $X = 25/Y$. Substitute the last equation into the first to get $25/Y = 3Y + 7$. Cross multiplying yields $25 = 3Y^2 + 7Y$ or $3Y^2 + 7Y - 25 = 0$. Applying the quadratic formula yields $Y = -4.28$ and $Y = 1.95$. Substituting these values of $Y$ into $X = 3Y + 7$ yields the corresponding values of $X$, $X = -5.84$ and $X = 12.85$.

*Equation of Line Through Two Points.* The equation of the straight line through points $(x_0, y_0)$ and $(x_1, y_1)$ is $y = y_0 - rx_0 + rx$ where $r = (y_0 - y_1)/(x_0 - x_1)$.

*Logarithms.* The symbol for the natural (base $e$) logarithm is ln. If $Y = aV^bW^c$, then $\ln Y = \ln a + b\ln V + c\ln W$. This application of logarithms is used to convert a power function into a linear equation.

## 2.2.2  Calculus Review

Calculus is primarily used to calculate numerical values for the maximums and minimums of profit and cost functions since optimization is generally concerned with maximizing profits or minimizing costs. A course in calculus is not a prerequisite for using this book to learn the basic theory and techniques of managerial economics. They are explained using graphs.

Students who have never taken a course in calculus should practice the rules in this section until they are proficient at taking the derivative of a power function. A power function is of the general form $Y = CX^N$, where $X$ and $Y$ are variables and $C$ and $N$ are constants. A polynomial is the sum of two or more power functions, such as $Y = aX^2 + bX + c$.

Calculus is a technique for calculating the rate at which one variable changes when there is a very small change in one or more of the other variables in a function or equation. The symbol $\Delta X$ means "calculate the difference between two values of $X$." That is, $\Delta X = X_2 - X_1$. The derivative is the limit of the ratio $\Delta Y/\Delta X$ where $\Delta X$ approaches zero, but never is actually equal to zero. The limit of this ratio as $X \to 0$ is defined as the derivative of the function. If the function is $Y = F(X)$, which is read "$Y$ is a function of $X$," then the symbol for the derivative is $dY/dX$. The expression $dY/dX$ is not read as "$dY$ divided by $dX$." Since it is a symbol, it is read as "the derivative of $Y$ with respect to $X$." The calculation of limits as $\Delta X \to 0$ is used to derive the formulas for taking derivatives. The formulas used in this book are provided in this section.

***Derivative of a Constant.*** If $Y = C$, where $C$ is a constant, the derivative is zero. Since a derivative measures a rate of change, and constants do not change, the derivative of a constant is zero.

***Derivative of a Power Function.*** If $Y = CX^N$ then $dY/dX = CNX^{N-1}$. This rule is frequently used in this book. It should be memorized and the student should practice the rule until it is second nature. For example, if $Y = 3X^2$, then $dY/dX = (3)(2)X^{(2-1)} = 6X$. If $Y = 2X^{0.5}$, then $dY/dX = (2)(0.5)X^{(0.5-1)} = X^{-0.5}$. In managerial economics, answers are never left with negative exponents; thus, $dY/dX = X^{-0.5} = 1/X^{0.5}$.

***Derivative of a Sum or Difference.*** The derivative of the sum or difference of two power functions is the sum or difference of the derivatives of each power function. The derivative of $Y = 3X^2 - 2X^{0.5}$ is $dY/dX = 6X - 1/X^{0.5}$.

***Partial Derivatives.*** Some equations contain two or more independent variables. When a partial derivative is taken with respect to one of the independent variables, the other independent variables are treated as constants. If $Q = 3W^{0.6}V^{0.8}$, then finding the derivative of $Q$ with respect to $W$, written as $\partial Q/\partial W$ to make clear that it is a partial derivative, amounts to treating $3V^{0.8}$ as the constant term. This partial derivative is $\partial Q/\partial W = (3V^{0.8})(0.6)W^{(0.6-1)} = 1.8V^{0.8}/W^{0.4}$. The partial derivative of $Q$ with respect to $V$ treats $3W^{0.6}$ as the constant term so that $\partial Q/\partial V = 2.4W^{0.6}/V^{0.2}$.

***Second Derivatives.*** The derivative of a derivative is called a second derivative. The symbol $d^2Y/dX^2$ differentiates the second from the first derivative, $dY/dX$. If $Y = X^2 + 3X - 9$, $dY/dX = 2X + 3$ and $d^2Y/dX^2 = 2$.

*Maximum or Minimum of a Function.* Take the first and second derivatives, set the first derivative equal to zero and solve for the variable, and substitute the solution values into the second derivative to determine if they are local maximum or minimum values. If the second derivative is negative, that value of the variable yields a local maximum value for the function. If the second derivative is positive, it yields a local minimum. As is shown in Figure 2.1, there may be more than one local maximum or minimum. If $Y = X^3 - 8X^2 + 20X - 100$, $dY/dX = 3X^2 - 16X + 20$ and $d^2Y/dX^2 = 6X - 16$. Setting $dY/dX = 0$ and factoring the resulting equation to solve it yields

$$3X^2 - 16X + 20 = 0$$

$$(X - 2)(3X - 10) = 0$$

$$X = 2, 10/3$$

Substituting $X = 2$ into $d^2Y/dX^2$ yields $6(2) - 16 = -4$; therefore, $X = 2$ when substituted into the function yields a local maximum of $Y = (2)^3 - 8(2)^2 + 20(2) - 100 = -84$. Substituting $X = 10/3$ into

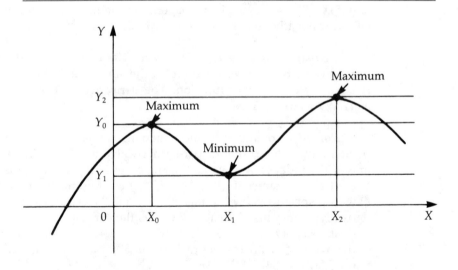

**Figure 2.1   Maximums and Minimum of a Function**

There are two local maximums and one local minimum for the curve graphed in this figure. One local maximum is at $(X_0, Y_0)$ and the other is at $(X_2, Y_2)$. The local minimum is at $(X_1, Y_1)$.

$d^2Y/dX^2$ yields $+4$; therefore $X = 10/3$ yields a local minimum. The student should become proficient at finding maximums and minimums.

## 2.3  *Statistical Inference*

Managerial economics is not simply the theoretical study of decision making; it also includes using observed data to estimate numerical values for the coefficients of the equations describing the decision problem. For example, to use the equation $TC = a + bQ$ to calculate a firm's total cost ($TC$) of producing $Q$ units of output, statistical estimates must be made of coefficients $a$ and $b$. These estimates make use of several statistical techniques. The coefficients are estimated on the basis of a sample, and not all of the possibly relevant variables are included in the analysis. Statistical methods are generally used because of the high cost, relative to management's perceptions of the benefits, of obtaining a larger sample or analyzing more variables.

*Population and Sample.* A population consists of all possible observations that could be gathered on a variable. A sample is a set of observations drawn from a population. For example, the population could be all 7,500 employees of a company, and a sample could be 100 of those employees. Statistical theory is based on random samples. A sample is random if each element of a population had an equal chance of being included in the sample. Random samples are obtained using a procedure ensuring that one observation in the sample cannot be used to predict that another observation in the population will also be in the sample. If the next observation can be predicted on the basis of knowledge of another observation in the sample, then the sample is not random. For the purposes of illustrating the use of statistical analyses in managerial decisions, it is assumed that the sample is random.

*Average and Standard Deviation of a Sample.* Once a random sample of $N$ observations on variable $X$ has been obtained, its average and standard deviation are expressed in equations 2.5 and 2.6, respectively.

$$\overline{X} = \Sigma X/N \tag{2.5}$$

$$\sigma_X = \sqrt{\Sigma(X - \overline{X})^2/(N - 1)} \tag{2.6}$$

The symbol $\Sigma$ means "add up the values of all of the observations in the sample." If a random sample of $N = 10$ observations is 11, 2, 3, 7, 4, 9, 8, 8, 2, 6, the sum of the observations is 60 and the sample

average is $60/10 = 6$. $\Sigma(X - \overline{X})^2 = (11 - 6)^2 + (2 - 6)^2 + \cdots +$
$(6 - 6)^2 = 88$, and $\sigma_X = \sqrt{88/9} = \sqrt{9.778} = 3.127$.

The average is a measure of the center of the sample. Since $\sigma_X$ is calculated from $(X - \overline{X})$ for each observation in the sample, the standard deviation measures the variation in the data about its average. The greater the variation in the data within a sample, the greater the standard deviation.

**The Coefficient of Variation.** The coefficient of variation, $CV = \sigma_X/\overline{X}$, is a measure of relative variation between samples. $CV$ is not used when $\overline{X} = 0$ or is relatively close to zero. The greater the coefficient of variation, the greater the variation in the observations of the sample relative to its average. If one sample has a greater $CV$ than another, it is the sample with the greater variability in its data.

**The Normal Distribution.** Unless stated otherwise, the assumption used throughout this book is that samples are drawn from a normally distributed population. Calculating probabilities with the normal distribution begins with standardizing the end points of the range of values of $X$ or $\overline{X}$ for which the probabilities are to be computed. The standardized variable, $Z$, is

$$Z = (X - \overline{X})/\sigma_X \qquad (2.7)$$

In Figure 2.2, the normal curve has been drawn for a population with an average of 100 and a standard deviation of 10. The normal curve is centered over the population average — the actual population average,

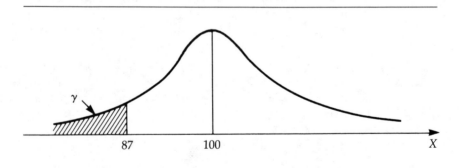

**Figure 2.2   Normal Distribution — One-Tail Probability Calculation**
The normal probability curve is centered over the population average, here 100. The probability that $X$ is less than 87 is represented by shaded area $\gamma$ under the normal probability curve.

a sample average estimating its value, or a hypothesized population average. If $X$ is a normally distributed random variable, then $\overline{X}$ is also normally distributed.

**EXAMPLE 2.1.**   Compute the probability that the next value of $X$ drawn from a population with an average of 100 and $\sigma_X = 10$ will be less than 87, which is the shaded area $\gamma$ in Figure 2.2. $Z$ for $X = 87$ is $(87 - 100)/10 = -1.30$. The minus sign on $Z$ indicates that $\gamma$ is in the left tail of the normal curve. Look up the probability $\gamma$ by going down the $Z$ column of Table 2.2 to 1.3 and then going across that row to the column headed by .00. The entry in that row and column is $\gamma = 0.0968$, or 9.68%. The probability that the next observation would be greater than 87 is $1 - \gamma = 1 - .0968 = 0.9032$, or 90.32%. The entire area under the normal curve is 1, or 100%.

**EXAMPLE 2.2.**   Example 2.1 was for a one-tail probability calculation. Other problems require calculation of the probability of being within a range of values having finite upper and lower limits. Assume that the sample size is $N = 60$, $\Sigma X = 1250$ and $\Sigma(X - \overline{X})^2 = 2401$. Compute the probability that the normally distributed random variable $X$ will be between 20 and 28. $\overline{X} = 1250/50 = 25$ and $\sigma_X = \sqrt{2401/(50 - 1)} = \sqrt{49} = 7$. The diagram is in Figure 2.3 with $\gamma$ between 20 and 28. The $Z$ values and corresponding probabilities for the two tails and for $\gamma$ are

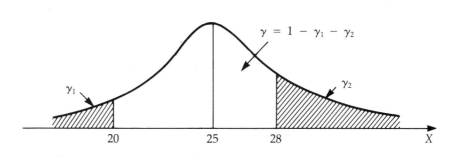

**Figure 2.3   Normal Distribution — Two-Tail Probability Calculation**

To calculate the probability that $X$ will be between 20 and 28, it is first necessary to calculate the areas $\gamma_1$ and $\gamma_2$ in the tails of the normal probability curve, since it is those areas that are provided in Table 2.2. Since the area under the curve is one, or 100 percent, the desired probability $\gamma = 1 - \gamma_1 - \gamma_2$.

## Table 2.2    Areas Under the Normal Curve

| % | .00 | .01 | .02 | .03 | .04 | .05 | .06 | .07 | .08 | .09 |
|-----|------|------|------|------|------|------|------|------|------|------|
| 0.0 | .5000 | .4960 | .4920 | .4880 | .4840 | .4801 | .4761 | .4721 | .4681 | .4641 |
| 0.1 | .4602 | .4562 | .4522 | .4483 | .4443 | .4404 | .4364 | .4325 | .4286 | .4247 |
| 0.2 | .4207 | .4168 | .4129 | .4090 | .4052 | .4013 | .3974 | .3936 | .3897 | .3858 |
| 0.3 | .3821 | .3783 | .3745 | .3707 | .3669 | .3632 | .3594 | .3557 | .3520 | .3483 |
| 0.4 | .3446 | .3409 | .3372 | .3336 | .3300 | .3264 | .3228 | .3192 | .3156 | .3121 |
| 0.5 | .3085 | .3050 | .3015 | .2981 | .2946 | .2912 | .2877 | .2843 | .2810 | .2776 |
| 0.6 | .2743 | .2709 | .2676 | .2643 | .2611 | .2578 | .2546 | .2514 | .2483 | .2451 |
| 0.7 | .2420 | .2389 | .2358 | .2327 | .2296 | .2266 | .2236 | .2206 | .2177 | .2148 |
| 0.8 | .2119 | .2090 | .2061 | .2033 | .2005 | .1977 | .1949 | .1922 | .1894 | .1867 |
| 0.9 | .1841 | .1814 | .1788 | .1762 | .1736 | .1711 | .1685 | .1660 | .1635 | .1611 |
| 1.0 | .1587 | .1562 | .1539 | .1515 | .1492 | .1469 | .1446 | .1423 | .1401 | .1379 |
| 1.1 | .1357 | .1335 | .1314 | .1292 | .1271 | .1251 | .1230 | .1210 | .1190 | .1170 |
| 1.2 | .1151 | .1131 | .1112 | .1093 | .1075 | .1056 | .1038 | .1020 | .1003 | .0985 |
| 1.3 | .0968 | .0951 | .0934 | .0918 | .0901 | .0885 | .0869 | .0853 | .0838 | .0823 |
| 1.4 | .0808 | .0793 | .0778 | .0764 | .0749 | .0735 | .0721 | .0708 | .0694 | .0681 |
| 1.5 | .0668 | .0655 | .0643 | .0630 | .0618 | .0606 | .0594 | .0582 | .0571 | .0559 |
| 1.6 | .0548 | .0537 | .0526 | .0516 | .0505 | .0495 | .0485 | .0475 | .0465 | .0455 |
| 1.7 | .0446 | .0436 | .0427 | .0418 | .0409 | .0401 | .0392 | .0384 | .0375 | .0367 |
| 1.8 | .0359 | .0351 | .0344 | .0336 | .0329 | .0322 | .0314 | .0307 | .0301 | .0294 |
| 1.9 | .0287 | .0281 | .0274 | .0268 | .0262 | .0256 | .0250 | .0244 | .0239 | .0233 |
| 2.0 | .0228 | .0222 | .0217 | .0212 | .0207 | .0202 | .0197 | .0192 | .0188 | .0183 |
| 2.1 | .0179 | .0174 | .0170 | .0166 | .0162 | .0158 | .0154 | .0150 | .0146 | .0143 |
| 2.2 | .0139 | .0136 | .0132 | .0129 | .0125 | .0122 | .0119 | .0116 | .0113 | .0110 |
| 2.3 | .0107 | .0104 | .0102 | .0099 | .0096 | .0094 | .0091 | .0089 | .0087 | .0084 |
| 2.4 | .0082 | .0080 | .0078 | .0075 | .0073 | .0071 | .0069 | .0068 | .0066 | .0064 |
| 2.5 | .0062 | .0060 | .0059 | .0057 | .0055 | .0054 | .0052 | .0051 | .0049 | .0048 |
| 2.6 | .0047 | .0045 | .0044 | .0043 | .0041 | .0040 | .0039 | .0038 | .0037 | .0036 |
| 2.7 | .0035 | .0034 | .0033 | .0032 | .0031 | .0030 | .0029 | .0028 | .0027 | .0026 |
| 2.8 | .0026 | .0025 | .0024 | .0023 | .0023 | .0022 | .0021 | .0021 | .0020 | .0019 |
| 2.9 | .0019 | .0018 | .0018 | .0017 | .0016 | .0016 | .0015 | .0015 | .0014 | .0014 |
| 3.0 | .0013 | .0013 | .0013 | .0012 | .0012 | .0011 | .0011 | .0011 | .0010 | .0010 |

The values in the table are the areas in the tail of the normal curve.

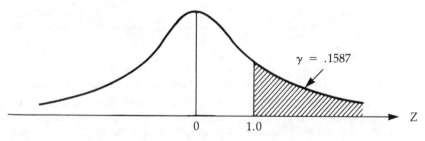

If the sign of Z is positive, the area is in the right tail; if Z is negative, the area is in the left tail.

*Source: Biometrika Tables for Statisticians*, vol. 1, 3rd ed. (1966). Reprinted with permission of the *Biometrika* Trustees.

$$Z(\gamma_1) = (20 - 25)/7 = -0.71 \text{ and } \gamma_1 = 0.2389$$

$$Z(\gamma_2) = (28 - 25)/7 = 0.43 \text{ and } \gamma_2 = 0.3336$$

$$\gamma = 1 - \gamma_1 - \gamma_2 = 1 - 0.2389 - 0.3336 = 0.4275$$

*Calculating Probabilities for the Sample Average.* If the random variable is the sample average and there are $N$ observations in the sample, the standard deviation of the sample average, $\sigma_{\overline{X}}$, is

$$\sigma_{\overline{X}} = \sigma_X/\sqrt{N} \tag{2.8}$$

where $\sigma_X$ is the standard deviation of the individual observations in the population. The reason $\sigma_{\overline{X}}$ is less than $\sigma_X$ is that in computing the sample average, relatively large observations are offset by relatively small observations, which reduces the variation in the sample averages. The larger the sample size for computing $\overline{X}$, the more likely these offsetting variations will occur and the smaller $\sigma_{\overline{X}}$ will be.

If the sample size is large, the normal distribution can be used to calculate the probability of observing a specified range of values of the sample average. The normal distribution is used when the sample size is large. The only difference from the calculations in examples 2.1 and 2.2 is that the standardizing formula becomes

$$Z = (\overline{X} - \mu)/\sigma_{\overline{X}} \tag{2.9}$$

where $\mu$ is the hypothesized population average.

**EXAMPLE 2.3.**   Assume that the population average is $\mu = 50$ and its standard deviation is $\sigma = 22$. Calculate the probability, $\alpha$, that the average of a sample of 70 observations will be less than $\overline{X}^* = 46$. The first step is to calculate

$$\sigma_{\overline{X}} = 22/\sqrt{70} = 2.63$$

Standardizing $\overline{X}^*$ yields

$$Z = (46 - 50)/2.63 = -1.52$$

Looking up in Table 2.2 the probability associated with $Z = 1.52$ yields $\alpha = 0.0643$ or 6.43% as the probability that $\overline{X}$ would be less than 46.

*Calculating Probabilities Using the t-Distribution.* When the sample size is less than $N = 50$, the *t*-distribution is used to calculate probabilities associated with the sample average. To compute probabilities with the *t*-distribution, three statistics are required: the average, standard deviation, and the degrees of freedom, $\phi$. The degrees of freedom are the minimum number of observations required to calculate the standard deviation of the variable. Since $\overline{X}$ is required to calculate $\sigma_X$, only $N - 1$ observations and $\overline{X}$ are required to calculate $\sigma_X$ — the *N*th observation can be calculated from $\overline{X}$ and the other $N - 1$ observations. The statistic *t* is calculated by replacing *Z* in equation 2.9 with *t*. To find the probability associated with a given value of *t*, (1) go down the left column of Table 2.3 to the degrees of freedom, (2) go across that row to the closest value of *t*, and (3) go up to the first row to find the probability in the tail corresponding to the specified value of *t*. For example, if the sample size is $N = 22$, $\phi = 22 - 1 = 21$ and the value of *t* calculated using equation 2.9 is 1.715, the probability in the right tail of the *t*-distribution is 0.05 or 5%.

**EXAMPLE 2.4.**  Assume that a sample of $N = 25$ observations will be drawn from a normally distributed population with a population average of 120 and standard deviation of $\sigma = 40$. What is the probability that this sample average will be greater than $\overline{X}^* = 140$? The standard deviation of the sample average is

$$\sigma_{\overline{X}} = 40/\sqrt{25} = 8$$

The standardized value of $\overline{X}^*$ is

$$t = (140 - 120)/8 = 2.5$$

For $\phi = 25 - 1 = 24$ degrees of freedom, go down the left column of Table 2.3 to 24 and then across that row to the *t* value closest to 2.5. It is 2.492. The probability that the sample average will be greater than 140 is $\alpha = 0.01$ or 1% at the top of the table.

*Linear Interpolation.* If the calculated value of *t* lies between two values in Table 2.3, linear interpolation can more precisely calculate the desired probability. To make a linear interpolation, find the percentage of the difference between the bracketing values in the table for the calculated value of *t* and the larger value in the table. For example, if the calculated *t* is 1.475, with $\phi = 20$, this percentage is $0.250/0.400 = 0.625$ or 62.5%.

| | |
|---|---|
| *t* for $\alpha = 0.05$ is 1.725 | *t* for $\alpha = 0.05$ is 1.725 |
| *t* for $\alpha = 0.10$ is <u>1.325</u> | calculated value of *t* <u>1.475</u> |
| 0.400 | 0.250 |

## Table 2.3    Areas Under the *t*-Distribution Curve

| $\alpha =$ .25 | .20 | .15 | .10 | .05 | .025 | .01 | .005 |
|---|---|---|---|---|---|---|---|
| $\phi$ | | | | | | | |
| 4    .741 | .941 | 1.190 | 1.533 | 2.132 | 2.776 | 3.747 | 4.606 |
| 5    .727 | .920 | 1.156 | 1.476 | 2.015 | 2.571 | 3.365 | 4.032 |
| 6    .718 | .906 | 1.134 | 1.440 | 1.943 | 2.447 | 3.143 | 3.707 |
| 7    .711 | .896 | 1.119 | 1.415 | 1.895 | 2.365 | 2.998 | 3.499 |
| 8    .706 | .889 | 1.108 | 1.397 | 1.860 | 2.306 | 2.896 | 3.355 |
| 9    .703 | .883 | 1.100 | 1.383 | 1.833 | 2.262 | 2.821 | 3.250 |
| 10    .700 | .879 | 1.093 | 1.372 | 1.812 | 2.228 | 2.764 | 3.169 |
| 11    .697 | .876 | 1.088 | 1.363 | 1.796 | 2.201 | 2.718 | 3.106 |
| 12    .695 | .873 | 1.083 | 1.356 | 1.782 | 2.179 | 2.681 | 3.055 |
| 13    .694 | .870 | 1.079 | 1.350 | 1.771 | 2.160 | 2.650 | 3.012 |
| 14    .692 | .868 | 1.076 | 1.345 | 1.761 | 2.145 | 2.624 | 2.977 |
| 15    .691 | .866 | 1.074 | 1.341 | 1.753 | 2.131 | 2.602 | 2.947 |
| 16    .690 | .865 | 1.071 | 1.337 | 1.746 | 2.120 | 2.583 | 2.921 |
| 17    .689 | .863 | 1.069 | 1.333 | 1.740 | 2.110 | 2.567 | 2.898 |
| 18    .688 | .862 | 1.067 | 1.330 | 1.734 | 2.101 | 2.552 | 2.878 |
| 19    .688 | .861 | 1.066 | 1.328 | 1.729 | 2.093 | 2.539 | 2.861 |
| 20    .687 | .860 | 1.064 | 1.325 | 1.725 | 2.086 | 2.528 | 2.845 |
| 21    .686 | .859 | 1.063 | 1.323 | 1.721 | 2.080 | 2.518 | 2.831 |
| 22    .686 | .858 | 1.061 | 1.321 | 1.717 | 2.074 | 2.508 | 2.819 |
| 23    .685 | .858 | 1.060 | 1.319 | 1.714 | 2.069 | 2.500 | 2.807 |
| 24    .685 | .857 | 1.059 | 1.318 | 1.711 | 2.064 | 2.492 | 2.797 |
| 25    .684 | .856 | 1.058 | 1.316 | 1.708 | 2.060 | 2.485 | 2.787 |
| 26    .684 | .856 | 1.058 | 1.315 | 1.706 | 2.056 | 2.479 | 2.779 |
| 27    .684 | .855 | 1.057 | 1.314 | 1.703 | 2.052 | 2.473 | 2.771 |
| 28    .683 | .855 | 1.056 | 1.313 | 1.701 | 2.048 | 2.467 | 2.763 |
| 29    .683 | .854 | 1.055 | 1.311 | 1.699 | 2.045 | 2.462 | 2.756 |
| 30    .683 | .854 | 1.055 | 1.310 | 1.697 | 2.042 | 2.457 | 2.750 |
| 40    .681 | .851 | 1.050 | 1.303 | 1.684 | 2.021 | 2.423 | 2.704 |
| 60    .679 | .846 | 1.046 | 1.296 | 1.671 | 2.000 | 2.390 | 2.660 |
| 120    .677 | .845 | 1.041 | 1.289 | 1.658 | 1.980 | 2.358 | 2.617 |
| $Z =$    .674 | .842 | 1.036 | 1.282 | 1.645 | 1.960 | 2.326 | 2.576 |

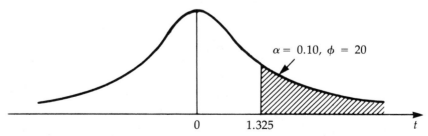

$\alpha = 0.10, \phi = 20$

0          1.325                              *t*

*Source:* Abridged from Table III in R. A. Fisher. and F. Yates, *Statistical Tables for Biological, Agricultural and Medical Research* (1976). Published by the Longman Group Ltd., London (previously published by Oliver and Boyd Ltd., Edinburgh) and by permission of the authors and publishers.

35

The difference between the bracketing values is $0.10 - 0.05 = 0.05$. The interpolated probability is $0.05 + (0.05 \times 0.625) = 0.08125$ or 8%, where the first 0.05 is the probability associated with the larger value in Table 2.3.

*Statistical Inference.* Assume that one of two mutually exclusive states of the world is true. Either hypothesis H1 is true or H2 is true. Statistical inference is the use of sample data to determine which hypothesis will be asserted to be true. The true state of the world generally will never be known with certainty; hence, it is possible to make a wrong assertion. The two types of errors are

Type I: Assert H2 is true when in fact H1 is true.
Type II: Assert H1 is true when in fact H2 is true.

The convention is to define the hypotheses so that the type I error is the more costly one. The type II error is not discussed here because it is not used in this book.

The procedure for determining the range of values of the sample average $\overline{X}$ that would lead to accepting H1 is as follows:

1. Assume that H1 is the actual state of the world. Draw the normal curve when H1 is the world's actual state as in Figure 2.4.
2. Determine the tail of the normal curve for the Type I error ($\alpha$)
   a. If H2 is of the "greater than" form, the type I error is in the right tail of the normal curve for H1.
   b. If H2 is of the "less than" form, the type I error is in the left tail of the normal curve for H1.
   c. If H2 is of the "not equal to" form, divide the type I error equally between the two tails. This is a "two-tail" test.
3. Use the $Z$ value for the type I error to calculate the critical values $\overline{X}_1^*$ and $\overline{X}_2^*$, which divide the values of $\overline{X}$ into two sets: those values of $\overline{X}$ for which it is asserted that H1 is true and those for which H2 is asserted to be true, as in Figure 2.4.

**EXAMPLE 2.5.** Assume that a sample of $N = 100$ observations will be drawn from a normally distributed population. The hypotheses are H1: $\mu = 25$ and H2: $\mu = 23$. The population standard deviation is $\sigma_X = 15$ and the type I error is not to exceed 5.0%. The first step is to calculate $\sigma_{\overline{X}} = \sigma_X/\sqrt{N} = 15/\sqrt{100} = 1.5$. The next step is to find in Table 2.2 or 2.3 the $Z$ value for 2.5% in the tail — 1.96. The standardization formula is used to calculate $\overline{X}_1^*$ and $\overline{X}_2^*$.

$$-1.96 = (\overline{X}_1^* - 25)/1.5 \Rightarrow \overline{X}_1^* = 22.06$$

$$+1.96 = (\overline{X}_2^* - 25)/1.5 \Rightarrow \overline{X}_2^* = 27.94$$

H1 is accepted for all values of $\overline{X}$ between 22.06 and 27.94.

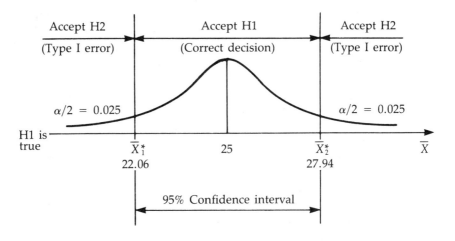

**Figure 2.4   Calculation of the Values of $\overline{X}$ for Which H1 Is Accepted**

Statistical inference is a procedure for finding the values of $\overline{X}$ for which hypothesis H1 will be accepted given the probability of committing the type I error, where $\alpha = 5\%$ in this example. Half of the type I error probability is placed in each tail of the normal curve and the critical values of $\overline{X}$, $\overline{X}_1^*$ and $\overline{X}_2^*$, calculated. The values of $\overline{X}$ between $\overline{X}_1^*$ and $\overline{X}_2^*$ are also referred to as 95 percent confidence interval.

*Confidence Interval.* The confidence interval is the range of values within which there is a specified probability that the sample average $\overline{X}$ will occur when a sample of $N$ observations is drawn from a normally distributed population. The confidence interval is calculated in the same manner as the critical values for a two-tailed statistical inference test. The probability associated with the confidence interval is 100 percent minus the probability of the type I error. In example 2.5, the range of values 22.06 to 27.94 is the 95 percent confidence interval when the population average is $\mu = 25$.

## 2.4   *Simple and Multiple Regression*

Regression is a technique used to estimate empirical relationships among variables that economic theory has identified as relevant for a particular decision. It is used to estimate the *b*-coefficients of the linear equation of the form

$$Y = b_0 + b_1X_1 + b_2X_2 + \cdots + b_nX_n \qquad \textbf{(2.10)}$$

The *b*-coefficients of the independent variables in equation 2.10 are also referred to as their slope coefficients. Simple regression has one independent ($X$) variable. Multiple regression is used when there is more than one independent variable. Regression analysis also includes methods for measuring the extent to which the regression equation fits the data and the statistical significance of its coefficients.

*The Error Term of the Regression Equation.* Assume that the "true" or population relationship between $X$ and $Y$ is $Y = A + BX$. Let $a$ and $b$ be the sample estimates of the population coefficients $A$ and $B$. In general, when $a$ and $b$ are computed from sample data, the estimated value of $Y$, which is $\hat{Y} = a + bX_0$ for a given value of $X = X_0$, is not equal to the actual sample value, $Y_0$. This error can be due to a number of factors, including omitted variables having an effect on $Y$, the true relationship's not being linear, measurement errors in the data, and random shocks on the system. The error is defined as $e = Y - \hat{Y}$. For most values of $X$, $e \neq 0$.

*Least Squares Formulas.* The least squares formulas for estimating $a$ and $b$ minimize the sum of the squared errors, $\Sigma e^2$, for all observations in the sample. The least squares formulas are

$$b = \Sigma(X - \overline{X})(Y - \overline{Y})/\Sigma(X - \overline{X})^2 \qquad (2.11)$$

$$a = \overline{Y} - b\overline{X} \qquad (2.12)$$

An alternative formula for calculating $b$ is

$$b = (n\Sigma XY - \Sigma X \Sigma Y)/[n\Sigma X^2 - (\Sigma X)^2] \qquad (2.13)$$

The least squares formulas do not require any assumptions about the probability distribution of the error terms.

Another way to view the problem of estimating the regression equation is to ask this question: Given the values of $X$ and $Y$ in the sample, what are the hypothesized population coefficients $A$ and $B$ that maximize the probability of obtaining the values of $a$ and $b$ calculated using the least squares method? This approach to the regression problem is called the Maximum Likelihood Principle. The least squares values of $a$ and $b$ are maximum likelihood estimates of $A$ and $B$ given the following assumptions about the probability distribution of the error terms: (1) $e$ is normally distributed, (2) the expected value of $e$ is zero, (3) the standard deviation of $e$ is constant for all values of $X$, and (4) $e_i$ is statistically independent of $e_j$ for all $i \neq j$. These assumptions are required to compute the confidence interval about the regression line or to test hypotheses about the significance of the regression coefficients.

*Standard Error of the Estimate.* The standard error of the estimate, $\sigma_{\hat{Y}}$, is the standard deviation of the actual values of $Y$ relative to their estimated values, $\hat{Y}$, using the regression equation. The first step in calculating $\sigma_{\hat{Y}}$ is to calculate the variance of the regression equation's error terms $\sigma_e^2$. The formula is

$$\sigma_e^2 = \Sigma(Y - \hat{Y})^2/(N - 2) \tag{2.14}$$

The denominator is $N - 2$ because that is the number of degrees of freedom in the estimation process. In order to estimate $Y$ using simple regression, two statistics must first be estimated, $a$ and $b$; hence, $N - 2$ is the minimum number of observations needed to compute $\sigma_e$. If $e$ is normally distributed with an expected value of zero, the normal probability curve for $Y$ given a specific value $X_0$ of the independent variable $X$ is centered over $\hat{Y} = a + bX_0$. The standard deviation of $\hat{Y}$, which is referred to as the standard error of the estimate, is

$$\sigma_{\hat{Y}} = \sigma_e\sqrt{(1/N) + ((X_0 - \overline{X})^2/\Sigma(X - \overline{X})^2)} \tag{2.15}$$

The further $X_0$ is from $\overline{X}$, the greater the value of $\sigma_{\hat{Y}}$.

**EXAMPLE 2.6. Reducing the 95 Percent Confidence Interval Using Regression Analysis.** Forecasting the price of a product based on the sample of 11 observations on past prices in Table 2.4 begins with calculating the average price and its standard deviation. The average price is \$2.67 and its standard deviation is $\sqrt{0.5848/(11 - 1)} = \$0.242$. If the probability distribution of prices is normal, there is a 95 percent probability that the actual price during the next period will be between $Y_1^* = \$2.20$ and $Y_2^* = \$3.14$. The range of the 95 percent confidence interval is \$3.14 − \$2.20 = \$0.94. To calculate $Y_1^*$,

$$-1.96 = (Y_1^* - 2.67)/0.242 \Rightarrow Y_1^* = 2.20$$

To reduce the range of the 95 percent confidence interval, an additional variable can be used and a simple regression calculated. This variable could be selected empirically or on the basis of economic theory. Since price has gradually increased over time, empirical observation indicates that the year can be used as the independent variable, $T$. The additional calculations for this regression are in Table 2.4. The regression coefficients and equation are

$$b = 7.58/110 = 0.069$$

**Table 2.4   Data for Price Projection**

| Price ($Y$) | $(Y - \bar{Y})$ | $(Y - \bar{Y})^2$ | $T$ | $(T - \bar{T})$ | $(T - \bar{T})^2$ | $(T - \bar{T})(Y - \bar{Y})$ |
|---|---|---|---|---|---|---|
| $2.38 | −0.29 | 0.0841 | 1 | −5 | 25 | 1.45 |
| 2.50 | −0.17 | 0.0289 | 2 | −4 | 16 | 0.68 |
| 2.47 | −0.20 | 0.0400 | 3 | −3 | 9 | 0.60 |
| 2.51 | −0.16 | 0.0256 | 4 | −2 | 4 | 0.32 |
| 2.55 | −0.12 | 0.0144 | 5 | −1 | 1 | 0.12 |
| 2.61 | −0.06 | 0.0036 | 6 | 0 | 0 | 0.00 |
| 2.65 | −0.02 | 0.0004 | 7 | 1 | 1 | −0.02 |
| 2.70 | 0.03 | 0.0009 | 8 | 2 | 4 | 0.06 |
| 2.87 | 0.20 | 0.0400 | 9 | 3 | 9 | 0.60 |
| 3.05 | 0.38 | 0.1444 | 10 | 4 | 16 | 1.52 |
| 3.12 | 0.45 | 0.2025 | 11 | 5 | 25 | 2.25 |
| $29.41 | | 0.5848 | 66 | | 110 | 7.58 |

$$a = 2.67 - (0.069 \times 6) = 2.256$$

$$\hat{Y} = 2.256 + 0.069T$$

The first three columns of Table 2.5 contain the data to calculate $\sigma_e^2$ and $\sigma_{\hat{Y}}$.

$$\sigma_e^2 = 0.0646/9 = 0.00718 \Rightarrow \sigma_e = 0.08472$$

For $T_0 = 12$, the first year after the data series,

$$\sigma_{\hat{Y}} = (0.08472)\sqrt{(0.09091) + ((12 - 6)^2/110)} = 0.055$$

The 95 percent confidence interval for $T = 12$ using $\sigma_{\hat{Y}}$ is

$$\hat{Y}(T = 12) = 2.256 + 0.069(12) = \$3.08$$

$$(\hat{Y}_1^* - 3.08)/0.055 = -1.96$$

$$\hat{Y}_1^* = 3.08 - 1.96(0.055) = \$2.97$$

$$\hat{Y}_2^* = 3.08 + 1.96(0.055) = \$3.19$$

The range of the 95 percent confidence interval is now $3.19 − $2.97 = $0.22, which is substantially less than the $0.94 range when it was based on the sample average and standard deviation. Adding the year as an independent variable and performing the simple regression

**Table 2.5  Calculation of Estimated Prices and Statistical Test Data**

| $\hat{Y}$ | $e = Y - \hat{Y}$ | $e^2$ | $\hat{Y} - \overline{Y}$ | $(\hat{Y} - \overline{Y})^2$ |
|---|---|---|---|---|
| 2.32 | 0.06 | 0.0036 | −0.35 | 0.1225 |
| 2.39 | 0.11 | 0.0121 | −0.28 | 0.0784 |
| 2.46 | 0.01 | 0.0001 | −0.21 | 0.0441 |
| 2.53 | −0.02 | 0.0004 | −0.14 | 0.0196 |
| 2.60 | −0.05 | 0.0025 | −0.07 | 0.0049 |
| 2.67 | −0.06 | 0.0036 | 0.00 | 0.0000 |
| 2.74 | −0.09 | 0.0081 | 0.07 | 0.0049 |
| 2.80 | −0.10 | 0.0100 | 0.13 | 0.0169 |
| 2.87 | 0.00 | 0.0000 | 0.20 | 0.0400 |
| 2.97 | 0.11 | 0.0121 | 0.27 | 0.0729 |
| 3.01 | 0.11 | 0.0121 | 0.34 | 0.1156 |
| | | 0.0646 | | 0.5198 |

made possible a more precise forecast. Additional independent variables, suggested by either empirical observation or economic theory, could be added to the analysis to attempt to further reduce the range of the 95 percent confidence interval and produce a better forecast. Adding more variables would require multiple regression.

*Coefficient of Determination.* The coefficient of determination, or $R^2$, measures the extent to which the regression equation fits the data. $R^2$ is the percentage of the total variation in the dependent variable, $Y$, that is "explained" by the regression equation. The greater the value of $R^2$, the better the regression line fits the data. The formula for computing $R^2$, which is the same for simple or multiple regression analyses, first requires calculation of the ratio

$$RR = \Sigma(\hat{Y} - \overline{Y})^2 / \Sigma(Y - \overline{Y})^2 \qquad \textbf{(2.16)}$$

and then substituting $RR$ into the formula

$$R^2 = RR - ((K - 1)(1 - RR)/(N - K)) \qquad \textbf{(2.17)}$$

where $K$ is the number of $b$-coefficients in the regression equation. This formula has been corrected for the increase in $R^2$ that results when the number of degrees of freedom declines with smaller samples.

*The F-Statistic.* The $F$-statistic is calculated using the formula

$$F = R^2(N - K)/(1 - R^2)(K - 1) \qquad \textbf{(2.18)}$$

Its purpose is to determine whether a statistically significant portion of the total variation in $Y$ has been explained by the independent variables. Since this is a significance test, use Table 2.6 to determine the critical value of $F$ above which the hypothesis that the regression is significant will be accepted given a 5 percent probability of making the type I error. Go down the left column of Table 2.6 to row $N - K$ and then across to the column headed by $K - 1$ to find the critical value of $F$. For example, if the number of observations is $N = 20$ and $K = 3$, $b$-coefficients are estimated using multiple regression, $F^* = 3.5915$. If the calculated value of $F$ is greater than $F^*$, the hypothesis is accepted that the independent variable explains a significant portion of the total variation in $Y$.

*Statistical Significance of the Slope Coefficients.* The final statistical test discussed here is determining whether the slope coefficients of the regression equation are significantly different from zero. A zero $b$-coefficient in equation 2.10 means that the variable has no influence on the value of $Y$. It should be dropped and the equation estimated again. The standard deviation of the slope coefficient of a simple regression is

$$\sigma_b = \sqrt{\sigma_e^2/\Sigma(X - \overline{X})^2} \tag{2.19}$$

where $X$ is the independent variable. $\sigma_b$ is referred to as the standard error of the coefficient. The standardization formula is

$$t = b/\sigma_b \tag{2.20}$$

To determine whether a slope coefficient is significant, start with the number of degrees of freedom, $\phi = N - 2$. Go down the left column of Table 2.3 to $\phi$, and then across that row to the $t$-statistic value for one-half of the type I error probability, which is $\alpha/2 = 0.025$ in this book. The resulting value of $t$ is the critical value $t^*$. For example, $\phi = 20$ and $\alpha = 0.05$, $t^* = \pm 2.086$. If the calculated value of $t$ for the coefficient using equation 2.20 is greater than $t^*$, then the slope coefficient is said to be significant. This procedure is equivalent to calculating the 95 percent confidence interval for the slope coefficient.

EXAMPLE 2.7.   The last two columns of Table 2.5 provide the data for calculating $R^2$ and the $F$-statistic and for testing the significance of the $b$-coefficient of the regression equation estimated in example 2.6. The coefficient of determination is

$$RR = 0.5198/0.5848 = 0.89$$

$$R^2 = 0.89 - ((2 - 1)(1 - 0.89)/(11 - 2)) = 0.88$$

**Table 2.6** **Critical Values of the *F*-Statistic: α = 5**

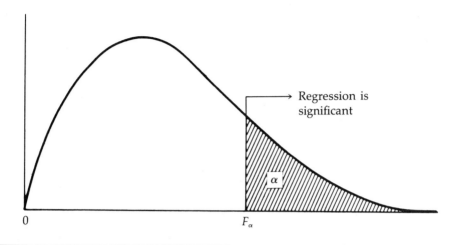

| $K-1$ <br> $N-K$ | 1 | 2 | 3 | 4 | 5 | 6 | 7 | 8 | 9 |
|---|---|---|---|---|---|---|---|---|---|
| 1 | 161.45 | 199.50 | 215.71 | 224.58 | 230.16 | 233.99 | 236.77 | 238.88 | 240.54 |
| 2 | 18.513 | 19.000 | 19.164 | 19.247 | 19.296 | 19.330 | 19.353 | 19.371 | 19.385 |
| 3 | 10.128 | 9.5521 | 9.2766 | 9.1172 | 9.0135 | 8.9406 | 8.8868 | 8.8452 | 8.8123 |
| 4 | 7.7086 | 6.9443 | 6.5914 | 6.3883 | 6.2560 | 6.1631 | 6.0942 | 6.0410 | 5.9988 |
| 5 | 6.6079 | 5.7861 | 5.4095 | 5.1922 | 5.0503 | 4.9503 | 4.8759 | 4.8183 | 4.7725 |
| 6 | 5.9874 | 5.1433 | 4.7571 | 4.5337 | 4.3874 | 4.2839 | 4.2066 | 4.1468 | 4.0990 |
| 7 | 5.5914 | 4.7374 | 4.3468 | 4.1203 | 3.9715 | 3.8660 | 3.7870 | 3.7257 | 3.6767 |
| 8 | 5.3177 | 4.4590 | 4.0662 | 3.8378 | 3.6875 | 3.5806 | 3.5005 | 3.4381 | 3.3881 |
| 9 | 5.1174 | 4.2565 | 3.8626 | 3.6331 | 3.4817 | 3.3738 | 3.2927 | 3.2296 | 3.1789 |
| 10 | 4.9646 | 4.1028 | 3.7083 | 3.4780 | 3.3258 | 3.2172 | 3.1355 | 3.0717 | 3.0204 |
| 11 | 4.8443 | 3.9823 | 3.5874 | 3.3567 | 3.2039 | 3.0946 | 3.0123 | 2.9480 | 2.8964 |
| 12 | 4.7472 | 3.8853 | 3.4903 | 3.2592 | 3.1059 | 2.9961 | 2.9134 | 2.8486 | 2.7964 |
| 13 | 4.6672 | 3.8056 | 3.4105 | 3.1791 | 3.0254 | 2.9153 | 2.8321 | 2.7669 | 2.7144 |
| 14 | 4.6001 | 3.7389 | 3.3439 | 3.1122 | 2.9582 | 2.8477 | 2.7642 | 2.6987 | 2.6458 |
| 15 | 4.5431 | 3.6823 | 3.2874 | 3.0556 | 2.9013 | 2.7905 | 2.7066 | 2.6408 | 2.5876 |
| 16 | 4.4940 | 3.6337 | 3.2389 | 3.0069 | 2.8524 | 2.7413 | 2.6572 | 2.5911 | 2.5377 |
| 17 | 4.4513 | 3.5915 | 3.1968 | 2.9647 | 2.8100 | 2.6987 | 2.6143 | 2.5480 | 2.4943 |
| 18 | 4.4139 | 3.5546 | 3.1599 | 2.9277 | 2.7729 | 2.6613 | 2.5767 | 2.5102 | 2.4563 |
| 19 | 4.3808 | 3.5219 | 3.1274 | 2.8951 | 2.7401 | 2.6283 | 2.5435 | 2.4768 | 2.4227 |
| 20 | 4.3513 | 3.4928 | 3.0984 | 2.8661 | 2.7109 | 2.5990 | 2.5140 | 2.4471 | 2.3928 |
| 21 | 4.3248 | 3.4668 | 3.0725 | 2.8401 | 2.6848 | 2.5757 | 2.4876 | 2.4205 | 2.3661 |
| 22 | 4.3009 | 3.4434 | 3.0491 | 2.8167 | 2.6613 | 2.5491 | 2.4638 | 2.3965 | 2.3419 |
| 23 | 4.2793 | 3.4221 | 3.0280 | 2.7955 | 2.6400 | 2.5277 | 2.4422 | 2.3748 | 2.3201 |
| 24 | 4.2597 | 3.4028 | 3.0088 | 2.7763 | 2.6207 | 2.5082 | 2.4226 | 2.3551 | 2.3002 |

**Table 2.6**  *(continued)*

| K − 1 / N − K | 1 | 2 | 3 | 4 | 5 | 6 | 7 | 8 | 9 |
|---|---|---|---|---|---|---|---|---|---|
| 25 | 4.2417 | 3.3852 | 2.9912 | 2.7587 | 2.6030 | 2.4904 | 2.4047 | 2.3371 | 2.2821 |
| 26 | 4.2252 | 3.3690 | 2.9751 | 2.7426 | 2.5868 | 2.4741 | 2.3883 | 2.3205 | 2.2655 |
| 27 | 4.2100 | 3.3541 | 2.9604 | 2.7278 | 2.5719 | 2.4591 | 2.3732 | 2.3053 | 2.2501 |
| 28 | 4.1960 | 3.3404 | 2.9467 | 2.7141 | 2.5581 | 2.4453 | 2.3593 | 2.2913 | 2.2360 |
| 29 | 4.1830 | 3.3277 | 2.9340 | 2.7014 | 2.5454 | 2.4324 | 2.3463 | 2.2782 | 2.2229 |
| 30 | 4.1709 | 3.3158 | 2.9223 | 2.6896 | 2.5336 | 2.4205 | 2.3343 | 2.2662 | 2.2107 |
| 40 | 4.0848 | 3.2317 | 2.8387 | 2.6060 | 2.4495 | 2.3359 | 2.2490 | 2.1802 | 2.1240 |
| 60 | 4.0012 | 3.1504 | 2.7581 | 2.5252 | 2.3683 | 2.2540 | 2.1665 | 2.0970 | 2.0401 |
| 120 | 3.9201 | 3.0718 | 2.6802 | 2.4472 | 2.2900 | 2.1750 | 2.0867 | 2.0164 | 1.9588 |
| ∞ | 3.8415 | 2.9957 | 2.6049 | 2.3719 | 2.2141 | 2.0986 | 2.0096 | 1.9384 | 1.8799 |

The regression equation explains 88 percent of the variation in the product's price over the past 11 years. This is an excellent fit of the data. The exact value of $R^2$ above which there is an adequate fit of the data is a matter of judgment on the part of the analyst. Another use of the $R^2$ statistic is in deciding between two or more alternative regression equations. In general, the regression equation with the highest $R^2$ value is preferred.

The F-statistic is

$$F = (0.88)(11 - 2)/(1 - 0.88)(1) = 66.0$$

To find the critical value of $F$, go down the left column of Table 2.6 to $N - K = 11 - 2 = 9$ and across the top row to $K - 1 = 1$. The critical value of $F$, $F^*$, is 5.1174. Since the critical value of $F$ is less than the value of $F$ calculated from the data, the independent variable ($T$) explains a significant portion of the total variation in $Y$.

Testing the significance of the b-coefficient of the regression begins with using equations 2.19 and 2.20 to calculate the values of $\sigma_b$ and $t$.

$$\sigma_b = \sqrt{(0.00718/110)} = 0.0081$$

$$t = 0.069/0.0081 = 8.52$$

Since this is a two-tail test, the critical value of $t$ for a 5 percent type

I error is in the $\alpha/2 = 0.025$ column and the $N - K = 9$ degrees of freedom row of Table 2.3. Since $t^* = \pm 2.262$, the hypothesis that the *b*-coefficient is not equal to zero is accepted because the calculated value of $t$ is greater than $t^*$. The coefficient is said to be significant.

## 2.5  *Regression Pitfalls*

Regression analysis appears to be a relatively straightforward method for analyzing data and finding relationships among variables; however, several problems can arise. The most commonly encountered problems — identification, serial correlation, multicollinearity, and heteroskedasticity — are briefly reviewed in this section.

*The Identification Problem.* All statistical techniques rely on data to provide the basis for identifying relationships between variables. Some relationships cannot be identified with the available data. Assume that the only data available are price and output points *A*, *B*, and *C* in Figure 2.5. These points were generated by a static curve *S* and shifts in curve *D*. With no additional information on the reasons for curve *D* shifting, these data are only capable of identifying curve *S*. The keys to being able to identify relationships are (1) the extent of the variability in the data and (2) the number of variables on which data have been gathered. The greater the variability in the data, the more likely that statistical techniques can be used to identify economic relationships. The greater the number of variables, the more likely the analyst will be able to identify the reasons for each curve to shift.

*Serial Correlation.* The fourth assumption required by the Maximum Likelihood Principle is that the error terms be statistically independent. That is, error term $e_i$ cannot be predicted on the basis of knowledge of one or more of the other error terms. When the error terms are not statistically independent, serial correlation exists. Serial correlation frequently occurs when time series data are used to fit the regression equation, although it can be encountered in any regression analysis. Serial correlation results in a bias in the standard error of the regression, $\sigma_e$, that can render invalid significance tests for the regression coefficients and the *F*-test of the significance of the entire regression. In general, the calculated value of $\sigma_e$ will be too small, and the coefficients and regression will appear to be significant when in fact they are not.

To test for the existence of serial correlation, use the Durbin-Watson statistic

$$d = \sum_{i=2}^{m}(e_i - e_{i-1})^2 \bigg/ \sum_{i=1}^{m} e_i^2 \qquad \textbf{(2.21)}$$

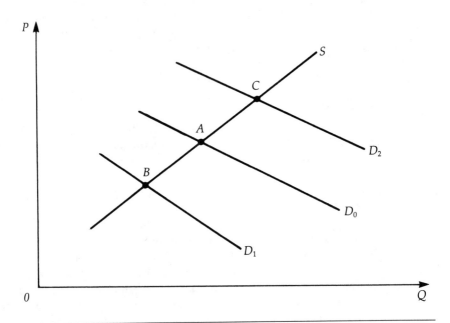

**Figure 2.5   The Identification Problem**

If curve $S$ does not shift but curve $D$ does shift, the resulting data points are only capable of "identifying" curve $S$. There is insufficient variation in the data to identify the $D$ curves since only one data point on each $D$ curve is available.

where $e_i$ is the error term associated with the $i$-th independent variable. If the value of the Durbin-Watson statistic is 2, the hypothesis that there is no first-order serial correlation in the residuals is accepted. First order serial correlation exists when $e_i = a + be_{i-1}$, which would violate the fourth assumption required by the Maximum Likelihood Principle. There is a range of values about $d = 2$ within which the hypothesis can be unambigously accepted. Its lower limit is entry $d_U$ in Table 2.7, and its upper limit is $4 - d_U$. For a simple regression of $k = 2$ with $N = 20$ observations, $d_U = 1.41$ and $4 - d_U = 2.59$. A regression equation with a calculated value of $d$ between 1.41 and 2.59 would lead to the conclusion that the first-order serial correlation is absent. For more information on use of the Durbin-Watson statistic, see a textbook in econometrics.[1]

---

[1]For example, see Michael D. Intriligator, *Econometric Models, Techniques, and Applications* (Englewood Cliffs, NJ: Prentice-Hall, 1978), section 6.4.

**Table 2.7  Critical Values of the Durbin-Watson Statistic**

Significance Points of $d_L$ and $d_U$: 5%

| $n$ | $k = 2$ | | $k = 3$ | | $k = 4$ | | $k = 5$ | | $k = 6$ | |
|---|---|---|---|---|---|---|---|---|---|---|
| | $d_L$ | $d_U$ | $d_L$ | $d_U$ | $d_L$ | $d_U$ | $d_L$ | $d_U$ | $d_L$ | $d_U$ |
| 15 | 1.08 | 1.36 | 0.95 | 1.54 | 0.82 | 1.75 | 0.69 | 1.97 | 0.56 | 2.21 |
| 16 | 1.10 | 1.37 | 0.98 | 1.54 | 0.86 | 1.73 | 0.74 | 1.93 | 0.62 | 2.15 |
| 17 | 1.13 | 1.38 | 1.02 | 1.54 | 0.90 | 1.71 | 0.78 | 1.90 | 0.67 | 2.10 |
| 18 | 1.16 | 1.39 | 1.05 | 1.53 | 0.93 | 1.69 | 0.82 | 1.87 | 0.71 | 2.06 |
| 19 | 1.18 | 1.40 | 1.08 | 1.53 | 0.97 | 1.68 | 0.86 | 1.85 | 0.75 | 2.02 |
| 20 | 1.20 | 1.41 | 1.10 | 1.54 | 1.00 | 1.68 | 0.90 | 1.83 | 0.79 | 1.99 |
| 21 | 1.22 | 1.42 | 1.13 | 1.54 | 1.03 | 1.67 | 0.93 | 1.81 | 0.83 | 1.96 |
| 22 | 1.24 | 1.43 | 1.15 | 1.54 | 1.05 | 1.66 | 0.96 | 1.80 | 0.86 | 1.94 |
| 23 | 1.26 | 1.44 | 1.17 | 1.54 | 1.08 | 1.66 | 0.99 | 1.79 | 0.90 | 1.92 |
| 24 | 1.27 | 1.45 | 1.19 | 1.55 | 1.10 | 1.66 | 1.01 | 1.78 | 0.93 | 1.90 |
| 25 | 1.29 | 1.45 | 1.21 | 1.55 | 1.12 | 1.66 | 1.04 | 1.77 | 0.95 | 1.89 |
| 26 | 1.30 | 1.46 | 1.22 | 1.55 | 1.14 | 1.65 | 1.06 | 1.76 | 0.98 | 1.88 |
| 27 | 1.32 | 1.47 | 1.24 | 1.56 | 1.16 | 1.65 | 1.08 | 1.76 | 1.01 | 1.86 |
| 28 | 1.33 | 1.48 | 1.26 | 1.56 | 1.18 | 1.65 | 1.10 | 1.75 | 1.03 | 1.85 |
| 29 | 1.34 | 1.48 | 1.27 | 1.56 | 1.20 | 1.65 | 1.12 | 1.74 | 1.05 | 1.84 |
| 30 | 1.35 | 1.49 | 1.28 | 1.57 | 1.21 | 1.65 | 1.14 | 1.74 | 1.07 | 1.83 |
| 31 | 1.36 | 1.50 | 1.30 | 1.57 | 1.23 | 1.65 | 1.16 | 1.74 | 1.09 | 1.83 |
| 32 | 1.37 | 1.50 | 1.31 | 1.57 | 1.24 | 1.65 | 1.18 | 1.73 | 1.11 | 1.82 |
| 33 | 1.38 | 1.51 | 1.32 | 1.58 | 1.26 | 1.65 | 1.19 | 1.73 | 1.13 | 1.81 |
| 34 | 1.39 | 1.51 | 1.33 | 1.58 | 1.27 | 1.65 | 1.21 | 1.73 | 1.15 | 1.81 |
| 35 | 1.40 | 1.52 | 1.34 | 1.58 | 1.28 | 1.65 | 1.22 | 1.73 | 1.16 | 1.80 |
| 36 | 1.41 | 1.52 | 1.35 | 1.59 | 1.29 | 1.65 | 1.24 | 1.73 | 1.18 | 1.80 |
| 37 | 1.42 | 1.53 | 1.36 | 1.59 | 1.31 | 1.66 | 1.25 | 1.72 | 1.19 | 1.80 |
| 38 | 1.43 | 1.54 | 1.37 | 1.59 | 1.32 | 1.66 | 1.26 | 1.72 | 1.21 | 1.79 |
| 39 | 1.43 | 1.54 | 1.38 | 1.60 | 1.33 | 1.66 | 1.27 | 1.72 | 1.22 | 1.79 |
| 40 | 1.44 | 1.54 | 1.39 | 1.60 | 1.34 | 1.66 | 1.29 | 1.72 | 1.23 | 1.79 |
| 45 | 1.48 | 1.57 | 1.43 | 1.62 | 1.38 | 1.67 | 1.34 | 1.72 | 1.29 | 1.78 |
| 50 | 1.50 | 1.59 | 1.46 | 1.63 | 1.42 | 1.67 | 1.38 | 1.72 | 1.34 | 1.77 |
| 55 | 1.53 | 1.60 | 1.49 | 1.64 | 1.45 | 1.68 | 1.41 | 1.72 | 1.38 | 1.77 |
| 60 | 1.55 | 1.62 | 1.51 | 1.65 | 1.48 | 1.69 | 1.44 | 1.73 | 1.41 | 1.77 |
| 65 | 1.57 | 1.63 | 1.54 | 1.66 | 1.50 | 1.70 | 1.47 | 1.73 | 1.44 | 1.77 |
| 70 | 1.58 | 1.64 | 1.55 | 1.67 | 1.52 | 1.70 | 1.49 | 1.74 | 1.46 | 1.77 |
| 75 | 1.60 | 1.65 | 1.57 | 1.68 | 1.54 | 1.71 | 1.51 | 1.74 | 1.49 | 1.77 |
| 80 | 1.61 | 1.66 | 1.59 | 1.69 | 1.56 | 1.72 | 1.53 | 1.74 | 1.51 | 1.77 |
| 85 | 1.62 | 1.67 | 1.60 | 1.70 | 1.57 | 1.72 | 1.55 | 1.75 | 1.52 | 1.77 |
| 90 | 1.63 | 1.68 | 1.61 | 1.70 | 1.59 | 1.73 | 1.57 | 1.75 | 1.54 | 1.78 |
| 95 | 1.64 | 1.69 | 1.62 | 1.71 | 1.60 | 1.73 | 1.58 | 1.75 | 1.56 | 1.78 |
| 100 | 1.65 | 1.69 | 1.63 | 1.72 | 1.61 | 1.74 | 1.59 | 1.76 | 1.57 | 1.78 |

*Note:* $n$ = number of observations; $k$ = number of explanatory variables, including the constant term.

*Source:* J. Durbin and G. S. Watson, "Testing for Serial Correlation in Least Squares Regression," *Biometrika*, Vol. 38 (1951), pp. 159–178. Reprinted with permission of the *Biometrika* Trustees.

*Multicollinearity.* A frequently encountered problem in multiple regression analyses is multicollinearity. Multicollinearity occurs when the independent variables are highly correlated, as often occurs when using time series data. The symptoms of multicollinearity are low $t$-statistics for the regression coefficients and a high $F$-statistic. When there is serious multicollinearity, the separate effects of each of the individual independent variables cannot be distinguished. The $b$-coefficients of the regression equations are not reliable estimators of their true values. One way to reduce multicollinearity problems is to calculate the $R^2$s between all of the independent variables. If independent variables $X_i$ and $X_j$ have a high $R^2$, it may be best to rerun the regression first with $X_i$ eliminated, and then with $X_j$ eliminated and $X_i$ included. If the symptoms of multicollinearity are reduced, then the regression with the higher coefficient of determination or $F$-statistic can be used. If the objective of the regression model is forecasting,

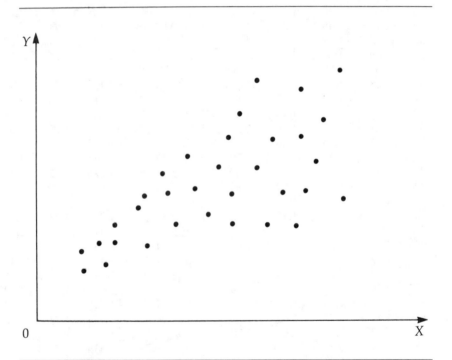

**Figure 2.6　Sample Data Exhibiting Heteroskedasticity**

As the value of $X$ increases, the range on the $Y$ axis of the data points becomes greater. Thus, the standard deviation of $Y$ for a given value of $X$ changes as the value of $X$ increases, giving rise to the heteroskedasticity problem.

good forecasts can generally be obtained despite the presence of multicollinearity.

*Heteroskedasticity.* Another problem is heteroskedasticity. The third assumption required for least squares estimates of the $b$-coefficients to be maximum likelihood estimates of the true coefficients is for the standard deviation of the error term to be constant for all values of the independent variable. Heteroskedasticity exists when this assumption does not hold for the sample used to estimate the regression coefficients. Again, the usual tests for the statistical significance of the regression and its coefficients are invalid. A simple test for heteroskedasticity is to plot the dependent variable on the vertical axis of a graph and the independent variable on its horizontal axis. If the scatter of the points becomes larger or smaller as the independent variable becomes larger, as occurs in Figure 2.6, heteroskedasticity should be suspected. Alternatively, the sample can be divided into two parts and the standard deviation of each part calculated. If the standard deviations are appreciably different, then heteroskedasticity is suspected.

One approach to reducing the effects of heteroskedasticity is to divide both sides of the regression equation by the independent variable for which heteroskedasticity is suspected. If the original regression equation is $Y = b_0 + b_1 X$, the new equation would be $(Y/X) = (b_0/X) + b_1$. Thus, the data for the regression would become $(Y/X)$ as the dependent variable and $(1/X)$ as the independent variable. This reformulation often works well where larger values of $X$ are associated with an increased standard deviation for $Y$.

## 2.6  *Summary*

Making decisions where costs, revenues, or profits are incurred in more than one planning period requires calculation of their present values. Present values are calculated by discounting dollar amounts in future planning periods using the appropriate interest rate or cost of capital. The rate of return is the interest rate that reduces to zero the present value of a time series of profits containing both positive and negative entries. In either case, the objective is to make dollars received or spent at different times in the future comparable by making all dollar amounts comparable to dollars spent or received at the present time.

The algebra review focused on solving equations and on the algebra of exponents. The calculus review covered the rules for taking the derivative of power functions. These rules are used in calculating the maximums of profit functions or the minimums of cost functions.

The statistical review concentrated on the methods for calculating probabilities with the normal distribution and using these probabilities to make decisions (test hypotheses). It also covered the methods for calculating a simple regression equation and the statistics used to evaluate the equation's fit of the data. These statistics are also used to evaluate a multiple regression equation, which is usually estimated using a computer program because of the large number of calculations required. Four of the principal problems with regression studies were also reviewed.

## Key Terms

| | | |
|---|---|---|
| average | identification problem | quadratic formula |
| coefficient of determination | independent variable | sample |
| | internal rate of return | serial correlation |
| coefficient of variation | midyear centering of the profit stream | simple regression |
| | | slope coefficient |
| confidence interval | multicollinearity | standard deviation |
| cost of capital | multiple regression | statistical significance |
| degrees of freedom | normal distribution | *t*-distribution |
| F-statistic | population | type I error |
| heteroskedasticity | present value | type II error |

## Review Questions

1. Why is it necessary to calculate present values before adding together profits in two or more time periods.

2. Define the term *cost of capital*. How is the cost of capital like an internal rate of return?

3. Why is the derivative of a constant equal to zero?

4. A bill will be introduced into the legislature to apply an excise tax to over-the-counter drugs. Comment on the argument of its supporters that the average adult spends only $5 per year for these drugs, and hence the tax will burden no one.

5. Do the majors of students in a managerial economics class constitute a random sample of all majors at the university? Why or why not?

6. Assume that there are two possible routes to get from city A to city B. Why would you expect the route with the greater standard deviation of arrival times to take, on the average, a shorter period of time than the other route?

7. What is meant by the term *multicollinearity*? What are the symptoms of multicollinearity?

8. Describe the identification problem. Why do a lack of variation in the data and an inadequate number of variables give rise to identification problems?

## *Problems and Applications*

1. Calculate the net present value at a 10 percent interest rate of an expenditure of \$1.5 million today and profits of \$0.4 million in 1 year, \$0.9 million in 2 years, \$0.7 million in 3 years, \$0.3 million in 4 years, and nothing thereafter. Calculate the internal rate of return of this profit series.

2. Recalculate the present value and internal rate of return for problem 1 using the midyear centering method.

3. Calculate the value of $Y = X^{0.3-1}$ when $X = 7$.

4. Calculate the value of $Y = (X)^2(X/V^{0.5})^2$ when $X = 4$ and $V = 25$.

5. Factor the expressions $2X^2 - 8X$ and $2X^2 - 2X - 12$ by inspection and using the quadratic formula. Verify the factors by multiplying them together.

6. Use the quadratic formula to solve the equations $2X^2 - 2X - 13 = 0$ and $X^2 + 14X + 33 = 0$.

7. Use cross multiplication to solve the equation $X^{0.25}/Y^{0.5} = 3Y^{0.5}/2X^{0.75}$.

8. Solve the equations $2X - Y = 4$ and $X^{0.5}Y^{0.5} = 5$ for $X$ and $Y$.

9. Find the equation of the straight line through the pair of points (160,100) and (196,20), where the $X$ coordinate is the first entry of the pair.

10. Find the equation of the straight line through (0,20) and (60,180).

11. Calculate the first and second derivatives of the following power functions: $Y = 4X^3$ and $Y = V^{0.5} + 2V^{0.25}$.

12. Calculate the first and second derivatives of $Y = 6X^2 - 5$ and $R = 0.5/T^2$.

13. Calculate the partial derivatives of $Q = 4X^{0.5}Y^{0.5}$ and $Q = 3X^{0.25}Y^{0.5}$.

14. Calculate the partial derivatives of $Z = 5X^{0.75}Y$.

15. Find the local maximum and minimum of $Y = X^3 - 8.5X^2 + 24X + 50$ and $Y = X^3/3 - 4X^2 - 48X - 12$.

16. Find the maximum and minimum of $Y = X^3/3 - 7X^2 - 16X + 20$.

17. Calculate the average, standard derivation, and standardized value of each observation for the sample: 19, 5, 17, 20, 12, and 14.

18. Calculate the average, standard deviation, and standardized value of each observation for the sample: 7, 14, $-4$, $-2$, 9, $-1$.

19. Assume that on the average it takes you 27.4 minutes to drive to the university and walk to class, with a standard deviation of 2.5 minutes. If the time is normally distributed, what is the probability of being late if you leave 30.0 minutes before class?

20. If $\overline{X} = -3.5$, $\Sigma(X - \overline{X})^2 = 40$, $N = 81$, and $X$ is normally distributed, compute the probability that $X$ will be greater than $-5.0$.

21. If $\overline{X} = 12.3$, $\Sigma(X - \overline{X})^2 = 494.3$, $N = 40$, and $X$ is normally distributed, compute the probability that $\overline{X}$ will be between 7.7 and 9.9.

22. An employer council claims that it pays minority laborers as much as it pays other laborers, who earn an average of $106 per week. A government agency found in a survey of 25 minority laborers the following sample data: $\Sigma X = \$2,600$ and $\Sigma(X - \overline{X})^2 = 245.76$. What is the probability that the agency would draw this sample if in fact minority laborers earned the same amount as other laborers? Assume the distribution of wages is normal.

23. The observed level of a pollutant has averaged 12.6 ppm with a standard deviation of 1.9 ppm for several years. How likely is it that a pollution control agency would draw a sample of 25 observations with an average of 13.1 ppm or more?

24. If, using the results of problem 23, such a sample were actually drawn, could you conclude that pollution in the river has risen? Explain why.

25. Let H1: $\mu = \$8,432$ and H2: $\mu \neq \$8,432$ where $N = 400$ and $\sigma_X = \$2,000$. What range of values of $\overline{X}$ would lead you to reject H1 with a probability of not more than 6 percent when H1 is in fact true?

26. Let H1: $\mu = 100$ and H2: $\mu > 100$. Compute the critical value of $\overline{X}$ that would lead you to reject H1 when $N = 12$, $\Sigma(X - \overline{X})^2 = 121$, $X$ is normally distributed, and the type I error is set at 10 percent.

27. Assume that the following are data on monthly sales and advertising, in thousands of dollars.

| Sales, Y | 110 | 106 | 120 | 130 | 126 | 122 | 121 | 103 | 98 | 80 | 97 | 112 |
|---|---|---|---|---|---|---|---|---|---|---|---|---|
| Adver., X | 5.2 | 5.3 | 6.0 | 6.3 | 5.7 | 4.8 | 4.2 | 3.0 | 2.9 | 2.7 | 3.2 | 4.0 |

Calculate the relationship between sales and advertising using the

linear regression $Y = a + bX$, the coefficient of determination, the
$F$-statistic, the 95 percent confidence interval for sales when advertising is $X = 5.5$, and determine whether the $b$-coefficient is
statistically different from zero.

28. Assume that an alternative independent variable for the regression
    in problem 27 is $P$, the price of the product. If the coefficient of
    determination for the regression equation $Y = a - bP$ is $R^2 = 0.803$, would you use $X$ or $P$ to project future sales? Explain why.

29. Use the regression equation calculated in problem 27 to calculate
    the level of sales if advertising is 7.0.

30. You have gathered the following data relating the number of workers,
    $X$, in your plant and the kilowatt hours of electricity, $E$, used to
    the output, $Y$, produced.

| Y | 112.6 | 87.6 | 150.3 | 131.2 | 94.0 | 110.0 | 144.7 | 167.4 | 120.6 | 155.9 | 134.1 | 127.8 |
|---|-------|------|-------|-------|------|-------|-------|-------|-------|-------|-------|-------|
| X | 12 | 9 | 17 | 14 | 10 | 12 | 15 | 20 | 14 | 18 | 14 | 15 |
| E | 110.6 | 111.2 | 144.7 | 131.1 | 101.8 | 116.0 | 137.2 | 162.6 | 104.0 | 151.2 | 126.2 | 119.3 |

a. Calculate the simple regressions $Y = a + bX$, $Y = c + dE$, and
   $X = e + fE$. Calculate the coefficient of determination and the
   $F$-statistic, and determine whether the slope coefficient is statistically different from zero for each regression. Which of the first
   two regressions fits the data better? Explain why.
b. Calculate the multiple regression $Y = a + bX + cX^2$ and its
   coefficient of determination. Does this multiple regression fit the
   data better than $Y = a + bX$? Explain why.
c. Calculate the multiple regression $Y = a + bX + cE$. Does this
   regression fit the data better than $Y = a + bX$, $Y = c + dE$, or
   $Y = a + bX + cX^2$? Explain why.
d. Do you have any evidence that there is a multicollinearity problem
   in the regression in part (c)? Explain.
e. Calculate the Durbin-Watson statistic for the regression in part
   (c). Is it likely that there is serial correlation?

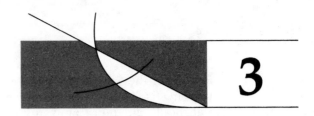

# Demand

Few, if any, factors are more important to a firm's success than the demand for its product, the quantity consumers are willing to buy at a given market price. If consumers will not buy enough of its product at a profitable price, even a well-managed firm with efficient production facilities will ultimately fail. Marketing involves the management of those factors that the firm can manipulate to influence demand and to create new products. Efficient marketing includes analyzing cost and profit changes resulting from utilizing one market strategy rather than its alternatives.

Demand can be the most difficult element of the profit function to estimate empirically. The direction of consumers' responses to changes in the firm's price or the price of a competitor's product can be predicted with great confidence — if everything else is held constant. However, everything else rarely stays constant as consumers and competitors alike adapt to the ever-changing circumstances in which they find themselves. Moreover, it is often prohibitively expensive to obtain all of the data that might permit management to estimate more precisely the level of demand. Data for estimating demand may be available from trade association or government reports in such an aggregated form or with such a long time lapse that intervening market changes may reduce their usefulness. Even though economists and business managers know a great deal about the direction and general nature of consumer responses to changes in prices, incomes, and other demand function variables, it can be difficult to make specific predictions for the next planning period, much less for several planning periods into the future.

Economists divide firms into two types, price-taker firms and price-searcher firms, when applying the results of demand studies. Only the price-searcher firm has the ability to influence prices.

A price-taker firm cannot influence the market price of its product. Its management is primarily interested in the level of the overall industry's demand. In general, the higher the level of industry demand, the greater the market price and the higher the output and profits of the price-taker firm. A price-taker firm generally has a profit incentive to join with other firms in the industry's trade association to use advertising, product quality standards, or other industry-wide strategies to increase consumers' demand. A management that refuses to pay its share of the industry's marketing campaign would enjoy the benefits without the costs. To eliminate this free rider problem, the trade association may enlist government support to force participation by all firms in its marketing efforts.

The management of a price-searcher firm, on the other hand, can influence the market price for its product. It is primarily interested in the demand for its own product. If the price-searcher firm produces a product that is differentiated from those of its competitors, its management must devise a wide range of advertising and other marketing strategies as means for profitably increasing the demand for its product. It must also set the price for its product, after evaluating the probable responses of its competitors to alternative prices that the firm could adopt.

The first two sections of this chapter focus on the direction and general nature of consumer responses to changes in the several major variables in the demand function. The demand curve, covered in the first two sections, is a function relating the maximum quantity of a good or service consumers are willing to purchase to its market price. All other factors affecting the consumer's decisions are held constant so that the effect of price changes on the quantity purchased can be isolated and measured. A change in demand occurs when something increases or decreases other than the firm's price and the quantity that is purchased at its market price. The prices of other products, consumer incomes, and advertising can influence the maximum quantity consumers are willing to purchase at a given price and thus change demand.

Sections 3.3 through 3.5 are concerned with using elasticities to measure consumer responses to changes in prices, incomes, and advertising expenditures. Section 3.6 discusses using elasticities to prepare sales forecasts. The chapter concludes with a discussion of elasticity changes over time after a price change. A case is presented based on determining whether two goods are substitutes.

## 3.1 *Fundamental Demand Relationships*

This section discusses the demand curve, which expresses the empirical relationship between price and the quantity sold of a good or service. Several reasons for a shift in the demand curve, which results in a change in the quantity sold at a given price, are also discussed. They are changes in the prices of related goods, income, advertising, and price expectations.

*Definition of Demand.* The demand curve is a function relating the maximum quantity of a good or service consumers are willing to purchase to its market price during a specified period of time. That is, the quantity demanded of a good or service is the maximum quantity that consumers are willing to purchase at a given price, holding constant everything except its price. For example, the prices of other goods and services, the level of consumer income, consumer preferences, and the level of advertising are held constant. The quantity demanded can be measured for individuals or for all persons buying the product. In the latter case, market demand at a given price is the sum of the quantity purchased by each consumer at that price. The quantity units may be expressed in terms of a time unit (such as pounds per week or bushels per year) or a stock of the product (such as 1,500 houses).

*The Downward Sloping Demand Curve.* As price increases, holding constant everything except its price, the quantity demanded of the good or service will decline. In other words, raise the price of a good and change nothing else, and consumers will purchase less of it. This inverse relationship between the price of a good and the quantity demanded is illustrated by demand curves $D$ and $D'$ in Figure 3.1. The downward sloping demand curves reflect this inverse relationship between price and quantity. This empirical relationship between price and quantity is referred to as the downward sloping demand curve. A movement along a demand curve, as when price increases from $P$ to $P''$ on demand curve $D'$, is referred to as a change in the quantity demanded of a good. It is not referred to as a change in demand. A change in demand, or in the quantity purchased at a given price, only occurs when something other than the price of the good changes, and the demand curve shifts to the right or left.

The inverse relationship between price and quantity is based on observations of consumer behavior under a wide range of market conditions. It applies equally well today as it did two hundred years ago. Yet, there are managers who choose to ignore this widely observed empirical relationship by claiming that price increases will have little or no impact on their sales volume. These managers believe that if their competitors were more "enlightened," they could all raise prices with

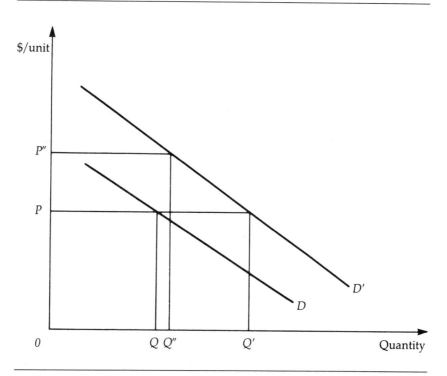

**Figure 3.1   The Demand Curve**

Demand curves *D* and *D'* are downward sloping, reflecting the empirical observation that price reductions result in a greater quantity sold. A price change from *P* to *P″* on *D'* illustrates movement along the demand curve and a change in the quantity demanded. Holding price constant at P and changing something affecting demand other than the good's price results in a shift in the demand curve itself (from *D* to *D'*, for example) and a change in consumer demand.

little or no loss in sales volume. Such thinking is unlikely to be supported by actual observations, which may be why their competitors are prone to hold prices down. The existence of substitutes for the good or service provides a reason to believe that price increases are likely to result, possibly after some period of time, in consumer responses leading to a lower demand for the product. When the price of a good or service goes up, consumers look for substitutes, and other business firms have profit incentives to make sure that consumers find substitutes in their products.

The downward sloping demand curve says nothing about how much less consumers will buy when price increases. That is an empirical matter that varies from product to product, and sometimes from one time period to the next. For some goods, consumers may be responsive to a price change because a wide range of substitute products is readily available. They may hardly respond to higher prices for other goods, at least immediately. But they will respond, and the direction — if not the magnitude — of their response is highly predictable. If price goes down, they will buy more; if price goes up, they will buy less.

What happens if something other than price changes? The inverse relationship between price and quantity remains unchanged, but the quantity purchased by consumers at each price may change. This is illustrated in Figure 3.1 by the demand curve's shifting from *D* to *D'* and the quantity purchased at price *P* rising from *Q* to *Q'*. The amount by which the quantity purchased changes is an empirical matter, with some quantity responses being relatively small and others being relatively large.

*Substitute Goods.* Consumer responses to a change in a good's price depend on the extent to which consumers are willing to substitute other goods for it. Goods X and Y are substitute goods when a change in the price of X results in an opposite change in the quantity of Y. There are one or more substitutes for every good. The substitute goods may not be intuitively obvious or immediately discernable, but at least one substitute always exists. The substitute good may be functionally unrelated to the good whose price is changing, as occurs when the consumer decides to purchase fewer ski lift tickets and substitute more drinks in the lodge when the price of ski lift tickets rises. Where substitutes are readily available, a price increase has a greater impact on the quantity demanded than if the substitutes are relatively imperfect. Where the consumer has few direct substitutes immediately available, as in the case of gasoline to power automobiles, and must seek entirely new goods or services to substitute for gasoline, the response to a price increase may be relatively slow. This is especially likely if the substitution process requires basic lifestyle changes, such as moving closer to work or using public transportation.

The relationship between the prices of substitute goods and the quantity purchased of the good under consideration can be illustrated using Figure 3.1. If the price of a substitute good increases and the price of the good under consideration remains unchanged at *P*, its demand will increase from *Q* to *Q'*. If the substitute goods relationship holds for all prices of the good under consideration, the demand curve shifts from *D* to *D'*.

*Independent Goods.* A change in the price of one good may result in no discernable response in the demand for another, in which case they are independent goods. A change in the price of an independent good does not shift the demand curve of the good under consideration.

If the demand for two goods has been independent in the past, they may not continue to be independent in the future. When the price of gasoline was relatively low and stable, gasoline and bicycles may have been independent goods in the sense that changes in their relative prices would not result in any discernible response in demand for the other good. Yet, when the price of gasoline rose sharply, the demand for bicycles increased. After the sharp increase in the price of gasoline, people came to view the bicycle as a suitable substitute for the automobile for some of their transportation.

*Complementary Goods.* Complementary goods generally have a functional relationship to the good under consideration. Classic examples of complementary goods are bread and butter, and gasoline and automobiles. If more of one good is purchased, the demand for its complementary good will increase as well, assuming the price of the complementary good is held constant. The downward sloping demand curve implies that when the price of a good increases, less of that good will be purchased and the demand curves for its complementary goods will shift to the left. This response is the opposite of that when an increase in the price of a substitute good occurs. If the price of a complementary good increases, so that consumers buy less of it and the good under consideration, the demand curve shifts from $D'$ to $D$ in Figure 3.1.

*Income Changes, Normal and Inferior Goods.* Income changes generally will shift the demand curve. If income increases and demand at price $P$ rises from $Q$ to $Q'$ in Figure 3.1, the good is a normal good. An increase in income, holding constant the price of the good, results in an increase in expenditures on the normal good. An increase in income of $1,000 per year could result in an increase in expenditures on a normal good of $22 per year. Examples of normal goods are consumer durables such as automobiles and home appliances. A good is an inferior good when an increase in income results in a decrease in demand, holding constant its price. Thus, when income increases, the demand curve shifts from $D'$ to $D$ in Figure 3.1. The quantity purchased at price $P$ will fall from $Q'$ to $Q$ as a result of the increase in income. Examples of inferior goods may be margarine and cheap clothing. When income goes up, people may prefer to consume butter and better quality, more attractive clothing. Inferior may or may not mean low in quality. Relatively low-quality goods may be normal goods in the sense that when income goes up, their demand goes up. A good is inferior only when its demand falls as a result of an increase in income, or rises when income falls.

Knowledge of the direction of consumer responses to income changes can be valuable when making marketing decisions. If the purchasing agent for a department store believes that incomes in the community are likely to decline because of layoffs at a large plant, the store's stocks of inferior goods should be increased and inventories of decidedly normal goods reduced. The store's management may advertise price reductions for its normal goods to reduce inventories quickly.

*Superior Goods.* A superior good is a special type of normal good. Like all normal goods, consumer purchases of superior goods rise when income rises. However, superior goods have the additional property that an increase in income of $1,000 per year will result in an increase in expenditures on the good of more than $1,000. That is, an increase in income of $1,000 could result in an increase in expenditures on the superior good of $1,500. Since there is now $500 less income available to spend on all other goods, all other goods, taken as a group, must be inferior. Superior goods are rare, although the market for single-family homes in southern California in the late 1970s may have provided an example for at least some middle-class families. If the family's income rose enough so that by cutting back on its expenditures on other "less important" goods and services it could then afford to buy the home, the new home was thought to be a superior good.

*Real Income.* In times of significant inflation, an increase in income may not result in an increase in consumer purchasing power. If incomes rise by 8 percent and all prices rise by 8 percent as well, consumers have simply broken even as far as their purchasing power is concerned. Only if incomes rise faster than prices will consumers enjoy an increase in real income that will affect their purchases of various goods and services. Thus, for the purpose of estimating how consumers will respond to income changes, it is generally necessary to use real income rather than income measured in terms of current dollars. In general, real income is measured by dividing current dollar income by an appropriate price index, such as the Consumer Price Index.

*Role of Advertising in Shifting Demand.* For many consumer goods, the level of advertising and sales promotion expenditures is a more important determinant of sales than price, provided that the price is reasonably competitive with substitute goods. The downward sloping demand curve is observed for heavily advertised goods. However, sales may rise more in response to a 10 percent increase in advertising expenditures than in response to a 10 percent decrease in price. Thus, it can be more profitable to stimulate sales by increasing advertising than by reducing prices. An example comparing price reductions to advertising increases as a means of reducing inventories is given in section 3.6. A further concern is that price increases following price reductions may meet with much more consumer resistance and lower sales than would result from an equivalent reduction in advertising expenditures.

One objective of advertising is to provide information to consumers about the characteristics and uses of the good, where it is sold, and its price and credit terms. Advertising makes the market function more efficiently by increasing competition and providing information that would be more costly if each individual consumer attempted to gather it without access to advertising. That is, some advertising serves the purpose of reducing transaction costs that would otherwise have to be incurred by the consumer. A second objective is to modify consumer preferences. Advertising attempts to influence consumer preferences so that the advertised good will be substituted for other goods. For example, advertising succeeded in selling laundry detergents by convincing consumers that they had to have a brighter, whiter wash than soap could produce. Advertising also attempts to convince people that they should use more of a product and that they should buy new items sooner rather than later.

In addition to direct advertising aimed at preference modification, there is indirect preference modification through lifestyle portrayals in the media. Examples are the middle-class, urban consumer lifestyle portrayed on television and the lifestyle-promoting stories in special interest magazines that attract advertising support from the industry.

Because it is potentially so profitable, most advertising is aimed at preference modification that shifts the demand curve to the right rather than at providing information to consumers about prices and product qualities.

*Price Expectations.* In periods of relatively rapid price inflation or deflation, consumers may behave in ways that appear inconsistent with a downward sloping demand curve. When there is a price increase, consumers may increase their purchases of the good because they believe that its price may rise further in the future. This increase in purchases is not the result of a movement along the demand curve; rather, the change in consumer expectations regarding future prices has shifted the demand curve itself. This kind of consumer behavior is most likely to be observed with respect to durable goods and goods that can be stored at low cost. Thus, consumer expectations of future price changes are held constant when the price of a good is changed. Advertising can influence consumer expectations about future price changes, as when a price rebate program is advertised as ending on a specified date. However, the information and mental processes used by consumers in forming their price expectations are not entirely understood. In general, it is believed that current price expectations are based on past changes in prices, with more recent price changes being given a greater weight in the mental process of arriving at a future price expectation.

## 3.2  *The Demand Function*

The downward sloping demand curve predicts the direction of consumer responses to a change in the price of a good or service. The magnitude of consumer responses to price, advertising or other marketing policies is needed for management to make profitable decisions. Management also must predict consumer responses to the prices and advertising programs of other firms and trends in consumer purchasing power or population in the company's market area. The first step in measuring the magnitude of these responses is to estimate the demand function.

*The Demand Function.* The demand function is an empirically derived relationship between the quantity demanded $Q_x$ and its price $P_x$; the prices of related goods — $P_y$, a substitute good, and $P_z$, a complementary good; consumer income $I$; the level of advertising expenditures $A$; and any other relevant independent variables. In functional notation, the demand function is

$$Q_x = F(P_x; P_y, P_z, I, A, \ldots) \tag{3.1}$$

*Linear Demand Function.* A linear demand function is

$$Q_x = 200 - 3P_x + 4P_y - 7P_z + 2I + 5A$$

where $I$ and $A$ are measured in thousands of dollars. This demand curve is downward sloping because the coefficient of $P_x$ is negative. The positive coefficient for $P_y$ implies that $X$ and $Y$ are substitutes because an increase in the price of $Y$ will result in an increase in purchases of $X$ as consumers substitute $X$ for $Y$. Goods $X$ and $Z$ are complements because an increase in the price of $Z$ will result in a decrease in demand for $Z$, which reduces the quantity purchased of $X$ because $X$ and $Z$ are used together. $X$ is a normal good because an increase in consumer incomes will result in an increase in the purchases of $X$. The positive coefficient for the advertising expenditures variable means that consumer preferences for the good are influenced by advertising. Studying the signs of the coefficients of the variables in a linear demand function provides information about the nature of the product. Since multicollinearity may result in coefficients that are unreliable estimates of their true values, testing for multicollinearity is necessary before demand function coefficients can be used to study the nature of the product.

*The Power Function As a Demand Function.* A linear demand function may not provide the best statistical fit of the data. The computer programs for performing multiple regression studies permit experimentation with a wide range of functional forms for the demand function. One form that may provide better fits of the data is the power function $Q_x = AP_x^{-b}P_y^c$, which is converted for statistical estimation into its log-linear form $\ln Q_x = \ln A - b\ln P_x + c\ln P_y$, where the symbol "ln" stands for the natural (base $e$) logarithm. Another form is the polynomial $Q_x = a - bP_x + cP_y - dP_y^2$. Whether $X$ and $Y$ are complementary depends on the relative magnitudes of coefficients $c$ and $d$ and on the value of the price of $Y$.

*Estimating the Demand Function.* The usual procedure in a demand study is to gather data on as many of the variables that might influence the demand for the product as the budget will allow. Multiple regression is then used to estimate the coefficients and calculate measures of statistical significance for several functional forms for the demand equation. Variables that are not statistically significant are removed from the demand equations and the coefficients estimated again until all variables in each demand equation are significant. The several demand equations are ranked by the magnitude of their respective coefficients of determination since $R^2$ measures the extent to which the demand equation fits the data. Each demand equation is checked to see if, for the range of data used to estimate the equations, the price coefficients yield estimates of the quantity demanded that are consistent with a downward sloping demand curve. The price coefficients of substitute goods are checked to determine if demand increases when the price of a substitute good rises.

Because of multicollinearity or the nature of the sample, a demand function with one or more implications that do not fit the analyst's beliefs about the nature of the product or its market may provide an excellent fit of the data. After the analyst's beliefs are double checked, these demand functions are either subjected to additional analysis or eliminated from the study. Two or more demand equations may provide an acceptably good fit of the data and coefficients that are statistically significant and reasonable with respect to their implications. To hold down the costs of preparing demand forecasts, the demand function requiring the least data to estimate is often the one that is chosen. Alternatively, two or more of the demand equations may be used in preparing the statistical basis for marketing policy recommendations. Chapter 4 is devoted to procedures for estimating and evaluating demand functions.

The demand function is part of the information required for determining the firm's profit-maximizing marketing and production plans. These demand functions need not be based on sophisticated statistical analyses. They may be based on the manager's intuitive judgment and "feel" for the market. But regardless of how the price and sales projections for future planning periods are developed, such projections are essential for managerial decision making. Demand functions form the basis for management's calculations of consumer responses to changes in prices, incomes, and other key variables.

## 3.3  *Price Elasticity*

The elasticity of demand measures the responsiveness of consumer purchases to a change in one of the independent variables in the demand function. It is independent of the units in which the quantities are measured. The same elasticity estimate can be used whether sales volumes are measured in gallons or barrels. For many goods, the elasticity of demand is relatively stable over time and among the various geographical areas where the product is marketed. This stability reduces the cost of preparing empirical estimates of the elasticity of demand since the estimates do not need to be prepared frequently or for all of the firm's marketing areas. When they are stable over time, elasticity estimates are particularly useful in preparing sales forecasts.

### 3.3.1  *The Elasticity of Demand*

The general formula for the elasticity of demand, $E$, is

$$E = (\% \text{ change in } Q)/(\% \text{ change in } X) \qquad \textbf{(3.2)}$$

All variables in the demand function except $X$ are held constant. The variable in the demand function which becomes $X$ in equation 3.2 depends on the decision to be made. For example, if management is interested in the responsiveness of gasoline sales to an increase in its price, price would become variable $X$ in equation 3.2. If gasoline sales fell by 5.7 percent when its price rose by 45.0 percent, the price elasticity of demand, $E_p$, was

$$E_p = -5.7\%/45.0\% = -0.127$$

The data for this calculation should be for a period of time when the other factors affecting gasoline demand were relatively constant; otherwise, the elasticity estimate would not be meaningful. Additional data on the other factors that have changed (for example, a drop in the purchasing power of consumer incomes) would be necessary to develop the demand function from which a better elasticity estimate could be calculated. An elasticity of demand this close to zero means that the quantity demanded of gasoline is unresponsive to price changes.

The arc-elasticity of demand can be calculated for any change in the independent variable. If the change is from $X_1$ to $X_2$, arc-elasticity is measured using the formula

$$E_x = (Q_2 - Q_1)X_1/(X_2 - X_1)Q_1 \qquad (3.3)$$

This formula generally yields a different elasticity value for an increase in variable $X$ from $X_1$ to $X_2$ than for a decrease from $X_2$ to $X_1$ because the base values for calculating the percentage changes are different. If the elasticity value is used with a change in $X$ in only one direction, this formula is applicable. If the arc-elasticity measure is to be the same for an increase or decrease in $X$, the average arc-elasticity is calculated using

$$E_x = (Q_2 - Q_1)(X_2 + X_1)/(Q_2 + Q_1)(X_2 - X_1) \qquad (3.4)$$

Use of equations 3.2, 3.3, or 3.4 assumes that the other independent variables in the demand function are held constant.

If $\Delta Q = Q_2 - Q_1$ and $\Delta X = X_2 - X_1$, equation 3.3 is

$$E_x = (\Delta Q/\Delta X)(X_1/Q_1)$$

As $\Delta X$ becomes smaller, $\Delta Q/\Delta X$ approaches the derivative $dQ/dX$ and in the limit as $\Delta X$ approaches zero is $dQ/dX$.[1] Thus, the elasticity of demand at a specific point on the demand function is

$$E = (dQ/dX)(X/Q) \qquad (3.5)$$

where the values of all independent variables except $X$ have been substituted into the demand function and incorporated into its constant term.[2]

### 3.3.2  *Calculating and Interpreting Price Elasticities*

The price elasticity of demand can be calculated using any of the three formulas in section 3.3.1. The formula to be used depends on the decision management is considering. For example, if the decision involves

---

[1]See section 2.2.2 for more on the relationship between $\Delta Q/\Delta X$ and the derivative $dQ/dX$.

[2]Alternatively, point-elasticity can be calculated using the partial derivative of the demand function, $\partial Q/\partial X$, and $E_X = (\partial Q/\partial X)(X/Q)$.

a small change in price, the point-elasticity formula in equation 3.5 would become

$$E_p = (dQ/dP)(P/Q) \tag{3.6}$$

The procedures for calculating the price elasticity of demand are illustrated in Example 3.1.

**EXAMPLE 3.1.**    The first step in calculating demand elasticities is to estimate the demand function. The demand function could include in its independent variables the price of the product ($P_x$), the prices of substitute and complementary goods ($P_y$ and $P_w$), consumer incomes ($I$), and advertising expenditures ($A$). Assume that the demand function is

$$Q_x = 50 - 22P_x + P_x^2 + 8P_y - 9P_w + 15I + 25A \tag{3.7}$$

This equation can be used to estimate elasticities associated with each of its independent variables.

To calculate the elasticity of demand, it is necessary to have values for each of the independent variables. These base values are those expected to exist prior to the change in the independent variable or variables under management's control, or which will change as a result of actions taken by the firm's competitors. The following base values are assumed: $P_x$ = \$4.00, $P_y$ = \$2.50, $P_w$ = \$3.00, $I$ = 10 (income is measured in thousands of dollars), and $A$ = 8 (advertising is measured in millions of dollars). Thus, the quantity demanded in the base period is

$$Q_x = 50 - 22(4.00) + (4.00)^2 + 8(2.50)$$
$$- 9(3.00) + 15(10) + 25(8) = 321 \text{ units} \tag{3.8}$$

If the range of observed prices for good $X$ was \$1 to \$9, equation 3.7 should not be used for calculating price elasticity at a price of \$25. That price would yield a positive price elasticity, which is not consistent with a downward sloping demand curve. If the values of the other independent variables are substituted into equation 3.7 and incorporated into the constant term, $dQ_x/dP_x$ and its value when $P_x$ = \$25 are

$$dQ_x/dP_x = -22 + 2P_x = -22 + 2(25) = +28$$

Since $Q_x$ and $P_x$ are always positive, a positive $dQ_x/dP_x$ means that $E_p$ is positive and the demand curve upward sloping. This inconsistency with the downward sloping demand curve is a manifestation of the general problems associated with extrapolations; however, its importance for marketing studies can be substantial. Policy changes may deliberately carry an independent variable beyond the range of the observations used to estimate the demand function. For example, management may wish to use the elasticity of advertising expenditures to calculate the effect on sales of a 200 percent increase in industry advertising expenditures. If this level of industry advertising expenditures has never been attained before, management may wish to temper its use of the elasticity estimate with its expert opinion judgement.[3]

The arc-elasticity of demand is calculated by specifying a price different from the base price while holding constant the other independent variables. If price rises to $5, the quantity demanded falls to 308 units, which is found by replacing the $4 with $5 in equation 3.8. The price arc-elasticity $E_p$, using equation 3.4, is $-0.186$:

$$E_p = (308 - 321)(5.00 + 4.00)/(5.00 - 4.00)(308 + 321)$$

$$E_p = (-13)(9)/(1)(629) = -.186 \qquad (3.9)$$

Calculating the point elasticity begins with substituting the base values of all independent variables except $P_x$ into the demand function.

$$Q_x = 50 - 22P_x + P_x^2 + 8(2.50) - 9(3.00) + 15(10) + 25(8)$$

$$Q_x = 393 - 22P_x + P_x^2$$

The next step is to calculate $dQ_x/dP_x$ and then use equation 3.6 and $P_x = \$4$ to calculate the point elasticity.

$$dQ_x/dP_x = -22 + 2P_x = -22 + 2(4.00) = -14$$

$$E_p = (-14)(4.00/321) = -56/321 = -0.174$$

Repeating this calculation for $P_x = \$5$ yields $E_p = -0.195$. The average of these two point elasticities is $-0.184$, which is very close to the average arc-elasticity calculated using equation 3.9.

*Inelastic Demand.* Demand is inelastic when the absolute value of $E_p$ is between 0 and 1. The absolute value is the unsigned value of the price elasticity, or 0.186 in equation 3.9. The terms *elastic* or *inelastic demand* always refer to the absolute value of the price elasticity. Demand

---

[3]See section 4.1 for a discussion of expert opinion forecasts.

is inelastic when the percentage change in price is greater than the resulting percentage change in the quantity demanded. When demand is inelastic, total sales revenues (*TR*) for the product go up when price is increased. Marginal revenue, *MR*, is the change in total revenue. Since *TR* increased when price went up, *MR* is positive for a price increase when demand is inelastic.

Inelastic demand: $P\uparrow$, $TR\uparrow$, and $MR > 0$ or $P\downarrow$, $TR\downarrow$, and $MR < 0$

(3.10)

**EXAMPLE 3.2.**   In example 3.1, when $P_x$ rose from \$4 to \$5, *TR* increased from \$4 $\times$ 321 units = \$1,284 to \$5 $\times$ 308 units = \$1,540. *MR* for this \$1 price increase is \$1,540 − \$1,284 = \$256. Similarly, if price declines from \$5 to \$4, *TR* would decline from \$1,540 to \$1,284, and *MR* would be −\$256.

*Elastic Demand.* Demand is elastic when the absolute value of $E_p$ is greater than 1. For an elastic demand, the percentage change in the quantity demanded is greater than the percentage change in price. A price increase is accompanied by a decrease in *TR*, and a price decrease by an increase in *TR*. Marginal revenue will be positive for a decline in price if demand is elastic. In symbol terms:

Elastic demand: $P\uparrow$, $TR\downarrow$, and $MR < 0$ or $P\downarrow$, $TR\uparrow$, and $MR > 0$

(3.11)

*Unitary Elasticity.* Demand is unitary elastic when $|E_p| = 1$, in which case an increase or decrease in price will leave *TR* unchanged. *MR* is zero when the elasticity of demand is unitary.

*Constant Elasticity Demand Function.* The log-linear form of the demand function yields point elasticities by inspection of the coefficients of the demand function. It is estimated by calculating the natural logarithms of the observations and then estimating the equation

$$\ln Q_x = a + b\ln P_x \qquad (3.12)$$

The coefficient of $\ln P_x$, $b$, is the price elasticity of demand. The log-linear demand function is derived from the power function $Q_x = aP_x^b$ and is a constant elasticity demand function. A small increase in the statistical fit of other forms of the demand function may not outweigh the convenience of the log-linear form when it comes to calculating elasticities.

### 3.3.3 *Reasons for Differing Elasticities*

The elasticity of demand need not remain constant as the price changes, although constant elasticity of demand functions often fit empirical data quite well. Nor is there any particular reason for demand to be elastic at low prices and then inelastic for higher prices, as is the case when the demand function is linear. The elasticity of demand for any good or service is an empirical matter. The three principal reasons for price elasticities differing among products are the availability of substitutes, whether the good is a necessity or luxury, and the percentage of the consumer's income spent on the good. These reasons are discussed in this section.

*Availability of Substitute Goods.* The most important reason for two goods having different price elasticities is generally the extent to which other goods can be substituted for the good under consideration as its price rises. As the price of a good increases, consumers purchase less of it because its price is now higher relative to the prices of all other goods. This is the response predicted by the downward sloping demand curve. This response is predicted regardless of substitution possibilities or whether demand is elastic or inelastic. However, if the price rise results in more of the substitute goods being purchased, the quantity demanded response will be greater. The change in the quantity demanded for a given percentage price change will now consist of the quantity reduction resulting from the higher price plus the additional reduction in quantity as consumers substitute other goods. With the percentage change in quantity greater for the given percentage change in price, the price elasticity of demand will be greater. Thus, more substitution opportunities mean that demand is more likely to be elastic.

Jojoba oil is a product whose demand is likely to be elastic if price decreases. It can be substituted for a wide range of oils and waxes ranging from relatively high-priced, low-volume sperm whale oil, carnauba wax, and beeswax to relatively low-priced, high-volume vegetable oils. This implies that as the price of jojoba oil declines, its demand will become more elastic, making jojoba cultivation more attractive than if its demand were likely to be inelastic. With an elastic demand, price declines resulting from greater production will be accompanied by increased industry revenues. With output increasing and total costs rising, increases in total revenues will be necessary if the industry is to be profitable at the lower price. Increases in industry revenues will be forthcoming if the demand for jojoba oil is elastic, although the increase in total revenue may not be great enough to maintain or increase profits for the typical firm.

There are virtually no substitutes for table salt; hence, its demand is likely to be inelastic with respect to price increases. An increase in price would increase the industry's total revenues. With price in the inelastic region of the demand curve, competition among the sellers of table salt keeps its price from rising until demand becomes elastic. Since table salt has few other uses, its demand is also likely to be inelastic with respect to price declines.

*Necessity or Luxury?* The second principal reason for demand elasticity differences results from the extent to which consumers view them as luxuries or necessities. Necessities, like small amounts of table salt, have relatively inelastic demands because consumers do not readily substitute other goods for them.

A good is not a necessity simply because it fulfills a particular biological requirement; there are many alternative ways to provide our bodies with food, water, shelter, and warmth. Goods and services are necessities relative to some particular lifestyle. Gasoline is a necessity if you live in the suburbs far enough from where you work and shop that you cannot walk and there is no public transportation. Gasoline is hardly a necessity if you live close to work and shopping, and public transportation is readily available. Thus, what constitutes a necessity is subject to change. Consumers do not change their basic lifestyles readily. However, over a period of time, their lifestyles may change in response to rising prices for goods that are necessities in their current lifestyles. If the price of gasoline and automobiles becomes high enough relative to the family's income, gas and cars may be converted from necessities to luxuries by the family's moving from a distant suburb to the city. Thus, the demand for gasoline, automobiles, and other goods associated with suburban living may become more elastic over time in response to price increases.

Luxuries generally have relatively elastic demands because there are many alternative ways to satisfy the desire for status, novelty, and avoiding the blues. Advertisers of luxury goods try to overcome the existence of many substitutes by creating and encouraging lifestyles that incorporate their product as an essential element. Once a good or service is incorporated into the consumer's lifestyle, it becomes more of a necessity, and its demand becomes more inelastic. This approach to making demand more inelastic is in addition to the advertiser's attempts to shift the demand curve to the right by getting consumers to prefer more of the good at any given price. Making demand more inelastic and shifting the demand curve to the right generally make the good more profitable.

*Percentage of Income Spent on the Good.* The elasticity of demand also depends on the percentage of the consumer's income spent on the good. If the consumer spends only a tiny percentage of his or her income on the good, demand tends to be inelastic. This is another reason why table salt has an inelastic demand. Spending 10 percent more for a good on which the consumer spends $1 per year is hardly worth spending much time seeking a substitute. Saving 10 cents per year is not worth more than one minute searching for a substitute if the consumer values his or her time at $6 per hour. A higher-income consumer will spend even less time and effort on shopping than a lower-income consumer. A consumer valuing his or her time at $12 per hour would not spend more than 30 seconds seeking a substitute, unless the consumer particularly enjoyed shopping and avoiding paying higher prices.

If the product requires a relatively large proportion of the consumer's income, demand is more likely to be elastic. The consumer will shop more extensively for high-priced items than for low-priced ones. Most people do not rush into a car dealer's showroom, checkbook in hand, and say "I'll take that one!" They shop carefully for big-ticket items and are more likely to evaluate thoughtfully the range of available substitute goods before making a purchase, making their demand relatively elastic because greater savings can be earned from an hour of shopping time.

## 3.4  *Income Elasticity*

This section provides the formulas for calculating income elasticity. The relationship between income elasticity and normal and inferior goods is also discussed.

*Income Elasticity Formulas.* The income elasticity of demand measures the responses of consumers to changes in their income.

$$E_I = (\% \text{ change in quantity})/(\% \text{ change in income})$$

The formulas for calculating the point and average income arc-elasticity of demand are

$$E_I = (dQ/dI)(I/Q) \tag{3.13}$$

$$E_I = (Q_2 - Q_1)(I_2 + I_1)/(Q_2 + Q_1)(I_2 - I_1) \tag{3.14}$$

**EXAMPLE 3.3.** Using the demand function in equation 3.7, the average income arc-elasticity for an increase in income from the base value of $10,000 per year ($I = 10$) to $12,000 per year ($I = 12$) is $+0.49$.

First calculate the quantity demanded at the higher income level with the other independent variables at their base values. For $I = 12$, $Q_x = 351$ units. At $I = 10$, $Q_x$ was 321 units. Substituting these values into equation 3.14 yields

$$E_I = (351 - 321)(12 + 10)/(351 + 321)(12 - 10) = +0.49$$

To calculate the income point-elasticity, first find the demand function after substituting in the base values of all independent variables except income.

$$Q_x = 50 - 22(4) + 4^2 + 8(2.50) - 9(3.00) + 15I + 25(8)$$
$$Q_x = 171 + 15I$$

Since $dQ/dI = 15$, point income elasticity at $I = 10$ is

$$E_I = 15(10/321) = +0.47$$

*Normal Goods.* Income elasticity can be used to determine if the product is a normal or inferior good. For a normal good, an increase in income results in a shift to the right in the demand curve and an increase in the quantity purchased at each price. Income elasticity is positive for a normal good since both the percentage change in quantity and the percentage change in income are in the same direction. Normal goods typically include consumer durables, better quality or more stylish personal items such as clothing or jewelry, and luxuries such as foreign vacations. At their existing income level, virtually all consumers are purchasing the basic goods and services required for their current lifestyle. When income rises, they can save a portion of the increase in the form of financial assets or acquire more goods and services. The goods they generally acquire will be those that improve the quality of their lives. These goods and services are normal goods relative to the consumer's lifestyle.

Normal goods can be divided into two groups depending upon the value of their income elasticity. A normal good with an income elasticity between zero and one is a necessity. A necessity has a less than one percent increase in the quantity purchased when income rises by one percent. Luxury goods have income elasticities greater than one. Since consumers generally distribute an increase in income among several or many goods and services, some may be necessities and others luxuries. Luxury goods should not be confused with superior goods. Both are special types of normal goods. A superior good is a luxury good, but a luxury good need not be superior. A good is superior if the dollar amount of the increase in expenditures on the good is greater than the increase in income. Many consumer durables are luxury goods. Superior goods are rare.

*Inferior Goods.* Less of an inferior good is consumed when income rises, and more of it is consumed when income declines. Income elasticity is negative for an inferior good because the percentage changes in quantity and income are in opposite directions. Because the sign of the income elasticity determines whether the product is an inferior good, its absolute value is never used. Inferior goods are not necessarily low in quality or poorly designed. With an increase in income, a middle-income man may switch his purchases from ordinary suits and fabrics at the local department store to the more stylish suits and fabrics available at a specialty shop. The ordinary suits and fabrics are inferior goods for him. Yet those same suits may be a normal good for a man at a lower income level with the same increase in income. The lower-income man might have been going to work in discount store sport coats and slacks, which then become his inferior good.

*Measuring Income.* In order to measure income elasticity, it is necessary to determine how the income variable in the demand function is to be measured. One measure is actual or estimated income in the current time period. This measure is applicable to most services and nondurable goods. For big-ticket durable goods like a house or car purchased on credit, expected future income may be a better measure. Future income will be used to make the principal and interest payments on the debt. One method of computing expected future income is to assume that the consumer will project past income trends in income into the future. The past trend in income may be calculated using unweighted past income or past incomes weighted using the distributed lag model.[4]

## 3.5 *Cross-Elasticity*

The cross-elasticity of demand measures the responsiveness of the quantity demanded of one good to changes in the price of another. The point and arc cross-elasticities are

$$E_{xy} = (dQ_x/dP_y)(P_y/Q_x) \tag{3.15}$$

$$E_{xy} = (Q_{x2} - Q_{x1})(P_{y2} + P_{y1})/(Q_{x2} + Q_{x1})(P_{y2} - P_{y1}) \tag{3.16}$$

---

[4]See section 4.6.2 for a discussion of the distributed lag model.

The $xy$ subscript denotes that there are two goods, $x$ and $y$, with good $y$ being the one whose price has changed. The sign of $E_{xy}$ is essential for determining whether good $y$ is a substitute or a complement to good $x$.

*Independent Goods.* If $E_{xy} = 0$, goods $x$ and $y$ are independent. Good $y$ should not be included in the demand function for good $x$.

*Substitute Goods.* When $E_{xy}$ is positive, the two goods are substitutes. When the price of $y$ rises, consumers purchase less of good $y$ and substitute the relatively cheaper good $x$ for some of the good $y$ that they are not consuming because of its higher relative price. This does not mean that consumers are spending on good $x$ the entire amount of money saved by reducing their purchases of $y$. They generally substitute more than one good for $y$ when its price goes up. If the demand for $y$ is inelastic, so that total expenditures on $y$ rise when its price goes up, both the net increase in expenditures on $y$ and the increased expenditures on its substitute $x$ are financed through a reduction in expenditures on other goods. Thus, all other goods, taken as a group, must be complementary with respect to good $y$.

*Complementary Goods.* Consider now another good, $w$. An increase in the quantity demanded of good $w$ when its price falls will result in an increase in the demand for its complements. The sign of $E_{xw}$ will be negative because $Q_x$ and $P_w$ change in opposite directions. Consumers use goods $x$ and $w$ together for technological or lifestyle reasons. For example, if the price of bread goes up, consumers will buy less bread and less butter, since bread and butter are used together in one of the major uses for bread: toast.[5] If the price of ski lift tickets goes up, people go downhill skiing less. The demand for ski lodge accommodations should go down if ski lift tickets and ski lodge accommodations are complementary. Of course, people may simply ski less and spend more time in the lodge's lounges or engage in more cross-country skiing, in which case the demand for ski lodge accommodations would be independent of the price of ski lift tickets and the cross-elasticity of demand would be zero.

**EXAMPLE 3.4.**    The demand function for good $x$ in equation 3.7 contains the prices of two other goods, $y$ and $w$. At the base values for $P_y$ and $P_w$, $Q_x = 321$ units. To calculate the cross-elasticity between

---

[5]To get this result, everything else is held constant. However, if consumers substitute potatoes for bread and drench their potatoes in butter, the demand for butter could rise even though the quantity of bread has fallen.

goods $x$ and $y$, first find the demand function after substituting in the base values of all independent variables except the price of $y$.

$$Q_x = 50 - 22(4) + 4^2 + 8P_y - 9(3.00) + 15(10) + 25(8)$$
$$Q_x = 301 + 8P_y$$

Since $dQ_x/dP_y = +8$, point cross-elasticity at $P_y = \$2.50$ is

$$E_{xy} = (+8)(2.50/321) = +0.062$$

Since $E_{xy} > 0$, goods $x$ and $y$ are substitutes. Substituting the base values of all independent variables except the price of $w$ into the demand function yields

$$Q_x = 50 - 22(4) + 4^2 + 8(2.5) - 9P_w + 15(10) + 25(8)$$
$$Q_x = 348 - 9P_w$$

Since $dQ_x/dP_w = -9$, point cross-elasticity at $P_w = \$3.00$ is

$$E_{xw} = (-9)(3.00/321) = -0.084$$

Since $E_{xw} < 0$, goods $x$ and $w$ are complements.

If the price of $y$ increases to \$3.00 from \$2.50, the arc-cross-elasticity, $E_{xy}$, is found by calculating the quantity of $x$ when $P_y = \$3.00$ and then substituting the relevant prices and quantities into equation 3.16:

$$Q_x = 301 + 8(3.00) = 325 \text{ units}$$
$$E_{xy} = (325 - 321)(3 + 2.5)/(3 - 2.5)(325 + 321) = +0.068$$

As before, $x$ and $y$ are substitutes since $E_{xy} > 0$. If the price of good $w$ falls from \$3.00 to \$2.00,

$$Q_x = 348 - 9(2.00) = 330$$
$$E_{xw} = (330 - 321)(2 + 3)/(2 - 3)(330 + 321) = -0.069$$

Goods $x$ and $w$ are complements over this price range.

## 3.6 *Using Elasticities in Sales Forecasts*

This section provides an example of how to calculate the percentage change in a firm's sales volume ($Q$) if two independent variables in its demand function are changed simultaneously. The firm has a larger inventory of its product than it wishes to hold. To clear out this excess inventory, its policy alternatives are to reduce its price, increase its advertising, or implement both policies simultaneously. Management has estimates of the demand elasticities for the product.

*Calculating the Percentage Change in Quantity.* The elasticity of demand can be used to estimate the change in the quantity purchased by consumers resulting from a given change in an independent variable. Equation 3.2 can be rewritten as

$$(\% \text{ change in } Q) = E \times (\% \text{ change in } X) \qquad (3.17)$$

If the independent variable is price, the signed value of $E_p$, and not its absolute value, is used in equation 3.17. The net effect of changing two independent variables is calculated by adding the two percentage changes in quantity.

$$(\% \text{ change in } Q) = [E_{X1} \times (\% \text{ change in } X1)] + (E_{X2} \times (\% \text{ change in } X2)$$

$$(3.18)$$

where $X1$ (price) is one independent variable and $X2$ (advertising) is another.

*Reducing Price by 10 Percent.* Assume that the present quantity demanded is 10,000 units per week and the price elasticity of demand is $-0.92$. If management is considering a 10 percent price reduction to reduce excess inventories, its sales gain, using equation 3.17, is (% change in $Q$) $= (-0.92)(-10\%) = +9.2\%$. A 10 percent price reduction would increase sales by 10,000 times 0.092 or 920 units per week. If the excess inventory is 2,000 units, reducing prices by 10% for 2.17 weeks will work off the excess inventory. Since demand is inelastic, total revenue will decline during the clearance sale period.

*Increasing Advertising by 10 Percent.* Assume that the advertising elasticity of demand is $+0.38$. Assume further that advertising expenditures are measured in thousands of dollars per week and present advertising expenditures are $10,000 per week. A 10 percent increase in advertising expenditures would increase sales of the company's product by $(+0.38)(+10\%) = +3.8\%$, or 380 units per week.

*Reducing Price and Increasing Advertising by 10 Percent.* A 10 percent reduction in the price of the product when combined with a

10 percent increase in advertising expenditures would increase sales by 9.2% + 3.8% = 13% or 1,300 units per week.

*Determining the Cost-Minimizing Method for Reducing the Inventory.* Management can determine whether it incurs lower cost to reduce its inventory using a price reduction or an increase in advertising. If its product sells for $10 per unit, a 10 percent price reduction would reduce revenues by $1 on every unit sold during the 2.17 week inventory reduction period. Total sales volume for the 2.17 weeks would be 10,920 units per week times 2.17 weeks = 23,696 units. Since revenues fall by $1 per unit during the price reduction period, the total cost to the company would be $23,696. If advertising expenditures are increased by 10 percent, or $1,000 per week, demand rises by 380 units per week if prices remain the same. Working off the 2,000-unit excess inventory would require 2,000/380 or 5.26 weeks. At $1,000 per week in additional advertising expenditures, the total cost to the company would be $5,260.

Using a 10 percent price reduction and a 10 percent increase in advertising expenditures increases sales by 1,300 units per week. The inventory would be worked off in 2,000/1,300 = 1.54 weeks. Total sales during this period would be 11,300 units per week for 1.54 weeks or 17,402 units. The $1 price reduction would cost $17,402. In addition, advertising expenditures would rise by $1,000 per week for 1.54 weeks or $1,540. The total cost of clearing the inventory in this manner is $17,402 + $1,540 = $18,942. This alternative is less expensive than the 10 percent price reduction ($23,696), but it is substantially more expensive than using greater advertising expenditures ($5,260).

## 3.7  *Elasticity Increases Over Time*

The downward sloping demand curve predicts that a change in the price of a good will result in a change in the opposite direction of its quantity demanded, holding constant everything but price. An additional prediction can be made regarding the direction of the change over time in $E_p$ (price elasticity) after a change in the price of the good. The prediction is that the absolute value of $E_p$ will increase over time after a price change. There is less empirical evidence of the existence of systematic increases in price elasticity, primarily because elasticity changes are more difficult to observe directly.

Similar empirical relationships between time and the elasticity of demand may be observed for other independent variables in the demand function, particularly income and advertising expenditures. This trend toward a more elastic demand is not based on demand's being elastic or even becoming elastic over time. Demand is more elastic if the absolute value of $E_p$ increases from 0.15 to 0.40. Moreover, there is no specific statement regarding the rate at which elasticity increases. Consistent with empirical observations, elasticity will increase slowly at first, then increase more rapidly, and finally increase slowly as $|E_p|$ approaches its maximum value. Alternatively, $|E_p|$ may increase rapidly at first with the rate of increase tapering off to zero as $|E_p|$ approaches its maximum value. The precise temporal pattern of price elasticity increases is an empirical matter.

### 3.7.1  *Reasons for Increasing Elasticity Over Time*

Three principal factors are responsible for the empirical observations underlying the increased price elasticity over time. They are consumer habits, the time it takes for consumers to realize price has changed, and the extent to which the good is used with relatively expensive and long-lived, complementary durable goods. The first two factors dominate the pattern of elasticity increases when elasticity reaches its maximum value in a short period of time. Where complementary durable goods are involved, price elasticity may increase over a relatively long period of time, even over several years.

*Consumer Habits.*  Consumers form habits for a good reason. Making decisions about which goods to consume requires time and effort that could be used to yield the consumer more benefits. Once formed, consumption habits may not be particularly responsive to price changes. However, as the consumer's interests and lifestyle change, and as the consumer becomes aware of price differences, new habits are formed. If the discarding of old habits is in response to a price increase, $|E_p|$ will increase because of a fall in the quantity demanded at the new price. With different consumers discarding old habits at varying times, the elasticity of demand for the product will increase over time. Firms can influence the rate at which consumers drop old habits and the nature of their new habits through specially designed advertising programs.

*Becoming Aware of a Price Change.*  The second factor is the rate at which consumers become aware of a price change and respond to it. Obtaining information about market prices, which is a major component of the transaction costs associated with using the market, is not free. Sellers do not make it easy for consumers to find out about price increases, and their advertising tends to promote the various qualities and uses of the product. This practice is intended to reduce the rate at which consumers respond to the price increase and keep $|E_p|$ low as long as possible. Sellers generally advertise price decreases to increase consumer awareness and reduce the cost of making price comparisons. "Sales" are almost always well advertised. The elasticity for consumer goods increases faster when there is a price reduction than when there is an increase. If the product is purchased infrequently, some time may be required before a large percentage of consumers are aware of a price change, delaying the adjustments in their lifestyle and buying habits. If the item is purchased frequently, $|E_p|$ will increase faster.

*Complementary Durable Goods.* The third factor is whether the good is used with long-lived durable goods. The connection may be technological, as would be the case for gasoline and an automobile, or it may result from the consumer's lifestyle choices, as may be the case between gasoline and a home in the suburbs. Consumers do not immediately make a large response to a price change if the cost of changing their stock of complementary consumer durables is high. This cost is partly a result of the transaction costs associated with selling an old durable good and buying a new one, and partly the result of the costs associated with lifestyle changes, such as breaking old habits and friendships and forming new ones. As durable goods wear out or become technologically obsolete, consumers respond to the price change by acquiring new goods that use more or less of the good whose price has changed. The consumer may also make significant lifestyle adjustments that further increase or decrease its use.

### 3.7.2  *Graphical and Numerical Examples*

Supply and demand curves can be used to illustrate graphically the impact of a rising elasticity of demand on the product's price. Two numerical examples complete this section.

*Graphical Analysis.* The increasing price elasticity implies that the demand curve for the firm will become flatter over time. This is illustrated in Figure 3.2, where $D_1$ is its demand curve one week after increasing its price and $D_4$ is its demand curve four weeks later. Demand curve $D_4$ illustrates the type of consumer behavior implied by a rising $|E_p|$ because for the price change from $P_0$ to $P_1$, the quantity falls by a greater amount (to $Q_3$) with $D_4$ than with $D_1$ (only to $Q_1$). Both demand curves go through point $(Q_0, P_0)$ because the initial condition is the price and quantity prevailing at the time of the price change. After a new equilibrium price has been attained, a new price change will not result in a movement along $D_1$ or $D_4$, but rather along a new set of demand curves emanating from the new equilibrium price and quantity.

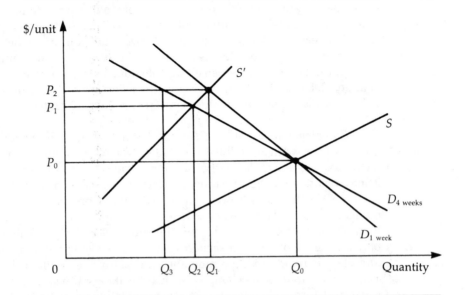

**Figure 3.2   Increasing Price Elasticity Over Time**
The initial equilibrium is at price $P_0$ and quantity $Q_0$. The supply curve shifts up to $S'$, leading to a price of $P_2$ in 1 week. The increase in the elasticity of demand over time is reflected in the shift of the demand curve to $D_{4 \text{ weeks}}$ and a decline in the market price to $P_1$ from its $P_2$ level 1 week after the supply curve shift.

**EXAMPLE 3.5.**   Assume that prices $P_0$, $P_1$, and $P_2$ in Figure 3.2 are \$10, \$12, and \$11.50, respectively, and that quantities $Q_0$, $Q_1$, and $Q_2$ are 120, 105, and 100, respectively. Using equation 3.3, arc-elasticity from $P_0$ to $P_1$ and from $P_0$ to $P_2$ is

$$E_p = (105 - 120)(\$10)/(\$12 - \$10)(120) = -0.625$$

$$E_p = (100 - 120)(\$10)/(\$11.50 - \$10)(120) = -1.111$$

The absolute value of $E_p$ increased from 0.625 to 1.111 as consumers adapted their consumption patterns.

**EXAMPLE 3.6.**   An empirical demand curve can be tested for consistency with a rising $E_p$. Assume that the demand curve, where T is the time in weeks after a change in $P_x$, is the power function $Q_x = 2TP_x^{-T}P_y$. Applying the point-elasticity formula in equation 3.6 yields

$$\partial Q_x / \partial P_x = -2T^2 P_x^{-T-1}(P_y)$$
$$E_p = (-2T^2 P_x^{-T-1} P_y)(P_x / Q_x)$$

Substituting $Q_x$ into the last equation yields $E_p = -T$. If $T$ equals 1, $|E_p| = 1$; if $T$ equals 2, $|E_p|$ is 2; and so on. Thus, $|E_p|$ increases over time.

## 3.8 *Summary*

The demand curve is a function relating the maximum quantity of a good or service consumers are willing to purchase to its market price. All other factors that affect the quantity consumers will purchase are held constant except price. The prices of substitute and complementary goods, income, consumer preferences and expectations of the future, and advertising expenditures are nonprice variables that are held constant. Changes in the quantity demanded occur when the price changes and there is a movement from one point on the demand curve to another. A change in demand, or in the quantity purchased at a given price, occurs when something other than price changes and the demand curve shifts to the left or right. The demand curve is empirically observed to be downward sloping to the right. At a lower price consumers will buy more of the good, assuming everything else is held constant.

The definitions of substitute, complementary, and independent goods assume that everything except the price of good $X$ is held constant. If the price of good $X$ increases, the quantity of substitute goods purchased by consumers will increase, and consumers will buy less of good $X$. If the price of good $X$ rises, the quantity demanded of good $X$ and the quantity purchased of all goods complementary to good $X$ will fall. Changes in the price of good $X$ have no effect on the quantity purchased of goods independent of $X$.

Income elasticity is measured holding constant the price of the good and all factors other than income. If income increases and the quantity purchased of good $X$ decreases, it is an inferior good. If income increases and the quantity purchased of $X$ increases, it is a normal good. Normal good $X$ is superior if an increase in income of $1,000 results in an increase of more than $1,000 spent on $X$. All other goods, taken as a group, are inferior to $X$.

The elasticity of demand measures the responsiveness of consumers to a change in variable $X$ in the demand function. It is defined as (% change in $Q$)/(% change in $X$) where all variables in the demand function except $X$ are held constant. Arc-elasticity is calculated for a change from one value of $X$ to another. Point-elasticity is calculated using the derivative of the demand function with respect to X and applies to a very small change in X.

Since the demand curve is downward sloping, price elasticity is always negative. Demand is inelastic if the absolute value of $E_p$ is less than one. When demand is inelastic, total revenue will change in the same direction as the price change. The absolute value of $E_p$ is greater than one if demand is elastic. Total revenue changes in the opposite direction from the price change when demand is elastic. If income elasticity is negative, the good is inferior. If it is positive, the good is normal.

Cross-elasticity is used to determine empirically if one good is a substitute for, complement to, or independent of another good. If two goods are substitutes, their cross-elasticity will be positive, because the percentage change in the quantity of X and the percentage change in the price of Y have the same sign when the goods are substitutes. If the goods are independent, their cross-elasticity is zero because there is no change in the quantity of X when the price of Y changes. If two goods are complements, their cross-elasticity is negative, because an increase in the price of good X reduces its quantity demanded and the quantity purchased of its complement.

A sales forecast is prepared from elasticities using the formula (% change in Q) = $E \times$ (% change in X). If two independent variables are changed at the same time, the net effect on the percentage change in quantity is calculated by adding the two percentage changes.

The absolute value of the price elasticity of some goods increases over time. It takes time for consumers to find out about price changes, respond to them, and change their habits. Also, the quantities consumers buy of relatively expensive and long-lived durable goods do not immediately change when the price of a complementary good changes.

| CASE | 1 | Is Beer Beer, or Do Brand Names Count? |
|------|---|----------------------------------------|

This case is concerned with determining if the observed level of the cross-elasticity of demand is sufficiently great to conclude that two products are substitutes.

### The Assignment

You work for a large accounting firm as a management consultant for its clients. A major client is a national brewery selling a heavily advertised brand of premium beer. The client is negotiating a merger with a regional brewery that produces a low-priced beer. Its advertising is limited to point-of-sale posters and a few billboards. The Federal Trade Commission contends that the merger will substantially reduce competition in the market for beer and hence violate Section 7 of the Clayton Antitrust Act. You are to determine if the available data support the client's position that the merger will not lessen competition because consumers do not treat the two brands as substitutes. The client believes that there are two markets for beer, not one as the government contends, and competition will not be reduced in either the premium or low-priced beer markets by the merger.

## The Statistical Study

You obtained both companies' average prices for sales of canned beer in 54 cities for a 3-month period. The large brewery also provided its sales (in thousands of cases) in each of these markets. Canned beer constitutes about 85 percent of the large brewery's and 100 percent of the small brewery's direct sales to consumers in these cities. You fitted a regression equation to these data and the population of each city in the last census, $C$, and obtained the demand function

$$Q_L = 5{,}455 - 12.2P_L + 2.1P_S + 1.6C \qquad R^2 = 0.92$$
$$\quad\;\; (2.7) \quad\;\; (1.4) \quad (0.1)$$

where the subscript $L$ refers to the large brewery and $S$ to the small one. The number in parentheses is the standard error of the coefficient. With $R^2 = 0.92$, the regression equation explains 92 percent of the variation in sales among the 54 cities, which means that the regression equation provides an excellent fit of the data. If the average values of $P_L$ and $C$ are substituted into this demand function and $dQ_L/dP_S$ calculated, the result is $dQ_L/dP_S = +2.1$. This will yield a positive cross-elasticity and the conclusion that the two brands of beer are substitutes. However, the standard deviation of the slope coefficient of $P_S$ is 1.4, and the calculated $t$-statistic is $t = 2.1/1.4 = 1.5$. For a 95 percent confidence interval (5 percent type I error), the critical value of $t$ is $t^* = \pm 2.0$. Since $t < t^*$, the slope coefficient of $P_S$ is not significantly different from zero.

## Conclusions

Statistical analysis of the available data implies that the cross-elasticity of demand is likely to be zero. Since the coefficient of $P_S$ is not significantly different from zero, $dQ_L/dP_S$ and $E_{LS}$ are also likely to be zero. That is, changes in the small brewery's price have an insignificant effect on the large brewery's sales. Thus, on the basis of the observed market behavior of consumers, the two brands of beer are independent goods. Acquisition of the small brewery is unlikely to reduce competition in the markets for either premium or low-priced beer. The statistical evidence indicates that there is no violation of the Clayton Act since the two companies do not compete in the same market.

---

## Key Terms

| | | |
|---|---|---|
| arc-elasticity | elastic demand | point-elasticity |
| complementary goods | elasticity | price elasticity |
| cross-elasticity | income elasticity | price-searcher firm |
| demand curve | independent goods | price-taker firm |
| demand elasticity | inelastic demand | substitute goods |
| downward sloping | inferior goods | superior goods |
|   demand curve | normal goods | unitary elasticity |

## Review Questions

1. Define and then compare and contrast these terms: *quantity demanded* and *shift in demand; substitutes* and *complements; normal* and *inferior goods.*

2. How does the existence of substitutes contribute toward a downward sloping demand curve?

3. Define the term *demand function.*

4. Why should the signs of the coefficients of a statistically estimated demand function be checked to see if they are reasonable? What are the possible pitfalls with such a procedure?

5. Define the term *elasticity.* What is the difference between point elasticity and arc-elasticity?

6. Define the terms *elastic* and *inelastic demand.* What is the relationship between the elasticity of demand and the firm's total and marginal revenue when it changes its price?

7. Explain why a decrease in price, holding the other independent variables constant, will result in an increase in total revenue if demand is elastic.

8. What are the three factors that tend to make demand elastic?

9. If a new product can be substituted for an increasingly wide range of other goods as its price declines, why is it likely to have an elastic demand?

10. Explain why the price elasticity of demand for airline tickets to overseas locations is likely to increase slowly at first, then increase rapidly, and finally taper off to little change. Is the rate and pattern of the elasticity change likely to be different for a price increase than for a decrease? Explain why.

## Problems and Applications

1. Calculate arc-elasticity when price declines from $10 to $9 and sales rise from 24 to 36 units. Is demand elastic or inelastic?

2. If the demand function is $Q = 450 - 0.8P - 2.5P^2$, is demand elastic or inelastic when $P = \$10$?

3. Your company produces a unique product for which there are no close substitutes. Its price is presently $P = \$84$, and its demand function is $Q = 5Y^{0.25}/P^{0.5}$ where $Y$ is income in thousands of dollars and presently is $16,000. Explain why you would recommend a price increase.

4. The demand function is $Q = 200 - 4.2P + 0.05P^2 + 10I$ where $I$ is income in thousands of dollars. Calculate price elasticity when price is $25 and income is $12,000. Is demand elastic or inelastic? Why?

5. The demand function is $Q = 500 - 0.9P + 25I - 0.8I^2$ where $I$ is income in thousands of dollars. Calculate income elasticity when $P = \$80$ and income is $14,000. Is this a normal or inferior good? Why?

6. If the demand function is $Q_x = 20 - 3P_x - 5P_y + 2P_y^2 + 0.8I$, is $Y$ a substitute for or complement to $X$ if $P_x = \$1$, $P_y = \$2$, and $I = 10$? Explain why.

7. If the demand function is $Q_x = 10 - 5P_xP_y^{0.5} + P_y$, calculate the cross-elasticity if $P_x = \$2$ and $P_y = \$100$. Are $X$ and $Y$ substitutes or complements? Explain why.

8. Explain why a cross-elasticity of $+1.45$ implies that the two goods are substitutes. By how much will the demand for one product change (holding constant its price) if the other product's price goes down by 3.5 percent?

9. The boss is contemplating a 5 percent price increase and a 10 percent increase in advertising expenditures. If $E_p = -1.1$ and $E_A = +0.8$, is this likely to result in an increase in total revenues? Why?

10. If, in problem 9, $E_p = -1.8$, would your conclusion be different? Why? Would it be different if $E_p = -2.8$? Why?

11. Demand for one week is $Q = 80 - 4P$ and six weeks later it is $Q = 85 - 5P$. If $P$ rises from $5 to $6, is price elasticity increasing over time? Why?

12. You are the marketing manager of a firm producing two nondurable consumer goods. The demand curve for product $X$ has been estimated as $Q_x = 225 - 5P_x + 12A_x - 2P_y$ where $Q_x$ is sales in thousands of units per month, $P_x$ is the price of the product (presently $P_x = $25$), $A_x$ is advertising expenditures in units of $100,000 per month (presently $A_x = 10$, or $1.0 million spent on advertising), and $P_y$ is the price of product $Y$ (presently $P_y = $35$). This demand curve applies to the first month after a change in $P_x$. For the second month, the $-5$ coefficient on $P_x$ becomes $-6.4$. None of the other coefficients change. The demand curve for product $Y$ is $Q_y = 500 - 8P_y$, where $Q_y$ is sales of product $Y$ in thousands of units per month. Executive management is contemplating increasing $P_x$ by 5 percent.

   a. Calculate the price, advertising, and cross elasticity of demand for product $X$ one month and two months after $P_x$ is increased by 5 percent.

   b. Based on the two price elasticities, what is your prediction of the percentage change in sales in the first month and in the second month? Why are the percentage changes different?

   c. Holding constant $A_x$ and $P_y$ at their present levels, calculate total revenue per month before the price increase, during the first month after the price change, and during the second month after the price change. Why do the three total revenues differ?

   d. Calculate the dollar amount by which advertising must be increased in the second month to maintain total revenue of product $X$ at the level of the first month after the price change.

   e. If advertising expenditures are increased by $100,000 per month at the start of the second month, calculate the dollar amount by which $P_y$ must be decreased in the second month to maintain total revenue of product $X$ at the level of the first month after the price change. Calculate the impact of the price reduction for product $Y$ on its total revenue.

   f. Which approach, the one in (d) or in (e), results in the greatest net gain in total revenues from $X$ and $Y$ after taking into consideration the cost of increased advertising and the revenue losses for product $Y$?

# 4

# Demand
# Forecasting

Chapter 3 concentrated on the basic nature of consumer demand and the use of elasticities to measure consumer responses to changes in the independent variables in the demand function. This chapter extends the analysis in two ways. First, it considers fluctuations in demand that are beyond the control of the firm or industry. These fluctuations are attributed to seasonal shifts in demand curves, economic growth, the business cycle, and the product life cycle. Second, methods for estimating demand curves using the regression technique are discussed. The chapter concludes with two cases illustrating the use of demand forecasts.

*Time Series Data.* The emphasis in this chapter is on using time series data to estimate the demand curve and shifts in the demand curve because of systematic factors such as changes in the seasons or growth in the economy and in population. Time series data are used in empirical studies because businesses and government agencies routinely gather information on a monthly or quarterly basis. Data from several geographical areas or markets and types of consumers are often aggregated and reported as one statistic by government agencies, trade associations, or the firm's accountants. Thus, the analyst may only have time series data for estimating demand curves. In many cases, there is little variation in prices, consumer incomes, and other independent variables in the demand function among geographical areas or markets. Without variation in the data, there is nothing for regression analysis to explain and no way for the analyst to learn about the relationships among the variables being studied. The existence of more variation in the independent variables when time series are used often makes regression analysis an efficient technique for estimating demand functions.

*Alternatives to Time Series Data.* There are alternatives to the use of time series data. Cross-section data are gathered during a specified time period from a number of separate markets, such as cities. If the independent variables vary among a sufficiently large number of geographical areas and markets, the use of cross-section data becomes practical. The statistical technique used with cross-section data, as with time series data, is regression. Other sources of data are consumer surveys and various types of market experiments. These sources may yield either time series or cross-section data. Because they are relatively expensive, consumer surveys and market experiments are generally used only when other data sources are not available or do not yield satisfactory estimates of the demand function.

Time series data are generally available at relatively low cost from routinely prepared accounting, management, or government agency reports. Therefore, techniques for using regression analyses of time series data to estimate demand relationships are discussed in this chapter.

## 4.1 *Demand Forecasting*

Forecasting means making predictions about the future. Forecasts are based on the knowledge and experience of the individuals preparing them, and they are also based on data describing the past values of the variables that the forecaster believes to be relevant. How these data are utilized in providing the statistical basis for the forecast and how the forecaster utilizes his or her knowledge and experience when introducing unquantified, and often unquantifiable, factors into arriving at predictions about the future varies from person to person, and even from day to day for the same person. One of the most difficult tasks facing anyone joining an organization is obtaining an understanding of how management views the future and how its views change in response to changes in prices, costs, competitor actions, government policies, and consumer preferences. Moreover, two equally experienced and respected managers can use the same information to arrive at different predictions.

*The Limited Information Problem.* Much remains to be learned about how managers can consistently make good forecasts on the basis of limited information, sometimes inaccurate information, and rising costs for additional information. Managers must sort out from the available information what they believe is relevant. They must ignore some possibly relevant information and relationships because they lack the time or are unwilling to bear the costs of obtaining and analyzing the data. They must accept their ignorance of information that they could use in arriving at their forecasts if they knew of its existence or understood its importance. Experience and judgment must often be substituted for more information and sophisticated analytical methods. Forecasting is more an art than a science. If their job involves forecasts, managers must be willing to take personal risks and trust their judgment.

Demand forecasts are among the more difficult forecasts that managers make. For even a small business, there may be hundreds or thousands of customers whose purchases constitute the sales of the firm, and a much larger number of potential customers. Large firms may deal with millions of customers, with different regional biases, income levels, and preferences. A multinational firm must deal with customers of several different nationalities and with different languages and cultures. Since people are generally unwilling or unable to reveal their preferences directly, information about consumer behavior is obtained indirectly through observations of how people have behaved in the past. Because many of the factors influencing consumer behavior may not have been measured, or even be measurable, and because the set of factors that have not been measured may be changing, forecasts are subject to errors.

*Formal Structure of a Forecast.* Forecasts contain two terms — the predicted level of the variable being forecast plus an error term. If sales volume, $Q_{ft}$, is being forecast for time $t$, actual sales volume, $Q_{at}$, is

$$Q_{at} = Q_{ft} + e_t \qquad (4.1)$$

where $e_t$ is the forecast error. The forecast error $e_t$ is not known when the forecast is made. Managers may provide opinions or information about likely forecast errors. A marketing manager might present three sales forecasts: a most likely forecast, an optimistic forecast, and a pessimistic forecast. The most likely forecast is $Q_{ft}$ in equation 4.1. The optimistic forecast provides the marketing manager's views on the extent to which favorable market or economic conditions may increase sales above $Q_{ft}$ and yield a positive value for $e_t$. The probability that the optimistic forecast will be observed may also be included. The pessimistic forecast predicts the extent to which unfavorable market or economic conditions could yield a negative value for $e_t$.

*Types of Forecasts.* Demand forecasts generally are a blend of expert opinion and persistence forecasts. Expert opinion forecasts use the minds of the firm's managers and consultants to arrive at predictions of sales, prices, and other variables. Persistence forecasts use data and various statistical techniques to make predictions. One type of persistence forecast is a trend forecast, which includes predicting the same percentage growth rate as occurred last year, extrapolation of the time trend of the variable, and distributed lag forecasts (to be discussed in section 4.6). Most forecasts start with a persistence forecast, which is then modified by expert opinion to reflect unmeasurable and judgmental variables, relationships, and data not included in the trend forecast.

Expert opinion is based on many areas of knowledge. One basis for an expert opinion forecast is the experienced manager's knowledge of the business. Knowledge of economic theory provides another basis. The theory of consumer behavior provides a menu of factors to examine when preparing an expert opinion forecast. Some of those factors are not always quantifiable; others may provide little more guidance than advising the manager to prepare lists of substitute and complementary goods. A knowledge of elasticities can be invaluable in adjusting trend extrapolations. If a competitor's price was particularly low last year and the cross-elasticity of demand between the competitor's price and the firm's sales volume is known, the manager has more guidance in revising a percentage growth forecast than if he or she had no understanding of cross-elasticity or of how to interpret a statistical estimate of its value. The methods used to make persistence forecasts range from simple ratios to multiple-equation econometric models requiring a knowledge of economic theory, great expertise to construct, and sophisticated statistical techniques. A knowledge of economic theory will not ensure success, but it can come in handy when a difficult forecasting problem is encountered.

**EXAMPLE 4.1.**   The percentage growth rate is

$$\% \text{ change} = \frac{(\text{latest month} - \text{month earlier}) \times 100}{\text{month earlier}}$$

If the latest month's sales were 11,400 units and the month-earlier sales were 10,860, the change in sales in terms of percentage growth rate is $[(11,400 - 10,860) \times 100]/10,860 = 4.97\%$. Applying this percentage to the latest month's sales yields a persistence forecast of $11,400 + (11,400 \times 0.0497) = 11,967$ units for the next month. If the weather last month was particularly bad and a competitor had just introduced a new line, the marketing manager might increase the persistence forecast to 6 percent and recompute the forecast for next month to 12,084 units. The reasons for converting the persistence forecast into an expert opinion forecast should be explained in the memo containing the forecast. The manager may also include information on the likely magnitude of the error term, $e_t$. For example, the actual percentage changes in sales between the latest month and the next month for the last five years may have been quite variable. Thus, the forecast 6 percent increase in sales could be subject to an error of plus or minus 2 percent.

## 4.2 *Seasonal Shifts in Demand Curves*

Shifts in the demand curve may be caused by seasonal factors. Seasonal shifts are generally the result of weather, holidays, or customs. Observations of sales, price, wage, or other economic data spanning several years are referred to as a time series. Seasonal shifts in demand take place within each year in a recurring pattern. If the time series contains annual data, there are no seasonal variations. When management works with monthly or quarterly data, as is generally the case when preparing operating budgets and plans, reasonably predictable seasonal variations must be taken into consideration.

*Examples of Seasonal Shifts.* Weather-induced seasonal shifts occur in the fertilizer industry. Farmers primarily apply fertilizers to their fields at or near planting time and during the growing season. The result is a relatively high demand for fertilizer during the spring and summer months. During the fall, the demand curve for fertilizer shifts to the left because the crops no longer need fertilization. During the winter, fertilizer demand to apply to crops is low; however, fertilizer dealers and farmers are beginning to build up their inventories in anticipation of next spring's requirements. With the coming of warm weather, the annual cycle begins again. Because of weather-induced changes in crop requirements, changes in inventory policies resulting from interest rate changes, changes in the prices of agricultural products, or other factors, the exact amount of the shift in fertilizer demand varies from year to year. The accumulation of inventories by dealers and farmers reduces the amplitude of seasonal cycles in the fertilizer demand, but it does not completely eliminate seasonal shifts. Inventories are costly to hold, and manufacturers are unlikely to find it profitable to reduce their prices enough to compensate for these costs. Thus, seasonal fluctuations in demand persist because it is not profitable to adopt inventory policies eliminating them.

Seasonal fluctuations can be important in the sales of consumer goods. The demand for overcoats is lower in spring than in the fall. As the weather warms up, the demand curve for overcoats shifts to the left; and as cold weather approaches in the fall it begins its seasonal shift to the right. With the seasonal shift to the left in the demand curve, stores may offer price reductions to clear their inventories of unsold coats. These reduced prices result in a movement down the demand curve that has already shifted because of the seasonal change.

The seasonal shift in the demand curve is not changed by the price reduction, although the quantity of overcoats demanded by consumers in late spring is increased by the price reduction. If price changes also occur on a seasonal basis, both the price and sales volume time series must be seasonally adjusted before estimating the demand curve.

Holidays are another factor leading to seasonal shifts in demand curves. The seasonal pattern of sales at department stores before and after Christmas is an example. It is customary for most people to take their vacations during the summer. This leads to seasonal shifts to the right in the demand curves for gasoline and the services of motels and restaurants along major highways and in resort areas.

The common element in these examples is the regular annual recurrence of the shifts in response to factors that occur on a predictable basis. Managements build these regular seasonal fluctuations in demand into operating plans and take advantage of them when maximizing the firm's profits and wealth.

*Seasonally Adjusted Time Series.* Many economic time series are available on a seasonally adjusted basis. The government agencies collecting and publishing the data perform the adjustments and regularly report seasonally adjusted data. Where a government agency does not report seasonally adjusted data, the unadjusted data generally do not show statistically significant seasonal patterns.

Seasonal adjustment indices must be used with a healthy degree of skepticism. They may not be appropriate because of significant, identifiable forces modifying this year's seasonal pattern. A temporary change in the seasonal index to management's best estimate of its value may be all that is required in the case of unusual weather. In other cases, it may be necessary to recompute periodically the seasonal indices. In the case of a new product, the several years of data required to compute the seasonal adjustment indices may not be available. The seasonal adjustment indices for similar products may be used as preliminary indices. Management's expert opinion can change these indices until enough data are available to compute them.

## 4.3  *Economic Growth*

The demand for virtually all industrial products and services has shown a long-term growth trend since the end of World War II and in many cases since 1900. There have been years when demand has not grown because of a general economic recession. However, when viewed on a decade-to-decade basis, the demand for most products has grown steadily. This long-term growth trend has mostly been a result of population growth, general economic growth, and technological change.

*Population Growth and Rising Per Capita Incomes.* One source of economic growth has been population growth. More people means greater demand for a wide range of products. Population growth has been accompanied by economic growth and growth in the volume of goods and services. Prior to the 1970s, real output grew faster than population, leading to rising per capita incomes. Since most goods and services have a positive income elasticity of demand, rising incomes have reinforced the demand-increasing effects of population growth. Most consumers prefer to use rising incomes to finance increases in their purchases of goods and services, rather than to increase their leisure time by working less. This desire to consume more has been cultivated by business managements through their advertising expenditures.

*Technological Change.* A major source of growing incomes is technological change, which generally leads to a rising output per hour.

Technological change takes on several forms. New and improved products have provided substantial growth opportunities for managements seeking profitable investments. Better ways have been found to lower the cost of production and to economize on increasingly scarce factors. Substituting less costly for more expensive materials and methods generally requires the development of new equipment and substantial investments in new facilities. The lower production costs made possible by these new technologies permit income to rise without upward pressures on prices. Where this type of technological progress is particularly rapid, prices fall, further stimulating economic growth. With larger markets, it is possible to build larger production facilities to take advantage of the economies of mass production. Low-cost transportation systems also make larger but more widely spaced plants more profitable investments.

As the experience of the 1970s demonstrates, rising money incomes in the form of wage or profit increases do not necessarily translate into growing output. Unless the capability of producing more goods at competitive prices is present, rising money incomes fuel inflationary price increases. With the exception of products utilizing the extraordinarily rapid advances in solid-state electronics, technological progress and greater economies from larger production facilities were virtually non-existent throughout the 1970s. Output per hour of labor hardly increased, but people's expectations of rising incomes changed little, so wages and other costs continued to rise.

The lack of productivity growth during the 1970s partly resulted from unprecedentedly sharp increases in energy prices. Other factors contributing to the relatively slow growth in productivity included a rising cost of capital and growing investments in environmental protection facilities that do not increase labor productivity.

*Economic Growth and the Demand Function.* Long-term trends in market demand can be incorporated into the demand function $Q_T = a - bP_T$ relating output at time $T$ to its price $P$ by introducing a second independent variable, $T$, representing time.

$$Q_T = a - bP_T + cT = (a + cT) - bP_T \qquad (4.2)$$

Incorporating the effects of economic growth on demand in this fashion amounts to shifting the vertical intercept of the demand function upward by a fixed amount, $c$, each year if $T$ is measured in years. An alternative equation is

$$Q_T = a - bP_T + c(1 + G)^T \qquad (4.3)$$

The quantity demanded depends upon the price of the product in year $T$ and the growth rate, $G$. $T$ is the number of years since some base period. If 1945 is the base period when $T = 0$, 1980 is $T = 35$. The expression $(1 + G)^T$ is used when demand grows at an average percentage rate. An alternative is to assume exponential growth by replacing $c(1 + G)^T$ with $ce^{GT}$.

One or more of the general measures of economic growth can also be used as independent variables in the demand function. Gross national product (GNP), personal income, average hourly wages of manufacturing production workers, or some other monthly series could be used. Since these series are generally highly correlated with time, using $T$ as an independent variable is likely to yield regressions providing predictions close to those of regressions using GNP or personal income as an independent variable. In addition, using $T$ is generally cost effective because it is not necessary to wait until the government agency publishes its GNP or personal income estimates or to obtain predictions of their likely future levels from economists.

## 4.4  *The Business Cycle*

Business cycles consist of two phases, an expansion phase and a recession phase.

*The Expansion Phase.* In the expansion phase, incomes are growing, and both consumers and businesses are optimistic. Times are good, unemployment is relatively low, and industrial plants are operating at or near capacity. Consumers are willing to borrow to buy big-ticket items such as automobiles, household appliances, new homes, and expensive vacations. Managers are willing to invest in new facilities to expand their capacity or produce new products because current operations are profitable and consumer demand is growing relatively rapidly. The construction of new facilities adds to demand and consumer incomes, which further increases the demand for income-elastic products.

*The Recession Phase.* Unfortunately, the happy scenario just described does not continue forever. Rising credit demands ultimately push up interest rates and the cost of capital. Inventory accumulation and additional investments in plant and equipment become less attractive. Rising interest rates reduce consumer demand for goods financed using long-term credit. Monthly payments rise with the interest rate, and interest costs are often a major portion of the price paid by consumers. Consumer stocks of many durable goods have reached their desired level given the family's current lifestyle and expectations of future income growth. The result is reduced growth in consumer demand, and then demand's declining in many industries. The economy has now entered the recessionary phase during which consumer incomes are falling because of rising unemployment and the loss of overtime pay. Business profits are falling, as is the rate of capacity utilization. Managers and consumers become pessimistic about the future and are less willing to undertake major future commitments. Business managers become more averse to risk, preferring to make short-term financial investments rather than riskier investments in plant and equipment.

During recessions, various government programs reduce the effects of rising unemployment on consumer incomes. Government purchases of goods and services may rise as various public works programs are started up. However, government fiscal and monetary policies to fight recessions and restore consumer and business confidence generally have not been highly successful. Public works projects take too long to start up and may not contribute to demand until the economy is already expanding. The historical record does not lead to much confidence on the part of business managers in government policies intended to prevent or end recessions. Some economists believe that these changes in government policies destabilize the economy rather than return it to full employment, and are a major source of inflationary price and wage increases.

*The Return to Expansion.* In spite of the growing pessimism on the part of consumers and business managers, falling incomes, and rising inventory/sales ratios, recessions ultimately end and a new expansion begins. Falling interest rates and reduced costs make new investments in production facilities and credit purchases more attractive. Population growth, the development of new products, new production methods, and various technological improvements can create a new expansionary phase. Increases in sales result in higher production levels to supply consumer demand and maintain desired inventory-to-sales ratios. Consumer and business confidence shifts to the optimistic side, and managers become less averse to risk. Government policies intended to end the recession begin to become effective in promoting demand growth. These, and a host of other factors, end the recession.

*The Business Cycle and Demand Forecasting.* Business cycle forecasting is basically an art rather than a science even with the availability of large data bases, highly efficient computers, and sophisticated econometric models. The track records of even the most respected analysts are not particularly good. Firms in cyclical industries face major risk management problems when making decisions near turning points. Since the number of months in each business cycle varies widely and any of a number of factors could reverse the cycle, forecasting turning points is a difficult art, and the resulting forecasts are subject to relatively large forecast errors.

In the demand function $Q = a - bP + c(1 + G)^T$, growth rate, G, represents the long-term trend in demand. Management may, however, believe that next year is likely to be a relatively good year because the business cycle is beginning another expansionary phase. Management could make an expert opinion forecast of the amount by which G is to be adjusted upward. If the average value of G is 4 percent per year (i.e., $G = 0.04$), management might increase G to 7 percent for the next year. Similarly, if the economy is entering a recession, management may forecast a decline in sales by using a negative value for G. This is only one of many methods for incorporating the business cycle into demand forecasting. Its advantages are simplicity and often, given the limited data available to management, practicality.

*The Leading Economic Indicators.* One or more leading economic indicators may be included in the variables used to estimate the demand curve. The government's index of leading economic indicators is published monthly. It predicts virtually all turning points in the business cycle approximately 6 months in advance of the turn. However, it also predicts false turning points, such as predicting an expansion when a recession still has a few more months to run its course. Demand forecasts using leading economic indicators are subject to the same kind of expert opinion scrutiny as other forecasts.

*Time Series Data and the Business Cycle.* Caution should be used when calculating growth rates using a time series that is subject to substantial business cycle fluctuations. The data should start and end at the same point in the business cycle. If the time series begins at the

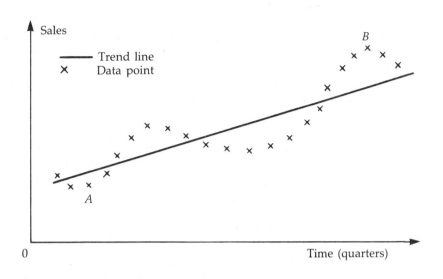

**Figure 4.1   Business Cycles and the Long-Term Trend**

Care must be taken when fitting trend lines to cyclical data to ensure that the first and last observation of the data set are from the same point in the business cycle. Otherwise the growth rate trend could be overstated, as from points *A* to *B*, or understated.

peak of a business cycle, the last observation should also be at a cyclical peak. Having the first observation at a trough and the last at a peak results in a higher growth rate than is actually the case. This point can be seen by placing a ruler across points *A* and *B* in Figure 4.1. Starting and ending at the same phase of the business cycle may result in not using some of the available observations in the time series; however, it is nonetheless a worthwhile precaution.

## 4.5   *The Product Life Cycle*

The product life cycle refers to systematic shifts in the demand curves for newly developed products from the time of their initial marketing until they become either mature products, whose growth in demand approximates the overall growth in the economy, or obsolete products replaced by substitutes. Although producer goods also exhibit product life cycles, this section focuses on consumer goods. Some capital goods do not exhibit the demand shift patterns of the typical product life cycles discussed here.

*The Rapid Growth Phase.* Product substitution and complementarity are the primary reasons for the demand curve shifts observed in the rapid growth phase of the typical product life cycle. A new product may fulfill consumers' desires for new, unusual, or high-status goods and services, leading some consumers to substitute this new product for others. If these consumers act as role models for other people, greater exposure to the product's advertising and comments on it in the media encourage increasingly larger numbers of consumers to adapt their consumption patterns and lifestyles to the new product. The rapid growth in demand and relatively profitable price will likely attract new firms into the industry, each providing its own version of the product. The increased volume of advertising and wide product choices continue to accelerate the growth in consumer demand. Throughout this phase of the cycle, the primary impetus to growth is to be found in the substitution of this product for other products already being used by consumers.

*Transition from the Rapid Growth Phase.* At some point, the growth in demand for the product begins to slow down. This principally results from its no longer being substituted for a wide range of alternative goods and services in many consumers' lifestyles. The product must now be sold to consumers who are more resistant to lifestyle changes and with relatively lower incomes. Lower-income consumers do not have as much discretionary income and spend a smaller percentage of their incomes on new or high-status products. Like higher-income consumers, they may like the product and want to buy it; however, they lack the purchasing power to do so at the prices that were attractive to higher-income consumers. If the new product is used with complementary products, some of which are relatively expensive, lower-income consumers may not buy the product because they cannot afford the complementary goods or services.

At this point in the new product's life cycle, its producers are faced with accepting a lower rate of growth in demand or developing lower-cost versions of the product. In either case, sales will not be as profitable as the earlier sales to higher-income consumers. The declining profits reduce the firms' incentives to develop more affordable versions of the product and market them with the aggressive advertising that accompanied the product's introduction and early growth. Even though a large potential market still exists, the firms may no longer find it profitable to devote significant resources to expanding the market. The product is now in its mature growth phase.

*The Mature Growth Phase.* The mature growth phase of a product's life cycle is characterized by growth in line with economic and population growth. If the product is a consumer durable, the demand for replacement of obsolete or worn-out models may become more important than the demand generated by new consumers or new uses for the product. Demand for the product also becomes more subject to fluctuations caused by the business cycle. In its high growth phase, income growth and consumer expectations regarding future prosperity were less important in consumer decisions to buy the product than their desire to substitute it for other products. With product substitution assuming a lesser role, business cycle factors become more important determinants of demand.

*The Decline Phase.* The mature growth phase can continue for a long time if a substitute for the product is not developed. In a technologically dynamic society where substantial profits can be earned from the marketing of new products, all consumer products are subject to eventual replacement by new, competitive products. Few discretionary products can expect a growing demand for long periods of time. Eventually, substitute products and lifestyles will be accepted by consumers and be more profitable to produce and market. The demand curve for the existing product will begin to shift to the left, and the decline phase will begin. Profits from producing and selling the product will decline, particularly as excess plant capacity appears and prices are reduced in an attempt to hold on to the market and maintain profits. Firms will leave the industry as their product assumes a minor place in consumer lifestyles or becomes unprofitable.

*The Product Life Cycle in Demand Forecasting.* Managements ignore the demand shifts associated with the product life cycle at the risk of making unprofitable operating and investment decisions. For example, the relatively high price and rate of growth in demand for a product during the first couple of years after its introduction should be projected for the third year only if the product will continue to be substituted at a relatively high rate for existing products. Management must assess carefully the potential for firms producing similar products entering the industry and existing producers expanding their production. Increased competition can reduce the firm's market share and markedly reduce its sales growth. Management must also be alert to new products that are potentially more attractive to consumers. These competitive products could lead to early onset of the mature growth or decline phases of the product's life cycle. Product life cycles are becoming shorter in those industries where the leading firms are seeking and showing dynamic growth through technological or marketing innovations. This can reduce the effectiveness of basing projections of the life cycle of a new product on the demand growth patterns of similar products in the past. However, in most practical situations, the best guide to future life cycle demand shifts is likely to be those of similar products.

## 4.6  *Trend Forecasts Using Regression*

Regression techniques are widely used in making persistence forecasts. The trend extrapolation and distributed lag models for making forecasts are discussed in this section. Trend extrapolation is used with annual data or seasonally adjusted monthly or quarterly data. Removing seasonal fluctuations from the data makes the regression statistics easier to interpret. Removing these predictable variations leaves the nonsystematic variations in the data due to the business cycle and various random influences about the estimated trend line. These cyclical and random factors are important determinants of the statistical significance of the estimated trend line.

### 4.6.1  *Trend Extrapolation*

This section discusses the formulation of linear extrapolation models, their estimation using regression analysis, and evaluation of the alternative models. A discussion of how to estimate forecasting errors is also provided.

   *Linear Extrapolation Models.*  Three regression equations are generally used in estimating the trend in a time series. Estimating the equation $Y = A + BT$ yields REGRESSION 1. $Y$ is the variable to be extrapolated using the trend equation, $T$ is time, and $A$ and $B$ are the coefficients to be estimated. This approach estimates the trend in terms of a fixed number of units of change, $B$, each year.

   Another approach is to assume that $Y$ changes by a constant percentage rate, $b$, each year so that the trend extrapolation equation becomes $Y = ae^{bt}$. The linear form of this equation is $\ln(Y) = \ln(a) + bT$, referred to as REGRESSION 2.

   These regression equations are subject to serial correlation. To reduce the serial correlation problem, first differences are calculated using the formula $\Delta Y = Y_T - Y_{T-1}$. The value of $\Delta Y$ is used in REGRESSION 3: $\Delta Y = A' + B'T$. An alternative to using first differences is to use percentage changes in the variable to be estimated.

   The second column of Table 4.1 contains the annual sales for a 10-year period. The fourth column contains the first differences in sales. The fifth column of Table 4.1 contains the estimated first differences calculated using REGRESSION 3. Table 4.2 contains the regression statistics for the three regressions and the trend extrapolation to

**Table 4.1  Annual Sales Data**

| Actual Sales | | First Differences | | | Lagged Actual Sales | |
|---|---|---|---|---|---|---|
| $T$ | Amount | $T$ | Actual | Estimated | One Period | Two Periods |
| 1 | 7,120 | — | — | — | — | — |
| 2 | 7,504 | 1 | 384 | 352.0 | 7,120 | — |
| 3 | 7,840 | 2 | 336 | 377.2 | 7,504 | 7,120 |
| 4 | 8,604 | 3 | 764 | 402.3 | 7,840 | 7,504 |
| 5 | 8,566 | 4 | 38 | 427.5 | 8,604 | 7,840 |
| 6 | 9,041 | 5 | 475 | 452.7 | 8,566 | 8,604 |
| 7 | 9,644 | 6 | 603 | 477.8 | 9,041 | 8,566 |
| 8 | 10,186 | 7 | 542 | 503.0 | 9,644 | 9,041 |
| 9 | 10,361 | 8 | 175 | 528.2 | 10,186 | 9,644 |
| 10 | 11,194 | 9 | 833 | 553.3 | 10,361 | 10,186 |
| 11 | — | 10 | — | 578.5 | — | — |
| 12 | — | 11 | — | 603.7 | — | — |

make persistence forecasts of sales in years 11 and 12. The extrapolations using REGRESSIONS 1 and 2 are straightforward. For example, estimated sales when $T = 11$ using REGRESSION 1 are $6,602u + (436u \times 11) = 11,398$. Using REGRESSION 3, the projected change in sales for the first year to be extrapolated is the estimated first difference for $T = 10$, or 578.5 units plus last year's sales, or a $T = 11$ sales projection of $11,194 + 578.5 = 11,772.5$ units. Adding the estimated first difference for $T = 11$ to this projection yields $11,772.5 + 603.7 = 12,376.2$ units as the $T = 12$ projection.

**Table 4.2  Regression Coefficients and Sales Projections: Trend Models**

| | Regression 1 | Regression 2 | Regression 3 |
|---|---|---|---|
| Intercept | 6,606 | 6,822 | 326.8 |
| Slope | 436 | 4.87%/year | 25.2 |
| | (17.3) | (0.17%/year) | (32.5) |
| $R^2$ | 0.984 | 0.987 | 0.062 |
| $F$-statistic | 508.5 | 631.1 | 0.467 |
| Standard error | 157.2 | 1.57%/year | 251.8 |
| Forecasts | | | |
| First year | 11,398 | 11,657 | 11,772 |
| Second year | 11,838 | 12,238 | 12,376 |

*Evaluating the Alternative Models.* The regression statistics in Table 4.2 give the impression that REGRESSIONS 1 and 2 are preferable to REGRESSION 3 since their $R^2$ values are very high while REGRESSION 3 explains only 6.2 percent of the variation in the first differences. The *F*-statistics are very high for REGRESSIONS 1 and 2, indicating that the regressions are statistically significant. The *t*-values for the slope coefficients indicate that they are significant at less than a 0.05 percent probability level. The standard deviation of the slope coefficient of REGRESSION 3 is almost one-third greater than the slope coefficient, which means that the slope coefficient is not statistically significant at even the 10 percent probability level. Nevertheless, the regression equations yield substantially the same trend extrapolation forecasts. The regression statistics differ because of the high level of serial correlation in REGRESSIONS 1 and 2. This serial correlation is largely removed in REGRESSION 3. When the trend extrapolation forecast will be modified by management's expert opinion, any of these regressions may be used; the business analyst generally is not too concerned with the levels of the various regression statistics. The slope and intercept coefficients are interpreted as average, or benchmark, values that serve as the basis for management's expert opinion forecast.

*Estimating Potential Forecasting Errors.* Good forecasting procedure also includes indicating the likely forecast errors and the conditions which may lead to them. The latter can be based on expert opinion or the confidence interval of the forecast. The standard error of the regression is calculated using equation 2.14 and the standard deviation of estimated sales using equation 2.15. For REGRESSION 1, $\bar{T} = 5.5$, $\Sigma(T - \bar{T})^2 = 82.5$, $N = 10$, and the standard error of the regression is $157.2u$. For $T = 11$,

$$\sigma_{\hat{Y}} = 157.2\sqrt{0.1 + [(11 - 5.5)^2/82.5]} = 107.4$$

For $T = 12$,

$$\sigma_{\hat{Y}} = 157.2\sqrt{0.1 + [(12 - 5.5)^2/82.5]} = 123.0$$

Expressed as a percentage of the projected value, $\sigma_{\hat{Y}}$ for $T = 11$ is $107.4/11,402 = 0.94\%$ and for $T = 12$ it is $1.04\%$. For a 5-year projection this percentage is $171.8/13,146 = 1.31\%$. If the regression error terms are normally distributed, there is a 68 percent probability that the actual sales will be within 1.31 percent on either side of the forecast level. Although the above percentages are small, they increase as the length of time increases over which sales are forecast. Because these percentages are small, the manager may conclude that the forecasts are subject to negligible errors even 5 years in the future. However, serial correlation reduces the value of the standard error of the regression, which yields a smaller confidence interval than may actually be the case.

If REGRESSION 3 is used, the standard error of the regression is 251.8$u$. On the assumption that the expected value of the errors for the years up to the forecast year is zero, the standard deviation of the growth in sales for $T = 11$ is

$$\sigma_{\hat{Y}} = 251.8\sqrt{0.11 + [(10 - 5)^2/60]} = 181.6u$$

This standard deviation is 181.6/11,772 = 1.54% of the sales forecast, which is greater than the 0.94% calculated using the REGRESSION 1 approach. Where serial correlation is likely to be a problem, it is advisable to use REGRESSION 3 if the probability of the forecast error is to be calculated. Thus, the marketing manager could report the persistence forecast of 11,772 units and a 68 percent probability that actual sales will be within 181.6 units of this forecast. A two-standard-deviation forecast (95 percent confidence interval) would be actual sales within 363.2 units on either side of 11,772 unit forecast.

The standard deviation of the forecast increases as the period to be forecast is put further into the future. This results from the increase in the $(T_0 - \overline{T})^2$ term in equation 2.15 as $T_0$ becomes larger. This increase in $\sigma_{\hat{Y}}$ ultimately limits the number of years into the future for which it is practical to make trend extrapolation projections. If for a 20-year forecast $\sigma_{\hat{Y}}$ is 50 percent of estimated sales, another forecasting method probably would need to be investigated. Alternatively, the persistence forecast might need to be hedged with a careful expert opinion analysis of likely market and economic conditions far into the future.

## 4.6.2  *Distributed Lag Models*

Another persistence forecast technique is the use of distributed lag extrapolations. A distributed lag model takes into account the fact that consumer demand changes are not instantaneous. The model predicts the effects of lags in consumer response and distributes those effects over one or more periods. One form of the distributed lag model is

$$Y_t = a + bY_{t-1} + cY_{t-2} + dY_{t-3} + \cdots \tag{4.4}$$

Consumer demand generally depends not only on current price and income levels but also on expectations of future price and income levels. Consumer expectations of the future depend in turn on both the current values of these variables and on past values, with the more recent values being given a greater weight. The effects of advertising on consumer preferences depend on cumulative exposure to the advertiser's messages, with more recent advertising expenditures having a greater effect than expenditures made further back in time. The effects of current price changes on consumer demand increase over time because of a response lag resulting from durable goods stocks with a positive economic life. Finally, consumption habits take time to break, and people do not find out about price changes immediately. These observations on consumer behavior provide a basis in economic theory for use of the distributed lag model.

*Two Alternative Models.* Two relatively simple forms of the linear distributed lag model are estimated using the data in Table 4.1. The first model is $Y_t = a + bY_{t-1}$. It assumes that sales in one year depend upon the level of sales in the preceding year. The second is the two-period distributed lag model $Y_t = a' + b'Y_{t-1} + c'Y_{t-2}$. It is estimated using the multiple regression. Additional lagged values of $Y$ could be added. Restricting the number of lags to one, two, or a few periods makes it feasible to estimate the coefficients of the equation while preserving enough degrees of freedom to yield statistically acceptable results. The data for the one-period model are obtained from the second and sixth columns of Table 4.1. The data for the two-period model are in the third, second, sixth, and seventh columns. The results of the regression analyses of these models are in Table 4.3.

*Evaluating the Alternative Models.* Both distributed lag models exhibit high values of $R^2$ and the $F$-statistic because of the general existence of serial correlation in time series data. The persistence forecasts prepared using distributed lag models are comparable to those prepared using the trend extrapolation models. Preparation of the forecasts for the second year uses the forecast value for $T = 11$ as one of the independent variables. That is, the $T = 11$ forecast using the one-period lag was 11,737u and the $T = 12$ forecast was calculated using the equation

$$(T = 12 \text{ sales}) = 140.2 + 1.036(11,737) = 12,300u$$

The regression statistics of distributed lag models may be overstated as a result of multicollinearity and/or serial correlation. Distributed lag models generally have overstated regression statistics caused by multicollinearity, since the value in one period of a variable subject to a time trend tends to be highly correlated with its values in other time periods. The two-period lag model has the low $t$-statistic ($0.692/0.426 = 1.62$) and high $F$-statistic, which is symptomatic of multicollinearity. A distributed lag model that generally does not have the statistical problems

**Table 4.3  Regression Coefficients and Sales Projections: Distributed Lag Models**

|  | Lagged 1 Period | Lagged 1 and 2 Periods |
|---|---|---|
| Intercept | 140.2*u* | 328.4*u* |
| Slope coefficients |  |  |
| 1 period lag | 1.036*u* | 0.354*u* |
|  | (0.079*u*) | (0.421*u*) |
| 2 period lag | — | 0.692*u* |
|  |  | (0.426*u*) |
| $R^2$ | 0.950 | 0.956 |
| *F*-statistic | 134.1 | 54.1 |
| Standard error | 257.2*u* | 277.3*u* |
| Forecasts |  |  |
| $T = 11$ | 11,737*u* | 11,461*u* |
| $T = 12$ | 12,300*u* | 12,132*u* |

of these simple models is the Koyck, or geometric lag, model in which the coefficients of the estimating equation decline geometrically. The Koyck model is discussed in advanced courses in forecasting.

## 4.6.3 *Selecting the Best Forecasting Equation*

With five regression models to choose from, which one is best for making the sales projections? All five yield roughly comparable forecasts. Based on the $R^2$ and *F*-statistics values of their regression statistics, REGRESSIONS 1 and 2 and the two distributed lag models are all comparable. From a statistical point of view, the first differences model of REGRESSION 3 appears to be decidedly inferior to the other four; yet its forecasts are comparable and it does not suffer from the problems of serial correlation that inflate the regression statistics of the other models. The standard errors are roughly comparable when converted into terms of the sales forecasts. If only a sales forecast is required, a pragmatic analyst could choose any one of them or could average them. If confidence interval estimates are required, the analyst should choose one of the models and present its 95 percent confidence interval. The persistence forecast is likely to be modified by management's expert opinion; hence, which model is chosen probably isn't critical since they all give comparable forecasts.

## 4.7 *Summary*

An expert opinion forecast is based on the knowledge and experience of the person preparing it. A persistence forecast is based on analysis of the available data, generally using statistical techniques. All forecasts involve errors. One objective of a forecasting procedure is to minimize forecasting errors, the difference between the forecast value and the actual value of the variable. Good forecasting procedures also provide an assessment of the potential magnitude of forecast errors and the probability of their occurrence.

Demand curves shift with the passage of time as a result of:

1. Seasonal factors, such as recurring weather patterns or holidays.
2. Economic growth caused by such long-term factors as population growth and technological change.
3. The business cycle with its expansion and recession phases.
4. The product life cycle with its rapid growth phase as the new product is substituted for existing products and consumers build up their stocks of complementary durable goods, followed by mature growth in line with overall economic growth, and a declining phase in which substitute goods make it obsolete.

One method for estimating the trend is to use simple or multiple regression. Linear and constant percentage rate growth trends are subject to serial correlation, making their regression statistics unreliable. A first differences trend is less subject to serial correlation. Trends can also be estimated using a distributed lag model. Distributed lag models can produce excellent forecasts; however, they are subject to serial correlation and multicollinearity problems that make their regression statistics unreliable. Estimated time trends are extrapolated to obtain persistence forecasts of the dependent variable. Confidence intervals for the forecast can be calculated from the standard deviation of the forecast to provide an estimate of possible forecast errors.

CASE   2     **Evaluating Alternative Marketing Strategies**

This case illustrates the use of both persistence and expert opinion forecasts. It begins with the marketing department's sales forecast being too low to utilize new manufacturing capacity. The marketing manager must then develop a strategy for expanding sales. This requires consideration of the elasticity of demand for the company's product, the extent to which marketing policy changes might shift the company's demand curve to the right, and the likely responses of its competitors.

## The Trend Projection of Next Year's Sales

Your department is responsible for marketing the gasoline produced by one of the company's refineries. A modernization project has increased by 15 percent its capacity to produce gasoline. Based on general trends in the industry, gasoline sales are projected to fall by 2 percent next year. If the year-to-year percentage changes in sales over the past five years are averaged, the annual sales decrease was 1.6 percent for the company and 1.7 percent for the industry. This trend projection was changed to a 2 percent decline next year to reflect three key economic factors. The first is the expectation that the economy will grow only slightly next year in a weak recovery from the current recession. Unemployment will remain high. Consumers are likely to remain pessimistic about future increases in their purchasing power and more interested in saving money and paying off their debts than in buying new cars and taking long driving vacations. The second is continuing consumer preferences for small, fuel-efficient cars, thus reducing the miles driven by large cars. The scrap rate for large cars is higher than for small, fuel-efficient cars. The third is that new-car sales are expected to remain at low levels. Since consumers generally put more miles on a car during its first year than during subsequent years, this is expected to depress gasoline demand. Hence, the expert opinion forecast is a 2 percent decline in sales for next year.

**The Demand Function.** The demand function for the company's gasoline sales has been estimated, using regression analysis, as $Q = 14.6 - 0.21P + 70.4(PC/P)$ where $Q$ is sales in thousands of barrels per day (abbreviated as $MB/D$), $P$ is the average retail price of gasoline at your stations in dollars per barrel, and $PC/P$ is the ratio of the average retail price of your major competitors divided by your average retail price. Given an average retail price of $45.06 per barrel and the normal $PC/P$ ratio of 0.98, this demand curve predicts sales averaging 74.13 $MB/D$. Adjusting its intercept to reflect the projected 2 percent decline in sales, this demand curve becomes $Q = 13.12 - 0.21P + 70.4(PC/P)$. If the average price is $45.06 per barrel and $PC/P$ is 0.98, next year's sales are projected at 72.65 $MB/D$, which is 2 percent less than the 74.13 $MB/D$ projected for this year.

Reducing price by 5 percent would not produce a sufficiently large sales increase to make the price change profitable or absorb the new refinery capacity. The 5 percent lower price of $42.81 per barrel yields projected sales of 73.12 *MB/D* next year using the above demand curve with $PC/P = 0.98$. The normal $PC/P$ ratio is used in this sales projection because it is likely that the company's competitors would immediately drop their prices to maintain the historical price ratio. Put another way, the demand for your gasoline is highly inelastic if your price reduction is met by your competitors. The average arc-elasticity for a range of prices 5 percent above and below the current $45.06 per barrel retail price is $-0.13$ for next year's demand curve if $PC/P = 0.98$. That is, if $P_1 = 1.05 \times \$45.06 = \$47.31$ and $P_2 = 0.95 \times \$45.06 = \$42.81$, $Q_1 = 72.18$ *MB/D* and $Q_2 = 73.12$ *MB/D*. Substituting these values into equation 3.4 yields

$$E_p = (73.12 - 72.18)(42.81 + 47.31)/(42.81 - 47.31)(73.12 + 72.18)$$

$$E_p = -0.13$$

## The Assignment

Given the 15 percent increase in refinery capacity, executive management requested an examination of the alternatives available for increasing sales in spite of the relatively poor outlook for the company and industry. In response to this request, three alternative courses of action were developed. The rejected alternatives were to emphasize service at the company's stations or to build new stations within the company's existing markets and in several new marketing areas. Neither of these alternatives was felt to be sufficiently profitable to warrant the investments required. Hence, executive management requested that an in-depth study be performed of the third alternative: to use heavily advertised price reductions and to eliminate credit cards. Your company would price its gasoline 2 or 3 cents per gallon below the average price of its competitors. This policy would reverse the previous policy of setting prices 2 or 3 cents per gallon above competitors' prices.

## Limitations of Only Reducing Prices Relative to Competitor Prices

What is needed is a marketing strategy that encourages your competitors to maintain their prices when your price is reduced so that the $PC/P$ ratio will rise. Reducing your price by 5 percent to $42.81 per barrel and having your competitors' average price 2% above your price would yield a sales projection of 75.94 *MB/D* for next year. This is 4.5 percent above the initial projection of 72.65 *MB/D*.

**Reasons for Eliminating Credit Cards.** Clearly, you need to develop marketing policies that will increase the elasticity of demand for your gasoline. This is the role of the proposed advertising campaign and the elimination of your company's credit card. Eliminating credit sales will save over $20 million per year in processing costs and credit losses, or $0.73 per barrel ($0.0174 per gallon) on sales of 75 *MB/D*. Assuming that people have credit cards to make gasoline purchases more convenient, they probably are not highly responsive to price reductions, that is, their demand is inelastic. This lack of demand elasticity increases profits when prices rise and reduces profits when prices fall. Customers placing a premium on credit card convenience will probably be lost to other companies. Since the other companies expect to gain these customers, they will continue their credit card sales. They probably will design their advertising to lure your credit card customers to their stations. Since these customers are not likely to be highly responsive to lower prices, the incentives of the other companies to reduce their prices is reduced.

**Increasing Price Elasticity Over Time.** The other companies will probably want to see the effects of your no-credit-cards policy on their credit sales before responding to your new marketing strategy. This will provide valuable time to build up sales to the other companies' cash customers. Cash customers are relatively price conscious. If you can attract cash customers to your stations with lower prices and then keep them coming back with consistently lower prices and highly visible advertising, you will have increased the elasticity of your company's demand curve. This increase in price elasticity results from the rate at which consumers obtain knowledge about price changes and change their buying habits in response to price differentials. A well-designed advertising campaign will increase the rate at which consumers find out about your lower prices and change their buying habits.

If it takes your competitors 90 days or more to respond to this new marketing strategy, the strategy should be highly successful. Since this approach to increasing sales has not been used previously, you do not have any direct evidence of its potential effects. Neither do your competitors, and that is to your advantage. You have sales data on a few test markets where your prices were below those of competitors for several months. There were no media advertising campaigns or prominent point-of-sale price advertising signs at these stations so the buildup of sales was not rapid. But sales did increase steadily and were roughly consistent with a 15 percent increase in the coefficient of the $PC/P$ term in the demand function. Virtually all of the increase came from new cash customers; credit card customers

increased their purchases only by 1.1 percent at the nearly 10 percent lower prices.

### The Demand Curve Shift

With the contemplated pricing and advertising strategy, your expert
opinion forecast is a 10 percent increase in the coefficient of the
$PC/P$ term and next year's demand function will become $Q = 13.12 - 0.21P + 77.4(PC/P)$. A 5 percent lower price for your gasoline and maintaining a price 2 percent lower than that of your com-
petitors yields sales of 83.12 $MB/D$, or a 14.4 percent increase in
sales over the 72.65 $MB/D$ expected next year. With the 5 percent
price reduction yielding a 14.4 percent increase in projected sales,
demand is elastic and total revenues will increase substantially.

### Conclusions

Since the proposed strategy of price reductions and elimination of
credit cards is forecast to increase sales by 14.4 percent, and greater
new-car sales than projected and a higher rate of economic growth
could add to the sales increase, your recommendation is that executive management adopt this bold strategy. Since your present market
share is 6.1 percent, and the 14.4 percent increase in sales will be
obtained more or less proportionately from all of your 16 competitors, you feel that this marketing strategy should not lead to a sustained price war if they believe you are willing to risk a costly price
war to maintain your avowed 2 percent price advantage. Hence,
having top executives give interviews to the media emphasizing the
company's commitment to low prices and determination to maintain
a price 2 cents per gallon below its major competitors is a part of the
overall strategy. If competitors' managements feel that gasoline
prices will rise in the future, they may be content with the added
credit card customers even if they lose a slightly greater number of
cash customers. You are not so certain that prices will rise, and you
prefer to build your position with price-conscious cash customers in
the event that lower crude oil prices allow you to make further price
cuts.

---

## CASE   3    Justifying an Increased Line of Credit

This case illustrates the use of multiple regression to estimate a company's demand function. The estimated demand function is used to

calculate the price and cross-elasticities of demand, and the regression coefficients of the advertising and time trend variables are analyzed. These elasticities and coefficients are then interpreted in terms of their bearing on whether its bank should increase the company's line of credit.

## The Assignment

You are the manager of a chain of 12 discount men's clothing stores. Sales have risen by 25 percent over the past 6 months and appear likely to remain at high levels. However, you are up against your credit limits and need a 25 to 30 percent increase in your line of credit to finance larger orders and inventories. The loan officer at the bank is not convinced that an increase is reasonable. If the high sales of the past 6 months cannot be maintained, serious inventory problems might result. About 18 months ago the bank had to provide an emergency 40 percent increase in your line of credit when sales fell unexpectedly. A clearance sale retired this added line of credit, but the company ran a loss that year. The banker feels that the extended line of credit must be justified through a study of the demand for your principal product, men's suits, including its response to changes in your price, your competitors' prices, and your advertising. He wants empirical evidence supporting your contention that present sales levels can be maintained with lower prices than those of your principal competitors and relatively little advertising. A department store executive recently told the banker that department store prices for men's suits were going to fall about 5 percent next year. This price decline is expected to increase department store sales at the expense of discount clothing chains. You were dubious of this, but had no evidence to support your view.

## The Available Data

The number of suits sold each month and their average price is in your monthly accounting reports. One section of each manager's monthly sales report deals with the store's competitive environment. Each store manager surveys prices at nearby stores selling comparable suits and records them in this section. You obtained a 36-month time series for the average prices of nearby discount and department stores. The account executive at your advertising agency provided the agency's estimates of your percentage of total discount clothing store advertising. You thought about gathering data on consumer incomes and general economic conditions. However, to save time and reduce costs you decided to first try the data you have already located.

These data are in Table 4.4. The average monthly sales of 12,778 suits for the last 6 months are substantially greater than for any other 6-month period in the last 3 years. Average sales for the other five 6-month periods, starting with the most recent one, were 9,782, 9,785, 10,950, 10,700, and 10,536. Your prices were below the

**Table 4.4   Demand Curve Data for Clothing Store Chain**

| Chain's Sales | Chain's Price | Competitor's Price | Department Store Price | Chain's Advertising | Time Trend |
|---|---|---|---|---|---|
| 11,127 | $89.90 | $91.48 | $147.12 | 14.0% | 1 |
| 8,250 | 92.60 | 92.64 | 143.08 | 14.6 | 2 |
| 11,370 | 94.22 | 89.43 | 138.22 | 20.0 | 3 |
| 9,064 | 99.35 | 104.45 | 139.10 | 10.7 | 4 |
| 10,172 | 90.10 | 89.75 | 142.46 | 17.0 | 5 |
| 13,231 | 95.46 | 97.29 | 141.00 | 19.1 | 6 |
| 10,111 | 99.05 | 97.63 | 131.51 | 19.7 | 7 |
| 8,690 | 98.91 | 95.05 | 133.05 | 13.5 | 8 |
| 13,029 | 93.66 | 98.32 | 140.88 | 13.9 | 9 |
| 12,331 | 93.54 | 98.81 | 133.02 | 11.1 | 10 |
| 9,380 | 90.36 | 87.57 | 147.46 | 13.6 | 11 |
| 10,662 | 89.57 | 96.27 | 139.08 | 17.1 | 12 |
| 10,533 | 101.30 | 91.83 | 150.94 | 20.4 | 13 |
| 11,451 | 99.26 | 97.68 | 144.81 | 17.2 | 14 |
| 8,722 | 95.88 | 89.33 | 148.11 | 12.4 | 15 |
| 9,921 | 98.62 | 97.16 | 143.17 | 17.5 | 16 |
| 12,737 | 90.04 | 97.20 | 136.94 | 13.6 | 17 |
| 12,333 | 90.41 | 89.13 | 135.15 | 13.6 | 18 |
| 10,793 | 93.11 | 86.35 | 146.91 | 17.5 | 19 |
| 9,897 | 105.74 | 96.94 | 135.66 | 14.5 | 20 |
| 8,467 | 104.12 | 99.41 | 137.74 | 17.7 | 21 |
| 6,820 | 105.70 | 96.67 | 140.60 | 12.0 | 22 |
| 11,841 | 94.92 | 98.45 | 139.11 | 14.3 | 23 |
| 10,892 | 102.69 | 104.96 | 143.86 | 11.2 | 24 |
| 10,087 | 100.50 | 95.63 | 132.08 | 19.7 | 25 |
| 7,512 | 107.60 | 101.74 | 147.62 | 13.6 | 26 |
| 8,207 | 101.70 | 97.42 | 144.02 | 14.0 | 27 |
| 9,667 | 102.81 | 96.16 | 145.44 | 19.7 | 28 |
| 13,531 | 96.40 | 97.21 | 152.00 | 16.3 | 29 |
| 9,687 | 103.11 | 100.80 | 141.15 | 12.6 | 30 |
| 14,692 | 90.92 | 97.88 | 148.05 | 16.9 | 31 |
| 11,072 | 100.03 | 100.11 | 146.12 | 11.8 | 32 |
| 12,657 | 92.61 | 98.63 | 155.71 | 17.2 | 33 |
| 13,728 | 89.96 | 99.33 | 147.54 | 15.5 | 34 |
| 12,388 | 99.44 | 99.68 | 140.81 | 12.6 | 35 |
| 12,134 | 97.80 | 101.73 | 144.11 | 10.1 | 36 |

average price for your competitors during the last 6 months. Over all 3 years, the average of your prices and those of your competitors are $96.98 and $96.39. Your advertising is below its average for the 3-year period — 14.0 percent in the last 6 months compared to 15.2 percent for the 3-year period. This makes the sales performance for the last 6 months seem all the more remarkable since advertising is generally felt to be very important in your business.

## Regression Analysis of the Data

You decided to use a 95 percent confidence interval to evaluate the significance of the $t$- and $F$-statistics for each regression equation. With $N = 36$ observations, $\phi = N - 2 = 34$ degrees of freedom, and a 2.5 percent area in each tail of the probability distribution, the critical value of the $t$-statistic for testing the significance of the slope coefficients of the regression equations is approximately $t^* = 2.03$ in Table 2.3. The critical values of the $F$-statistic depend on the number of independent variables in the regression and range from approximately 19.5 when there are two independent variables to approximately 4.5 when there are five. Critical values of the $F$-statistic are obtained from Table 2.5.

**The Simple Trend Regression.** The first regression you tried was a simple trend projection. Sales, $Y$, was the dependent variable and time, $T$, was the independent variable. The equation is $\hat{Y} = 10019.1 + 39.8T$; the standard deviation of the $T$ coefficient is 30.0, and its $t$-value is 1.33. This $t$-value is not statistically significant; hence, the coefficient for $T$ is likely to be zero. Since $R^2 = 0.05$, this regression explains only 5 percent of the variation in sales. Since $F = 1.76$, the regression is not significant.

**Competitors' Prices in the Demand Function.** All of the regression equations for estimating the demand function contain your price, $X1$, as an independent variable. This regression also includes your competitors' price, $X2$, as an independent variable.

$$\hat{Y} = 19286.1 - 281.3X1 + 194.5X2$$
$$(50.2) \qquad (58.4)$$

The numbers in parentheses under the $X1$ and $X2$ coefficients are the standard errors of those coefficients. Since $t = 281.3/50.2 = 5.6$ and $t = 194.5/58.4 = 3.33$ are greater than $t^* = 2.03$, both coefficients are significant. The $R^2$ value is 0.49, and the $F$-statistic is 16.0, both of which are significant improvements over the time trend projection's values. The $R^2$ between $X1$ and $X2$ is only 0.22, so multicollinearity is not a problem. This equation confirms your belief that both your price and your competitors' prices are important determinants of sales. You were surprised by the lack of a strong correlation between your price and the prices of your competitors. Although the average prices are very close, none of the chains serves as an effective price leader in the sense that changes in its prices are quickly matched by its competitors, which would result in a high $R^2$ value between $X1$ and $X2$.

**Adding Department Store Prices and Advertising to the Demand Function.** The next regression added the average price of comparable suits at department stores, $X3$, and your percentage of industry advertising, $X4$, as independent variables.

$$\hat{Y} = 7595.4 - 296.6X1 + 249.5X2 + 35.2X3 + 187.0X4$$
$$(48.1) \qquad (59.7) \qquad (38.3) \quad (80.6)$$

Although $R^2 = 0.58$, the coefficient of $X3$ is not significant. Its $t$-statistic is $35.2/38.3 = 0.92$, which is less than the critical value. There is no significant relationship between your sales and the average prices of comparable suits at department stores. Your customers are highly price-conscious, and department store customers are more service- and credit-oriented. The other coefficients are statistically significant. The $F$-statistic is 10.6, which is significant when there are 4 independent variables and 31 degrees of freedom.

**Removing Department Store Prices from the Demand Function.** Since the coefficient of $X3$ was not significant, you eliminated $X3$ from the regression equation.

$$\hat{Y} = 13106.2 - 300.3X1 + 248.1X2 + 187.1X4$$
$$(47.9) \qquad (59.5) \qquad (80.4)$$

All of the coefficients of this regression equation are significant. Its $R^2$ value is 0.57 and its $F$-statistic is 13.9, which means that the regression is significant. The $X4$ coefficient is more than half of the magnitude of your price's coefficient and three-fourths of the competitor's price coefficient; yet the average level of your percentage of industry advertising expenditures (15.2 percent) is less than one-sixth the average level of prices (about $96). This means that your sales are relatively insensitive to your percentage of industry advertising, which is why advertising is not your principal means for increasing sales or protecting your market share.

**Adding the Time Trend.** With $X1$, $X2$, and $X4$ in the regression equation, introducing $T$ may further improve the regression statistics.

$$\hat{Y} = 18824.1 - 309.6X1 + 188.4X2 + 177.4X4 + 59.9T$$
$$(44.3) \quad (57.7) \quad (74.9) \quad (21.7)$$

The coefficients of this regression equation are significant. Since $R^2 = 0.64$, it explains 64 percent of the variation in sales. The $F$-statistic is 13.9. You accept the hypothesis that the coefficients and variables on the right side of the equation explain the variation in sales, because the critical value for the $F$-statistic is 5.75. The $t$-statistics are relatively high, so multicollinearity is not a problem. The standard error of estimate is 1,202.3 suits. As a final test, you ran the regression residuals through the Durbin-Watson test for serial correlation. This regression has a $d$-statistic of 2.14, which does not support the hypothesis of first-order serial correlation in the regression residuals. With neither multicollinearity nor serial correlation likely, the regression statistics are reliable indicators of the ability of this regression equation to explain the observed variations in sales.

Your sales have been growing at an average of 60 suits per month over the past 3-year period, which is the coefficient of $T$ in the regression equation. This growth trend is strongly influenced by the exceptionally good sales in the past 6 months. There was no sales growth during the preceding year when economic conditions in your market area were depressed because of the nationwide recession. This sales trend will add 720 suits to monthly sales after a year.

**Adding Other Variables.** You could try other independent variables to explain more of the variation in sales; however, you would have to introduce consumer income and general business conditions variables into your regression equations. You introduced some of their effects by adding the time trend variable $T$ because the income and general economic conditions variables are more or less correlated with $T$. Besides, you do not feel that further improvements in the regression equation and statistics from introducing more variables will add much to your knowledge of the factors responsible for your large sales increase.

**Demand Elasticities.** Holding constant your competitors' average price at $100 and your share of industry advertising at 14.0 percent, the absolute value of the average price arc-elasticity of demand for prices between $92 and $102 is 2.435 in month $T = 37$. Thus, your demand curve is highly elastic within the normal range of prices. The arc-cross-elasticity of demand when your price is $97 and your competitors' price is varied between $95 and $105 is +1.45. Your suits are good substitutes for those of your competitors since a 1 percent increase in your competitors' price will increase your sales by 1.45 percent. This high cross-elasticity provides a major reason for the highly elastic demand for your suits. Your conclusion is that sales can be maintained in the range of 12,000 to 13,000 suits per month by paying close attention to the prices of your competitors. The highly elastic demand and large cross-elasticity will make it relatively easy to reduce inventories with a clearance sale. This will make the bank's loans more liquid because you can quickly convert excess inventories into cash.

**Advertising.** The large swings in your share of industry advertising result more from changes in your competitors' advertising expenditures than from changes in your advertising expenditures. Except for occasional reduced-price sales when you increase your price advertising on radio and TV to shorten the time necessary for potential customers to learn about your lower prices, you maintain a fairly constant advertising budget. You could increase your advertising expenditures from 14.0 percent to 15.0 percent; however, this would only add an average of 177 suits to your monthly sales. Moreover, your competitors are more responsive to changes in your advertising expenditures than to changes in your prices, and they may increase their advertising expenditures. Your conclusion is that your advertising expenditures need not change significantly to support higher sales.

## Conclusions

The banker agreed that your aggressive price policy is likely to result in maintaining recent sales levels. The insignificant relationship between your sales and department store prices was very interesting to him because it reduced the risk that lower department store prices would substantially reduce your sales. The banker feels that increasing your line of credit by 30 percent is justified by your potential sales and does not expose the bank to significantly greater risks. Since a large portion of your operating costs are fixed and do not change if your sales go up by 10 or 20 percent, your profits are likely to increase sharply, making the additional credit even more secure. You realize that too, but then that's another story.

## Key Terms

business cycle expansion    persistence forecast    technological
business cycle recession    product life cycle      change
distributed lag forecast    seasonally adjusted   trend extrapolation
expert opinion forecast     time series        trend forecast
first differences

## Review Questions

1. Why would managers not increase their spending on the preparation of forecasts if the result will be a smaller error term for the forecast?
2. What is the difference between a persistence forecast and an expert opinion forecast?
3. Over the past 15 years, sales in the second quarter have averaged 10 percent more than in the first quarter. What information would you need to determine if this is a seasonal variation in demand?
4. Would price changes reduce seasonal fluctuations in the demand for hotel rooms in a resort area? Why or why not?
5. Why are technological change and the economies of mass production important sources of economic growth?
6. Why is economic growth important to industries producing products with a positive income elasticity of demand?
7. How does the expansion phase of the business cycle differ from the recession phase?
8. Describe the roles of product substitution and complementarity in the rapid growth, mature growth, and decline phases of the product life cycle.
9. In Case 2, the ratio $PC/P$ was used in the demand function. Why is this a reasonable variable to use in the demand function for estimating sales?

## Problems and Applications

1. Sales in January for the last 8 years, starting with the most recent year, were 8,600; 8,430; 8,160; 7,960; 8,100; 7,840; 7,600; and 7,680 units. Calculate the percentage change in sales from one year to the next and the average percentage change. Explain how you would use these data in making a sales forecast.

2. Assume that the good in the time series in problem 1 has a positive income elasticity. When was the economy in an expansion phase and when was it in a recession phase? What other information do you need to increase the probability that sales of this good can be used to identify the current business cycle phase?

3. Sales for the past 12 years, starting with the most recent year, were 8,600; 8,430; 8,160; 7,960; 8,100; 7,840; 7,600; 7,680; 7,440; 7,360; 7,400; and 7,260. Calculate the trend in this time series using REGRESSION 1 and REGRESSION 2. Which equation fits the data best?

4. Use the equations calculated in problem 3 to prepare a forecast for 3 years in the future and calculate the 95 percent confidence interval for REGRESSION 1.

5. Use the data in problem 3 to calculate REGRESSION 3. Compare how this equation fits the data to the fit of the data provided by REGRESSIONS 1 and 2. Why might REGRESSION 3 be preferred over the other two regressions? Prepare a forecast for 3 years in the future.

6. Use the data in problem 3 to calculate the coefficients of the one- and two-period distributed lag models. Compare the fits of the data and 3-year forecasts of these models to REGRESSIONS 1, 2, and 3. Are there symptoms of multicollinearity in the two-period distributed lag model? Calculate its Durbin-Watson statistic.

7. Calculate the Durbin-Watson statistic for REGRESSION 1 and REGRESSION 3. Which regression shows the least likelihood of serial correlation?

8. The marketing department has collected data for 23 of its stores on sales (in units per day), $Q$; price, $P$; average income per full-time worker residing in the neighborhood of the store, $I$; and advertising in each community (in hundreds of dollars per week), $A$. These data are provided in Table 4.5. Management is considering whether to enter a new market where $I = 12$. When the company enters a new market it generally sets $P = \$30$ and $A = 40$ and then makes incremental adjustments in these two variables to meet competition and obtain sales of 275 units per week or more. As the data in Table 4.5 illustrate, the company is not always successful at meeting this sales goal. In an attempt to better predict the changes in sales resulting from price and advertising changes, management has requested that regression analyses be performed on the data in Table 4.5 and their implications explored for this potential new market.

   a. Calculate the simple regression $Q = a - bP$ and its $R^2$, $F$-statistic and test its significance, and $\sigma_b$ and test the significance of the $b$-coefficient. Evaluate this regression equation as a predictor of the value of $Q$ given $P$.

Table 4.5    Data for Demand Forecast

| Market | Q | P | I | A |
|--------|------|----|----|----|
| A | 284.6 | 36 | 19 | 51 |
| B | 344.3 | 25 | 9 | 31 |
| C | 221.2 | 37 | 15 | 53 |
| D | 322.8 | 26 | 12 | 31 |
| E | 358.7 | 27 | 8 | 34 |
| F | 344.9 | 28 | 9 | 36 |
| G | 322.4 | 26 | 5 | 33 |
| H | 370.9 | 30 | 19 | 52 |
| I | 187.0 | 39 | 20 | 55 |
| J | 384.7 | 32 | 23 | 52 |
| K | 330.2 | 32 | 20 | 51 |
| L | 231.6 | 38 | 16 | 60 |
| M | 387.9 | 23 | 10 | 37 |
| N | 419.8 | 31 | 21 | 53 |
| O | 277.5 | 36 | 23 | 54 |
| P | 329.0 | 35 | 24 | 59 |
| Q | 290.7 | 35 | 21 | 52 |
| R | 344.6 | 34 | 19 | 57 |
| S | 435.0 | 30 | 16 | 60 |
| T | 324.4 | 29 | 13 | 36 |
| U | 303.9 | 29 | 9 | 32 |
| V | 386.9 | 23 | 8 | 33 |
| W | 252.2 | 36 | 20 | 52 |

b. Calculate the 95 percent confidence interval for $Q$ using both the data for $Q$ and the simple regression equation in part a. Did the 95 percent confidence interval fall when price was added as an independent variable?

c. Calculate the multiple regression $Q = a - bP + cI + dA$. Calculate and evaluate its $R^2$ and $F$ and determine if the $b$, $c$, and $d$ coefficients are significant. Calculate the 95 percent confidence interval for $Q$. In what sense is this a better or worse forecasting equation than the simple regression in part b?

d. Calculate the point price elasticity when $P = \$30$ and $A = 40$. Is demand elastic or inelastic? If $A$ is increased to 50, what happens to the price elasticity of demand? Repeat the elasticity calculation for $A = 60$. What effect does increasing advertising expenditures have on the elasticity of demand? Would you recommend that advertising expenditures be increased above the normal $A = 40$? Explain why or why not.

e. If $A = 60$ and $P$ is increased to $P = \$35$ as the initial price, calculate the price elasticity at this price. Would you recommend that price be increased beyond $35? Explain why or why not.

f. If competition in the new market is likely to require a price of $26, would you recommend that advertising be increased or decreased? Explain why.

g. If there is another market in which $I = 10$, explain why demand will be more elastic in this market than in the one in which $I = 12$. Use $P = \$30$ and $A = 40$ as their base values.

h. Continuing with the problem in part g, calculate the amount by which advertising must increase to yield the same price elasticity as when $P = \$30$, $I = 12$, and $A = 40$.

# 5

# *Production*

Costs depend on the productivity of labor, capital, and the other factors of production used to produce the good or service. Fundamental to all measurements of productivity is the production function. The production function relates the input quantities to the output of the product. Production functions may be for the short-run time period when some factors are fixed in amount or for the long-run period when all factors are variable. In most cases, labor and raw materials are the variable factors of production in the short run, and capital (plant, equipment, and so on) is the fixed factor. Production functions are generally estimated using simple or multiple regression.

The principal use for production functions is to estimate the quantities of the variable factors required to produce a given output. Since more than one combination of the variable factors of production generally can produce a given output, the production function is used to find the combination of factors that minimizes production cost. The required input quantities are multiplied by their unit costs to estimate the total cost of producing the specified output. In this chapter, the emphasis is on how to estimate factor productivity using the production function. The procedures for making cost calculations are discussed in the next chapter.

## 5.1 *Long Run and Short Run*

Managers make decisions involving plans for operating their existing facilities for periods ranging from a few days or weeks to several months. They plan plant and equipment commitments affecting profits for many years. The terms *long run* and *short run* differentiate between these two types of planning decisions. Short-run decisions are concerned with optimal operation of a given physical facility, marketing department, or other unit of the company. They are made within constraints imposed by the company's existing plant and equipment, sales force, or other productive factors that management decides will not be varied during the planning period. In the short run, one or more factors of production are fixed in amount. In the long run, there are no fixed factors of production. The long run is sufficiently long that all factors of production, including plant and equipment, can be profitably varied. In the short run, management may not vary one or more factors of production because it believes that doing so is not profitable.

***Reasons for the Existence of Fixed Factors.*** In general, the fixed factors are those that management believes to be unprofitable to change within the planning period. Examples of fixed factors are plant and equipment and highly skilled labor. Attempting to vary fixed factors within a short time period will result in increases in their prices. Variable factors can be changed during the planning period without significant effects on the price paid by the firm to acquire them. Examples are relatively unskilled labor and most raw materials. Since their prices are not significantly affected by the quantity purchased by the firm, the profits from employing more of a variable factor depend on changes in its productivity. That is, the decision to hire another unit of unskilled labor depends on the value of the output it produces, since the worker's wage is unaffected by the company's decision to hire one more worker.

In the short run, management believes that it must pay a price for additional units of the fixed factor that is too high to be profitable; thus, additional quantities of the "fixed" factor will not be purchased during the next planning period. Since fiber optics engineers are rarely unemployed, hiring one or several of them within one week would likely require paying a substantially greater salary to get them to leave their present jobs. This higher salary, and the likely need to pay the company's existing engineers the higher salary, can make it unprofitable to hire more fiber optics engineers next week. However, if the company's personnel department has more time, it can search for engineers who are unhappy with their existing jobs or looking for new challenges and hire them at a lower, and more profitable, salary.

The length of time within which the firm is operating under short-run conditions is basically a matter of managerial judgment. Some factors of production are never fixed. Electrical power and water obtained over the company's existing lines are rarely fixed factors, because enough excess capacity is generally designed into them to meet any conceivable demands that the production activity may place on them. Unskilled labor is another factor that is readily available in most urban areas. Hiring or firing additional unskilled laborers will have no appreciable impact on their wages or the numbers of such workers seeking employment; hence, unskilled labor is a variable factor of production. Purchased components, such as nuts, bolts, washers, and many other off-the-shelf hardware items, are variable factors since their dealers or manufacturers maintain substantial inventories relative to the maximum quantity of the factor that one firm might desire to purchase.

The quantities of specialized or custom components may be fixed for one or more planning periods at the amount previously ordered because suppliers cannot produce more within a short period of time unless they are paid a higher price to cover their increased costs. Because the item is not a standard off-the-shelf one, the supplier may not maintain inventories of it. After two or three planning periods, the supplier can provide additional quantities of the component at the normal price, and it again becomes a variable factor. Contractual obligations may make a purchased component a fixed factor for one or more planning periods. Even if the company would prefer to use fewer units of the item, the cost may be lower to accept delivery than to defend against a breach of contract lawsuit.

*Plant and Equipment As a Fixed Factor.* The most commonly cited example of a fixed factor is the firm's plant and equipment. For many industries, it takes one to several years to construct a new plant. It may take 10 years to obtain the required regulatory approvals and construct a nuclear power plant, 4 or 5 years to open an underground coal mine, 2 or 3 years to build a metals fabricating plant, and 18 to 24 months to launch an oil tanker. Granted that it is technically feasible to build these facilities in a shorter period of time, construction costs would be higher and profits from the plant would be reduced. It is often expensive to expand these plants in a short period of time. Thus, plants in these capital-intensive industries are fixed factors for long periods of time.

Not all industries or departments of a firm use production facilities that are so time-consuming to build or expand. A new fast-food restaurant or gas station can be built in a month or two. A 2,000-foot oil well can be completed in a few days. A general-purpose machine or assembly shop can be set up in a few weeks if standardized equipment held in manufacturer or dealer inventories is used. Used equipment can be purchased within a short period of time. Buildings suitable for light industry or offices can often be built within 6 months, and in most urban areas suitable buildings are readily available for lease or purchase.

Thus, the long run can be a relatively short period of time because it is possible to vary all factors of production within a few weeks or months.

*Operating and Capital Budgets.* Even when it is possible to vary all factors of production within a short period of time, management normally separates the budgets for operating existing facilities from those for acquiring new facilities. The operating budget is concerned with decisions relating to operation of the company's existing plant and equipment. Thus, the methods of short-run analysis are applicable because management treats as fixed the quantity of capital. The capital budget is concerned with decisions to expand existing production or marketing facilities or build new ones. Capital is treated as a variable and the techniques of long-run analysis are utilized.

## 5.2  *The Production Function*

The production function provides the maximum output obtainable from specified quantities of the inputs into the production process. Production function $Q = Q(K,L,M)$ expresses the empirical relationship between output ($Q$) and inputs of capital ($K$), labor ($L$), and raw materials ($M$). This equation is read as "The quantity produced is a function of the quantities of capital, labor, and raw materials." The productivity of a factor is the rate at which output increases when the factor is increased. Although it is possible to increase the use of one factor to the point that adding another unit will reduce output, management presumably knows enough about its production facilities to avoid such situations. That is, within the range of quantities of the variable factors relevant for the company's budgeting process, an increase in a factor will always increase output.

*Short- and Long-Run Production Functions.* Production functions may be either long-run or short-run. Short-run production functions are special cases of the long-run production function where one or more factors are held constant. When the firm is considering whether to build a new plant and deciding on its capacity, the long-run production function is relevant because all factors of production are variable. Once the plant has been built, it will contain one or more fixed factors that are, for some period of time, too costly to vary. These fixed factors are generally capital items such as buildings and heavy machinery. The short-run production function is used to measure the productivity of the factors that are variable after the plant is built.

*Empirical Basis for Production Functions.* The production function
is an empirical relationship estimated using data obtained from the
company's accounting records or calculated by its engineers. Long-run
production functions are generally developed in engineering studies of
alternative plant designs and capacities. Short-run production functions
are obtained from engineering studies or statistical analyses of actual
production runs.

Estimating short-run production functions using operating data
can be difficult and costly. Accounting records are kept on a cumulative
and summary basis. Production records are often unaudited and incomplete because job tickets were not used or carefully filled out. To
estimate the production function, management may have to rely on
engineering estimates, rules of thumb accumulated by operating managers, or relatively costly special studies. Computerized information
systems, with their more disciplined approach to gathering and recording
data, generally contain the information necessary to calculate production
functions.

In principle, production functions can be estimated for operations
other than those involving the company's tangible products. In practice,
it may not be feasible to do so. For example, the quantity of services
provided by an attorney or accountant is difficult to measure because
the qualitative nature of their activities differs greatly. The lines of
contract language written per week is not a good measure of an attorney's
productivity; contracts vary widely with respect to the legal knowledge
and creativity required. The attorney may perform other duties, such
as answering questions, giving verbal interpretations of contract language,
and bargaining with persons having claims against the company. Another
problem with measuring service productivity can be the uneven flow
of work over the day or the year. The intensive work of accountants
during the monthly closing and when income tax returns are being
prepared is generally balanced by a slower work pace the rest of the
year. Similar problems arise in measuring the productivity of retail
clerks when customers arrive in erratic numbers at various times of the
day and where the clerks handle a wide range of products. Although
these measurement problems can be overcome by using relatively complex
models, production functions generally are best applied to manufacturing
and some routine clerical operations.

*Power Functions As Production Functions.* Establishing the functional form of the production function is based on regression analyses
of empirical data. The production functions utilized in this book are
power functions of the form $CX^N$ where $C$ is a constant, $X$ is the quantity
of the factor, and $N$ is the exponent. Linear functions are power functions

where $N = 1$. Where there are two or more variables in the production function, the Cobb-Douglas form of the power function will generally be used. Its general form is $Q = CX^aY^b$ where $C$ is a constant, and $X$ and $Y$ are the quantities of the two factors. An example of a Cobb-Douglas production function is

$$Q = 10K^{0.5}L^{0.5} \tag{5.1}$$

Although power functions are often used in empirical studies, other functional forms may provide a better fit of the data. In this book, the use of power functions is primarily motivated by a desire to simplify calculations of factor productivity and keep the calculus to the level in section 2.2. The methods for using factor productivity estimates to calculate costs can be utilized with any functional form of the production function and are not restricted to power functions.

**EXAMPLE 5.1. Standard Cost Tables.**     Linear production functions in the form of standard cost tables have long been used by industrial engineers and managers. For example, the standard cost table for a drill press may indicate that 1.43 minutes are required to place a part in the vise, drill a hole of a specified depth and diameter, and remove the drilled part. The setup and cleanup time for the drill press, 12.0 minutes, can also be obtained from the standard cost table. The fixed factor is the drill press. The variable factor is the labor to machine the part. The linear short-run production function, where $L$ is in minutes, for this machining operation would be

$$Q = (L - 12.0)/1.43 = 0.7L - 8.4 \tag{5.2}$$

If obtaining a new drill press and its tooling take one month, the short run is one month. If one month is available, both capital and labor are variable and management could make a long-run decision. The setup and cleanup time and the time to drill one part depend on the size, horsepower, and tooling of the drill press. They are generally summarized in the production function by the amount of money (in hundreds of dollars), $K$, invested in the drill press. The production function for a new drill press may be

$$Q = (L - 59.6/K)/(7.1/K) = 0.14KL - 8.4 \tag{5.3}$$

If $K = 5$, equation 5.3 is the same as equation 5.2. Since capital is variable, equation 5.3 is a long-run production function. The short-run production function for a drill press costing $800 is $Q = 1.12L - 8.4$. Using the $500 drill press, one hour of labor produces $Q =$

(0.7)(60) − 8.4 = 33.6 units. The same amount of time applied to the $800 drill press would yield 58.8 units.

*Materials in the Production Function.* Production functions also include the quantities of the various raw materials and purchased components necessary to produce the product. Assume that a fixture requires four bolt, nut, and washer sets. These are generally purchased components because they can be made at a lower cost by a firm specializing in their manufacture. Let $W = 4Q$ be the number of sets required to produce one unit of the product. Output is the independent variable because the purchased components are required as a result of producing the product. If there is no fixed relationship between the raw materials or purchased components and output, these factors are included in the production function with labor and capital. Energy is often included in the production function.

## 5.3 *Variable Factor Proportions*

Because the firm is faced with competition, management seeks to minimize the cost of producing and marketing goods and services. Technology is the way in which factors of production are combined to produce a good. Once the available technologies have been identified, the managerial problem becomes one of finding the lowest-cost technology. If the price of the product is determined by competitive market forces, maximizing profits requires minimizing production costs.

There is more than one technology for producing virtually every good or service. Even where chemical reactions are involved, more than one raw material is generally available, and the reactions can take place under different conditions of temperature, pressure, or Ph; different catalysts or equipment can be used. A primary job assignment for the company's engineering staff is to monitor technological developments and find lower-cost production methods. Firms producing equipment and components used in manufacturing the company's products also are important sources of technological information.

EXAMPLE 5.2.   One technology for producing threaded studs is a general-purpose lathe and a skilled machinist. This technology combines relatively low-cost equipment with hand labor by a highly paid skilled worker. Another technology is an automatic lathe together with a skilled machinist to make the tooling and set the machine up, and a machine operator with average skills to run it. An automatic lathe is more expensive than a general-purpose lathe. Capital is increased and labor inputs are reduced because its operating rate is much faster than that of a general-purpose lathe. A third technology is a numerically controlled lathe, which results in combining a great deal of capital with relatively little highly skilled labor and a machine operator. The managerial problem is to determine which is the lowest-cost technology.

If the cost of capital is low relative to the cost of labor, the numerically controlled lathe might be the lowest-cost technology for producing 10,000 or more studs. The numerically controlled lathe economizes on the use of labor by substituting relatively low-cost capital for it. If the production run is only 50 studs, the general-purpose lathe may be lowest cost. If it is 1,000 studs, the automatic lathe may involve the lowest cost. If capital is expensive and the cost of labor is low, the automatic lathe may produce 10,000 studs at a lower cost than the numerically controlled lathe. The lower-cost factor will be substituted for the relatively higher-cost factor whenever a feasible technology is available. The availability of opportunities to substitute one factor for another gives rise to the varying proportions of capital, labor, and raw materials observed in virtually all production processes.

*Development of New Technologies.* Although there may be only one technology for producing a new good or service at the time it is invented, over time additional ways of producing it will be found by the firm inventing it or by its competitors. When engineers and scientists are assigned the task of developing a new technology, they do not seek ways of using more of the relatively expensive factors. They seek new techniques for utilizing more of the low-cost factors of production and economizing on relatively expensive inputs. With continuing research into new technologies, the range of technological options for producing a good or service expands. The prospects for earning profits from this kind of research and development effort are relatively attractive. The increasingly diverse technologies result from the efforts of scientists and engineers seeking lower-cost production methods. With more than one way available to produce any given good or service, and with research and development likely to result in new technologies, the firm is continually forced to seek the lowest-cost production method to remain competitive.

## 5.4  *Marginal and Average Product*

Business managers are interested in three basic measures of productivity: total output, the average products of each of the fixed and variable factors, and the marginal products of each of the variable factors. Total output (or total product, $TP$) is found by substituting the quantities of the factors into the production function. The average product of factor $X$ is defined as $APX = Q/X$. The marginal product of variable factor $X$ is defined as the change in total output when the factor is changed by a small amount, or $MPX = \Delta Q/\Delta X$. If $\Delta X$ approaches zero in the limit, $MPX = dQ/dX$. Marginal product can be calculated only for variable factors. Since the managerial decision-making process must include changes in costs, revenues, and profits when a variable under management's control changes, marginal products are particularly important measures of factor productivity. The total average and marginal product curves are graphed in Figure 5.1: $MPL$ is the marginal product of labor, and $APL$ is the average product of labor.

As long as $MPL$ in Figure 5.1 is above $APL$, $APL$ is increasing. This is analogous to a student's receiving 100% on an examination when his or her average on the previous three exams is 80%. Since the marginal grade is greater than the average grade, the average grade will go up to 85% if the exams are weighted equally. Similarly if $MPL < APL$, $APL$ is decreasing. When $MPL$ is positive, total output is rising.

**EXAMPLE 5.3. Calculating *TP*, *APL* and *MPL*.** The production function is

$$Q = 100L + 74L^2 - L^3 \qquad (5.4)$$

where $L$ is the number of workers and $Q$ is output per hour. If there are 20 workers, $L = 20$ and $Q = 100(20) + 74(20)^2 - (20)^3 = 23{,}600$ units per hour. Since capital does not appear in equation 5.4, it is a short-run production function. Calculating the marginal product of labor, $MPL$, involves finding the derivative of the production function with respect to $L$ and evaluating the derivative at the desired quantity of labor. Taking the derivative of equation 5.4 when $L = 20$ yields

$$dQ/dL = MPL = 100 + 148L - 3L^2 \qquad (5.5)$$
$$MPL = 100 + (148)(20) - 3(20)^2 = 1{,}860 \text{ units/hr.}$$

The average product of labor, $APL$, is found by dividing output by the quantity of labor.

$$APL = Q/L = (100L + 74L^2 - L^3)/L = 100 + 74L - L^2 \qquad (5.6)$$

For $L = 20$,

$$APL = 100 + (74)(20) - (20)^2 = 1{,}180 \text{ units/hr.}$$

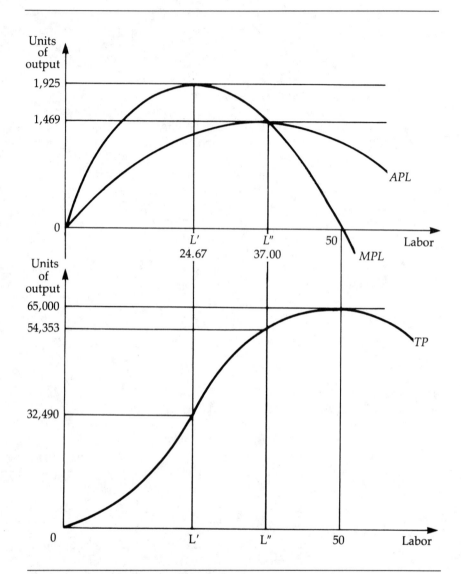

**Figure 5.1  Total, Average, and Marginal Products**

The upper graph contains the average and marginal product curves for a plant exhibiting both increasing and diminishing returns. The corresponding total product curve is in the lower graph. *TP* reaches its maximum point where $MPL = 0$.

**EXAMPLE 5.4. Finding the Maximum** *TP, APL,* **and** *MPL* **(optional).**
The maximum points of the TP, MPL, APL functions are found by
taking their derivatives, setting them equal to zero, solving for $L$, and
substituting that value of $L$ into the function. Since the derivative of
the *TP* function is the *MPL* function in equation 5.5, setting it equal to
zero and using the quadratic formula (equation 2.4) to solve it yields
the maximum point of the *TP* curve.

$$MPL = 100 + 148L - 3L^2 = 0 \Rightarrow L = -0.67 \text{ or } 50$$

Since a negative value of $L$ has no managerial significance, maximum
total product occurs at $L = 50.$[1] Output when $L = 50$ is $Q = 100(50) +
74(50)^2 - (50)^3 = 65,000$ units. The first step in finding the maximum
of the *MPL* function is to take its derivative.

$$dMPL/dL = d^2Q/dL^2 = 148 - 6L \qquad (5.7)$$

Setting equation 5.7 equal to zero and solving for $L$ yields the value of
$L$ at which *MPL* is maximized.[2]

$$dMPL/dL = 148 - 6L = 0 \Rightarrow L = 24.67$$

$$Q = 100(24.67) + 74(24.67)^2 - (24.67)^3 = 32,490 \text{ units}$$

$$MPL = 100 + 148(24.67) - 3(24.67)^2 = 1,925 \text{ units}$$

Taking the derivative of equation 5.6, setting it equal to zero, and
solving for $L$ yields the quantity of labor maximizing APL.[3]

$$dAPL/dL = 74 - 2L = 0 \Rightarrow L = 37$$

$$Q = 100(37) + 74(37)^2 - (37)^3 = 54,353 \text{ units}$$

$$APL = 100 + 74(37) - (37)^2 = 1,469 \text{ units}$$

---

[1]A more general method for determining which value of L maximizes total product
is to calculate the second derivative of the *TP* function. This is done in equation 5.6.
Substituting each value of $L$ into equation 5.6 yields

$$d^2Q/dL^2 \text{ for } L = -0.67 \text{ is } +152; TP \text{ is minimized}$$
$$d^2Q/dL^2 \text{ for } L = 50 \text{ is } -152; TP \text{ is maximized}$$

[2]To check for a maximum calculate the second derivative of the *MPL* function.
Since $d^2MPL/dL^2 = -6$, MPL is maximized.

[3]Since $d^2APL/dL^2 = -2$, APL is maximized.

## 5.5 *Short-Run Increasing and Diminishing Returns*

In the short run, at least one factor of production is held constant. In general, capital is the fixed factor and labor is variable. When the marginal product of a variable factor is rising, there are increasing returns to the factor. When its marginal product is declining, there are diminishing returns.

*The Law of Diminishing Returns.* The marginal products of variable factors always exhibit diminishing returns after some rate of use of the factor. That is, beyond some quantity of the variable factor, its marginal product will decline. In Figure 5.1, *MPL* begins to decline after *L'* workers. In some production processes, marginal product begins to decline after the first unit of the variable factor. Although empirically observed short-run production functions always exhibit diminishing returns after some quantity of labor, production functions generated by engineering studies often exhibit a range of increasing returns when the variable factor is increased from zero. However, diminishing returns eventually occur as the variable factor increases beyond some level. The *MPL* curve in Figure 5.1 exhibits increasing returns up to *L'* workers and diminishing returns thereafter.

Diminishing returns is a fact of life that managers learn to cope with. It is generally profitable to take advantage of all specialization opportunities that result in an increasing *MPL* because rising productivity means lower costs. Given the product's price, a lower cost for producing the next unit of output means it yields a greater profit. Profit maximization requires that it be produced. Rising marginal production costs due to diminishing returns eventually reduce to zero the profit earned on the next unit of output. Once the next unit of output yields a negative profit (a loss), the firm will cease to increase its output. Thus, firms will produce in the range of output where there are diminishing returns. It is these rates of output and labor utilization that provide the data which are used to fit empirical production functions and yield good fits of the data for production functions that exhibit only diminishing returns.

*Reasons for Increasing Returns.* The production function in Figure 5.1 could have been developed by industrial engineers studying how to best operate a new plant. Increasing returns to labor are primarily the result of specialization and the division of labor. As the number of production workers increases, the opportunities for the division of labor and for greater specialization increase. Specialization is impossible if only one production task, such as hoeing weeds, is to be performed.

As the number of production tasks increases, there are more opportunities to assign to each worker the tasks best suited to the worker's skills, temperament, and interests. Production of industrial goods requires thousands of different tasks and creates many opportunities for the division of labor. As the number of workers rises, productivity increases because of the greater specialization associated with the reduction in the number of tasks performed by each worker. Rising productivity from greater specialization declines as the number of workers increases. The first tasks assigned to specialized workers will be those with the greatest prospects for increasing productivity. As more tasks are assigned to specialized workers, the gains in productivity fall because the tasks with the greatest productivity gains were specialized first.

*Reasons for Diminishing Returns.* The principal reason for the diminishing returns segment of any *MPL* curve is to be found in the ratio of fixed to variable factors of production. If capital is fixed, as labor increases, the capital/labor ratio ($K/L$) decreases. Since each worker has less capital to work with, *MPL* falls. Alternatively, labor productivity can be increased by increasing the $K/L$ ratio. Since diminishing returns applies to the situation in which there is a fixed amount of capital, the $K/L$ ratio must fall as the quantity of labor increases. Once the *MPL* reductions from the declining $K/L$ ratio become greater than the increases in *MPL* because of further specialization, diminishing returns begin and *MPL* falls.

The management pyramid provides a secondary reason for the declining *MPL* as more production workers are added. The management pyramid results from the increasingly greater numbers of supervisory, coordination, and staff workers as the number of production workers increases. Each foreman may supervise up to 10 production workers and perform the necessary clerical activities to account for their work. Once there are two or three foremen, a supervisor will be necessary to control and coordinate their activities. The supervisor's greater clerical responsibilities will require a clerk or secretary. Once there are a sufficiently large number of production workers, foremen and supervisors, a third level of management is required — the superintendent and a staff of secretaries, clerks, accountants, expediters, and engineers. The larger staff is required because the superintendent's span of control and coordination is larger. The administrative tasks required are more numerous and complex at each additional level of management. As the number of production workers rises, the number of supervisory and staff workers per production worker will increase. Eventually, this increase in the relative number of staff and supervisory workers results in diminishing returns to additional production workers.

*Constant Returns.* Constant returns to the variable factor, labor, exist when increasing the quantity of labor results in no change in *MPL*. If *MPL* = 20 when *L* = 10, 11 and 12, the production function exhibits constant returns for that range of labor inputs. Presumably, there would be increasing returns for quantities of labor up to *L* = 10 and diminishing returns for quantities of labor greater than *L* = 12. Constant returns could result when productivity increases resulting from greater labor specialization are precisely offset by productivity decreases resulting from the smaller *K/L* ratio as *L* increases. Point-constant returns are always observed at the maximum point of the *MPL* curve. The linear production function $Q = A + BL$ has *MPL* = *B* and constant returns for all *L*.

**EXAMPLE 5.5. Diminishing Returns and the Cobb-Douglas Production Function.**   The Cobb-Douglas production function exhibits diminishing returns if the exponent of *L* is less than 1.

$$Q = 10K^{0.5}L^{0.5}$$

$$MPL = \partial Q/\partial L = 5K^{0.5}/L^{0.5}$$

As *L* increases, *MPL* declines because labor is in the denominator and *K* is fixed in the short run. For example, if *K* is fixed at 100 and *L* = 4, then $MPL = (5)(100^{0.5})/(4^{0.5}) = 50/2 = 25$. When *L* is increased to 16, *MPL* falls to 50/4 or 12.5. If the exponent for *L* is greater than one, *MPL* will increase as *L* increases, and there will only be increasing returns. If the exponent of *L* equals 1, there will be constant returns for all quantities of labor.

## 5.6   *Short-Run Factor Substitution*

Short-run production functions may have two or more variable factors of production. One of the variable factors can be substituted for the other. More than one combination of the variable factors can be used to produce a given output. The most notable exception is where the engineering design of the product calls for a specified number of certain purchased components for each unit produced. In this case, there are no managerial decisions to be made once the engineering design of the product has been made final.

*Isoquant Curves.* Isoquant curves are used to represent production functions in which there are two variable factors. The isoquant curve is found by using the production function to calculate all combinations of the variable factors that produce the specified output. The isoquant curve is the locus of all the combinations of the two variable factors producing a specified output given the quantities of the fixed factors.

Since two variable factors generally are not perfect substitutes, the isoquant curve is convex to the origin of the graph, as in Figure 5.2, where $L$ and $W$ represent two types of labor. A curve is convex if its curvature is away from the origin of the graph rather than toward the origin, as occurs when the curve is concave. If two factors are perfect substitutes, the isoquant is a straight line.

*Marginal Rate of Technical Substitution.* The slope of the isoquant is called the marginal rate of technical substitution ($MRTS$). If two factors

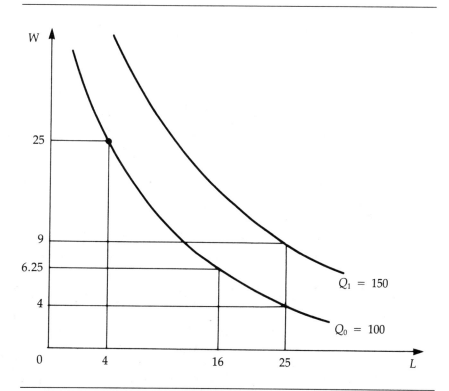

**Figure 5.2  Short-Run Isoquant Curves**

In the short run, there is a fixed factor, usually capital. Short-run isoquant curves provide the minimum quantity of one variable factor, given the quantity of the other variable factor, that is capable of producing a specified output. The isoquant for a higher output lies to the right and above the isoquant for the lower output. The production function for plotting this graph is $Q = 10L^{0.5}W^{0.5}$.

are not perfect substitutes, MRTS will vary along the isoquant. If they are perfect substitutes, the MRTS will be a constant. Like the demand elasticities discussed in chapter 3, the MRTS can be measured between two specified factor combinations on the isoquant (arc-MRTS) or at a given point on the isoquant (point-MRTS).

The point-MRTS = $dW/dL$. Finding the point-MRTS requires, in most cases, use of the total differential method of calculus. The total differential of production function $Q = Q(L,W)$ is defined as

$$dQ = (\partial Q/\partial L)dL + (\partial Q/\partial W)dW$$

The change in quantity, $dQ$, is zero along an isoquant curve. Since $\partial Q/\partial L = MPL$ and $\partial Q/\partial W = MPW$, this equation can be rewritten as

$$0 = (MPL)dL + (MPW)dW$$

$$MRTS = dW/dL = (-MPL/MPW) \qquad \textbf{(5.8)}$$

That is, the rate at which the two variable factors can be substituted for each other with no change in output depends upon the ratio of their marginal products. If $L$ and $W$ are both subject to diminishing returns as their quantities increase, an increase in $L$ will result in MPL's declining. Since the increase in $L$ will reduce the amount of $W$ necessary to maintain output at $Q_0$, MPW will increase. Thus, as $L$ increases, MRTS will increase from, say, $-1$ to $-0.5$, and the isoquant curve will get flatter as $L$ increases. This is the reason for the isoquant curve's being convex to the origin.

**EXAMPLE 5.6.** If the short-run production function is $Q = 10L^{0.5}W^{0.5}$, an output of $Q_0 = 100$ units per hour could be produced with 25 hours of type $L$ labor and 4 hours of type $W$ labor. $L = 16$ and $W = 6.25$ also could be used to produce 100 units per hour. Thus, it is possible to substitute $6.25 - 4 = 2.25$ units of type $W$ labor for $25 - 16 = 9$ units of type $L$ labor and maintain a production rate of 100 units per hour. The isoquant curve for a higher output $(Q_1)$ lies above the $Q_0$ isoquant curve. If $Q_1 = 150$ units per hour, 25 units of type $L$ labor and 9 units of type $W$ labor will be required.

The arc-MRTS for a shift from factor combination $L = 25$ and $W = 4$ to $L = 16$ and $W = 6.25$ is

$$MRTS = (4 - 6.25)/(25 - 16) = -2.25/9 = -0.25$$

The MRTS is negative because the isoquant is a downward sloping curve.

The first step in finding the point-*MRTS* is to find *MPL* and *MPW*. The partial derivatives of the production function $Q = 10L^{0.5}W^{0.5}$ are

$$MPL = \partial Q/\partial L = 5W^{0.5}/L^{0.5}$$

$$MPW = \partial Q/\partial W = 5L^{0.5}/W^{0.5}$$

Substituting these partial derivatives into equation 5.8 yields

$$dW/dL = (-5W^{0.5}/L^{0.5})dL/(5L^{0.5}/W^{0.5})$$

$$dW/dL = MRTS = -W/L \qquad (5.9)$$

The point *MRTS* at $L = 25$ and $W = 4$ is $dW/dL = (-4/25)$ or $-0.16$. The arc- and point-*MRTS*'s are not equal because they are calculated for a different change in factor *L*.

To interpret this result, rewrite equation 5.9 as

$$dW = (MRTS)dL = (-W/L)dL \qquad (5.10)$$

If $L = 25$ and $W = 4$, $MRTS = -0.16$. If management adds one unit of type *L* labor ($dL = 1$), the reduction in the number of type *W* workers that will leave output unchanged is 0.16 units, because $dW = -0.16$. At another combination of *L* and *W*, the *MRTS* and the rate at which one type of labor could be substituted for the other would be different. For example, if $L = 16$ and $W = 6.25$, $MRTS = (-6.25/16) = -0.39$ and a one-unit increase in type *L* labor would permit a 0.39 unit reduction in the quantity of type *W* labor with no change in output. Thus, the *MRTS* is the rate at which one type of labor can be substituted for the other with no change in output.

## 5.7 *Long-Run Returns and Factor Substitution*

When the planning period is sufficiently long that all factors of production are potentially profitable to vary, management becomes concerned with the long-run production function. The long-run isoquant is the locus of all the combinations of capital and labor that produce a given output. Capital can be substituted for labor and the specified output maintained. In Figure 5.3, $Q_0$ units of output can be produced using $L_0$ units of labor and $K_0$ units of capital, or by using the combination $L_1$ and $K_1$. Since capital-labor ratio $K_0/L_0$ is greater than $K_1/L_1$, the technology that permits the production of $Q_0$ units of output with factor combination $L_0$, $K_0$ is relatively capital intensive. Alternatively, the technology associated with factor combination $L_1$, $K_1$ is relatively labor intensive.

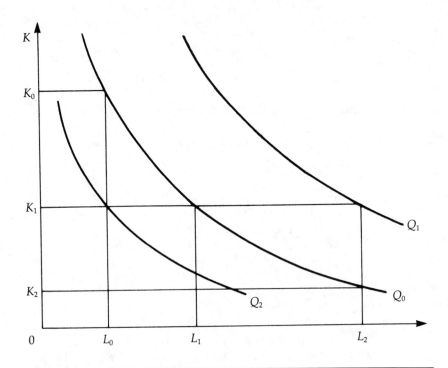

**Figure 5.3   Long-Run Isoquant Curves**

In the long run, all factors of production — including capital, $K$ — are variable. With capital fixed at $K_1$, the isoquant diagram shows the quantity of labor required in the short run to produce a given output.

The equipment used in a capital-intensive technology is different from that for a labor-intensive technology. A numerically controlled lathe is a much different technology than a general-purpose lathe; the former utilizes electronic control devices to replace the hands and eyes of a skilled machinist. Another example is provided by ditch digging. Factor combination $L_2$, $K_2$ could be a large group of workers with shovels and wheelbarrows for capital and $L_0$, $K_0$ could refer to two workers with a backhoe-equipped tractor. Although the technologies at the various points along the isoquant may differ substantially in the nature of the capital equipment used, they all share one common characteristic. At the time when they are drawn, each isoquant curve provides the minimum quantity of one factor required to produce the specified output given the quantity of the other factor.

The isoquant curve is not restricted to the technologies currently used to produce the product. The currently used technologies were the most profitable of the alternatives available at the time each plant was built. The isoquant curves that are relevant to current planning decisions reflect the technological options available today. With new technologies being developed, with changes in the relative prices of labor and capital, and with changes in competitive market conditions, technologies that were profitable in the past need not be profitable today. Because they incorporate new and existing technologies, long-run isoquants are generally constructed from data provided in engineering studies.

*Returns to Scale.* Long-run production functions can also be described in terms of their returns to scale. A change in scale means all factors of production are increased or decreased by the same proportion. A production function exhibits increasing returns to scale when doubling each factor of production results in output's more than doubling. The production function $Q = 5K^{0.75}L^{0.5}$ exhibits increasing returns because output is 125.74 when $K = 10$ and $L = 20$ and 299.07 when $K = 20$ and $L = 40$. Both factors were doubled, yet output increased by 2.38 times. Constant returns to scale exist when doubling the factors results in exactly doubling the output. $Q = 5K^{0.5}L^{0.5}$ is a constant returns-to-scale production function. Decreasing returns to scale exist when a doubling of all factors results in output increasing by less than double the previous amount. If $Q = 5K^{0.5}L^{0.25}$ is the production function and $K = 10$ and $L = 20$, output is 33.44. If $K$ and $L$ are doubled, output rises to 56.23, which is only 1.68 times 33.44.

*Factor Substitution in the Long Run.* Business managers seldom find the returns to scale of a production function to be useful in their planning decisions. They are rarely interested in producing more output by increasing all factors of production proportionately. To minimize costs, they seek technologies using more of the lower-cost factors and less of those factors that are relatively expensive. When real labor costs were rising over time and the cost of capital showed no long-term upward time trend, managements promoted the development of new technologies with a higher $K/L$ ratio. These new technologies economized on the use of labor. When a larger plant was to be built, it would be designed to use proportionately more capital than labor. Since energy is generally a complementary factor with capital, and real energy costs were generally trending downward between 1900 and 1970, there was a concurrent increase in plants' energy intensity. To keep costs as low as possible, business managers sought technological opportunities to substitute capital and energy for labor, rather than increasing all three factors proportionately.

   With capital and energy relatively low-cost factors of production, economic incentives for creating and using technologies substituting capital for labor were present for a century prior to 1970. The end result of this long period of factor substitution is the highly capital- and energy-intensive economies that exist today in industrial nations. However, with the cost of energy and capital trending upward and the purchasing power of wages showing no trend since the late 1960s, the economic incentives for substituting capital and energy for labor are not as great today as they were prior to 1970 and may not exist except in such technologically dynamic industries as electronics.

The long-run *MRTS* is the rate at which labor can be substituted for capital while maintaining a specified output. This *MRTS* is equal to the ratio of the marginal products, or $-MPL/MPK$ where *MPK* is the marginal product of capital. *MPK* is relevant in the long run because capital is variable.

**EXAMPLE 5.7.**   If the production function is $Q = 10KL^{0.25}$,

$$MPL = \partial Q/\partial L = 2.5K/L^{0.75}$$

$$MPK = \partial Q/\partial K = 10L^{0.25}$$

$$MRTS = -(2.5K/L^{0.75})/(10L^{0.25}) = -K/4L$$

Assume that management is presently considering factor combination $K = 10$ and $L = 10$ and wants to calculate the number of workers that can be replaced with one more unit of capital, holding constant output. Since $MRTS = dK/dL$, $dK/dL = -K/4L$ and $dL = (-4L/K)dK$. Substituting in the given values of $K$ and $L$, and $dK = +1$, yields $dL = (-40/10)dK = -4(+1) = -4$. Thus, one unit of capital can be substituted for four units of labor with no change in output.

Whether this substitution of capital for labor will be profitable depends upon their relative prices. If one unit of capital costs $100 and a unit of labor costs $10, it would not be profitable to replace four units of labor (costing $40) with one unit of capital. The relative price is 10 units of labor for one unit of capital, which is greater than the *MRTS*. If the cost of a unit of capital was $25, it would pay to make this substitution. Thus, the *MRTS* can be used in determining the cost minimizing combination of the two factors.

*Relationship Between Long- and Short-Run Production Functions.* Once management decides to build a plant and it is constructed, management returns to making short-run decisions. Substituting the quantity of capital into the long-run production function yields the short-run production function. The long-run production function is used when the decision is to determine the optimum quantity of capital to invest in the plant. This is no longer relevant once the quantity of capital is fixed. If the quantity of capital is fixed, $MPK = 0$ and the $MRTS$ of labor for capital no longer exists.

The shift from the long-run production function to the short-run production function is illustrated in Figure 5.3. With capital fixed at $K_1$, output depends on the quantity of labor. To find the output produced by a given quantity of labor, find the isoquant curve that intersects the horizontal $K_1$ line. With capital equal to $K_1$, the quantity of labor required to produce $Q_1$ units of output in Figure 5.3 is $L_2$ and for $Q_2$ it is $L_0$. This amounts to substituting the quantity of capital into the long-run production function to find the short-run production function and solving for the quantity of labor given output.

**EXAMPLE 5.8.**   If the long-run production function is $Q = 10KL^{0.25}$, the short-run production function when $K$ is fixed at 8 units is $Q = (10)(8)L^{0.25} = 80L^{0.25}$. This short-run production function can be used to calculate the output produced by a given quantity of labor. If $L = 20$, $Q = 80(20)^{0.25} = 80(2.115) = 169.2$ units. The number of workers required to produce $Q = 200$ units of output is found by solving the equation $80L^{0.25} = 200$ for $L$. The solution is $L^{0.25} = 200/80 = 2.5$ and $L = (2.5)^4 = 39$ workers.

## 5.8 *Summary*

The short run is that period of time during which one or more factors of production are held constant. They are fixed because it would be unprofitable to change them during the current planning period or because management wants to focus its attention on the operation of existing facilities. The long run is the minimum period of time required to profitably change all factors of production. In the long run there are no fixed factors.

The production function expresses the empirical relationship between output (total product) and inputs of capital, labor, and raw materials into the production process. The long-run production function has no fixed factors; short-run production functions contain one or more fixed factors. The marginal product of a variable factor is the change in output when the factor is changed by one unit or a very small amount. The average product of a fixed variable factor is output divided by the total quantity of the factor.

If the quantity of labor is increased and $MPL$ rises, there are increasing returns to labor, generally resulting from increased labor specialization when many tasks are performed to produce the product. If the quantity of labor is increased and $MPL$ falls, there are diminishing returns to labor. Diminishing returns generally result from a declining

$K/L$ ratio, where $K$ is the fixed variable. They may also result from the increasing number of supervisory and administrative workers required as the number of production workers increases. All short-run production functions eventually exhibit diminishing returns as labor increases.

There is more than one combination of capital, labor, and raw materials for producing a specified output of almost all goods and services. The isoquant curve is the locus of all combinations of variable factors that can be used to produce a specified output given the quantities of the fixed factors. Its slope is the marginal rate of technical substitution, which is equal to minus the ratio of the marginal products of the two factors.

Regression analysis can be used to estimate empirical production functions and test their statistical validity. Alternatives to regression analyses are engineering studies, standard cost tables, and rules of thumb developed by operating managers.

## CASE 4    Estimating the Production Function

This case illustrates the use of simple regression to estimate the firm's short-run production function. The estimated production function is then used to estimate the number of production workers the firm must use to produce the output rate ordered by management.

### The Assignment

The boss wants you to review the assignment of production workers to manufacturing one of the company's products. Production runs of varying quantities are made when inventories fall to a predetermined order point. For the first few production runs, the number of workers was based on the recommendations of the engineering company that designed the plant. The boss wants you to estimate the relationship between the number of production workers and output since the plant manager finished experimenting with changing the number of workers required to produce a specified output. There are 22 production runs for which the data are complete. The data on hourly output ($Q$) and the number of production workers ($W$) are provided in Table 5.1.

### The Data

The equipment has not changed since the plant was built, and management has no plans to change it in the foreseeable future. Since the plant and equipment are fixed factors, the short-run production

Table 5.1  Input/Output data

| Production Run | Output per Hour | Number of Workers | Production Run | Output per Hour | Number of Workers |
|---|---|---|---|---|---|
| 1 | 23.8 | 5 | 12 | 25.7 | 7 |
| 2 | 32.1 | 17 | 13 | 33.4 | 17 |
| 3 | 31.7 | 15 | 14 | 26.3 | 8 |
| 4 | 29.4 | 13 | 15 | 33.0 | 15 |
| 5 | 29.2 | 10 | 16 | 29.4 | 12 |
| 6 | 36.4 | 28 | 17 | 30.0 | 16 |
| 7 | 35.0 | 24 | 18 | 33.8 | 21 |
| 8 | 37.2 | 27 | 19 | 28.8 | 13 |
| 9 | 32.5 | 21 | 20 | 34.3 | 24 |
| 10 | 37.0 | 30 | 21 | 35.7 | 28 |
| 11 | 36.0 | 19 | 22 | 31.1 | 15 |

function is being estimated. The purchased components and raw materials used in the production process are in a fixed ratio to output; thus, it is not necessary to include them in the production function. Their amounts are determined from the product's engineering specifications. The only exception might be electrical energy. Since extracting the data on the number of kilowatt-hours of electricity used is rather time-consuming, you decide to estimate the production function with labor as the independent variable. If the resulting production function is not statistically significant or does not provide a good fit of the data, you will dig out the energy use data and reestimate it.

## The Statistical Analysis

The next step is to decide on the functional form of the production function. Power functions often provide excellent statistical fits of empirical data on the inputs into and outputs from production processes. You decide to estimate the power function $Q = CW^n$, which is converted into a linear equation by taking the natural logarithm of both sides.

$$\ln Q = \ln C + n\ln W \qquad (5.11)$$

Using the data in Table 5.1 to estimate equation (5.11) yields

$$\ln Q = 2.74387 + 0.256825\ln W \qquad R^2 = 0.94, F = 314 \qquad (5.12)$$
$$(0.04071) \quad (0.0145)$$

The coefficient of determination, $R^2$, measures the percentage of the total variation in the dependent variable, $\ln Q$, explained by the right side of the regression equation. Since $R^2 = 0.94$, the right side of equation 5.12 explains 94 percent of the variation in $\ln Q$. The estimated production function provides a very good fit of the data. Management can have considerable confidence in using equation 5.13 to calculate the number of workers required to produce a given hourly output. Because of the high $R^2$ value, it probably would not be cost-effective to include energy in the production function.

The F-statistic is 314. The F-statistic tests whether equation 5.12 provides a statistically significant explanation of the variation in its dependent variable. If the estimated F-statistic is greater than its critical value, the hypothesis is accepted that the independent variables explain the variation in $\ln Q$. Given a 95 percent confidence interval and 1,20 degrees of freedom, the critical value of the F-statistic is $F^* = 4.35$. The calculated value of $F$ is greater than $F^*$, so the regression is significant.

The last step is to determine if the intercept and slope coefficients of equation 5.12 are statistically significant. With a 95 percent confidence interval and $22 - 2 = 20$ degrees of freedom, the critical value of the t-statistic is $t^* = 2.086$. The calculated t-statistic for the intercept of equation 5.12 is $2.74387/0.0407 = 67.4$. For the slope coefficient, $t = 0.256825/0.0145 = 17.7$. The t-values for both coefficients are larger than the critical value; hence, both coefficients are statistically significant.

To convert equation 5.12 into the power function form, take the antilogs of both sides. Using a hand-held calculator, enter 2.74387 into the register, press the inverse (INV) and $\ln X$ keys, and read the value of $C$ in the display. It is 15.547, rounded off. The coefficient of $\ln W$ is $n$.

$$Q = 15.547W^{0.26} \tag{5.13}$$

## Conclusions

Since the estimated production function fits the data so well and is statistically significant, your recommendation to management is that equation 5.13 be used to assign production workers to the plant. Equation 5.13 would probably be presented to management in tabular form as a Standard Cost Table. The first column of the table would have the number of workers and the second column would have their output calculated using equation 5.13. Once management decides on the output to be produced, the second column is scanned to find the output closest to the desired rate and the number of production workers needed. For two workers, output is $Q = (15.547)(2)^{0.26} = (15.547)(1.1975) = 18.62$ units per hour. Output for 10 workers is 28.29 units, and for 20 workers it is 33.88 units. Since doubling the number of workers from 10 to 20 results in less than twice as much output as when $L = 10$, the production function exhibits diminishing returns.

## Key Terms

| | | |
|---|---|---|
| average product | increasing returns | marginal rate of technical substitution |
| constant returns | isoquant curve | |
| decreasing returns | long run, | production function |
| factors of production — fixed, variable | short run | returns to scale |
| | marginal product | total output |

## Review Questions

1. How does the long run differ from the short run?
2. Why is the short-run period only a few weeks for some technologies and several years for others?
3. Why might skilled engineers be a fixed factor for 2 weeks and a variable factor after 6 months?
4. Define the terms *productivity* and *production function.*
5. How does a long-run production function differ from a short-run production function?
6. How does the goal of profit maximization contribute to the development of new technologies for producing a product?
7. If a factor of production, such as energy, is increasing in cost, why will engineers seek new technologies that economize on the use of energy?
8. How do the definitions of the *average product of labor* and the *marginal product of labor* differ?
9. Define the terms *increasing returns, constant returns,* and *diminishing returns.*
10. Why do empirical estimates of short-run production functions generally exhibit diminishing returns?

11. As the quantity of labor increases, how do increasing specialization and the declining capital/labor ratio interact to yield diminishing returns?

12. Define the terms *isoquant* and *marginal rate of technical substitution*.

13. How do capital-intensive technologies differ from labor-intensive ones?

14. Define the term *returns to scale*. How do increasing returns to scale differ from decreasing returns to scale?

15. How do the terms *diminishing returns* and *decreasing returns to scale* differ?

# Problems and Applications

1. How can a production function like equation 5.2 be used to measure the average and marginal productivity of labor when the time spent drilling a part is increased from 480 minutes per day to 540?

2. If the long-run production function is $Q = 10KL^{0.25}$, what is the short-run production function if $K = 10$?

3. Calculate the total, average, and marginal products of labor if the production function is $Q = K^2L + 0.4KL^2 - 0.2L^3$, the quantity of capital is 10 units, and the quantity of labor is 15 workers.

4. Calculate the quantities of labor at which the total, average, and marginal products of labor are maximized using the production function and quantity of capital in problem 3.

5. Does labor productivity rise if the quantity of capital rises from 10 to 11 units in the production function in problem 3? Explain why or why not.

6. For which quantities of labor does the production function in problem 3 yield diminishing returns?

7. Calculate $MPL$ for the production function $Q = 2K^{0.25}L^{1.5}$. Does this production function exhibit increasing or diminishing returns?

8. Does the production function $Q = 4KL^{0.25}$ exhibit increasing or diminishing returns when $L = 16$? Explain why.

9. If the production function is $Q = 2L^{0.25}W^{0.25}$, calculate two combinations of $L$ and $W$ that can produce $Q_0 = 100$ units of output.

10. Calculate the formula for $MRTS$ using the production function in problem 9.

11. Calculate the $MRTS$ for the two factor combinations in your answer to problem 9. Explain why the two $MRTS$s imply that the isoquant curve is convex to the origin.

12. Use the production function $Q = 5KL^{0.5}$ to calculate the short-run production function if $K = 10$ and find the output produced by $L = 5$ workers.

13. Assume that the long-run production function is $Q = 4KL^{0.5}$. Calculate its *MRTS* if $K = 10$ and $L = 20$ and determine whether it would reduce costs to substitute capital for labor if one unit of capital costs $50 and one unit of labor costs $15.

14. The company is presently negotiating a new contract with the union at one of its production facilities. The union claims that its members deserve a 10 percent wage increase because the average product of labor during the previous contract was 1.82 units per worker and now is approximately 2 units per worker. The data supporting the union's claim are provided in Table 5.2. These data are for the 26 production runs during the present (expiring) contract. The company has made a few capital improvements in the facility's plant and equipment during the present contract, which could have shifted its production function upward. Your assignment is to determine the validity of the union's claim.

    a. Calculate $L$, the average number of workers, and $Q$, the average output, per production run. The union's claim is based on this ratio, which was used to calculate the *APL* of 1.82 for the previous contract. Have they done their arithmetic correctly?

    b. The average number of workers per production run during the previous contract was 43.1. Use the average number of workers per production run and the likely existence of diminishing returns to argue that the observed increase in the plant's *APL* was caused by the smaller average number of workers and not greater efforts and more efficiency on the part of the union's members.

    c. The union's negotiating team does not accept your argument. They insist that you demonstrate that diminishing returns exist at the plant, rather than constant returns and that they are great enough to account for the observed average productivity increase. Write a brief explanatory memo to the union explaining the statistical methodology, based on simple regression estimates of the production functions $Q = a + bL$ and $Q = aL^b$, to demonstrate whether the union's or the company's position is supported by the data in Table 5.2.

    d. Estimate $a$ and $b$ for the two regression equations $Q = a + bL$ and $Q = aL^b$, calculate their $R^2$ and *F*-statistics, and test the significance of the regressions and their slope coefficients. Which regression is preferable based on its regression statistics? Explain why.

    e. Use the regression of the form $Q = aL^b$ to calculate *APL* for the average number of workers during the present contract and for

**Table 5.2  Production Run Data**

| Run | $Q$ | $L$ | Run | $Q$ | $L$ |
|-----|------|-----|-----|-------|-----|
| 1 | 54.5 | 23 | 14 | 67.1 | 32 |
| 2 | 55.1 | 20 | 15 | 80.6 | 47 |
| 3 | 52.9 | 23 | 16 | 110.0 | 55 |
| 4 | 55.7 | 22 | 17 | 44.5 | 17 |
| 5 | 104.2 | 48 | 18 | 88.0 | 39 |
| 6 | 100.0 | 54 | 19 | 58.8 | 27 |
| 7 | 100.0 | 53 | 20 | 54.9 | 17 |
| 8 | 68.8 | 32 | 21 | 88.3 | 47 |
| 9 | 82.9 | 41 | 22 | 114.6 | 60 |
| 10 | 109.7 | 60 | 23 | 68.6 | 33 |
| 11 | 112.6 | 58 | 24 | 94.0 | 47 |
| 12 | 44.4 | 19 | 25 | 77.4 | 49 |
| 13 | 30.2 | 12 | 26 | 78.1 | 48 |

43.1 workers. Explain how these estimates of *APL* refute or support the union's claim that they deserve a 10 percent pay increase.

15. Your company has recently completed a prototype plant with a significantly improved technology for producing the company's principal product. One of the purposes of this plant is to determine the relationship between the numbers of skilled and unskilled workers operating the plant and its output. The company plans to build upwards of 100 of these plants throughout the United States. Twenty-

**Table 5.3  Output Produced by Different Crews**

| Crew | Skilled | Unskilled | Output | Crew | Skilled | Unskilled | Output |
|------|---------|-----------|--------|------|---------|-----------|--------|
| A | 8 | 8 | 41.9 | M | 11 | 6 | 52.0 |
| B | 8 | 10 | 48.7 | N | 11 | 8 | 51.0 |
| C | 8 | 12 | 50.2 | O | 11 | 10 | 55.1 |
| D | 8 | 14 | 58.8 | P | 11 | 12 | 58.5 |
| E | 9 | 7 | 51.5 | Q | 12 | 5 | 48.7 |
| F | 9 | 9 | 47.2 | R | 12 | 7 | 64.6 |
| G | 9 | 11 | 58.1 | S | 12 | 9 | 58.9 |
| H | 9 | 13 | 60.2 | T | 12 | 11 | 57.4 |
| I | 10 | 6 | 54.6 | U | 13 | 5 | 56.8 |
| J | 10 | 8 | 51.7 | V | 13 | 7 | 53.1 |
| K | 10 | 10 | 54.5 | W | 13 | 9 | 68.3 |
| L | 10 | 12 | 59.5 | X | 13 | 11 | 61.1 |

four crews from the company's existing plants were given the same one-week course on operating the plant, after which they actually ran the plant for a 2-week period. The number of skilled and unskilled workers in each crew and its average daily output is recorded in Table 5.3.

a. Fit a production function of the form $Q = aS^bL^c$ to these data using multiple regression, statistically evaluate the regression, and plot the isoquants for outputs of 50 and 60 units per day.

b. Calculate the *MRTS* for crews with 8 and 10 unskilled workers and outputs of 50 and 60 units per day.

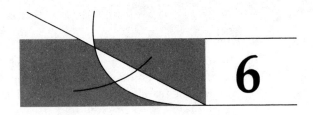

# Cost

Costs depend on the productivity of the factors of production used to produce the good or service. Higher productivity among those factors means lower product costs if the factors' prices are unchanged. Costs also change as a result of changes in the unit prices of the factors of production. Whether the quantity of a factor is fixed or can be varied by management within the planning period is an important determinant of costs, as is the rate at which factor prices change when the firm varies the quantity it purchases.

This chapter begins with definitions of the several cost concepts used in managerial economics. Sections 6.2 and 6.3 focus on estimating short-run costs when there is one variable factor. Estimating short-run costs when there are two variable factors is covered in sections 6.4 and 6.5. Sections 6.6 and 6.7 discuss long-run costs when there are no fixed factors of production. The first of these sections concentrates on deriving the long-run average cost curve and the second on the relationship between the long-run and short-run cost curves. The last section discusses the relationship between the long-run average cost curve and the number of firms in the industry. The chapter concludes with a case on statistical cost estimation.

## 6.1  Cost Concepts

This section provides definitions and explanations of the principal measures of costs. The opportunity cost of a factor of production is the most general cost concept used in managerial economics. In detailed analyses, there are several alternative breakdowns of opportunity costs.

One depends on whether the firm purchases the factor in the current planning period or has previously acquired it. Another depends on whether the quantity of the factor is fixed for the planning period or varies when the firm changes its output. The existence of fixed factors determines whether short- or long-run cost analysis is being performed. The last cost breakdown discussed in this section depends on whether one or several distinct products are jointly produced.

## 6.1.1  *Opportunity Cost*

The opportunity cost of activity *A* is the value of the next best alternative that could have been undertaken if the resources were not applied to activity *A*. This fundamental concept underlies all managerial assessments of costs. When management makes a decision, it incurs costs because it has committed resources to carrying out that decision. It cannot put those same resources to other uses at the same time; hence, the firm has incurred a cost.

*Explicit Costs.* Most of the costs incurred by a firm are explicit opportunity costs. An explicit cost arises whenever the firm purchases a factor of production during the current planning period for use during that period. If the firm spends $100 on labor, it cannot spend that $100 on some other factor of production. The explicit cost of the labor is $100. The firm's accounting system records all of the explicit costs incurred by the firm.

*Implicit Opportunity Costs.* An implicit opportunity cost arises when the firm already owns a resource and does not pay money in the current planning period to acquire it. If the firm uses a building it owns, it cannot rent the building to another firm. The implicit opportunity cost of using the building in its production operations is the rent it would have received. Managerial economics includes both explicit and implicit costs in its cost functions. Accountants do not include implicit costs in their profit-and-loss statements. Measuring an implicit cost is not as precise or objective as the measurement of an explicit cost like wages. However, managers use a broader measure of costs than accountants since managers are interested in optimal use of all of the firm's resources, including those resources that were previously purchased by the firm.

## 6.1.2  *Fixed Costs*

Fixed costs are the costs of those factors of production that do not change with changes in the firm's output during the current planning period. Examples of fixed costs are plant and equipment costs, the value of raw material and finished goods inventories at the start of the planning period, managerial salaries, the cost of liability and casualty insurance, and property taxes. These costs are incurred whether the firm produces 10 units of output or 1,000 units. Some fixed costs, such as salaries or insurance premiums, are explicit costs measured by the amount of money the firm will pay during the current planning period to acquire the factors. Other fixed-cost items, most notably plant and equipment, were acquired in the past and have economic lives spanning several or many planning periods. The cost of the firm's plant and equipment in the current planning period is an implicit fixed cost.

*Accounting Estimates of Implicit Fixed Costs.* The fixed costs of factors of production with economic lives spanning several planning periods are implicit costs because the firm does not purchase them during the current planning period. They are measured differently by economists and accountants. Accountants allocate to fixed costs in the current planning period some portion of the asset's historical cost as a depreciation allowance. An asset costing $100,000 at the time it was purchased and having an expected economic life of ten years has a cost of $10,000 per year using the straight-line depreciation method. The straight-line depreciation allowance is the historical cost of the asset divided by its expected economic life. The asset's economic life is the number of years the firm expects to use the asset in producing its product.[1]

This approach is reasonable when there is no significant price inflation or deflation in the economy and the cost of capital is low. However, depreciation allowances based on historical costs may not reflect opportunity costs. The ten-year asset's depreciation allowance would be zero if it were profitable to use for an eleventh year; however, the cost of the firm's using the asset is not zero. The firm's opportunity cost is the amount of money that could also be obtained by renting the asset. The implicit cost of the asset is the market value of its services and will not be zero if the asset is still profitable to use.

*Managerial Estimates of Implicit Fixed Costs.* Two alternative methods are used for measuring the opportunity costs of assets having economic lives greater than the length of the current planning period. These methods are most applicable when the asset is not highly specialized or site-specific. If the asset is highly specialized, there may not be a

---

[1]The economic life of an asset generally differs from the number of years over which the asset is depreciated for the purposes of calculating the firm's income tax liability. See section 14.1 for the income tax treatment of depreciation.

market price to use as its opportunity cost. Moreover, the price at which the firm can sell or rent a specialized factor is often sensitive to the amount of time allowed to make the sale and the costs the firm is willing to incur in searching for a buyer, negotiating the sale or rental, and obtaining the required financing.[2] In this case, management must apply its best judgment as to the opportunity cost for the asset.

*Current Replacement Cost Method.* This method starts with an estimate of the asset's current replacement cost, which is denoted by the symbol $K$. The remaining economic life of the asset is then projected. If the planning period is one month, its fixed cost is the monthly payment necessary to amortize $K$ over its remaining economic life at an interest rate equal to the firm's cost of capital. This procedure measures the opportunity cost as the monthly or annual payment that would be required by a lender if the company were to purchase the asset and finance 100 percent of its cost. The estimate of the asset's opportunity cost is independent of the financing method actually used to acquire the asset and its original historical cost. As the current replacement cost, cost of capital, or expected economic life of the asset change, management can adjust its opportunity cost accordingly.

*Equipment Rental Method.* This method assumes that the company is either renting or leasing the asset. Comparable rental rates are obtained if the asset is a building. Leasing costs are generally available when the asset is a relatively standard piece of equipment that leasing companies handle on a regular basis, such as a truck, a computer, a general-purpose machine tool, or office equipment. Specialized equipment can also be leased, although the interest rate may be somewhat higher if the resale market is limited. The monthly rental or lease payment is the asset's fixed cost. This method has the disadvantage that the rental or lease payment may not reflect the firm's cost of capital. The interest charge in the rental or lease payment reflects the lessor's cost of capital and assessment of the risk of default on the lease payments inherent in the firm's finances and trends in its industry.

## 6.1.3  Variable Costs

The firm's variable costs consist primarily of the costs of production workers (labor), raw materials, and purchased components. The quantities of these factors of production vary when the firm changes its output. Producing more output generally requires hiring more labor and buying additional quantities of materials; hence, the costs of labor and materials

---

[2]Transactions costs are discussed in section 8.6.

are variable with respect to changes in output. Most variable costs are explicit costs.

*Labor Costs.* The unit cost of labor is the wage rate $w$, the hourly wage paid to the workers plus the hourly cost of employee benefits provided by the firm. Employee benefits may range from 20 to 50 percent of the wage rate. Throughout this book, it is assumed that the wage rate does not vary with the number of workers.

Since most labor costs are paid to workers who are not owners of the firm, these costs are explicit costs. If the owners of the firm also work for the firm, as is common with many small businesses, the owners may pay themselves a relatively low wage and take the remainder of their earnings in the form of profits and luxuries paid for by the company. In this case, the wages paid to the owners do not reflect the opportunity cost of their labor. Although the firm's owners may obtain tax or financing advantages from paying themselves wages below what they could earn in their next-best alternative occupation, their labor costs should include an implicit charge equal to the difference between the opportunity cost of their labor and the wages they actually pay themselves. Otherwise, their decisions may be biased toward labor-intensive production and marketing methods because they have made the cost of labor artificially low relative to capital or materials.

*Materials Costs.* In all production and marketing processes, raw materials and purchased components are used along with labor. These materials include energy, metals, and plastics produced by other firms or in another division of the same firm. They also include parts such as fasteners and electrical or electronic components or supplies like paper and typewriter ribbons. For firms processing natural resources, they include crude oil, ores, timber, and agricultural products. These materials may be included in the production function along with labor and capital or included in a separate function relating the quantity of the material to the output of the good or service.

The prices paid for materials purchased from other firms are explicit costs. The general assumption in this book is that their unit prices do not depend upon the quantity purchased by the firm. That assumption, however, is not always realistic; the sellers of many materials routinely offer quantity discounts. If, as a result of increasing its output, the firm is able to obtain a greater quantity discount, this lower price should be used when the firm exceeds the threshold output for its product. If the firm uses four nut, bolt, and washer sets in each unit of its product and the price is $0.50 each for the first 10,000 sets and $0.45 each for all sets over 10,000, the threshold output is 2,500 units. Its costs up to 2,500 units of output are based on the $0.50 price. When output is above 2,500 units, its costs decline by $0.05 to reflect the lower cost of materials.

***Transfer Prices.*** If a component or raw material is produced by another division of the company, the price charged the division using the material is called the transfer price. In principle, the transfer price should represent the opportunity cost of the material to the firm. If the material is also sold to other firms, its price is one measure of its opportunity cost. If the division using the material buys a portion of its requirements from other firms, the price it pays them also represents an opportunity cost. If the material is bought or sold in a competitive market, the firm will produce the profit-maximizing output if the transfer price is its market price. If the component or raw material is not bought or sold in a competitive market, determination of the appropriate transfer price becomes more complex. We assume in this book that management can estimate the appropriate transfer price from the material's market price.

### 6.1.4  *Semivariable Costs*

Although economists generally utilize only fixed and variable costs in their analyses, some decisions involve consideration of semivariable costs. Semivariable costs are constant when output varies within a specified range; they increase or decrease only if output moves out of that range. The principal semivariable cost is the cost of supervisory and administrative labor, or the cost of the management pyramid.

Firms generally use a staffing formula to determine the number of supervisory and administrative workers required when hiring more production workers. A sample staffing formula is provided in Table 6.1. The total cost of supervisory and administrative costs goes up in increments as the number of production workers rises. Total cost is fixed for the range of output produced by a group of one to ten production workers and then becomes variable when the eleventh worker is added and more supervisory and administrative workers are required. For example, between 51 and 60 production workers, semivariable costs are $68 per hour. When the firm hires the sixty-first production worker, semivariable costs jump to $171 per hour because of the addition of a new layer of management. This cost does not change, however, when the sixty-second production worker is hired. When the seventy-first production worker is hired, the semivariable cost again increases.

For the most part, the theory of managerial decision making will be explained without explicit reference to semivariable costs. In effect, such costs will be included with fixed costs. There is, however, one notable exception: larger plants generally require more production workers

**Table 6.1   Representative Staffing Formula**

| Number of Production Workers | Foremen | | Supervisors and Staff | | Superintendent and Staff | | Total Cost |
|---|---|---|---|---|---|---|---|
| | Number | Cost | Number | Cost | Number | Cost | |
| 1–10 | 1 | $ 8/hr | 0* | $ 0/hr | 0 | $ 0/hr | $ 8/hr |
| 11–20 | 2 | 16 | 0* | 0 | 0 | 0 | 16 |
| 21–30 | 3 | 24 | 3 | 20 | 0** | 0 | 44 |
| 31–40 | 4 | 32 | 3 | 20 | 0** | 0 | 52 |
| 41–50 | 5 | 40 | 3 | 20 | 0** | 0 | 60 |
| 51–60 | 6 | 48 | 3 | 20 | 0** | 0 | 68 |
| 61–70 | 7 | 56 | 6 | 40 | 8 | 75 | 171 |
| 71–80 | 8 | 64 | 6 | 40 | 8 | 75 | 179 |
| 81–90 | 9 | 72 | 6 | 40 | 8 | 75 | 187 |

*The manager of the production facility supervises the first two foremen. One supervisor and a staff consisting of a secretary and clerk are required when the third foreman is hired and another supervisor and staff are required when the seventh foreman is hired.
**The manager of the production facility manages the first supervisor. One superintendent and a staff of seven administrative workers are required when the second supervisor is hired.

to operate them, and more production workers require proportionately greater numbers of supervisory and administrative workers. For most production technologies, the increase in semivariable costs ultimately leads to rising costs per unit of output and a limit on the size of the plant or firm.[3]

## 6.1.5  *Joint Costs*

When the firm produces more than one product, accountants allocate among the several products those costs that cannot be identified with only one of the products and refer to them as joint costs. If the products are produced in separate areas of the plant or are produced serially over time, it is not particularly difficult to make the required cost allocations. They can be allocated on the basis of the proportion of the building area or the time used to produce each product. It is when the products are produced at the same time and use the same production facilities that the portion of total cost to allocate to each product becomes difficult to determine. If two products are produced in fixed proportions so that ten units of product A must be produced with eight units of product B, economists treat the two products as if they were a single product. This eliminates arbitrary and inappropriate cost allocations

[3]Section 6.6.4 contains a more detailed discussion of this point.

that lead to suboptimal pricing and output decisions. When two or more products are produced under conditions of variable output proportions, it is generally possible to calculate a cost to apply to each of the products. To simplify the cost functions used in this book, we generally assume that the firm produces a single product.[4]

### 6.1.6  *Short- and Long-Run Costs*

The short run is the period of time during which there are one or more fixed factors in the firm's production function. Those factors may be fixed because management believes that they are unprofitable to change during the current planning period. Alternatively, management may choose to plan its operations for the current planning period by treating its existing production facilities as fixed factors even though it would be possible to expand them during the current planning period. In either case, when there are fixed factors of production, management is concerned with estimating short-run costs. When all factors of production are variable, the emphasis is on estimating long-run costs.

## 6.2  *Short-Run Cost Functions*

In the short run, there is at least one fixed factor. Producing more output requires increasing the variable factors, primarily labor and materials. The several cost functions relate output to the levels of total, average, and marginal cost. These cost functions may be derived from the production functions discussed in Chapter 5 or from statistical cost studies. The graphs of the cost functions are referred to as cost curves.

### 6.2.1  *Total Cost Function*

The total cost function provides the relationship between output and its total cost. Both the explicit costs in the company's accounting statements and the implicit opportunity costs of factors owned by the firm are included in the total cost function. The short-run total cost function includes both fixed costs and variable costs. All of the costs relevant to management's profit- or wealth-maximizing decisions are provided in the firm's total cost function.

The short-run total cost function, *SRTC*, is the sum of the fixed costs, *FC*, and total variable costs, *TVC*.

---

[4]Chapter 7 provides examples of cost calculations where there are joint costs and fixed proportions among the several products.

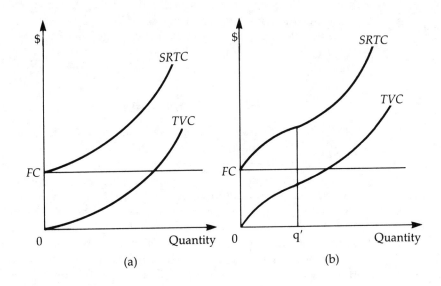

**Figure 6.1  Total Cost Curves**

The total cost and total variable cost curves rise as output increases. Both *TC* and *TVC* have the same slope at a given output. Fixed cost is represented by a horizontal line because fixed costs do not change as output increases. In part (a), there are only diminishing returns as labor is increased to produce more output. In part (b), there are increasing returns up to output $q'$ and diminishing returns thereafter.

$$SRTC = FC + TVC \qquad\qquad (6.1)$$

Since fixed costs do not change with output, the graphs of fixed costs in Figure 6.1 are horizontal lines. Total variable costs consist of the total cost of labor, *TCL*, and the total cost of materials, *TCM*.

$$TVC = TCL + TCM \qquad\qquad (6.2)$$

*Total Cost and Factor Productivity.* If the unit costs of labor and materials do not change with output and if the quantity of materials per unit of output is a constant, then the shape of the *TVC* curve depends on the marginal product of labor as output increases. If there are increasing returns as the quantity of labor is increased from zero, and then diminishing returns, the *TCL* curve reflects the shape of the total product of labor curve.[5] The *TCL* curve starts from zero, rises at

---

[5]A typical total product curve is graphed in Figure 5.1.

a decreasing rate until output $q'$ is reached and increasing returns cease, and then rises at an increasing rate reflecting diminishing returns to labor. If the unit cost of materials is constant, *TVC* has the same shape as the *TCL* curve. The *TVC* and *SRTC* curves where there are both increasing and diminishing returns are graphed in Figure 6.1 as *TVC* and *SRTC*. Both *TVC* and *SRTC* have an inflection point at output $q'$. Output $q'$ is produced by $L'$ units of labor. The *SRTC* curve starts at the level of fixed costs and rises as output and the quantity of labor increase. The *TVC* and *SRTC* curves at a given output have the same slope.

**EXAMPLE 6.1.**   Management is interested in the total cost of producing 100 units of output per hour in a plant with fixed costs of $120 per hour. Assume that the wage rate is $5.00 per hour and the cost of materials is $1.50 per unit of output. If the average product of labor is *APL* = 12.5 units, producing the 100 units of output requires 8 production workers at a total cost of labor of $40 per hour. The total cost of materials is $1.50 per unit times 100 units of output, or $150 per hour. *TVC* = $40 + $150 = $190 per hour and *SRTC* = $190 + $120 = $310 per hour.

Assume now that a change in work rules results in an increase in *APL* to 14.3 units. This productivity increase will reduce to seven the number of production workers required to produce 100 units per hour. The total cost of labor falls to $35 per hour, and short-run total cost falls to $305 per hour. If, however, the work rule changes were accompanied by an increase in the wage rate to $6.00 per hour, the total cost of labor would rise to $42 per hour and *SRTC* to $312 per hour. Thus, the total cost of the product depends on the productivity of the factors and their unit costs.

## 6.2.2  *Average Cost Functions*

The graphical analysis of short-run costs is generally carried out using average and marginal cost curves. The profit-maximizing output is easier to identify with average and marginal cost curves than with the corresponding total cost curves. This subsection covers the average cost functions. Marginal cost is discussed in the next subsection.

Dividing both sides of equation 6.1 by output yields the short-run average total cost (*SRATC*), which consists of the average fixed cost (*AFC*) and the average variable cost (*AVC*).

$$SRATC = AFC + AVC \qquad\qquad (6.3)$$

where $SRATC = SRTC/Q$, $AFC = FC/Q$, and $AVC = TVC/Q$. Dividing both sides of equation 6.2 by output yields

$$AVC = ACM + ACL \qquad (6.4)$$

where *ACL* is the average cost of labor and *ACM* is the average cost of materials. A fixed proportions function relating output to the required quantities of materials is $M = gQ$, where $g$ is the number of units of materials per unit of output. If the unit cost of materials is $m$, equation 6.4 is

$$AVC = mg + ACL \qquad (6.5)$$

since $ACM = mgQ/Q$. *ACM* in the right graph of Figure 6.2 is a horizontal line at level $mg$ if neither $m$ nor $g$ depends on output.

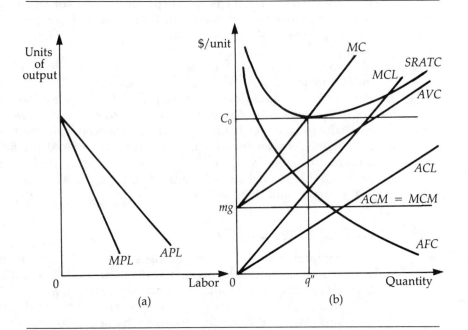

**Figure 6.2   Average and Marginal Cost Curves: Diminishing Returns**

The *AVC* and *MC* curves start from the level of the horizontal $ACM = MCM$ line. The rate at which *ACL* and *MCL* rise depends on the rate at which *APL* and *MPL* decline since $ACL = w/APL$ and $MCL = w/MPL$. The *SRATC* is U-shaped and *MC* goes through its minimum point. *SRATC* approaches *AVC* as output increases because *AFC* approaches zero.

*Average Variable Cost.* Average variable cost depends on the average costs of labor and materials. $ACL$ is calculated by dividing the wage rate by $APL$. Since total labor cost is $TLC = wL$ and $APL = Q/L$, $ACL = wL/Q = w/(Q/L) = w/APL$. Thus, equation 6.4 becomes

$$AVC = ACM + (w/APL) \qquad (6.6)$$

The shape of the $AVC$ curve depends on whether the production function first exhibits increasing returns or whether it exhibits only diminishing returns. In Figure 6.2 there are only diminishing returns, so that the $APL$ curve is always downward sloping and the $AVC$ curve is upward sloping. The $APL$ curve when there are both increasing and diminishing returns is in the left-hand graph of Figure 6.3. From equation 6.6, a rising $APL$ implies that $ACL$ and $AVC$ are declining, and a declining

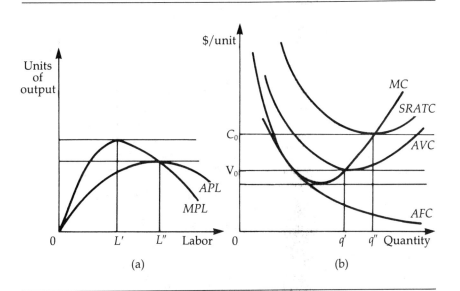

**Figure 6.3 Average and Marginal Cost Curves: Increasing and Diminishing Returns**

The $AFC$ curve is downward sloping because $AFC = FC/q$ and $q$ is increasing. The cost of materials is assumed to be constant; hence, the slopes of the $AVC$ and $MC$ curves depend upon the slopes of the $APL$ and $MPL$ curves. Since $ACL = w/APL$ and $MCL = w/MPL$, the shapes of $AVC$ and $MC$ ultimately depend on $APL$ and $MPL$. $SRATC$ is U-shaped because $AVC$ eventually rises at a higher rate than $AFC$ declines. $MC$ goes through the minimum points of the $AVC$ and $SRATC$ curves.

*APL* implies that *ACL* and *AVC* are increasing. Thus, the *AVC* curve is U-shaped. Output $q''$ in the right graph of Figure 6.3 is produced by $L''$ units of labor in the left graph.

*Average Fixed Cost.* The *AFC* curve in the right graph of Figures 6.2 or 6.3 is a rectangular hyperbola. If output is low, *AFC* is high because there are few units of output over which to spread the fixed cost. As output rises, AFC falls because the denominator of $FC/Q$ rises and the numerator is a constant. If $FC = \$200$, $AFC = \$200/10 = \$20/$unit when $Q = 10$, and $AFC = \$2/$unit when $Q = 100$. As output increases, AFC approaches zero. Although AFC declines as output increases, increasing output will not necessarily increase profits, because the reduction in *AFC* may be more than offset by an increase in *AVC*. In Figures 6.2 or 6.3, the *SRATC* curve is U-shaped. As output increases from zero, the decline in *AFC* will initially be more rapid than the increase in *AVC*. However, beyond $q''$ diminishing returns as labor increases eventually result in *AVC* increasing at a faster rate than *AFC* is declining. A manager cannot make a judgment with respect to the impact of higher output on total costs and profits without considering both *AFC* and *AVC*.

**EXAMPLE 6.2.** Calculate *AVC* and *SRATC* for an output of $Q = 20$ units per hour assuming that the firm's production function is $Q = 2L^{0.5}$, the wage rate is $w = \$8$ per hour, the cost of materials is $ACM = \$25$ per unit of output, and fixed costs are $FC = \$600$ per hour.

$$APL = Q/L = 2L^{0.5}/L = 2L^{0.5}$$
$$ACL = w/APL = \$8/(2/L^{0.5}) = \$4L^{0.5}$$

Solving the production function yields $L^{0.5} = 0.5Q$.

$$ACL = \$4(0.5Q) = \$2Q$$
$$AVC = ACM + ACL = \$25 + \$2Q$$
$$AVC = \$25 + \$2(20) = \$65/\text{unit}$$
$$AFC = FC/Q = \$600/20 = \$30/\text{unit}$$
$$SRATC = AFC + AVC = \$30 + \$65 = \$95/\text{unit}$$

### 6.2.3 *Marginal Cost Function*

Marginal cost, *MC*, is defined as the change in total cost or total variable cost when output changes by a small amount. *MC* can be calculated as the change in total cost or total variable cost when output is increased by one unit from $Q_0$.

$$MC = TC(Q_0 + 1) - TC(Q_0) = TVC(Q_0 + 1) - TVC(Q_0) \quad \text{(6.7)}$$

In this book, $MC$ is generally calculated by taking the derivative of the total cost or total variable cost function.

$$MC = dTC/dq = dTVC/dq$$

Marginal cost equals the marginal cost of labor, $MCL$, plus the marginal cost of materials, $MCM$, or $MC = MCL + MCM$. If there are fixed proportions between output and materials and their unit cost does not change with output, $TCM = mgQ$ and $MCM = d(TCM)/dQ = mg$. The graph of $MCM$ is a horizontal line at level $mg$. Since $TCL = wL$, $MCL = d(TCL)/dQ = w(dL/dQ) = w/(dQ/dL) = w/MPL$. Marginal cost is

$$MC = MCM + MCL = MCM + (w/MPL) \quad \text{(6.8)}$$

*The Marginal Cost Curve.* If the production function first exhibits increasing and then diminishing returns, as in the left-hand graph of Figure 6.3, $MPL$ has an inverted U shape and the $MC$ curve has the U shape in the right graph of Figure 6.3. In the right graph of Figure 6.3, $q'$ is the output produced by $L'$ units of labor in the left graph. Since the $MPL$ curve goes through the maximum point on the $APL$ curve at $L'$ units of labor, the $MCL$ curve goes through the minimum point of the $ACL$ curve at $q'$ units of output. The $MC$ curve also goes through the minimum points of the $AVC$ and $ATC$ curves.

If the production function exhibits only diminishing returns when labor is increased from zero, the $MC$ curve is always rising from $mg$, as is the $AVC$ curve. If $AVC$ is rising, $MC$ must lie above $AVC$, because an average will increase only if the marginal is greater than the average. When the $MPL$ curve is downward sloping, the $MC$ curve is upward sloping, as in Figure 6.2.

**EXAMPLE 6.3.** Management wishes to find the marginal cost of increasing output by one unit. Assume that total cost when $Q = 100$ is \$1,450 and is \$1,465 when $Q = 101$. $MC = \$1,465 - \$1,450 = \$15$ for the one-unit change in output. If fixed costs are \$200, then $TVC = \$1,250$ when $Q = 100$ and \$1,265 when $Q = 101$. $MC$ is again equal to \$15 since $MC = \$1,265 - \$1,250$.

**EXAMPLE 6.4.** Assume that the firm's total cost function is $TC = \$750 + \$15Q + \$2Q^2$. The marginal cost function is $MC = dTC/dQ = \$15 + \$4Q$. If output is $Q = 10$ units, $MC = \$15 + \$4(10) = \$55$.

**EXAMPLE 6.5.** Calculate marginal cost for an output of five units per hour assuming that the firm's production function is $Q = 0.5L^{0.5}$, the wage rate is $w = \$5$ per hour, and the cost of materials is $MCM = \$150$ per unit of output.

$$MPL = dQ/dL = 0.25/L^{0.5}$$

$$MCL = w/MPL = \$5/(0.25/L^{0.5}) = \$20L^{0.5}$$

Solving the production function for $L^{0.5}$ yields $L^{0.5} = 2Q$ and substituting this result into the $MCL$ function yields

$$MCL = \$20(2Q) = \$40Q$$

$$MC = MCM + MCL = \$150 + \$40Q$$

$$MC = \$150 + \$40(5) = \$350$$

## 6.3   *Calculating Short-Run Costs**

This section provides examples of two techniques for calculating points on the cost curves discussed in the previous section. The first example assumes that the analyst has estimated the firm's production function, either from an engineering study or from a statistical study of actual operations similar to the one in section 5.8. The second example assumes that the analyst has statistically estimated the firm's total cost function.

### 6.3.1   *Calculating Short-Run Costs from the Production Function*

**EXAMPLE 6.6.** The Cobb-Douglas production function is used in statistical studies of labor productivity because it generally provides good empirical fit to actual data. It also exhibits diminishing returns as the quantity of labor increases from zero. Assume that the production function has been estimated as $Q = K^{0.5}L^{0.5}$ where output $Q$ is in units per hour. The amount of capital is fixed in the short run at $K = 100$ units; thus, the production function becomes

$$Q = (100)^{0.5}L^{0.5} = 10L^{0.5} \text{ or } L^{0.5} = 0.1Q \qquad \text{(6.9)}$$

*This section may be omitted without loss of continuity.

*Average Fixed Cost.* Assume that the implicit opportunity cost of each unit of capital has been estimated at $2 per hour and the explicit costs of the other fixed factors used in the production process are $100 per hour. Thus, fixed costs are $FC = (\$2)(100) + \$100 = \$300$/hour. Average fixed costs are

$$AFC = \$300/Q = \$300/10L^{0.5} = \$30/L^{0.5}$$

*Average Variable and Average Total Cost.* Assume that the wage rate is $5.00 per hour, the cost of materials is $m = \$0.25$ per unit, and $g$ = four units of materials required per unit of output. The average product of labor is

$$APL = Q/L = 10L^{0.5}/L = 10/L^{0.5}$$

The average cost of labor is

$$ACL = w/APL = w/(10/L^{0.5}) = 0.1wL^{0.5}$$
$$ACL = 0.1(\$5.00)L^{0.5} = \$0.50L^{0.5} = \$0.05Q$$

since, from equation 6.9, $L^{0.5} = 0.1Q$. Since $ACM = mg = (\$0.25)(4) = \$1.00$ per unit of output,

$$AVC = ACM + ACL = \$1.00 + \$0.05Q$$
$$SRATC = AFC + AVC = \$300/Q + \$1.00 + \$0.05Q$$

*Marginal Cost.* Calculating MCL begins with the equation for MPL obtained by differentiating the production function in equation 6.9 with respect to labor. The basic equation relating MCL to MPL is $MCL = w/MPL$. The derivative of the production function is

$$MPL = dQ/dL = 5/L^{0.5}$$

Since the wage rate is $5.00 per hour,

$$MCL = \$5L^{0.5}/5 = \$L^{0.5} = \$0.10Q$$

Since neither the unit cost nor the quantity of materials required to produce one unit of output varies with output, the marginal cost of materials, MCM, equals $mg$.

$$MC = MCM + MCL = mg + L^{0.5} = \$1.00 + \$0.10Q$$

*Graphing the Cost Curve.* These cost equations can be graphed by constructing a table relating the quantities of labor and output to the several measures of cost. When these cost functions are graphed, they yield cost curves similar to those in Figure 6.2.

*Calculating Minimum* **SRATC.** The *SRATC* curve in Figure 6.2 has a minimum point. At first, as $Q$ increases, *AFC* declines by more than *AVC* increases, so that *ATC* declines. As output continues to increase, *AFC* ultimately declines by less than *AVC* increases, so that *SRATC* increases. The output at which *SRATC* is minimized can be found using differential calculus. The equation for *SRATC* is differentiated with respect to output, and the resulting derivative set equal to zero. Solving this equation yields the output at which *SRATC* is minimized.

$$SRATC = \$300Q^{-1} + \$1.00 + \$0.05Q$$

To find the minimum point,[6] $dSRATC/dQ = \$-300/Q^2 + \$0.05 = 0.$

$$\$300/Q^2 = \$0.05 \text{ or } Q^2 = 300/0.05 = 6{,}000 \text{ units}$$
$$Q = (6{,}000)^{0.5} = 77.46$$

Average total cost when $Q = 77.46$ units is

$$SRATC = \$300/77.46 + \$1.00 + (\$0.05)(77.46) = \$8.74/\text{unit}$$

## 6.3.2 *Calculating Short-Run Costs from the* **TC** *Function*

**EXAMPLE 6.7.** Management wishes to calculate the *SRATC*, *AFC*, *AVC*, and *MC* functions for the firm and find the outputs at which *AVC* and *SRATC* are minimized. Assume that a statistical cost study has estimated the firm's short-run total cost function as

$$TC = \$Q^3 - \$9.50Q^2 + \$50Q + \$500$$

This TC function can be broken down into two components:

$$FC = \$500$$
$$TVC = \$Q^3 - \$9.50Q^2 + \$50Q$$

---

[6]To determine if *SRATC* is minimized, take the second derivative of the *SRATC* function and substitute 77.46 for $Q$.
$$d^2SRATC/dQ^2 = 600/Q^3 = 600(77.46)^3 = +0.0013$$
Since the second derivative is positive, *SRATC* is minimized.

*The Average Costs.* Average total cost, average fixed cost, and average variable cost are

$$SRATC = TC/Q = \$Q^2 - \$9.50Q + \$50 + \$500/Q$$

$$AFC = FC/Q = \$500/Q$$

$$AVC = TVC/Q = \$Q^2 - \$9.50Q + \$50$$

If the unit cost of materials does not change with output, the $50 term in *SRATC* and *AVC* is the unit cost of materials. The first two terms in the equations for *SRATC* and *AVC* are the average cost of labor.

*Marginal Cost.* Marginal cost is the derivative of the total cost or total variable cost function. When $Q = 5$,

$$MC = d(TVC)/dQ = \$3Q^2 - \$19Q + \$50$$

$$MC = \$3(5)^2 - \$19(5) + \$50 = \$30$$

The $50 term in the *MC* function is the marginal cost of materials if *MCM* does not change with changes in output. The other two terms are the marginal cost of labor.

*Minimizing* **AVC** *and* **SRATC.** The minimum point on the *AVC* curve is found by taking the derivative of AVC with respect to output, setting it equal to zero, and solving for *Q*.

$$d(AVC)/dQ = \$2Q - \$9.50 = 0 \Rightarrow Q = 4.75 \text{ units}$$

Substituting this output into the *AVC* function yields the minimum level of *AVC* of $27.44.

To find the minimum point on the *SRATC* curve, rewrite the *SRATC* function as

$$SRATC = \$Q^2 - \$9.50Q + \$50 + \$500Q^{-1}$$

Taking this function's derivative, setting it equal to zero, and multiplying both sides by $Q^2$ yields

$$dSRATC/dQ = 2Q - 9.50 - 500/Q^2 = 0$$

$$2Q^3 - 9.5Q^2 - 500 = 0$$

This cubic equation can be solved by trial and error by finding the value of *Q* that yields a value of zero for the left side of the equation.

Since *AVC* is minimized at $Q = 4.75$ units and *SRATC* is minimized at a greater output than *AVC*, try $Q = 7$ as the first trial value:

$$2(7)^3 - 9.5(7)^2 - 500 = -279.5$$

Thus, $Q = 7$ is too low an output to minimize *SRATC*. Trying $Q = 8$ yields $-84.0$ and $Q = 8.5$ yields $+41.875$. The sign change between these last two values indicates that *SRATC* is minimized between $Q = 8$ and $Q = 8.5$. Next try $Q = 8.3$, which yields $-10.881$. $Q$ must be increased. Setting $Q$ equal to 8.34 yields $-0.59$. $Q = 8.34$ is probably close enough to the value of $Q$ that actually minimizes *SRATC* to use for cost estimation purposes.[7] When $Q = 8.34$,

$$SRATC = \$(8.34)^2 - \$9.50(8.34) + \$50 + \$500/8.34 = \$100.28 \text{ per unit}$$

## 6.4 *Cost Minimization with Two Variable Factors*

Cost minimization involves finding the greatest output that can be produced with a given expenditure on the variable factors of production. In this section, there are two variable factors whose proportions can be varied by the firm's management.[8] The first step in this planning procedure is to specify the budget — the amount of money to be spent on the two factors. The next step is to use the production function to find the quantity of each factor that produces the maximum output for that budget. Average and marginal cost can then be calculated for that output. Finally, alternative budget levels can be specified and the process repeated to provide the costs associated with a range of possible outputs for the firm.

### 6.4.1 *The Labor Budget and Isocost Curve*

Decision-making centers within a firm, institution, or public agency have a budget. The budget is the maximum amount that the manager is authorized to spend to attain a specified goal, such as producing a given output during the planning period. A business manager or public administrator becomes a decision maker when he or she is assigned a

---

[7]The second derivative of *SRATC* is

$$d^2 SRATC/dQ^2 = 2 + 100/Q^3 = 2 + 1,000/8.34^3 = +3.72$$

Since the second derivative is positive, *SRATC* is minimized.

[8]In the preceding two sections, labor was the only variable factor on which management had to make a decision since materials were used in fixed proportions with output.

budget and given discretionary authority to make choices within the confines of that budget. The budget is a constraint on the decision maker's authority.

Assume that the labor budget for producing a specified output is to be minimized. The two types of production labor are skilled labor, $S$, and unskilled labor, $L$. If the labor budget is $B$ dollars, $W$ is the symbol for both types of labor, and output is $Q$, the average cost of labor, $ACW$, is $ACW = B/Q$. In calculating $ACW$, $B$ and $Q$ must have the same time units. If $Q$ is output per hour, then $B$ is the hourly budget. Minimizing $ACW$ requires that $B$ be the smallest budget sufficient to purchase the quantities of skilled and unskilled labor capable of producing output $Q_0$. Alternatively, if the budget is specified, minimizing $ACW$ requires that $Q$ be maximized. Since minimizing $B$ when $Q$ is given yields the same quantities of skilled and unskilled labor as when $Q$ is maximized and B is given, either method may be used.[9]

*The Isocost Curve.* The isocost curve is the locus of all combinations of skilled and unskilled labor that can be purchased with a specified total expenditure (budget) on labor. If the amount of skilled labor is $S$ and its wage rate is $s$, the amount spent on skilled labor is $sS$. Similarly, if the amount of unskilled labor is $L$ and its wage rate is $w$, the amount spent on unskilled labor is $wL$. The budget equation is $B = sS + wL$. The graph of the budget equation is referred to as the isocost curve or the budget constraint.

If the entire labor budget, $B_0$, is allocated to the purchase of unskilled labor, so that $S = 0$ in the budget equation, the maximum quantity of unskilled labor that can be purchased is $L' = B_0/w$. If all of the labor budget is allocated to skilled labor, the maximum quantity of skilled labor is $S' = B_0/s$. These points are graphed in Figure 6.4. Since the budget equation is linear, the maximum quantity of skilled labor that can be purchased given the quantity of unskilled labor is on the straight line connecting $L'$ and $S'$. This straight line is the isocost curve for a budget of $B_0$ dollars. If $L_0$ unskilled workers are hired, a maximum of $S_0$ skilled workers can be hired given the labor budget of $B_0$ dollars. The expenditures on skilled labor are $sS_0$ dollars per hour and on unskilled labor are $wL_0$ dollars per hour.

*Shifting the Isocost Curve.* The intercept-slope form of the budget equation is $S = (B/s) - (w/s)L$. Its slope is $dS/dL = -(w/s)$ and its vertical intercept is $(B/s)$. If the budget is changed, the intercept of the isocost curve changes in the same direction, but its slope is unchanged.

[9]Maximizing $Q$ when $B$ is given is referred to as the "dual" of minimizing $B$ when $Q$ is given.

When the budget changes, the isocost curve shifts up or down parallel to the original isocost curve. Isocost curve $B_1$ in Figure 6.4 is obtained by increasing the budget from $B_0$ to $B_1$. An increase in the wage rate for unskilled workers from $w_0$ to $w_1$, with no change in the wage rate for skilled workers or in budget $B_0$, leaves the vertical intercept unchanged. However, the horizontal intercept shifts to the left to $L'' = B_0/w_1$. This isocost curve is steeper because the numerator of the expression for its slope has increased. If the wage rates for skilled and unskilled workers change by the same percentage, the slope of the isocost curve is un-

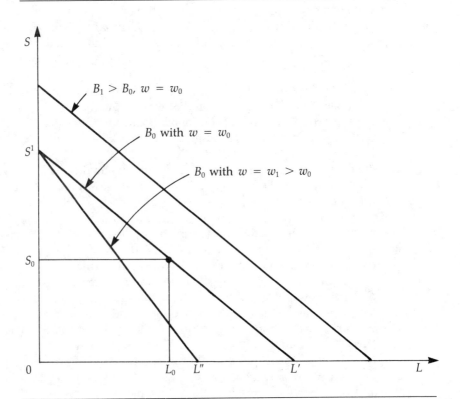

**Figure 6.4  Isocost Curves**

The skilled labor wage rate is held constant in this diagram. The initial isocost curve is $B_0$ with $w = w_0$, the initial value of the unskilled labor wage rate. When $w$ rises to $w_1$, the vertical ($S'$) intercept of the isocost curve is unchanged, but its horizontal intercept shifts from $L'$ to $L''$ because budget $B_0$ will now buy less unskilled labor. If the budget is increased to $B_1$ and $w = w_0$, the isocost curve shifts up parallel to the initial isocost curve because more of both types of labor can now be purchased.

changed, but it shifts parallel to the original isocost curve. If the two wage rates increase by 5 percent, the isocost curve will shift to the left because higher wage rates mean that a given budget can buy less of each type of labor.

EXAMPLE 6.8. Assume that the labor budget is $B_0 = \$1,000$ per hour. If unskilled labor costs $10 per hour, the maximum number of unskilled workers that the firm can hire is $L' = \$1,000/\$10 = 100$ workers. Similarly, if the hourly cost of skilled labor is $20, $S' = \$1,000/\$20 = 50$ skilled workers. Points $L_0$ and $S_0$ in Figure 6.4 could be for $L_0 = 50$ unskilled workers at an hourly cost of $500 and $S_0 = 25$ skilled workers also at an hourly cost of $500, for a total expenditure of $B_0 = \$1,000$. If the wage rate for unskilled workers rises to $12.50 per hour, $L'' = \$1,000/\$12.50 = 80$ workers. If the budget were increased to $B_1 = \$1,200$ per hour, budget line $B_1$ in Figure 6.4 would have its intercepts at 120 unskilled workers and 60 skilled workers at wage rates of $10 and $20 per hour, respectively.

## 6.4.2 *The Production Function and the Isoquant Curve*

Finding the combination of skilled and unskilled labor that minimizes the cost of producing a given output requires knowledge of the production function for the good or service. The production function yields all combinations of skilled and unskilled labor capable of producing output $Q_0$ given the capital invested in the plant and its technology. The isoquant curve is the graphical representation of the production function.[10] It is found by specifying the output to be produced and then using the production function to calculate all combinations of the variable factors producing this output. The isoquant curve in Figure 6.5 is the locus of all combinations of skilled and unskilled labor that can produce $Q_0$. Since unskilled labor is not a perfect substitute for skilled labor, and diminishing returns to each factor are widely observed, the isoquant curve is convex to the origin of the graph. The slope of the isoquant curve, the marginal rate of technical substitution, varies along the isoquant curve.

## 6.4.3 *Maximizing Output Given the Budget*

Cost minimization requires that the firm produce as much output as possible given its budget because this will minimize the average cost of labor ($ACW = B/Q$). Finding the combination of $S$ and $L$ that minimizes

---

[10]For a more complete discussion of the isoquant curve see section 5.6. The special case of linear isoquant curve is discussed in section 7.1.

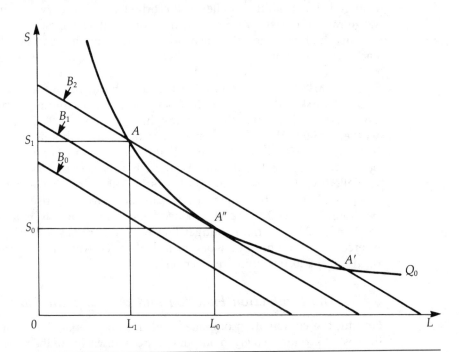

**Figure 6.5   Finding the Optimum Combination of $L$ and $S$**

Isoquant curve $Q_0$ graphs all combinations of $L$ and $S$ capable of producing output $Q_0$. All combinations of $L$ and $S$ along isocost curve $B_0$ are inadequate for producing $Q_0$. Isocost curve $B_2$ can finance the production of $Q_0$ but it represents a greater budget than is necessary. Budget $B_1$, yielding the iso-cost curve tangent to the $Q_0$ isoquant, minimizes the cost of producing $Q_0$ and provides the optimum combination of $L$ and $S$ at point $A''$.

the average cost of labor requires finding the lowest isocost curve capable of supplying the quantities of $L$ and $S$ that can produce $Q_0$ units of output. All of the isocost curves in Figure 6.5 are for the same wage rates. Budget $B_0$ cannot buy enough $L$ and $S$ to produce $Q_0$ because it lies entirely below the $Q_0$ isoquant curve. Budget $B_2$ is a larger budget than is necessary for producing $Q_0$. The combinations of $L$ and $S$ on $B_2$ at points $A$ and $A'$ are capable of producing $Q_0$. Budget $B_1$ yields the isocost curve that is tangent to isoquant $Q_0$ at factor combination $L_0$ and $S_0$ (point $A''$). $B_1$ is the smallest budget that can be used to produce $Q_0$; a lower budget than $B_1$ would, like $B_0$, not touch the $Q_0$ isoquant curve at any point. Thus, the budget that minimizes the average cost of labor used to produce a given output is found at the point of tangency between an isocost curve and the given isoquant curve.

This point of tangency also yields the cost-minimizing combination of unskilled and skilled labor $(L_0, S_0)$ for producing $Q_0$. If budget $B_2$ in Figure 6.5 is used to produce $Q_0$, factor combination $L_1, S_1$ at point $A$ could produce $Q_0$. Reducing skilled labor from $S_1$ to $S_0$ would reduce expenditures on skilled labor by $s(S_1 - S_0)$. Factor combination $L_1$ and $S_0$, however, will not produce $Q_0$. To get output up to $Q_0$, unskilled labor must be hired until factor combination $L_0$ and $S_0$ at $A''$ is obtained. The new budget would be $B_1 = B_2 - s(S_1 - S_0) + w(L_0 - L_1)$, and $B_1$ would be less than $B_2$ if $s(S_1 - S_0)$ is greater than $w(L_0 - L_1)$.

**EXAMPLE 6.9.** If the production function is $Q = 10L^{0.25}S^{0.5}$, point $A$ in Figure 6.5 is factor combination $L = 16$ and $S = 25$, and $Q_0 = 100$. If the wage rates are $w = \$5$ and $s = \$10$, $B_2 = (16 \times \$5) + (25 \times \$10) = \$330$. Another combination of $L$ and $S$ to produce 100 units of output is $L = S = 21.544$. At the above wage rates, $B_1 = (21.544 \times \$5) + (21.544 \times \$10) = \$323.16$, which is less than $B_2$. Reducing skilled labor from 25 to 21.544 units reduced the labor budget by $\$10(25 - 21.544) = \$34.56$, and increasing unskilled labor from 16 to the 21.544 units now necessary to produce $Q_0 = 100$ increased the labor budget by $\$5(21.544 - 16) = \$27.72$. On balance, the labor budget was reduced by $\$34.56 - \$27.72 = \$6.84$, which is the difference between $B_2$ and $B_1$. The average cost of labor if the labor budget is $\$323.16$ is $ACW = \$323.16/100 = \$3.23$.

### 6.4.4. *Cost Minimization Using Marginal Cost*

The tangency of the isoquant and isocost curves that yields the cost-minimizing quantities of $S$ and $L$ can also be interpreted in terms of marginal cost. In section 5.6, it was demonstrated that

$$MRTS = dS/dL = -MPL/MPS \qquad (6.10)$$

The slope of the isocost curve is

$$dS/dL = -w/s \qquad (6.11)$$

The two slopes are equal when the isocost and isoquant curves are tangent.

$$-MPL/MPS = -w/s$$
$$w/MPL = s/MPS \qquad (6.12)$$

Since marginal cost is the unit cost of the factor divided by its marginal product, equation 6.12 implies that when labor costs are minimized,

$$MCL = MCS \tag{6.13}$$

where $MCL$ is the marginal cost of producing one more unit of output using unskilled labor. Labor costs are minimized when the increase in total cost is the same whether output is increased by adding skilled or unskilled labor.

**EXAMPLE 6.10.**  Assume that at an output of $Q_0$, producing one more unit by adding unskilled labor results in a marginal cost of $MCL =$ $120, and adding skilled labor results in a marginal cost of $MCS =$ $100. The cost of producing the product has not been minimized at the factor combination yielding these marginal costs. Using more skilled labor and less unskilled labor will reduce total cost. Reducing output by one unit $Q_0$ by reducing the quantity of unskilled labor will reduce total cost by $120. Output is now, however, one unit less than $Q_0$. Producing this additional unit of output by increasing the quantity of skilled labor adds $MCS =$ $100 to total cost, resulting in a cost reduction of $20. These reductions in production costs continue until the two marginal costs are equal.

**EXAMPLE 6.11.**  This example uses equation 6.12 and the budget equation to calculate the cost-minimizing quantities of skilled and unskilled labor. These amounts are then used to calculate output and the average and marginal costs of labor. Assume that the budget assigned to the plant is $900 per hour, the unskilled wage is $5 per hour, the skilled wage is $10 per hour, and the plant's production function is $Q = 2L^{0.5}S$. The first step is to calculate the marginal costs of unskilled and skilled labor:

$$MPL = \partial Q/\partial L = S/L^{0.5}$$
$$MCL = w/MPL = \$5/(S/L^{0.5}) = \$5L^{0.5}/S$$
$$MPS = \partial Q/\partial S = 2L^{0.5}$$
$$MCS = s/MPS = \$10/2L^{0.5}$$

Since cost minimization requires that $MCL = MCS$,

$$\$5L^{0.5}/S = \$5/L^{0.5} \Rightarrow L = S$$

For the firm to minimize its average cost of labor, it uses the same quantities of skilled and unskilled labor. The budget equation is

$$\$5L + \$10S = \$900$$

Substituting $L = S$ into the budget equation yields

$$5L + 10(L) = 900$$

$$15L = 900$$

$$L = S = 60 \text{ workers}$$

Output and the average cost of labor are

$$Q = 2(60)^{0.5}(60) = 2(60)^{1.5} = 929.5 \text{ units}$$

$$ACW = B/Q = \$900/929.5 = \$0.97 \text{ per unit}$$

Since $MCL = MCS$, the marginal cost of labor is

$$MCW = MCS = \$5/(60)^{0.5} = \$0.65$$

*Graphical Illustration of Cost Minimization Through Equating* **MCL** *to* **MCS.** Assume that the marginal product curves for both factors are downward sloping, as in Figure 6.6, and that $MCL > MCS$. This is represented by point $A$ on each graph. $L_0$ units of unskilled and $S_0$ units of skilled labor are presently planned for the production facility. Since $MCL$ is greater than $MCS$, common sense indicates that the quantity of skilled labor should be increased. Spending more on skilled labor must result in less spending on unskilled labor if the total cost is to be reduced. When more skilled labor is used, and the amount of skilled labor rises to $S_1$, $MPS$ falls to $B$ because there are diminishing returns. The $MPL$ curve shifts upward from $MPL(S_0)$ to $MPL(S_1)$ because each unit of unskilled labor now has more skilled labor to work with it, making the unskilled workers more productive. If total cost is to be reduced, unskilled labor must fall from $L_0$ to $L_1$ and $MPL$ must rise to $B$. The MPS curve shifts downward from $MPS(L_0)$ to $MPS(L_1)$ because each unit of skilled labor now has fewer units of unskilled labor to assist it, thus reducing skilled labor productivity. $MPS$ falls to point $C$, and $MCS$ rises because $MCS = s/MPS$, and the skilled labor wage rate is unchanged. The increase in $MCS$ moves it closer to $MCL$ and the cost-minimizing quantities of skilled and unskilled labor where $MCS = MCL$. Similarly, $MPL$ rises to point $C$ and $MCL$ falls, which is in the right direction to attain $MCL = MCS$ and cost minimization because $MCL$ was greater than $MCS$.

A change in either $L$ or $S$ when $MCL = MCS$ will result in an increase in total cost. Increasing one factor beyond the quantity where $MCL = MCS$ will result in its marginal product declining and its marginal cost rising. With more money being spent on the factor that has been increased, the quantity of the other factor must be reduced and its

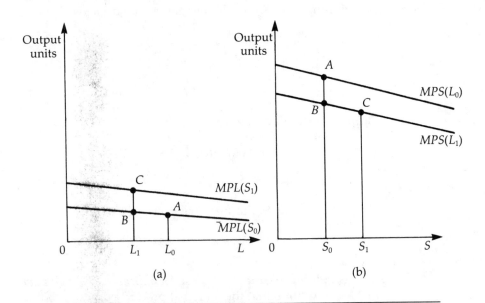

**Figure 6.6  Marginal Product Curves When Factor Quantities Change**

The initial condition is at point $A$ on both diagrams. Since $MCL > MCS$, the quantity of unskilled labor is reduced to $L_1$, yielding point $B$ on diagram (a). The $MPS$ curve on diagram (b) shifts down to $MPS(L_1)$ reflecting the reduced productivity of skilled labor when there are fewer unskilled workers. With less being spent on $L$, more can be spent on $S$, yielding point $C$ on both diagrams and the upward shift in the $MPL$ curve. The result is a lower $MCL$, since $MCL = w/MPL$, and an increased $MCS$, leading toward making $MCL$ and $MCS$ equal.

marginal product must rise. The higher marginal product will reduce the marginal cost of that factor. The two marginal costs are now unequal, and the argument presented in the preceding paragraph can be used to demonstrate that total cost is reduced by reversing the changes in the quantities of the two factors. Thus, costs are minimized where $MCL = MCS$.

*Role of the Diminishing Returns Assumption.* The $MPL$ and $MPS$ curves in Figure 6.6 are downward sloping because there are diminishing returns to both types of labor. The existence of diminishing returns is crucial to this demonstration of costs being minimized when $MCL = MCS$. It is analogous to the calculus condition for a minimum — that the second derivative of the function be positive.

## 6.5 *Calculating the Cost-Minimizing Factor Combination\**

This section provides two additional examples of the cost minimization procedure developed in the previous section. In both examples, the goal is to calculate the average and marginal cost of labor. Management has estimated the production function for its plant and knows the hourly cost of skilled and unskilled labor. In example 6.12, it wishes to find the smallest budget capable of producing 100 units of output per hour. In example 6.13, management has specified a labor budget of $540 per hour and wishes to find the maximum output of the plant. Example 6.13 uses several of the calculations performed in solving example 6.12.

### 6.5.1 *Minimizing the Budget Given Output*

**EXAMPLE 6.12.** Assume that the production function is

$$Q = 10L^{0.25}S^{0.5} \tag{6.14}$$

*MPL* and *MPS* are found by taking the partial derivatives of this production function.

$$MPL = \partial Q/\partial L = 2.5S^{0.5}/L^{0.75}$$

$$MPS = \partial Q/\partial S = 5L^{0.25}/S^{0.5}$$

The marginal rate of technical substitution is the slope of the isoquant curve:

$$MRTS = dS/dL = -MPL/MPS = -(2.5S^{0.5}/L^{0.75})/(5L^{0.25}/S^{0.5}) = -S/2L$$

Assume that $w = \$5$ and $s = \$12$. The budget function is $B = 5L + 12S$, or $S = B/12 - (S/12)L$. The slope of the isocost curve is

$$dS/dL = -5/12$$

Equating the slopes of the isoquant and isocost curves yields

$$-S/2L = -5/12$$

Using cross-multiplication (see section 2.2) and solving for $L$ yields

$$5L = 6S \Rightarrow L = 1.2S \tag{6.15}$$

Equation 6.15 provides one equation for finding the cost-minimizing combination of $L$ and $S$. Because there are two unknowns, a second relationship between $L$ and $S$ is necessary. If the objective is to find the combination of $L$ and $S$ that minimizes the budget required to produce $Q_0 = 100$ units per hour, the production function provides the second equation. Substituting equation 6.15 into 6.14 yields

$$Q = 10(1.2S)^{0.25}S^{0.5} = 10(1.2)^{0.25}S^{0.75}$$

$$S^{0.75} = Q/(10)(1.047) = Q/10.47$$

Since $S^{0.75} = S^{3/4}$, solving this equation involves taking the 4/3rds root of both sides because $(S^{3/4})^{4/3} = S^1$:

$$S = (Q/10.47)^{4/3}$$

$$S = (100/10.47)^{1.33} = 20.11 \text{ workers}$$

$$L = 1.2(20.11) = 24.13 \text{ workers}$$

$$B = (24.13)(\$5) + (20.11)(\$12) = \$362/\text{hour}$$

$$ACW = \$362/100 = \$3.62/\text{unit}$$

The marginal cost of labor, $MCW$, can be found by substituting the above values of $L$ and $S$ into either $MCL = w/MPL$ or $MCS = s/MPS$ because the two marginal costs are equal when total cost is minimized.

$$MCW = w/MPL = 5/(2.5S^{0.5}/L^{0.75}) = 2L^{0.75}/S^{0.5}$$

$$MCW = 2(24.14)^{0.75}/(20.11)^{0.5} = \$4.86/\text{unit}$$

$MCW$ is greater than $ACW$; therefore, $ACW$ will rise if output is increased. If $ACM = MCM = \$3.00/\text{unit}$ for all rates of output, $AVC = ACM + ACW$, and $MC = MCM + MCW$. For $Q = 100$, $AVC = \$3.00 + \$3.62 = \$6.62$, and $MC = \$3.00 + \$4.86 = \$7.86$. If fixed costs are \$1,000 per hour, $AFC = \$1,000/100 = \$10.00$ and $SRATC + AVC = \$10.00 + \$6.62 = \$16.62$.

## 6.5.2  *Maximize Output Given the Budget*

**EXAMPLE 6.13.** If the objective is to find the combination of $L$ and $S$ that maximizes the output produced by a specified budget, equation

6.15 provides the first equation, and the budget constraint provides the second. Since the budget is $540 per hour, the budget equation is

$$540 = 5L + 12S$$

Substituting equation 6.15 into this equation yields

$$540 = 5(1.2S) + 12S \Rightarrow S = 30 \text{ workers}$$

$$L = 1.2(30) = 36 \text{ workers}$$

$$Q = 10(36)^{0.25}(30)^{0.5} = 134.16 \text{ units per hour}$$

$$ACW = \$540/134.16 = \$4.02 \text{ per unit}$$

$$MCW = s/MPS = 12/(5L^{0.25}/S^{0.5}) = 2.4S^{0.5}/L^{0.25}$$

$$MCW = 2.4(30)^{0.5}/(36)^{0.25} = \$5.37/\text{unit}$$

As predicted after the calculation of *MCW* for an output of 100, the increase in output to 134 units resulted in an increase in *ACW*.

# 6.6 *The Long-Run Average Cost Curve*

In the long run, all factors of production are variable. Once the planning period is long enough for the firm to profitably change all factors of production, it can make long-run decisions involving new equipment at existing plants, expansion of their capacity, or construction of new plants. The firm never actually operates its facilities under long-run conditions. Once a new facility is constructed, the quantity of capital is fixed and the firm is operating under short-run conditions until it is again profitable to change the amount of capital. Long-run analysis involves planning for new facilities.

## 6.6.1 *The Long-Run Average Cost Curve*

The long-run average cost (*LRAC*) curve provides the lowest unit cost of producing a given output. With all factors of production variable, management can find the lowest-cost combination of factors to produce the desired output at minimum average total cost, *ATC*. Isoquant curve $q_0$ in Figure 6.7 provides the combinations of capital, *K*, and labor, *L*, capable of producing $q_0$ units of output. Finding the combination of *K* and *L* that minimizes the *ATC* of producing $q_0$ is equivalent to finding the isocost curve tangent to isoquant curve $q_0$. In Figure 6.7, this is $B_0$. The *LRAC* of producing $q_0$ is $B_0/q_0$ in Figure 6.8. To find other points

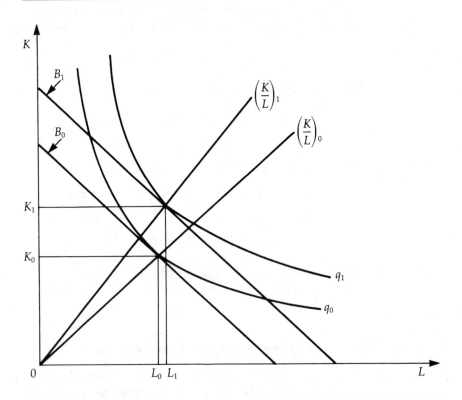

**Figure 6.7  Long-Run Cost Minimization**

The cost-minimizing quantities of $K$ and $L$ occur where the isocost and iso-quant curves are tangent. The capital-to-labor ratio is represented by a straight line from the origin through the isocost–isoquant tangency point, with the $K/L$ ratio generally rising as output increases. Long-run average cost is the ratio $B_i/q_i$.

on the *LRAC* curve, specify another output, $q_1$, find the isocost curve ($B_1$) tangent to the $q_1$ isoquant in Figure 6.7, and plot the point ($q_1$, $B_1/q_1$) in Figure 6.8.

### 6.6.2  *Economies of Mass Production*

In Figure 6.8, the *LRAC* curve declines for all outputs up to $q_2$. There are economies of mass production when the *LRAC* curve declines as output increases. The principal reason for *LRAC*'s declining is to be found in the different technologies used to produce larger outputs. When the firm produces a low output, it generally uses a labor-intensive

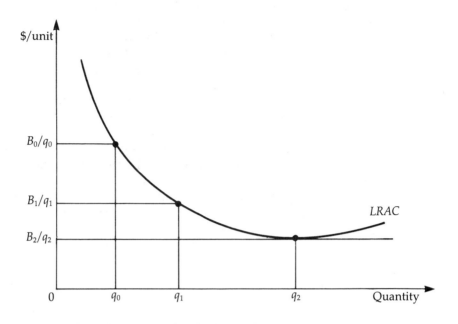

**Figure 6.8   The Long-Run Average Cost Curve**

The *LRAC* curve is derived from the isocost-isoquant diagram in Figure 6.7 by plotting for each output its $LRAC = B_i/q_i$. The *LRAC* curve is downward sloping to output $q_2$, reflecting lower average production costs with increasing capital intensity. After $q_2$, the *LRAC* curve becomes upward sloping because the lower average production costs are more than offset by rising average administrative costs as additional layers of management are added because more production workers are required to produce the greater output.

technology. As output rises, the firm uses increasingly capital-intensive technologies. In Figure 6.7 this shift to a more capital-intensive technology is illustrated by the capital-to-labor ratio rising from $(K/L)_0$ to $(K/L)_1$.

**EXAMPLE 6.14.**   A firm may use a hand-operated lathe and skilled machinist to produce 25 parts per hour. If it plans to produce 10,000 parts per hour, the firm may use numerically controlled lathes. This use of a more capital-intensive technology with increasing output primarily results from the total volume of output to be produced. An output of 25 parts per hour for a 2,000-hour year yields 50,000 parts. With this volume of output, the firm is unlikely to spend much on sophisticated tooling and specialized machinery. The high fixed costs would result in a relatively high average fixed cost. The firm may be unprofitable if its competitors use a more labor-intensive technology with sharply lower fixed costs and only modestly higher variable costs.

Assume that sophisticated tooling would cost $500,000 and result in labor costs of $80,000 to produce 50,000 parts. Total cost using this capital-intensive technology, where the ratio of capital to labor costs is $500,000/$80,000 or 6.25 to 1, would be $580,000. *ATC* is $580,000/50,000 = $11.60, and labor cost is $1.60 per part. Use of a labor-intensive technology may result in tooling costs of $40,000 and labor costs of $120,000 for an *ATC* of $160,000/50,000 = $3.20 and a labor cost of $2.40 per part. The ratio of capital to labor costs in this case is $40,000/$120,000 or 0.33 to 1. However, if 2 million parts are produced with the same tooling and unit labor cost, *ATC* using the sophisticated tooling falls sharply and it becomes the lower-cost technology. *ATC* using the more capital-intensive technology is now $500,000/2,000,000 + $1.60 = $1.85. *ATC* using the labor-intensive technology is now $40,000/2,000,000 + $2.40 = $2.42.

### 6.6.3   *Avoiding Short-Run Diminishing Returns in the Long Run*

With capital variable in the long run, the firm may not be faced with the declining $K/L$ ratio that is characteristic of higher outputs in the short run. This declining $K/L$ ratio was the primary reason for short-run diminishing returns and rising marginal costs as output increased. In the long run, the $K/L$ ratio can be maintained, or even increased, if suitable technologies are available. Thus, the principal reason for short-run diminishing returns when output rises may not exist in the long run.

There are limits to the extent that the $K/L$ ratio can be increased. These limits are imposed by the availability of suitable capital-intensive technologies and by the slope of the isocost curve. The available technologies determine the slope (*MRTS*) at each point on the isoquant curve. The slope of the isocost curve is $-w/k$, where $w$ is the wage rate and $k$ is the unit cost of capital. As $w$ rises relative to $k$, the isocost curve becomes steeper. It is now cost-minimizing to use a more capital-intensive technology if one is available. This is illustrated in Figure 6.9, where $k$ is held constant at $k_0$ and the wage rate increases from $w_0$ to $w_1$. At $w_0$, a budget of $B_0$ produces $q_0$ at minimum cost. If the wage rate increases to $w_1$, $B_0$ is no longer large enough to produce $q_0$ because the isocost line with $w = w_1$ does not touch $q_0$. This requires increasing the budget to $B_0'$ so that the isocost line is tangent to $q_0$. The quantity of capital increases from $K_0$ to $K_1$, the quantity of labor decreases from $L_0$ to $L_1$, and the $K/L$ ratio rises. However, the technologies with the

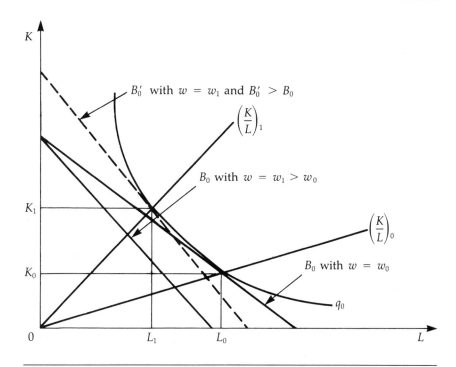

**Figure 6.9   Long-Run Implications of an Increased Relative Cost of Labor**
The unit cost of capital is held constant for this diagram. The initial condition is for a wage rate of $w_0$ and $LRAC$ of $B_0/q_0$. If the wage increases to $w_1$, budget $B_0$ is inadequate to produce $q_0$. The budget must be increased to $B_0'$ to produce $q_0$ and the capital-to-labor ratio rises from $(K/L)_0$ to $(K/L)_1$. It would not be cost minimizing for $K/L$ to rise above $(K/L)_1$ if $w$ equals $w_1$.

higher $K/L$ ratios on isoquant curve $q_0$ above point $(L_1, K_1)$ are not cost-minimizing if the slope of the isocost curve is $-w_1/k_0$. The $LRAC$ of producing $q_0$ has risen from $B_0/q_0$ to $B_0'/q_0$, shifting the $LRAC$ curve from $LRAC_0$ to $LRAC_1$ in Figure 6.10.

## 6.6.4 *Diseconomies from Rising Supervisory and Administrative Costs*

The $LRAC_0$ curve becomes upward sloping at $q_2$ in Figure 6.10. Increases in the number of production workers as output rises are accompanied by proportionately greater increases in the cost of supervisory and

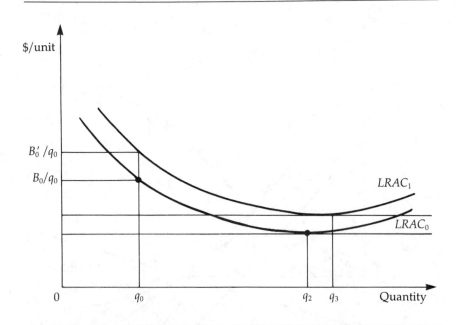

**Figure 6.10   Upward Shift in *LRAC* Curve When the Wage Rate Rises**

$LRAC_0$ is the *LRAC* curve when the wage is at its initial level, $w_0$. If the wage rises to $w_1$, the budget necessary to produce a given output rises (for example, to $B_0'$ to produce $q_0$) and *LRAC* rises to $LRAC_1$. The minimum point on $LRAC_1$ is to the right of $LRAC_0$ because the higher wage rate results in a higher $K/L$ ratio and a larger output before increases in average administrative costs exceed the decreases in average production costs, with $q$ and $K/L$ going up.

administrative workers.[11] The total cost of managing the firm rises faster than output. As the number of levels of supervisors and staff departments rises, it becomes increasingly difficult to manage and coordinate the activities of the firm and fix the responsibility for managerial failures. This reduces efficiency and further increases cost. After $q_2$ on the $LRAC_0$ curve in Figure 6.10, declining production average costs caused by a rising $K/L$ ratio are more than offset by increasing administrative average costs. That is, between $q_2$ and $q_3$ on $LRAC_0$, production average costs may fall by \$0.02 per unit and administrative average costs may rise by \$0.05 per unit, resulting in a net increase in *LRAC* of \$0.03 per unit.

$LRAC_1$ resulted from an increase in wages over those prevailing

---

[11]See sections 5.5 and 6.1, especially Table 6.1, for the relationship between output and administrative costs.

for $LRAC_0$, with the cost of capital held constant. The minimum point on $LRAC_1$ is to the right of that $LRAC_0$, resulting, in part, from use of a more capital-intensive technology when producing the higher output. However, when the wage rate rises relative to the unit cost of capital, fewer production workers are used to produce a given output at minimum costs; thus, fewer supervisory and administrative workers are required. This reduction in administrative costs at $q_2$ on $LRAC_1$ relative to $LRAC_0$ means that more output can be produced before increases in administrative average costs offset the reduction in production average costs. This is the principal reason for $LRAC_1$ not beginning to increase until $q_3$.

The $LRAC$ curve need not decline up to relatively large outputs. The industry's technology may be such that beyond some relatively small output rate, higher outputs are associated with rising long-run average costs. This is likely to occur when the industry is labor-intensive because of a lack of suitable capital-using technologies. An example is strawberry harvesting, which is done entirely by hand. As the farm gets larger, the larger numbers of field workers results in increasingly higher supervisory costs. The result is a rising $LRAC$ curve if the farm is larger than a relatively small acreage. Thus, strawberry farms are much smaller than the capital-intensive farms growing wheat or soybeans.

### 6.6.5 *Downward Sloping and Horizontal* **LRAC** *Curves*

The $LRAC$ curve may be downward sloping for all outputs, as occurs when greater outputs are produced with more capital and little change in the quantity of labor. For example, a larger-diameter natural gas pipeline increases output but requires no more labor to operate it. It is also possible for the $LRAC$ curve to be horizontal for outputs within a given range. In this case, the lower production average costs associated with a greater output are exactly offset by the higher administrative average costs required by the larger number of production workers needed to produce it. Some manufacturing industries may have $LRAC$ curves with a substantial range of constant costs because large firms do not appear to have significant cost advantages over their smaller rivals. Whether the $LRAC$ curve is U-shaped or one of the other alternatives is an empirical matter.

### 6.6.6 *The Planning Curve*

Industrial engineers refer to the $LRAC$ curve as the planning curve. The curve is generally developed using a case study method. Several outputs are specified by management. The company's engineering staff and their consultants then examine the technological alternatives for producing each output, which amounts to developing the isoquant curve for each output. The next step is to find which technological alternative has the lowest cost. Its *ATC* is then calculated, yielding a point on the *LRAC* curve. Given the minimum *LRAC* for each output, the final step is to determine which output offers the lowest *ATC*. Once the lowest cost plant has been identified, the firm's engineers can proceed with the detailed design of that plant.

## 6.7  *Relationship Between Long-Run and Short-Run Cost Curves*

The *LRAC* curve provides the lowest possible average cost of producing a specified output, $q_0$. Once the plant producing output $q_0$ at minimum average cost is built, the firm is operating in the short run with a fixed amount of capital which cannot be profitably changed as market conditions change. Since the market price for a product may change from time to time, the firm may not find it profit-maximizing to produce $q_0$. At the time management is doing its long-run planning, it also estimates the short-run cost curves associated with the lowest-cost plant for producing $q_0$. These short-run cost curves determine the firm's response to fluctuations in the market price for its product.

In Figure 6.11, the short-run average and marginal cost curves associated with outputs $q_0$ and $q_1$ on the *LRAC* curve are illustrated. For every output, there exists a set of short-run average and marginal cost curves in which the *SRATC* (short-run average total cost) curve is tangent to the *LRAC* curve.

### 6.7.1  *Derivation of the* **SRATC** *Curve from an Isoquant/Isocost Diagram*

Both the *LRAC* curve and the short-run cost curves are derived from the isoquant/isocost diagram. In Figure 6.12, output $q_0$ is produced at an average cost of $B_0/q_0$ using $L_0$ units of labor and $K_0$ units of capital. As long as isoquant curve $q_0$ is tangent to isocost line $B_0$, point $A$ represents (that is, "maps into") point $A'$ on the *LRAC* curve in Figure 6.13. If capital is fixed at $K_0$, point $A'$ is also on the *SRATC* curve. The *LRAC* and *SRATC* curves are tangent at point $A'$, and all other points on the *SRATC* curve lie above the *LRAC* curve. In Figure 6.12, if capital is variable, the *LRAC* of producing $q_1$ is $B_1/q_1$ at point $B$ in Figure 6.12 and $B'$ in 6.13. With capital fixed at $K_0$, budget $B_1$ is capable of purchasing only $L_2$ units of labor. To produce $q_1$, the budget must be increased above $B_1$ by $w(L_3 - L_2)$ to $B_1' = B_1 + w(L_3 - L_2)$. Since $B_1'$ is greater

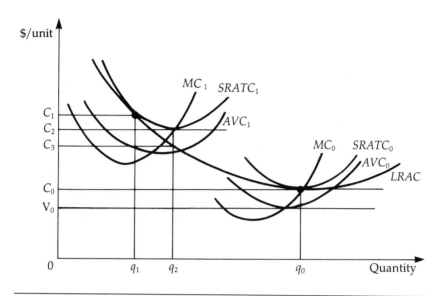

**Figure 6.11  Long- and Short-Run Cost Curves**

At each output on the *LRAC* curve, there is a different set of short-run cost curves. At output $q_0$, *LRAC* is minimized and tangent to the minimum point of the *SRATC*$_0$ curve for the plant producing $q_0$ at minimum cost. For the smaller output $q_1$, the *LRAC* and *SRATC*$_1$ curves are tangent at an output to the left on the minimum of *SRATC*$_1$, which is at output $q_2$.

than $B_1$, the *SRATC* of producing $q_1$ is greater than its *LRAC*. Thus, *SRATC*$(K = K_0)$ lies above the *LRAC* curve at output $q_1$. A similar situation exists for all outputs except $q_0$ when capital is fixed at $K_0$. Thus, the *SRATC* curve lies above the *LRAC* curve except at $q_0$, where the two cost curves are tangent.

Once the *SRATC* curve for a specified output has been determined, the *AVC* and *MC* curves can be found using the techniques in section 6.3. Assume that output is $q_i$, which is not equal to $q_0$. If capital is the fixed factor and its unit cost is $k$, $FC = kK_0$ and $AFC = kK_0/q_i$. *AVC* for output $q_i$ is equal to *SRATC* at $q_i$ minus *AFC* at $q_i$. Marginal cost at $q_i$ is found by taking the derivative of the short-run total cost function and evaluating that derivative at $q_i$.

### 6.7.2  *Tangency of the* **LRAC** *and* **SRATC** *Curves*

A *SRATC* curve is tangent to each point on the *LRAC* curve. The *LRAC* curve is the envelope of the *SRATC* curves. The *LRAC* curve is tangent to the *SRATC* curves to the left of their minimum points when the

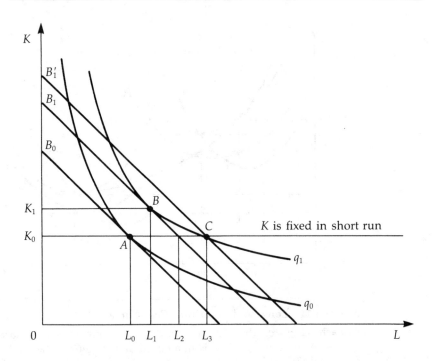

**Figure 6.12  Finding the Short-Run Quantity of Labor**

The initial condition is at point $A$, where the firm has built the plant with $K_0$ units of capital, which becomes the fixed factor in the short run. In the long run, if the firm were to produce $q_1$, it would build the plant at point $B$; but it cannot do this in the short run. With $K_0$ units of capital, producing $q_1$ requires $L_3$ units of labor and a larger budget ($B_1'$) than would be necessary to produce $q_1$ in the long run. Hence, the *SRATC* of producing $q_1$, which is $B'/q_1$, is greater than its *LRAC*, which is $B_1/q_1$.

*LRAC* curve is downward sloping because the two curves must have the same slope at their point of tangency. The *LRAC* curve is only tangent at the minimum point of a *SRATC* curve where the *LRAC* curve is horizontal or at its minimum point, as is the case for $SRATC_0$ in Figure 6.11. The minimum point of $SRATC_1$ is at output $q_2$. However, $q_2$ can be produced at a lower *LRAC*, $C_3$, by using more capital than was used for the plant with $SRATC_1$. When the *LRAC* curve is upward sloping, the *SRATC* curves are tangent to the *LRAC* curve where each *SRATC* curve is upward sloping.

**EXAMPLE 6.15.**  This example illustrates two points. The first is the procedure for calculating the *LRAC* for two outputs ($Q = 100$ and

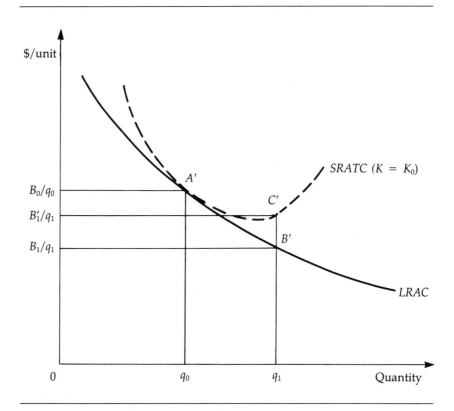

**Figure 6.13   Short- and Long-Run Average Cost Curves**
Points $A'$, $B'$, and $C'$ are plotted points $A$, $B$, and $C$, respectively, in Figure 6.12. $A'$ is the short- and long-run average cost of producing $q_0$ units of output with $K_0$ units of capital. $B'$ is the *LRAC* of producing $q_1$ when capital is variable, and $C'$ is the *SRATC* of producing $q_1$ when capital is fixed at $K_0$.

$Q = 150$ units). The second is that when the amount of capital used in calculating the *SRATC* is not equal to the amount of capital that would be used in the long run, the *SRATC* of a given output is greater than its *LRAC*.

**LRAC *of 100 Units of Output.*** Assume that the production function is $Q = 0.8KL^{0.5}$, the cost of a unit of capital is $k = \$40$, and the wage is $w = \$10$. The average cost of production is minimized when *MRTS* (the marginal rate of technical substitution, or the slope of the isoquant curve) equals the ratio of the unit costs of the two variable factors of production (the slope of the isocost line). That is, $MRTS = -w/k$. For this production function,

$$MPK = \partial Q/\partial K = 0.8L^{0.5}$$

$$MPL = \partial Q/\partial L = 0.4K/L^{0.5}$$

$$MRTS = -MPL/MPK = -(0.4K/L^{0.5})/0.8L^{0.5} = -K/2L$$

Thus, the cost minimizing combination of $K$ and $L$ is

$$-K/2L = -\$10/\$40 \qquad\qquad\qquad \textbf{(6.16)}$$

$$K = 0.5L$$

To find the *LRAC* of producing 100 units of output, substitute $Q = 100$ and equation 6.16 into the production function:

$$100 = 0.8(0.5L)L^{0.5}$$

$$100 = 0.4L^{1.5}$$

$$L^{1.5} = 100/0.4 = 250 \text{ and } L = 39.7 \qquad\qquad \textbf{(6.17)}$$

$$K = 0.5(39.7) = 19.85$$

The budget required to produce *100* units of output and its *LRAC* are

$$B = wL + kK = (\$10)(39.7) + (\$40)(19.85) = \$1,191$$

$$LRAC = B/Q = \$1,191/100 = \$11.91 \text{ per unit}$$

**LRAC of 150 Units of Output.** The *LRAC* of producing 150 units of output is found by replacing the 100 in equation 6.17 with $Q = 150$.

$$L^{1.5} = 150/0.4 = 375 \text{ and } L = 52.0$$

$$K = 0.5(52.0) = 26.0$$

$$B = (\$10)(52) + (\$40)(26) = \$1,560$$

$$LRAC = \$1,560/150 = \$10.40/\text{unit}$$

**SRATC of 150 Units of Output Using 19.85 Units of Capital.** If capital is fixed at 19.85 units, the quantity of labor to produce $Q = 150$ is

$$150 = 0.8(19.85)L^{0.5}$$

$$L^{0.5} = 150/15.88 = 9.446 \text{ and } L = 89.2 \text{ workers}$$

The short-run budget and *SRATC* are

$$B' = (\$10)(89.2) + (\$40)(19.85) = \$1,686$$

$$SRATC = \$1,685/150 = \$11.24 \text{ per unit}$$

Thus, the *SRATC* of producing 150 units of output with $K = 19.85$ is greater than the *LRAC*, which required that $K = 26.0$ units. These average costs correspond to points $A'$, $B'$, and $C'$ in Figure 6.13.

## 6.8  *Long-Run Average Cost and the Number of Firms*

The number of firms in an industry depends on the relationship between output at the minimum point of the *LRAC* curve and the industry's demand curve. The *LRAC* curve provides the minimum average total cost of producing a given output when all factors of production are variable. The shape of the *LRAC* curve depends upon the technologies and administrative structures specific to the industry. The *LRAC* curve differs among industries with respect to the output produced at its minimum point. The minimum point of the *LRAC* curve is one factor having an important bearing on the number of firms in the industry. The level of demand at prices in the neighborhood of minimum *LRAC* for the typical firm ($C_0$ at output $q_0$ in Figure 6.14) is also important.

### 6.8.1  *Demand and the Number of Firms*

Demand curve $D_1$ in Figure 6.14 results in a relatively small number of firms in the industry. Assume that each firm in the industry has one plant and produces a product that is a perfect substitute for the products of the other firms. The typical firm will build the plant that minimizes *LRAC*. Minimizing *LRAC* will result in the plant's having the lowest possible *SRATC* curve (see Figure 6.11). Failure to build the plant producing $q_0$ at minimum *LRAC* increases the probability that the firm will be unprofitable. The other firms will likely build the cost-minimizing plant, giving them a cost advantage over firms without the *LRAC*-minimizing plant. With demand at $D_1$, there will not be one large firm in the industry because its *LRAC* would be at $C_1$ if it built the plant to produce demand $q_1$ at a price equal to $C_1$. At a price equal to $C_0$, market demand is equal to $Q_0 = Kq_0$. There is room in the industry for $K = Q_0/q_0$ firms, each with one *LRAC*-minimizing plant.

If the industry's demand curve shifts to $D_2$ in Figure 6.14, the number of firms in the industry will rise to $M$ if the *LRAC* curve does

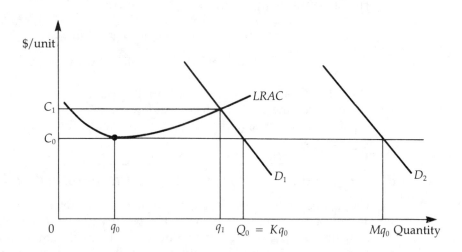

**Figure 6.14   Demand, *LRAC*, and the Number of Firms**

The firm generally builds the plant at the minimum point of the *LRAC* curve so that its competitors will not have a cost advantage. Building the plant with $LRAC = C_1$ to produce $q_1$ would result in higher costs for the firm than a smaller plant designed to produce $q_0$ at $LRAC = C_0$. If each firm has one plant to produce $q_0$ at minimum cost, there can be $K$ firms with demand curve $D_1$ and a greater number of firms, $M$, if demand is $D_2$.

not shift. If $M$ is large, there are many firms in the industry because its technology is such that *LRAC* begins to increase at an output that is small relative to the level of industry demand. Even when there are multiple-plant firms, the industry will have many firms if demand is large relative to $q_0$ because there are limits to the cost savings available to multiple-plant firms.

## 6.8.2   *Technical Change and the Number of Firms*

Assume that a cost-reducing new technology is developed that cannot be incorporated into existing plants. This new technology shifts the minimum point of the *LRAC* curve for new firms down and to the right. Unless demand is relatively elastic, so that industry sales rise substantially at a price equal to the new technology's minimum *LRAC*, the number of firms will likely decline. If the minimum point on $AVC_1$ in Figure 6.15 is below the minimum point of the new technology's *LRAC* curve, the existing plants will be competitive with a new plant. Even though the *ATC* of a new plant is below that of an existing plant,

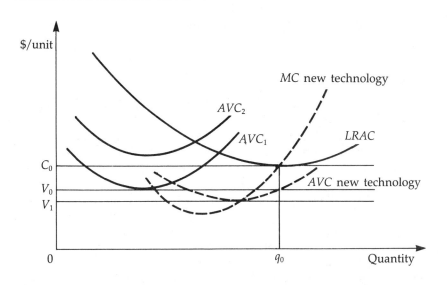

**Figure 6.15   Cost Advantages of New Plants**

A new technology results in the *LRAC* curve for new plants and the dashed-line *AVC* and *MC* curves. $AVC_1$ and $AVC_2$ are the *AVC* curves of two old plants. As soon as price falls below the minimum point of $AVC_2$, that plant will be forced to shut down because its revenues are less than the cost of its labor and raw materials. If price falls below $V_0$ but remains above $V_1$, the old plant with $AVC_1$ will be forced to shut down but the plant with the new technology can continue to operate.

the non-cash fixed costs of the existing plant are sunk costs having no bearing on the decision to operate it. However, if *AVC* for the existing firms is $AVC_2$ in Figure 6.15, new plants will be able to operate profitably at prices less than minimum *AVC* for plants with the higher-cost, old technology. The old plants will shut down once price falls below their minimum *AVC*.

If the *AVC* of a new plant is significantly below $AVC_1$, it may pay a new firm to enter the industry even if price will fall below $V_0$ in Figure 6.15, because the existing plants will then be abandoned. The new plant will suffer losses as long as price is below $C_0$, but it can continue to operate as long as price is above $V_1$. Once the existing plants are abandoned, price will rise. If price rises above $C_0$ for some period of time, the present value of the profits is compared to the present value of the losses before the existing plants were abandoned to determine if it is wealth-maximizing for the new firm to enter the industry.[12] If the new plants are significantly larger than those that are abandoned, the number of firms in the industry will decline.

## 6.9 *Summary*

The opportunity cost of a factor of production is the value of that factor in its best alternative use. Money paid to acquire factors of production are explicit costs because the firm no longer can use that money to acquire other factors. Implicit opportunity costs are the amounts of money that the firm would have received if it had sold or rented a factor it owns to another firm.

Production costs depend on factor productivities and their unit cost. The greater a factor's marginal or average product, the lower the cost of producing the good or service. Short-run costs are developed when one or more of the factors of production are fixed in amount for the planning period. Fixed costs are the costs of those factors that do not change with changes in output. Variable costs are the costs of those factors that must be increased if output is increased. Examples are production labor, raw materials, and purchased components. Semivariable costs are the costs of those factors that do not change for some range of output, but then increase if that range is exceeded. Examples are administrative and supervisory labor.

Average fixed cost is equal to fixed cost divided by output. *AFC* declines as output increases. Average variable cost is equal to total variable cost divided by output. It consists of two elements, the average cost of labor (*ACL*) and the average cost of materials (*ACM*). *ACL* = $w/APL$ where $w$ represents the wage rate. Average total cost is the sum of average fixed and average variable cost at the specified output. Marginal cost is the change in total cost (or total variable cost) when output is changed by a very small amount. The derivative of *TC* or *TVC* is used to calculate *MC*. Marginal cost includes the marginal cost of labor (*MCL* = $w/MPL$) and the marginal cost of materials. Although increasing returns may result in marginal cost's falling for some outputs, the existence of diminishing returns in all short-run production processes means that marginal cost becomes upward sloping beyond some output, and average variable cost also becomes upward sloping.

There are two basic approaches to developing empirical estimates of the firm's short-run costs for various outputs. One begins with a production function from which average and marginal product, and then average variable and marginal cost, can be calculated. Data on

[12] Wealth-maximizing decisions of this type are discussed at greater length in section 9.2.

fixed costs permit calculation of average fixed and average total cost. The other approach, statistical cost estimation, begins with accounting data and prepares statistical estimates of the cost curves using regression techniques. Which approach is used depends upon the data available and management's assessment of which approach will yield the desired planning and budgeting data at lowest cost.

Minimizing the cost of producing a given output, or maximizing the output produced with a specified budget, occurs at the combination of variable factors for which the isocost and isoquant curves are tangent. The calculus solution is to find the slopes of the isoquant and isocost curves, equate them, and substitute the resulting equation into either the budget equation or the production function. Since the slopes of two curves are equal at their point of tangency, the graphical and calculus techniques are equivalent.

In the long run, all factors of production are variable. The minimum cost of producing a given output $q_i$ is found at the point of tangency of the isocost and isoquant curves. The resulting average total costs $(B_i/q_i)$ are plotted to yield the long-run average cost (*LRAC*) curve of the typical firm considering entering the industry. The plant producing the output at which the *LRAC* curve is minimized is the one that a competitive firm must build if it is to be a low-cost producer and have the best chance of being profitable. The number of firms in an industry depends on the relationship between the industry's demand curve and the minimum cost and output on the *LRAC* curve of the typical firm.

| CASE | 5 | Statistical Cost Estimation |

There are at least two basic approaches to statistical cost estimation. Where limited accounting data are all that is available, the total cost or average total cost function is generally estimated and the other cost functions derived from it. Where records of production and overhead costs are available, the total variable cost or average variable cost function can be estimated. In this case, the firm's accounting records permitted estimating *AVC* and fixed cost. *SRATC* and *MC* were then calculated and the implications of the observed high *MC* relative to *SRATC* explored.

## The Assignment

You are an accountant for a food processing company. A little over 9 months ago, the company began producing a new confectionary product. Your assignment is to prepare a statistical estimate of the plant's *AVC*, *MC*, and *SRATC* at various outputs. Prices fluctuate substantially from week to week in this industry. Since the product is perishable, it cannot be held in inventory for more than a few days. Management feels that it would better be able to respond to these price changes if it had more up-to-date cost estimates than the *SRATC* projections prepared on the basis of an engineering study shortly after the plant was completed. You are to make these cost estimates for outputs of 120, 140, 160, and 180 cases per hour.

## The Available Data

By examining the plant's accounting records, you were able to extract the plant's fixed and total variable costs for the past 32 weeks. Wage and material costs have not changed since the start of the 32 week data series, so you do not have to adjust the data. The substantial output fluctuations during these 32 weeks resulted from management's responses to price fluctuations. The average hourly output and cost data for each week are in Table 6.2.

## Estimating Average Variable Cost

You decide to estimate the *AVC* function using the linear and second-degree polynomial equations $AVC = a + bQ$ and $AVC = A + BQ + CQ^2$. If neither of these equations gives an acceptably good fit of the data, you will try other functional forms.

The linear regression equation for output and *AVC* is

$$AVC = 0.72Q - 48.44$$
$$(0.07)$$

where the 0.07 under the coefficient of $Q$ is its standard error. Its $R^2$ is 0.75, and the *F*-statistic is 88.72. The *t*-statistic for the slope coefficient is $0.72/0.07 = 10.29$. These regression statistics indicate that the regression is significant at the 5 percent probability level. Serial correlation is likely to have increased the significance of these regression statistics since the data are a time series. However, this equation provides a useful basis for preparing a persistence forecast of the *AVC* of producing a given output.

The estimate of the second-degree polynomial equation is

$$AVC = 119.644 - 1.8903Q + 0.0095Q^2$$
$$(0.1384) \qquad (0.0005)$$

Its $R^2$ value is 0.98, and the *F*-statistic is 763.41. The *t*-statistics for

Table 6.2   Fixed and Variable Cost Data

| Week | Output | Fixed Cost | Variable Cost | AVC |
|------|--------|-----------|---------------|-----|
| 1  | 100 | $2,986.66 | $2,460.00 | $24.60 |
| 2  | 70  | 3,039.42 | 2,371.60 | 33.88 |
| 3  | 100 | 3,030.43 | 2,504.00 | 25.04 |
| 4  | 63  | 3,044.62 | 2,453.85 | 38.95 |
| 5  | 125 | 3,048.71 | 3,912.50 | 31.30 |
| 6  | 131 | 3,019.20 | 4,443.52 | 33.92 |
| 7  | 133 | 3,040.46 | 4,253.34 | 31.98 |
| 8  | 124 | 3,019.25 | 4,154.00 | 33.50 |
| 9  | 111 | 2,977.86 | 3,112.44 | 28.04 |
| 10 | 141 | 3,003.73 | 5,678.07 | 40.27 |
| 11 | 165 | 3,013.83 | 10,741.50 | 65.10 |
| 12 | 165 | 2,942.15 | 11,972.40 | 72.56 |
| 13 | 177 | 3,030.43 | 15,195.45 | 85.85 |
| 14 | 189 | 3,026.93 | 19,499.13 | 103.17 |
| 15 | 171 | 3,009.40 | 11,759.67 | 68.77 |
| 16 | 190 | 3,041.54 | 22,518.80 | 118.52 |
| 17 | 125 | 3,041.18 | 4,253.75 | 34.03 |
| 18 | 113 | 2,976.34 | 2,895.06 | 25.62 |
| 19 | 112 | 3,013.59 | 3,198.72 | 28.56 |
| 20 | 190 | 3,039.89 | 19,144.40 | 100.76 |
| 21 | 152 | 2,999.67 | 8,463.36 | 55.68 |
| 22 | 198 | 2,961.18 | 24,195.60 | 112.20 |
| 23 | 136 | 2,958.16 | 4,878.32 | 35.87 |
| 24 | 188 | 3,004.94 | 18,662.76 | 99.27 |
| 25 | 139 | 3,007.17 | 6,455.16 | 46.44 |
| 26 | 158 | 2,986.08 | 8,626.80 | 54.60 |
| 27 | 144 | 3,014.95 | 6,451.20 | 44.80 |
| 28 | 123 | 2,998.02 | 3,800.70 | 30.90 |
| 29 | 172 | 3,001.59 | 12,688.44 | 73.77 |
| 30 | 138 | 3,009.60 | 5,714.58 | 41.41 |
| 31 | 126 | 3,113.36 | 4,416.30 | 35.05 |
| 32 | 131 | 3,111.00 | 4,788.05 | 36.55 |

the $Q$ and $Q^2$ coefficients are both greater than 10. This equation provides a better fit of the data than the linear equation. However, since the coefficient of determination for $Q$ and $Q^2$ is 0.977, some of the improvement in the regression statistics could result from multicollinearity. On balance, it is likely that the second-degree polynomial provides a better fit of the data than the linear equation.

Another, nonstatistical, test of the two equations is to calculate the value of *AVC* that each equation projects for outputs near the lower and upper ends of their range. If $Q = 70$, the linear equation projects an $AVC$ of $1.96, and the second-degree polynomial equation projects an $AVC$ of $33.87. The actual value of $AVC$ for $Q = 70$ was $33.88. For $Q = 190$, the linear equation projects an $AVC$ of $88.36, and the second-degree polynomial equation projects an $AVC$ of $103.44. The actual value of $AVC$ for $Q = 190$ was $100.76. These results reinforce the conclusion arrived at on the basis of the regression statistics that the second-degree polynomial provides a better fit of the data. This test of extreme values should not be used as the sole basis for choosing between two regressions. The regression statistics should always provide the primary basis for deciding which equation to use in preparing a persistence forecast.

## Estimating Fixed Costs

The regression equation for the relationship between output and fixed cost is

$$FC = 3044.41 - 0.20Q$$
$$(0.19)$$

Its $R^2$ value is 0.035, and the $F$-statistic is 1.09. The $t$-statistic for the coefficient of $Q$ is 1.05. These regression statistics indicate that the relationship between output and fixed costs is not statistically significant. The conclusion is that the cost categories included under fixed costs are truly fixed costs.

The final issue was whether there is a statistically significant time trend in the fixed-cost data that should be considered when projecting future fixed-cost levels. The regression equation for the relationship between fixed cost and time where the first week is $T = 1$, the second week $T = 2$, and so on, is

$$FC = 3011.39 + 0.28T$$
$$(0.69)$$

The $R^2$ value for this regression is virtually zero (0.005), and the $F$-statistic is 0.15. The $t$-statistic for the coefficient of $T$ is 0.41. Because these statistics are insignificant, there is no significant time trend in fixed costs. Your forecast of fixed costs is the average value for the data period, or $3,015.98 per hour.

## Your Cost Estimates and Recommendations

You are now ready to present your cost projections. You calculated the marginal cost equation from the estimated $AVC$ equation.

Table 6.3  Statistical Cost Projections

|  | Alternative Output Rates | | | |
|---|---|---|---|---|
|  | Q = 120 | Q = 140 | Q = 160 | Q = 180 |
| FV | $3,015.98 | $3,015.98 | $3,015.98 | $3,015.98 |
| TVC | 3,553.20 | 5,768.00 | 9,664.00 | 15,694.20 |
| TC | $6,569.18 | $8,783.98 | $12,679.00 | $18,710.18 |
| AFC | $25.13 | $21.54 | $18.85 | $16.76 |
| AVC | 29.61 | 41.20 | 60.40 | 87.19 |
| ATC | $54.74 | $62.74 | $79.25 | $103.95 |
| MC | $76.34 | $148.96 | $244.35 | $362.54 |

$$TVC = AVC \times Q = 119.644Q - 1.8903Q^2 + 0.0095Q^3$$
$$MC = dTVC/dQ = 119.644 - 3.7806Q + 0.0285Q^2$$

You then substituted each output into the cost equations to calculate *AVC, TVC, ATC, TC,* and *MC.* You sent this information in Table 6.3 to the boss together with a memo explaining the sources of your data, the distribution of line items in the accounting reports between fixed and variable costs, and the results of your regression analyses.

The boss was intrigued by your study and its recommendations. Price fluctuates between $150 and $200 per case. When price is at the high end of its range, the company's customers are clamoring for more of the product. To accommodate them, the company hires considerably more unskilled labor at the plant to increase its output. These workers perform materials-handling tasks normally performed by the equipment operators or are used to create higher stacks of raw material or finished goods inventories in the plant's limited refrigerated floor space. Spillage rates are higher, and it is more difficult to package the product in the limited space. Supervisory personnel are temporarily borrowed from other facilities operated by the company. Since a $200 price is substantially above the average total cost of $105 estimated by the engineering study, the boss had viewed the higher output rates as being profitable. However, your recommendation is that output be held to no more than 150 cases per hour. When the plant is operating at 180 cases per hour, producing another case costs $362.54, yet it will be sold for only $200. This is without a doubt unprofitable even though your estimate of average total cost at 180 cases per hour is $103.95.

# Key Terms

| | | |
|---|---|---|
| average cost of labor | joint costs | planning curve |
| average variable cost | long-run average | semivariable cost |
| explicit cost | cost curve (*LRAC*) | short-run average |
| fixed cost | marginal cost | total cost (*SRATC*) |
| implicit opportunity | marginal cost of | total cost |
| cost | labor | total variable costs |
| isocost curve | materials costs | transfer price |
| isoquant curve | opportunity cost | |

# Review Questions

1. Define the term *opportunity cost*. How does an implicit opportunity cost differ from an explicit opportunity cost?

2. Your company purchased 10 light trucks 2 years ago for $100,000. They should provide excellent service for 5 more years. How should the opportunity cost of these trucks be calculated?

3. Define the terms *fixed cost, variable cost,* and *semivariable cost*. Provide an example of each.

4. Why do marginal cost and average variable cost depend on the productivity of labor and its unit cost?

5. If the *APL* curve declines after output $Q'$, explain why increasing output will eventually result in *AVC*'s increasing faster than *AFC*'s decreasing and in *SRATC*'s increasing.

6. Draw the graphs of the marginal and average variable cost curves where there are increasing and then diminishing returns to labor. Describe the relationship between the minimum points on the *MC* and *AVC* curves and the maximum points on the *MPL* and *APL* curves.

7. Explain why the *MC* curve must go through the minimum points of the *AVC* and *SRATC* curves.

8. Why does a change in the budget result in a parallel shift in the isocost curve, and a change in the price of a variable factor change the slope of the isocost curve?

9. Define the terms *isoquant* and *isocost*. Explain why output is maximized subject to a budget constraint, and the budget is minimized subject to an output constraint, where the isoquant and isocost curves are tangent.

10. Explain why costs are minimized when the marginal cost of one variable factor equals the marginal cost of the other variable factor. Assume that diminishing returns result when either factor is changed.

11. If $MCL$ = \$4.50 and $MCS$ = \$4.00, are costs being minimized? Why? Which factor should be increased and which one should be reduced? Why?

12. Why does a firm never operate its plant under long-run conditions?

13. Derive the $LRAC$ curve from an isocost/isoquant diagram.

14. How does the firm avoid in the long run the diminishing returns to additional units of labor that led to rising short-run $AVC$ and $SRATC$ curves?

15. Why does the capital intensity of production processes generally rise with increases in planned total output? Are there practical limits to increases in capital intensity? Explain why.

16. Explain why supervisory and administrative costs may result in the $LRAC$ curve's becoming upward sloping as output increases. For what kinds of technologies is the $LRAC$ curve likely to be downward sloping for all planned outputs?

17. Under what conditions is the $LRAC$ curve likely to be horizontal for some outputs?

18. Use the proper graphs to explain how to derive the $SRATC$ curve that is tangent to the minimum point of the $LRAC$ curve. Once you have the $SRATC$ curve, explain how to obtain its $AVC$ and $MC$ curves.

# *Problems and Applications*

1. The production function is $Q = 4L^{0.5}$ where $Q$ is in units per hour, the wage rate is \$6 per hour, materials cost \$7 per unit of output, and fixed costs are \$500 per hour. Management has decided to hire 25 units of labor. Calculate $Q$, $APL$, $MPL$, $ACL$, $AVC$, $MCL$, $MC$, $AFC$, and $SRATC$.

2. Explain why the production function in problem 1 exhibits only diminishing returns and why the graphs of the average and marginal cost curves will resemble those in Figure 6.3.

3. The production function is $Q = 0.4KL^2 + K^2L$, the wage rate is \$50 per day, and the quantity of capital (the fixed factor) is 10 units. If each unit of capital costs \$60, materials cost \$5 per unit of output, and management decides to use 10 units of labor, calculate $Q$, $APL$, $MPL$, $ACL$, $MCL$, $AVC$, $MC$, $AFC$, and $SRATC$.

4. The production function is $Q = 0.5K^{0.5}L^{0.25}$ where $Q$ is in units per hour and capital is fixed at $K = 25$ units. The wage rate is \$10 per hour and materials cost \$220 per unit of output. The cost of a unit of capital is \$40 and other fixed costs are \$2,000 per hour. Calculate

$L$, $APL$, $MPL$, $ACL$, $MCL$, $AVC$, $MC$, $AFC$, and $SRATC$ for an output of 10 units per hour.

5. Using the production function and data in problem 4, calculate $Q$, $APL$, $MPL$, $ACL$, $MCL$, $AVC$, $MC$, $AFC$, and $SRATC$ if there are $L = 81$ production workers at the plant.

6. Using the production function and data in problem 5, find the output at which $SRATC$ is minimized. Calculate the level of $SRATC$ at this output.

7. Assume that two purchased components, one costing $80 and the other costing $140, are used to produce the good in problem 4. If the manufacturer of the component costing $140 offers a $20 per unit quantity discount if the firm purchases 2,000 units of the component each month, describe how this offer will affect its cost curves. Assume that the plant operates for 200 hours per month.

8. Assume that the company's engineers have discovered a new technology that can be incorporated into its existing plant with a negligible capital investment. The new production function is $Q = 0.2K^{0.5}L^{0.5}$. The new technology also requires the use of a third purchased component costing $150 per unit. Calculate $L$, $APL$, $MPL$, $ACL$, $MCL$, $AVC$, $MC$, $AFC$, and $SRATC$ for an output of 10 units per hour. Would you recommend that this new technology be adopted by the firm in problem 4? Why?

9. The firm's production function is $Q = 14KL + 0.125K^2L^2 - (L^3/3)$ where $Q$ is output per hour and the firm has $K = 10$ units of capital.
   a. If $L = 20$, does this production function exhibit increasing or diminishing returns?
   b. How many production workers will maximize $MPL$?
   c. If the firm hires $L = 20$ production workers and pays $10 per hour for its labor and $1.50 per unit of output for its materials, calculate $Q$, $APL$, $MPL$, $ACL$, $MCL$, $AVC$, and $MC$.
   d. If fixed costs are $100 per unit of capital and $2,000 for all other fixed costs, calculate $AFC$ and $SRATC$.

10. Using the data in problem 9, find the maximum points on the $MPL$ and $APL$ curves and the minimum points on the $MCL$, $MC$, $ACL$, $AVC$, and $SRATC$ curves.

11. If the wage rate in problem 4 rises to $11, recalculate $ACL$, $MCL$, $AVC$, $MC$, and $SRATC$ for an output of 10 units per hour; find the outputs at which $AVC$, $MC$, and $SRATC$ are minimized; and explain how the cost curves in Figure 6.3 will shift.

12. Assume that the production function is $Q = KL + 0.5L^2 - 0.03L^3$, where $K = 10$, $L = 10$, the cost per unit of capital is $10, the wage

rate is $5 per hour, and the cost of materials is $0.50 per unit. Calculate $Q$, $APL$, $ACL$, $AVC$, $AFC$, $SRATC$, $MPL$, $MCL$, and $MC$. Is $MC$ upward or downward sloping at this output?

13. A statistical cost study has estimated the firm's short-run total cost function as $TC = \$0.2Q^2 + \$20Q + \$1,000$. Calculate $SRATC$, $AFC$, $AVC$, $ACL$, $MC$, $MCL$, and the unit cost of materials when output is $Q = 10$ units. Calculate the outputs at which $MC$, $AVC$, and $SRATC$ are minimized. Is this total cost function consistent with a production function exhibiting decreasing returns for all quantities of labor? Explain why or why not.

14. A statistical cost study has estimated the firm's short-run total cost function as $TC = \$2Q^3 - \$12Q^2 + \$80Q + \$800$. Calculate $SRATC$, $AFC$, $AVC$, $ACL$, $MC$, $MCL$, and the unit cost of materials when output is $Q = 10$ units. Calculate the outputs at which $MC$, $AVC$, and $SRATC$ are minimized.

15. The plant's production function is $Q = 5L^{0.5}$ where $L$ is the number of production workers and $Q$ is in units per hour. The wage rate is $10 per hour for production workers. The company's staffing formula requires one foreman costing $15 per hour for every ten production workers (11 production workers would require two foremen) and one supervisor and two clerks costing $35 per hour for every five foremen. The plant manager, engineer, accountant, personnel officer, and their clerical support staff cost $300 per hour. The opportunity cost of plant and equipment is $140 per hour, and other fixed costs are $60 per hour. Materials cost $80 per unit of output. Management is considering producing 50 units of output per hour at the plant. Calculate the number of production and supervisory workers required to produce this output, $ACL$ for production and supervisory workers, $AVC$, $AFC$, and $SRATC$.

16. Management is considering increasing output to 51 units per hour at the plant in problem 15. Calculate the marginal cost of production labor, the marginal cost of supervisory labor, and the marginal cost of the additional unit of output. Is $MC$ greater or less than the $SRATC$ of 50 units of output? Calculate $SRATC$ if the plant produces 51 units of output.

17. A new technology at the plant in problem 15 requires relatively little capital investment (opportunity cost of plant and equipment rises to $142 per hour) and results in a new production function, $Q = 5.2L^{0.5}$. Calculate the effect of this new technology on the $SRATC$ of producing 50 units of output, the $MC$ of the 51st unit of output, and the $SRATC$ of 51 units of output.

18. The production function is $Q = 4SL^{0.5}$ where $L$ and $S$ are variable

factors. If the budget is $1,200, the cost of an hour of skilled labor is $10, and the cost of an hour of unskilled labor is $5, calculate the combination of skilled and unskilled labor that minimizes the average cost of labor, output, the average cost of labor, and the marginal cost of labor.

19. The production function is $Q = 0.1S^{0.75}L^{0.25}$ where $L$ and $S$ are variable factors and $W$ is the general symbol for labor. If the budget is $900, the cost of $S$ is $15, and the cost of $L$ is $10, calculate the cost-minimizing combination of $L$ and $S$, $Q$, $ACW$, and $MCW$.

20. The production function is $Q = 0.2K^{0.5}S^{0.75}L^{0.5}$ where $Q$ is output per hour, $L$ and $S$ are variable factors, and $W$ is the general symbol of labor. $K = 16$ units is the fixed factor of production and a unit of $K$ has an opportunity cost of $50. The budget is $1,200, the cost of a unit of $S$ is $12, the cost of a unit of $L$ is $8, and the cost of fixed factors other than $K$ is $200 per hour. Each unit of $Q$ requires materials costing $15. Calculate $Q$, the minimum $ACW$, $AVC$, $MCW$, $MC$, $AFC$, and $SRATC$.

21. The production function is $Q = 0.5K^{0.5}L^{0.5}$, the cost of a unit of capital is $k = \$30$, and the wage rate is $w = \$8$.
    a. Calculate the $LRAC$ of producing $Q = 16$ and $Q = 25$ units.
    b. Assume that the firm builds a plant with $K = 20$ units of capital. Calculate the $SRATC$ of producing $Q = 16$ and $Q = 25$ units of output. What is the relationship between the short-run and long-run average costs of producing those outputs?

22. The production function is $Q = 0.4KL^{0.25}$, the unit cost of capital is $k = \$5$, the wage rate is $w = \$10$, and the budget is $1,000.
    a. Calculate the cost-minimizing quantities of $K$ and $L$, the output they produce, and the resulting $LRAC$.
    b. Repeat the calculations in part (a) using a budget of $1,200. Are there economies to producing the larger output even though the $K/L$ ratio is unchanged?
    c. If the quantity of capital is fixed at the amount calculated in part (a), calculate the quantity of labor required to produce the output in part (b) and the $SRATC$ of that output.

23. Repeat parts (a), (b), and (c) of problem 22 using the production function $Q = 2K^{0.25}L$, a unit cost of capital of $k = \$10$, a wage rate of $w = \$4$, and a budget of $1,000 for part (a).

24. Continuing with example 6.15 at the end of section 6.7, assume that there are no materials costs. Calculate $AVC$ and $MC$ at an output of $Q = 150$ units with $K = 19.85$. Based on the values of $SRATC$ and $MC$, would $SRATC$ increase or decrease if output were increased? Explain why.

25. Assume that the long-run average cost function for the typical firm interested in entering an industry is $LRAC = 32,200 - 60q + q^{1.5}$ and that industry demand is $Q = 20,000 - 4P$. Calculate the number of firms in this industry in long-run equilibrium.

26. Assume that the $LRAC$ function is that in problem 25, and that the demand curve is $Q = 38,000 + 2,000T^{0.5} - 40P$ where $T$ is the number of years from now. How many firms are likely to be in the industry in year $T = 1$ and in year $T = 11$?

27. Assume that a new technology shifts the $LRAC$ function to $LRAC = 32,175 - 60q + q^{1.5}$. Given the demand curve in problem 26, what will now be the number of firms in the industry in year $T = 11$?

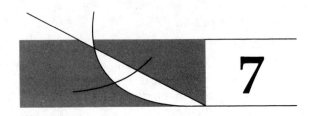

# Linear
# Programming

Calculus-based techniques for finding the cost-minimizing combination of two variable factors permit the use of power functions and other nonlinear functions for either the production function or the constraint. In many practical situations, however, the production function can be closely approximated by a linear equation. Moreover, many decisions are subject to more than one constraint, and many constraints are inequalities.

For example, in the short run it is not profitable to change the equipment in a machine shop. More than the available number of lathes cannot be scheduled for use during the short run. Since all of the available lathes need not be used, this constraint is a less-than-equal-to inequality. Given the unit costs of the various factors of production, the available machines and skilled workers, and the nature of the product, it may cost less not to utilize all of the lathes.

When it is practical to utilize models consisting of linear equations and inequalities, linear programming (LP) is a more efficient technique than calculus for finding solutions. Linear programming has been applied to a wide range of managerial problems in both the private and public sectors of the economy. It was one of the first management science techniques to be widely applied by managers.

One of the earliest applications was to transportation problems. For example, assume that the firm has several warehouses and a larger number of stores to which it will be shipping products from its warehouses. Management's goal is to minimize the cost of shipping its products from the warehouses to the stores. The diet problem was another early application of LP. In this case, the goal is to produce an animal feed at minimum cost that meets several product specifications, such as a minimum percentage of protein or a vitamin. Manufacturing problems, which are also referred to as activity analysis problems, have as their goal either maximizing profits or minimizing costs given factor productivities and the constraints imposed by fixed factors or desired output levels. This is only a partial list of the potential uses of linear programming. The goal of this chapter is to introduce the formal structure of an LP model and to illustrate a few of its applications.

The first section reviews the nature of linear economic models using a graphical model of a cost-minimization problem. In most problems, however, there are too many variables for graphical solutions. Section 7.2 discusses the general structure of a linear programming model. The next section discusses the SIMPLEX method and illustrates its use in solving the problem presented in section 7.1. The economic information that can be obtained from the solution to an LP model is discussed in section 7.4. The chapter concludes with two cases illustrating the use of linear programming in maximizing profits and minimizing costs. Although the LP models in these cases can be solved using the SIMPLEX method, it would be a tedious process with many repetitive calculations; the discussion of these cases is based on use of a computer program for solving LP problems.

## 7.1 *Graphical Solution of a Linear Programming Model*

Linear programming is utilized where there are multiple constraints on managerial decisions and the constraints are inequalities. Its use requires that the problem be stated in terms of linear equations and that all variables be nonnegative (zero or positive). In many practical problems, the relationships between inputs and outputs, and the various elements of the constraints, are linear equations (like the budget constraint) or can be approximated with linear equations within the range of variation contemplated by management. Restricting the decision variables to non-negative values normally does not present any problems in business applications of linear programming. When there are only two decision variables, linear programming models can be solved using graphical techniques.

*The Objective Function.* As with all optimization techniques, the first step is to specify the goal to be attained. In linear programming, the goal is referred to as the objective function, which must be expressed as a linear equation. If unskilled labor, $L$, and machines, $M$, are the two variable factors, the budget equation is $B = mM + wL$, where $m$ and $w$ are the unit costs of the factors of production. If the goal is to minimize the cost of producing a specified output, the objective function is

$$\text{Minimize: } B = mM + wL \qquad (7.1)$$

*The Constraints.* The second step is to specify, using linear equations, the constraints faced by management when it is searching for the cost-minimizing factor combination. In the short run, at least one constraint is caused by fixed factors that are unprofitable to change. For example, it may not be profitable to increase the number of machines beyond the present number of 30. This constraint, in equation form, is

$$M \leq 30 \qquad (7.2)$$

Equation 7.2 is an inequality because it may not be cost-minimizing to use all of the available machines to produce the output desired by management. From the earlier discussions of marginal products, the constraint is an inequality because it is possible that after using, say, 15 machines, the marginal product of the next machine becomes negative. Presumably, additional units of unskilled labor can be obtained in the short run so the quantity of unskilled labor is not subject to a constraint.

Another constraint on the quantity of each factor results from its productivity. This requires consideration of the production function. Assume that the production function is $0.5M + 0.1L = q_0$, where $q_0$ is the output to be produced. If $q_0$ is 20 units per hour, the production function is

$$0.5M + 0.1L = 20 \qquad (7.3)$$

Linear programming problems include in their constraints a requirement that all variables must be nonnegative. Thus,

$$M, L \geq 0 \qquad (7.4)$$

The signs of the objective function and constraint coefficients can generally be specified so that the variables are nonnegative.

*The Solution.* Equations 7.3 and 7.4 are graphed in Figure 7.1. Only the first quadrant of the graph is shown because $M$ and $L$ are nonnegative (equation 7.4). The relevant portion of the production isoquant is below the $M_0 = 30$ constraint. Any combination of $L$ and $M$ between points $A$ and $B$ on the isoquant are capable of producing 20

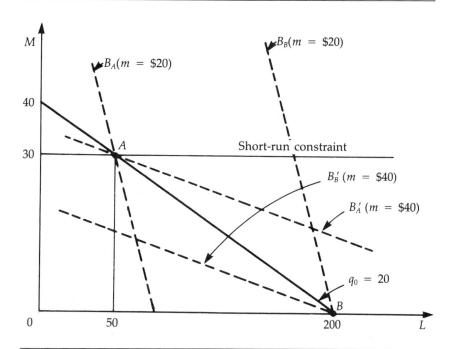

**Figure 7.1   Graphical Solution of an LP Model**

Since the maximum number of machines is 30, only that portion of the production isoquant between $A$ and $B$ is relevant. $B_A$ and $B_B$ are the isocost curves at points $A$ and $B$, respectively. Since $B_A$ is the lowest isocost curve that can produce 20 units of output, the firm would use 30 machines and 50 workers. Isocost curves $B_A'$ and $B_B'$ are drawn for a cost of $40 per machine, with $B_B'$ being the lowest isocost curve under this machine cost assumption.

units of output. Management's problem is to determine which combination of $L$ and $M$ minimizes the budget (equation 7.1). A theorem of linear programming states that the optimal solution is one of the "corner" points, which are points $A$ and $B$ in Figure 7.1. In the terminology of linear programming, points $A$ and $B$ are referred to as "basic feasible solutions" to the problem.

The variable cost of operating one machine is $m$ dollars per hour, and the cost of an hour of labor is $w$. Once the values of $m$ and $w$ have been specified, the quantities of $L$ and $M$ at points $A$ and $B$ can be substituted into equation 7.1 and the combination with the lower budget selected. If $m = \$20$ and $w = \$5$, equation 7.1 becomes

$$\text{Minimize: } B = \$20M + \$5L \qquad (7.5)$$

The objective function values at points $A$ and $B$ are

$$B_A = \$20(30) + \$5(50) = \$850$$
$$B_B = \$20(0) + \$5(200) = \$1,000$$

The decision would be to use 50 unskilled workers and all 30 machines. The objective function is an isocost curve. In Figure 7.1, the isocost curves going through points $A$ and $B$ are graphed as $B_A$ and $B_B$.

If the cost of a machine-hour is $m = \$40$, the budget at point $A$ is

$$B_A' = \$40(30) + \$5(50) = \$1,450$$

The budget at point $B$, $B_B'$, is unchanged. These isocost curves are graphed in Figure 7.1 as the steeper straight lines through points $A$ and $B$. Given isocost curves $B_A'$ and $B_B'$, the decision is to use 200 production workers and none of the machines.

This example illustrates the principles for constructing a linear model of the cost minimization problem. It could be solved using a graph because it involved only two variables, $L$ and $M$. It could also be solved by calculating the budgets associated with each factor combination at a corner point. However, as the number of variables rises above two, the number of corner points rises rapidly. This makes it too costly to identify each corner point, calculate the value of the objective function for each corner point, and then find the solution maximizing or minimizing the objective function. Linear programming is a valuable technique because there exist methods for solving very large and complex linear models involving several hundred variables and constraints. One of these techniques is the SIMPLEX method discussed in section 7.3.

## 7.2  *Formal Structure of a Linear Programming Model*

Linear programming (LP) models can be formulated as maximization or minimization problems. They are generally formulated as maximization problems because the SIMPLEX method for solving them maximizes the objective function. This maximization formulation is generally referred to as the primal problem. For example, the primal problem can be maximizing output given a budget constraint (and whatever other constraints management feels are appropriate). The dual problem for a maximization problem is its reformulation into a minimization problem. Thus, the dual problem to maximizing output given the budget is minimizing the budget given output as a constraint. LP problems can be solved as maximum or minimum problems, with the choice primarily depending on which formulation is more convenient to analyze.

Linear programming is also referred to as activity analysis. The firm undertakes a number of activities to attain its goals. One activity might involve the use of machinery, labor, and raw materials to produce the firm's product. Others might be transporting its product to a central warehouse and advertising the product on radio. The company's operations are broken down into the activities performed in the process of producing and marketing its product. A decision variable is assigned to the level of each activity. $X_1$ may represent output at the plant and $X_7$ the number of one-minute radio commercials. The LP model analyzes each activity, its interrelationships with other activities, and its effects on the firm's resource constraints to determine the level of each activity that best attains management's goal.

An LP model consists of the objective function and the constraints. If management's goal is to maximize profits, the objective function is a linear equation for calculating the profit from each activity the firm undertakes. The constraints are linear equalities or inequalities defining the alternatives that management can choose to attain its goal. In the short run, one or more of the constraints are fixed resources. The number of machines or skilled workers can provide fixed resource constraints. The constraint equation provides a means for calculating the relationship between the level of each activity and the required number of machines or skilled workers. Other constraints may reflect contractual commitments, budget decisions, and various policies adopted by the firm.

*Formal Statement of an LP Model.* Assume that the firm's production and marketing operations can be broken down into four activities: $X_1$, $X_2$, $X_3$, and $X_4$. There are three constraints on the alternatives that management can choose among. The levels of these constraints that cannot be exceeded are $b_1$, $b_2$, and $b_3$. If there are 20 of the first type of machine, $b_1$ would be equal to 20. The goal is to maximize the firm's profits. The contribution to profit resulting from increasing activity $X_j$ by one unit is $c_j$. If the product produced by activity $X_1$ is sold at a profit of \$12.40 per unit, then $c_1 = 12.40$. The equations describing this LP model are

$$\text{Maximize: } Z = c_1X_1 + c_2X_2 + c_3X_3 + c_4X_4$$

$$\text{Subject to: } a_{11}X_1 + a_{12}X_2 + a_{13}X_3 + a_{14}X_4 \leqslant b_1$$

$$a_{21}X_1 + a_{22}X_2 + a_{23}X_3 + a_{24}X_4 \leqslant b_2$$

$$a_{31}X_1 + a_{32}X_2 + a_{33}X_3 + a_{34}X_4 \leqslant b_3$$

$$\text{All } X_j \geqslant 0$$

The $a_{ij}$ coefficients of the constraints are equal to the increase in use of the resource of constraint $i$ resulting from a one-unit increase in the level of activity $j$ ($X_j$). For example, $a_{11}$ is equal to 2 if producing one unit of product $X_1$ requires use of two of the first type of machine. Alternatively, $a_{11}$ is the inverse of the productivity of the first type of machine in manufacturing product $X_1$. If $a_{11} = 2$, one machine would produce $1/a_{11} = 1/2$ unit of $X_1$. These examples of the interpretation of $a_{ij}$, $b_j$, and $c_i$ coefficients of a linear programming problem are in terms of a manufacturing problem. The interpretations of the coefficients of other types of linear programming problems are similar.

When management's goal is to minimize $Z$, the objective function is

$$\text{Maximize: } -Z = -c_1X_1 - c_2X_2 \cdots -c_nX_n$$

Assume that there are four possible values for total cost: 23, 37, 14, and 46. The goal is to minimize total cost. By inspection, the third value (14) is the minimum total cost. But if you can only maximize numbers, multiplying all of the values by ($-1$) and then picking the algebraically largest value will yield the same answer. Thus, $-14$ is greater than $-23$, $-37$, or $-46$.

*Slack and Artificial Variables.* The constraints of a linear programming model can be either equalities or inequalities. The techniques for finding solutions to systems of linear equations are based on the constraints being equalities. Less-than-or-equal-to inequalities are converted into equalities by adding slack variables. The inequality $M \leqslant 30$ can be converted into an equality by rewriting it as $M + S_1 = 30$, where the slack variable $S_1$ is nonnegative. If all 30 machines are used in the production process, then $S_1 = 0$ and $M = 30$. If only 10 of the machines are used, the equation is solved with $M = 10$ and $S_1 = 20$. In effect, the slack variable measures the excess machine capacity. Inequalities of the greater-than-or-equal-to type can be converted into equalities by assigning a coefficient of ($-1$) to the slack variable. If management imposes the constraint that the number of machines used be greater than or equal to 10, then the inequality is $M \geqslant 10$ and the constraint is $M - S = 10$. $S$, like all linear programming variables, must be nonnegative. If $S = 0$, $M = 10$, and if $S = 1$, $M = 11$. Thus, as $S$ increases from zero, the number of machines increases from 10 and $M = 10$ is the minimum number of machines.

When the constraint is of the greater-than-or-equal-to type or an equality, an artificial variable is introduced into the constraint equation and the objective function. To make certain that this artificial variable does not enter into the final solution, its objective function coefficient is set equal to a very large negative number. For example, assume that a constraint is the equality $X_2 = 5$. Adding artificial variable $A_1$ to this equation converts the constraint into $X_2 + A_1 = 5$. To make certain that the value of the artificial variable is zero in the final solution, the coefficient of $A_1$ in the objective function is set equal to a large negative number. This ensures that the objective function can be increased by eliminating $A_1$ from the solution. If the constraint is an equality, it is not necessary to have a slack variable with a $(-1)$ coefficient because the artificial variable in the equality can be used to find the initial solution to the model.

*Formulating Linear Programming Models.* This is a rather bare-bones description of the formal structure of a linear programming model. The best way to learn how to use linear programming is to set up and work out relatively simple examples. Applying linear programming to business decisions is as much an art as it is a science. There are no pat formulas for setting up an LP model. Every practical model has its unique features. Often there is more than one way to formulate the model. Linear programming gives precise answers whether or not the problem is correctly formulated and its parameters estimated with a reasonable degree of accuracy. As with all of the economic tools discussed in this book, there is no substitute for the analyst's seasoned judgment and willingness to be creative.

## 7.3 *The SIMPLEX Method*

A linear programming model is a system of linear equalities in which all variables are nonnegative. The SIMPLEX method is an iterative technique for solving systems of linear equalities where the variables are nonnegative and there is an objective function to guide the procedure toward a final solution.

Assume that there are $M$ constraint equations and $M + K$ variables. When there are $K$ more variables than equations, $K$ of the variables can be set equal to zero and the system of equations solved for the remaining $M$ variables, which are referred to as the basis variables. Because there is a slack or artificial variable with a coefficient of 1 in each constraint equation, these variables provide the initial solution to the model when the other variables (the $X_j$'s) are set equal to zero. The SIMPLEX method provides a procedure for determining which of the variables that had been set equal to zero increases the objective function's value more than the others and adds that variable to the solution set. Since there are now $M + 1$ nonzero variables, one of the other variables must be set equal to zero and deleted from the solution set. The SIMPLEX method deletes the variable that most limits the level of the variable to be added. This provides an efficient technique for going from one trial solution to the next. The optimal solution has been found when none of the variables outside the solution set (i.e., the variables set equal to zero) will increase the value of the objective function by more than the reduction in the objective function's value resulting from deleting one of the solution variables.

*Using the SIMPLEX Method to Solve the Example in Section 7.1.* The manufacturing example that was solved graphically in section 7.1 can be solved using the SIMPLEX method. Adding the slack and artificial variables to convert equations 7.1 through 7.4 to equalities yields the formal statement of the linear programming model:

$$\text{Maximize: } -B = -20M - 5L + 0S_1 - 1,000A_1$$

$$\text{Subject to: } M + S_1 = 30$$

$$0.5M + 0.1L + A_1 = 20$$

$$M, L \geqslant 0$$

The objective function is negative, because equation 7.1 calls for minimizing the budget used to produce 20 units per hour. Slack variable $S_1$ converts the constraint on the number of machines into an equality. Since positive values of the slack variable mean that some of the machines are not being used, and have no variable costs, the objective function coefficient on $S_1$ is zero. The production function contains artificial variable $A_1$ because it is an equality. The objective function coefficient on $A_1$ is the very high cost, $-1,000$ dollars, to ensure that the final solution to the model will not contain $A_1$ as one of the nonzero variables.

These equations are translated into the initial SIMPLEX table in Table 7.1. The top row of the table contains the column ($j$) indexes for the variables, with the variables in the first basis (solution set) carrying a $B$ after the variable number. The second row contains the objective function coefficient for each variable. The two basis variables and their objective function coefficients are in the second and third columns of the table. The $b_i$ column contains the constraint levels from the number of machines and production function equations. The next four columns of the table contain the $a_{ij}$ coefficients of the constraint equations. If a variable does not appear in a constraint equation, its $a_{ij}$ coefficient is zero. The remainder of the numbers in the table are calculated from the $a_{ij}$, $b_i$, and $c_j$ entries.

The $Z_j$ and ($C_j - Z_j$) rows are used to determine which variable should be added to the basis at the next iteration of the SIMPLEX

**Table 7.1  First SIMPLEX Table**

| | | | | $j =$ | 1 | 2 | 3B | 4B | |
|---|---|---|---|---|---|---|---|---|---|
| First Basis Variables | | | | $C_j =$ | $-20$ | $-5$ | 0 | $-1,000$ | |
| $i$ | $j$ | $K_i = C_j$ | $b_i$ | | $M$ | $L$ | $S_1$ | $A_1$ | $N_i$ |
| 1 | 3 | 0 | 30 | | 1 | 0 | 1 | 0 | 30 |
| 2 | 4 | $-1,000$ | 20 | | 0.5 | 0.1 | 0 | 1 | 40 |
| | | $Z_j$ | $-20,000$ | | $-500$ | $-100$ | 0 | $-1,000$ | |
| | | $C_j - Z_j$ | — | | 480 | 95 | 0 | 0 | |
| | | Action $\longrightarrow$ | | | Add to basis | | Delete from basis | Keep in basis | |

method. The $Z_j$ row of Table 7.1 is calculated using the following formulas:

$$Z_0 = \sum_{i=1}^{m} b_i K_i = (30)(0) + (20)(1,000) = -20,000 \qquad (7.6)$$

to calculate the value of the objective function and

$$Z_j = \sum_{i=1}^{m} a_{ij} K_i \qquad (7.7)$$

If $j = 1$, $Z_1 = (1)(0) + (0.5)(-1,000) = -500$. The $(C_j - Z_j)$ row provides the key numbers for determining which variable is to be added to the basis. For $j = 1$, $C_j - Z_j = -20 - (-500) = +480$. $(C_j - Z_j)$ measures the increase in the objective function's value from adding one unit of variable $j$. A positive value for $(C_j - Z_j)$ means that adding one unit of variable $j$ will increase the value of the objective function by $C_j - Z_j$. In Table 7.1, $(C_j - Z_j)$ is greatest for variable $j = 1$. Adding one machine will add more to the objective function value (i.e., reduce costs by a greater amount) than adding one unit of labor. Hence, the action is to add variable $M$ to the basis.

The next step is to determine which variable is to be deleted from the initial set of basis variables. This requires calculation for each constraint equation of the number of units, $N$, of the variable entering the basis that can be added without violating any of the constraints. If $k$ is the number of the variable to be added to the basis ($k = 1$ in Table 7.1), the maximum number of units of the variable that can be added without violating constraint $i$ is

$$N_i = b_i/a_{ik} \qquad (7.8)$$

For the first constraint ($i = 1$), $N_1 = 30/1 = 30$. The variable to be deleted is the basis variable in the row with the smallest positive value of $N$. Negative values of $N$ are ignored because they imply that adding one unit of the variable reduces the requirements for the constrained resource rather than increasing its demand as when $N$ is positive. In this example, this is the $i = 1$ row, and the basis variable to be deleted is $S_1$ because ($a_{31} = 1$) denotes that the first constraint equation was used to solve for the value of $S_1$. Thus, the basis variables for the first iteration of the SIMPLEX method are $M$ and $A_1$.

*First SIMPLEX Iteration.* The SIMPLEX table for the first iteration is Table 7.2. The first two rows of Table 7.2 are unchanged from Table 7.1 except that the basis variable designation $B$ has been moved from variable 3 to 1. The second basis variables, first row, are $j = 1$ and $K_1 = C_1 = -20$. The next step is to calculate the solution values of $b_i$ and $a_{ij}$. This amounts to solving simultaneously the two constraint equations for the basis variables $M$ and $A_1$. Assume that the number of the variable being added to the basis is $j = k$ and the number of the row of the variable being deleted from the basis is $i = L$. The new basis variable is solved for when $a_{Lk} = 1$ and all other coefficients in that column are zero. That is, solving for basis variable $M$ in the first ($i = 1$) constraint equation requires that $a_{11} = 1$ and $a_{21} = 0$. For the second constraint equation ($i = 2$), the basis variable being solved for is still $A_1$ so $a_{24} = 1$ and $a_{14} = 0$ are the desired coefficient values in the fourth column.

**Table 7.2  Second SIMPLEX Table**

| | Second Basis Variables | | $j =$ | 1B | 2 | 3 | 4B | |
|---|---|---|---|---|---|---|---|---|
| | | | $C_j =$ | $-20$ | $-5$ | $0$ | $-1,000$ | |
| $i$ | $j$ | $K_i = C_j$ | $b_i$ | $M$ | $L$ | $S_1$ | $A_1$ | $N_i$ |
| 1 | 1 | $-20$ | 30 | 1 | 0 | 1 | 0 | $\infty$ |
| 2 | 4 | $-1,000$ | 5 | 0 | 0.1 | $-0.5$ | 1 | 50 |
| | | $Z_j$ | $-5,600$ | $-20$ | $-100$ | 480 | $-1,000$ | |
| | | $C_j - Z_j$ | — | 0 | 95 | $-480$ | 0 | |
| | | Action $\longrightarrow$ | | Keep in basis | Add to basis | | Delete from basis | |

Inspection of Table 7.1 shows that the first constraint equation already has $a_{11} = 1$ and $a_{14} = 0$. To solve the second constraint equation, multiply each element of the first constraint equation by 0.5 and subtract the result from the corresponding element of the second equation. Each element of the constraint equation must have the same operation performed on it to maintain the equation that is represented in the SIMPLEX table by the coefficients in that row. This yields $b_2 = 20 - (0.5)(30) = 20 - 15 = 5$ and $a_{21} = 0.5 - (0.5)(1) = 0$. The value of $a_{24}$ continues to be 1, because $a_{14} = 0$. The results of these calculations are in Table 7.2. The $Z_j$, $(C_j - Z_j)$, and $N_i$ values in Table 7.2 are calculated using equations 7.5, 7.6, and 7.7.

The value of $Z_0$ in Table 7.2 is $-5,600$. Because $M = b_1 = 30$ is the solution value for $M$ from the first constraint equation, the objective function value has been increased by $30 \times 480 = 14,400$ and the objective function value in Table 7.2 is the objective function value in Table 7.1 plus 14,400, or $-20,000 + 14,400 = -5,600$. The largest of the $(C_j - Z_j)$ values in Table 7.2 is $+95$ in the $j = 2$ column. Thus, $L$ is to be added to the basis. The smallest value of $N_i$ is $N_2 = 50$; hence, $A_1$ is to be deleted from the basis. The basis variables for the third SIMPLEX table are $M$ and $L$.

*Second SIMPLEX Iteration.* The calculations necessary to prepare the second iteration of the SIMPLEX method in Table 7.3 are similar to those for the first iteration. The simultaneous equations calculations in this case are to yield $a_{21} = 0$ and $a_{22} = 1$, which was accomplished by multiplying each element of the second constraint equation by 10. Because $(C_j = Z_j)$ is either zero or negative for all $j$, the solution to the linear programming model has been found. The solution values are $M = 30$ from the $i = 1$ constraint equation and $L = 50$ from the

**Table 7.3   Third SIMPLEX Table**

| i | j | $K_i = C_i$ | $b_i$ | M | L | $S_1$ | $A_1$ |
|---|---|---|---|---|---|---|---|
| | | Third Basis Variables | $j =$ | 1B | 2B | 3 | 4 |
| | | | $C_j =$ | $-20$ | $-5$ | 0 | $-1,000$ |
| 1 | 1 | $-20$ | 30 | 1 | 0 | 1 | 0 |
| 2 | 2 | $-5$ | 50 | 0 | 1 | $-5$ | 10 |
| | | $Z_j$ | $-850$ | $-20$ | $-5$ | $+5$ | $-50$ |
| | | $C_j - Z_j$ | — | 0 | 0 | $-5$ | $-950$ |
| | | Action $\longrightarrow$ | | Solution Variables | Solution Variables | | |

$i = 2$ constraint equation. These are the same solution values that were found using the graphical technique in section 7.1.

*General Applicability of the SIMPLEX Method.* The preceding example could be solved using the graphical method because it had only two decision variables. The SIMPLEX method is not restricted to two decision variables. It is a general method that can be applied to any number of variables and constraint equations. Virtually all practical managerial problems involve more than two decision variables; therefore, the SIMPLEX method is appropriate for solving them. Because many iterative calculations are required to solve a linear programming model with more than two or three constraint equations using the SIMPLEX method, a computer is normally used to solve the model. The cases at the end of this chapter are solved using a computer program based on the SIMPLEX method.

## 7.4 *Analyzing the Solution to a Linear Programming Model*

The solution to an LP model contains at least four elements: the maximum value of the objective function, the solution values of each decision variable, the solution values of each of the slack variables, and the shadow prices.

*The Objective Function.* The objective function's value is obtained by substituting into it the solution values of the decision values. It is the greatest value of the objective function that can be obtained given the $a_{ij}$ coefficients of the constraint equations and the quantity of each resource, the $b_i$s. In the example in section 7.3, the solution value of the objective function was $Z_0 = -850$. Because this was a minimization problem, the minimum cost is $-Z_0 = \$850$. Any combination of $M$ and $L$ besides $M = 30$ and $L = 50$ would require a budget higher than $850 to produce $Q_0 = 20$ units of output.

Because $Q = 20$ units of output, the average variable cost of producing the product is $AVC = B/Q = \$850/20 = \$42.50$ per unit. If fixed costs are $400 per hour, $AFC = \$400/20 = \$20$/unit and $SRATC$ is $20 + \$42.50 = \$62.50$ per unit. Additional points on the firm's $SRATC$ curve could be found by changing $b_2$ to another level of output and again solving the LP model. If the change of output is one unit, as from $b_2 = 20$ to $b_2 = 21$, the marginal cost of producing the additional unit of output is the change in the budget (the objective function's value). Performing the SIMPLEX with $b_2 = 21$ yields an objective function value of $-900$ and solution values of $M = 30$ machines and $L = 60$ workers. The budget is $B = \$900$; hence, the marginal cost of producing the 21st unit of output is $\$900 - \$850 = \$50$. When $Q = 21$ units, $AVC = \$900/21 = \$42.86$, $AFC = \$400/21 = \$19.05$, and $SRATC = \$61.91$ per unit.

*Slack Variables and Shadow Prices.* The slack variable values provide the amount of each resource that is not utilized in the solution to the model. If for constraint $i$, $b_i = 40$ and the slack variable is 25, only 15 units of the constrained resource are used to obtain the optimal solution to the LP model. When the slack variable is zero, as was the case for $S_1$ in the solution to the model in section 7.3, the constraint limits the level that the objective function can attain. The shadow price of a constraint with a slack variable equal to zero is the amount by which the objective function would increase if the level of the constraint were increased by one unit. The shadow price is equal to $Z_j$ for the slack variable. For the example in section 7.3, adding one more machine would reduce the overall budget (the objective function) by \$5. If the slack variable is positive, its shadow price is zero; otherwise, another unit of the resource could be utilized to increase the objective function. There is no economic interpretation of the value of the artificial variable or its $Z_j$ value.

## 7.5  *Summary*

The use of linear programming to solve management problems requires that all equations describing the model be linear and all variables be restricted to nonnegative values. The primary advantage of LP over calculus is that it can be used when there are many variables and resource constraints, and the constraints are inequalities.

If the isoquant and isocost functions are linear, the two-variable factor problem can be solved graphically where there is more than one constraint. The solution technique involves evaluating each of the corner points where two constraints intersect to determine which corner point is the optimum one. The optimum corner point maximizes or minimizes the linear objective function expressing management's goal.

Linear programming is generally used when there are more than two variables, making graphical solution of the problem impractical. Management's goal is expressed as a linear function referred to as the objective function. The constraints on management's choices are expressed as linear inequalities or equalities. The variables are restricted to nonnegative values. Since the SIMPLEX method for solving linear programming models is an iterative process, computers are normally used to solve them.

The solution to a linear programming model provides the value of the objective function, the values of the variables of the model and the slack variables, and the shadow price associated with each constraint with a zero slack variable. The slack variable measures the extent to which a resource is not fully utilized. The shadow price provides the amount by which the objective function will change if the constraint is increased by one unit.

## CASE  6    The Machine Shop

A machine shop produces four specialty automotive products sold to speed shops and custom car shops. Each week it decides which products to produce based on the expected profit margin for each product. The shop has limited numbers of three of the types of machines used to produce these products. Its other types of equipment are never used to capacity and hence are not a constraint on the production decision. The three constraining machines are labeled $X$, $Y$, and $Z$ and the four products $A$, $B$, $C$, and $D$. There are 20 type $X$ machines, 25 type $Y$ machines and 22 type $Z$ machines. The time required on each machine to produce one unit of each product and its unit profit are as follows:

| Product | Unit Profit | Time Required (Hours) | | |
|---------|-------------|-----------|-----------|-----------|
|         |             | Machine $X$ | Machine $Y$ | Machine $Z$ |
| $A$ | $9.00 | 0.5 | 0.8 | 0.4 |
| $B$ | 8.00 | 0.3 | 0.9 | 1.0 |
| $C$ | 7.00 | 0.6 | 0.9 | 0.9 |
| $D$ | 5.00 | 0.0 | 0.4 | 0.5 |

**The Linear Programming Model.** The number of units of product $A$ is variable $X_1$, of product $B$ is $X_2$, of product $C$ is $X_3$, and of product $D$ is $X_4$. Because the goal is to maximize the machine shop's profits, the objective function is

$$\text{Maximize: } Z = \$9X_1 + \$8X_2 + \$7X_3 + \$5X_4$$

The next step is to set up the constraints. The number of machines of each type constrain the number of parts that can be produced by the shop, so $b_1 = 20$, $b_2 = 25$, and $b_3 = 22$. The $b_i$ are the number of machine hours available during one hour of shop time, and the constraints are of the less-than-or-equal-to type because the $b_i$ cannot be exceeded. The three constraints are

$$0.5X_1 + 0.3X_2 + 0.6X_3 + 0.0X_4 \leqslant 20$$
$$0.8X_1 + 0.9X_2 + 0.9X_3 + 0.4X_4 \leqslant 25$$
$$0.4X_1 + 1.0X_2 + 0.9X_3 + 0.5X_4 \leqslant 22$$

**Solving the LP Model Using a Computer.** Because only two iterations are required, this LP model could be solved using a hand calculator and the SIMPLEX method. The SIMPLEX tables for this LP model are provided in the appendix, page 227.

A computer is used for solving complex LP models, and an interactive computer program is used to solve the model in this case. The first two questions provide the computer program with the number of constraints and variables. The questions are, together with the appropriate answers for this problem:

```
            CONSTRAINTS AND VARIABLES
    NUMBER OF CONSTRAINTS (MAX OF 10)? 3
     NUMBER OF VARIABLES (MAX OF 20)? 4
```

The next series of questions provides the objective function.

```
                OBJECTIVE FUNCTION
    TYPE OF PROBLEM (1 = MAX, −1 = MIN)? 1
            COEFFICIENT FOR VAR 1? 9
            COEFFICIENT FOR VAR 2? 8
            COEFFICIENT FOR VAR 3? 7
            COEFFICIENT FOR VAR 4? 5
```

The coefficients of each constraint equation are entered next.

```
            CONSTRAINT NUMBER 1
        COEFFICIENT FOR VAR 1? 0.5
        COEFFICIENT FOR VAR 2? 0.3
        COEFFICIENT FOR VAR 3? 0.6
        COEFFICIENT FOR VAR 4? 0.0
            CONSTRAINT VALUE? 20
    TYPE 1 FOR <= ; 2 FOR = ; 3 FOR >= ? 1
            CONSTRAINT NUMBER 2
        COEFFICIENT FOR VAR 1? 0.8
        COEFFICIENT FOR VAR 2? 0.9
        COEFFICIENT FOR VAR 3? 0.9
        COEFFICIENT FOR VAR 4? 0.4
            CONSTRAINT VALUE? 25
    TYPE 1 FOR <= ; 2 FOR = ; 3 FOR >= ? 1
```

```
        CONSTRAINT NUMBER 3
      COEFFICIENT FOR VAR 1? 0.4
      COEFFICIENT FOR VAR 2? 1.0
      COEFFICIENT FOR VAR 3? 0.9
      COEFFICIENT FOR VAR 4? 0.5
        CONSTRAINT VALUE? 22
   TYPE 1 FOR <=; 2 FOR =; 3 FOR >= ? 1
```

**The Solution.** Once the last constraint has been entered, the program proceeds with solving the LP model. The solution to the model appears next.

```
     OBJECTIVE FUNCTION VALUE 297.09 - SOLUTION VALUES
     VARIABLE         VALUE        VARIABLE         VALUE
     X1               15.41        X2               0
     X3               0            X4               31.66
```

The objective function value is its profit if the shop produces the indicated quantities of each product. If 15.41 units of product *A* and 31.66 units of product *D* are produced each hour, the hourly profit will be $279.09. Products *B* and *C* will not be produced this week because their expected unit profit is not sufficiently great for them to be more profitable than products *A* and *D*. Even though the unit profit of product *D* is less than that of products *B* and *C*, it is more profitable to produce because it uses less machine time.

The values of the slack variables and shadow prices are:

```
                        SHADOW PRICES
                     SHADOW                           SHADOW
CONST.    SLACK      PRICE      CONST.    SLACK        PRICE
1         12.29      0          2         0            10.42
3         0          1.67
```

This table provides two essential pieces of information. The first is that 12.29 type *X* machines are not used and $22 - 12.29 = 9.71$ machines are used each hour. The 12.29 type *X* machines are the shop's excess capacity. This excess capacity exists because the shop does not have enough type *Y* and *Z* machines to use all of the available type *X* machines. If the number of type *Y* machines were increased by 1, the objective function's value would rise by $10.42 per hour. If another type *Y* machine could be leased for $5 per hour, it would be profitable because profits would rise by $5.42 more than the cost of the machine. Leasing a type *Z* machine at a cost of $5.00 per hour would not be profitable since it would only add $1.67 to profits.

| CASE | 7 | **Fertilizer Mixing** |

A plant that custom mixes fertilizers to a farmer's specifications has received an order for 100 sacks of fertilizer with the following specifications: Each sack is to weigh 100 pounds, with a minimum nitrogen content of 6 pounds per sack, a minimum phosphorous content of 10 pounds per sack, and a maximum sodium content of 1.0 pounds per sack. Its inventory contains four compounds to use in formulating this fertilizer. Their analyses yield the following information:

| Compound | Cost/lb. | Nitrogen | Phosphorous | Sodium |
|---|---|---|---|---|
| A | $0.048 | 4% | 6% | 0.8% |
| B | 0.072 | 2% | 16% | 0.6% |
| C | 0.084 | 5% | 14% | 0.2% |
| D | 0.100 | 12% | 2% | 0.2% |

The goal is to minimize the cost of producing this fertilizer.

**The LP Model.** The first step is to set up the objective function. This requires defining the variables. Let $X_1$ be the number of pounds of compound A blended into a 100-pound sack of the fertilizer. $X_2$, $X_3$, and $X_4$ are the quantities of compounds B, C, and D, respectively. The goal is to minimize the cost, so the objective function is as follows:

$$\text{Maximize: } -Z = -0.048X_1 - 0.072X_2 - 0.084X_3 - 0.100X_4$$

The next step is to set up the constraints. One constraint is that the number of pounds of each component add up to 100 pounds. That is,

$$X_1 + X_2 + X_3 + X_4 \leq 100$$

If the product specifications can be met with less than 100 pounds of these compounds, sand will be blended in to bring the sack weight up to 100 pounds. The constraints on nitrogen and phosphorous content are of the greater-than-or-equal-to type.

$$0.04X_1 + 0.02X_2 + 0.05X_3 + 0.12X_4 \geq 6$$

$$0.06X_1 + 0.16X_2 + 0.14X_3 + 0.02X_4 \geq 10$$

The constraint on its sodium content is of the less-than-or-equal-to type.

$$0.008X_1 + 0.006X_2 + 0.002X_3 + 0.004X_2 \leqslant 1.0$$

**The Solution.** The solution to the model, using the same computer program as in Case 6, is

```
OBJECTIVE FUNCTION VALUE 7.83529 — SOLUTION VALUES
VARIABLE        VALUE        VARIABLE        VALUE
X1            23.5294        X2            0
X3            58.8235        X4            17.6471
```

The values of the variables are the number of pounds of each component to use in preparing 100 pounds of fertilizer. The objective function value is its cost. The materials cost of a 100-pound sack is $7.84 and for 100 sacks is $784. If the labor cost of processing the fertilizer is $80 and the cost of bags is $50, the total variable cost of producing the fertilizer is $914. If the fertilizer sells for $12 per sack, total revenue is $1,200 and the gross margin before fixed costs is $286.

The values of the slack variables and shadow prices are:

| CONST. | SLACK | SHADOW PRICE | CONST. | SLACK | SHADOW PRICE |
|---|---|---|---|---|---|
| 1 | 0 | 0.006 | 2 | 0 | 0.824 |
| 3 | 0 | 0.347 | 4 | 0.624 | 0 |

The slack variables and shadow prices are interpreted relative to the constraint equation. The shadow price $0.006 for the first constraint means that if another pound of fertilizer were added to each sack, it would cost 0.6 cents. Since only 100 pounds goes into a sack, this is not a useful piece of information. If the minimum nitrogen content of the fertilizer rises from 6 percent to 7 percent, the shadow price for the second constraint indicates that the materials cost of a sack of fertilizer will rise by 82.4 cents. Similarly, the cost of increasing the phosphorous content to 11 percent is 34.7 cents per 100-pound sack. If the farmer was not certain as to whether his crops need the 6%/10% fertilizer or a somewhat richer one, the shadow prices provide the cost information necessary to make the decision. Since the fourth constraint's slack variable is 0.624, the sodium content of the fertilizer is only 1% − 0.624% = 0.376%. If the plant has a somewhat lower-cost compound with a higher sodium content, it may wish to make another run of the linear programming model including the higher sodium content compound in the set of variables because its costs may be lower.

---

# Key Terms

| | | |
|---|---|---|
| activity analysis | corner point | primal problem |
| artificial variable | dual problem | shadow price |
| basic feasible solution | linear programming | SIMPLEX method |
| basis variables | objective function | slack variable |

# Review Questions

1. Define the terms *objective function, constraint, slack variable, artificial variable,* and *shadow price.*

2. How do the variables in a solution (basis) differ from the variables that are not in a solution?

3. When going from the first SIMPLEX table to the second, why is it necessary to solve the system of equations for the new variable that is being added to the basis? Why is it not necessary to solve the system of equations for the variables that are being kept in the basis?

4. When solving the system of equations to construct the next SIMPLEX table, why must the same multiplication or division operation be performed on $b_I$ and on $a_{Ij}$ for all $j$, where $i = I$ is the row of the table?

5. Why is there a nonzero shadow price when the value of a slack variable is zero, and a zero shadow price if the slack variable is positive?

# Problems and Applications

1. Reduce the desired output in equation 7.3 to $Q = 19$ units. Find the solution to the problem in section 7.1 using (a) the graphical method in section 7.1 and (b) the SIMPLEX method in section 7.3. Assuming that fixed costs are $400 per hour, calculate *AFC, AVC,* and *SRATC* for $Q = 19$ units and *MC* for the 20th unit of output.

2. Use the SIMPLEX method to verify that increasing the number of

machines to 31 will reduce the budget for producing $Q = 20$ units of output by $5.

3. The production function is $Q = 1.2M + 3.0L$ where $Q$ is output per hour, $M$ is the number of machines, and $L$ is the number of production workers. The company has 10 machines and can hire up to 20 production workers. If the operating cost of a machine is $20 per hour and the cost of a production worker is $5 per hour, use (a) the graphical method and (b) the SIMPLEX method to find the cost-minimizing combination of machines and workers to produce 66 units of output.

4. If the cost of production workers was $10 per hour in problem 3, would the answer change? Why or why not?

5. A company produces four products using two types of machines. It has 30 type $A$ machines and 20 type $B$ machines. The time required to produce $X_1$ is 0.3 hours of $A$ and 0.5 hours of $B$, $X_2$ is 0.6 hours of $A$ and 0.4 hours of $B$, $X_3$ is 0.7 hours of $A$ and 0.2 hours of $B$, and $X_4$ is 0.6 hours of $A$ and 0.3 hours of $B$. The unit profit for $X_1$ is $20, for $X_2$ is $21.50, for $X_3$ is $19.50, and for $X_4$ is $19. Calculate the profit-maximizing quantities of each product and the maximum profit attainable if fixed costs, which are not included when calculating unit profits, are $600 per hour.

6. Continuing with problem 5, the company can lease another type $A$ machine for $23 per hour, or another type $B$ machine for $25. Is either of these leases profitable? Why?

7. Continuing with problem 5, the customer for product $X_4$ is desperate! The customer is willing to pay enough for product $X_4$ to yield the company a unit profit of $22 if it can get 30 units. (a) Will this change the company's production plans? (b) Is either of the machine leases in problem 6 profitable at the higher unit profit for product $X_4$?

8. A company blends six different meals to produce its all-age mash. This chicken feed must have not less than 18.0 percent protein and 2.4 percent fat, and not more than 6.3 percent fiber and 12.5 percent ash. The analyses of the meals and their cost per 100 pounds are given in the table. Calculate the combination of meals that minimizes the cost of producing the feed.

| | Meal 1 | Meal 2 | Meal 3 | Meal 4 | Meal 5 | Meal 6 |
|---|---|---|---|---|---|---|
| Protein | 23.0% | 21.0% | 16.5% | 17.2% | 13.5% | 8.5% |
| Fat | 1.4% | 1.9% | 2.6% | 3.0% | 2.0% | 4.2% |
| Fiber | 2.1% | 8.8% | 5.4% | 6.0% | 6.6% | 8.0% |
| Ash | 8.1% | 9.6% | 11.0% | 13.0% | 14.0% | 15.0% |
| Cost | $11.30 | $10.70 | $ 9.00 | $ 9.60 | $ 8.10 | $ 7.20 |

9. Management is considering increasing the protein content of the feed in problem 8 to 19 percent. By how much will its cost rise?

10. A plant produces three products using the same machinery. The variable cost of producing product *A* is $20.50 per unit. For product *B*, it is $24.00 per unit. When the output of product *C* exceeds 20 units per hour, its variable cost rises from $30 to $35 per unit. (Hint: Create two variables for product *C*.) There are 40 machines in the plant, with 5 percent normally out of service at any time. One unit of product *A* requires 0.5 hour of machine time, one unit of *B* requires 0.20 hour, and one unit of *C* requires 0.25 hour. The plant has 7,000 square feet with 5,000 square feet being taken up by the machines. The remaining 2,000 square feet are used as general work space. Each unit of product *A* requires 10 square feet, and each unit of *B* requires 8 square feet. When the output of *C* is less than 20 units per hour, each unit requires 40 square feet. When the output of *C* exceeds 20 units per hour, each unit requires 25 square feet, because more labor is hired to stack the raw materials and work in progress higher. The price of product *A* is projected at $25.25 next month, that of product *B* at $28.40 and that of product *C* at $39.60. Calculate the profit-maximizing quantity of each product.

11. Continuing with problem 10, it would cost $12 per hour to hire another worker to clean, lubricate, and adjust machines and reduce their out-of-service rate to 2.5 percent. Would it be profitable to hire this worker?

12. Continuing with problem 10, explain why product *A* is not profitable to produce given its current market price and why product *C*, which is twice as profitable per unit as product *B*, is not produced in larger amounts.

# Appendix
## *SIMPLEX Tables for Case 6*

The solution to the LP model in Case 6 was obtained using an interactive computer program. This appendix contains the three SIMPLEX tables (7A.1, 7A.2, 7A.3) that result from using the method in section 7.3. The small differences between the solution values in the computer output and the SIMPLEX are caused by rounding-off errors.

**Table 7A.1  First SIMPLEX Table: Case Six**

| First Basis Variables | | | | $j =$ 1 | 2 | 3 | 4 | 5B | 6B | 7B | |
|---|---|---|---|---|---|---|---|---|---|---|---|
| | | | $C_j =$ | 9 | 8 | 7 | 5 | 0 | 0 | 0 | $N_i$ |
| $i$ | $j$ | $K_i = C_i$ | $b_i$ | $X_1$ | $X_2$ | $X_3$ | $X_4$ | $S_1$ | $S_2$ | $S_3$ | |
| 1 | 5 | 0 | 20 | 0.5 | 0.3 | 0.6 | 0 | 1 | 0 | 0 | 40.00 |
| 2 | 6 | 0 | 25 | 0.8 | 0.9 | 0.9 | 0.4 | 0 | 1 | 0 | 31.25 |
| 3 | 7 | 0 | 22 | 0.4 | 1.0 | 0.9 | 0.5 | 0 | 0 | 1 | 55.00 |
| | | $Z_j =$ | 0 | 0 | 0 | 0 | 0 | 0 | 0 | 0 | |
| | | $C_j - Z_j =$ | — | 9 | 8 | 7 | 5 | 0 | 0 | 0 | |
| | | | | Add to basis $\longrightarrow$ | | | | Keep in basis | Delete from basis | Keep in basis | |

Action

**Table 7A.2  Second SIMPLEX Table: Case Six**

| Second Basis Variables | | | | $j =$ 1B | 2 | 3 | 4 | 5B | 6 | 7B | | |
|---|---|---|---|---|---|---|---|---|---|---|---|---|
| | | | $C_j =$ | 9 | 8 | 7 | 5 | 0 | 0 | 0 | | |
| $i$ | $j$ | $K_j = C_j$ | $b_i$ | $X_1$ | $X_2$ | $X_3$ | $X_4$ | $S_1$ | $S_2$ | $S_3$ | $N_i$ | Note |
| 1 | 5 | 0 | 4.375 | 0 | -0.2625 | 0.0375 | -.25 | 1 | -0.0625 | 0 | NEG. | 2 |
| 2 | 1 | 9 | 31.25 | 1 | 1.125 | 0.125 | 0.5 | 0 | 0.125 | 0 | 62.5 | 1 |
| 3 | 7 | 0 | 9.5 | 0 | 0.55 | 0.45 | 0.3 | 0 | -0.0625 | 1 | 31.67 | 3 |
| | | $Z_j =$ | 281.25 | 9 | 10.125 | 10.125 | 4.5 | 0 | 1.125 | 0 | | |
| | | $C_j - Z_j =$ | — | 0 | -2.125 | -3.125 | 0.5 | 0 | -1.125 | 0 | | |
| | | Action → | | Keep in basis | | | Add to basis | Keep in basis | | Delete from basis | | |

*Notes:*

1. Divided $i = 2$ constraint equation in Table 7A.1 by 0.8 to convert $b_2$ to 31.25, $a_{21}$ to 1, $a_{22}$ to 1.125, etc. in Table 7A.2.
2. Multiplied $i = 2$ constraint equation in Table 7A.2 by 0.5 and subtracted it from the $i = 1$ constraint equation in Table 7A.1 to convert $b_1$ to 4.375, $a_{11}$ to 0, $a_{12}$ to −0.2625, etc. in Table 7A.2.
3. Multiplied $i = 2$ constraint equation in Table 7A.2 by 0.4 and subtracted it from the $i = 3$ constraint equation in Table 7A.1 to convert $b_3$ to 9.5, $a_{31}$ to 0, $a_{32}$ to 0.55, etc. in Table 7A.2.

**Table 7A.3** Third SIMPLEX Table: Case Six

| Third Basis Variables | | | $j =$ | 1B | 2 | 3 | 4B | 5B | 6 | 7 | |
|---|---|---|---|---|---|---|---|---|---|---|---|
| | | | $C_j =$ | 9 | 8 | 7 | 5 | 0 | 0 | 0 | Note |
| $i$ | $j$ | $K_i = C_j$ | $b_i$ | $X_1$ | $X_2$ | $X_3$ | $X_4$ | $S_1$ | $S_2$ | $S_3$ | |
| 1 | 5 | 0 | 12.292 | 0 | 0.196 | 0.4125 | 0 | 1 | 0.0415 | 0.833 | 2 |
| 2 | 1 | 9 | 15.4165 | 1 | 0.0285 | 0.375 | 0 | 0 | 0.1165 | -0.1665 | 3 |
| 3 | 4 | 5 | 31.667 | 0 | 1.833 | 1.500 | 1 | 0 | -0.208 | 3.333 | 1 |
| | $Z_j =$ | | 297.08 | 9 | 9.4215 | 10.875 | 5 | 0 | 0.0085 | 15.1665 | |
| | $C_j - Z_j =$ | | — | 0 | -1.4215 | -3.875 | 0 | 0 | -0.0085 | -15.165 | |

*Notes:*
1. Divided $i = 3$ constraint equation in Table 7A.2 by 0.3 to obtain values in Table 7A.3.
2. Multiplied $i = 3$ constraint equation in Table 7A.3 by 0.25 and added it to the $i = 1$ constraint equation in Table 7A.2 to obtain the $i = 1$ constraint equation in Table 7A.3.
3. Multiplied $i = 3$ constraint equation in Table 7A.3 by 0.5 and subtracted it from the $i = 2$ constraint equation in Table 7A.2 to obtain the $i = 2$ constraint equation in Table 7A.3.

# 8

# *Competitive Markets*

Supply is a function relating the market price of a good or service to the maximum quantity that the firm or industry is willing to sell, holding constant everything except price. A competitive firm cannot influence the market price; therefore, the firm compares price to its *MC* (marginal cost) and *AVC* (average variable cost) to determine its profit-maximizing output and whether its revenues exceed its variable costs. Once the profit-maximizing output at each price has been estimated for all firms, the industry supply curve can be estimated. By comparing demand and supply at a given price, it can be determined whether there is excess demand or supply, or a market-clearing price where demand equals supply.

This chapter begins with a discussion in section 8.1 of the nature of competitive markets and the pricing behavior of competitive firms. The next two sections are devoted to determining the profit-maximizing output for a competitive firm. Sections 8.4 and 8.5 discuss the industry supply curve and how it is used with the demand curve to find the market clearing price. Section 8.6 discusses transaction costs — the costs of using the market to buy and sell goods. The last two sections cover the long-run supply curve and price and output in long-run equilibrium. The case for this chapter discusses how marketing and production cost data are used to determine the firm's profit-maximizing operating budget. The appendix covers breakeven output and price analysis.

## 8.1  *Competitive Markets*

The term *competition* has a special definition when it is used by economists to describe the market for a good or service. A market consists of all consumers and firms who engage in the buying or selling of a specified good, service, or factor of production. Whenever or wherever there is an exchange of money for goods or productive factors, there is a market. Competition exists when firms selling goods in the market believe that changes in their output cannot influence the market price.

*Product Characteristics.* The firms in a competitive market produce goods or services that are close or perfect substitutes. Products that are produced to an industry specification are perfect substitutes. Examples are agricultural products traded on the commodity exchanges, fasteners such as nuts and bolts, and many electrical or electronic components. Other products may be outwardly different in some respects; yet consumers view them as being close substitutes for each other. If the price cross-elasticities among the firms' products are sufficiently great, the products are perfect substitutes. Whether two products are good substitutes depends on the behavior of consumers and not on the differences in the products as alleged by their manufacturers.

*Price-Taker Firms.* Firms in a competitive market are price takers who treat the observed market price as a given when deciding how much to buy or sell. Whether the competitive firm produces 100, 200, or 500 units of output per hour, it will receive the same market price. The firm can change its output and have no measurable impact on the market price of the good or service. Because the firm cannot influence the market price, it takes the market price as a given and adjusts its output to the level that maximizes profits.

In actual market situations, the output decisions of a competitive firm probably do have some impact on the market price. However, a firm's impact on the market price may not be discernible by its management because the actions of other firms or random variations in consumer purchases obscure the relationship between changes in the firm's output and changes in the market price. If a large number of firms sell the same good or service, variations in market prices resulting from changes in one firm's output may be relatively small when compared to the variations in prices resulting from shifts in consumer demand. A reduction in a firm's output may increase the market price by 0.1 percent. However, a reduction in the price of a substitute good may have resulted in a 5 percent decrease in the quantity demanded of the product and a 6 percent decrease in its price. Thus, management cannot determine whether its firm's output changes have resulted in price changes.

Whether a particular market is competitive is an empirical matter that the management of each firm must determine on the basis of its observations of the behavior of consumers and the managements of the other firms. If management finds that its output decisions have little discernible effect on the market price, then the firm will be a price taker even if there are few firms in the market. The existence of many firms producing goods that are close or perfect substitutes generally means that the market is competitive. When all firms in an industry are price takers, the industry is competitive.

*Additional Assumptions.* When economists evaluate the efficiency of competitive markets, they include in their definition of competition two additional characteristics: (1) firms and the resources they employ may enter into or exit from the industry at little or no cost, and (2) buyers and sellers have perfect knowledge of the market prices of the product and the resources used to produce it. These last two characteristics are not necessary to understand the profit-maximizing behavior of managers of competitive firms; they are primarily used by economists to simplify their models of price behavior. The need for these assumptions results from the costs of making market transactions (discussed in section 8.6), rather than from the existence of price-taker firms. The existence of many firms producing products that are close or perfect substitutes is adequate to predict price-taker behavior by the firms in the market.

## 8.2 *Profit-Maximizing Output — Graphical Method*

A price-taker firm believes that it cannot influence the market price for its product. Regardless of the firm's output, the market price of its product will not be affected in a systematic manner that can be identified by management. The firm's output can vary from zero up to the physical production capacity of its plant with no change in the market price.

*The Profit Maximization Goal.* The competitive model presented in this chapter assumes that the firm's goal is to maximize its profits. Attaining this goal requires that the price-taker firm's management find the output that maximizes profits. Because it is assumed that profits in subsequent planning periods do not depend on decisions made with respect to output in the current planning period, maximizing the value of the firm amounts to maximizing profits. If decisions for the current planning period affect the level of profits in future planning periods, wealth maximization must be used to evaluate alternative output plans for the several planning periods. Use of the wealth-maximization model by competitive firms is discussed in the next chapter.

Profit, $\Pi$, is the difference between total revenue, *TR*, and total cost, *TC*, both of which are a function of output.

$$\Pi = TR(Q) - TC(Q) \tag{8.1}$$

The profit-maximizing competitive firm produces each unit of output for which the price of the product is greater than its marginal cost. Assume that management has decided to produce ten units of output. Because the firm cannot change the market price by producing another unit of output (the 11th), its marginal revenue is equal to the market price. If price is $10, the change in the firm's total revenue if it sells one more unit of output is $MR = \$10$. Marginal cost is the change in total cost if the firm produces one more unit of output. If $MC = \$7$ for the eleventh unit of output, the eleventh unit will add $MR - MC = \$10 - \$7 = \$3$ to the firm's profits. Since the goal of the firm is to maximize its profits, the 11th unit should be produced because it will increase profits by $3.

This situation is illustrated in Figure 8.1. The *MR* curve is horizontal at the $10 market price, reflecting the assumption that the firm is a price taker. The *MC* curve is upward sloping for all rates of output. At $Q = 11$ units, the difference between the *MR* and *MC* curves is the marginal profit from producing the 11th unit of output. If the marginal profit is positive, the firm can increase its profits by producing that unit of output. In Figure 8.1, the firm maximizes its profits at $Q = 17$ units because each unit of output up to the 17th has a positive marginal profit and increases the firm's total profits. The firm would not increase its profits by producing more than 17 units of output. Producing the 20th unit of output adds $12.50 to *TC* and only $10 to *TR*, which reduces profits by $2.50. The firm maximizes its profits by producing the output where $MC = MR$, which is 17 units in this example.

*The Average Variable Cost Test.* When the *MC* curve is upward sloping as in Figure 8.1, $MR = MC$ is the only condition required to determine the firm's profit-maximizing output. If its production process exhibits both increasing and diminishing returns, so that the *MC* curve is U-shaped as in Figure 8.2, two additional conditions must be met before the firm will have a positive profit-maximizing output. The first condition is that the *MC* curve be upward sloping at output $q''$ where $MR = MC$. Output $q'$, where *MC* is downward sloping, is not profit-maximizing because no profits have been earned on any of the units of output between 0 and $q'$. The second condition is that at the profit-maximizing output, price must be greater than *AVC*. In Figure 8.2, *AVC* is $V_0$ at output $q''$. As long as price is greater than *AVC*, the firm's revenues exceed its labor and materials costs. If the firm is unable to

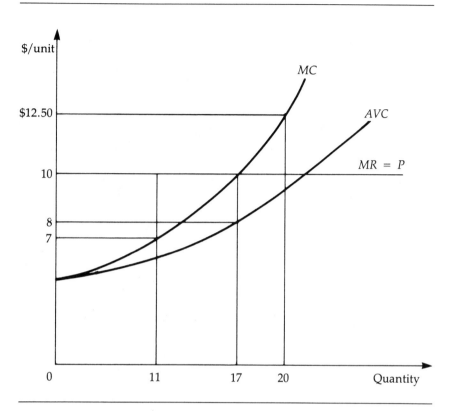

**Figure 8.1 Profit-Maximizing Output, Upward Sloping Marginal Cost Curve**

An upward sloping *MC* curve results when the production function exhibits diminishing returns. At an output of 11 units, *MC* is $3 less than price; hence, it is definitely profitable to produce 11 units. It is even more profitable to produce 17 units because the difference between price and *MC* is positive and is added to total profit. Profits are reduced if 20 units are produced; *MC* is greater than price, reducing profits, for all outputs in excess of 17 units.

earn enough revenues to pay its labor and materials costs, as would occur if price were less than the minimum *AVC*, the firm should shut down and produce nothing. Every unit of output produced when price is at less than the minimum *AVC* will reduce the firm's cash balances and ultimately lead to its bankruptcy. If the *MC* curve is U-shaped, the profit-maximizing output, $q''$, occurs where $MR = MC$, *MC* is upward sloping, and *AVC* at $q''$ is less than price.

The definition of *AVC* needs to be expanded for the purposes of determining when to shut down a production facility. Fixed costs are those costs that do not change when output changes. However, if some

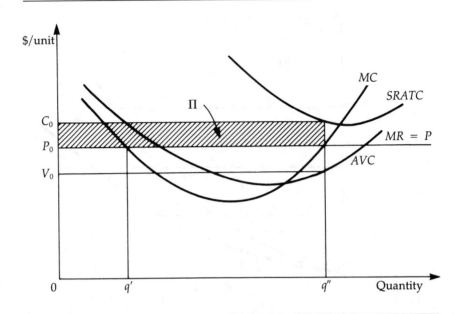

**Figure 8.2  Profit-Maximizing Output, U-Shaped MC Curve**
The $MC$ curve is U-shaped when the production function exhibits increasing and then diminishing returns. Output $q'$ is profit-minimizing since $MC > P$ for all output up to $q'$, yielding a loss on each unit of output. For outputs between $q'$ and $q''$, $MC < P$, and each unit of output adds to profits. Output $q''$ is profit-maximizing because each unit beyond $q''$ has an $MC$ greater than price, which reduces profits. The firm's unit profit is $P_0 - C_0$, and is a loss here because $C_0 > P_0$.

portion of the fixed production costs can be avoided when the firm shuts down its plant, those "fixed" costs become variable with respect to the decision to shut down the plant and produce nothing. The costs of supervisory and administrative workers are an example of a cost that becomes variable when the plant is shut down. Those costs that are variable with respect to the shutdown decision are included in $AVC$ when it is compared to price to determine whether to shut down the plant. Average variable cost for making the shutdown decision is usually greater than $AVC$, as it is normally calculated when the decision is whether to increase or decrease output.

*The Level of Profits.* To determine whether the firm is making a profit at output $q''$, the average total cost curve, $SRATC$, must be considered. The firm's total profit, which is actually a loss in Figure 8.2, is $\Pi = (P_0 - C_0)q''$. This amount is represented by the shaded area between $P_0$ and $C_0$.

Even though the firm is producing its profit-maximizing output at $q''$ in Figure 8.2, it is not earning a profit because price is below its *SRATC* at $q''$. However, from the point of view of the managerial decision process, the actual level of profit is strictly a memo item. The competitive firm cannot influence the market price. If the firm is minimizing the cost of its profit-maximizing output, it cannot earn a greater profit. It has done the best it can to maximize its profits given the market price. The firm may contribute to the cost of trade-association-sponsored advertising to stimulate demand and raise the market price and its profits. The firm may also support its trade association's political (lobbying) efforts to enact legislation or government regulations that favor profits by raising the market price or reducing costs. But the firm acting by itself cannot influence the market price.

As long as price is greater than $AVC(q'')$, producing $q''$ will increase the value of the firm. If $P > AVC(q'')$, cash flow is positive, and at least some portion of its fixed costs are being paid from revenues. If the firm were to shut down because $P < ATC(q'')$ and it was not making a profit, it would have to pay all of its fixed costs that could not be avoided if output were zero by drawing down its assets to pay these costs. Thus, the firm would produce $q''$ units of output because its assets would be reduced by a smaller amount than if it produced nothing.

## 8.3  *Profit-Maximizing Output — Calculus Method*

Finding the profit-maximizing output involves calculating the first and second derivatives of the profit function, setting the first derivative equal to zero, and solving the resulting equation for $q$. The values of $q$ that solve the first derivative equation are then substituted into the second derivative to determine which output is profit-maximizing. If the second derivative is negative, the profit function has a local maximum at that value of $q$. Given the normal assumptions relating to the nature of production costs and the demand function, more than one local maximum will not occur.

Taking the first derivative of equation 8.1 yields

$$d\Pi/dq = dTR(q)/dq - dTC(q)/dq \qquad (8.2)$$

Since marginal revenue is defined as $dTR(q)/dq$ and marginal cost is $dTC(q)/dq$, equation 8.2 can be written as

$$d\Pi/dq = MR(q) - MC(q) \qquad (8.3)$$

Taking the second derivative yields

$$d^2\Pi/dq^2 = dMR(q)/dq - dMC(q)/dq \qquad \textbf{(8.4)}$$

Setting the first derivative $d\Pi/dq$ equal to zero yields

$$MR(q) - MC(q) = 0 \text{ or } MR(q) = MC(q) \qquad \textbf{(8.5)}$$

This is the first condition for finding the profit-maximizing output, $q''$, that was demonstrated graphically in the previous section.

Because the competitive firm is a price taker, its marginal revenue is equal to the market price. Thus, equation 8.5 becomes

$$MC(q'') = P \qquad \textbf{(8.6)}$$

if the firm is to maximize its profits at output $q''$. $P$ is a constant for the price-taker firm and $MR(q) = P$; therefore, $dMR(q)/dq = 0$, and equation 8.4 becomes

$$d^2\Pi/dq^2 = 0 - dMC(q'')/dq \qquad \textbf{(8.7)}$$

The quantity $q''$ yields maximum profits if $d^2\Pi/dq^2$ is negative; thus, $dMC(q'')/dq$ must be positive. This is the second condition for a profit-maximizing output, that the $MC$ curve be upward sloping. The third condition, that $P > AVC(q'')$, is not demonstrated using calculus.

**EXAMPLE 8.1.** The marketing department has projected a market price of $180 for the next planning period. Because the market is competitive, management believes that it can sell all of its output at that price. Total revenue is $TR = \$180q$. The accounting department has estimated the total cost function as

$$TC = (\$1/12)q^3 - (\$1/2)q^2 + \$100q + \$800$$

where $q$ is output per hour. Total profit is

$$\Pi = 180q - q^3/12 + q^2/2 - 100q - 800$$
$$\Pi = -q^3/12 + q^2/2 + 80q - 800$$

The first derivative of the profit function is

$$d\Pi/dq = -q^2/4 + q + 80$$

Setting $d\Pi/dq$ equal to zero, multiplying both sides of the equation by 4, and factoring it yields

$$-q^2 + 4q + 320 = 0 \qquad\qquad (8.8)$$

$$(q + 16)(20 - q) = 0$$

$$q = -16, 20$$

In this example, it is not necessary to evaluate the second derivative of the profit function because a negative output ($q = -16$) cannot be profit-maximizing.[1] At $q = 20$, profit is

$$\Pi = -(20)^3/12 + (20)^2/2 + 80(20) - 800 = \$333.33$$

The total cost function can be divided into two parts, total variable cost (*TVC*) and fixed cost. Fixed cost is $800 per hour, and

$$TVC = q^3/12 - q^2/2 + 100q$$

Marginal cost is the derivative of *TVC* with respect to $q$, or

$$MC = dTVC/dq = q^2/4 - q + 100$$

Equating marginal cost to price yields

$$q^2/4 - q + 100 = 180$$

Performing some algebra on this equation yields equation 8.8. The first method (maximizing $\Pi$) facilitates calculating profits after the profit-maximizing output has been calculated.

Average variable cost at $q = 20$ is

$$AVC = TVC/q = q^2/12 - q/2 + 100$$

$$AVC = (400/12) - (20/2) + 100 = \$123.33$$

Thus, the firm will produce 20 units of output because *AVC* is less than the $180 price. Average fixed cost is $AFC = \$800/20 = \$40$, and *ATC* is $123.33 + $40.00 = $163.33. Profit per unit of output is $180.00 − $163.33 = $16.67, and total profit is $333.40. The difference in the two profit calculations is attributable to round-off errors.

---

[1]Since $d^2\Pi/dq^2 = -q/2 + 1$, $d^2\Pi/dq^2 = -9$ when $q = 20$; thus, $q = 20$ maximizes profits. When $q = -16$, $d^2\Pi/dq^2 = +9$; thus, $q = -16$ is where profits are minimized.

The last step is to calculate the quantity of labor required to produce 20 units per hour of the product. Average variable cost consists of two elements, labor cost and materials cost. If the cost of materials is $13.33 per unit of output and the wage rate is $5.50 per hour, the number of production workers required to produce one unit of output is

$$L = (\$123.33 - \$13.33)/\$5.50 = 20$$

Because 20 units of output are produced each hour, a total of 400 production workers are required to produce the profit-maximizing output.

## 8.4   *Short-Run Supply Curve*

The supply curve is a function relating the market price of a product or service to the maximum quantity that the firm or industry will offer for sale, holding constant all variables except price. The variables held constant include wages, the unit cost of materials, and each firm's production function. The variables that are held constant are those that shift the $MC$ curve of the firm.

### 8.4.1   *Supply and Shifts in Supply Curves*

This section contains discussions of the typical firm's supply curve and the supply curve of a competitive industry. The types of changes that result in shifts in supply curves are also discussed in this section.

*The Supply Curve.* The $MC$ curve above its $AVC$ curve is the firm's supply curve; the firm finds its profit-maximizing output by equating the market price to the upward sloping portion of its $MC$ curve. When the market price rises, the firm will supply more output because it is profit-maximizing to do so. If price is below the minimum point on its $AVC$ curve, its profit-maximizing output is zero. The supply curve of the firm is the portion of the $MC$ curve in the left-hand graph of Figure 8.3.

If all firms in a competitive industry have identical $MC$ curves, industry supply is found by multiplying the profit-maximizing output of the typical firm by the number of firms in the industry. If $M$ is the number of firms, industry supply at price $P_0$ is $Q_0 = Mq_0$. The industry supply curve under this assumption is in the right-hand diagram of Figure 8.3. If the firms in the industry do not have identical $MC$ curves, industry supply is found by adding up their profit-maximizing outputs at each market price.

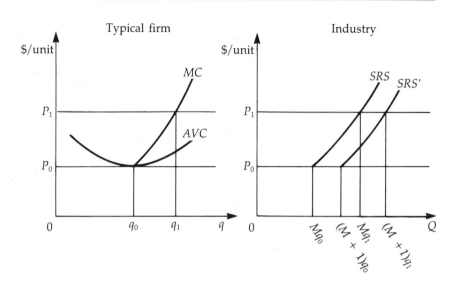

**Figure 8.3  Short-Run Supply Curves, Increase in Number of Firms**

The *MC* curve above the *AVC* is the profit-maximizing firm's supply, because the firm will supply the quantity on the *MC* curve at each price. To find the industry supply curve, multiply the output of the typical firm at each price by the number of firms, *M*. If another firm enters the industry, output of the typical firm at each price is multiplied by *M* + 1 to find industry supply. The typical firm and the industry will supply nothing at a price below $P_0$ because price would then be less than *AVC*.

*Changes in the Number of Firms.* A change in the number of firms shifts the industry supply curve. When a new firm enters a competitive market, the industry supply curve shifts to the right by the quantity at each price on the *MC* curve of the new entrant. If all firms, including the new entrant, have identical *MC* curves, industry supply in Figure 8.3 at price $P_0$ will become $(M + 1)q_0$. If a firm were to withdraw from the market, the industry supply curve would shift to the left by the amount at each price that the firm leaving the industry had been supplying.

*Changes in Factor Prices or* **MPL.** The effect of changes in factor prices or production functions on the short-run supply curve of a firm, and then on the supply curve of the industry, is determined from the basic equation for marginal cost:

$$MC = (wage/MPL) + MCM \qquad (8.9)$$

where *MCM* is the marginal cost of materials. An increase in either the wage rate or *MCM* will increase marginal cost at every output. The *MC* curve for the typical firm in Figure 8.4 will shift up from *MC* to *MC'*, and the industry supply curve will also shift up from *SRS* to *SRS'*. Only that portion of the *MC* curve above $V_0$, the minimum point of the *AVC* curve, is drawn in Figure 8.4 because the remainder of the firm's *MC* curve is not part of its supply curve. The impact of this upward shift in the *MC* curve on the quantity supplied by the firm can be viewed in two ways. The upward shift in the *MC* curve means that it now costs more to produce $q_0$ units of the good; hence, the firm will produce that amount only if the market price rises to $P_1$. If the market price were to remain unchanged at $P_0$, the firm would supply only $q_1$ units of output. The supply curves for the firm and industry, if all firms in the industry are similarly affected, will shift upward as a result of the increase in the wage rate or the unit cost of materials.

Shifts in the supply curve of the firm or industry can also occur as a result of changes in the marginal product of labor (*MPL*). Changes in *MPL* result from shifts in the production function. Shifts in the production function can result from changes in the technology of the firm's plant and equipment; however, these changes generally occur

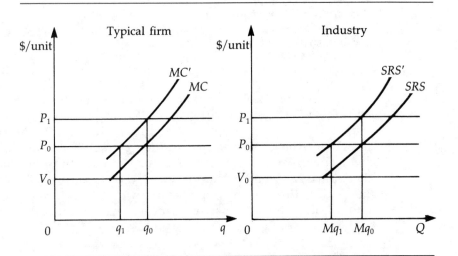

**Figure 8.4   Short-Run Supply Curves, Increase in Wage Rate**

An increase in the wage rate increases *MCL* and *MC*, shifting the typical firm's *MC* curve up to *MC'*. At price $P_0$, the typical firm will reduce its output from $q_0$ to $q_1$, and industry supply would fall from $Mq_0$ to $Mq_1$, shifting from *SRS* to *SRS'*.

in the long run. In the short run, production function shifts can occur from organizational changes that result in employees' working harder or more efficiently, or from using fewer or more productive raw materials. Short-run shifts in the production function can also occur as a result of changes in government regulations or a new collective bargaining agreement that changes work rules or job descriptions. An increase in *MPL* will reduce marginal cost and shift the *MC* curve down, from *MC'* to *MC* in Figure 8.4. The reduction in *MC* can be seen in equation 8.9 as a result of the denominator of its first term becoming larger. The downward shift in the *MC* curve also results in a downward shift in the short-run supply curve from *SRS'* to *SRS* if the increase in labor productivity occurs throughout the industry. More output will be supplied at each market price when the *SRS* curve shifts to the right.

*Changes in Prices of Other Products.* The supply curve of a firm or competitive industry will also shift if there are changes in the prices of other goods that could be produced by the firm. If a farm has been planting wheat and rye, a rise in the price of rye, holding constant the price of wheat, is likely to result in a reduction in the acreage planted to wheat. The firm will supply less wheat at its present market price because the price of rye has risen, making rye more profitable. Similarly, assembly and machine shops have the capability of supplying a wide range of services to manufacturers. If the price they can charge for one line of services rises, holding constant the prices they can charge for other services, these firms will concentrate more of their efforts on the now more profitable services and supply more of them. If their plants are operating at capacity, they must reduce their supply of the less profitable services.

*Changes in Management Expectations.* A change in management's expectations with respect to future prices, wages, or other cost elements can also shift the firm's supply curve. If similar expectations are held by most or all managers in the industry, the industry supply curve will also shift. Assume that increased imports are expected in one of the company's markets. If imports are lower-priced than the firm's product, or of higher quality, the firm's managers would expect future prices to decline. This would lead them to look for other products to produce and to plan for a lower output of the current product. Similarly, expectations of higher future prices, caused possibly by the enactment of import controls, would likely result in an increase in the quantity that the firm plans to produce. This would result in more raw materials being ordered from suppliers, new workers being hired, and inventories being accumulated to take advantage of the expected higher prices. These actions would shift the firm's supply curve to the right.

244    Competitive Markets

## 8.4.2  Calculating the Supply Function

This section contains two examples of calculating the typical firm's supply curve and that of the industry. In the first example, the supply curves are obtained from an estimate of the typical firm's $AVC$ function. In the second example, an estimate of the typical firm's production function provides the basis for estimating the supply curves.

**EXAMPLE 8.2. Supply Curve from the $AVC$ Function.**  If the $AVC$ function of the typical firm is known, the industry's supply curve can be calculated. Assume that there are $M = 40$ identical profit-maximizing firms in a competitive industry. The average variable cost curve for the typical firm is

$$AVC = 20 + 0.2q^2 \tag{8.10}$$

where $q$ is output per hour. Equation 8.10 most likely would be obtained from a statistical cost study of the firm's accounting records. Marginal cost is found by multiplying $AVC$ by $q$ and then differentiating the resulting total variable cost function.

$$TVC = (AVC)(q) = (20 + 0.2q^2)q = 20q + 0.2q^3$$
$$MC = dTVC/dq = 20 + 0.6q^2 \tag{8.11}$$

The typical firm's profit-maximizing output is found by setting $MC$ equal to the market price, $P$, and solving the resulting equation for $q$:

$$MC = 20 + 0.6q^2 = P$$
$$q = \sqrt{(P - 20)/0.6} \tag{8.12}$$

Industry supply, $Q$, at price $P$ is

$$Q = 40q = 40\sqrt{(P - 20)/0.6} \tag{8.13}$$

The typical firm will not sell any output unless price is greater than $AVC$. All outputs greater than the output at which $AVC$ is minimized are on the firm's supply curve. This output is zero for the $AVC$ curve in equation 8.10. The minimum $AVC$ is $20 per unit if $q = 0$. Thus, the industry supply curve is $Q = 40\sqrt{(P - 20)/0.6}$ for all positive rates of output and all prices greater than $20. Industry output is zero at prices less than $20. If $P = \$100$, the typical firm would supply $q = \sqrt{(100 - 20)/0.6} = 11.55$ units and industry supply would be $Q = (40)(11.55) = 462$ units.

**EXAMPLE 8.3. Supply Curve from the Production Function.** Assume that the typical firm has the production function

$$q = 10L^{0.5} \tag{8.14}$$

where $q$ is output per hour and $L$ is the number of production workers. The first step is to calculate the $MC$ function for the typical firm. Assume that the wage rate is \$8 per hour. $MPL$ and $MCL$ are

$$MPL = dq/dL = 5/L^{0.5}$$

$$MCL = wage/MPL = \$8/(5/L^{0.5}) = \$1.60L^{0.5}$$

If $MCM = \$15$ per unit, then

$$MC = \$15 + \$1.60L^{0.5}$$

From equation 8.14, $L^{0.5} = 0.1q$; therefore,

$$MC = \$15 + \$0.16q$$

Average variable cost is found in a similar manner. $APL$ and $ACL$ are

$$APL = q/L = 10/L^{0.5}$$

$$ACL = w/APL = \$0.80L^{0.5}$$

Because $ACM = MCM$ under the constant cost assumption, $AVC$ is

$$AVC = \$15 + \$0.80L^{0.5} = \$15 + \$0.80q$$

$AVC$ and $MC$ are minimized when $q = 0$ at \$15.00 per unit. The minimum points of the supply curves are at \$15.
To find the firm's supply curve, set $MC = P$.

$$P = \$15 + \$0.16q$$

$$q = (P - \$15)/\$0.16$$

If there are $M = 40$ firms, industry supply is

$$Q = 40q = 40(P - \$15)/\$0.16 = 250(P - \$15)$$

At a market price of \$63, the typical firm would supply

$$q = (\$63 - \$15)/\$0.16 = 300$$

units of output, and industry supply would be 12,000 units.

The advantage of starting with the production function when estimating industry supply is that it facilitates estimating the impact of changes in wage rate, material cost, and production function on industry supply. In the above example, if the wage rate were to rise to $10 per hour, $MC$ and $AVC$ for the typical firm would become

$$MC = \$15 + \$0.20q$$

$$AVC = \$15 + \$0.10q$$

Minimum $AVC = \$15$ when $q = 0$. The supply curve of the typical firm is

$$q = (P - \$15)/\$0.20$$

and the industry supply curve is

$$Q = 40q = 200(P - \$15)$$

At a market price of $63, the typical firm would now supply 240 units, and industry supply would be 9,600 units.

## 8.5  *The Market-Clearing Price*

Economists divide into two categories the factors that have been found in empirical studies to influence price in a competitive market: demand and supply. The interaction of demand and supply determines the market-clearing price. The market-clearing price is that price at which the market is in equilibrium: There are no systematic market forces leading to higher or lower prices.

*Demand and Supply.* The demand curve relates the market price of a good or service to the maximum quantity that consumers are willing to purchase, holding constant the prices of substitute and complementary goods, consumer incomes, consumer preferences, and any other factors that influence the willingness of consumers to buy the product. The demand curve expresses the relationship between price and the quantity demanded at each price. There is a movement along the demand curve when price changes. When something other than price changes, the demand curve shifts to the right or the left. For a discussion of the reasons for demand curve shifts, see chapter 3.

The supply curve relates the maximum quantity firms are willing to sell to its market price — holding constant wage rates, the cost of materials, the production function, and the number of firms in the industry. When the price of the product changes, there is a movement along the supply curve to the new quantity supplied. When factor prices or productivities change, there is a shift in the supply curve.

*Market Equilibrium.* In Figure 8.5, the market-clearing price is the price $P_0$ at the point where the demand and supply curves $D_0$ and $S_0$ intersect. Consider first a price, such as $P_1$, below the market-clearing price. At $P_1$, the quantity demanded by consumers is greater than the quantity supplied to the market by business firms. There is excess demand at price $P_1$ equal to the difference between the quantities demanded and supplied. This difference, which is $Q'_1 - Q_1$ in Figure 8.5, is the shortage at price $P_1$. With the quantity demanded greater than the quantity supplied, current production is not adequate to fill the demand for the product, and the inventories of its producers and mar-

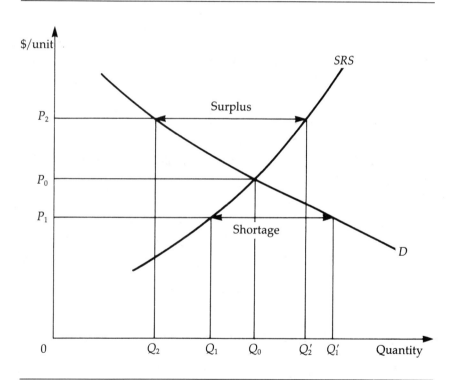

**Figure 8.5    Shortage, Surplus, and Market Equilibrium**

At price $P_1$ there is a shortage equal to $Q'_1 - Q_1$ because $D$ is greater than $SRS$ at $P_1$. At price $P_2$ there is a surplus of $Q'_2 - Q_2$. At price $P_0$, the demand and $SRS$ curves intersect, yielding a market equilibrium at output $Q_0$.

keters will decline. This inventory decline signals the sellers that there is a shortage and that price should be increased. Other signals would be increasing new order backlogs and lines of customers waiting to buy the good or service. The shortage will be reduced as the market price rises and will become zero once price has risen to $P_0$. The shortage leads to increases in the market price until equilibrium price $P_0$, where the demand and supply curves intersect, is attained.

Assume now that the market price is $P_2$ in Figure 8.5. At price $P_2$, the quantity demanded is less than the quantity supplied, and there is an excess supply of the product. The difference between the quantities demanded and supplied, $Q'_2 - Q_2$ in Figure 8.5, is the surplus at price $P_2$. With the quantity demanded less than that supplied, inventories will be increasing. This signals the firms to reduce their price. Until the market price has fallen to $P_0$, there will be a surplus and continued inventory buildups. Once price has fallen to $P_0$, the quantities demanded and supplied are equal, and there are no further incentives to reduce price. The market is in equilibrium. Other symptoms of a surplus are falling backlogs and a lack of customers waiting to buy the product.

Assume now that the market is in equilibrium at price $P_0$ and industry output $Q_0$, as in Figure 8.6. After this market-clearing price and output have been established, the demand curve shifts to the right. This shift could occur, for example, because the price of a substitute good went up or consumer incomes rose and this product is a normal good. There is a shortage at price $P_0$ because the quantity demanded has risen to $Q'_0$, and the quantity supplied is unchanged at $Q_0$. The shortage is $Q'_0 - Q_0$ because consumers want to buy that much more than firms are willing to sell at price $P_0$. The result is falling inventories and a rising backlog of new orders. Price will increase until it has risen to $P_1$ and the quantity demanded is again equal to that supplied, at industry output $Q_1$. If demand were to have shifted to the left, there would first have been a surplus of the product at price $P_0$ and then price reductions until a lower market clearing price was established.

**EXAMPLE 8.4.** If statistical or other estimates of the demand and supply functions for an industry are available, it is possible to calculate the market-clearing price. Assume that management has estimated the market demand and supply functions for its product:

$$\text{Demand: } Q = 10,000 - 30P$$

$$\text{Supply: } Q = 8,000 + 20P$$

Finding the market-clearing price amounts to solving simultaneously these two equations for price. Equating the quantities demanded and

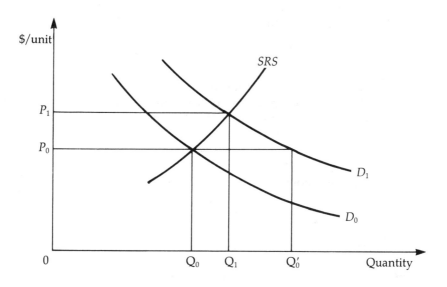

**Figure 8.6   Changes in the Market Equilibrium Price**
The initial equilibrium is at price $P_0$ and $Q_0$ where the $D_0$ and $SRS$ curves intersect. If demand shifts to the right to $D_1$, a shortage equal to $Q_0' - Q_0$ is created. This shortage puts upward pressure on prices until the market price rises to $P_1$ where the $D_1$ and $SRS$ intersect. $P_1$ is the new equilibrium price.

supplied yields an equilibrium price of $40:

$$8{,}000 + 20P = 10{,}000 - 30P$$
$$50P = 2{,}000 \text{ or } P = \$40$$

Industry output is found by substituting $P = \$40$ into either the demand or supply equation (both quantities being equal). Substituting $P = \$40$ into the demand equation yields

$$Q = 10{,}000 - (30)(40) = 8{,}800$$

The market-clearing price is $40, and industry output is 8,800 units. If there are $M = 40$ identical firms in the industry, the output of each firm is $q = Q/M = 8{,}800/40 = 220$ units.

**EXAMPLE 8.5.**   The general analytical model of this and the preceding section provides a market research strategy for a firm that is attempting to determine its profit-maximizing output. Its marginal and average variable cost curves are those in equations 8.10 and 8.11. Management has estimated the market demand curve for the product to be

$$P = 2,400 - 0.08Q^2$$

where $Q$ is output of the 40 identical firms. The first step is to calculate the supply curve of the typical firm and the industry. This has been done in equations 8.12 and 8.13. The industry supply curve is

$$Q = 40\sqrt{(P - 20)/0.6}$$

Squaring both sides of this equation yields

$$Q^2 = 1,600(P - 20)/0.6$$

Substituting this equation into the demand function yields

$$P = 2,400 - 0.08(1,600)(P - 20)/0.6$$
$$P = 2,400 - 213.33P + 4,266.67$$
$$214.33P = 6,666.67 \text{ or } P = \$31.10$$

$P = \$31.10$ is the market-clearing price. Industry output is 172 units (from equation 8.13), and the profit-maximizing output of the typical firm is 4.3 units. If fixed costs are $25.00 per hour, the profits of the typical firm are

$$\Pi = (P - AVC)q - FC \qquad (8.15)$$
$$\Pi = (31.10 - 20 - 0.2(4.3))(4.3) - 25.00 = \$19.03 \text{ per hour}$$

## 8.6 *Transaction Costs*

Transaction costs are the costs of buying and selling goods and services using the market. They are also referred to as *ICP* costs — information (*I*), contracting (*C*), and policing (*P*) costs. Transaction costs also include sales taxes.

Information costs are the costs associated with determining the market price for a good or service. These costs may be very low relative to the price of the product. The cost of a phone call to a stockbroker to find the current price of a listed security is a low transaction cost. Information costs may be relatively high when a considerable amount of time and gasoline is spent searching for the best price on a certain model of car. Purchasing agents are specialists at quickly and cheaply finding the lowest-cost sources of anything the company may wish to purchase. The salary and expenses of the purchasing agent are transaction costs incurred by the firm.

Contracting costs are the costs of concluding a sale. They may be low when buying a cartful of groceries at the market, or several hundred dollars in escrow and title fees when buying a home. Preparing the contract for the sale of a complex technology may require several attorneys and engineers and cost $50,000 or more.

Policing costs arise when there is a dispute over the terms of a contract or one party fails to fulfill its terms. The costs of a lawsuit or repossessing property securing a loan are examples of policing costs.

*Minimizing Transaction Costs.* Transaction (*ICP*) costs benefit neither the seller nor the buyer; they are, rather, the result of making a market transaction that benefits them both. It is in the best interest of both sellers and buyers to develop methods of doing business that minimize transaction costs. Organized stock and commodity exchanges, with their rapid market price quotations, low brokerage fees, and standard contracts, exist because they are the lowest-cost method available for making these transactions. Price advertising, especially when the seller wants potential customers to learn quickly about price reductions, is a way to reduce buyers' transaction costs. Supermarkets' advertising of reduced-price specials in the food section of the Wednesday or Thursday newspaper reduces consumers' costs of finding the lowest prices for food items. Locating automobile dealerships along freeways or together in "automobile rows" reduces the costs of comparison shopping, thereby increasing customer traffic at the dealerships. Because the price of a new or used car is large relative to most consumers' income, people shop several dealers before making a decision. Isolated dealerships are expensive for many consumers to comparison shop at.

More examples of actions taken by firms to reduce transaction costs could be cited. The point is that production, marketing, and distribution costs are not the only costs that management must pay attention to. Reducing variable transaction costs borne by the company can shift its marginal cost down and increase profits in much the same way as a technological change. Any innovation by one firm resulting in higher profits is likely to be quickly emulated by other firms. With the marginal cost curves of all firms shifting down, the industry supply curve will shift to the right and price will fall. Similarly, a reduction in fixed transaction costs borne by the company can increase profits, although it will not increase the firm's profit-maximizing output or shift the industry supply curve to the right. Ultimately, the increase in profits caused by a reduction in fixed transaction costs will attract additional firms into the industry, which will shift the supply curve to the right and reduce the profits from the innovation.

Developing a marketing strategy that reduces the transaction costs borne by consumers can make it possible for the company to charge a higher price for its product and still be competitive with other sellers. Again, adoption of this marketing strategy by all firms in the industry will affect the industry's supply curve, its price, and the profits to be earned by the firms. Enactment of a new law or government regulation that reduces consumer transaction costs incurred by the customers of an industry will have a similar effect.

In Figure 8.7, consumer preferences for the product yield industry demand curve $D$. However, since consumers must bear transaction costs of $T$ dollars per unit of the product, their effective demand curve for the product is $D^T$, which is found for each output by subtracting $T$ from the price on demand curve $D$. With supply curve $S$, the market

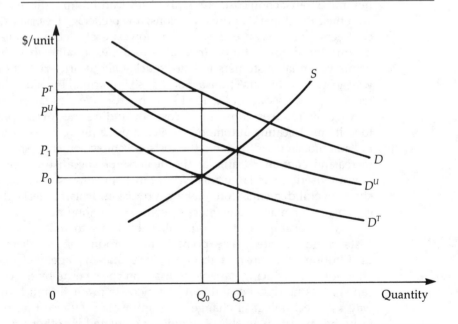

**Figure 8.7  Demand Curve Shifts with Transaction Cost Changes**

Consumer demand for the product is $D$, but consumers must pay transaction costs equal to $P_T - P_0$, which reduce their effective demand curve to $D^T$. If the sellers are able to reduce transaction costs to $P_u - P_1$, the effective demand curve rises to $D^U$, increasing the price received by the firms to $P_1$ and sales to $Q_1$ in the new market equilibrium.

price is $P_0$, and the difference between $P_T$ and $P_0$ is the transaction cost of $T$ dollars. Assume that a marketing innovation reduces the transaction costs incurred by consumers from $T$ to $U$ dollars. The result is an upward shift in the effective demand curve from $D^T$ to $D^U$, which increases the market-clearing price from $P_0$ to $P_1$. The difference between $P_1$ and $P_U$ is the transaction cost of $U$ dollars still incurred by consumers. If the firms in the industry incur no increase in their marginal costs as a result of the innovation, their profits will rise.

*Alternative to Transaction Costs.* The alternative to incurring the costs of making a market transaction is for the firm or the consumer to produce the item. This alternative requires the firm to incur the costs of producing the item and managing its production. The costs of managing the item's production within the firm are administrative costs. If the item is subject to sales taxes, the firm or consumer can save the sales tax by producing it. Income taxes also provide incentives for consumers to perform some services for themselves; at a 50 percent marginal income tax rate, the consumer must work two hours to hire one hour of labor earning the same wage rate as the consumer. It is not always the case that firms or consumers should buy an item on the market and incur the resulting transaction cost. It may cost less, when the transaction cost is considered, for the consumer or firm to produce the item itself.

## 8.7  *The Long-Run Supply Curve*

The supply curve for a competitive industry, whether short-run or long-run, is a function relating the maximum quantity of the good or service offered for sale to its market price, holding constant the relevant non-price variables. The variables held constant are those that shift the firm's *LRAC* curve. They include the wage rate, the unit costs of capital and materials, and the production function. If the wage rate and unit cost of capital do not change as the number of firms in the industry changes, the firm's *LRAC* curve will not shift. In order not to have higher costs than the other firms, a firm contemplating entry into a competitive industry must build its plant at the minimum point of the *LRAC* curve. Once the *LRAC*-minimizing plant is constructed, its short-run cost curves are $SRATC_0$, $AVC_0$, and $MC_0$ in Figure 6.11.

*Normal Profit.* The minimum price that will lead a firm to build a plant and enter an industry is equal to *SRATC* at the minimum point on the *LRAC* curve. In Figure 6.11, this *SRATC* is $C_0$. Because $C_0$ includes the unit cost of capital, the firm is covering all of its costs and earning a normal profit on its equity investment. A normal profit is equal to the implicit opportunity cost of its resources that firm commits to building the plant. If the firm invests \$1.0 million of its equity funds in the plant and can earn \$100,000 per year on those funds in its most profitable alternative investment, then the unit cost of capital must reflect that opportunity cost. Interest on debt capital used to finance the plant is an explicit cost included in the unit cost of capital. Thus, the firm will be able to increase its profit (value) whenever price is greater than $C_0$.

*Slope of the LRS Curve.* In Figure 8.8, the long-run supply (*LRS*) curve is horizontal at a price equal to $C_0$. Such an industry is referred to as a constant-cost industry. When the first firm enters, *LRS* is $q_0$ at a price equal to $C_0$. If a second firm enters, *LRS* is $2q_0$ and so forth as additional firms enter the industry because price is greater than $C_0$. The total number of firms in the industry depends on the level of demand. In Figure 8.8, *LRS* equals demand at output $Mq_0$, where there are $M$ firms in the industry. If another firm enters the industry, demand

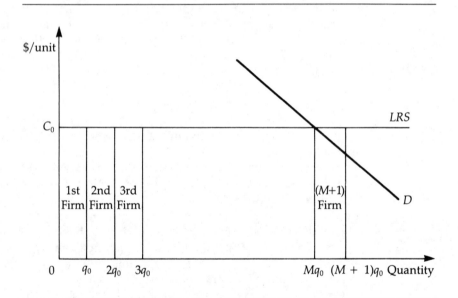

**Figure 8.8   Horizontal *LRS* Curve (Constant-Cost Industry)**
The minimum point on the *LRAC* curve for the typical firm is at $C_0$. If price is equal to or greater than $C_0$, price is equal to or greater than the firm's average explicit and implicit opportunity costs; hence, it will enter the industry. If the *LRAC* curve does not shift upward with additional firms entering the industry, the *LRS* curve is horizontal. The number of firms in the industry in long-run equilibrium where *LRS* = *D* is *M*.

is less than supply at a price equal to $C_0$, which implies a market price below $C_0$. This would result in the last, $(M + 1)$, firm's earning less than a normal profit. It would not enter the industry because it can earn the opportunity cost of its equity capital in some other industry.

The *LRS* curve need not be horizontal. Its slope depends on the slope of the factor (labor and capital) supply curves. If the factor supply curves are upward sloping, entry of another firm will increase the demand for both factors and increase their prices. Increases in factor prices shift the isocost curve inward, increasing the budget required to produce a specified output. The result is an increase in the *LRAC* of producing that output and an upward shift in the *LRAC* curve. As each firm enters the industry and the *LRAC* curve shifts upward, the *LRS* curve becomes upward sloping as in Figure 8.9, because a higher market price is required to make entry profitable for an additional firm. An industry with an upward sloping *LRS* curve is called an increasing-cost industry.

The long-run supply curve is downward sloping when increases in the number of firms result in lower factor prices. This results when factor supply curves are downward sloping. The lower factor prices shift down the *LRAC* curve and result in a downward sloping *LRS* curve as the number of firms increases. The industry is referred to as a decreasing-cost industry. When the industry buying a component is

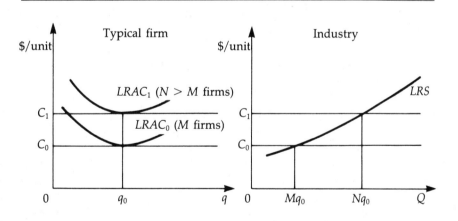

**Figure 8.9   Upward Sloping *LRS* Curve (Increasing-Cost Industry)**

As more firms enter the industry, factor prices rise and the *LRAC* curve of the typical firm shifts upward, with the minimum point of the *LRAC* curve shifting upward. A higher price is required if another firm is to enter the industry and the *LRS* curve is upward sloping.

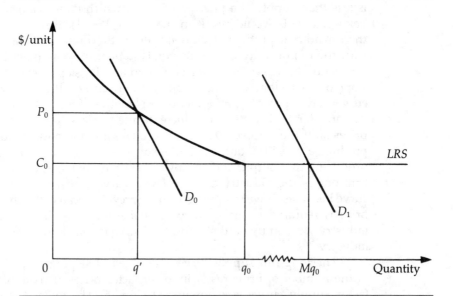

**Figure 8.10** *LRS* **Curve with Declining Initial Segment**

With industry demand at $D_0$, the *LRS* curve follows the *LRAC* curve of the one firm in the industry. As demand shifts to the right, the firm can build a larger plant and earn a normal profit at a lower price. Once demand shifts beyond point ($q_0$, $C_0$), the slope of the *LRS* curve depends on the response of factor prices to the greater demand for factors as the industry grows. The *LRS* curve becomes horizontal after $q_0$ if factor prices are unchanged.

in the earliest stage of its product life cycle, demand is at $D_0$ in Figure 8.10 and the one firm supplying the component has a plant on the downward sloping portion of its *LRAC* curve. This firm would probably be using a relatively labor-intensive technology. As the industry buying the component grows, the firm supplying the component will eventually find it profitable to build the more capital-intensive plant at the minimum point of its *LRAC* curve. As demand for the component continues to grow, new plants producing $q_0$ at minimum *LRAC* will be built and the component's price will no longer decline as the industry buying the factor grows. The horizontal segment of the *LRS* curve occurs when demand for the component is great enough that each firm builds the plant that minimizes its *LRAC*.

**EXAMPLE 8.6.** The impact of rising factor prices on the *LRAC* and *LRS* curves is illustrated in this example. Assume that the production function is $Q = 0.8KL^{0.5}$, the unit cost of capital is $k = \$40$, and the wage rate is $w = \$10$. In example 6.15, it was shown that the *LRAC* of producing 100 units of output under these conditions is \$11.91 per unit. Assume now that as more firms enter the industry, the unit cost of labor rises to $w = \$15$ and the unit cost of capital to \$50. Under these assumptions, equation 6.16 becomes $K = 0.6L$. The quantities of labor and capital for $Q = 100$ are

$$100 = 0.8(0.6L)L^{0.5}$$

$$100 = 0.48L^{1.5}$$

$$L^{1.5} = 100/0.48 = 208.33 \text{ and } L = 35.1$$

$$K = 0.6(35.1) = 21.1$$

The budget for $q = 100$ and its *LRAC* are

$$B = (\$15)(35.1) + (\$50)(21.1) = \$1{,}581.50$$

$$LRAC = \$1{,}581.50/100 = \$15.82 \text{ per unit}$$

The *LRAC* of producing 100 units is greater than the \$11.91 per unit prevailing when there were fewer firms in the industry; therefore, the *LRS* curve is upward sloping.

## 8.8 *Price and Output in Long-Run Equilibrium*

The long-run equilibrium price is the price at the industry output where the *D*, *LRS*, and *SRS* curves all intersect. Market price changes generally restore short-run equilibrium; however, changes in the number of firms in the industry ultimately restore long-run equilibrium. This section discusses the restoration of long-run equilibrium when there are shifts in the demand and short-run supply curves.

*Demand Curve Shifts.* Assume that a constant-cost industry is in long-run equilibrium where $D_0 = LRS = SRS_0$ at price $P_0$ in Figure 8.11. Each of the $M$ identical firms is producing $q_0$ units of output. If the demand curve shifts to the right, a shortage exists at price $P_0$. In the short run, additional firms will not be able to enter the industry. The market price will rise until the short-run equilibrium price $P_1$ is established where $D_1 = SRS_0$. At the higher price, it is profit-maximizing for each of the existing $M$ firms to produce $q_1$, with industry supply being $Mq_1$.

Price $P_1$ is greater than *LRS* at an output of $Mq_1$. This means that price is greater than the minimum average cost on the *LRAC* curve of

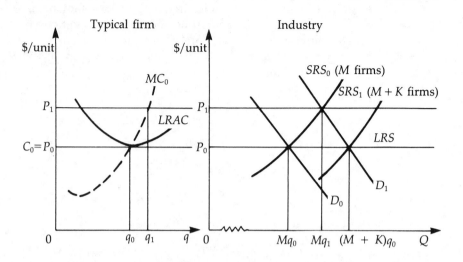

**Figure 8.11    Short- and Long-Run Responses to a Demand Shift**
The initial equilibrium is the point at which the $D_0$, $SRS_0$, and $LRS$ curves
intersect. When demand shifts to right, there is a shortage at price $P_0$ leading to price's increasing to $P_1$, where short-run equilibrium is reestablished.
Because $P_1$ is greater than $C_0$, the industry is not in long-run equilibrium.
When $K$ firms enter the industry, shifting the $SRS$ curve to $SRS_1$, long-run
equilibrium is restored; thus, $S_1$, $SRS_1$, and $LRS$ all intersect again.

the typical firm. With price greater than minimum $LRAC$, entry into
the industry will yield an economic profit. An economic profit occurs
when price exceeds the average cost, including all implicit opportunity
costs, of producing the good. The opportunity to earn an economic
profit will attract new firms into the industry, shifting the short-run
supply curve to the right. Holding demand constant at $D_1$, this will
result in the market price declining from $P_1$. The declining market price
makes it unprofitable for more than $K$ firms to enter the industry. Once
$K$ firms have entered, the short-run supply curve is $SRS_1$, as shown in
Figure 8.11. At price $P_0$, $D_1 = LRS = SRS_1$ and the industry is again
in long-run equilibrium. Each firm produces $q_0$ units of output and the
$M + K$ firms produce $(M + K)q_0$.

   **EXAMPLE 8.7.**   Assume that $LRAC = \$168 - \$24q + \$4q^{1.5}$ for
the typical firm. If this is a constant-cost industry, the $LRS$ curve would
be horizontal at the level of minimum $LRAC$.

$$dLRAC/dq = -24 + 6q^{0.5} = 0 \Rightarrow q^{0.5} = 4 \text{ and } q = 16$$

$LRAC = C_0 = \$168 - \$24(16) + \$(16)^{1.5} = \$40$ per unit is the level of the *LRS* supply curve.[2] If the demand function is $Q = 1,600 - 12P$, *LRS* equals demand ($P = C_0$) at an industry output of $Q = 1,600 - 12(40) = 1,120$ units. The typical firm produces $q_0 = 16$ units of output, so in long-run equilibrium there will be $M = 1,120/16 = 70$ firms.

Assume now that the demand function shifts to $Q = 1,680 - 12P$ and that the *SRATC* function for the plant that produces $q_0 = 16$ units at minimum *LRATC* is $SRATC = 296 - 32q + q^2$. This *SRATC* function has its minimum point at $q = 16$ and $SRATC = \$40$. To find the *MC* function, multiply *SRATC* by $q$ and then differentiate *SRTC*.

$$SRTC = 296q - 32q^2 + q^3$$

$$MC = dSRTC/dq = 296 - 64q + 3q^2$$

If $q = 16$, $MC = \$40$, and if $q = 20$, $MC = \$216$. A straight line fitted through these two points approximates the upward-sloping portion of the *MC* function above the minimum point of the *SRATC* curve for the purpose of calculating the equation of the *SRS* curve to use with shifts in demand of the amount assumed for this example. The straight-line fitting method in section 2.2.1 yields

$$MC = 44q - 664$$

The first step in calculating the equation of the *SRS* curve is to find the profit-maximizing output of the typical firm.

$$MC = P \Rightarrow P = 44q - 664 \Rightarrow q = 0.0227P - 15.091$$

The industry *SRS* function for the 70 firms is

$$Q = 70q = 70(0.0227P - 15.091) = 1.589P - 1,056.37$$

The short-run market-clearing price is where $D = SRS$,

$$1,680 - 12P = 1.589P - 1,056.37 \Rightarrow P = \$201.37$$

Because this price is above minimum *LRAC*, it will result in the entry of new firms into the industry. In the new long-run equilibrium, price will fall to \$40 and industry output will be $Q = 1,680 - 12(40) = 1,200$ units. Since each firm produces $q_0 = 16$ units in long-run equilibrium, the number of firms will rise to $M' = 1,200/16 = 75$.

[2] *LRAC* is minimized at $q = 16$ because $d^2LRAC/dq^2 = 3/q^{0.5} = +0.75$.

*Entry of New Firms When Demand Shifts Are Unpredictable.* In actuality, the responses of firms entering the industry may differ somewhat from the idealized description at the beginning of this section. For example, if the increase in demand is highly predictable, it will be anticipated and new plants will be constructed as demand grows. Price will not rise much above *LRS* as demand grows. Managements generally have varying views of the rate at which demand is likely to grow, and the rate of growth in demand is rarely highly predictable. Thus, the short-run equilibrium price is likely to vary above or below the price equal to *LRS*. Also, potential new entrants may not be aware of the construction plans of other firms. A shift in demand may result in the entry of more than the $K$ firms required to restore long-run equilibrium in Figure 8.11, and in a market price below $P_0$. In Figure 8.12, this is price $P_2$ where $SRS_2$ intersects $D_1$ after the entry of $K + J$ firms. With industry output at $Q_2$, price would have to rise to $P_0$ for the firms to earn a normal profit. Too many new entrants have resulted in depressed prices and not in profitable operations from the growing demand.

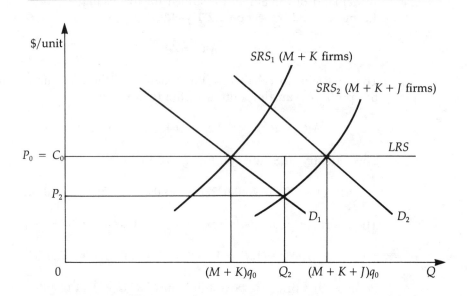

**Figure 8.12   Disequilibrium Resulting from Excessive Entry**

$D_1$, $SRS_1$, and $LRS$s all intersecting would result in long-run equilibrium; however, $J$ more firms have entered the industry and the actual $SRS$ curve is $SRS_2$. The short-run equilibrium price is now at $P_2$, which is below the long-run equilibrium price of $P_0$. If demand continues to grow, when it reaches $D_2$, long-run equilibrium will again be restored.

This situation is not uncommon in growing industries producing products that are perfect substitutes, especially during the expansionary phase of the business cycle when managers tend to be optimistic. It results from the entry of new firms with limited information about the intentions of other firms and the desire of managements to take advantage of apparently profitable opportunities. If demand continues to grow and more new firms do not enter the industry, profitable operations will be restored once demand reaches $D_2$ in Figure 8.12 and price has risen to $P_0$. Also contributing to restoration of profitable prices can be the closing of existing plants for which price is no longer above *AVC*. As plants age, their *AVC* generally rises. As plants are closed, *SRS* shifts to the left, increasing the market price and helping to restore profitable operations for the remaining firms.

There is a time dimension to long-run decisions that is not made explicit by the graphical analysis of demand and supply curves. Long-run responses to demand and supply curve shifts take time. In some industries, technology may be such that the long run is a period of a few weeks or months. In others, the long run may be several years and commitments to build new facilities may be made in anticipation of demand conditions 5 or more years in the future. When the industry's technology is highly capital-intensive, *AVC* is a relatively small percentage of *ATC* and plant closings due to a rising *AVC* are rare. Uncertainty about future demand and the number of firms entering the industry increases the risk associated with decisions to build new facilities. Procedures for explicitly taking into consideration the expected future course of prices, and the risks associated with an uncertain future, are treated in chapters 12 through 14.

## 8.9  *Summary*

A firm is a price-taker when its management believes that it cannot affect the market price for its product by changing its output. The firms in a competitive market take the market price as given. The products of the firms in a competitive industry are very close or perfect substitutes for one another, and there are many firms in the industry.

The goal of the firm is to maximize its total profit, $\Pi$, which is the difference between its total revenue and total cost. The conditions for finding the profit-maximizing output, $q''$, are $P = MR(q'') = MC(q'')$, *MC* at $q''$ is upward sloping, and $P > AVC(q'')$. The profit-maximizing output can be found by taking the first and second derivatives of the profit function, setting the first derivative equal to zero and solving it for output, and then substituting the values of $q$ into the second derivative to determine which $q$ has the negative second derivative.

The supply curve of a profit-maximizing, competitive firm is its *MC* curve above its *AVC* curve. If all firms in an industry have identical *MC* curves, industry supply at price $P_0$ is found by multiplying the profit-maximizing output for the typical firm by the number of firms. If the firms do not have identical *MC* curves, each firm's profit-maximizing output at price $P_0$ is added up to find industry supply at that price. Shifts in the supply curve of a firm or industry occur when there are changes in the number of firms, wage rates or materials prices, the firm's production function, the relative prices of the different products that can be produced by the firm, and management's expectations of future prices.

The short-run equilibrium, or market-clearing, price for a competitive industry occurs at the price at which the quantity demanded is equal to the quantity supplied. If the quantity demanded is greater than the quantity supplied at a given market price, there is a shortage and price will rise. If the quantity supplied is greater than the quantity demanded at a given market price, there is a surplus and price will decline. That is, at the short-run equilibrium price, $D = SRS$.

Transaction (*ICP*) costs are the information, contracting, and policing costs incurred by the consumer or the firm when a good or service is purchased on the market. Transaction costs benefit neither buyer nor seller, and both parties to a transaction have incentives to reduce them. The alternative to incurring transaction costs is to produce the item and accept the resulting administrative costs.

The long-run supply (*LRS*) curve is based on the minimum point on the *LRAC* curve of the typical potential new entrant. If it is a constant-cost industry, the unit costs of the factors of production will not change as additional firms enter the industry. The *LRS* curve will be horizontal, and shifts in the demand curve will not change the long-run equilibrium price. If factor prices change with the entry of new firms, the *LRS* curve will be upward or downward sloping.

The long-run equilibrium price occurs where $D = LRS = SRS$. Until the long-run equilibrium price is attained, the market price is determined by the intersection of the demand and *SRS* curves. As new firms enter the industry, the *SRS* curve shifts to the right and the market price falls until enough firms have entered to yield the new long-run equilibrium price.

With the normal uncertainties associated with future demand growth, factor prices, technological change, and the intentions of other firms that may enter the industry, the new long-run equilibrium price may not be established as smoothly as the graphs would indicate. When demand grows faster than was generally anticipated and the economy is in the expansionary phase of the business cycle, more firms may enter than would yield the long-run equilibrium price. The result is a lower price, and depressed profits or economic losses. Whether entering the industry will increase the value of the firm depends on whether the present value of the annual economic profits and losses is positive. If it is, the firm may enter the industry even if it expects one or more periods of economic losses.

## CASE   8   Determining the Profit-Maximizing Output

You are the plant manager for a small manufacturing company. You, the marketing manager, and the boss are meeting to plan the company's operations for next month. The goal of today's meeting is to determine the plant's profit-maximizing output. As is customary in such meetings, you begin by presenting four alternative operating plans for the plant. The marketing manager then reviews market conditions and provides a price projection. The boss concludes the meeting by making the output decision.

### *Your Presentation*

The company has signed a new contract with the union. Wages are going up from $5.50 to $6.00 per hour. Components cost has risen from $1.10 to $1.20 per unit of output. A reduction in raw material prices will reduce their cost from $5.95 to $5.80 per unit of output. The plant's production function is $Q = 2K^{0.25}L^{0.5}$, where $Q$ is the output produced in one hour and $L$ is the number of production workers. Capital invested in the plant is $K = 256$ units. Substituting this quantity of capital into the production function yields $Q = 2(256)^{0.25}L^{0.5} = 8L^{0.5}$. The implicit opportunity cost of a unit of capital is estimated at $0.20 per hour. This equation is used to calculate the output produced by a specified number of production workers. Your four alternative plans are based on hiring 25, 36, 49, or 64 production workers, which will result in production rates of 40, 48, 58, and 64 units per hour.

There are four categories of fixed costs. The implicit cost of plant and equipment is the 256 units of capital multiplied by $0.20 or $51.20 per hour (rounded off to $51 in Table 8.1). Managerial salaries, rent on the building in which the plant is located, and the other explicit fixed expenses are in Table 8.1. Total fixed cost at the plant is $116 per hour.

The wages of the foremen, supervisors, and clerks required to supervise the activities of the production workers are semivariable

**Table 8.1   Four Alternative Operating Budgets**

| Category | Output 40 Units | 48 Units | 56 Units | 64 Units |
|---|---|---|---|---|
| Fixed costs | | | | |
| Plant and equipment | $ 51/hr | $ 51/hr | $ 51/hr | $   51/hr |
| Managerial salaries | 40 | 40 | 40 | 40 |
| Building rental | 15 | 15 | 15 | 15 |
| Other expenses | 10 | 10 | 10 | 10 |
| Subtotal | $116/hr | $116/hr | $116/hr | $  116/hr |
| Semivariable costs | | | | |
| Supervisory salaries | $ 44/hr | $ 75/hr | $113/hr | $  142/hr |
| Other expenses | 16 | 20 | 27 | 33 |
| Subtotal | $ 60/hr | $ 95/hr | $140/hr | $  175/hr |
| Variable costs | | | | |
| Production workers | $150/hr | $216/hr | $294/hr | $  384/hr |
| Raw materials | 232 | 278 | 325 | 371 |
| Purchased components | 48 | 58 | 67 | 77 |
| Subtotal | $430/hr | $552/hr | $686/hr | $  832/hr |
| TOTAL COST | $606/hr | $763/hr | $942/hr | $1,122/hr |
| Average total cost | $ 15.15 | $ 15.90 | $ 16.82 | $   17.53 |
| Average fixed cost | $  2.90 | $  2.42 | $  2.07 | $    1.81 |
| Average semivariable cost | $  1.50 | $  1.98 | $  2.50 | $    2.73 |
| Average variable cost | $ 10.75 | $ 11.50 | $ 12.25 | $   13.00 |
| Marginal cost | $ 14.50 | $ 16.00 | $ 17.50 | $   19.00 |

costs. The number of supervisory workers is obtained from the company's standard staffing formula, which also provides the other expenses generally resulting from each type of supervisory worker. For example, if 25 production workers are hired, the staffing formula calls for four foremen, one supervisor, and two clerks at an hourly cost of $44 per hour and other expenses of $16 per hour. These costs for the other numbers of production workers are in Table 8.1.

Variable costs consist of production worker and material costs. Production labor costs are equal to the number of production workers multiplied by the wage rate of $6 per hour. Materials costs are equal to their unit costs multiplied by output.

The average costs in Table 8.1 are found by dividing the appropriate total cost by the output at the top of the column. For example, $AVC$ for 40 units of output is $430/40 = $10.75 per unit. Calculating $MC$ requires taking the derivative of the production function to find $MPL$, $MCL$, and $MC$.

$$MPL = dQ/dL = 4/L^{0.5}$$

$$MCL = W/MPL = \$6/(4/L^{0.5}) = \$1.5L^{0.5}$$

$$MC = MCM + MCL = \$7.00 + \$1.5L^{0.5}$$

Because 25 production workers are required to produce 40 units of output, its $MC = \$7.00 + \$1.5(25)^{0.5} = \$14.50$. Your presentation ends with a brief discussion of the costs of producing each of the four outputs.

## The Marketing Manager's Presentation

The firm's product is produced by 54 other companies and faces competition from several substitutes. Whenever price rises above $19.00, consumers begin to shift their purchases to a substitute product. This results in a shift to the left in the industry's demand curve toward the "normal" demand curve that yields a market price of $19.00. Similarly, whenever price falls below $19.00, consumers begin to substitute the firm's product for those produced by other industries. This shifts the demand curve to the right and reestablishes the customary $19.00 price.

The supply curves of the firm and industry shift with changes in the unit costs of labor and raw materials and with the entry or exit of firms from the industry. Immediately after a supply curve shift, there will be a new market-clearing price. With labor costs rising more than the $0.05 net reduction in materials costs, the industry's supply curve will be shifting to the left and its price will rise. If a similar increase in variable costs does not occur for the industries producing substitute products, demand for the firm's product will shift to the left, toward reestablishing the customary $19.00 price. If the prices of substitute goods rise because of similar labor and materials cost increases, the leftward shift in the demand curve will be reduced or will not occur.

The market price last month was $18.50. With wages rising about 9 percent and materials cost decreasing $0.05 per unit of output, costs will be higher next month. This will result in a shift to the left in the industry's supply curve and in a higher price. Because price was below its customary level last month, there is likely to be a shift to the right in the demand curve as consumers substitute the firm's product for those of other industries. With the industries producing substitute products also incurring rising labor costs, the marketing manager projects an average price of $19.50 for next month. The marginal and average variable cost of marketing and distributing the product is $2.00 per unit.

### The Boss's Conclusions

The boss begins by accepting the marketing manager's projection of next month's price. The next step is to compare the price less the MC of marketing the product, or $19.50 - $2.00 = $17.50, to the marginal cost projections in the last row of Table 8.1. The profit-maximizing output is 56 units per hour because the $17.50 net price equals marginal cost. Assume that average semivariable cost ($2.50) and average variable cost ($12.25) are the average variable manufacturing costs ($14.75) with respect to the shut-down decision. The marketing costs that are fixed with respect to output, but variable with respect to the plant shut-down decision, are $30 per hour. Average variable marketing cost is $30/56 + $2.00 = $2.54. Thus, average variable cost of supplying the product is $2.54 + $14.75 = $17.29, which is less than the $19.50 projected market price.

Average fixed cost, which is not variable with respect to the plant shut-down decision, is $2.07 per hour. Thus, for the combined manufacturing and marketing operations, average total cost is $17.29 + $2.07 = $19.36 per unit of output. This yields a unit profit of $19.50 - $19.36 = $0.14, or an hourly profit of $(0.14)(56) = $7.84. This is a slim profit margin, and it makes only a nominal contribution toward the company's overhead costs and profit. The marketing manager comments that the market price is likely to rise further in subsequent months as higher labor costs are more fully reflected in prices. A price of $20.25 within 2 or 3 months is not unlikely. You add that the higher cost of labor may make profitable new, labor-saving equipment. The boss ends the meeting by requesting that you prepare an analysis of the new equipment for next year's capital budget and orders preparation of next month's budgets.

## Key Terms

administrative costs
competition
constant-cost
  industry
decreasing-cost
  industry
factor supply curve
increasing-cost
  industry

long-run equilib-
  rium price
long-run supply
  curve
market
market-clearing
  price
normal profit

price-taker firm
short-run equilibrium
  price
short-run supply curve
supply
transaction costs: information costs, contracting
  costs, policing costs

# *Review Questions*

1. Define the terms *market, competition, price-taker,* and *market-clearing (or equilibrium) price.*

2. What are the two basic characteristics of a competitive market? How do these characteristics lead to all firms in the market being price-takers?

3. Assume that the industry is competitive and that the firm's *MC* curve is upward sloping for all outputs. Explain why the firm maximizes its profits where *MC* = Price using (a) a numerical example and (b) a graph.

4. If the *MC* curve is U-shaped as in Figure 8.2, explain why output $q'$ is not profit-maximizing and $q''$ is profit-maximizing.

5. As long as $P = MC$ at output $q''$ and $P > AVC(q'')$, the firm is maximizing its profits and should produce $q''$ even if $P < SRATC(q'')$ and the firm is running a loss. Explain why this statement is true if *AVC* includes all costs that can be avoided if the firm shuts down its plant.

6. Why do changes in factor prices or productivities result in shifts in the short-run supply curve of the typical firm and competitive industry? Why will a change in the typical firm's fixed costs have no effect on its short-run supply curve?

7. Define the terms *shortage* and *surplus.* Use these terms to explain why the intersection of the demand and supply curves yields the market-clearing price for the industry.

8. Why are transaction costs also referred to as *ICP* costs? How do transaction costs differ from administrative costs?

9. Some state and local governments require gasoline stations to post their prices prominently. How does price posting affect consumers' transaction costs, and why might it lead to a lower average gasoline price than would result if price posting weren't mandatory?

10. How does a long-run supply curve differ from a short-run supply curve?

11. Why does long-run supply include a normal profit in the costs of a firm entering the industry? Define the term *normal profit.*

12. Why does the competitive firm build the plant that produces the product at minimum *LRAC*, rather than a larger or smaller plant?

13. If there is no change in factor prices as new firms enter the industry, why is the *LRS* curve horizontal? What determines the number of firms in the industry in long-run equilibrium? Draw the relevant graphs to explain your answer.

14. Assume that the unit cost of raw materials used by a competitive industry falls by 50 percent as a result of a new technology for producing them. This is a constant-cost industry. What will happen to the number of firms in this industry (a) in the short run and (b) in the new long-run equilibrium? Carefully state your assumptions and explain your answers.

## *Problems and Applications*

1. Assume that a competitive firm's product sells for $150 and that its total cost function is $TC = \$q^2 + \$6q + \$4,500$, where $q$ is output per hour. Calculate the firm's profit-maximizing output and total profit.

2. A competitive firm sells a product with a market price of $80. Its fixed costs are $250 and its $AVC = q^2/3 - 2q + 20$, where $q$ is output per hour. Calculate the firm's profit-maximizing output and total profit.

3. Assume that the firm's production function is $q = 4L^{0.5}$ where $q$ is output per hour, the wage rate is $8 per hour, the cost of materials is $14 per unit of output, fixed costs are $500 per hour, and price is $40. Calculate the firm's profit-maximizing output, total profit, and the number of workers necessary to produce the profit-maximizing output.

4. Assume that there are $M = 100$ identical firms in an industry with each firm having fixed costs of $500 per hour and $AVC = 50 + 0.1q$, where $q$ is output per hour. Calculate the supply curve of the typical firm and the industry. What would be the profit-maximizing output of the typical firm and industry supply at a price of $80? Calculate the typical firm's hourly profit when $P = \$80$.

5. Assume that the typical firm's production function is $q = 4L^{0.5}$, the wage rate is $10 per hour, and the cost of materials is $20 per unit of output. If there are $M = 80$ identical firms, calculate the typical firm's and industry's supply curves. Calculate the number of workers employed by the industry if the product sells for $60.

6. Continuing with problem 5, if a new collective bargaining agreement results in a wage increase to $12 per hour and foreign competition holds the industry's price to $60, calculate the number of employees that will be laid off throughout the industry as a result of this wage increase.

7. If demand is $Q = 12,000 - 15P + 500(T - 1)$ and supply is $Q = 2,000 + 25P$, calculate the market clearing price in year $T = 1$ and industry output. In year $T = 3$, what will be the market-clearing price?

8. Assume that there are $M = 60$ identical firms in an industry with each firm having fixed costs of $400 per hour and $AVC = 40 + 0.2q$, where $q$ is output per hour. Calculate the industry supply curve and the market-clearing price if the industry demand curve is $Q = 10,000 - 10P$. Also calculate the output and profits of the typical firm.

9. What will happen to the market-clearing price if five firms decide to exit the industry in problem 8 by converting their plants to produce another product?

10. Continuing with problem 6, use a demand/supply graph to explain why the existence of foreign competition that holds price at $60 will result in more laid-off workers than if there were no foreign competition.

11. The $LRAC$ function for the typical firm is $LRAC = \$q^3/3 - \$15q^2 - \$400q + \$19,000$. Find the output at which $LRAC$ is minimized, minimum $LRAC$, and the number of firms in the industry in long-run equilibrium if the industry demand curve is $Q = 3,200 - 6P$.

12. Assume that the industry demand curve in problem 11 shifts right to $Q = 3,400 - 6P$.
   a. Draw a graph showing what will happen to the number of firms in this industry in the new long-run equilibrium. Draw a typical short-run supply curve and explain how price changes influence the entry of new firms into the industry.
   b. Calculate the number of firms that will enter the industry to bring it back into long-run equilibrium.
   c. Assume that the short-run supply curve prior to the shift in demand can be approximated by $Q = 9P - 1,800$. Immediately after the demand curve shift and before any new firms enter the industry, what will be the new short-run equilibrium price? Will this price attract entry into the industry?
   d. Is a short-run supply curve of $Q = 9P - 1,600$ after long-run equilibrium has been reestablished by the entry of new firms consistent with both long-run and short-run equilibrium? Why?

13. Assume that the $AVC$ curve for the new plant that minimizes $LRAC$ is $AVC = \$50 + \$0.05q$ where $q$ is output per week and that weekly fixed costs are $112,500. The product's price is normally $200 but has risen to $230 recently because of an unanticipated shift to the right in the industry's demand curve. A new plant will cost $200,000 and take one year to construct.
   a. At a price of $230, will one or more new firms be attracted into the industry? Why?
   b. If the company decides to build a new plant and enter this industry, management expects price to average $225 for its first operating year, $190 for its second and third operating years,

and $200 thereafter. If the cost of capital is 15 percent, can management expect to increase the firm's wealth if it builds this new plant? Explain why.

c. Assume that this is a constant-cost industry. Explain why management is predicting the pattern of prices in part (b).

14. A constant-cost, competitive industry with 50 identical firms is presently in long-run equilibrium at a price of $100, with the typical firm producing 100 units per day. A new technology shifts the $LRAC$ curve of the typical firm from $LRAC = \$1,100 - \$30q + \$2q^{1.5}$ to $LRAC' = \$1,411 - \$33q + \$2q^{1.5}$. The arc-elasticity of demand for this industry is $|E_p| = 1.534$ when calculated using equation 3.3 with $X = P$.

a. Verify that the long-run equilibrium price is $100 for this industry before invention of the new technology and calculate the long-run equilibrium output of this industry.

b. Draw the demand/supply graph illustrating how the industry's long-run equilibrium output will change in response to the shift in its $LRS$ curve resulting from this new technology.

c. Calculate the number of firms in the new long-run equilibrium after this technology has been adopted by all firms in the industry.

# Appendix
# *Breakeven Output and Price Analysis*

## *Breakeven Output*

Managers are often interested in the breakeven output for their product. Assume that management can predict the market price with considerable accuracy, as when competition among the firms in the industry is for markets. The established (or "customary") price for the product rarely changes, but the quantity sold by the firm fluctuates from month to month. To maximize its profits, the firm would not sell additional units of output if their marginal cost were greater than the market price. However, the firm may have to sell less than the profit-maximizing output because it cannot obtain sufficient numbers of customers. Thus, management accepts the established market price as a given and wishes to find the lowest output at which it will cover its fixed and variable costs of production.

In Figure 8.13, $P_0$ is the established market price. To maximize its profits, the firm would like to sell $q''$ units of output; however, competition for customers may be such that it will not be able to sell $q''$. At output $q'$, price $P_0$ equals the $ATC$ of producing that output. The firm would

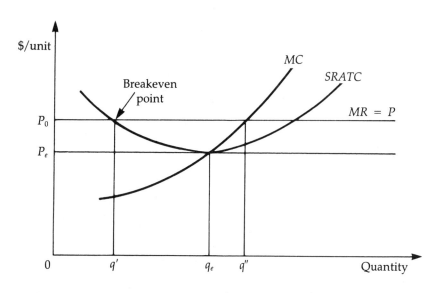

**Figure 8.13    Breakeven Output, Breakeven Price**

Breakeven output: If the established market price is $P_0$, the firm's breakeven output is $q'$ where $P_0 = SRATC(q')$. The profit-maximizing price is at $q''$, but there may not be sufficient demand at price $P_0$ for the firm to sell $q''$. Breakeven price: If the market price cannot be predicted accurately, management can set output at $q_e$ where $SRATC$ is minimized. If price is greater than $P_e$, the firm will be profitable at output $q_e$.

break even if it sells $q'$ units of output. It would earn a marginal profit on each unit of output sold in excess of $q'$ because $MC$ is less than price for all units of output between $q'$ and $q''$. As long as management believes that it can sell more than $q'$ units of output, it is willing to produce the additional output because it can increase its profits.

**EXAMPLE 8.8.**    Assume that the firm provides computer repair services. A statistical study of its past operations yielded the $AVC$ function

$$AVC = \$25 + \$0.25q + \$0.05q^2$$

where $q$ is the number of units repaired per hour. Its cash fixed costs that cannot be avoided even if the firm repairs nothing are $1,275 per hour (mostly building and equipment rental and salaries). The industry-wide charge for servicing and repairing a unit is $125. The firm's profit-maximizing output is found by calculating its marginal cost, setting $MC = P$, and solving for $q$.

$$MC = \$25 + \$0.05q + \$0.15q^2$$

$$MC = P \Rightarrow 0.15q^2 + 0.50q + 25 = 125$$

$$0.15q^2 + 0.50q - 100 = 0 \Rightarrow q = 24.2$$

Thus, the profit-maximizing number of units to service each hour is 24.2. If $q = 24.2$,

$$AVC = \$25 + \$0.25(24.2) + \$0.05(24.2)^2 = \$60.33$$

$$AFC = \$1,275/24.2 = \$56.69$$

$$\Pi = (\$125 - \$60.33 - \$56.69)(24.2) = \$193.12 \text{ per hour}$$

The profit-maximizing number of units is the largest number that the firm will service in one hour. It may, however, have to service a smaller number because fewer than 24.2 units per hour are delivered to the firm by its customers. To find the breakeven number of units, find the number of units at which profits are zero. This amounts to solving the equation $P - AVC(q) - AFC(q) = 0$ for $q$. Substituting the $AVC$ function and $AFC = \$1,275/q$ into this equation and simplifying it yields the third-degree polynomial $\$100q - \$0.25q^2 - \$0.05q^3 - \$1,275 = 0$. This equation is best solved by trial and error. If $q = 18$, its left-hand side (profit) is $152.40. Profits are still positive, so $q = 18$ is more than the breakeven number of units. If $q = 15$, its left-hand side is $0.00; hence, $q = 15$ is the breakeven number of units for the firm to service. If $q$ is less than 15 units per hour, $AFC$ would be so high that the firm would lose money. Thus, the firm would keep its service facility open if management felt reasonably confident that at least 15 units per hour will be delivered by its customers.

## Breakeven Price

An alternative situation arises when the market price for the firm's product cannot be predicted with a reasonably high degree of accuracy. Supply and demand conditions are such that prices fluctuate considerably from month to month. Management can set its output for the planning period; however, it cannot accurately predict the price at which it can sell the output it produces.

The breakeven price, $P_e$, equals the firm's average total costs when it produces its profit-maximizing output under the assumption that the market price will be $P_e$. If the actual price exceeds $P_e$, the firm's operations will be profitable. Finding the breakeven price requires solving simultaneously these equations:

$$P_e = MC(q) \tag{8A.1}$$

$$P_e = AVC + AFC \tag{8A.2}$$

The first equation yields the profit-maximizing output. Equation 8A.1 presumes that the upward sloping portion of the *MC* curve above the *AVC* curve is used to calculate $P_e$. The second equation is the profit function with profit set equal to zero. The only point on the firm's *SRATC* curve that meets the conditions in equations 8A.1 and 8A.2 is its minimum point. If the firm plans to produce output $q_e$ in Figure 8.13 at which its *SRAC* curve is minimized, it will break even if price is equal to *SRATC* at $q_e$.

**EXAMPLE 8.9.** Assume that $q$ is in units per hour, the production function is $q = 8L^{0.5}$, the wage rate is $6.40 per hour, and materials cost $25 per unit of output. The *AVC* function is found by calculating *APL*, *ACL*, and then *AVC*.

$$APL = q/L = 8L^{0.5}/L = 8/L^{0.5}$$

$$ACL = w/APL = \$6.40/(8/L^{0.5}) = \$0.80L^{0.5}$$

Since $L^{0.5} = q/8 = 0.125q$,

$$ACL = \$0.10q$$

$$AVC = ACM + ACL = \$25 + \$0.10q \tag{8A.3}$$

Assume that the firm has fixed costs of $FC = \$90$ per hour. The *SRATC* function is

$$SRATC = AVC + AFC = 25 + 0.1q + 90/q \tag{8A.4}$$

To find its minimum, differentiate the *SRATC* function, set it equal to zero, and solve for $q$.

$$dSRATC/dq = 0.1 - 90/q^2 = 0$$

$$q^2 = 900 \Rightarrow q = 30$$

$$SRATC = 25 + 0.1(30) + 90/30 = \$31 = P_e$$

If management believes that price will be above $31.00 next month, it expects to earn a profit if it produces 30 units of output per hour. It can then order the materials and hire the necessary labor for an output of 30 units per hour. With output set at 30 units per hour,

$$AVC = \$25 + \$0.1(30) = \$28.00$$

As long as price is above $28.00, the firm will earn at least enough to cover the cost of its labor and materials.

Assume that price is a normally distributed random variable with an expected value of $30 and a standard deviation of $2. To calculate the probability that the actual price will exceed $31 next month, calculate area $\delta$ under the normal curve in Figure 8.14.

$$Z_\delta = (31 - \$30)/\$2 = 0.5$$

From Table 2.2, $\delta = 0.3085$ or 31 percent. That is, there is a 31 percent probability that the actual price will exceed the breakeven price. The probability that the actual price will exceed the $28 necessary for the firm to cover the cost of its labor and materials is area $1 - \gamma$ in Figure 8.14.

$$Z_\gamma = (\$28 - \$30)/\$2 = -1.0$$

From Table 2.2, $\gamma = 0.1587$ and $1 - \gamma = 0.8413$. Thus, there is an 84 percent probability that the actual price will be great enough for the firm to cover the cost of its labor and materials. Whether these probabilities

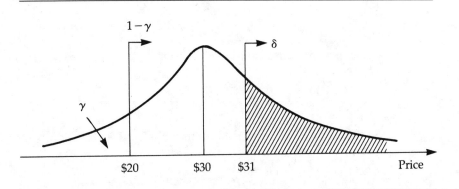

**Figure 8.14  Probability of the Breakeven Price**

When the market price is normally distributed random variable with an average of $30, $\delta$ is the probability that the market price will exceed breakeven price of $31 and $1 - \gamma$ is the probability that price will exceed $AVC$ at output $q_e$.

are great enough for the firm to produce this product is a decision that management must make as part of its risk-management program. If management requires at least a 25 percent probability that the actual price will equal or exceed the breakeven price, this project would be approved.

## *Breakeven Price for Overtime Operations*

If the actual market price during the next month turns out to be greater than $31 in Example 8.9, the firm may find it profitable to expand output beyond the planned 240 units per day that an output of 30 units per hour for 8 hours would produce. This increase in output could be accomplished by having the plant work one or more hours of overtime. Finding the breakeven price for the overtime output requires calculation of its *SRATC* and comparing it to the likely market price for the product. Having workers work overtime involves paying time-and-a-half wages. Some of the firm's materials suppliers may not have adequate inventories or scheduled production rates to supply increased purchases of their products. They may require the firm to pay a premium price for additional materials. These factor price changes must be incorporated into the calculation of *SRATC* for the overtime output.

There is a limit to the number of hours of overtime that a crew can work. In general, as more hours of overtime are worked, declining labor productivity will shift the production function downward and *ACL* upward, eventually making another hour of overtime unprofitable.

**EXAMPLE 8.9 (Continued).** To produce 30 units per hour, management must hire 14 workers, because from the production function, $L^{0.5} = 30/8 = 3.75$ and $L = (3.75)^2 = 14$. Assume that management decides to assign its 14 production workers to overtime to produce more than the 240 units of output produced in an 8-hour shift. Each hour of overtime by the 14 workers will produce another 30 units of output. The overtime wage is $1.5 \times \$6.40$ per hour $= \$9.60$ per hour.

The first step in finding the breakeven price for the hour of overtime is to calculate its *ACL*.

$$ACL = \$9.60/(8/L^{0.5}) = 1.2L^{0.5}$$

Since $L^{0.5} = 3.75$, $ACL = 1.2(3.75) = \$4.50$ per unit

$$AVC = \$25 + \$4.50 = \$29.50 \text{ per unit}$$

Fixed costs for straight-time hours are $90 per hour. Assume that $40 per hour of the fixed costs cover items whose costs do not change if the plant works overtime (for example, the opportunity cost of its equipment, property taxes, and insurance). Assume further that $50 per hour are fixed costs with respect to output that are incurred if the plant works one hour of overtime (for example, supervisory and administrative costs and energy for heating and illuminating the working areas).

$$AFC = \$50/30 = \$1.67 \text{ per unit}$$

The breakeven price for one hour of overtime is equal to its *SRATC*, which is $29.50 + $1.67 = $31.17, or $0.17 more than the breakeven price for straight-time hours. This is why firms are often willing to put their workers on overtime when demand is high. If the fixed costs that do not change when the plant works overtime are a large percentage of total fixed costs, and fixed costs are a significant percentage of total costs, working overtime is a profitable means of producing more output.

## Problems

1. Assume that management knows with certainty that the market price next month will be $100. Its fixed costs are $1,200 per hour and its $AVC = \$36 + \$0.2q$. Calculate its breakeven and profit-maximizing outputs.

2. Assume that the firm's fixed costs are $500 per hour and its $AVC = \$40 + \$0.2q$ where $q$ is output per hour. Calculate the breakeven price and the profit-maximizing output at that price.

3. Continuing with problem 2, assume that management requires that there be at least a 75 percent probability that a price equal to or greater than the breakeven price will occur in the next planning period. If price is a normally distributed random variable with an expected value of $64 and a standard deviation of $4, calculate the probability that price will exceed the breakeven price. Also calculate the probability that price will be high enough to cover the cost of the firm's labor and materials.

4. Assume that the production function is $q = 0.5K^{0.5}L^{0.5}$ where $q$ is output per hour, the firm's plant has $K = 4$ units of capital, each unit of capital has an implicit opportunity cost of $80, other fixed costs are $100 per hour, materials cost $25 per unit, and the wage rate is $8 per hour. Calculate the breakeven price, the profit-maximizing output at that price, and the number of production workers to hire.

5. Continuing with problem 4, calculate the breakeven price if the production workers are to work one hour of overtime per day and are paid 1.5 times their regular wage. Fixed costs for one hour of overtime are $80.

6. Continuing with Example 8.9, show why it would not be profitable for the firm to put the plant on a second hour of overtime if the production function becomes $q = 7L^{0.5}$ and the market price is $34.

# 9

# *Wealth Maximization*

In the previous chapter, short-run profit maximization was the firm's goal because it was assumed that decisions made for the current planning period would have no discernible impact on profits in subsequent planning periods. Either profits in the planning periods were independent, or management was aware of no cost-effective method for predicting the impact of decisions made for the current planning period on future profits. In either case, decisions were made with respect to output, the quantities of variable factors, and so forth one planning period at a time using the short-run profit maximization model.

This chapter extends the procedures used in short-run profit maximization analyses to situations in which management can predict the impact of its decisions on profits for more than one planning period. The short-run profit maximization model is applied to each planning period. One new element in the analysis is explicit recognition of the linkages between decisions made in one planning period and profits in subsequent planning periods. The finished goods inventory created in one planning period and carried over to the next planning period for sale to consumers is an example of a linkage between planning periods. The other new element is calculation of present values.

Wealth maximization occurs when the present value of short-run profits over several planning periods is maximized. Management uses wealth maximization as its goal when decisions made for the current planning period have a predictable impact on the level of profits in subsequent planning periods.[1] Profits received in one planning period are made comparable with profits received in other planning periods by calculating the present value of profits in each period and totaling

---

[1]See section 1.5 for a discussion of the firm's goals.

to find the change in the firm's wealth resulting from each alternative decision. The alternative with the highest present value of profits is the wealth-maximizing decision. Wealth maximization is used when product prices, factor prices, and factor productivity are likely to vary in subsequent planning periods. Examples of decisions utilizing the wealth maximization model include decisions about inventory levels, maintenance expenditures, and abandoning a plant.

Most of the economic theory used in this chapter has been covered in previous chapters. Although several new theoretical concepts are introduced, the emphasis is on applications of the theory of the firm. Most of the chapter consists of examples using the wealth maximization model to plan the firm's operations for the current planning period in the context of projected prices, costs, sales, and profits in subsequent planning periods.

Section 9.1 discusses the wealth maximization model and provides an example of calculating the present value of profits when the linkage is a fixed total output in the two planning periods. Section 9.2 provides an introduction to inventory management. Inventory buildup links the current planning period with subsequent periods, when the inventory will be sold. Section 9.3 is concerned with the decision to abandon a plant. Section 9.4 provides a discussion of the relationship between plant capacity and the expected rate of growth in demand. The three cases for this chapter provide additional examples of use of the wealth maximization model. Case 9 discusses the conditions under which it is profitable to build a new plant and enter an industry. Case 10 extends the plant abandonment model to consideration of whether to temporarily shut down a plant. The last case provides a discussion of maintenance expenditures and their impacts on current and future profits.

## 9.1   *Wealth Maximization*

This section begins with a general discussion of the wealth maximization model and the basic procedures used when finding the wealth-maximizing alternative. The section concludes with an example illustrating the procedures for applying the wealth-maximizing model to a relatively simple production rate problem. More complex problems are covered in subsequent sections.

### 9.1.1   *Elements of the Wealth Maximization Model*

The wealth maximization model consists of four principal elements. The first two are the projections of profits in each planning period and the relationship between profit in one period and the others. The third element is the cost of capital to use in calculating present values. Calculation of the present values, and determining which alternative has the highest present value, is the final element.

*The Profit Projection.* The first step is to project profits for each planning period. This involves a forecast of market prices and the firm's cost functions for each period. Given the price and cost projections, the firm's profit-maximizing output and profit are calculated using the procedures in chapter 8.

*Linkages Between Planning Periods.* Inherent in the decision to use the wealth maximization model is management's belief that profits in subsequent periods depend on decisions made for the current planning period. For example, if a higher output in the current planning period results in a lower output in the second and subsequent periods, this linkage must be taken into consideration when calculating profits. Identifying the linkages between planning periods can result from abstract reasoning based on economic theory, statistical studies, and expert opinion forecasts. The linkages are used in developing profit projections for planning periods subsequent to the present one.

*Cost of Capital.* The firm's cost of capital is used as the interest rate for calculating the present value of profits in each planning period. The cost of capital is defined as the rate of interest that equates the present value of the firm's profits to the market value of its debt and equity securities. It is, in effect, the "breakeven" rate of return on the company's capital. Estimating the cost of capital for a firm is discussed in section 13.2.

*Calculating the Present Value.* The procedures for calculating the present value of a time series of profits are discussed in section 2.1. Calculating present values makes comparable all dollar amounts, regardless of how many planning periods they are projected into the future. Each profit projection is reduced to the amount of money that would have to be invested at time zero at a compound interest rate equal to the cost of capital to yield the projected profit. For example, the present value of a profit of $110 in one year at a 10 percent cost of capital is $100 because $100 can be invested for one year to yield $110. The sum of the present values of a time series of profits is the maximum amount of money an investor would be willing to pay for that time series of profits if he or she were able to obtain capital at the firm's cost of capital. Wealth maximization as the firm's goal requires that management make the decision that maximizes the present value of the firm's projected future profits.

## 9.1.2 *Wealth Maximization Where Output in the Second Planning Period Depends on Output in the First*

**EXAMPLE 9.1.** In this example, the firm's output in the first planning period determines output in the second. The linkage between the two planning periods is based on total output in the two periods being equal to a specified amount. Producing one unit of output in the first period means that one less unit can be produced in the second. Three alternative operating plans are analyzed, one for each first-period output rate that management wishes to consider. The plan with the highest present value is the wealth-maximizing one.

*General Assumptions.* Assume that two alternatives for a gravel pit operator are to maintain output at 100,000 cubic yards in each of two years, or to produce 150,000 cubic yards the first year, which is equal to the capacity of the company's equipment, and 50,000 cubic yards the second year. The price is $6 per cubic yard regardless of the output rate, and annual fixed costs for either decision are $40,000. Average variable cost for any year is $AVC = \$3.50 - \$0.01Q$ where the units for $Q$ are 1,000 cubic yards. The company's cost of capital is 15 percent. The linkage between the two output rates is that the pit has reserves of 200,000 cubic yards. Producing more in the first year means that there will be less gravel for the next year's production.

*Operating Plan One.* For an output of 100,000 cubic yards, $AVC = \$3.50 - \$0.01(100) = \$2.50$ per cubic yard and $TVC = \$2.50 \times 100,000 = \$250,000$. Total revenue is $\$6.00 \times 100,000 = \$600,000$ and profit is $\$600,000 - \$250,000 - \$40,000 = \$310,000$ each year. Using the mid-year centering method, the present value of profits is

$$PV_1 = \$310,000/(1.15)^{0.5} + \$310,000/(1.15)^{1.5} = \$540,447$$

Thus, producing 100,000 cubic yards per year would add $540,447 to the wealth of the firm operating the gravel pit.

*Operating Plan Two.* For an output of 150,000 cubic yards in the first year, $AVC = \$3.50 - \$0.01(150) = \$2.00$ per cubic yard and $TVC = \$2.00 \times 150,000 = \$300,000$. Total revenue is $\$6.00 \times 150,000 = \$900,000$ and profit is $\$900,00 - \$300,000 - \$40,000 = \$560,000$. For an output of 50,000 cubic yards in the second year, $AVC = \$3.50 - \$0.01(50) = \$3.00$ per cubic yard and TVC $= \$3.00 \times 50,000 = \$150,000$. Total revenue is $\$6.00 \times 50,000 = \$300,000$ and profit is $\$300,000 - \$150,000 - $

$40,000 = $110,000. The present value of profits is

$$PV_2 = \$560,000/(1.15)^{0.5} + \$110,000/(1.15)^{1.5} = \$611,399$$

Thus, the second operating plan has the higher present value.

*Operating Plan Three.* Additional investment in the facilities for operating the pit is not required in either of the above cases. However, the company can lease additional equipment for $120,000 ($10,000 per month) that would permit it to extract 200,000 cubic yards in one year. With the more efficient new equipment, the $AVC$ curve becomes $AVC = \$3.50 - \$0.008Q$. $AVC$ for 200,000 cubic yards is $3.50 - $0.008(200) = $1.90 per cubic yard and total variable cost is $1.90 × 200,000 = $380,000. Total revenue is $6.00 × 200,000 = $1,200,000 and profit is $1,200,000 - $380,000 - $40,000 - $120,000 = $660,000. The present value of profits is $PV_3 = \$660,000/(1.15)^{0.5} = \$615,453$.

*Conclusion.* Operating plan three increases the firm's wealth by more than either of the other two alternatives. The wealth-maximizing output is 200,000 cubic yards in the first year.

## 9.2  *Inventory Policy When Price Changes Are Forecast*

There are several reasons for inventories to be accumulated. Only one reason is discussed in this section — the accumulation of inventories in response to a projection of higher prices in the subsequent planning period. Inventories are accumulated by producing more in the current period than is sold. Inventories are reduced by producing less than is currently being sold. Expectations of higher prices in the future generally lead to inventory accumulation, and inventories are reduced when lower prices are expected. The amount by which inventories change is a management decision that provides a linkage between two time periods.

This section provides a method for calculating the wealth-maximizing output in the current period when management believes that the market price in future planning periods will be higher or lower than the current price. Although the output policies of price-taker firms do not significantly affect the market price, their managements can respond to expected price changes in future planning periods by accumulating or drawing down inventories. The managements of other firms will, of course, have their expectations with respect to future prices, and price expectations will differ among firms. If the firm is correct in its price projections, it can earn substantial profits on its inventory decisions.

## 9.2.1 *A Two-Period Inventory Accumulation Model*

This model is based on maximizing the present value of profits in two planning periods. To simplify our understanding of the model, we will assume that management makes its decisions as if its price projections will occur with certainty. The firm has already contracted to sell during the next year its profit-maximizing output. In Figure 9.1, this output is $q_0$ and price is $P_0$. The firm must sell $q_0$ next year unless it wishes to incur the costs of lawsuits by its customers. Price is expected to rise to $P_1$ by the end of next year, which will be its contract price in the second year. Management is contemplating whether to increase its

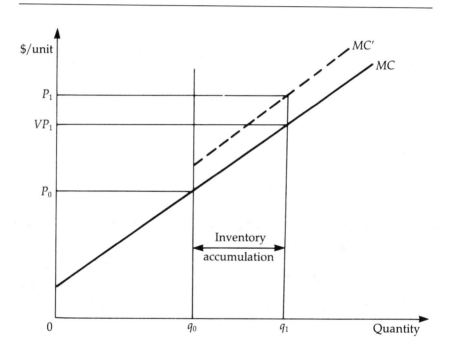

**Figure 9.1 Finding the Wealth-Maximizing Rate of Inventory Accumulation**

At $P_0$ in the current planning period, the profit-maximizing output is $q_0$. If price in the next period is expected to be $P_1$, the wealth-maximizing output in the current planning period is $q_1$, with $q_1 - q_0$ added to inventory. One way to find $q_1$ is to calculate the present value of $P_1$, $VP_1$, and equate $VP_1$ to MC. The other is to increase MC by the cost of carrying the inventory, shifting MC to MC'.

inventory by producing more than $q_0$ next year. The output added to inventory will be sold in precisely one year.

*Zero Carrying Costs.* Assume that the marginal cost of carrying the inventory for one year is zero. Providing a storage area and security involves no additional costs beyond those already incurred, and the product does not deteriorate. One solution is to calculate the present value of price $P_1$, which is $VP_1 = P_1/(1 + k)$ where $k$ is the cost of capital, and find the output where $VP_1$ is equal to $MC$. This yields output $q_1$ in Figure 9.1 and additions to inventories of $q_1 - q_0$. Alternatively, multiply the marginal cost of the output added to inventory by $(1 + k)$ to reflect the interest cost of the working capital invested in the inventory. This shifts up the $MC$ curve after $q_0$ to $MC'$. $MC'$ is equated to $P_1$ to find the wealth-maximizing output, which is again $q_1$.

The wealth-maximizing additions to inventory are the same whichever method is used. To demonstrate this point, assume that the firm's marginal cost function is $MC = 10 + 0.1q$. Equating $MC$ to the present value of $P_1$ and solving the $q_1$ yields

$$10 + 0.1q_1 = P_1/(1 + k) \qquad \textbf{(9.1)}$$

$$q_1 = 10P_1/(1 + k) - 100$$

where $q_1$ is the wealth-maximizing output. Multiplying $MC$ by $(1 + k)$ to reflect the interest costs yields

$$(10 + 0.1q_1)(1 + k) = P_1$$

Dividing both sides of this equation by $(1 + k)$ yields equation 9.1; therefore, the two outputs are equal.

*Positive Carrying Costs.* If additional storage and security costs are incurred when inventories are held, these costs are added to marginal cost, shifting the $MC$ and $MC'$ curves in Figure 9.1 upward. The result is a lower output and smaller additions to inventories when there are positive carrying costs.

**EXAMPLE 9.2.**    Assume that $MC = \$10 + \$0.1q$ before marginal storage costs of \$3 per unit, the current price is \$40, next year's price is projected at \$55, and the cost of capital is $k = 0.15$. Output for sale in the current period, $q_0$, is found by equating $MC$ without storage costs to the \$40 price.

$$\$10 + \$0.1q_0 = \$40$$

$$q_0 = 300 \text{ units per day}$$

Total output, $q_1$, in the current period is found by equating $MC$ plus marginal storage costs to the present value of next year's price.

$$\$13 + \$0.1q_1 = \$55/(1.15) = \$47.83 \qquad (9.2)$$

$$\$0.1q = \$47.83 - \$13 = \$34.83$$

$$q_1 = 348.3 \text{ units per day}$$

The amount added to inventory for sale in one year is $q_1 - q_0 = 348.3 - 300 = 48.3$ units per day.

*Relationship Between Rate of Price Change and the Cost of Capital.* Assume that price in one year is expected to be $P_1 = (1 + g)P_0$, where $g$ is the rate of change in price and $P_0$ is the current price. The present value of the future price is

$$VP_1 = (1 + g)P_0/(1 + k) \qquad (9.3)$$

If $g > k$, the present value of the future price is greater than the current price, and it will be wealth-maximizing to accumulate an inventory for sale in one year. If $g < k$, it is not wealth-maximizing to accumulate an inventory since the current price, $P_0$, is greater than the present value of the future price. Existing inventories should be sold at the current price.

## 9.2.2 Impact of Inventory Accumulation on the Future Market Price

Management's price projection for next year is based on its analysis of supply and demand that takes into account the accumulation of inventories. In Figure 9.2, the supply curve based on the marginal cost curves of the $M$ identical firms in this industry intersects the demand curve for this year, $D_0$, at a price of $P_0$. The demand curve for next year is expected to be $D_1$. If inventories are not accumulated, price next year will be $P_3$ where the $SRS$ curve based on $MC$ intersects $D_1$. Inventories accumulated in the current year by the $M$ firms in the industry shift the $SRS$ curve to the right by $M(q_1 - q_0)$, yielding "$SRS$ with inventory accumulation." This new supply curve intersects $D_1$ at $P_2$. Other points on the "$SRS$ with inventory accumulation" curve are found by inserting other possible future prices into equation 9.2, calculating the wealth-maximizing amount of inventory accumulation, multiplying it by the number of firms, and adding the result to $SRS$ based on $MC$. The minimum point on the "$SRS$ with inventory accumulation" curve occurs at price $P_1$ where $g = k$ in equation 9.3. Below that price, inventories are not accumulated and the supply curve is $SRS$ based on $MC$.

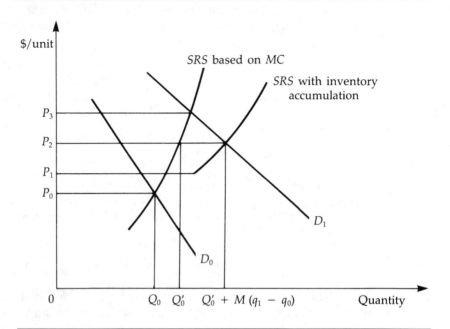

**Figure 9.2   The Market Price with Inventories Accumulated in the Previous Year**

$P_0$ is the projected price for the current planning period. In the next planning period, demand is expected to shift to $D_1$, yielding a market price of $P_3$ if inventories are not accumulated. If the wealth-maximizing inventory is accumulated by all firms in the industry, supply shifts to the right, and next year's price falls to $P_2$.

## 9.3   *The Plant Abandonment Decision*

A plant is abandoned when management decides to close it and sell or otherwise dispose of its assets. In section 9.3.1, the behavior of *AVC* as the plant ages is discussed. Since its *AVC* generally rises over time, an older plant will eventually be abandoned because its *AVC* has become greater than price. The year when the plant will be abandoned, which is referred to as its economic life, is based on management's current expectations as to future prices and costs. Section 9.3.2 discusses the role of the plant's salvage value in the abandonment decision. Previous discussions of the abandonment decision assumed that salvage value was zero. When salvage value is not zero, the abandonment decision requires use of the wealth-maximization model.

### 9.3.1  *Behavior of Average Variable Cost Over Time*

The discussion of production functions and cost curves in the previous chapters was based on the assumption that they do not shift over time. Although this assumption is a useful first approximation, management must consider systematic shifts in its cost curves that can be projected with reasonable certainty. These shifts in cost curves provide a linkage between planning periods that requires use of wealth maximization as the firm's goal.

Upward shifts in the *AVC* curve ultimately lead to abandonment of a plant. The first two reasons for shifts in the *AVC* curve — the learning curve and technological change — do not lead to abandonment of a plant but rather make it more profitable. They are included in this section to provide a more complete discussion of shifts in the *AVC* curve. The last two reasons — increases in factor prices and wear and tear on plant and equipment — can lead to abandoning a plant.

*The Learning Curve.* The learning process that generally accompanies startup and operation of a new plant shifts the *AVC* curve downward. These shifts are referred to as the learning curve effect. Unless the new plant is virtually an exact copy of other plants that have been in operation for a few years, errors will occur in its design. Some of the equipment cannot be used at its design capacity because of bottlenecks elsewhere in the production process. These relatively lower-capacity bottlenecks are discovered as the plant is operated. Their removal, which often requires only a relatively small investment, results in a reduction in *AVC*. The interview and job experience review process used to assign workers is rarely perfect, and the formal job descriptions may not have accurately described the plant's labor requirements. Some workers can have their responsibilities increased; others need to have theirs reduced. Some workers are effective in teamwork settings; others perform best on individual assignments. Successive reorganizations of the workforce, as more experience is gained with the labor requirements of the production process and with the capabilities of the plant's employees, can reduce *ACL* and *AVC*. New raw materials or purchased components may become available, because of technical change in their industries, and require integration into the production process. Since cost reductions caused by the learning curve effect are only available to new plants, their impact on a competitive industry's price is generally minimal.

*Technological Change.* Another reason for the *AVC* curve to shift downward is a time trend in *APL* due to the continual development of new technologies that can be incorporated into the firm's production process without constructing a new plant or making significant capital investments. These new technologies increase $APL$ and shift $AVC$ downward. Since $MPL$ and $MC$ also shift downward, the firm's profit-maximizing output increases. If the new technologies are available to all firms in the industry, its supply curve will shift to the right, leading to a reduction in the market price.

*Changes in Wages and the Unit Cost of Materials.* The $AVC$ curve can shift with changes in wage rates, $w$, and the unit costs of raw materials, $m$. Since $AVC = w/APL + mg$ and $MC = w/MPL + mg$, where $g$ is the number of units of the raw material used to produce one unit of the product, a time trend in either $w$ or $m$ will cause both curves to shift. Thus, projecting the short-run cost curves requires a projection of both $w$ and $m$ for each planning period.

Projecting changes in $w$ and $m$ for other firms is necessary to estimate the impact of these cost trends on the industry supply curve. If these trends are related to general trends in the economy, there may be shifts in the industry's demand curve. Both the supply and demand curve shifts will affect the market price for the firm's product. The market price will likely show a similar trend as $w$ and $m$, although it may change at a faster or slower rate. When $AVC$ shifts up faster than price, the difference between $P$ and $AVC$ lessens and ultimately disappears, resulting in abandonment of the plant.

*Wear and Tear.* The average product of labor changes over time because of the normal wear and tear resulting from use of the plant. As the plant ages, it requires more maintenance, reducing $APL$. Increased maintenance also requires more skilled labor; thus, the ratio of skilled to unskilled labor rises, and skilled labor receives a higher wage. Higher maintenance levels also require more spare parts. The increased cost of spare parts, and the possibility that it may take several days to obtain a part, shifts the $AVC$ curve upward. $AVC$ also may rise over time because of an increase in unscheduled shutdowns as the plant ages. These breakdowns can have major impacts on the average product of labor and labor costs, and hasten the time when $AVC$ becomes greater than price.

**EXAMPLE 9.3.** This example illustrates the procedures used in calculating the present value of profits when $AVC$ rises over time. Assume that the price is expected to be $150 per unit for the next 10 years and that $AVC = \$0.5q + \$20T$, where $T$ is the year in which the plant is operated (that is, now is $T = 0$, the first year is $T = 1$, the second $T = 2$, and so on). The cash fixed costs[2] that must be paid each year the plant operates are $2,000; hence, they are variable with respect to the decision to abandon the plant. The cost of capital is $k = 20$ percent. The profit-maximizing output for year $T$ is found by calculating $MC$ from $AVC$ and equating $MC$ to price ($150).

$$TVC = AVC \times q = \$0.5q^2 + \$20Tq$$

$$MC = (dTVC)/(dq) = \$q + \$20T = \$150$$

$$q = 150 - 20T$$

Total revenue, total cost, and profit at time $T$ are

$$TR = (150 - 20T)150 = 22,500 - 3,000T$$

$$TC = \$2,000 + \$0.5(150 - 20T)^2 + \$20T(150 - 20T)$$

$$TC = 13,250 - 200T^2$$

$$\Pi = TR - TC = \$9,250 - \$3,000T + \$200T^2$$

Profits are calculated for each year until profits become negative, at which time the plant is abandoned. These calculations are in Table 9.1. The discount factor is $1/1.2^T$. The present value of profits from operating 4 years is $9,590. The plant is abandoned in the fifth year because profits are negative.

**Table 9.1   Present Value of Profits**

| Year | Output | Profit | Discount Factor | Present Value |
|------|--------|--------|-----------------|---------------|
| 1 | 130 | $6,450 | 0.8333 | $5,375 |
| 2 | 110 | 4,050 | 0.6944 | 2,812 |
| 3 | 90 | 2,050 | 0.5787 | 1,186 |
| 4 | 70 | 450 | 0.4823 | 217 |
| 5 | 50 | (750) | — | — |
| | | | Total present value | $9,590 |

[2]Cash fixed costs are explicit costs such as managerial salaries, property taxes, and insurance premiums. Implicit opportunity costs are not cash costs.

## 9.3.2  *The Role of Salvage Value*

In chapter 8, the profit-maximizing output was zero if the market price of the product was less than minimum *AVC*. An implicit assumption of this rule was that the plant's salvage value is zero. This section applies the wealth maximization model to the plant abandonment decision when there are nonzero salvage values.

*Managerial Definition of Salvage Value.* Salvage value is the amount of money that the firm realizes when it sells an abandoned plant. The salvage value may result from sale of all or part of the equipment, buildings, or land. Alternatively, some of these assets may be transferred to other divisions of the company, in which case the salvage value is their value in the alternative use. Until the asset is sold or otherwise disposed of, its salvage value is an implicit opportunity cost. Estimating salvage value involves appraising the market value of the plant's assets as they age. The salvage values of some assets, such as highly specialized equipment, may decline rapidly and then remain at a low value for the remainder of their useful life. Others, such as buildings or standardized equipment, usually decline slowly in value. Land may appreciate and have a rising salvage value. Salvage value is negative if it costs more to clean up the plant site to meet governmental regulations than the land and used equipment can be sold for.

*Differences Between Managerial and Accounting Definitions of Salvage Value.* The managerial definition of salvage value differs from that of the accountant. The accountant sets the salvage value as low as the government will allow when depreciation allowances are based on the difference between the asset's historical cost and its salvage value. The lower the salvage value, the higher the depreciation allowances and the lower the company's income tax liabilities.[3] Depreciation allowances are also used to calculate book value, which is the asset's historical cost less accumulated depreciation. Companies may overstate salvage values to obtain relatively high book values for their balance sheet assets, which may be used by lenders in evaluating loan applications. Book value generally is useless for estimating the asset's value if it is sold or transferred to another division of the company. Also, there generally is a systematic relationship between salvage value and the planned level of maintenance. The level of maintenance is subject to managerial control and can have a significant impact on an asset's salvage value and the length of its useful life.

---

[3]The *ACRS* depreciation method does not consider the asset's salvage value — see section 14.1.

*Calculating a Plant's Economic Life.* If management's goal is to maximize the firm's wealth, determining a plant's economic life involves determining the year when the cumulative present value of the profits from operating the plant plus its salvage value are maximized. The plant will be abandoned when it reaches the end of its economic life. Even though it may be physically possible to continue to operate the plant, its economic life is over because it is more profitable to sell the plant for its salvage value than to operate it. The economic life of a plant can change from year to year with changes in the market price of the product, in the factors leading to shifts in the *AVC* curve, or in the prices of substitute or complementary products.

EXAMPLE 9.4.   The calculations in example 9.3 implicitly assumed that the plant's salvage value was zero. This example uses the same price, cost, and cost of capital assumptions as example 9.3 but adds the assumption that salvage value is positive.

Finding the year when the present value of profits is maximized requires extending Table 9.1 to include the present value of the plant's salvage value in the firm's revenues. Column 1 of Table 9.2 is the present value column of Table 9.1. Cumulative present value is found by summing up the annual present values of the current and previous years. The estimated salvage value for each year in column 3 was prepared by the company's engineers and accountants based on information currently available about the condition of the physical facilities, planned maintenance expenditures, and the likely sale prices for the equipment and other facilities. In the fourth column, the present values of the salvage values are calculated by multiplying the salvage value by the discount factor in Table 9.1. The present value of the plant is the cumulative present value of the profits from operating the plant plus the present value of its salvage value.

Table 9.2   Determining When to Abandon a Plant

| End of Year | PV of Profits | | Salvage Value | | Cumulative Present Value |
|---|---|---|---|---|---|
| | Annual | Cumulative | Amount | Present Value | |
| | (1) | (2) | (3) | (4) | (2) + (4) |
| 1 | $5,375 | $5,375 | $4,500 | $3,750 | $ 9,125 |
| 2 | 2,812 | 8,187 | 3,000 | 2,083 | 10,270 |
| 3 | 1,186 | 9,373 | 2,000 | 1,157 | 10,530 |
| 4 | 217 | 9,590 | 1,000 | 482 | 10,072 |
| 5 | — | — | 500 | — | — |

The plant's present value is maximized if it is operated for 3 years and then sold for its $2,000 salvage value. If its salvage value were zero, the plant would be operated for 4 years, at which time it would be abandoned because profits become negative in the fifth year. The plant is abandoned at the end of the third year since the reduction in salvage value is greater than the operating profit for the fourth year. In general, when salvage values are positive, it is wealth-maximizing to abandon the plant and sell it for its salvage value prior to the time when the price of the product becomes less than minimum *AVC*.

*Negative Salvage Value.* A negative salvage value occurs, for example, when it costs more to restore a strip mined area to meet government regulations than can be obtained from selling the reclaimed land and mining equipment. In general, when salvage value is negative, the company will operate the plant beyond the time when the rising *AVC* equals price.

**EXAMPLE 9.5.**  Assume that an operating loss of $100,000 is expected if a firm produces the minimum output required for an operating strip mine. Salvage value is negative: An expenditure of $1.0 million to restore the stripped area is required when the mine is abandoned. If the company does not abandon the mine, it can lend out the $1.0 million at a 15 percent interest rate and earn $150,000 in interest. By continuing to operate the mine and accepting the $100,000 operating loss, the company adds $50,000 to its profits.

**EXAMPLE 9.6.**  The previous examples assumed stable prices. Prices may also vary over time in a predictable manner. When there are downward pressures on prices, upward pressures on operating costs hasten the time when the plant will be abandoned. If price at time $T$ is $P_T = \$150 - \$5T$ and the assumptions relating to the plant's costs are those in section 9.4.1, the profit-maximizing output is

$$MC = P = \$q + \$20T = \$150 - \$5T$$

$$q = 150 - 25T$$

Total revenue, total cost, and profit are

$$TR = (\$150 - \$5T)(150 - 25T) = \$22{,}500 - \$4{,}500T + \$125T^2$$

$$TC = \$2{,}000 + \$0.5(150 - 25T)^2 + \$20T(150 - 25T)$$

$$TC = 13{,}250 - 750T - 187.5T^2$$

$$\Pi = TR - TC = \$9{,}250 - 3{,}750T + 312.5T^2$$

Under these assumptions, the plant will be operated for 3 years because there is a loss of $750 if the plant is operated for the fourth year. The present value of profits for the 3 years is $9,625.

## 9.4 *Demand Growth and New Plant Capacity*

This section discusses the reasons for relatively rapidly growing industries' building plants with excess capacity. The capacity of a plant is generally defined as the output at which its *SRATC* is minimized.[4] Excess capacity exists when the firm is producing less than the output at which its *SRATC* is minimized. The existence of excess capacity generally requires that the firms in the industry be reluctant to reduce their average price below *SRATC*. This kind of price behavior is unlikely to be observed in competitive markets. The model discussed in this section applies to firms selling in markets that are not competitive.

### 9.4.1 *Reasons for Excess Plant Capacity*

The basic assumption of this section is that the *LRAC* curve is downward sloping so that larger plants have lower average costs. The firm is likely to find that building a larger plant with excess capacity relative to demand at the current market price is wealth-maximizing if demand is growing and the cost of capital is low.

*Role of a Growing Demand.* When demand is expected to grow and the *LRAC* curve is downward sloping, firms generally design their plants with some excess capacity. As demand grows, the excess capacity will gradually disappear and *SRATC* will fall. When the firm builds its next plant, excess capacity will also be designed into it. Some rapidly growing industries have been plagued with excess capacity over a number of years as the firms built for future demand growth and were tempted to cut prices to utilize the excess capacity.

Petroleum refining in the 1950s and early 1960s and the organic chemical and ammonia industries in the 1960s provide examples of growing industries with relatively weak prices. The firms would attempt to sell their incremental production (that is, output above sales to their normal customers) in such a way that prices in their regular markets were not affected. However, when most firms are making incremental sales to other firms' customers, the cut-rate price soon becomes the market price. With the general slowdown in demand growth in the

---

[4]The ultimate capacity of a plant occurs at the output where *MPL* = 0. Capacity can also be defined as the output where the slope of the *MC* curve is so steep that a large price increase would be necessary for the firm to increase its output by one unit.

1970s for products based on petroleum, caused principally by sharply higher prices, new plant construction virtually ceased, excess capacity disappeared, and these industries have enjoyed greater price stability and more profitable operations.

*Role of the Cost of Capital.* Since management's goal is to maximize wealth, the rate of interest is an important factor affecting decisions to build excess capacity into new plants. The interest rate is an important element in the firm's cost of capital. A higher interest rate increases the cost of capital and reduces the present value of future profits. Interest rates were relatively low in the 1950s and 1960s; thus, the present value of the profits from building excess capacity would more likely exceed its cost than after 1970, when interest rates were much higher. This is another reason for excess capacity gradually disappearing from industries producing products based on petroleum. It no longer was profitable to incur the cost today of building excess capacity that will not be needed for several years when the present value of the profits from the excess capacity are low and less than the capital cost of the additional facilities.

## 9.4.2  *Which Plant Capacity Is Wealth-Maximizing?*

**EXAMPLE 9.7.**   Assume that a firm has a downward sloping *LRAC* curve like that in Figure 9.3. A downward sloping *LRAC* curve generally results when the profitable technologies become increasingly capital intensive as output rises. If demand is expected to grow steadily for a number of years, management must decide on the scale of plant to build. The larger the plant, the lower *ATC* will be. If demand is at level $D_1$ in Figure 9.3, it is a matter of time before it will grow to $D_2$ and then to still higher levels in the future. Based on today's demand curve, the plant with $SRATC_0$ would be the lowest-cost one to construct. Yet, in five years when demand reaches $D_2$, the plant with $SRATC_2$ would involve still lower costs and presumably be more profitable.

Assume that the company's engineers have estimated construction costs and the average cost curves for two plant designs. In the context of this example, average cost, *AC*, is defined as the average cost of production exclusive of the cost of constructing the plant, which is excluded from *AC* since the plant's cost is a separate item in calculating its net present value (*NPV*). The *AC* curves are similar to the *SRATC* curves in Figure 9.3.

*Present Value of the Smaller Plant's Profits.* The smaller plant, which requires $4.8 million to construct, produces at minimum *AC* the

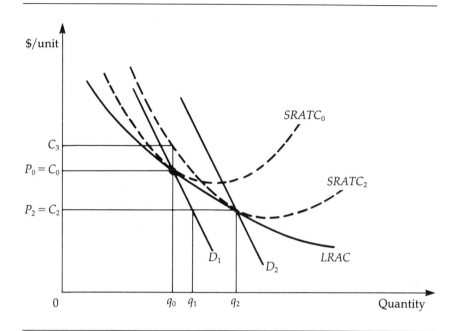

**Figure 9.3　Alternative Plant Capacities and Costs**

Management is considering building one of two plants with $SRATC_0$ and $SRATC_2$ as their $SRATC$ curves. Demand is expected to grow over time. It will be at level $D_1$ in one year and at $D_2$ at some time in the future. If the plant with $SRATC_0$ is built, it will reach capacity in one or two years. Building the plant with $SRATC_2$ will result in excess capacity in its early years of operation.

400 units per day the company expects to sell in the first year after the plant is completed. Although demand is expected to grow at 5 percent per year, output will not be increased beyond the 403 units per day where its $MC$ equals the projected market price of $110. The $AC$ curve for this plant is $AC_0 = 900 - 6q + 0.2q^{1.5}$, which has its minimum $AC$ of $100 per unit at $q = 400$ units per day. Output rises to 403 units per day in the second year and remains at that level until the plant must be shut down after 10 years of operation. The plant will be operated for 260 days per year. The calculations of the present value of profits are summarized in Table 9.3. The present value of the profits at a 15 percent cost of capital is $5.618 million, and its net present value is $818,000.

***Present Value of the Larger Plant's Profits.*** The larger plant's $AC$ curve is $AC_2 = 1159.8 - 6.6q + 0.2q^{1.5}$ and its construction cost is $5.2

**Table 9.3    Present Value of Profits (Thousands of dollars)**

| Time* | Smaller Plant | | | Larger Plant | | |
|---|---|---|---|---|---|---|
| | Profit | PV at 15% | PV at 6% | Profit | PV at 15% | PV at 6% |
| 0 | ($4,800) | ($4,800) | ($4,800) | ($5,200) | ($5,200) | ($5,200) |
| 1 | 1,042 | 972 | 1,012 | (960) | (895) | (932) |
| 2 | 1,044 | 847 | 957 | 127 | 103 | 116 |
| 3 | 1,044 | 736 | 902 | 1,022 | 721 | 883 |
| 4 | 1,044 | 640 | 851 | 1,644 | 1,008 | 1,341 |
| 5 | 1,044 | 557 | 803 | 1,895 | 1,010 | 1,458 |
| 6 | 1,044 | 484 | 758 | 1,896 | 879 | 1,376 |
| 7 | 1,044 | 421 | 715 | 1,896 | 764 | 1,298 |
| 8 | 1,044 | 366 | 674 | 1,896 | 665 | 1,225 |
| 9 | 1,044 | 318 | 636 | 1,896 | 578 | 1,155 |
| 10 | 1,044 | 277 | 600 | 1,896 | 503 | 1,090 |
| | NPV = | $ 818 | $3,108 | NPV = | $ 136 | $3,810 |

*To calculate the mid-year centered present values, except for time 0, use the formula $(Profit)/(1 + k)^{T-0.5}$ because it is assumed that the plant starts up at time 0 and earns the profit at a constant rate over the year.

million. This plant has its minimum $AC$ at $q = 484$ units per day and a minimum $AC$ of $95 per unit. Its annual profits and their present values are also provided in Table 9.3. Capacity operations are not achieved until the fifth year. This is a loss of $960,000 in its first year. Over the ten-year period, this larger capacity plant has a present value of profits of $5.336 million and an $NPV$ of $136,000 at a 15 percent cost of capital. Therefore, the wealth-maximizing plant to build is the smaller one because it has the greater $NPV$.

*A Lower Cost of Capital and Plant Capacity.* The present value of profits at a 6 percent cost of capital is provided for both plants in Table 9.3. If the cost of capital is 6 percent, the larger plant maximizes the present value of profits. Its profits would have a present value of $9.010 million, which is $1.1 million greater than the $7.908 million present value of the smaller plant. Since the difference in construction costs is $400,000, the larger plant's $NPV$ is $700,000 greater than the smaller plant's. The larger plant has a higher $NPV$ because it earns substantially higher profits once it attains capacity operations. The relatively greater present value of the sixth to tenth year profits at the 6 percent cost of capital more than offsets the substantial profit advantages of the smaller plant in the first 2 years of operations.

*Additional Considerations.* More than two plants would be analyzed before making a decision. Other factors, such as the location of the plant, would likely be taken into consideration. The *AC* curves of the plants and the price, cost of capital, and output projections are nonetheless important elements in the plant capacity decision. It need not be wealth-maximizing to build a larger plant with a lower *AC* once it reaches capacity. A smaller plant may be preferable if capital costs are relatively high or the growth in output is expected to be relatively slow. Gradually declining future prices, however, generally favor larger plants with their lower unit costs.

# 9.5 *Summary*

Wealth maximization is the goal of the firm when actions taken in the current planning period predictably influence profits in subsequent planning periods. The linkages between actions taken in one planning period and profits in subsequent planning periods are specified as part of the wealth maximization model. Present values of profits, revenues, and costs make dollars received at one point in time comparable to dollars received at another point in time. The firm's cost of capital is used in calculating present values. Maximizing the firm's wealth amounts to maximizing the present value of its future profits.

The wealth maximization model can be applied to many managerial decision problems. One such decision is whether to increase production above current sales to add to inventories to be sold in the future. Inventory accumulation is wealth maximizing if the future price is sufficiently above the current market price to cover the marginal cost of the additional production, the costs of holding the inventory, and the cost of the capital tied up in the inventory. Another set of decision problems is concerned with whether to abandon a plant when *AVC* rises, price declines, and there are nonzero salvage values. These problems provide examples of use of the wealth maximization model when profits fluctuate over time. The last example involved calculating whether it would be wealth-maximizing to build a larger plant when entering an industry that is not competitive.

An assumption of the wealth maximization model discussed in this chapter was that management was willing to base its decisions on a single forecast of the future. This amounts to behaving as if the future were known with certainty. Basing decisions on certainty models is not an unusual business practice. However, when the information to do so is available, decision making generally can be improved by explicitly considering the alternative outcomes of a decision and their probabilities of occurrence. This is the subject of chapter 12.

| CASE | 9 | Will Entry Increase the Value of the Firm? |

Section 8.8 posed the question of whether entering an industry will increase the value of the firm when price first rises above *LRAC*, falls below it for some period of time, and then returns to being equal to *LRAC*. The value of the firm will rise if the present value of the projected profits is positive when discounted at the firm's cost of capital. In this case, the linkage between the planning periods is the price projection for each period, which is based on management's price projection for the first period and its expert opinion as to future price trends. Since the present value is positive, the value of the firm will increase if it goes ahead with the project.

**The Assignment.** Your company has been considering entering an industry showing relatively steady growth over the past few years. Recent technological developments have resulted in an unexpectedly large shift to the right in the industry's demand curve. Since this shift was not anticipated, firms in or entering the industry have not constructed the new capacity necessary to supply it. Price has risen 21 percent in the past few weeks from its normal average of $95. To produce this new product the manufacturing department has completed its plans for converting a plant that presently makes an unprofitable product. Your assignment is to convince executive management of its financial feasibility.

**Cost Projections.** The average variable cost function for the converted plant is $AVC = \$35 + \$0.02q$ and marginal cost is $MC = \$35 + \$0.04q$, where $q$ is output per week. Fixed costs, excluding the cost of newly purchased equipment, are $45,000 per week. The unit costs of factors are unchanged with changes in the number of firms in the industry, making this a constant-cost industry. The new equipment will cost $150,000 and take 6 months to install. The opportunity costs of the building and several pieces of equipment already owned by the company are included in fixed costs. The cost of capital for calculating the present value of future profits is 20 percent.

**Price Projections.** Management expects an average price of $110 during the first year of operations, $80 during the second year caused by expected overbuilding of new capacity as a result of the present high price, and $90 during the third year as demand growth and plant abandonments reduce excess capacity in the industry.

Starting in the fourth year price is expected to average $95 for the remainder of the plant's life. The $95 price is equal to the minimum of the plant's *LRAC* and *SRATC* curves.

**Calculating Profits.** The first year profit-maximizing output is found by equating *MC* to the price projected by management.

$$P = MC \Rightarrow \$110 = \$35 + \$0.04q$$

$$q = 1{,}875 \text{ units per week}$$

$$AVC = \$35 + \$0.02(1{,}875) = \$72.50 \text{ per unit}$$

$$AFC = \$45{,}000/1{,}875 = \$24.00 \text{ per unit}$$

$$SRATC = AVC + AFC = \$96.50 \text{ per unit}$$

$$\Pi = (\$110 - \$96.50)(1{,}875) = \$25{,}313.50 \text{ per week}$$

Because the plant is shut down for 2 weeks each summer for employee vacations, it operates for 50 weeks each year.

$$\Pi = \$25{,}312.50/\text{week} \times 50 \text{ weeks} = \$1{,}265{,}625 \text{ per year}$$

Using the same calculation method, there are losses of $984,375 and $359,562.50 in the second and third years and a zero profit thereafter.

**Calculating the Present Value of Profits.** If management were to make its decision on the basis of its undiscounted profits projection, it would not convert the plant to this new product. The total profit for the 3 years is $1,265,625 − $984,375 − $359,562.50 = −$78,312.50, which is a loss on an undiscounted basis. However, since the profits and losses occur at different times, their present values should be calculated to determine if the project will increase the value of the company. The mid-year centered annual present values are

$$PV_1 = \$1{,}265{,}625/(1.2)^{1.0} = \$1{,}054{,}687.50$$

$$PV_2 = \$(-984{,}375)/(1.2)^{2.0} = -\$683{,}593.75$$

$$PV_3 = \$(-359{,}562.50)/(1.2)^{3.0} = -\$208{,}080.15$$

The net present value of profits is $PV_1 + PV_2 + PV_3 = \$163{,}013.60$. The value (wealth) of the company will increase by $163,013.60 − $150,000 = $13,013.60 if it invests the $150,000 in the plant.

**Conclusions.** Assume that there are no other alternative uses of the plant. The plant will be abandoned if it is not converted to producing the new product. If this is the case, the wealth of the firm would rise by $13,013.60 if the plant is converted and, presumably, by nothing if it is abandoned. It is wealth-maximizing, given the alternatives, to convert the plant to the new product.

<br>

**CASE  10    The Shutdown Decision**

This case extends the discussion in section 9.3 to the kinds of decisions management makes when it considers whether to shut down a plant for, say, 1 year. After 1 year, demand and prices are expected to return to profitable levels; hence, the company does not want to abandon the plant.

**The Assignment.** Your company rebuilds valves used in petroleum refineries and chemical plants. The current recession has resulted in cancelation of several major new plants and reduced maintenance at existing plants. This has increased competition for the remaining business and has driven down the average price to $98 per unit. Management expects the present situation to last about one year. Demand is then expected to increase substantially and price rise to the normal average of $150 per unit. You are to determine whether the company should shut down the plant for 1 year or continue to operate it.

**Costs of Shutting Down the Plant.** When the plant is shut down, the company's contract with the union requires a lump sum payment of $1,000 to each of the 18 laid-off workers with more than 5 years' seniority. The equipment mothballing cost is $10,000. Plant maintenance and security will cost $60,000 during the year when the plant is shut down. When the plant is reopened, the cost of replacing those workers who have found new jobs is expected to be $10,000. Putting the moth-balled equipment back into operation will require $40,000. The present values of these costs at a 25 percent cost of capital are in Table 9.4. They total $121,666.

**Cost of Operating the Plant.** To determine whether it is wealth-maximizing to shut down the plant, management must calculate the present value of the operating loss if it is not shut down. Assume that the production function is $Q = L^{0.5}$ where $Q$ and $L$ are

**Table 9.4   Present Value of Shutdown/Startup Costs**

|  |  | Dollar Costs | |
|---|---|---|---|
| Time | Cost Category | Amount | Present Value |
| 0.0 | Worker payments | $ 18,000 | $ 18,000 |
| 0.0 | Equipment mothballing | 10,000 | 10,000 |
| 0.5 | Plant security | 60,000 | 53,666 |
| 1.0 | Worker replacement | 10,000 | 8,000 |
| 1.0 | Equipment startup | 40,000 | 32,000 |
| | Totals | $138,000 | $121,666 |

hourly rates. Raw materials and purchased components cost $50 per unit of output, and cash fixed costs that can be avoided if the plant is shut down (which makes them variable relative to the shutdown decision) are $152 per hour.

$$APL = Q/L = 1/L^{0.5}$$

$$ACL = W/APL = WL^{0.5} = WQ$$

$$AVC = WQ + 50 + 152/Q$$

where $W$ is the wage rate. Marginal cost is $MC = 2WQ + 50$. The number of workers is found by solving the production function for $L = Q^2$.

The minimum point of the $AVC$ curve is found by taking its derivative, setting it equal to zero, and solving for $Q$.

$$dAVC/dq = W - 152/Q^2 = 0$$

$$Q = (152/W)^{0.5}$$

If $W = \$8$ per hour, $Q = (152/8)^{0.5} = 4.36$ units per hour and $L = Q^2 = 19$. That is, 19 production workers are employed at the output where $AVC$ is minimized. The minimum point on the $AVC$ curve is at $119.74.

**Operating Loss If the Plant Is Not Shut Down.** The profit-maximizing output is found by equating $P$ to $MC$ and solving for $Q$.

$$98 = 2WQ + 50 \text{ or } Q = 3.0 \text{ units per hour}$$

The quantity of labor required is $L = 3^2 = 9$ production workers. Since the plant has not been shut down, the $1,000 payment to each of the 9 laid-off senior workers is not required. For an output of $Q = 3$,

$$AVC = (8)(3) + 50 + 152/3 = \$124.67/\text{unit}$$

The operating loss is $124.67 − $98 = $26.67 per unit times 3.0 units of output or $80 per hour. The plant is operated for one 8-hour shift for an average of 43 weeks per year or 1,720 hours. The operating loss is $80 per hour times 1,720 hours or $137,600. Since the operating loss is incurred at a constant rate over the year, its present value at a 25 percent cost of capital is $123,073.

**Conclusions.** If the undiscounted costs are compared, the greater loss results from shutting down the plant. However, since the costs are incurred at different times, it is necessary to calculate their present values before determining which alternative is wealth-maximizing. The present value of the operating loss is $123,073 − $121,666 = $1,407 greater than the present value of the costs of shutting down the plant. The wealth-maximizing decision is to shut down the plant.

## CASE 11 Determining the Level of Maintenance Expenditures

This case is concerned with determining the wealth-maximizing level of maintenance expenditures for a competitive firm's aging plant. Maintenance expenditures add to total costs, but they also increase output relative to its level if maintenance expenditures were lower. Since today's maintenance expenditures affect future output, the wealth maximization goal is used to find the optimal maintenance program.

**The Assignment.** The boss has requested that next year's operating plan address the increasing costs of maintenance and the more frequent equipment breakdowns. Several maintenance service company sales representatives have called during the past few months, because they know the equipment is now old enough to make their service plans attractive. You are considering whether to hire a maintenance service company to do the increasing amount of regular maintenance.

**Costs of the Maintenance Contracts.** For the first year, the basic contract costs $250 per week and the extended contract costs $900 per week. Both contracts increase in cost by 10 percent in each subsequent year. With the basic contract, output is likely to fall by 4 percent per year. With the extended contract, output is likely to fall by 2 percent per year. If the company continues its current maintenance procedures, output will likely fall by 8 to 10 percent per year from this year's average of 150 units per week. Maintenance at a sufficiently high level to maintain output at 150 units per week would be prohibitively expensive.

**Profits with Each Contract.** Either of the two contracts is more profitable than the company's present procedure (see problem 13). The present value of profits for each contract are in Table 9.5. For both alternatives, the total cost of operating the plant is projected at $9,000 per week plus the cost of the maintenance contract. The marketing department has projected the market price of the product at

**Table 9.5  Present Maintenance Contract**

*Basic Maintenance Contract*

| Year | Output | Total Cost | ATC | Profit per Week Undiscounted | Present Value |
|---|---|---|---|---|---|
| 1 | 144.00 | $ 9,250 | $64.24 | $ 6,589 | $ 6,015 |
| 2 | 138.24 | 9,275 | 67.09 | 5,932 | 4,513 |
| 3 | 132.71 | 9,302 | 70.09 | 5,296 | 3,358 |
| 4 | 127.40 | 9,333 | 73.26 | 4,681 | 2,473 |
| 5 | 122.31 | 9,366 | 76.58 | 4,088 | 1,800 |
| | | | | $25,586 | $18,158 |

*Extended Maintenance Contract*

| Year | Output | Total Cost | ATC | Profit per Week Undiscounted | Present Value |
|---|---|---|---|---|---|
| 1 | 147.00 | $ 9,900 | $67.35 | $ 6,270 | $ 5,723 |
| 2 | 144.06 | 9,990 | 69.35 | 5,856 | 4,455 |
| 3 | 141.18 | 10,089 | 71.46 | 5,441 | 3,449 |
| 4 | 138.36 | 10,198 | 73.71 | 5,039 | 2,662 |
| 5 | 135.59 | 10,318 | 76.10 | 4,596 | 2,024 |
| | | | | $27,202 | $18,313 |

$125. *AVC* for the marketing department is $15 per unit; thus, the average revenue at the plant is $110 per unit. The undiscounted profit is $\Pi = (\$110 - AVC_t)q_t$ where $t$ is the year after the contract is awarded. The controller estimates the cost of capital at 20 percent. Weekly profits are used to make the decision since in each year the weekly profit would be multiplied by the same constant (52), which has no effect on the totals relative to each other.

**Conclusions.** The extended service contract has the higher present value; hence, it is the wealth-maximizing maintenance program. Although it shows a lower weekly profit than the basic contract for the first 2 years, it is substantially more profitable in the last 3 years. Moreover, the higher profits in the third through fifth years will be particularly valuable because the company will be seeking financing for a new plant. The boss will also find the lower rate of decline in output attractive, because the marketing department has been concerned about losing some key customers if output declines at the 8 to 10 percent rate projected for the plant without more maintenance.

---

# Key Terms

cost of capital      learning curve effect      technological change
excess capacity      salvage value              wealth maximization
learning curve

# Review Questions

1. When can the firm use short-run profit maximization as its goal and when must it use wealth maximization?

2. Define the term *cost of capital*. Why will an increase in the market value of its securities reduce a firm's cost of capital?

3. Why does the accumulation of inventories this year for sale next year require calculating present values?

4. Why would a firm with a 15 percent cost of capital want to reduce its inventories now if it believes that price will rise by 10 percent?

5. Why does an increase in the marginal cost for storing a product lead to a lower level of inventory accumulation?

6. Why are fixed costs not used when calculating the wealth-maximizing amount to add to inventory?

7. Show graphically why a reduction in inventories in anticipation of a price decline will result in a decline in the market price.

# Problems and Applications

1. Assume that the operator of the gravel pit in section 8.1 had a cost of capital of 8 percent. Would the wealth-maximizing operating plan change? Explain why.

2. $AVC$ for a competitive firm is $AVC = \$28 + \$0.3q$ where $q$ is output per day and fixed costs are \$2,400 per day. The plant operates 300 days each year. The market price of the product is $\$106 - \$6T$ where $T = 1$ is the first operating year, $T = 2$ the second, and so on. The firm's cost of capital is 15 percent. Calculate the present value of operating the plant for 3 years.

3. A construction company has received a contract to provide the labor and equipment to build a 90,000-foot-long concrete lined ditch. The customer will pay the cost of all materials. To provide an incentive for early completion, the customer will pay \$38 per foot if it is completed in 2 years and a bonus of \$3.60 per foot at the end of the project if it is completed in 18 months. The project costs for each operating day are projected as follows:

| | 225 feet/day | 300 feet/day |
| --- | --- | --- |
| Opportunity cost of equipment | \$3,000 | \$ 3,000 |
| Leased equipment | — | 1,000 |
| Fuel | 500 | 600 |
| Wage labor | 2,000 | 4,000 |
| Other fixed costs | 2,100 | 2,700 |
| Total cost | \$7,600 | \$11,300 |

If the project is completed in 18 months, the company will be able to lease its equipment out for \$3,000 per day for 100 days during the last 6 months of the 2-year period and will earn a profit of \$1,000 per day. Revenues from the contract are received at the end of each 6-month period and costs are incurred on a weekly basis (center these costs on the middle of each 6-month period). The company's cost of capital is 20 percent. Is it wealth-maximizing for the firm to complete the project in 18 months?

4. Continuing with problem 3, if the company were able to lease out its equipment for only 50 days during the 6-month period after completing the project, would the wealth-maximizing decision be different? Explain why.

5. If a firm's $AVC = \$30 + \$0.3q$ and $q$ is output per day, calculate the wealth-maximizing amount to add to its inventory in the next 30-day period if the present price of its product is \$90 and the price next year is expected to be \$105. The firm's cost of capital is 20 percent. Assume that the firm first ships its oldest product from inventory.

6. Assuming that salvage value is zero, calculate the year when the plant in problem 2 will be abandoned.

7. Assume that the firm's production function is $q = 2L^{0.5}/T^{0.25}$ where $q$ is output per hour and $T = 1$ is the first operating year, $T = 2$ is the second, and so on. The wage rate is \$6 per hour, materials cost \$10 per unit of output, cash fixed costs are \$195 per hour, and the market price of the product is $\$50 + \$2T$. The plant operates for 2,000 hours per year. Calculate the number of years the firm will operate this plant. (Hint: Calculate the profit-maximizing number of workers for each year to use in calculating $q$ and $AVC$.)

8. Assume that the plant in problem 7 has a salvage value of \$400,000 at the end of its first year of operations and that its salvage value declines by \$50,000 per year to a minimum of \$50,000. When will the plant be abandoned given this salvage value assumption?

9. Continuing with problem 7, in the year that the plant is to be abandoned, its workers offer to take a wage cut to \$5 per hour if management will keep the plant open for 2 more years. Will management accept this offer?

10. An oil well has suffered a mechanical failure costing \$90,000 to repair. In the first year after the repair, the well will produce 6,000 barrels of oil, and production will decline by 20 percent each year thereafter. Cash fixed costs are \$40,000 per year and rising at 10 percent per year. $AVC = MC = \$4$ per barrel and are expected to be constant over time, as is the \$20 price for the oil. The cost of capital is 25 percent and the present values are calculated using the mid-year centering method. Will the firm be maximizing its wealth if it makes this repair?

11. If the price of oil in problem 10 were to rise to \$25, would it then be wealth-maximizing to repair the well? Explain why.

12. Continuing with the example in section 9.4, a third possible plant has the short-run average total cost curve of $SRATC = \$1,849.6 - \$7.80Q + \$0.20Q^{1.5}$. If the cost of capital is 15 percent, is this plant the wealth-maximizing one if its construction cost is \$6.4 million?

13. Calculate, using the data in Case 11, the present value of performing no additional maintenance at the company's plant under the assumption that output will fall by 8 percent per year. Explain why this level of maintenance is not wealth-maximizing.

14. Continuing with Case 11, another maintenance service company has offered a contract that costs $2,000 per week and guarantees that output will fall by no more than 1 percent per year. This contract increases in cost by 12 percent per year. Should the company purchase this contract rather than one of the other two contracts? Explain why.

# 10

# *Monopoly and Monopolistic Competition*

Monopoly and monopolistic competition are price-searcher markets. A firm in a price-searcher market cannot set its price by referring to a market price established by the interaction of supply and demand in impersonal competition among firms. Some price-searcher firms market differentiated products. Others produce products that have close substitutes, but there are only a few firms in the market, and their rivals are immediately identifiable. A monopolized product has no close substitutes. Management must search for its profit-maximizing price.

Monopoly and monopolistic competition are relatively rare market structures. The principal reason for their rarity is to be found in the efforts of firms to discover and exploit profit opportunities in a technologically dynamic world. Research and development efforts to create substitutes for a monopolized product are likely to be relatively profitable. Market research designed to find profitable markets also contributes to the evolution of monopoly and monopolistic competition into oligopoly. Oligopoly is the dominant market structure in the manufacturing sector of the U.S. economy. Monopoly and competition are primarily studied because they are at the extremes of the possible range of market structures. The behavior of firms in monopolistic competition and oligopoly contains common elements with these simpler market structures. For example, monopolistic competition is primarily a transitional market structure as a product group, which started out as a monopoly held by an innovating firm, evolves into an oligopoly.

Section 10.1 discusses the nature of monopoly. The next two sections are devoted to finding the profit-maximizing price and output for a monopoly. Sections 10.4 and 10.5 discuss natural monopoly and price discrimination. In section 10.6, the theory of monopolistic competition is presented. In section 10.7, monopolistic competition is treated as a transitory stage in the evolution of a new product group into an oligopoly. Oligopoly is discussed in chapter 11. The case at the end of the chapter describes applying the principles of monopoly pricing to determining whether a firm should close one of its plants to increase its profits.

## 10.1 *The Nature of Monopoly*

A firm is a monopoly when no other firm produces a close substitute for its product. The monopolist's product is not simply a variation of a good or service produced by other firms, as is the case for automobiles, toothpaste, or television sets. When several firms produce branded products that differ in several of their characteristics but all serve the same purpose, the products are said to be differentiated. A monopolist does not produce a differentiated product but rather one for which no close substitutes exist.

With no direct competition for the available market, a monopoly is free to search for the market price that maximizes its profits without having to consider the prices or competitive reactions of other firms. This search for maximum profits is not free of constraints. The management of a monopoly must still deal with the reactions of firms producing complementary products to its pricing and marketing policies. However, since no other firm produces a close substitute for its product, management can focus its attention on its demand and production costs.

***Determining Whether a Firm Is a Monopoly.*** When estimating its demand function, the monopolist can determine whether there are good substitutes for its product by including the prices or sales of possible substitutes in its demand function. The firm can act as a monopolist if it has not found other products with sufficiently high cross-elasticities of demand to warrant considering them as substitutes. The cross-elasticity of demand is measured, using the estimated demand function, as

$$E_{xy} = (\% \text{ change in monopolist's } Q)/(\% \text{ change in other firm's } P)$$

In a cross-elasticity study, the monopolist's sales volume is the dependent variable of the demand function. The independent variables include the prices of possible substitutes, the prices of the monopolist's product and complementary products, consumer incomes, and other variables believed to be related to the level of demand. The demand function is estimated using multiple regression, and the statistically insignificant variables are removed from the equation. If the statistically significant variables include the prices of possible substitutes, the cross-elasticity of demand is calculated for specified prices of the monopolist's product and the possible substitute products. If no product has a sufficiently high cross-elasticity to warrant its consideration as a close substitute, the firm can act as a monopolist and set its price and other marketing policies to maximize its profits.

What constitutes, however, a "sufficiently high cross-elasticity"? Is it $E_{xy} = +5$, or $+1$, or $+0.5$, or $+0.1$? Unfortunately, there is no pat answer. This determination is a matter of managerial judgment. The cross-elasticity formula can be rewritten as

(% change in monopolist's $Q$) = ($E_{xy}$)(% change in other firm's price)

$E_{xy} = +5$ would signal the existence of a substitute product because a 1 percent change in its price would result in a 5 percent change in sales and lead management to conclude that it is not monopolist. But what about $E_{xy} = +0.2$? If a 10 percent price change results in a 2 percent sales change, is this an unrelated product? This level of consumer reaction may be within the normal, unexplained fluctuations in consumer demand.

*Elasticity of the Monopolist's Demand Curve.* From the consumer's point of view, no good or service is so inherently unique or valuable that substitutes do not exist. The extent to which consumers are willing to substitute other goods for the monopolist's good depends on its price. At relatively high prices, consumers will likely find a wider range of substitutes for the monopolist's product. The monopolist, like all firms, must compete for the consumer's limited income. The elasticity of the monopolist's demand curve depends on the extent to which consumers are willing to substitute unrelated goods or services for its product. As the percentage of income spent on the monopolist's product increases, the demand curve will become more elastic because consumers will have stronger incentives to find alternatives. Even though there may be no close substitutes in a functional sense, consumers will become increasingly willing to seek alternatives as the price of the monopolist's good rises. The result is an elastic demand curve above some price for the monopolist's product.

As price increases, the elasticity of demand increases because consumers prefer to use their limited incomes to buy other goods and services. The level and elasticity of the monopolist's demand curve also depend on the prices of complementary goods and services. Relatively long-lived complementary durable goods can influence the extent to which the monopolist's product will remain a necessity in the consumer's lifestyle. Cars getting 5 miles to the gallon were not immediately junked when the price of gasoline doubled and tripled. These low-mileage cars, which are complementary goods to gasoline, maintained the demand for gasoline even though its price had risen sharply. If its product is used by the producers of a complementary good or service, management cannot ignore the impact of its price on their prices. A jet fuel monopoly could not ignore the effect of jet fuel prices on airline fares. A higher price for jet fuel leading to higher air fares and fewer flights will result in a lower demand for jet fuel. Thus, the existence of complementary goods constrains the price policy and other marketing policies of monopolists.

*Transitory Nature of Monopoly.* Will a monopoly, once created, remain a monopoly for a long time? In spite of marketing folklore and the rhetoric of some politicians, monopolies are rare. This primarily results from the research and development or marketing activities of other firms that are attracted by the monopolist's profits to create substitutes for its product. These attempts to earn economic profits by creating close substitutes for the monopolist's product occur even when the monopolist has patent protection or an exclusive franchise. This is an economic fact of life that the managements of monopolies must accept as part of living in a free society, although monopolists are by no means so high-minded as to forego attempts to use the powers of government to preserve their monopolies. Patents, copyrights, and legal protection of trade secrets are means by which firms can use the regulatory powers of government to lengthen the life of their monopoly.

New technologies for producing or improving existing goods are unlikely to lead to monopoly because the older technologies will provide close substitutes. A monopoly is generally the result of developing a revolutionary new technology or consumer good. It takes time for other firms to develop their version of a radically different new product. The faster other firms try to create and market substitutes for a new product, the higher their production and distribution costs and the less likely their substitute product will be competitive. They will stretch their research and development program over several months or even years to keep their costs down. This leaves the firm that developed the new technology with a monopoly for some period of time during which it can search for price and marketing policies that maximize its profits and prolong its monopoly.

## 10.2 *Profit Maximization — Graphical Method*

Finding the firm's profit-maximizing output requires that marginal revenue be equated to its marginal cost. For a competitive firm, marginal revenue equals price because management believes that it cannot influence the market price by changing its output. The monopolist, however, is the only producer in the market. Its demand curve is the downward-sloping market demand curve. If the monopolist produces more output, the market price must be reduced to sell it.

*Marginal Revenue.* Marginal revenue is the change in total revenue, $TR$, when the firm sells one more unit of output. Marginal revenue can be expressed as

$$MR = P_1 - (P_0 - P_1)Q_0 \qquad \text{(10.1)}$$

where $P_0$ and $Q_0$ are the original price and output before reducing price to $P_1$ to sell one more unit. Area $A_1$ in Figure 10.1 is the addition to $TR$ from selling one more unit and is equal to $P_1 \times 1 = P_1$. Area $A_2$ is the reduction in $TR$ resulting from reducing the price of $Q_0$ units of output from $P_0$ to $P_1$. The net effect of these two changes determines whether $MR$ will be positive or negative. For demand curve $D_0$, if $Q_0 = 10$, $P_0 = \$30$ and $P_1 = \$29.50$, then $MR = \$29.50 - (\$30 - \$29.50)(10) =$

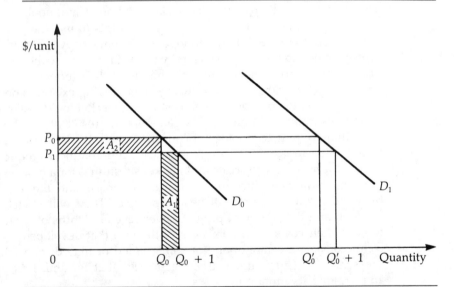

**Figure 10.1   Shifts in Demand, Marginal Revenue, and Demand Elasticity**

Reducing price from $P_0$ to $P_1$ on demand curve $D_0$ adds area $A_1$ to $TR$ from sale of the last unit of output. Area $A_2$ is the reduction in $TR$ from reducing price to $P_1$ on the $Q_0$ units of output sold before the price reduction. If $A_1$ is greater than $A_2$, $TR$ increases and demand is elastic. As the demand curve shifts to the right, area $A_2$ increases and $A_1$ remains unchanged; thus, $TR$ eventually decreases and demand becomes inelastic.

$29.50 - $5.00 = $24.50. Since *MR* is positive when price is reduced, demand is elastic. If for demand curve $D_1$, $Q'_0 = 100$ and the two prices are $30 and $29.50, *MR* = $29.50 - ($30 - $29.50)(100) = $29.50 - $50.00 = $-20.50. Demand is inelastic because the $0.50 price reduction resulted in a decrease in *TR*. In terms of Figure 10.1, area $A_1$ is unchanged but area $A_2$ is much larger for $D_1$ than for $D_0$, and *MR* is thereby reduced. For any straight-line demand curve, *MR* is positive as output increases from zero because $A_2$ is small relative to $A_1$. As price is reduced, $A_2$ rises because its base ($Q_0$) becomes larger. Area $A_1$ becomes smaller because its height ($P_1$) is declining. The net effect is to reduce *MR*. Eventually $A_2$ becomes larger than $A_1$ and *MR* is negative. This occurs at prices less than $P_0$ in Figure 10.2.

The *MR* curve has the same vertical intercept as the demand curve and twice its slope. At every price the *MR* curve lies halfway between the vertical axis and demand curve. If the demand curve is $P = a - bQ$,

$$TR = PQ = aQ - bQ^2$$

$$MR = dTR/dQ = a - 2bQ$$

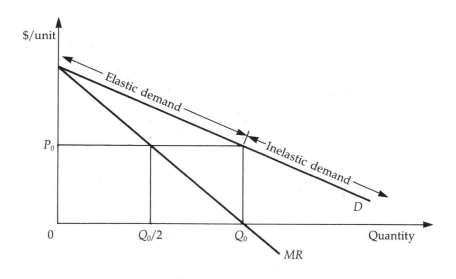

**Figure 10.2  Marginal Revenue and Demand Elasticity**

The *MR* curve is half the distance between the demand curve and vertical axis. If demand is elastic, *MR* is positive and above the horizontal axis. If demand is inelastic, *MR* is negative and below the horizontal axis.

In Figure 10.2, at $P_0$ the quantity demanded is $Q_0$, and the $MR$ curve passes through $(Q_0/2, P_0)$. The $MR$ curve is the straight line from the vertical intercept, $(0, a)$, through this point.

*Profit-Maximizing Output and Price.* The monopolist will not set its price where demand is inelastic. Setting price where demand is inelastic means that the monopolist has failed to exploit an opportunity to raise its price. When demand is inelastic, an increase in price will increase total revenue. At the higher price, output will be lower. Since marginal cost is always positive, producing less output means total cost must fall. Profits must increase if $TR$ goes up and $TC$ declines. However, if demand is elastic, an increase in price reduces $TR$. As long as $TR$ declines by less than $TC$, profits will rise. When demand becomes sufficiently elastic, $TR$ will decline by more than $TC$ and profits will fall.

The profit-maximizing output is where $MR = MC$. This is output $Q_1$ in Figure 10.3. At $Q_0$, $MR = MC$, but $MC$ has always been above $MR$, and profits are minimized at $Q_0$. Between $Q_0$ and $Q_1$, $MC < MR$, and every unit of output adds more to $TR$ than to $TC$. Profits are increasing. At $Q_1$, profits are maximized; producing more than $Q_1$ will result in $MC > MR$. When $MC > MR$, $TC$ is increasing faster than $TR$, and profits are declining. The maximum price the monopolist can charge for $Q_1$ is $P_1$. The monopolist cannot arbitrarily set both price and output. It can determine its profit-maximizing output, or it can find the profit-maximizing price and set output to meet the quantity demanded at that price. For $Q_1$ to be profit-maximizing, price must be greater than $AVC$. At $Q_1$, $AVC = V_1$, which is less than $P_1$; thus, $Q_1$ is profit-maximizing. The monopolist's profit is found using the $ATC$ curve. At $Q_1$, $ATC$ is $C_1$. In Figure 10.3, $P_1 - C_1$ is negative, and the monopolist has a loss. The total loss is $(P_1 - C_1)Q_1$, which is the shaded area in Figure 10.3. There is no reason why a monopolist should always earn a profit.

# 10.3  *Profit Maximization Using Calculus*

Calculus is used to calculate the profit-maximizing price and output for a monopolist if estimates of the relevant demand, production, and cost functions are available. This use of calculus is illustrated in the three examples that follow. In the first example, a statistical cost study of the firm's total cost function has been performed by its accounting staff. The second example is based on the firm's engineering staff's having prepared a statistical study of its production function, with labor as the variable factor of production. In the third example, the change in profits from increasing advertising expenditures is calculated.

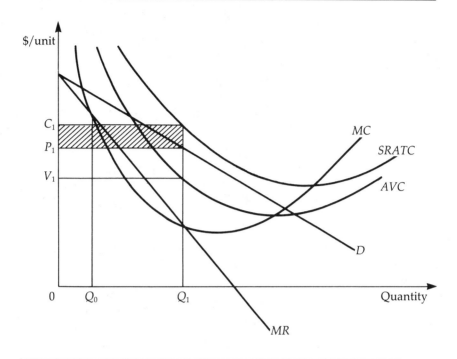

**Figure 10.3   Profit-Maximizing Output and Price**

The monopolist maximizes profit at output $Q_1$, where the $MR$ curve intersects its $MC$ curve and the $MC$ curve cuts the $MR$ curve from below. The
monopolist's price is found on the demand curve above $Q_1$ and its average
total cost on the $SRATC$ curve above $Q_1$. The monopolist is incurring a loss
in this graph because $C_1$ is greater than $P_1$.

Calculation of the short-run profit-maximizing output and price
assumes that the level of the monopolist's demand curve is independent
of the price set by the monopolist. There are no complementary goods
whose prices or sales depend on the monopolist's price. Also, the rate
at which other firms will engage in substitute-creating research and
development marketing activities is independent of the monopolist's
price. Under these assumptions, the monopolist can estimate an unambiguous demand curve for its product.

**EXAMPLE 10.1.**   The demand function is $P = 50 - Q$, and the
total cost function is $TC = 10 + 6Q + Q^2$. $Q$ is output per hour. Fixed
costs are \$10 per hour and $TVC = 6Q + Q^2$. To calculate the profit-
maximizing output, compute $MR$ and $MC$, equate them, and solve for
$Q$.

$$TR = PQ = 50Q - Q^2$$

$$MR = dTR/dQ = 50 - 2Q$$

$$MC = dTC/dQ = 6 + 2Q$$

$$MR = MC \Rightarrow 50 - 2Q = 6 + 2Q \Rightarrow Q = 11 \text{ units}$$

The profit-maximizing price is found by substituting $Q = 11$ into the demand function and solving for $P$.

$$P = 50 - 11 = \$39 \text{ per unit}$$

Total profit is the difference between $TR$ and $TC$ when $Q = 11$.

$$TR = (\$39)(11) = \$429 \text{ per hour}$$

$$TC = 10 + (6 \times 11) + (11)^2 = \$197 \text{ per hour}$$

$$\Pi = TR - TC = \$429 - \$197 = \$232 \text{ per hour}$$

An alternative is to calculate the profit function, find its derivatives, and check its second derivative to determine which output is profit-maximizing. Using the above $TR$ and $TC$ functions,

$$\Pi = 50Q - Q^2 - 10 - 6Q - Q^2 = -2Q^2 + 44Q - 10$$

$$d\Pi/dQ = -4Q + 44$$

$$d^2\Pi/dQ^2 = -4$$

Therefore, the value of $Q$ will be a maximum because $d^2\Pi/dQ^2$ is negative. Setting the first derivative equal to zero yields

$$-4Q + 44 = 0 \Rightarrow Q = 11 \text{ units}$$

Checking the second derivative was not important in this example because there was only one $Q$ value. If the $TC$ function is a third degree polynomial or the demand function contains a $Q^2$ term, check the sign of the second derivative.

**EXAMPLE 10.2.** A statistically fitted $TC$ function does not permit direct calculation of the profit-maximizing factor quantities. This example illustrates calculating the profit-maximizing output when labor is the variable factor and there are fixed proportions between output and the quantities of various raw materials. The short-run production function is $Q = 4L^{0.5}$, the wage rate is $6.00 per hour, and raw materials cost $7.00 per unit of output. The $MPL$ and $MC$ are

$$MPL = dQ/dL = 2/L^{0.5}$$

$$MC = w/MPL + \$7.00 = \$6.00/(2/L^{0.5}) + \$7.00$$

$$MC = \$3L^{0.5} + \$7$$

The demand function is $P = 70 - 0.5Q$ and $TR = 70Q - 0.5Q^2$. $MR$ in terms of the quantity labor is found by calculating $dTR/dQ$ and substituting the production function for $Q$.

$$MR = 70 - Q = 70 - 4L^{0.5}$$

The quantity of labor maximizing the monopolist's profit is found by equating $MR$ to $MC$ and solving for $L$.

$$70 - 4L^{0.5} = 3L^{0.5} + 7$$

$$L^{0.5} = 63/7 = 9 \text{ and } L = 81 \text{ workers}$$

Substituting $L = 81$ into the production function yields a profit-maximizing output of $4(81)^{0.5} = 36$ units. Substituting $Q = 36$ into the demand function yields a price of $P = 70 - 0.5(36) = \$52$. Total revenue is $(\$52)(36) = \$1,872$ per hour. Total variable cost of $738 equals labor costs of $486 (81 workers at $6/hour) plus raw material costs of $252 (36 units at $7 per unit). If fixed costs are $500 per hour, total cost is $738 + \$500 = \$1,238$ per hour. The monopolist's total profit is $1,872 per hour $-$ \$1,238 per hour $= \$634$ per hour.

**EXAMPLE 10.3.** Monopolists devote resources to advertising and other sales promotion policies intended to shift their demand curves to the right. This example illustrates calculating the profits from increased advertising. The demand function is $P = 220 - Q + 15A$ where $A$ is the number of its television commercials per day. The firm airs two commercials per day at a cost of $1,000 each. The demand function is $P = 220 - Q + 15(2) = 250 - Q$. The total cost function is $TC = 4,600 + 10Q + Q^2$. Total cost includes manufacturing, marketing, distribution and administrative costs, but not advertising costs. $Q$ is output per day. The profit-maximizing output is 60 units per day.

$$\Pi = 250Q - Q^2 - 4,600 - 10Q - Q^2 = 240Q - 2Q^2 - 4,600$$

$$d\Pi/dQ = 240 - 4Q = 0 \Rightarrow Q = 60$$

$$d^2\Pi/dQ^2 = -4.$$

Therefore $Q = 60$ is a maximum. The market clearing price is $P = 250 - 60 = \$190$ per unit. Daily profits are $240(60) - 2(60)^2 - 4,600 - 2(1,000) = \$600$.

The advertising agency recommends that the number of commercials be increased to six per day ($A = 6$). Television stations will run six commercials per day for $5,500, which will shift the demand curve to $P = 220 - Q + 15(6) = 310 - Q$. The profit-maximizing output is now 75 units per day.

$$\Pi = 310Q - Q^2 - 4,600 - 10Q - Q^2 = 300Q - 2Q^2 - 4,600$$
$$d\Pi/dQ = 300 - 4Q = 0 \Rightarrow Q = 75$$
$$d^2\Pi/dQ^2 = -4$$

Therefore $Q = 75$ is a maximum. The market clearing price is $P = 310 - 75 = \$235$ per unit. Profits are $300(75) - 2(75)^2 - 4,600 - 5,500 = \$1,150$ per day. Management should implement the advertising agency's recommendation because profits will increase by $550 per day.

## 10.4  *Natural Monopoly*

Monopoly exists when one firm produces a product with no close substitutes. Monopolies generally exist because of government protection against competition (from patents and franchises, for instance), exclusive ownership of a resource, or one firm's being the lowest-cost producer of the product. The firm is a natural monopoly when minimizing average cost requires that there be only one firm in the industry.

Natural monopoly exists when the demand curve intersects the *LRAC* curve to the left of its minimum point. This situation is illustrated in Figure 10.4, in which the demand curve intersects the *LRAC* curve at output $q_0$ and long-run average cost $C_0$. If the firm builds the plant that produces $q_0$ at the lowest possible *ATC*, its cost curves are the dashed-line curves in Figure 10.4. The monopoly's profit-maximizing output is at $q_1$ (where $MR = MC$), and its price is at $P_1$ on the demand curve. Its *SRATC* of producing $q_1$ is $C_1$, and its profit is $(P_1 - C_1)q_1$.

*Economic Profits and Entry of a Rival.*  With the monopoly earning an economic profit, another firm may be tempted to enter the industry. If the potential entrant builds a larger plant than one producing $q_0$ at *LRAC* $C_0$, its short-run costs will be higher than those of the monopolist. This supposition is illustrated in Figure 10.5, showing that the new firm builds the plant producing $q_2$ at $C_2$ *LRAC* and has *SRATC$_2$* as its average cost curve. The monopoly can reduce its price to $P_0$ and earn a normal profit if it has 100 percent of the market. The new entrant

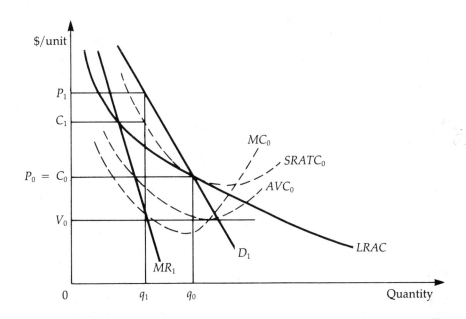

**Figure 10.4   Natural Monopoly**

The firm is a natural monopoly if the demand curve for its product intersects the *LRAC* curve where *LRAC* is declining. If the firm builds the plant that produces $q_0$ at minimum average cost, its *MC* curve will be $MC_0$. Its profit-maximizing output is $q_1$, where $MR_1$ and $MC_0$ intersect and its price is $P_1$ on the demand curve. $SRATC_0$ is the short-run average cost curve for this plant, and the firm's total profit is $(P_1 - C_1)q_1$. The firm would break even if it were forced to lower its price to $P_0$ to keep a rival from entering the industry by producing a close substitute product.

will have an economic loss at $P_0$ equal to $(P_0 - C_3)$ even if it can obtain 100 percent of the market. If the new firm sets a price like $P_2$, it still would not have lower average costs than the existing firm because $SRATC_2$ lies above $SRATC_0$ at $q_1$, the quantity demanded at $P_2$ with demand curve $D_1$. A similar situation exists if the potential entrant builds a plant smaller than the one at $SRATC_0$. Its plant will have higher costs than the existing firm's.

*Wealth Maximization and Maintaining a Monopoly.* The only way a new firm could enter the industry would be for it to build the plant at $SRATC_0$ and set its price below $V_0$ in Figure 10.4. At this price both firms would have a negative cash flow, which would ultimately bankrupt the firm with the smaller financial resources. Thus, the new firm would need to have greater financial resources than the existing firm. Even

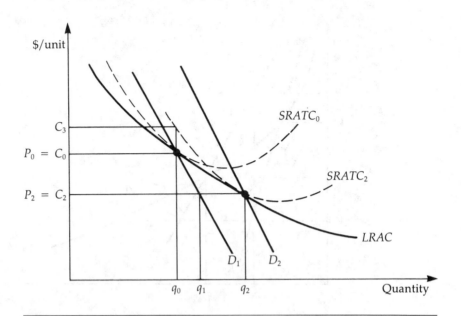

**Figure 10.5  Alternative Plant Capacities and Costs**

Assume that the initial firm in the industry builds the plant with $SRATC_0$. Another firm will not find it profitable to build the larger plant with $SRATC_2$ as long as demand is at $D_1$, because it will always have higher costs than the initial firm. If demand shifts to $D_2$, another firm could build the plant with $SRATC_2$ and have lower costs than the initial firm and possibly drive it out of business.

if the potential new entrant can drive the existing firm into bankruptcy, the victory may not be wealth-maximizing. The new entrant would need to compare the present value of its losses during the price war with the present value of its profits after the existing firm is bankrupt. Moreover, the new entrant may be financially weakened to the point that another, well-financed firm could buy the bankrupt firm's plant and then keep price low enough to drive the new entrant into bankruptcy.

The likelihood of a potential new entrant's increasing its wealth by entering a natural monopoly is generally so low that existing firms are unlikely to be challenged. This conclusion, however, is based on the assumption that the demand curve does not shift to the right in the future. If the demand curve shifts to $D_2$ shortly after the new firm enters the industry, its plant at $SRATC_2$ would be of lower cost. This cost advantage would reduce the losses required to drive the existing firm into bankruptcy. The cost advantage may also increase the profits of the new firm after it has established itself as a monopolist. The new entrant would be relatively protected from another firm's buying the bankrupt firm's plant and continuing the price war because the plant at $SRATC_0$ is no longer an economical plant. Expanding the plant at $SRATC_0$ to produce $q_2$ is unlikely to yield an average cost curve below $SRATC_2$ and probably will yield an $SRATC$ curve lying above $SRATC_2$. The reason is that the existing plant is a fixed factor that imposes constraints on the expansion. In general, the existence of constraints imposes costs on the firm relative to when it is unconstrained. The $LRAC$ curve applies where there are no constraints on the new plant's design and the lowest-cost combination of resources can be used.

**EXAMPLE 10.4.** If $LRAC = 1,700 - 80q + q^2$ and the demand curve is $P = 1,900 - 50q$, is this industry likely to be a natural monopoly? At the intersection of the $LRAC$ and demand curves, $P = LRAC$.

$$1,900 - 50q = 1,700 - 80q + q^2$$
$$q^2 - 30q - 200 = 0$$

Applying the quadratic formula yields $q = 35.62$ as the output where the two curves intersect. This output yields an $LRAC$ of $119.18 at the intersection of the two curves. To determine if the $LRAC$ curve is downward sloping, take its derivative, substitute $q = 35.62$ into the derivative, and see if the derivative is negative. Since $dLRAC/dq = -80 + 2q = -80 + 2(35.62) = -8.76$, the demand curve intersects the $LRAC$ curve where it is downward sloping. The industry is a natural monopoly.

## 10.5 *Price Discrimination*

A profitable marketing policy for a monopolist is price discrimination. Price discrimination occurs when two customers are charged different prices for the same product, or the same customer pays a different price for additional units. Price discrimination is rare in competitive industries because the customer paying the higher price has the alternative of seeking another seller who will charge the lower price. In competition, price differences primarily result from consumers' incurring different transaction and transportation costs when buying from one firm than from its competitors. Price discrimination can be profitable for a monopoly because consumers cannot buy a similar product from another firm.

*Conditions for Profitable Price Discrimination.* Two conditions are required for profitable price discrimination. The first is that consumers buying at low prices cannot resell to others who are charged a higher price. This separation of consumers can result from the relatively high transaction costs associated with resales of consumer goods. Automobiles, television sets, and appliances are examples of consumer goods with high transaction costs for resales, although they are not sold by monopolists. Perishable products and services provided directly to the consumer are expensive or impossible to resell. Medical services provided to one patient cannot be resold to another. Sometimes price discrimination is facilitated by government regulations, such as prohibitions against selling electricity across lot lines by anyone other than the local franchised electric utility.

The second condition is that the elasticity of demand in each market is different. The profit-maximizing price is higher in the market with the *relatively* more inelastic demand. One market has a more inelastic demand than the other when $|E_p| = 1.6$ and $|E_p| = 1.2$. The market with $|E_p| = 1.2$ has the more inelastic demand. For example, the only electronic repair service in a town may have a local monopoly because the nearest firm providing the same service is 60 miles away. Customers who rarely leave town have a more inelastic demand for the service than customers who commute to work in the city, where there are several similar businesses. If the manager knows the likelihood that the customer may travel to the city frequently, the monopolist may be able to practice price discrimination. People who rarely leave the town are unlikely to make a 120-mile round trip if they are charged $10 more on a repair bill than the going rate in the city.

**EXAMPLE 10.5.**   Assume that a monopolist can divide its market into two segments with different demand elasticities and identify which segment is appropriate for any consumer. Demand in one market is $P_1 = 150 - 2Q_1$ and demand in the other is $P_2 = 100 - 0.5Q_2$. Total revenue in the combined markets is

$$TR = P_1Q_1 + P_2Q_2 = (150 - 2Q_1)Q_1 + (100 - 0.5Q_2)Q_2$$

Because the same product is sold in both markets, there is only one total cost function. Assume that it is

$$TC = 2,500 + 20(Q_1 + Q_2) + 0.10(Q_1 + Q_2)^2$$

where fixed costs are $2,500. The total profit function is

$$\Pi = TR - TC = 150Q_1 - 2Q_1^2 + 100\,Q_2 - 0.5Q_2^2 - 2,500 - 20Q_1$$
$$- 20Q_2 - 0.1Q_1^2 - 0.2Q_1Q_2 - 0.1Q_2^2$$

To maximize the firm's profits, take the partial derivatives of the total profit function, set them equal to zero, and solve the two equations for $Q_1$ and $Q_2$. Since the partial derivatives are the marginal profits in each market, profits are maximized when the two marginal profits are zero.

$$\partial\Pi/\partial Q_1 = 150 - 4Q_1 - 20 - 0.2Q_1 - 0.2Q_2$$
$$\partial\Pi/\partial Q_1 = 130 - 4.2Q_1 - 0.2Q_2 = 0$$
$$Q_1 = (130 - 0.2Q_2)/4.2$$
$$\partial\Pi/\partial Q_2 = 100 - Q_2 - 20 - 0.2Q_1 - 0.2Q_2 = 80 - 1.2Q_2 - 0.2Q_1 = 0$$
$$Q_1 = (80 - 1.2Q_2)/0.2$$

Equating the two expressions for $Q_1$ yields

$$(130 - 0.2Q_2)/4.2 = (80 - 1.2Q_2)/0.2 \Rightarrow Q_2 = 62$$
$$Q_1 = [130 - 0.2(62)]/4.2 \Rightarrow Q_1 = 28$$

Therefore, the firm's profits are maximized if it sells 28 units in market one and 62 units in market two. Price in each market is found by substituting these quantities back into the demand functions.

$$P_1 = 150 - 2Q_1 = 150 - 2(28) = \$94$$
$$P_2 = 100 - 0.5Q_2 = 100 - 0.5(62) = \$69$$

The point-elasticity of demand at each of these prices is found from the formula $E = (\partial Q/\partial P)(P/Q)$. To find these derivatives, the demand functions are rewritten as $Q_1 = 75 - 0.5P_1$ and $Q_2 = 200 - 2P_2$.

$$E_1 = (-0.5)(94/28) = -1.68$$
$$E_2 = (-2)(69/62) = -2.23$$

Market one has the more inelastic demand and the higher market price. By practicing price discrimination, the firm's profit is

$$\Pi = (94 \times 28) + (69 \times 62) - 2{,}500 - (20 \times 90) - (0.1 \times 90^2)$$
$$\Pi = \$1{,}800$$

If the firm did not separate its customers into two groups, its demand curve would be found by horizontally adding the two demand curves. This procedure is illustrated in Figure 10.6. When price is between

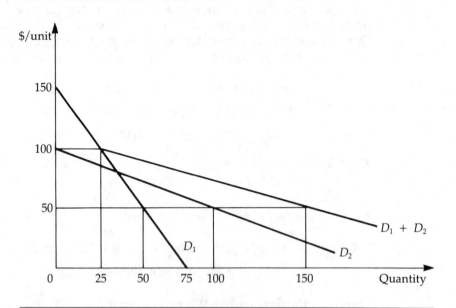

**Figure 10.6   Horizontal Addition of Demand Curves**

To add demand curves horizontally, find the quantity demanded on each demand curve at each price and then add together the two quantities. At a price of $50, 50 units are demanded on $D_1$ and 100 units on $D_2$ for a total of 150 units on the $D_1 + D_2$ demand curve.

$100 and $150, the demand of the second ($D_2$) group of customers is zero. At a price of $100, 25 units are demanded by customer group one and nothing by the second group. At a price of $50, $D_1$ is 50 units and $D_2$ is 100, for a total demand of 150 units. The slope of a straight line through these two points is $(100 - 50)/(25 - 150) = -0.4$. The equation of the line ($D_1 + D_2$) through these two points is $P = 110 - 0.4Q$ where $Q = Q_1 + Q_2$. Total revenue is $TR = 110Q - 0.4Q^2$ for outputs greater than 25 and $MR = 110 - 0.8Q$. Differentiating the total cost function yields a marginal cost function of

$$MC = 20 + 0.2Q$$

Setting *MR* equal to *MC* yields the profit-maximizing output if the firm doesn't practice price discrimination.

$$110 - 0.8Q = 20 + 0.2Q \Rightarrow Q = 90$$

Substituting $Q = 90$ into demand curve $D_1 + D_2$ yields

$$P = 110 - 0.4(90) = \$74$$

Total profit without price discrimination is

$$\Pi = (74 \times 90) - 2{,}500 - (20 \times 90) - (0.1 \times 90^2) = \$1{,}550$$

Therefore, price discrimination increases the firm's profits by $\$1{,}800 - \$1{,}550 = \$250$.

*Other Types of Price Discrimination.* Quantity discounts not related to differences in the costs of producing or selling the greater quantity are another form of price discrimination. For example, an electric utility may establish a rate schedule by which the incremental price falls as the quantity of electricity used (in KWH) rises. If the average residence uses 450 KWH per month, it may pay ($\$0.118 \times 400$ KWH) + ($\$0.092 \times 50$ KWH) = \$51.80 per month, or an average of $\$51.80/450 = \$0.115$ per KWH. If the average industrial customer purchases 25,000 KWH per month, it may pay \$1,413.20 per month, or an average of $\$1{,}413.20/25{,}000 = \$0.0565$ per KWH. The average rate for the industrial customer is lower even though the cost of service difference may be less than $\$0.115 - \$0.0565 = \$0.0585$ per KWH. The reason for the lower rate for industrial customers could be that their demand for electricity is more elastic than that of residential customers. Industrial customers are more likely to generate their own electricity or use some other source of energy than residential consumers. These substitutes make demand more elastic for industrial customers. The utility must also make sure that its residential customers cannot resell power to their neighbors to increase the quantity they use and lower their average rate.

Another form of price discrimination occurs when the firm sells more than one product. Tying contracts require the purchaser to buy certain supplies exclusively from the seller of a monopolized piece of equipment. The supplies are sold at a substantial markup over cost so that the seller earns larger profits from heavier uses of the equipment. The equipment is then priced as low as feasible to discourage research and development on the part of potential competitors and encourage its use by as many customers as possible. The results are higher profits than would be earned without the tying contract because it discriminates against the heaviest users who probably have fewer options. Smaller users could use hand methods or less sophisticated equipment. They buy the more advanced equipment because its cost is relatively low.

As the small firms grow, they will probably use the equipment more and find more uses for it. They end up with fewer choices as they grow and eventually become very profitable customers because the tying contract increases the monopolist's profits as utilization of the equipment rises.

*Role of High Transaction Costs.* The conditions for profitable price discrimination can sometimes be met by price-searcher firms that are not monopolists. High transaction costs can separate customers and keep them from reselling the product. Product modifications can differentiate products to make them appeal to different groups of consumers with different demand elasticities. For example, affluent consumers may be too busy and high-paid to do much comparison shopping, and have a relatively inelastic demand. Retired persons with more time may receive senior citizen discounts at off-peak-times or on bare-bones merchandise, with affluent consumers paying higher prices at prime times or for more stylish versions of the product. Low-income consumers may pay more for the same product at a neighborhood store than higher-income suburban consumers at a store owned by a chain. Higher-income consumers are more mobile and can afford to comparison shop.

## 10.6  *Monopolistic Competition*

Monopolistic competition can be a transitional stage in a new industry's evolution from a monopoly into an oligopoly. Its primary characteristics are differentiated products and each firm's ignoring the reactions of its rivals to its pricing and other marketing policies. This section discusses these characteristics and determination of price and output by firms in monopolistic competition.

*Product Differentiation.* There are few, if any, goods for which no good substitutes exist. On the other hand, relatively few goods are perfect substitutes. Most consumer and many industrial products are differentiated. Differentiated products are substitutes for one another, but they are heterogeneous rather than homogeneous. Homogeneous products are perfect substitutes for each other. Heterogeneous products are unique, with differences intended to reduce the substitution of one firm's product for another's. The objective of product differentiation is to give the firm some measure of monopoly power over its price and to permit the firm to use advertising to increase the demand for its product. If the product differentiation strategy succeeds, the firm can earn higher profits.

When products are differentiated, firms producing close substitutes are aggregated into a product group. The cross-elasticity of demand can be used to determine which goods or services are in the same product group, although setting a value for the cross-elasticity above which the differentiated products are felt to be in the same product group is basically arbitrary. Most marketers look more to functional relationships than to cross-elasticities to determine whether two products are in the same product group. For example, the minitruck product group consists of firms producing trucks of a certain range of sizes, horsepowers, and other characteristics. Each brand of minitruck differs from the others. However, with respect to the functions of minitrucks, they differ less among themselves than from cars and other trucks. Hence, minitrucks are a distinguishable "product group." Other product groups can be distinguished within the automobile product group by their characteristics. The automobile product group is an aggregation of several distinctive product groups that are more related to one another than they are to aircraft or boats. Although the term *industry* is often treated as being synonymous with *product group,* economists generally reserve the term *industry* for use when the products are perfect or very close substitutes.

*Firm Ignores Rivals' Reactions to Its Policies.* In monopolistic competition, the firm sets its price and marketing policies by assuming that the other firms in its product group will not react by changing their present (or projected) price and marketing policies. Management treats its demand curve as being stable because it assumes that the other firms will not respond by changing their prices even though they produce products that are more or less good substitutes. This assumption differentiates monopolistic competition from oligopoly. In oligopoly, management explicitly takes the probable reactions of its competitors into consideration when setting its pricing or marketing policies.

The principal reason for management's ignoring the reactions of its competitors has to do with the size of the firm relative to the market. If there are many roughly equal-sized firms in the product group, each firm will produce a small percentage of total output. Because it produces a differentiated product, the firm must seek its own price but believes that the effect of the price it sets on each of its competitors will be so small that they will not react to it. The other firms may not react because random variations in consumer demand are greater than any impact on their demand resulting from changes in another firm's price. If random variations in consumer demand are relatively large, or if the product is a new one with only a small accumulation of data about consumer behavior, this assumption may be observed even if there are few firms in the product group. Another reason for management's assuming that other firms will not react to its policies is that new firms are entering the product group and old firms are leaving it. This makes it difficult to identify the potential responses of specific firms since there is insufficient experience on which to base a prediction. Management may also believe that the cost of the market research necessary to identify the probable responses of competitors is greater than the likely profit increases from better demand forecasts. Thus, management ignores the possible reactions of its competitors because doing so is cost-effective.

*Profit-Maximizing Price and Output.* Since the firm produces a differentiated product, its demand curve, *d*, in Figure 10.7 is downward sloping. This demand curve is elastic because the other products are good substitutes. Demand curve *d* will be more elastic than the demand curve for the product group. This difference in elasticities results from the lower degree of substitutability between the product group and other product groups than within it. A minitruck is not a good substitute for a family sedan; hence, minitrucks are in a different product group.

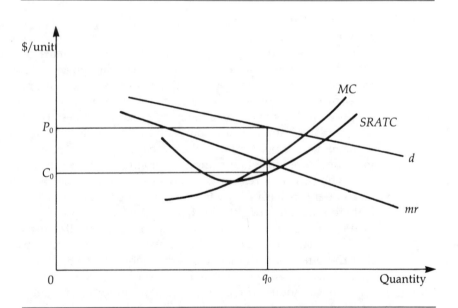

**Figure 10.7   Short-Run Profit Maximization in Monopolistic Competition**
The firm perceives its demand curve as *d* because there are substitutes for its differentiated product. The marginal revenue curve for *d* is *mr*. The firm maximizes its profits at output $q_0$ where *MC* and *mr* intersect and sets price $P_0$ on *d* over $q_0$. The firm's *SRATC* are at $C_0$ and its profits $(P_0 - C_0)q_0$.

The demand curve for minitrucks is less elastic than the demand curve for a specific make of minitruck because other makes are good substitutes.

Firms in monopolistic competition do not recognize the effects of their price changes on the other firms, nor do the other firms react to their policies in an identifiable manner. Management attempts to set its price, output, and other policies in the same way as a monopolist. To maximize short-run profits, the firm calculates marginal revenue from its demand function, which may include a term for the prices of substitute products. For example, its demand function may be $Q_x = a - bP_x + cP_y$ where $P_y$ is the average price of other goods in the product group. The important point is that the firm in monopolistic competition does not predict the level of $P_y$ on the basis of its price, $P_x$. However, once its competitors react to the firm's profit-maximizing price, its demand function shifts and management discovers that it has misjudged the market. This outcome leads to using the new value of $P_y$ observed in the market to calculate the firm's profit-maximizing price for the next planning period. But so long as the firm's management has not discovered the reasons for its failure to judge the market with acceptable accuracy and continues to attribute its errors to random fluctuations in market conditions, its estimate of $P_y$ will not be based on its price, $P_x$, but rather on only the past prices of other firms in the product group.

To find its profit-maximizing output and price, the firm finds the marginal revenue curve, *mr* in Figure 10.7, relative to demand curve *d*. The intersection of its *MC* curve and *mr* yields its profit-maximizing output, $q_0$, and price, $P_0$, on *d*. In this sense, the firm is acting as a monopolist over its differentiated product. Yet because the firm's demand curve is relatively elastic, its ability to earn an economic profit is limited by consumers substituting for its product others in the product group. In Figure 10.7, the firm expects to earn a substantial economic profit since its profit-maximizing price, $P_0$, is above its *SRATC* for output $q_0$, which is $C_0$. However, the firm probably has not determined its equilibrium price and output because subsequent reactions of its rivals to price $P_0$ will result in shifts in demand curve *d* that change the firm's profit-maximizing price. Once they observe $P_0$, the firm's rivals will find that they have not correctly estimated its price. They will recompute $P_y$ in their demand functions, which will shift their demand curves. Their profit-maximizing prices will likely change in response to $P_0$, shifting demand curve *d*. As a result, $P_0$ is an equilibrium price for the firm for only the relatively short period of time before the other firms recompute their profit-maximizing prices.

***Market Equilibrium.*** The difficulties of attaining an equilibrium in monopolistic competition should now be apparent. Management cannot correctly estimate its demand curve until it more accurately predicts the prices of other firms in the product group. Demand curve *d* is based on management's belief that its product differentiation and advertising policies have made its demand curve less than perfectly elastic. Because management does not take into consideration the reactions of the other firms, it cannot directly discover the true demand curve for its product, which can be estimated only if the firm accurately estimates the reactions of other firms to its price and marketing policies. Yet as long as the other firms are relatively numerous, new firms are entering the product group, and no institutions exist that permit the firms to signal their reactions to each other, accurate predictions of their competitors' responses are unlikely, and the assumptions of monopolistic competition will describe market conditions.

The equilibrium in Figure 10.7 is based on a fixed number of firms in the product group. If the firm is earning an economic profit equal to $(P_0 - C_0)q_0$, where $C_0$ is the *SRATC* of producing $q_0$, new firms may be attracted into the product group. The existence of economic profits is a signal that building a plant to produce another (differentiated) version of the group's product may be profitable. The entry of new firms will destabilize the product group and result in unpredicted shifts in the firm's demand curves. Even when new firms are not entering the industry, it is unlikely that the conditions for market equilibrium will be met for all firms at any time because of random shifts in consumer demand.

## 10.7   *The Transitory Nature of Monopolistic Competition*

The theory of monopolistic competition was developed in the 1930s to study markets for differentiated goods. Mass media advertising, brand names, and lifestyles built around new consumer goods had ushered in modern marketing concepts and systems. The dynamics of markets in which there is technical progress and creative marketing generally lead to monopolistic competition's being only a transitional stage in the evolution of a product group. Monopolistic competition is based on an assumption, unlikely to persist, about responses to the pricing policies of the producers of good substitutes. Ignoring the reactions of competitors to its policies for a sustained period of time implies that management will make a series of erroneous judgments about the demand for its product. But this is unlikely because business managers do not get or hold their jobs by consistently making mistakes. Modern marketing research techniques will be applied to find the reasons for demand forecasting errors. This market research is likely to lead to the development of strategies and information systems that reduce forecasting errors to an acceptable level. In the process, the firms' market research activities are likely to lead to a transition from monopolistic competition to oligopoly.

*Identification of Rivals and Predicting Their Reactions.* There may be a period of time when relatively good substitutes for a previously monopolized good or service are more or less constantly being introduced. This situation has likely existed in a number of high-tech product groups such as hand-held calculators and personal computers. Firms coming into competition with each other may not immediately recognize who are their rivals. Once they identify their rivals, it may take additional time before each firm understands how the others react to its pricing or marketing policies. In the absence of information on the behavior of the new rivals, the existing firms may make their price and other marketing decisions as if the new competitors did not exist. Once a firm in monopolistic competition identifies other firms in its product group, its management may assume that the competitors will adopt pricing and other policies similar to its own. At this point, the basic assumption of monopolistic competition is no longer viable and the product group becomes an oligopoly.

When the number of firms is expanding through imitation of a successful innovator, the leading firms may form a trade association or become a section of an existing trade association. A trade journal devoted to the product group may also be published. These are institutions that collect and convey information about developments in the product group. The statistical information they provide permits marketing research departments to develop better predictions of how the firm's rivals will behave. Speeches at trade association meetings, interviews of executives in trade journals, and editorials and articles prepared by the trade journal's staff all further the transition into oligopoly. This transition is likely to occur even if the number of firms is relatively large.

As a product group enters the transitional monopolistic competition phase, managements can expect a period of relatively chaotic pricing. Advertising, product quality, and other marketing policies may change frequently as the firms adapt to unpredictable shifts in demand. The length of time during which these unsettled market conditions will persist depends on a wide range of factors, many of which are probably specific to each product group. These chaotic conditions create incentives for the managers of firms, trade associations, and trade journals to develop, disseminate, and analyze information about market conditions.

*Technological Changes.* Production-oriented forces may also hasten the movement toward oligopoly. Many product groups have gone through a period of continued technological innovation once a new product has been successfully marketed. These innovations result in expanding markets as more consumers incorporate the product into their life. Production costs may fall with the development of new technologies and expanding markets. These innovations generally reduce production costs by making larger plants economical. If the rate at which the capacities of new plants with lower operating costs significantly exceeds the increase in the quantity demanded as prices fall, the number of firms in the product group will decline. This decrease can occur through bankruptcy or shutdown of firms that have become too high-cost or technologically unable to keep up with market developments. Decreasing numbers can also occur through acquisitions of weak or failing firms by successful firms, who may find acquiring these firms a lower-cost means of expanding their markets than augmenting their existing marketing staffs. With fewer firms in the product group, it is less costly for one firm to take into consideration the reactions of other firms, and the likelihood of making errors about their responses is further reduced.

## 10.8    *Summary*

Price-searcher firms can determine or influence the price of their product. Monopoly, monopolistic competition, and oligopoly are market structures under which the firms are price searchers. A monopoly produces a unique product for which there are no close substitutes. Its management does not consider the reactions of other firms to its pricing and marketing policies. A firm in monopolistic competition produces a differentiated product that has close, but not perfect, substitutes. The firm in monopolistic competition does not take into consideration the reactions of other firms to its pricing and other marketing policies. As a result, equilibrium is elusive in a product group subject to monopolistic competition, which eventually becomes an oligopoly in which the potential reactions of the firm's rivals are taken into consideration and become relatively predictable.

The three conditions for determining the price and output of a monopoly are (1) $MC = MR$, (2) $MC$ intersects $MR$ from below, and (3) $P > AVC$ at the profit-maximizing output. A monopoly's demand curve at its profit-maximizing price is always elastic because $MC$ is always positive and $MR$ is positive only when demand is elastic. A natural monopoly exists if one firm has lower average costs than if two or more firms share the market. Most monopolies are not natural monopolies, but rather result from government policies such as patents or public utility franchises. Price discrimination can be used by a monopolist to increase profits if groups of customers with different demand elasticities can be separated so that the group paying the lower price will not resell to the other.

In monopolistic competition, the demand curve for the product group is less elastic than the demand curve of the typical firm. The reason is that other goods are relatively poor substitutes for the product group's product, and products included in the product group are relatively good substitutes for each other. The firm in monopolistic competition equates marginal revenue from its perceived demand curve to its *MC* to find its profit-maximizing output and price. This price, however, is unlikely to be an equilibrium price for a long period of time. The firm's rivals are likely to change their prices in response to the firm's price, whereas the firm sets its price on the assumption than its rivals will not respond to its price. Once its rivals change their prices, the firm will reestimate its demand curve and change its price.

Monopoly and monopolistic competition are likely to be transitory, early phases in the evolution of a new industry. The creation of substitutes for the monopolist's product generally ends the monopoly phase. Management's responses to errors in forecasting demand, resulting from ignoring its rivals' responses to its price and other marketing policies, generally end the monopolistic competition phase. Oligopoly is the normal end result of the evolution of a new industry.

## CASE 12   Should a Plant Be Closed?

This case discusses the impact on the price and output of a product produced by an industry that is monopolized through a merger. The increase in profits from monopolization is also calculated. The case concludes with determining whether profits would be further increased by closing one of the monopolist's plants and producing the profit-maximizing output for the remaining plants.

### The Assignment

Your company is acquiring its five competitors. The merged company will be a monopoly. There has been a substantial decrease in demand for the industry's product because a superior substitute has been developed for one of its uses. No close substitutes exist for your product in the remainder of its uses. Since three of the firms have filed for bankruptcy, the Justice Department is not opposing the mergers. You have detailed accounting and other information about the companies to be acquired. Their plants have essentially the same production and cost functions as yours. The merged company will have six plants — four in St. Louis, one in Columbus, and one near Dallas. The boss wants you to determine whether one of the St. Louis plants should be closed.

## Market Price and Profit Prior to the Merger

Prior to the merger, none of the companies acted as if it could significantly influence the price of the product. The firms submitted sealed bids for the several hundred contracts up for bid each year. The industry's demand curve is $P = 983.8 - 0.5Q$ where $Q$ is output per day. For the typical plant, $AVC = 190 + 0.6q$ and $MC = 190 + 1.2q$, where $q$ is its daily output. When the industry was competitive, $MC$ was set equal to price, solved for $q$, and $q$ was multiplied by 6 to find the industry's supply curve. Equating $MC$ to $P$ yields $P = 190 + 1.2q$, and a firm supply curve of $q = (P - 190)/1.2$. Industry supply is $Q = 6q$, or $Q = 5P - 950$.

Equating demand and supply yields the market-clearing price if the industry were not merged into one company. Substituting the demand function for $P$ in the supply function yields

$$Q = 5(983.8 - 0.5Q) - 950$$

$$3.5Q = 3,969 \Rightarrow Q = 1,134 \text{ units per day}$$

$$P = 983.8 - 0.5(1,134) = \$416.80 \text{ per unit}$$

The typical plant produced one-sixth of industry demand or $1,134/6 = 189$ units per day. $TR = \$416.80 \times 189 = \$78,775.20$, $AVC = 190 + 0.6(189) = \$303.40$ per unit and $TVC = \$303.40 \times 189 = \$57,343.50$. The cash fixed costs of production, marketing, and administration were \$18,600 per day. Profit was \$2,831.70 before depreciation of \$7,650 per day. The typical firm lost \$4,818.30 per day. From the demand curve, $dP/dQ = -0.5$ and $dQ/dP = -2$. The elasticity of demand was $E_P = (-2)(416.80)/(1,134) = -0.735$. When it was competitive, the industry was unable to raise prices to obtain the increase in $TR$ resulting from the inelastic demand curve. One incentive for the firms to merge is to take advantage of the inelastic demand by raising price.

## Market Price and Profit After the Merger

After the merger, demand and supply will no longer determine the industry's price. Price will be determined by finding the marginal revenue curve, equating $MR$ to $MC$ to find the profit-maximizing output, and using the industry's demand curve to find the highest price at which that output can be sold. The merged firms' marginal cost curve will shift to the left if one of the plants is shut down. Cash fixed costs will be reduced by eliminating redundant administrative staffs, facilities, and sales representatives.

The first step in preparing the operating plan after the merger is to calculate marginal revenue. $TR = PQ = (983.8 - 0.5Q)Q = 983.8Q - 0.5Q^2$ and $MR = dTR/dQ = 983.8 - Q$. The marginal cost curve when the monopoly operates six plants is the supply curve for the industry before it was monopolized with $P$ replaced by $MC$ and the equation rearranged: $MC = 190 + 0.2Q$. Equating $MR$ to $MC$ yields a profit-maximizing output with six plants of 661.5 units per day and a price of $652.55 per unit. The elasticity of demand is $E_P = (-2)(652.55)/(661.5) = -1.973$. Demand is now elastic. Total revenue is $TR = \$652.55 \times 661.5 = \$431,661.82$. Output at each plant is $q = 661.5/6 = 110.25$ units per day and $AVC = 190 + 0.6(110.25) = \$256.15$ per unit. Total variable cost is $TVC = \$256.15 \times 661.5 = \$169,443.22$. Since cash fixed costs are $85,000 per day, total profit is $177,217.60 per day before depreciation of $45,900. Before-tax profit is $131,317.60 per day. When the industry was competitive, the six firms had a profit before depreciation of $2,831.70 \times 6 = \$16,990.20$ per day and a before-tax loss of $4,818.30 \times 6 = \$28,909.80$.

If a plant is closed, the firm's marginal cost curve is $Q = 5q = 5(MC - 190)/1.2$, or $MC = 190 + 0.24Q$. Equating $MR$ to $MC$ yields a profit-maximizing output of 640 units per day, a price of $663.72, and total revenues of $424,781 per day. Output at each of the five operating plants is $q = 640/5 = 128$ units per day, $AVC$ is $190 + 0.6(128) = \$266.80$ per unit, and $TVC$ is $\$266.80 \times 640 = \$170,752$. Closing one plant would reduce cash fixed costs by $5,000, to $80,000 per day. Profit before depreciation would now be $424,781 - \$170,752 - \$80,000 = \$174,029$ and profit after depreciation would be $174,029 - \$45,900 = \$128,129$, because though the plant was closing the depreciation allowances would still be incurred.

## Conclusions

Closing the plant is not profitable. Cash fixed costs would have to fall by an additional amount equal to the difference in the two profit rates, or $177,217.60 - \$174,029 = \$3,188.60$, before it would be profitable to shut down one plant. One reason it is not profitable to close one plant is that demand is elastic at the profit-maximizing output with six plants operating. Thus, reducing output does not add to total revenues, but rather they fall from $431,661.82 to $424,781, or by $6,880.82 per day. Another is that each plant produces where $AVC$ is rising so that the higher output at each of the five plants results in an increase in *TVC* of $1,363.76 per day. Your recommendation is that none of the plants be closed.

The conclusion that it is unprofitable to close one of the plants does not apply to all marginal cost curves. If the *MC* curves were U-shaped with a minimum point to the right of the profit-maximizing output, it might be profitable to close one plant to take advantage of the increasing returns at the remaining plants. Whenever another unit of output can be produced at a lower *MC*, total cost can be reduced by producing one more unit at one plant and reducing output by one unit at another. If *MC* = $25 at each plant when they produce 40 units and *MC* = $22 if either plant produces 41 units, having one plant produce 41 units adds $22 to total cost and reducing output to 39 units at the other reduces total cost by $25, resulting in a $3 cost savings. In general, it pays to close down plants until the firm's remaining plants are producing at a point where marginal cost is increasing.

## Key Terms

| | | |
|---|---|---|
| differentiated products | monopoly | price-searcher market product |
| full-line forcing | natural monopoly | differentiation |
| market equilibrium | oligopoly | product group |
| monopolistic competition | price discrimination | tying contract |
| | price-searcher firm | |

## Review Questions

1. Define the terms *price-searcher market, monopoly, monopolistic competition, differentiated products,* and *product group.*

2. Describe the constraints on the pricing policy of a monopolist. Why do these constraints increase the elasticity of demand as the monopolist's price increases?

3. Why do monopolies generally not last for a long time?

4. Why is the marginal revenue curve for a monopolist downward sloping? If the demand function is $P = 150 - 5Q$, calculate the marginal revenue function and find the output where $MR = 0$.

5. Why will the monopolist set its profit-maximizing output where demand is elastic?

6. Assume that the demand curve for a monopolist shifts to the right.

Show graphically what will happen to the monopolist's profit-maximizing price and output.

7. How does a natural monopoly differ from a monopoly that exists because of patent protection?

8. Explain why the *LRAC* and demand conditions leading to a natural monopoly imply that one firm will minimize the average costs of producing the product.

9. Define the term *price discrimination* and describe the conditions under which price discrimination will be profitable.

10. How can transaction costs keep consumers separate so that competitive firms like car dealers can practice some measure of profitable price discrimination?

11. Assume that the firm sells several products. One of the products is in high demand and monopolized by the firm. The others are sold under competitive conditions. To limit the creation of substitute products by other firms, management believes that it is wealth-maximizing to establish a form of price discrimination referred to as "full-line forcing." In order for a customer (generally a retailer) to buy the high-demand, monopolized product at a relatively low price, the firm requires the customer to buy specified numbers of its products that are sold in competitive markets, and possibly pay more than the normal market price for those products. Explain why full-line forcing may be a wealth-maximizing policy for the firm. Use a very popular model of car or motorcycle as an example.

12. Why does a firm in monopolistic competition not consider the potential reactions of other firms when determining its price?

13. Why is the firm in monopolistic competition unlikely to be able to forecast demand accurately enough to find its profit-maximizing equilibrium price?

14. Why is monopolistic competition likely to be a transitional market structure that will evolve into oligopoly? How do trade associations and trade journals serve to speed the transition to oligopoly?

15. Why is it unlikely that a firm with several plants would find it profit-maximizing to operate all of its plants at an output where their *MC* curves are downward sloping?

## *Problems and Applications*

1. The monopolist's demand function is $P = 405 - 5Q$, where $Q$ is output per hour, its *AVC* function is $AVC = 20 + 0.5Q$, and its fixed costs are $6,037.50 per hour. Calculate the monopolist's profit-maximizing output, price, and total profit.

2. Continuing with problem 1, assume that the monopolist's demand function shifts to $P = 400 - 4.5Q$. Calculate the monopolist's new profit-maximizing output, price, and total profit.

3. Calculate the point-elasticity of demand at the monopolist's profit-maximizing output in problem 1. Is demand elastic?

4. A monopoly's demand function is $Q = 24 - 4P + 2Y$ where $Y$ is per capita income in thousands of dollars. Its $AVC$ function is $AVC = Q^2 - 19.75Q + 101$, and its total fixed cost is $100. Calculate its profit-maximizing output, price, and profit or loss when $Y = 10$.

5. The production function is $Q = 8L^{0.5}$ where $Q$ is output per hour, $w = \$8$ per hour, and materials cost $24 per unit of output. The monopolist's demand function is $P = 434 - 5Q$ and fixed costs are $7,500 per hour. Calculate the profit-maximizing output, price, total profit, and number of workers.

6. The monopolist in problem 5 has just signed a new contract with the union that calls for a wage increase to $9 per hour and work rules changes that shift the production function to $Q = 8.1L^{0.5}$. What will be the effect of this contract on the monopolist's profit-maximizing output, price, total profit, and number of workers?

7. During the negotiations for the new contract in problem 6, management suggested that the union accept a pay cut to $7.20 per hour. Management supported this proposition by arguing that it would lead to the employment of more workers. How many more workers would the monopolist employ at this lower wage, assuming that the new work rules are also adopted into the contract?

8. The union rejected the pay cut proposal in problem 7 because it believes that unemployment among its members is caused by the low level of demand in the current recession. It believes that the recession is ending and that next year the monopolist's demand function will be $\$500 - 5Q$. Calculate the effect of this demand curve shift on employment at the plant under the new contract in problem 6.

9. The $LRAC$ function for the typical firm in an industry is $LRAC = 500 - 41Q + Q^2$. The demand function is presently $P = 280 - 10Q$. Is this industry likely to be a natural monopoly? Explain why.

10. Assume that the demand curve for the industry in problem 9 is expected to shift to $P = 480 - 6Q$ in 10 years. How many firms are likely to be in this industry in 10 years?

11. Assume that a monopolist can separate its customers into two groups. The demand curve for group one is $P_1 = 400 - 5Q_1$ and the demand curve for group two is $P_2 = 300 - 2Q_2$. Marginal cost is constant for all outputs at $MC = AVC = \$20$ and fixed costs are $1,000.

Calculate the profit-maximizing output, price, total profit, and point-elasticity in each market. Then horizontally add the demand curves in each market and calculate the profit-maximizing output, price, total profit, and point-elasticity in the combined market. Is price discrimination profitable?

12. Assume that the monopolist's total cost function is $TC = 1,000 + 20Q + 0.2Q^2$ where $Q = Q_1 + Q_2$ and that the demand curves for each of two separable markets are those in problem 11. Perform the calculations requested in problem 11.

13. Assume that in problem 11 it costs $5 per unit sold to group two to prevent group one consumers from buying the product sold to group two. Is price discrimination still profitable?

14. Assume that a competitive industry has a demand curve of $Q = 10,000 - 30P$ and a supply curve of $Q = 8,000 + 20P$, with a market-clearing price of $40 and output of 8,800 units. If this industry is monopolized, what will be the monopolist's profit-maximizing output and price? Why might consumers oppose this industry's being monopolized?

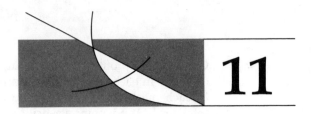

# Oligopoly

Neither monopoly nor monopolistic competition is likely to be a stable, price-searcher market structure over a long period of time. The generally capital-intensive production technologies of monopolies or firms in monopolistic competition imply that these market structures are unlikely to evolve into price-taker markets. The economies of mass production and the extensive market served by the large plants imply that most manufacturing industries evolve into oligopolies dominated by a few large firms. Much smaller firms may also compete with the giants in local markets or produce specialty products appealing to consumers wanting distinctive styling or higher-quality goods than those mass produced by the giants. However, the behavior of the large firms dominates determination of profit-maximizing outputs, prices, and marketing policies.

A monopolist's product has no close substitutes. A firm in monopolistic competition produces a differentiated product that is a close substitute for those of its rivals. The firms in an oligopoly produce homogeneous or differentiated products. In the case of homogeneous products, the industry is an oligopoly because of the economies of mass production relative to the size of the plant's market, which is determined in part by transportation costs. In the case of differentiated products, both the economies of mass production and the marketing opportunities open to large firms (for example, low-cost national advertising on television) contribute to the existence of oligopoly.

It is not the nature of the product, its production technologies, or its marketing that necessarily results in the existence of oligopoly but rather the recognized interdependences among the firms. Oligopolistic behavior is as likely among several hardware stores in a single city as among industrial giants. To maximize its profits and reduce the probability of unacceptably large losses, each hardware store takes into consideration the reactions of the other stores to its pricing and marketing policies. Thus, each hardware store acts as an oligopolist.

The first section of this chapter discusses the characteristics of oligopolistic markets. The next section uses the duopoly model to illustrate the importance of market strategies and management's predictions of its rival's responses in obtaining equilibrium in an oligopolistic market. The next three sections cover the characteristics of dominant-firm and price-leadership oligopolies. The chapter concludes with a discussion of the nature of multiple-plant firms and two cases. One case applies the duopoly model to a public administration problem, and the other discusses the use of markup pricing in an oligopolistic market.

## 11.1 *Nature of Oligopoly*

In a competitive market, the homogeneous products are perfect substitutes. Consumers can substitute the product of one firm for another and not notice any differences. Some oligopolies produce homogeneous products, for example, the steel, aluminum, copper, and chemical industries. Many of their products are produced to industry-wide specifications established by trade associations or engineering societies. Other oligopolies produce differentiated products that are not perfect substitutes. They differ in one or more attributes and are identified with the manufacturer's brand name. Firms producing relatively close substitutes are in the same product group. The goods or services included in a product group are better substitutes for one another than they are for other products. Most oligopolistic firms produce a wide range of goods and services in a number of related product groups.

Oligopolies typically consist of two or more large firms each producing, say, 5 percent or more of the market. A few oligopolies consist of one dominant firm producing more than 50 percent of the market and several smaller firms. Mainframe computers is an example of a dominant-firm oligopoly, with IBM as the dominant firm. If the oligopoly consists of two large firms, it is a duopoly. Several or even a relatively large number of small firms may be in an oligopoly. These small firms generally produce specialty products tailored to the requirements of a small segment of the market (Rolls-Royce, for example) or are regional firms with established market positions (for instance, local supermarkets or retailers competing with national chains). The large firms generally produce standardized products to obtain the economies of national advertising and mass production. Since consumers have differing preferences, smaller regional or specialty firms can prosper even if their costs are somewhat higher.

*Oligopolistic Rivalry and Interdependency.* Oligopolies are characterized by intensely "personal" rivalry in the market place. In a competitive industry, competition is impersonal. The firm does not compete for market share (sales) with specific other firms, but rather with all of the other firms. For example, investors buying or selling a common stock listed on the New York Stock Exchange do not know who is bidding to buy or sell a stock. All the investor knows is its market price. In an oligopoly, the firm knows the identities of its rivals and a fair amount about their past decisions and strategies. Continuing with the stock market example, oligopoly exists when two or more firms make tender offers for a company's stock. Rivalry between the bidders is often intense, with the competing managements countering each other's moves and developing new offers that take into consideration their rival's likely responses. That is, the managements of oligopolies exhibit strategic behavior with respect to their rivals. Strategic behavior is absent in competition, but is endemic to oligopoly.

A firm's market share is its total sales divided by the total sales of all firms in the industry or product group. Competition for market share is particularly important in an oligopoly. These firms typically use capital-intensive technologies with high fixed costs. Thus, up to a high percentage of their plant capacity, profits increase with increases in their market share and output. The largest firm may earn a greater share of the industry's profits than its market share, and the smallest large firm a lesser share of industry profits than its market share. Since price decreases are readily matched, or even exceeded, by the firm's rivals, changes in advertising, packaging, product design, and various product promotion policies may be the primary form of rivalry. Successful product promotion policies are more difficult, time-consuming, and costly for other firms to replicate than price changes. This provides each firm with strong incentives to initiate changes in product promotion policies to see if they will result in an increase in its market share.

The recognized interdependencies among the firms need not result in intense rivalry. Intense rivalry of competitive stock tenders is relatively rare in manufacturing and services. Rivalry is usually limited to product characteristics, service, or credit terms. There may be little rivalry in product pricing or tacit cooperation in other dimensions, such as warranties or product specifications. The aspects of the product or market where there is rivalry may change as firms embark on new strategies intended to increase their market shares, and the firms may engage in cooperative behavior when they perceive an opportunity to shift the industry's demand curve to the right.

*Oligopolistic Cooperation.* In competition, market communication among firms primarily takes the form of quantities offered for sale at the market price. Since a number of possible aspects of market rivalry or cooperation appear among oligopolistic firms, market communication becomes especially important and covers a wider range of market aspects than publishing list prices. For example, although list prices may be unchanged, oligopolists can signal their assessment of how "firm" the market is by changing their published charges for services or their credit terms. Higher charges for services or more stringent credit terms could be a signal to raise prices. The other firms' going along with higher service charges could be a signal to reassess list prices and raise them in accordance with each firm's assessment of market conditions. If the "trial balloon" of higher service charges is ignored, then the signal is that now is not an appropriate time to raise prices.

Many possible forms of market communication can be used by the firms in an oligopoly, and many responses are possible. Alternatively, the firms may engage in explicit collusion and set prices and marketing policies. Such collusion is illegal, and a number of cases have been prosecuted over the years by the Department of Justice. Explicit collusion, including formal cartels such as OPEC, is legal in many nations and practiced with or without government supervision. Collusion reduces the uncertainties associated with one firm's assessment of the reactions of other firms to changes in its pricing and marketing policies. However, since any firm in a collusive agreement can profit from "cheating" on its terms, collusive agreements generally do not have long lives. They may fall apart, be reinstated, and fall apart again. Collusive agreements enforced by governments or cartels where governments are parties to the agreements may have longer lives. Since the profits obtained from cheating are often large, the participants have strong incentives to find loopholes in the agreement or create legal entities allowing them to circumvent the cartel. For example, a member of a raw materials or components cartel can merge with a firm producing the finished product to circumvent the cartel's limits on its output. Collusive agreements and cartels do not eliminate predicting the actions and responses of the other oligopolists. Management simply has another set of actions and responses to consider. These actions and responses may be more tractable than the previous ones, but the uncertainties characteristic of oligopolies are still present.

Because there is a wide range of possible strategies with respect to each market aspect, oligopolists face a great deal of uncertainty as to their rivals' responses, and hence, their own best market strategy. Given these interacting uncertainties, profit maximization takes on added dimensions, and analysis of the market behavior of oligopolistic firms becomes complex. In fact, the crux of the theory of oligopoly lies in the information and procedures used by each of the firms in setting its pricing and marketing strategies. There are many possible theories of oligopoly because of the large number of market aspects involved and possible reactions on the part of rival firms.

## 11.2  *Duopoly*

Duopoly exists when the oligopoly consists of just two firms. For analytical convenience, it is assumed that the two firms have equal financial and other resources and that they produce perfect substitutes. There is a wide range of possible solutions to the problem of determining price, output, and other market variables for a duopoly. Each solution results from assuming different market strategies for one firm and behavioral responses by its rival to these strategies. The essence of oligopoly is rivalry between firms who study the strategies and reactions of their rivals.

*Monopoly Price and Output.* Assume that initially one firm controls an industry. For simplicity, assume the monopolist has zero marginal cost and that the market demand function is $Q = a - bP$. The profit-maximizing output is found by calculating the $MR$ function, setting $MR = 0$, and solving for $Q$.

$$P = a/b - Q/b \tag{11.1}$$

$$TR = PQ = aQ/b - Q^2/b$$

$$MR = dTR/dQ = a/b - 2Q/b = 0$$

$$Q = a/2 \tag{11.2}$$

$$P = a/b - (a/2)/b = a/2b \tag{11.3}$$

If $a = 500$ and $b = 10$, $Q = 250$ and $P = \$25$.

*Marketing Rivalry.* Assume now that a second firm begins producing a perfect substitute for this product and that it also has zero marginal costs. The second firm could have been attracted into this industry by the monopolist's profits. How should the new entrant price its product, and what is its profit-maximizing output? The management of the new firm must take into consideration the several possible reactions of the existing firm to its entry. One is to assume that the existing firm will maintain its output, $Q_1$, at 250 units and match the new firm's price. Given this reaction, the new entrant's demand curve is

$$Q_2 = a - bP - a/2 = a/2 - bP$$

where $Q_2$ is its quantity demanded. The profit-maximizing output and price for the second firm are

$$Q_2 = a/4 = 500/4 = 125 \qquad \text{(11.4)}$$

$$P_2 = a/4b = 500/4(10) = \$12.50 \qquad \text{(11.5)}$$

The initial firm will continue to produce 250 units of output but will reduce its price to \$12.50. At a market price of \$12.50, total industry output is $500 - 10(12.50) = 375$ units.

This price and output do not establish a profit-maximizing equilibrium. The initial firm is no longer producing its profit-maximizing output. With the new firm producing $a/4$ units, the initial firm's demand function is

$$Q_1 = a - bP - a/4 = 3a/4 - bP$$

After the initial firm begins producing its new profit-maximizing output and sets its price at the profit-maximizing level, the new entrant matches this price. However, the new firm is no longer producing *its* profit-maximizing output. Thus, a profit-maximizing equilibrium for both firms has not been found.

The process of price and output adjustments continues until both firms are producing $a/3 = 500/3 = 167$ units of output and the market price is $a/3b = 500/30 = \$16.67$. How do we know this is a profit-maximizing equilibrium? Assume that the initial firm produces $a/3$ units of output. The demand curve facing the new firm is

$$Q_2 = a - bP - a/3 = 2a/3 - bP$$

Solving this equation for $P$, finding total revenue, marginal revenue, and the profit-maximizing output for the new firm yields

$$P = 2a/3b - Q_2/b$$
$$TR = PQ_2 = 2aQ_2/3b - Q_2^2/b$$
$$MR = dTR/dQ_2 = 2a/3b - 2Q_2/b = 0$$
$$Q_2 = a/3$$

Thus, both a demand-equals-supply and a profit maximization equilibrium exist because the firm's profit-maximizing price and output are equal to the values assumed when the other firm maximizes its profits.

*Collusion and Cheating.* Although both firms are maximizing their profits given the assumption that the other firm will maintain output and match its price, total industry profits are below the monopoly profit of 250 × $25 = $6,250 (assuming that fixed and variable costs are zero). The total profit of the duopoly is 167 × 2 × $16.67 = $5,567.78. If the two firms collude, set a price of $25 and each produces 125 units, each firm earns a profit of 125 × $25 = $3,125. This is $341.11 more than their present profit of 167 × $16.67 = $2,783.89. Since collusion is illegal, the courts would not enforce a contract requiring each firm to sell 125 units at a price of $25. But the additional profits earned by secretly colluding are tempting to their managements. They may enter into an informal agreement each to sell 125 units at a price of $25.

Although greater profits can be earned through collusion, still greater profits can be earned through cheating on the agreement. Since $MC = 0$, each firm can earn a greater profit by offering the other firm's customers the following deal: "If you keep it a secret, I will sell you one unit of the product for $20." The customer could accept this offer or counter it by agreeing to keep the price concession secret only if the price is $10. The firm offering the secret price concession would increase its profits by $10 by accepting the counteroffer. Since both firms have an incentive to offer secret price concessions, the agreement soon breaks down. Both firms end up at the duopoly price and output of $16.67 and 167 units. The only practical way to remove the temptations to cheat on price-fixing agreements is for the two firms to merge.

*Price Wars.* Assume that the new firm sets its output and price at 125 units and $12.50. One alternative would be for the other to respond by setting a lower price, say $10. At this price the initial firm would sell all of the market demand and the new entrant would sell nothing. The new entrant would be forced to match the price of the initial firm. If the initial firm persists in setting a price below the new entrant's, the result is a classic price war. Price eventually reaches zero! Since the firms have equal financial resources, neither firm can drive the other out of business using this tactic. Both managements would soon realize their folly. By increasing its price to $16.67 and producing 167 units, one firm could signal the other that the price war should end. Since its profits are higher if it cooperates and sets the same price and output, the other firm would probably be willing to raise its price to $16.67 and end the price war. However, this price may not be stable because each firm could still offer profitable secret price concessions to the other firm's customers, which would touch off another price war.

After a few price wars, one firm could decide that this price instability is reducing the value of its common stock to levels well below that attainable if it could drive the other firm out of business in one big winner-takes-all price war. For this strategy to be effective, the other firm must incur cash fixed and variable costs that drain its assets when price is below average total cost. This firm could merge with a larger, well-financed firm; or, it could arrange for additional financing. Moreover, it may need only to acquire greater resources than the other firm, threaten a ruinous price war, and then buy it out. Once the other firm is out of business, the surviving firm would charge the monopoly price of $25 to make the price war and acquisition profitable for its investors. Its having driven one rival out of business may deter other firms from attempting to compete in this market.

*Evolution of a Duopoly.* The evolution of a duopoly need not follow any of these patterns. In each case, the market equilibrium depended upon each firm's maintaining its assumption about the other's behavior in spite of evidence to the contrary. That is, once one firm chose its profit-maximizing price and output under the assumption that the other firm would not change its output, the other firm would change its output to its new profit-maximizing level. Maintaining this assumption about the other firm's behavior until the common profit-maximizing output and price are reached would require each firm to ignore reality, something successful managers do not do.

## 11.3 *Dominant-Firm Oligopoly*

Dominant-firm oligopoly exists when there are two or more firms and the leading firm is much larger than the second largest firm. "Larger" in this context can be measured by the firms' sales or assets. The dominant firm is three to five or more times larger than its largest rival. For example, the dominant firm may sell 80 percent of industry output, with none of five smaller firms selling more than 10 percent. This industry is an oligopoly because the dominant firm must weigh the reactions of the smaller firms when setting its price. The smaller firms must also examine the reaction of the dominant firm if they plan to set their price at some level other than that set by the dominant firm. If the firms produce differentiated products or if the small firms serve geographical markets where the dominant firm has a small market share, the small firm considers the reaction of the dominant firm when contemplating setting a price above or below the dominant firm's price. If a small firm customarily sets its price at 95 percent of the dominant firm's, it would try to determine the possible reaction of the dominant firm when setting its price at 92 percent of the dominant firm's price.

*Price Leadership.* The dominant firm is the industry's price leader. The price leader initiates all price changes, and the price followers change their prices only in response to the change initiated by the price leader. Since only one firm initiates price changes, prices are more predictable than if they were initiated by any of the firms. Dominant-firm oligopoly is the simplest form of price leadership to analyze because it focuses on the price-searcher behavior of the dominant firm. The smaller firms, particularly if they are numerous and have only a small share of the market, are price takers because their managements believe that they cannot significantly influence the market price by changing their output. The smaller firms may also take the dominant firm's price as a given because they fear the response of the large firm to an independent price change. These smaller firms are large enough to influence the market price; however, their production, marketing, and financial resources are sufficiently smaller than those of the dominant firm that they are unwilling to risk triggering a price war that could bankrupt them.

*Profit-Maximizing Price and Output.* The dominant-firm oligopoly model assumes that the firms produce a homogeneous product and are profit maximizers. The small firms are price takers who find their profit-maximizing output by equating their $MC$ to the dominant firm's price. Assume that the typical small firm produces $q_0$ at price $P_0$ set by the dominant firm. $M$ identical small firms supply $Mq_0$ units of output at price $P_0$. Since the $MC$ curve of the typical small firm is upward sloping, the firms produce more output at prices above $P_0$. If the dominant firm sets a price below $P_1$, the small firms would supply nothing because $P_1$ is less than their minimum $AVC$.

The quantity demanded of the dominant firm's product at each price is found by deducting the output of the small firms from the market demand curve. The dominant firm's demand curve is $D'$ in Figure 11.1, and its marginal revenue curve is $MR'$. The profit-maximizing output for the dominant firm is $Q_0'$, where its $MC$ curve intersects $MR'$, and $P_0$ is its profit-maximizing price on demand curve $D'$. The small firms take price $P_0$ as a given and produce output $Mq_0$. Thus, market demand at price $P_0$, $Q_0$, is produced by the industry. If the market demand curve, production costs, or the number of small firms changes, the dominant firm would reconsider its price. Since the small firms are price followers, they would not change their prices unless the dominant firm first changed its price.

This model applies to the situation in which the products are perfect substitutes. Price differences among the firms would be attributable to their locations relative to the industry's customers. If the firms produce differentiated products, the dominant firm must look at this differentiation when setting its price. With differentiated products, the prices of the firms may vary. However, as is the case when firms producing a homogeneous product are in different locations, the prices of the several firms generally maintain a proportional relationship. Thus, when the

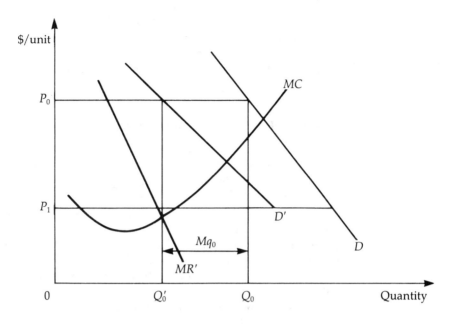

**Figure 11.1   The Dominant Firm**

To find $D'$, the demand curve for the dominant firm, choose a price and find the quantity supplied by the small firms. At $P_0$, the small firms supply $Mq_0$. Market demand is $Q_0$ and demand for the dominant firm is $Q_0' = Q_0 - Mq_0$. Marginal revenue for the dominant firm is the $MR'$ curve, which intersects the $MC$ curve at its profit-maximizing output $Q_0'$. Its profit-maximizing price is $P_0$.

price leader raises its price by 3 percent, the other firms raise their prices by 3 percent, although some of the small firms may raise their prices by slightly more or less than 3 percent depending on competitive conditions in their local markets.

*Frequency of Price Changes.* The model described above assumes that the dominant firm can correctly estimate the market demand curve and the $MC$ curves of the small firms. If the dominant firm incorrectly estimates these curves, its price will not be profit-maximizing because it will have incorrectly estimated its demand curve. This error in estimating $D'$ does not directly affect the small firms because they maximize profits at the output where their $MC$ equals the dominant firm's price. However, the dominant firm may wish to adjust its price from time to time to correct for errors in estimating $D'$. Their frequency depends on the costs of making price adjustments relative to the expected increase in profits. Alternatives to adjusting price are adjusting advertising expenditures, credit terms, or other marketing variables. Which approach will be used depends on management's assessment of the relative costs and of the additions to profits resulting from each option.

## 11.4  *Price Leadership to Increase Price Stability*

The conclusion of the duopoly model was that prices are likely to be unstable as the firms attempt to maximize their profits given the rival's predicted responses. This price instability can also be demonstrated for oligopolies in which there are more than two firms with approximately the same resources. The instability exists because, in the absence of collusion with its rivals, a firm cannot be certain of its rival's reactions to its price and other marketing policies. This uncertainty is compounded where there are more than two firms, because each rival may react differently to the firm's strategies. Uncertainty about rivals' reactions can make it costly and time-consuming to reach a price and output approximating the profit-maximizing levels. Moreover, the necessity to work out a new equilibrium price and output after changes in consumer demand or production costs can lead to additional price fluctuations. The result is a lower average profit than could otherwise be earned and a lower market value for the firm.

Unstable prices do more than depress profits and increase investor risks. Managerial time and effort must be devoted to making pricing decisions. This time is, as a consequence, not available for the company's top management to devote to other areas, such as new product development, that promise to be more lucrative. Fluctuating prices and profits make long-term planning more difficult. With long-term investments in plant and equipment made riskier, less capital-intensive production processes tend to be used. More capital-intensive processes could yield lower average costs and provide protection against the possibility of the entry of a new firm with lower costs. Capital-intensive businesses generally obtain a significant proportion of their investment funds from traditionally risk-averse commercial and investment bankers, insurance companies, pension funds, and other financial institutions. Thus, the increased risk caused by fluctuating prices and profits increases their cost of capital. Finally, their customers may prefer to buy products whose prices are relatively stable and thus may be more receptive to substitute products with more stable prices.

*Price Leadership.* Since cartels and collusive agreements are illegal, the firms in an oligopoly must seek other ways to stabilize prices and production volumes. This circumstance generally amounts to finding an industry-wide approach to pricing that trades off the benefits of greater price stability against the incremental increases in profits that might be possible if the firm fine tunes its prices to its perceptions of market conditions and the expected reactions of its rivals. Price leadership provides one approach to reducing the price instability inherent in oligopolies. Price leadership is not a formal institution adopted by the firms after much deliberation and bargaining and then embodied in a contract creating an agency to perform the functions of the price leader; a formal agreement is unnecessary. Price instability can be reduced if all but one of the firms become price takers, accepting the price leader's price as a given and adjusting their price and output policies accordingly.

Many oligopolies consist of several large firms managed by skilled professionals. These firms have low-cost plants and the financial strength to make it unlikely that one firm could drive another large firm into bankruptcy. A number of smaller companies may coexist with the large companies because of locational advantages or consumer acceptance of their differentiated products. They exist because the larger firms find it unprofitable to compete directly with the smaller. The larger firms may find producing for mass consumer markets more profitable than marketing a broader range of products.

The large firms have profit incentives to accept the price leadership of one of the other large firms. The interdependencies of their demand curves make it difficult for each firm to set independently its profit-maximizing price unless it can predict the reactions of the other large firms. Price leadership provides a noncollusive way to reduce the uncertainties associated with the reactions of the other large firms. To be effective at reducing price instability, price leadership does not require each firm to raise or lower prices by precisely the same amount or percentage as the price leader. Each firm can respond to the price leader's moves in accordance with its assessment of the market. Price leadership requires merely that the price-follower firms change their prices in a predictable manner when the price leader changes its price.

The largest firm is generally the price leader. It sells in most of the industry's markets and usually has large, geographically diverse production facilities. Its management is likely to have the expertise to set both the timing and magnitude of its price changes so that the other firms will find its price leadership profitable. However, there is no inherent reason for the largest firm always to be the price leader. One of the other large firms may have a skilled and dynamic management that is highly respected. Because of its business acumen, this firm may be accepted as the price leader. The price leader may change as market conditions change. For example, the price leader may enjoy such great consumer acceptance that new entrants and relatively rapidly expanding small firms will not have been reducing its market share appreciably. If the other large firms are losing an unacceptable portion of their market share, they may accept as the price leader the firm that lowers its price to discourage new entrants and expanding small firms. When the former price leader raises its price, the other large firms may not follow. The result may be more uncertainty with prices than the firms would prefer; however, they may be willing to trade off an increase in price fluctuations for a lower price that protects their future market shares and profits.

*Maximizing Industry Profits.* The price leader generally sets its price at the level that maximizes industry profits. There are strong incentives for the price leader to maximize industry profits. The managers of each large firm will evaluate the performance of the price leader by its ability to set a price that is likely to maximize their own firm's profits. The other large firms must believe that they can earn greater profits as price followers than if they set their prices without reference to the timing and amount of the price leader's price changes. By setting its price to maximize industry profits, the price leader can maximize the probability that the other large firms will follow its lead. In principle, the procedure for arriving at the price that maximizes industry profits is similar to that used by a dominant firm oligopolist. At each price, the profit-maximizing quantity supplied by the price-taker small firms is subtracted from market demand to yield the demand curve for the large firms. The *MR* curve is calculated from this demand curve and equated to the estimated *MC* curve for all of the large firms to find the industry's profit-maximizing price. The price leader then sets this as its price and the other large firms follow this price.

The ability of the price leader to set a price acceptable to the other large firms is basically an empirical matter. These cost and revenue functions are difficult to estimate. They are subject to considerable errors, and each firm may develop differing estimates. The desire for stable prices at profitable levels may be sufficiently strong that the other large firms may accept the price leader's price even though they believe that a higher or lower price would yield greater profits.

*Limit-Entry Pricing.* One constraint on the ability of the price leader to set the price that maximizes industry profits is imposed by the likelihood that other firms will enter the industry if it is profitable for them to do so at the price set by the price leader. Similarly, at a sufficiently high price, small firms already in the industry will expand their facilities. Because the profits of the large firms are sensitive to their market shares, they are unlikely to adopt a price that results in the entry of new firms or the expansion of existing small firms. The large firms may find it wealth-maximizing to set a price below that which maximizes industry profits because it will stabilize their market shares. Furthermore, the lower price is likely to be a more stable price because industry capacity is more predictable. Such a price is called the limit-entry price.

Limit-entry pricing is wealth-maximizing when the existing firms have a cost advantage over new firms considering entering the industry. For example, an existing firm may have established a high level of brand name identification with consumers and a reputation for supplying high-quality products. The advertising expenditures necessary for a new firm to establish a competitive brand name and product quality reputation may significantly increase its costs of entering the industry. An existing firm may have a lower-cost plant because new firms must locate in higher-cost areas and are subject to additional environmental protection costs. New firms, even if they have a somewhat superior product, generally cannot obtain capital at as low a cost as existing firms. The result is an *LRAC* curve for the potential new firm that lies above the *SRATC* curve of an existing firm, as in Figure 11.2. If the profit-maximizing

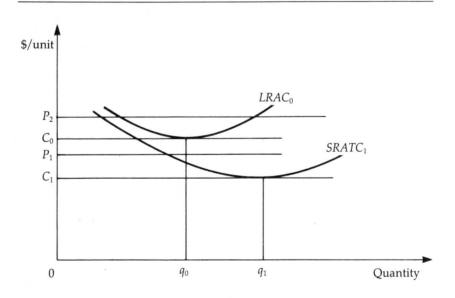

**Figure 11.2 Limit-Entry Pricing**

$LRAC_0$ is the *LRAC* curve of a potential new entrant in an oligopoly, with its minimum average cost at $C_0$. $SRATC_1$ is the *SRATC* curve of the typical firm already in the industry. Assume that $P_2$ is the price that maximizes industry profits for the oligopoly. At $P_2$, there would be entry into the industry because $P_2 > C_0$. Price $P_1$ is a limit-entry price because $P_1 < C_0$, yet it is profitable for the existing large firms because $P_1 > C_1$.

price was $P_2$, the new firm would be able to build the plant, minimizing its *LRAC* and earning an economic profit. However, if price is set at $P_1$, the new firm will not enter the industry since $P_1 < C_0$.

*Behavior of the Weakest Firm.* Another constraint on the price leader's pricing decisions results from the behavior of the least profitable large firm. This firm generally has the smallest market share or has suffered a substantial decline in its market share because of poor management or bad marketing decisions. If the weak firm believes that it will go bankrupt if it does not increase its market share, the price leader's price may not be followed by the weakest firm. Because it has nothing to lose when facing bankruptcy, the weak firm lowers its price in the hope that the other large firms will maintain their prices. The results are likely to be countering price reductions by the other large firms and a period of price instability and reduced profits for all firms. To keep the weak firm from upsetting the desired price stability, the price leader may set a somewhat higher price that will keep the weakest firm marginally profitable. The hope is that the weak firm will be acquired by a stronger firm to remove this potential source of price instability. If, however, the probability of the failing firm's being acquired within a reasonable period of time is low, the price leader may find it wealth-maximizing to set a price so low that the weak firm is quickly driven out of the industry. The other large firms may find such a price acceptable because it promises more stable and profitable prices in the future. Evaluating whether to set prices to support the weakest firm or drive it out of business requires use of the wealth maximization goal.

*Nonprice Competition.* Once the price leader and other large firms have set their prices, rivalry within the oligopoly does not cease. The firms compete for a greater market share and increased profits using product differentiation, advertising, and a host of other marketing policies. The reason for favoring nonprice competition is that price reductions can quickly be met by their rivals, making the profits from price reductions small or nonexistent. Successful marketing programs are more difficult and time-consuming for their rivals to counter. Small firms and potential new entrants may find it difficult to respond to the product development and other marketing programs of their larger, well-established rivals. Thus, the large firms may believe that they can add more to their profits through investment in marketing programs than through price reductions.

*Antitrust Implications.* Price leadership runs the risk of antitrust prosecution. Although price leadership has not been found to be unlawful, the behavior of firms in a price-leadership oligopoly may be watched closely by the Department of Justice for possible violations of the law.

If the large firms act independently and base their pricing and marketing decisions on a wider range of considerations than the leader's price, it is unlikely that they will be charged with antitrust violations.

## 11.5 *The Kinked Demand Curve*

The kinked demand curve theory describes the behavior of large price-follower firms once the price leader has set its price. This theory is not the only possible explanation of price-follower behavior, and the available empirical evidence is not always consistent with its implications. The kinked demand curve theory is presented here because it provides an explanation of the reluctance of a price-follower firm to change its price independently when its marginal cost curve shifts.

*Profit-Maximizing Price and Output for the Price-Follower Firm.* Assume that the price leader has set its price at $PL$, as in Figure 11.3. Industry demand at price $PL$ is $Q_0$. For the typical price-follower firm, output at price $PL$ is its normal market share, $S$, times industry demand, or $SQ_0$. If a price-follower firm cuts its price, the kinked demand curve theory holds that the other large firms will cut their prices proportionately to protect their market shares and profits. A price reduction to $P_1$ will result in its output being $SQ_1$, with no gain in market share. For price reductions below $PL$, the demand curve of the price-follower firm is $D_2$, and its marginal revenue curve is $MR_2$. If industry demand is inelastic below price $PL$, a relatively small increase in output and a decline in $TR$ occur for both the firm and the industry. $MR_2$ is negative for prices below $PL$.

An increase in the price follower's price above $PL$ will not, according to this theory, be followed by the other large firms. They believe that the price leader has set the appropriate price and do not accept the price-follower firm's judgment as to most profitable price for the industry. The result is a loss in its market share as consumers shift to the products of the other firms. The amount of this loss depends on consumer preferences if its product is differentiated, any locational advantages it may have, and the slopes of the $MC$ curves of the other large firms. The $MR$ curve for $D_1$, $MR_1$, is positive at outputs less than $SQ_0$ because $D_1$ is elastic.

Assume that $MC$ in Figure 11.3 is the marginal cost curve of the price-follower firm. Given the $MC$ and $MR$ curves in Figure 11.3, the firm's profit-maximizing price is $PL$. Because $MC$ does not intersect $MR_1$ or $MR_2$, the firm has no profit incentive to set a price other than $PL$. The price leader's price is profit-maximizing if the other large firms respond to its setting a price other than $PL$ in the manner assumed by

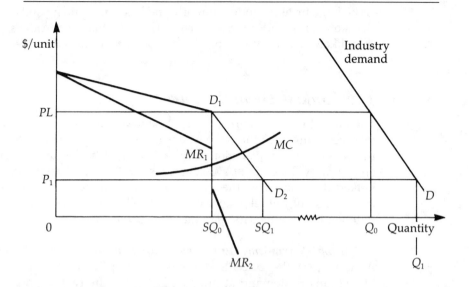

**Figure 11.3   The Price-Follower Firm**

At the price leader's price, $PL$ industry demand is $Q_0$ and the price-follower firm's demand is its market share, $S$, times $Q_0$. If the price follower lowers its price, the other firms will reduce their prices rather than lose their market share, yielding demand curve $D_2$ and its marginal revenue curve $MR_2$. If the price-follower firm raises its price above $PL$, the other firms will not raise their price, yielding $D_1$ and $MR_1$ for the price follower. Its profit-maximizing price is $PL$ if its $MC$ curve lies between $MR_1$ and $MR_2$ as in the diagram.

the kinked demand curve theory. Moreover, as long as changes in wage rates, raw material costs, and labor productivity do not shift the $MC$ curve to above point $A$ in Figure 11.3, they will not result in a change from $PL$ in the price follower's profit-maximizing price.

*Changes in the Price Leader's Price.* Even though shifts in one price-follower firm's $MC$ curve may not lead to that firm's adopting a price different from $PL$, this need not be the case if costs change for the entire industry. If costs rise for all firms, the price leader will reevaluate its price. If the cost increase is small and if additional increases are likely within a short period of time, the price leader may wait before raising its price to the level maximizing industry profits. Frequent price changes are generally avoided because they increase the probability that one of the price-follower firms may not adopt the price change.

When price changes are made in response to significant cost increases, the probability that all of the large firms will adopt the price increase is greater. A price reduction by the price leader, caused by declining costs or a desire to limit entry, will be followed by the other large firms because otherwise they would lose market share.

# 11.6   *Multiple-Plant Firms*

The preceding sections have focused on the managerial problems of single-product, single-plant firms. This section addresses the economics of multiple-plant firms. Its emphasis is on some of the principal reasons why firms find it wealth-maximizing to have multiple plants. The three situations discussed here are horizontal integration, vertical integration, and conglomerates. The same firm may be horizontally and vertically integrated and a conglomerate besides. Many oligopolies contain multiple-plant firms.

## 11.6.1   *Horizontal Integration*

Horizontal integration occurs when the firm acquires or constructs more than one facility serving similar functions. A supermarket or department store chain is horizontally integrated because the firm has more than one store. An auto manufacturer is horizontally integrated when it has more than one assembly plant. Virtually all large firms are horizontally integrated, especially if they serve national markets.

   Where there are cost incentives for horizontal integration, the likelihood that the industry will be an oligopoly is increased. Monopoly can increase profits for a multiple-plant firm, and acquisition of a monopoly can make price discrimination profitable. However, horizontal integration need not be the result of management's attempt to obtain a monopoly and higher profits. Seeking a monopoly can be a reason for horizontal integration, but the cost savings available to multiple-plant firms can be a more important reason.

   ***Reducing Transportation Costs.*** If the firm's sales are more than twice output at minimum *LRAC*, it generally reduces transportation costs to have plants located throughout the country. Even if sales are not more than twice output at minimum *LRAC*, transportation cost savings may make two plants in different locations more profitable than one plant. The transportation cost advantages of a two-plant firm can be illustrated with a relatively simple example. A firm sells in three markets, with the market price and quantity demanded being equal to

$2q_0/3$ in all markets. Total demand is $2q_0$. Transportation costs of $X$ dollars are incurred for shipments between adjacent markets.

$$B \overset{\$X}{\longleftrightarrow} A \overset{\$X}{\longleftrightarrow} C$$

A single plant located at $A$ produces $2q_0$ at an $SRATC = \$98$. It ships $2q_0/3$ to markets $B$ and $C$ at a transportation cost of $4q_0/3$ times $X$ dollars. If $q_0$ is 300 units and $X = \$5$, the total cost of serving all three markets is $(600u) \times (\$98/u) + (400u) \times (\$5) = \$60{,}800$ ($\$98/u$ is $\$98$ per unit of output). If there are two plants, one located at $B$ and the other at $C$, each plant produces $q_0$ at an $SRATC$ of $\$100$. Each plant ships $q_0/3$ to market $A$ to meet its demand of $2q_0/3$. These two plants serve all three markets at a total cost of $(600u) \times (\$100/u) + (200u) \times (\$5) = \$61{,}000$. Thus, the single plant located at $A$ is the lower-cost alternative. However, if the transportation cost were $\$10$, the two plants at $B$ and $C$ would have a total cost of $\$62{,}000$, or $\$800$ less than the $\$62{,}800$ for the plant at $A$. As transportation costs increase, larger product cost advantages are required for the single plant to be the more profitable alternative.

*Reducing Advertising Costs.* Horizontal integration can be profitable for reasons other than transportation cost savings. Having more than one store can yield a retailer significant savings in advertising costs. Advertising media covering larger market areas generally are lower in cost per potential consumer than ones covering smaller areas, and the larger audience generally justifies more sophisticated message presentations. If the firm does not have outlets in areas served by these advertising media, a portion of its messages will reach consumers who are unlikely to be customers. If the firm has outlets serving only a portion of the area receiving its messages, the cost per potential customer rises to levels making less effective advertising media more economical. But if other firms have a sufficiently large number of stores to make the lower-cost media economical, they will have a cost advantage over the firm with fewer outlets.

*Reducing Average Fixed Costs.* Spreading the firm's fixed overhead expenses over a larger number of units of output or sales is another reason for horizontal integration. The company's executive management team may be able to manage a larger number of production facilities or stores at no or only a small increase in total cost, with $AFC$ and $ATC$ both falling. Some staff and support functions need to have some minimum number of employees before a sufficiently wide range of specialties will be represented to make the overall operation highly efficient. An engineering support group may need to have electronic, electrical, mechanical, and industrial engineers before it can handle the company's engineering problems. One or two plants may not generate enough engineering work to support the smallest efficient engineering department. One or two plants would result in the company's having to use consulting engineers at higher costs (in terms of fees and co-ordinating costs) than engineers employed by the company. If engineering costs are significant, the company may need to have several plants before it can attain the cost levels of its larger rivals.

## 11.6.2 *Vertical Integration*

Most products are the result of many production activities, ranging from raw material extraction, to manufacturing components and the final product, to marketing to consumers through retail stores. In between each of these activities may occur a transportation activity. A firm that performs more than one of these activities for itself is vertically integrated. A steel company is vertically integrated if it obtains iron ore and coal from company-owned mines, moves them in company-owned ships, produces raw steel in its furnaces, and finishes it in its own rolling mills. An oil company is vertically integrated if it drills for oil, produces oil, ships it to its refineries in its own pipelines or tankers, and sells gasoline and other products through its own gas stations and bulk plants. A firm does not need to perform all of the production activities to be vertically integrated. An oil company owning just a refinery and gas stations is vertically integrated.

    ***Transaction Cost Savings.*** One motivation for vertical integration could be to obtain a monopoly over one or more production activities or to protect the firm from another firm's raw materials or marketing monopoly. There are cost reasons, however, for a firm's becoming vertically integrated. If the firm purchases a raw material, it must incur the transaction costs associated with that market purchase; that is, it must incur the costs of locating sellers of the raw material, ascertaining its market price, making the necessary purchase contracts, and policing the contract terms with respect to timely delivery and product quality. The firm can avoid these transaction costs by becoming vertically integrated and producing the raw material itself. Doing so means that it must incur the costs of administering the additional production activity and the transfer of the raw material to its processing plant. Assuming that the integrated firm is as efficient at producing the raw material as a firm specializing in its production, then if these administrative costs are less than the transaction costs, vertical integration will reduce its costs. Many firms are vertically integrated, so administrative costs are likely to be less than transaction costs in a number of industries.

***Production Economies.*** Production costs also play a major role in the extent to which firms are vertically integrated. The examples cited above from steel and oil assumed that production costs were the same whether each activity was performed by separate companies or by one company. However, the average cost curves of the several production activities need not have their minimum points at outputs that make vertical integration feasible. Assume that two production activities are required. In Figure 11.4, activity A involves production of a component that will be assembled into a final product in activity B. One unit of the component is required to produce one unit of the product. If the firm builds the plant that minimizes the *LRAC* of producing the final product, it will produce $B_0$ units and require $A_0$ units of the component. If it then builds the plant that produces $A_0$ units of the component, its ATC will be $a_0$, and the *ATC* of the final product will be $b_0$.

Assume that transaction costs are equal to administrative costs, so that the decision to build the component plant depends only on its production costs. A firm specializing in producing the component could build the plant that minimizes its *LRAC*. This firm could offer $2A_0$ units

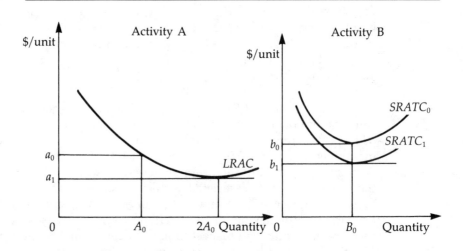

**Figure 11.4   Costs of Two Production Activities**

Production activity A provides a component used in activity B. If the firm produces the output that minimizes the *SRATC* of activity B, it would require $A_0$ units of the component. It can acquire A at lower cost than that of a plant designed to produce $A_0$ at minimum cost if it builds the plant that produces $2A_0$ or buys the component from another firm with the plant minimizing the *LRAC* of producing A. The lower cost for the component shifts the *SRATC* of activity B down to $SRATC_1$.

for sale at a price of $a_1$ and earn a normal profit from the plant. If the firm assembling the final product buys the component at $a_1$, its *ATC* would fall to $b_1$. To minimize its costs, the firm would either buy the component from another company or it would build the component plant producing $2A_0$ units and sell $A_0$ units on the market. Cost differences of this nature are common for firms producing standardized components parts and in the provision of specialized services to many individuals by CPAs, attorneys, and other professionals.

### 11.6.3 *Conglomerates and Diversified Firms*

A firm is a conglomerate when it has two or more plants producing products that are not good substitutes for one another. That is, a conglomerate produces in separate facilities products sold by two or more industries or product groups. Diversified firms are similar to conglomerates in that they both produce several product lines; however, diversified firms generally produce products that are related with respect to their technology or outlets for sales to consumers. Most large industrial companies are diversified, and many are also conglomerates. Large companies often grow by taking on new product lines and becoming conglomerates because it is more costly to grow by gaining a larger share of their present markets. Firms generally diversify or become conglomerates by merging with other firms presently producing the new product line. Building new plants to produce a new product is the other alternative, but it generally is less expensive to buy and expand an existing firm than to start up a new one.

*Acquire New Products.* Acquiring a monopoly over another industry is probably an unimportant reason for becoming a conglomerate. The firms that can be acquired are rarely the largest firms in the industry. The principal reason for becoming a diversified or conglomerate firm is to take advantage of the earnings growth potential of new products and technologies. These new products and technologies may offer more attractive investments for its capital than the firm's existing product lines. If the firm can hire or acquire through merger the necessary management and marketing expertise, investment in new product lines may increase earnings substantially faster than similar investments in existing product lines.

*Reduce Earnings Fluctuations.* Additional product lines can reduce fluctuations in earnings. If one product line is not profitable because the business cycle is in the recessionary phase, another product line may be doing well because it is not sensitive to the business cycle. Similarly, if one product line comes into stiff competition from a new technology, the impact on overall earnings can be reduced by profits from product lines unaffected by the new technology. The firm with several product lines may not grow as rapidly as one that concentrates its resources on a particularly profitable product line. Given the uncertainties associated with choosing in advance the product line that will grow most rapidly, investing in several offers a greater likelihood that the firm will benefit from at least one rapidly growing product line. The resulting reductions in earnings fluctuations reduces the financial risks associated with investing in the firm. Risk-averse sources of debt capital prefer investments in which there is steady growth in earnings to ones in which there is the same average rate of growth in earnings but much wider fluctuations. Thus, a conglomerate may have a lower cost of capital and a higher value than a single-product firm with the same average earnings level and growth rate.

*Other Reasons for Acquiring New Product Lines.* Another reason for the creation of conglomerates is related to the prospects for synergism. Synergism is described as two plus two equaling five. Combining two unrelated firms may result in the transfer of marketing, technological, or managerial expertise between the two product lines that makes them both substantially more profitable. It is like successful cross-pollination between plants, which yields a stronger offspring than inbreeding the separate strains. Acquisition of a firm that has well-established markets but has not had a dynamic management is generally felt to provide opportunities for synergism when the acquiring firm has been successful with its current product lines.

Acquiring new products, reducing earnings fluctuations, and synergism do not exhaust the possible sources of profits for diversified or conglomerate firms. Having the same sales force sell two unrelated products to the same outlet can reduce costs. Substantial tax savings may be possible if an acquisition is carefully structured and financed. The tax savings provide immediate benefits, and the other benefits of the additional product lines, which take some time to establish, provide the prospects for future earnings growth. Consolidating administrative and other support services can also add to the earnings from acquiring an unrelated company.

## 11.7   *Summary*

Oligopoly exists when each firm recognizes that it cannot profitably set its price and marketing policies without considering the reactions of its rivals. The products sold by oligopolies may be either homogeneous or differentiated. There usually is intense rivalry among the firms, although nonprice competition is normally preferred because it is more time-consuming and costly to counter than price reductions are. Oligopolists are particularly concerned with maintaining their market share because profits generally rise faster than the firm's market share.

An inability to predict the responses of the firm's rivals can make prices and profits unstable and lead the firms to engage in collusive price behavior. Since cheating on formal or tacit price agreements is highly profitable, such agreements tend to be short-lived. Price leadership is an alternative that can result in price stability and maximization of industry profits. In oligopolies dominated by a single giant firm, the dominant firm is the price leader. Industries with several large firms may follow the largest or the most successful firm as the price leader. The other large firms and the small firms then become price followers.

Multiple-plant firms may be horizontally or vertically integrated, conglomerates, or some combination of the three. Horizontally and vertically integrated firms have more than one production facility producing the same product (horizontally) or components for the production of a given product (vertically). Conglomerates produce two or more unrelated products, generally in separate facilities. Horizontal integration may result from a desire to obtain cost savings or to increase the firm's monopoly power. Vertically integrated firms and conglomerates are primarily created to obtain cost savings, although vertical integration can possibly enhance a firm's monopoly position by controlling a scarce resource. Many of the cost incentives for multiple-plant firms apply to competitive firms.

## CASE 13   Duopoly on the Beach

You work for the city's Parks and Recreation Department. Your job is to supervise 2 miles of city-owned beach. Two firms operate one skid-mounted hot dog stand each, one located north of the lifeguard station and the other to the south. The firms pay a concession fee of five cents per hot dog and soft drink (HDSD) sold. People visiting the beach spread themselves evenly along it. The cost of buying an HDSD from the consumer's point of view is the price paid at the stand plus the value of the time spent walking to the stand and back. To minimize the cost of buying an HDSD and to maximize the department's revenues, the stands are located one-half mile north and south of the lifeguard station.

The operator of the north stand wants to increase sales and profits by gaining a larger market share. He recognizes that all customers north of his stand are captive customers. The walk to the south stand is so far that they will never choose it. But if he secretly moves his stand 100 yards south of its present location, he will attract customers who are up to 50 yards south of the lifeguard station. So the operator of the north stand requests permission to bring a forklift onto the beach to repair the plumbing under its floor. You sign the pass and go back to observing rip tides and directing your lifeguards. That moonless, foggy night, the north stand is moved 100 yards to the south.

The operator of the north stand is pleased with the gradual increase in sales as people south of the lifeguard station realize that his stand is closer. The operator of the south stand has noted a gradual decline in sales; however, he attributes it to random variations. But one day, one of his employees reports that cups from the north stand are in the trash bin just south of the lifeguard tower, and people on the beach south of the lifeguard station are walking to and from the north stand. Checking further, he finds the north stand to be 126 paces closer to the lifeguard station. After verifying this information, the operator storms into your office and demands that the north stand be moved back to its proper location. So you call in the operator of the north stand. After going through the motions of checking its location, he is most apologetic. The forklift operator must have lost his bearings in the fog and put the stand in the wrong place. He agrees to move it back at dawn if you will place a stake in the proper place.

The operator of the south stand decides to recoup some of his lost sales. So he sneaks onto the beach at midnight and moves the stake 50 yards to the north. He talks his nephew, who starts operating the beach sweeper at 4 A.M., into pulling his stand 50 yards to the north and covering up the tracks. He reasons that the operator of the north stand will not notice the two 50-yard moves and attribute his decline in sales to the move and random variations in crowds and weather. Thus, the operator of the north stand will not react to his strategy and sales at the south stand should rise to above 50 percent of the market.

It is almost the end of the season before the operator of the north stand notices that something is amiss. Cups from the south stand are appearing in trash bins north of the lifeguard stand and his sales are not as high as before his original move. It looks like the stands are as far apart as they were originally. But one day he paces off the distances from each stand to the lifeguard station. Both stands are fifty yards north of their proper locations. So this time, you personally supervise moving of the stands and order your beach patrols to be sure that the stands are not moved again.

To eliminate the costs of supervising the locations of these stands, you decide to allow the operators to place their stands wherever they wish on their section of the beach. When the beach opens for the new season, both hot dog stands are 30 feet on either side of the lifeguard station! Each operator assumed that the other would place his stand at the center of his area of the beach. Using this as the reaction of the other operator, both operators thought they could obtain a larger market share by placing their stand next to the lifeguard station. Even if the other operator moved his stand to the lifeguard station the next day, the operator already at the lifeguard station would obtain a larger share of the sales to the huge opening day crowd and would not incur the $100 cost of moving his stand. Thus, from each operator's point of view, the best strategy was to locate adjacent to the lifeguard station, even though to maximize their *combined* sales they should be at the center of their concession areas. Since neither operator trusts the other, there is no incentive to come to an agreement as to where each stand should be located. And any agreement can be enforced only in court, where the operators must incur the costs of hiring attorneys and paying court fees.

To obtain the budgeted revenues from the concessions, you need to get them to move their stands to the center of their concession areas and stay there. So first thing on Monday morning you call up the city attorney. He promises to see if the city can force the operators to stay at the center of their concession areas. Having one operator own both stands would immediately solve the problem, but the city's charter requires at least two concessions. Having a larger number of concession operators would reduce the oligopolistic strategy/response problem, but the smaller size of each concession area would probably make the stands unprofitable. So he will look for another solution.

Each operator of a concession granted by the city must post a $25,000 performance bond as security for meeting the terms of the concession contract. Although the bond is intended to ensure that the operators pay all monies due to the city in a timely manner, the performances required could be enlarged to include locating the stands at the center of the concession area. Then if an operator moved his or her stand, the bond would be forfeited upon the department's proving that the stand was not in the center of its concession area. Since the incremental profits from moving a stand are nowhere near $25,000, this would keep them in the locations maximizing the department's revenues. Both operators are willing to include location of the stands in the performances required in their concession contracts. The next day both stands are at the center of their concession areas.

## CASE  14    The Yard Goods Store

For the past 5 years you have owned and operated a yard goods store in a small town about 25 miles from the city where you live. You have developed a marketing strategy that should be highly profitable in other areas. This strategy is based on competitive prices plus service-oriented clerks who are experienced in sewing and trained in providing advice to their customers. Your goal is to establish a chain of yard goods stores using your marketing techniques.

You have just leased a store in a new shopping center located on the edge of the city's central shopping area. There are five yard goods stores in the city, all of which appear to be prospering. A few variety stores and department stores also sell yard goods, but they provide little service and sell only a couple of product lines.

You have applied to your bank for a line of credit of $25,000 to finance the store's inventory of fabrics and other items. The loan application package requires a discussion of your pricing policies and a monthly profit projection. Since the yard goods store business in the city is an oligopoly, your pricing policies are based on your estimate of the reactions of the other store owners to your price and other marketing policies.

### Pricing at Your Present Store

There is no local competition at your yard goods store in the small town for most of its fabrics. The exceptions are plain broadcloth and cotton prints, which are sold at a nearby variety store. You must meet its competition in these product lines, which normally allows a 50 percent markup over their cost. That is, if a bolt of broadcloth costs $1.50 per yard from the manufacturer, you multiply the $1.50 by 1.5, which equals $2.25 per yard. This price is increased to $2.29 so that it ends in 9. This procedure normally results in a price that is no more than 10 percent above the variety store's. The rest of your yard goods, notions, and patterns are priced using a 100 percent markup. A stretch denim costing you $2.30 per yard would be priced at $4.69 per yard — $2.30 × 2 = $4.60 plus the increase of $0.09 to yield a price ending in 9. You occasionally run sales to clear slow-moving items or to attract new customers. Sale prices are based on a 25 percent to 35 percent markup.

### Pricing in the City

You have surveyed the five yard goods stores presently in the city. Prices at the shopping center stores are comparable for the same goods. The older stores in the strip commercial areas have prices 10 to 20 percent lower than the other stores. Their clientele appears to be mostly lower-income, older women. The shopping center stores cater to younger women and have customers from both lower- and middle-income families. Each of the three shopping center stores has at least one prominently displayed specialty line that is not stocked with such a wide variety of fabric patterns and colors by the other stores.

There appear to be three markup levels at these stores. The most heavily advertised, high-volume product lines apparently carry markups of 20 to 35 percent. These low markups apparently result from the high level of rivalry among the stores for this market, and from competition from variety stores. The second level is a 50 percent markup on the high-quality, high-fashion, and decorator product lines that you will emphasize. The third level is approximately a 100 percent markup on the store's specialty line. The apparent tacit agreement among the shopping center store owners not to compete vigorously with the other stores' specialty lines makes this high markup possible. Notions, patterns, and other products appear to carry 50 to 75 percent markups.

Competition for the high-quality, high-fashion, and decorator fabrics markets that you will emphasize is greatest among the shopping center stores. Although their selling skills were adequate, none of these clerks was particularly knowledgeable about sewing techniques or willing to spend a couple of minutes giving detailed advice on how best to cut or sew a pattern. Their emphasis was on how a particular fabric would look on the customer and on how much a bargain its price is. These clerks' lack of sewing experience should make it difficult for them to respond quickly to your use of experienced seamstresses as sales clerks.

## Your Conclusions Regarding Markups at the Shopping Center Stores

Your first conclusion is that the high-volume, relatively low-priced product lines are priced more on the basis of meeting the other stores' prices than on the basis of a customary markup. The higher-quality product lines show a consistent markup pattern among the shopping center stores, although the markup is much lower than at your small-town store. There is considerable advertising and in-store sales promotion of these fabrics, which probably accounts for the relatively low markups. The specialty line markup is the "customary" 100 percent for the business. The specialty line at your small-town store is fabrics for outdoor living. Since this line is not emphasized by any of the stores in the city, you decide to make it your specialty line. You will advertise this as your specialty line to signal the other stores that you expect them to respect your 100 percent markup. Moreover, you will stock only a small selection of their specialty items, not display them prominently, and price them using a 100 percent markup to signal the other stores that you will respect their specialty lines.

## Profit Projection

The first step is to use the markup data to calculate the gross margin on each of the store's four major product lines. This is done in Table 11.1, where the markup is multiplied by the average monthly sales volume projection to yield its gross margin. The gross margin projection for notions and other products is 15 percent of the projected gross margin for the fabric lines.

The store's monthly expenses for rent, labor, advertising, utilities, and other cost items are in Table 11.2. The labor projection is based on the store's being open 250 hours per month. On the average, there are two employees in the store and their cost (wages, em-

**Table 11.1  Gross Margin Projection**

| Product Line | Manufacturer's Price (per yard) | Markup (%) | Markup ($) | Monthly Volume (yards) | Gross Margin ($) |
|---|---|---|---|---|---|
| Regular quality | $1.15 | 25 | $0.34 | 2,400 | $ 816 |
| High quality | 2.00 | 50 | 1.09 | 2,000 | 2,180 |
| Specialty | 2.30 | 100 | 2.39 | 600 | 1,434 |
| Notions and other | | | | | 663 |
| | | | Total gross margin | | $5,083 |

**Table 11.2  Monthly Expense Projection**

| | |
|---|---|
| Rent | $ 650 |
| Labor | 2,200 |
| Advertising | 400 |
| Utilities | 300 |
| Other | 225 |
| Total expenses | $3,775 |

### Table 11.3 Monthly Profit Projection

| | | |
|---|---|---|
| Gross margin | | $5,083/month |
| Monthly expenses | | 3,775 |
| Net margin | | $1,308/month |
| Interest on inventory | | 262 |
| Accounting profit | | $1,046/month |
| Implicit costs | | 694 |
|    Your investment | $194 | |
|    Your labor | 500 | |
| Profit | | $352/month |

### Table 11.4 Capital Requirements Projection

| Product Line | Inventory (yards) | Manufacturer's Price (per yard) | Cost |
|---|---|---|---|
| Regular quality | 7,200 | $1.15 | $ 8,280 |
| High quality | 6,000 | 2.00 | 12,000 |
| Specialty | 1,800 | 2.30 | 4,140 |
| Notions and other | | | 3,600 |
| | | Total | $28,020 |
| | | Financed (85%) | 23,817 |
| | | Inventory investment | $ 4,203 |
| | | Fixtures investment | 4,500 |
| | | Working capital | 1,000 |
| | | Total investment | $ 9,703 |

ployee benefits, and payroll taxes) per hour averages $4.40. Your labor is accounted for under implicit costs in the profit projection in Table 11.3. The other expense categories are based on your rental contract and plans for operating the store.

The capital requirements projection is in Table 11.4. This projection consists of the cost of the store's normal inventory and its fixtures, and working capital. The inventory requirement for fabrics is 3 months' sales, and the cost of the notions and other products inventory is estimated at $3,600. The bank is expected to finance 85 percent of the store's inventory cost, yielding your inventory investment of $4,203. The store's fixtures cost $4,500, and the working capital required is $1,000. Your investment in the store is $9,703.

The monthly profit projection, provided in Table 11.3, can now be prepared. The gross margin and monthly expenses projections are from Tables 11.1 and 11.2. The interest rate on the bank loan to finance the store's inventory is 1.1 percent per month, or $262 per month. The accounting profit is $1,046 per month. The implicit cost of your $9,703 investment is based on the 2 percent per month average rate of return you have earned on your common stock and other investments. You estimate the opportunity cost of your time spent managing the store at $10 per hour for 50 hours per month. After deducting these implicit opportunity costs, the (economic) profit from operating the store is projected at an average of $352 per month for the first year of operations. You expect profits to grow by 20 to 50 percent per year as your store becomes better known and the city's population and per capita income rises.

In the final analysis, you consider the store to be an acceptably good investment of your time and capital. The bank's loan officer agrees and has authorized a line of credit of $25,000 secured by the store's inventory and fixtures.

## Key Terms

| | | |
|---|---|---|
| cartel | horizontal integration | price-leadership |
| conglomerate | kinked demand curve | oligopoly |
| diversified firm | limit-entry price | price war |
| dominant-firm oligopoly | nonprice competition | synergism |
| duopoly | price leadership | vertical integration |

## Review Questions

1. Compare and contrast oligopoly and monopolistic competition.

2. How does market communication among firms in an oligopoly differ from that of a competitive industry?

3. Although collusion can reduce some of the uncertainties associated with the response of one oligopolist to another's prices, there still exist significant destabilizing uncertainties. What are they and why do they lead to periodic price wars?

4. Why are small firms able to coexist with large firms in an oligopoly? Why do they generally act as price-taker firms?

5. Show graphically the impact on the dominant firm's price of (a) a

shift to the right in the market demand curve and (b) the entry of additional small firms.

6. Define the term *duopoly*. Explain how both firms in a duopoly would be able to increase their profits by colluding if there were some way to ensure that neither firm would cheat. Why will cheating lead to a price war?

7. Define the term *price leadership*. Why might an oligopoly with four or five large firms find price leadership attractive?

8. Describe the criteria that might be used by the price leader in determining its price so that there is a high probability that the other firms will follow its price.

9. Do the price followers necessarily set exactly the same price as the price leader? Why or why not?

10. Another term for a price leadership oligopoly is *shared monopoly*. Why might this term be appropriate?

11. Why do the large firms in an oligopoly prefer to compete using product differentiation, advertising, or other forms of nonprice competition?

12. Why might limit-entry pricing be acceptable to the large firms in an oligopoly even if it reduces profits in the next planning period?

13. How would the price leader determine the price that would limit (discourage) the entry of new firms into the industry?

14. What kind of behavior on the part of the large price-follower firms in a price-leadership oligopoly does the kinked demand curve theory explain?

15. Use the kinked demand curve theory to explain why a price-follower firm that develops a new technology reducing its variable costs by 5 percent is unlikely to lower its price.

16. Assume that the new technology in problem 15 was instead developed by a firm supplying equipment to the industry. Would this new technology lead to a lower industry price? Explain why or why not.

17. Define the terms *horizontal integration, vertical integration, conglomerate,* and *diversified firm.*

18. Why might a firm prefer to be horizontally integrated with two or more plants in different regions of the country than to have only one plant near the center of the United States?

19. Describe the cost savings that are potentially available to vertically integrated firms.

20. Assuming that both attorneys are equally skillful, why might a firm

prefer to hire an attorney in private practice rather than have an attorney on its staff to handle specialized litigation?

21. Why would a firm that is seeking earnings growth diversify or become a conglomerate in preference to seeking a larger share of its existing markets?

## *Problems and Applications*

1. The market demand curve for a dominant-firm oligopoly is $P = 1,000 - 5Q$, and the supply curve for the price follower firms is $P = 20 + 4Q$. The marginal cost curve for the dominant firm is $MC = 20 + 0.2Q$. Calculate the equation for the dominant firm's demand curve, its profit-maximizing output and price, and the output of the price-follower firms. Calculate the market share of the dominant firm.

2. Assume that $MC = \$10$ for all units of output and that the market demand function is $P = 500 - 5Q$.
   a. Calculate the profit-maximizing output, price, and total profit if this industry is a monopoly.
   b. Assume that a second firm that is identical to the monopolist enters the industry, making it a duopoly. Assume that the behavioral response of the initial firm is to maintain its output at the profit-maximizing level in part (a) and match the price of a new entrant. Calculate the profit-maximizing output and price of the new entrant firm.
   c. Is the price resulting in part (b) profit-maximizing for the initial firm? Why or why not?
   d. Calculate the equilibrium profit-maximizing output and price for both firms under the behavioral response assumed in part (b).
   e. If the two firms collude, what will be the price and output for each firm in collusion?
   f. Why do both firms have strong incentives to cheat on the collusion agreement?

3. The demand function for an oligopoly's homogeneous product is $P = 920 - 6Q$ where $Q$ is output per hour. The marginal cost curve for all firms, individually and collectively, is $MC = AVC = \$440$. There are four identical firms in the industry, each with fixed costs of $\$1,800$ per hour.
   a. Assume that the price leader maximizes industry profits. Calculate the profit-maximizing output and price for the industry.
   b. Calculate the hourly output and profit of each firm on the assumption that it has a 25 percent market share.

c. Calculate the point-elasticity of demand at the industry's profit-maximizing price and output. Is demand elastic?

d. It can be shown that $MR = (1 + 1/E_P)P$. Use this relationship to explain why a price-follower firm would not adopt a price different from the price leader's if management believes that its elasticity of demand is $-2.5$ for price reductions below the price leader's and $E_P = -5.0$ for price increases.

4. Assume that marginal cost in problem 3 rises to $MC = \$500$.

   a. Calculate the impact of this increase in $MC$ on the typical firm's profits.

   b. Explain why a price-follower firm would not independently change its price with this increase in marginal cost.

   c. Explain why the price-leader firm would raise its price as a result of this increase in marginal cost.

5. Continuing with problem 3, assume that one of the price-follower firms develops a new technology that shifts its $MC$ curve down to $MC = \$400$. None of the other firms has this new technology. Would this result in the price-follower firm's reducing its price? Explain why or why not. Use the equation for $MR$ in problem 3(d) to calculate the profit-maximizing price for the price-follower firm.

6. Assume that each of the 60 firms in a competitive industry has been producing 100 units per hour of a component for their product using a production facility with no fixed costs and $AVC = 650 - 15q + q^{1.5}$. A division of a large manufacturing company has developed a new technology for producing this component that has the average cost function $SRATC = \$256,100 - 120q + q^{1.5}$.

   a. What is the $AVC$ of producing this component for each of the competitive firms?

   b. Why will the 60 firms cease producing the component and buy it from the firm with the new technology if the component producer sets its price using a 25 percent markup above its $SRATC$?

   c. Assume that the competitive firms incur transaction and transportation costs of \$15 per unit if they buy the component from the large firm. Will this affect their decision to buy the component?

# 12

# *Risk Management*

One common element in all business decisions is the existence of uncertainty. Future prices, wage rates, raw material costs, factor productivities, and so forth are never known with certainty. Managers make decisions with incomplete information about the future because the cost of obtaining the additional information that might yield better forecasts is believed to be greater than the resulting increase in profits. When uncertainties about the future are converted into statements about the probabilities of events occurring, risk management can be applied to making business decisions.

Making decisions when there is risk means evaluating tradeoffs between greater risks and higher profits. Moreover, managers and investors have varying attitudes toward risk and the tradeoffs they are willing to make. Each decision maker has a risk preference function that relates the level of his or her utility to alternative combinations of risk and return. It is subjective, but if the decision maker can specify the risk preference function, the utility-maximizing alternative can be determined.

A wide variety of risk management techniques are available. This chapter introduces a few of these techniques and their application to several types of problems. The problems include choosing the utility-maximizing output for a competitive firm and deciding whether to add to inventories in anticipation of a possible price increase. Risk management techniques include casualty insurance, hedging, and options.

## 12.1  *Measuring Risk*

When the value of a variable is not known with certainty, it is a random variable. The sun's rising is an event that can be predicted with certainty. The price of wheat in July cannot be predicted with certainty; it is a random variable. Each value that the random variable can assume is referred to as an event or outcome. The market price of a product in the next planning period is a random variable, and the several prices that management believes are possible are events. Only one event, say, a price of $21.05, will actually occur. Yet managements must be able to evaluate in a systematic manner all of the possible outcomes and make decisions about output, the number of workers to hire, and so forth when price cannot be predicted with certainty.

*Estimating Probabilities.* The methods presented in this chapter for analyzing situations where the actual outcome cannot be predicted with certainty assume that the events are mutually exclusive. If event *A* is a price between $20.00 and $20.99, event *B* cannot be a price between $20.50 and $21.49 because the price ranges contain a common interval, $20.50 to $20.99. The probabilities associated with each event must add up to one if all possible outcomes are considered. When flipping a coin, the probability of a head, $Pr(H)$, plus the probability of a tail, $Pr(T)$, must add up to one. If $Pr(H) = Pr(T) = 0.5$, then $Pr(H) + Pr(T) = 1$. The events *H* and *T* are mutually exclusive. When probabilities can be estimated by dividing the number of possible outcomes into one, they are *a priori* probabilities. Random variables where probabilities can be specified *a priori* rarely occur in business decision making.

The probabilities associated with some random variables can be estimated on the basis of past experience. Assume that the random variable is the percentage of defective parts produced by a manufacturing process. Each event is a specified percentage of defective parts. The firm's quality assurance department has sampled 100 production runs, determined the percentage of defective parts in each run, and arranged the results in Table 12.1. The relative frequency column is the number of runs with the specified percentage of defective parts divided by the total number of runs. The relative frequency of each event is an estimate of its probability. If the relative frequencies of the events are not changed significantly by sampling, say, another 50 production runs, management can be reasonably confident that the relative frequencies are good estimates of the probability of each event. Regression analysis can also be used to estimate the probability that a random variable (the dependent variable of the regression equation) will take on a specified range of values. If probabilities can be estimated using relative frequencies, regression analysis or some other data-based technique, decisions based

**Table 12.1   Relative Frequency of an Event**

| Percent Defective | Number of Runs | Relative Frequency |
|---|---|---|
| 0% | 0 | 0.00 |
| 1% | 4 | 0.04 |
| 2% | 11 | 0.11 |
| 3% | 67 | 0.67 |
| 4% | 14 | 0.14 |
| 5% | 2 | 0.02 |
| 6% | 2 | 0.02 |
| Over 6% | 0 | 0.00 |
| | 100 | 1.00 |

on the random variable are subject to risk. Risk exists where the probabilities of the events can be specified.

The probabilities associated with some random variables cannot be estimated using the relative frequency method. Uncertainty exists when management believes that it cannot estimate, using the available data, the probability of an event's occurring. For example, the potential sales of a unique new product are highly uncertain. What basis does a manager have for asserting that the probability of sales of 10,000 units or more at a $20 price is 50 percent if the advertising budget is $25,000? If a similar product has never been marketed, the manager must guess the probability based on his or her experience and judgment. Thus, the 50 percent probability is referred to as a subjective probability. When there is uncertainty about the probabilities of each possible event, management must estimate them using a subjective reasoning process. Once subjective probabilities have been assigned to each event, uncertainty no longer exists.[1] The uncertain situation has been converted into one of risk.

A major problem faced by young or new managers is developing the ability to assess subjective probabilities in a manner acceptable to their superiors. Managers have their own ways of arriving at subjective probabilities and may not be able to articulate them in a clear and consistent manner. Their subordinates generally must learn how to assess subjective probabilities through observation of how the boss arrives at decisions and by the boss's reactions to their decisions.

---

[1]There exist truly uncertain cases where not even the set of possible outcomes is known or knowable. Such cases cannot be analyzed using the risk management techniques discussed in this chapter.

*Expected Value and Standard Deviation.* Once the probabilities associated with each possible event have been specified, the expected value and standard deviation of the random variable can be calculated. Let $R_i$ be the value of the event $i$ and $Pr_i$ be its probability. The formulas for calculating the expected value and standard deviation of random variable $R$ are

$$\overline{R} = \Sigma(R_i)(Pr_i) \tag{12.1}$$

$$\sigma_R = \sqrt{\Sigma(R_i - \overline{R})^2(Pr_i)} \tag{12.2}$$

Assume that management has prepared the price and probability forecasts in the second and third columns of Table 12.2. Calculation of the expected price is in the fourth column. Columns five through seven contain the steps for calculating the standard deviation of the price forecast. $\overline{R}$ and $\sigma_R$ are $20.40 and $2.46, respectively.

Interpretation of the expected price is straightforward. It measures the central tendency inherent in management's price predictions. When calculated using equation 12.1, the expected price is a weighted average in which the weights are the probabilities of each projected price. The expected value provides the reference point from which the standard deviation is calculated. Interpretation of the standard deviation involves consideration of the variation in the data. The variance measures the average variation of each price prediction from the expected value. ($R_i - \overline{R}$) is the amount by which $R_i$ varies from $\overline{R}$. By squaring ($R_i - \overline{R}$), the variations become positive. When multiplied by the probability and summed, the result is the weighted average of the squared variations. This average is the variance of the forecast. Since the units of the variance are dollars-squared, its square root is taken to yield a measure of variation with the same units (dollars) as the price projections and their expected value.

**Table 12.2　Calculating the Expected Value and Standard Deviation**

| $i$ | $R_i$ | $Pr$ | $R_iPr_i$ | $(R_i - \overline{R})$ | $(R_i - \overline{R})^2$ | $(R_i - \overline{R})^2(Pr_i)$ |
|---|---|---|---|---|---|---|
| 1 | $25 | 0.2 | $ 5.0 | $4.6 | $21.16 | $4.232 |
| 2 | 20 | 0.5 | 10.0 | −0.4 | 0.16 | 0.080 |
| 3 | 18 | 0.3 | 5.4 | −2.4 | 5.76 | 1.728 |
|  |  |  | $\overline{R}$ = $20.4 |  |  | $6.040 |
|  |  |  |  |  |  | $\sigma_R$ = $2.46 |

*Measuring Relative Risk.* For a given expected value, the larger the standard deviation, the greater the average variation in the price projections. The standard deviation measures the level of risk associated with a forecast. If two forecasts have the same expected value, the greater the average variation in the projections, the higher the inherent risk. When the standard deviation is zero, there is no risk and the value of the variable is known with certainty. Risk decreases when the probability increases that the actual value of the random variable will be within a specified range about the average. Assume that management has two possible investments with the same expected return and wishes to determine which investment involves greater risk. This amounts to determining which investment has the wider confidence interval. The confidence interval is the range of values about the expected value within which the actual value will occur with a specified probability. Investment $A$ has an expected rate of return of $\overline{R} = 18\%$ and a standard deviation in its rate of return of $\sigma_A = 4.7\%$. Investment $B$ has the same rate of return and $\sigma_B = 8.1\%$. Assume that management specifies a 75 percent probability for the confidence interval. If the probability distribution of the rates of return is normal, the 75 percent probability confidence interval is $\overline{R} \pm 1.15\sigma$.[2] For investment $A$ the confidence interval is $18\% \pm 1.15(4.7\%)$, or 12.595% to 23.405%. For investment $B$ it is $18\% \pm 1.15(8.1\%)$, or 8.685% to 27.315%. Investment $B$ is riskier because the confidence interval within which there is a 75 percent probability of the actual value's occurring is larger. There is a greater probability that investment $B$ will reduce the value of the firm. If the firm's cost of capital is 12 percent, investment $A$ has a greater than 75 percent probability of earning more than the cost of capital and increasing the value of the firm. Investment $B$ has less than a 75 percent probability of increasing the value of the firm because rates of return between 8.685 percent and 12 percent are included in its 75 percent confidence interval.

The standard deviation is used to measure risk when the expected values of the alternatives under consideration are equal. When the expected values are not equal, risk can be measured by the coefficient of variation, which is defined as $CV = \sigma_R / \overline{R}$ where $\overline{R} > 0$. An increase in $CV$ means that the alternative is riskier since $\sigma_R$ has risen relative to $\overline{R}$, which reduces the probability that the actual value will occur within a given range of values about $\overline{R}$. In the analysis that follows in this chapter, it is not necessary to use $CV$ as the measure of risk.

These procedures for calculating and interpreting the expected value and standard deviation are no better than the underlying forecasts

---

[2]The 1.15 coefficient on $\sigma$ is found from Table 2.2 as the Z value for $\alpha = 0.125$, because a 75 percent confidence interval implies that there is a probability of 12.5 percent in each tail of the normal distribution.

of prices or rates of return and their probabilities. As the computer people put it — garbage in, garbage out. If past data are used to prepare the forecasts, the data gathering and analysis phase is crucial. If management's experience and judgment play a major role in preparing the forecasts, the final decision maker must have confidence in the analysts who prepared them. All methods of risk management depend on the quality of the work that has gone into preparing the underlying forecasts.

## 12.2  *Risk Preference*

Uncertainty and risk are faced by managers and investors when they make decisions. Yet people differ with respect to their willingness to accept risk. When given the same return and risk level, one decision maker accepts the project and another rejects it. Some people seek out risky situations because they offer the chance, however small the probability, to earn phenomenal profits. Others abhor risks and cannot sleep at night when faced with making a high-risk decision or awaiting its outcome. Most managers and investors are somewhere in between these extremes, though few are neutral with respect to risk.

Risk preference curves are subjective representations of the manager's attitudes toward risk. They are not directly observable but may be inferred from the manager's past decisions if the risk and return information used by the manager are available. Particularly perceptive top managers may provide their subordinates with rules of thumb that approximate a risk preference function. The subjective attitudes of managers toward risk are formed over time through the interaction of a wide range of factors including the managers' temperament, training, past experiences with risky situations, influence of other managers they have worked with, and their dealings with bankers and financiers. Their risk preferences may change over time. Professional managers who are top executives at large corporations are usually risk-averse, although they may have managers on their staffs who are risk seekers. These risk-averse top managers will approve a few highly risky projects as part of the corporation's operating or capital investment plans because the overall plan fits their risk-averse preferences and the highly risky projects provide the prospects for major new areas of corporate growth if they turn out to be successful.

For the purpose of analyzing situations involving risk, managers and investors are viewed as possessing a risk preference, or *RP*, function. The *RP* function is a tradeoff function that has risk and the expected return as its variables. The graph of a decision maker's *RP* function is an indifference curve. An indifference curve consists of all opportunities leaving the decision maker equally well-off, and hence indifferent among them. Whether the decision maker is risk-averse, -neutral, or -seeking depends on the slope of the *RP* curve.

**Risk-Averse.** The risk preference curves for a risk-averse individual are upward sloping indifference curves. A risk-averse *RP* function occurs when the decision maker must be compensated with a higher expected return to take on a higher level of risk. Point *A* in Figure 12.1 is one combination of risk and return that an individual is willing to accept. If offered a second opportunity with the same return and a higher level of risk, as at point *B*, the risk-averse person will prefer opportunity *A*. For this decision maker to be indifferent between opportunity *A* and opportunity *C* with risk level $\sigma_1$, the return must rise to $\overline{R}_1$. The increase in return required, $\overline{R}_1 - \overline{R}_0$, will differ among decision makers, depending upon the extent to which they are risk-averse. A decision maker who is indifferent between opportunities *A* and *C* is willing to trade off an

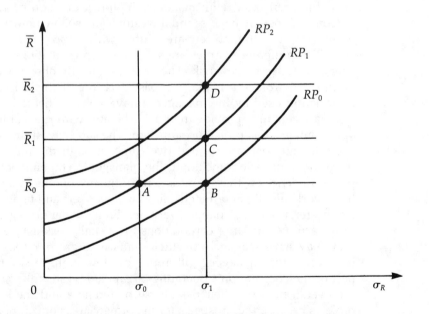

**Figure 12.1   Risk-Averse Preference Curves**

The decision maker is indifferent between points *A* and *C*; hence, they are on the same *RP* curve. Point *A* is preferred to point *B* because it has less risk (a smaller $\sigma$) for the same expected return. To compensate for the added risk of point *B*, the risk-averse decision maker requires an increase in the expected return from $\overline{R}_0$ to $\overline{R}_1$. Point *D* is preferred to *C* because it has a higher return for the same risk.

increase in risk, $\sigma_1 - \sigma_0$, for the increase in return $\overline{R}_1 - \overline{R}_0$. This same individual, if offered opportunity $D$, would prefer it to $A$ or $C$ because $D$ has the same level of risk as $C$ but a higher return. Opportunities $A$ and $C$ are on the same risk preference curve, $RP_1$; whereas opportunity $D$ is on the higher curve $RP_2$ and opportunity $B$ is on the lower curve $RP_0$. The decision maker would prefer a higher $RP$ curve.

**Risk-Neutral.** If the decision maker is risk-neutral, the RP curve is horizontal, as is the case for $RP_0$ and $RP_1$ in Figure 12.2. The individual is indifferent between opportunities $A$ and $B$, which have the same return but different risk levels. The risk-neutral decision maker would prefer $RP_1$ to $RP_0$ because $RP_1$ has a higher return for any level of risk.

**Risk-Seeking.** $RP_2$ in Figure 12.2 is the risk preference curve for a risk-seeking decision maker who is willing to trade off a lower return

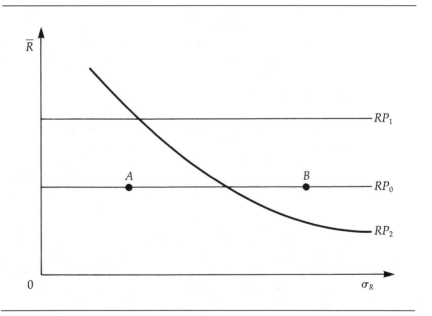

**Figure 12.2   Risk-Neutral and Risk-Seeker Preference Curves**

$RP_0$ and $RP_1$ are the horizontal preference curves of a risk-neutral decision maker because their level depends only on the expected return. $RP_1$ is preferred to $RP_0$ since it has a greater expected return for each level of risk. $RP_2$ is the preference curve of a risk-seeking decision maker who is willing to trade a lower expected return for a greater level of risk; hence, the risk preference curve is downward sloping.

for a higher level of risk. This may seem pathological to a risk-averse person; however, the risk-seeker places a high premium on the chance to obtain the very high return that a project with a large variation in outcomes provides. This person is seeking a higher probability of earning profits significantly above average, a sort of get-rich-quick, make-it-big attitude towards risk. Some persons, such as wildcat oil drillers and investors in R & D oriented companies, are relatively strong risk-seekers.

## 12.3 *Maximizing Utility When There Is Risk*

A risk preference curve is the locus of all combinations of risk and return that yield the decision maker the same level of well-being or utility. When prices or productivities are not known with certainty, the risk-averse decision maker cannot simply choose the alternative that maximizes profits or wealth, because the alternatives differ with respect to their risk level. Only a risk-neutral manager could behave in that manner since, by definition, a risk-neutral person is one who is indifferent to varying levels of risk. The risk-averse decision maker is willing to make some tradeoffs between risk and return, and not others. The decision maker includes both risk and return in the parameters to be considered when using his or her *RP* function to decide which alternative is utility-maximizing.

*The Risk-Return Curve.* The curve that plots the expected return of each alternative decision with its risk is the risk return, or *RR*, curve. In general, the risk return curve has the inverted U shape shown in Figure 12.3. The alternatives with the lowest risk have the lowest expected returns. As management is willing to take on more risk, the expected return rises. However, the expected return does not continue to rise as the risk level rises. At some level of risk, the expected return will reach its peak and then decline as the level of risk continues to rise. That is, highly risky projects offer a lower expected return than less risky ones, but they do offer a higher probability that the firm will earn an exceptionally high return if the outcome of accepting the high-risk project is very favorable. This relationship between risk and return as the risk level increases results from measuring risk with the standard deviation of the return. An example of how to calculate points on the risk-return curve is provided in the next section. The remainder of this section is devoted to finding the decision maker's utility-maximizing combination of risk and return given the risk return curve calculated for each of the alternative decisions.

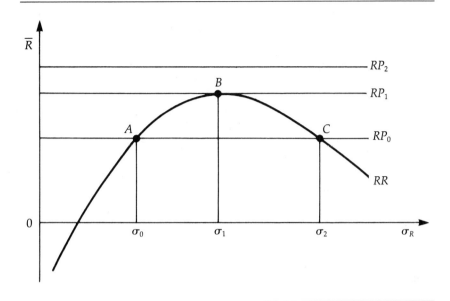

**Figure 12.3   Utility Maximization for a Risk-Neutral Manager**

*RR* is the firm's risk return curve. Each point on *RR* provides the combination of risk and expected return that occurs when the firm makes a specific decision. If the manager makes the decision yielding point *A*, the *RP* curve is $RP_0$. Successively higher utility levels can be attained by moving along *RR* from point *A* to *B*. At point *B*, the manager's utility is maximized. Moving beyond point *B* results in the manager's being on a lower *RP* curve.

*Utility Maximization.* Consider first the decision of a risk-neutral manager with the horizontal risk preference curves in Figure 12.3. The decision maker could attain utility level $RP_0$ with alternatives *A* or *C* on the *RR* curve. However, he or she would prefer to obtain a higher return if it were available. A higher return is available with alternative *B*. It yields a higher utility level because $RP_1$, which contains point *B*, lies above $RP_0$. The manager would prefer to choose a point on $RP_2$; however, the available alternatives are only those on the *RR* curve, and $RP_2$ is unattainable. Alternative *B* is the one that the risk-neutral manager will choose. Profit-maximizing managers are risk-neutral managers when variables involved in the profit calculation are not known with certainty, because the profit-maximizing manager will always choose point *B* in Figure 12.3 regardless of its risk level.

Most managers are risk-averse. The decision alternatives open to a risk-averse manager are the same as before and are plotted as the

*RR* curve in Figure 12.4. Risk preference curve $RP_0$ is attainable with either alternative *A* or *C*; however, alternative *B* lies on the higher *RP* curve $RP_1$ and is preferred to *A* or *C*. Alternative *D*, where the *RR* curve reaches its maximum, offers a higher expected return than *B*; however, the decision maker is risk-averse and willing to trade off a reduction in risk of $\sigma_1 - \sigma_0$ for an expected return that is $\overline{R}_1 - \overline{R}_0$ lower. Hence, the *RP* curve tangent to the *RR* curve at point *B* lies above the *RP* curve passing through point *D*. Risk preference curve $RP_2$ is not attainable given the available alternatives on the *RR* curve.

The utility-maximizing combination of risk and return occurs where the *RR* curve is tangent to an *RP* curve. This is a general condition for maximizing or minimizing one function subject to a constraint. The risk management problem is expressed as maximizing the decision maker's

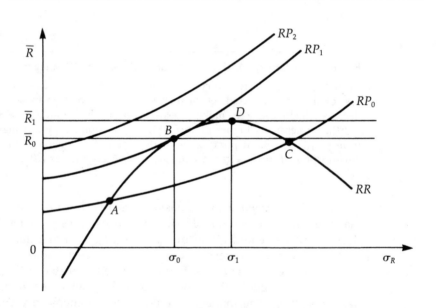

**Figure 12.4   Utility Maximization for a Risk-Averse Manager**

*RR* is the firm's risk return curve relative to the decision at hand. The manager can attain a more preferred combination of risk and expected return than point *A* on $RP_0$. By moving along the *RR* curve toward point *B*, the manager's utility rises until point *B* on $RP_1$ is reached. The decision yielding point *B* is utility-maximizing since continuing to move along the *RR* curve towards points *D* and *C* yields points that are on *RP* curves below $RP_1$.

utility subject to the constraint imposed by the combinations of risk and return inherent in the available alternatives. This structure of the decision problem provides a strategy for calculating the utility-maximizing combination of risk and return when the equations for the two functions are specified. Calculate the slopes of each function, equate them, and solve for the risk level and expected return that maximize the decision maker's utility.

**EXAMPLE 12.1.**   Assume that the risk return function is

$$\overline{R} = -20 + 11.3\sigma - 0.5\sigma^2$$

A risk-averse manager has the risk-preference function

$$\overline{R} = U + 0.5\sigma + 0.1\sigma^2$$

where $U$ is the manager's utility level.[3] This manager is risk-averse because increases in risk ($\sigma$) must be accompanied by an increase in $\overline{R}$ if the manager's utility level ($U$) is to be unchanged. Their derivatives are

$$d\overline{R}/d\sigma = 11.3 - \sigma$$
$$d\overline{R}/d\sigma = 0.5 + 0.2\sigma$$

Equating these derivatives and solving for $\sigma$ yields

$$11.3 - \sigma = 0.5 + 0.2\sigma$$
$$\sigma = 9$$

The expected return is found by substituting $\sigma = 9$ into the *RR* function

$$\overline{R} = -20 + 11.3(9) - 0.5(9)^2 = 41.2$$

Thus, the risk-averse manager would accept the alternative with $\sigma = 9$ and $\overline{R} = 41.2$. Had the manager been risk-neutral, the derivative of the risk return function would have been set equal to zero and solved for to yield $\sigma = 11.3$ and $\overline{R} = 43.845$.

---

[3]A more conventional way to write the risk-preference function would be as $U = \overline{R} - 0.5\sigma - 0.1\sigma^2$ to reflect the fact that for a risk-averse decision maker, an increase in $\overline{R}$ will increase his or her utility or an increase in risk ($\sigma$) will decrease it.

## 12.4  *Calculating the Utility-Maximizing Output*

Assume that the price at which a competitively produced product is sold is a random variable. The other variables used to calculate the profit-maximizing output are assumed to be known with certainty. When one of the variables in the profit function is not known with certainty, it would seem that profit maximization could be replaced with maximizing the expected value of profits. The firm would produce the output that maximizes its expected profits. However, this goal can be used only if the decision maker is risk-neutral. If the manager is risk-averse, the risk return function must be calculated, the manager's risk preference function specified, and the output maximizing the manager's utility determined. In this section, an example is used to illustrate assessment of the risks inherent in alternative output rate decisions.

*Making the Output Decision Without Considering the Standard Deviation of Profits.* Assume that the firm's product is perishable and cannot be stored for more than a day or two before it must be sold. The market price of this product is not known with certainty, but its probability distribution has been estimated by the market research department on the basis of a supply/demand study. Assume that there are two possible prices, $12 or $16 per unit.[4] The profit-maximizing output is $q_0$ in Figure 12.5 if price is $12 and $q_1$ if price is $16. The four possible profit outcomes, given the two possible prices and the two profit-maximizing outputs, are summarized in Table 12.3.

After examining Table 12.3, a conservative manager might decide to produce $q_0$, the profit-maximizing output if price is $12. This manager would prefer to avoid the loss of profits represented by area $A$ in Figure 12.5 if $q_1$ was chosen as the firm's output. An aggressive manager might prefer producing $q_1$ because if the actual price is $16 area $B$ will be added to profits. If these two types of managements both exist, the firms producing the profit-maximizing output for the actual market price would earn greater profits than the others. If some managers are more skilled than others in predicting the actual market price, their firms will be consistently more profitable. This could lead to relatively risky industries attracting high-quality managers. The ability to make correct judgments about the future is more likely to be rewarded in a relatively risky industry than in an industry where there is little fluctuation in market prices or other variables in the firm's profit function.

An astute manager may decide to avoid either extreme and produce

---

[4]These are the only outcomes that management believes are possible, or at least that it is willing to consider in its planning. Actual market conditions may yield other prices.

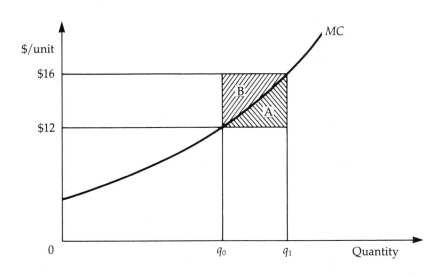

**Figure 12.5   Profit-Maximizing Output**
The firm finds its profit-maximizing output where $MC = P$. If the firm sets
its output at $q_0$, it will produce the profit-maximizing output if price turns
out to be $12 and will not earn the additional profits represented by area $B$
if price turns out to be $16. If the firm produces $q_1$, it will maximize its prof-
its if price is $16 but will lose profits equal to area $A$ if price turns out to be
$12, because $MC > P$ for all outputs between $q_0$ and $q_1$.

**Table 12.3   Decision/Outcome Table**

| Actual Market Price Resulting from Demand/ Supply Interaction | Decision: Produce the Profit-Maximizing Output Assuming Price Will Be: | |
|---|---|---|
| | $P_1 = \$12$ | $P_2 = \$16$ |
| $P_1 = \$12$ | Optimal decision | Produced too much; profits reduced by some output being sold at a price less than marginal cost |
| $P_2 = \$16$ | Produced too little; loss of potential profits because additional output could be produced at a marginal cost less than price. | Optimal decision |

the output that maximizes profit at the expected price. Let $E(X)$ be the expected value of variable $X$ where

$$E(X) = \Sigma(X_i)(Pr_i) \tag{12.3}$$

The equation for calculating the firm's profit is $\Pi = Pq - AVC(q)q - FC$. The expected profit is

$$E(\Pi) = E(P)q - AVC(q)q - FC \tag{12.4}$$

if price is the only random variable. To calculate the expected price, management must specify the probability of each possible price. The "true" probabilities will generally not be known, and may not be discernible even if the planning process is repeated for many planning periods. As the number of planning periods increases, the number of times a \$12 price has occurred divided by the total number of planning periods approaches the "true" probability of $P = \$12$. However, the rate at which this relative frequency probability approaches the "true" one is unknown and for a number of planning periods it may diverge from the "true" probability. All management can do is use the available data on price trends, likely demand/supply conditions in the next planning period, and its judgment and experience to specify what it believes are the correct probabilities.

Assume that the probability of $P = \$12$ is 0.6 and of $P = \$16$ is 0.4. Substituting these values into equation 12.3 yields an expected price of (\$12 $\times$ 0.6) + (\$16 $\times$ 0.4) = \$13.60. Assume that $AVC = \$2.50 + \$0.02q$ and $FC = \$400$. Marginal cost is $MC = \$2.50 + \$0.04q$. The profit-maximizing output for the expected price is found by equating $MC$ to \$13.60 and solving for $q$:

$$\$2.50 + \$0.04q = \$13.60$$

$$q = 277.5 \text{ units}$$

Substituting this value of $q$ into equation 12.4 yields an expected profit of \$1,140 for the next planning period. Thus, even though the actual price will be either \$12 or \$16, on the average over many planning periods the firm can expect to have a profit of \$1,140 if it produces 277.5 units of output.

*Calculating the Risk Return Function.* The preceding discussion was based on consideration of alternative prices to use in calculating profits. The decision-making process can generally be improved by

**Table 12.4  Calculating the Standard Deviation of Profits (Output is 277.5 and expected profit is $1,140)**

| Price | Prob-ability | Profit | $\Pi - E(\Pi)$ | $[\Pi - E(\Pi)]^2$ | $[(\Pi) - E(\Pi)]^2$ (Probability) |
|-------|---------|--------|---------|---------|---------|
| $12   | 0.6     | $  696 | $-444   | $197,136 | $118,282 |
| 16    | 0.4     | 1,806  | 666     | 443,556  | 177,422  |
|       |         |        |         | Variance = | $295,704 |
|       |         |        |         | Standard deviation = | $543.79 |

explicitly measuring the risk inherent in each possible output decision. The measure of risk used here is the standard deviation of profits at each possible output rate. For example, to find the standard deviation of profits when $q = 277.5$, calculate the firm's profits at $q = 277.5$ if price is $12 and if price is $16. When $P = \$12$, $\Pi = \$696$ and when $P = \$16$, $\Pi = \$1,806$. The standard deviation of profits when $q = 277.5$ units is $544. The details of this calculation are in Table 12.4.

Similar calculations of the expected profit and its standard deviation can be made for outputs other than 277.5 units. In Table 12.5, the expected profit and its standard deviation have been calculated for outputs ranging from 162.5 units to 437.5 units in increments of 25 units. The entries for $q = 277.5$ are also included in Table 12.5. The expected profit peaks at $q = 277.5$. As output rises, the standard deviation of profit also rises. Higher outputs are associated with higher levels of risk. The increasing risk results from the increasing difference in profits at the two possible market prices as output rises. Plotting the expected profit and standard deviation of profits for each possible output yields the risk return curve.

***Using the Risk Return Curve to Make the Output Decision.*** The policy of the conservative manager was to produce the profit-maximizing output for a price of $12, which is 237.5 units. From Table 12.5, the expected profit is $1,108 with a standard deviation of $465. This manager is risk-averse because the lower profit is compensated for by the lower risk. The aggressive manager chose the output that maximized profits at a price of $16, which is 337.5 units. This manager's expected profits are $1,068 with a standard deviation of $661. Like the conservative manager, the aggressive manager was willing to accept a lower expected profit than the astute manager; however, the lower expected profit was accepted because the probability of high profits was greater. At an actual price of $16, the astute manager would earn only $1,806; whereas

**Table 12.5  Expected Profits and Standard Deviations**

| Output | Projected Profits | | Expected Profit | Standard Deviation |
|--------|------------|------------|---------|-----------|
|        | P = $12    | P = $16    |         |           |
| 162.5  | $616       | $1,266     | $  876  | $318      |
| 187.5  | 676        | 1,428      | 978     | 367       |
| 212.5  | 716        | 1,566      | 1,055   | 416       |
| 237.5  | 728        | 1,678      | 1,108   | 465       |
| 262.5  | 716        | 1,766      | 1,135   | 514       |
| 277.5  | 696        | 1,806      | 1,140   | 544       |
| 287.5  | 678        | 1,828      | 1,138   | 563       |
| 312.5  | 616        | 1,865      | 1,116   | 612       |
| 337.5  | 528        | 1,878      | 1,068   | 661       |
| 362.5  | 416        | 1,866      | 996     | 710       |
| 387.5  | 278        | 1,828      | 898     | 759       |
| 412.5  | 116        | 1,766      | 776     | 808       |
| 437.5  | -72        | 1,678      | 628     | 857       |

the aggressive manager would earn $1,878. As Table 12.5 shows, it is possible to be too aggressive; at outputs beyond 337.5 units the profit at $P = \$16$ declines (because the rising $AVC$ is not compensated for by a higher price). In terms of section 12.2, the aggressive manager is a risk-seeker.

Assume now that the decision maker is risk-averse. Would this manager necessarily choose the conservative manager's output of 237.5 units? The answer is no. Once the manager has specified the risk preference function, the next step is to use the data in Table 12.5 to plot the risk return function in Figure 12.6. Since the manager's risk preference curve is tangent to $RR$ at a risk level of $514 and an expected profit of $1,135, the decision would be to produce $q = 262.5$ units. If the manager's $RP$ curves were steeper, the point of tangency would have been to the left of point ($514, $1,135) in Figure 12.6, and a lower output would have been utility-maximizing.

Calculating the risk-return curve is more complex if more of the variables entering into the profit function are random variables. However, the principles remain the same. Once the necessary probabilities have been estimated, either subjectively or using some method based on data, the expected profit and its standard deviation can be calculated for each output that management is considering. As long as the decision maker can articulate the tradeoffs between risk and expected profits, the method described here can be applied.

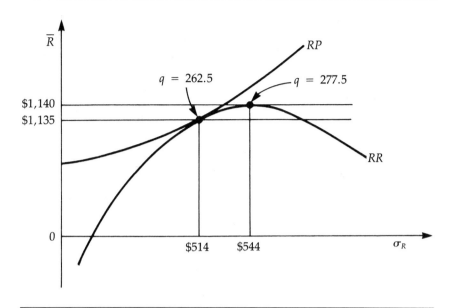

**Figure 12.6   Maximizing the Manager's Utility**

Each point on the risk return curve is the combination of risk and expected return that results from producing a specified output. The risk-averse manager maximizes his or her utility by producing the output where the manager's risk preference curve is tangent to the $RR$ curve, which is at an output of 262.5 units. The firm's expected profits are maximized at $q = 277.5$, but the manager believes that the greater risk is not compensated for by the $5 increase in $\overline{R}$, expected profits.

## 12.5  *Inventory Management Under Risk*

When two or more planning periods are being analyzed, the decision process involves calculating present values and determining which alternative maximizes the value of the firm. The example in this section is concerned with risk management when there are two planning periods. Management is deciding whether to increase production next year to add to its inventories for sale in 2 years. The price at which the inventory will be sold is a random variable because it cannot be predicted with certainty. Management does believe, however, that it has reasonable forecasts of the probability of each price's occurring.

Assume that the firm is weighing two alternative inventory policies. One is to maintain inventories at the minimum level necessary to conduct its business in a normal manner. The other is to add to inventories in anticipation of a price increase at the end of next year. Management's

**Table 12.6  Management's Price and Profit Forecasts
(Thousands of dollars)**

| Price Forecast | | Profit Forecast | |
|---|---|---|---|
| Price | Probability | Minimum Inventory | Add to Inventory |
| $10 | 0.1 | $105 | $ 50 |
| 11 | 0.2 | 155 | 140 |
| 12 | 0.5 | 200 | 210 |
| 13 | 0.1 | 240 | 280 |
| 14 | 0.1 | 275 | 340 |
| | | Expected profit   $207 | $220 |
| | | Standard deviation   $ 44.5 | $ 77.6 |

price forecast is in the first two columns of Table 12.6. The next two columns contain the profit forecasts for the second year under each inventory policy. The expected values and standard deviations of the profit forecasts are also provided. If the investors in the firm were risk-neutral, the decision could be made by finding the policy with the greater profit, in which case management would adopt for next year the production program that adds to inventories. In this section, it is assumed that investors in the firm's securities are risk-averse.

*The Risk-Adjusted Cost of Capital.* Risk preference functions can be expressed for investors in a firm as well as its managers. Investors in the firm's debt and equity securities and various short-term lenders like banks provide the capital for carrying inventories. If these investors are risk-averse, the firm will incur a greater cost of capital if its inventory policies result in greater investor risks. The amount by which the cost of capital rises when the firm takes on a higher level of risk depends upon the investors' risk preferences. Assume that the investors' risk preference function is $k' = 0.15 + 0.001\sigma$ where $k'$ is the risk-adjusted cost of capital. When the project is risk-free (that is, when $\sigma = 0$), the cost of capital is $k' = 0.15$. As risk rises, $k'$ rises. Investors require a higher cost for capital as the project's risk increases; hence, the investors in the firm are risk-averse.[5]

The data in Table 12.6 can be used to calculate the risk-adjusted cost of capital for each inventory policy. The risk-adjusted cost of capital if the minimum inventory is maintained is 19.45 percent because $\sigma = 44.5$:

$$k' = 0.15 + 0.001(44.5) = 0.1945$$

[5]Investor risk preferences are discussed at greater length in section 13.3.

If the firm adds to its inventories, the risk-adjusted cost of capital is 22.76 percent. These estimates of the risk-adjusted cost of capital are used to calculate the present value of the firm's expected profits from each inventory policy.

*Maximizing the Present Value of Expected Profits.* Once the risk-adjusted costs of capital have been calculated, the present value of the expected profits using each inventory policy can be calculated. Using mid-year centered discount factors on the assumption that the inventory is sold off at a constant rate during the second year, the respective risk-adjusted present values of the expected profits are $158.56 and $161.75:

$$V_1 = \$207/(1.1945)^{1.5} = \$158.56$$
$$V_2 = \$220/(1.2276)^{1.5} = \$161.75$$

Thus, given the investors' risk preference function, it is wealth-maximizing to add to inventories next year.

If the investors were more strongly risk-averse and had the risk preference function $k' = 0.15 + 0.002\sigma$, the wealth-maximizing decision would be to maintain the minimum level of inventories, because the present values would be $V_1 = \$150.09$ and $V_2 = \$147.54$. If the investors were risk-seekers, the decision could be made without calculating the present values since both the expected profit and standard deviation are greater for the "add to inventory" alternative.

There are a number of operating decisions for which management may make wealth-maximizing decisions when one or more of the profit variables are subject to probability distributions. The level of maintenance expenditures is a decision for which the use of risk-adjusted present values may be used. If a higher level of maintenance expenditures would reduce the probability of a future major breakdown, the standard deviation of profits and the risk-adjusted cost of capital should fall. Most of the use of risk-adjusted present values occurs with respect to investment projects and capital budgeting decisions.

## 12.6  *Risk and Insurance*

Risk and uncertainty are facts of life. The preceding sections have discussed how to measure risk and adapt the goals of the firm to situations where there is risk. This section discusses one institution for reducing the risks borne by firms. This institution is insurance, where in exchange for a premium payment an insurance company will protect the firm against specified types of losses up to the limits of the policy.

In exchange for the premium the insurance company agrees to assume specified risks. Insurance companies will not assume all risks. Examples of insurable risks are losses caused by fires and various kinds of accidents, loss of life, and theft losses. A generally uninsurable risk is damage resulting from an act of war or civil disturbance. Management may not insure against all possible risks. It may prefer to self-insure some risks because the premiums are too high relative to the potential loss.

*The Utility of Profits Function.* The decision to buy insurance involves a tradeoff. With insurable risks, the tradeoff is between the expected value of a risky situation and a certainty after paying the premium. The standard deviation of the risky situation is not discussed in the model here. This model is based on management's subjective evaluations of alternative profit levels, with management selecting the alternative maximizing its expected utility. Management's utility of profits function is not directly observable, although it can possibly be inferred from past decisions.

Assume that management's utility of profits function has been specified. Management prefers higher to lower profits, although the rate at which management's utility rises declines as profits increase. The marginal utility of a given increase in profits goes down as the level of profits rises. Management's utility of profits curve is curve $U$ in Figure 12.7. This curve becomes flatter as profits increase because the marginal utility of profits (its slope) declines.

*Maximizing the Utility of Profits.* Assume that management is thinking about insuring against the risk of a fire. If it does not insure against this risk and there is no fire, profits will be $\Pi_0$ and management's utility level $U_0$. If there is a fire, profits will fall to $\Pi_1$ and management's utility will be $U_1$. Neither of these events is a certainty. Let $Pr$ be the probability that the plant will not burn down, and $(1 - Pr)$ be the probability that it burns down. $\Pi_0$ and $\Pi_1$, together with their respective probabilities, are referred to as an uncertain prospect. The expected values of profits and utility are $E(\Pi) = Pr\Pi_0 + (1 - Pr)\Pi_1$ and $E(U) = PrU_0 + (1 - Pr)U_1$. The point $[E(\Pi), E(U)]$ is on a straight line between points $A$ and $B$ on the total utility curve because the expected value equations are linear with respect to $Pr$. As $Pr$ varies, the point $[E(\Pi), E(U)]$ moves along the straight line between $(\Pi_0, U_0)$ and $(\Pi_1, U_1)$. This straight line lies below the utility of profits curve $U$ in Figure 12.7 because a certain profit of, say, $1,000 would be preferred by a risk-averse manager to an uncertain prospect with a $1,000 expected profit. An uncertain prospect with an expected profit of $1,000 has a lower utility level than $1,000 with certainty.

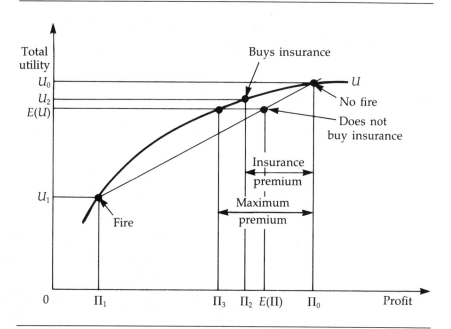

**Figure 12.7 Utility of Profits When Risk Is Insurable**

The manager's utility of profits curve $U$ yields the utility level of a specified level of profit. If the firm does not insure against a fire, its expected profit is $E(\Pi)$ and the manager's expected utility is $E(U)$. By buying fire insurance and paying a premium equal to $\Pi_0 - \Pi_2$, the manager's utility level is $U_2$ because the firm's profit level is now $\Pi_2$ with certainty. Because $U_2 > E(U)$, the firm will buy the fire insurance.

The points $(\Pi_0, U_0)$ and $(\Pi_1, U_1)$ comprise an uncertain prospect of two possible outcomes that has been reduced to a single point by calculating their expected values. Management can decide whether to insure the risk by comparing $E(U)$ to its utility if it pays the insurance premium. The insurance company will pay the firm the amount of its loss (which is $\Pi_0 - \Pi_1$) if a fire occurs. Thus, if it buys the insurance policy, the firm will have with certainty profit level $\Pi_0$ less the amount of the premium. The premium is a cost of doing business just like wages or the cost of electric power. If the premium is $R$ dollars, the firm has profit level $\Pi_2 = \Pi_0 - R$ and utility level $U_2$ if it buys the insurance policy.

In Figure 12.7, management would prefer to insure the risk and have profits of $\Pi_2$ with certainty. Although the expected profits $E(\Pi)$ are greater than profits after paying the insurance premium, the utility of $\Pi_2$, which is $U_2$, is greater than management's expected utility if it does not insure the risk. The relative utility levels determine which policy option will be taken. Management will buy the insurance policy if it can increase its utility.

*Insurance Company Profits.* Is it possible for the insurance company to earn a profit if it charges insurance premium $R$? That is, is the premium greater than the insurance company's expected loss on the policy? The expected loss $E(L)$, of the insurance company is

$$E(L) = Pr \times 0 + (1 - Pr)(\Pi_0 - \Pi_1)$$

$$E(L) = \Pi_0 - (Pr\Pi_0 + (1 - Pr)\Pi_1) = \Pi_0 - E(\Pi)$$

In Figure 12.7, the insurance company's expected loss is less than the premium. As long as the insurance company's operating costs are less than the difference between its premium and expected loss, it can expect to make a profit. However, the insurance company must make accurate predictions of the probability of loss if it is to set its premiums at profitable levels. It must also have sufficient capital to absorb losses that are bunched together so that the insurance company does not become bankrupt before the law of averages takes effect, bringing the average loss back to the expected loss. The probability of the insurance company's going bankrupt, given its capital, depends upon the standard deviation of its losses. This probability can be calculated using the method discussed near the end of section 12.1 if the losses are statistically independent. If the probability of one loss depends upon the occurrence of another loss, then the two losses are not statistically independent. This is the kind of event that can occur in a war, large-scale civil disturbance, earthquake, or major flood — all of which are generally viewed by private insurance companies as uninsurable without government participation.

What is the maximum premium that the insurance company can charge that will be acceptable to the purchaser of the policy? This question is answered by comparing management's utility level if it does not insure the risk, $E(U)$, to its utility level if it does insure it, $U(\Pi_0 - R)$. The maximum premium would have utility level $E(U)$. The maximum premium is $R = \Pi_0 - \Pi_3$ because $\Pi_3$ has the same utility level as the uncertain prospect, $E(U)$. Actually, premium $R$ would leave management indifferent between insuring and not insuring; thus, the insurance company would charge a slightly lower premium than $R$. Since there is competition among insurance companies, premiums will end up somewhere between $R$ and $\Pi_0 - E(\Pi)$. The potential margin of profit for the insurance company exists because the insured management's utility function exhibits diminishing marginal utility of profits. Managements with diminishing marginal utility for profits below their maximum uninsured profit will insure at least some risks.

EXAMPLE 12.2.   Management's utility of profits function is $U = 10 + \Pi^{0.25}$. This function exhibits a diminishing marginal utility of profits since $MU = dU/d\Pi = 0.25/\Pi^{0.75}$, which declines as $\Pi$ increases. If the uninsured profit is $\Pi_0 = \$100$, an insurable loss will reduce profits to $\Pi_1 = \$20$, and the probability of the loss is $Pr = 5\%$, then $U_0 = 13.1623$, $U_1 = 12.1147$, $E(\Pi) = \$96$, and $E(U) = 13.1099$. These results can be verified by substitution into the equations for $U$ and the expected values. Calculating the maximum premium is a little more complicated. The expected utility of the uncertain prospect is substituted into the utility of profits function, $13.1099 = 10 + \Pi_3^{0.25}$, which is then solved to yield $\Pi_3$. This implies that $\Pi_3 = \$93.5376$. The maximum premium the insurance company can charge is $\Pi_0 - \Pi_3 = \$100 - \$93.5376 = \$6.4624$. The insurance company's expected loss is $E(L) = \$100 - \$96 = \$4$. If the premium is $\$5$, the insurance company has a margin of $\$1$ to cover its operating costs and provide a profit to its investors. Management would find this premium acceptable because its utility after paying the premium would be $U_2 = 10 + 95^{0.25} = 13.1220$, which exceeds its expected utility of 13.1099 if it self-insures the risk.

## 12.7  *Hedging to Reduce Risk*

Insurance is not the only institution available to reduce the firm's risks by shifting them to others. Hedging by buying or selling futures contracts on the commodities exchanges is another risk management technique. Hedging provides at least some protection against adverse price changes for raw materials, foreign currencies, and common stocks; and adverse interest rate changes. All of the risk cannot be eliminated by hedging; however, hedging can reduce risks when futures prices and cash prices maintain more or less stable relationships over time.

*Hedging Operations in Risk Management.* Futures contracts are agreements to buy or sell a commodity at a specified time in the future. The contracts are for a specific commodity or financial investment to be exchanged at a specified time and place. Most futures contracts do not result in an actual transaction's taking place. Before delivery is to take place, the exchange will extinguish all contracts to sell with offsetting contracts to buy the commodity. Contracts that have not been extinguished by an offsetting contract are referred to as "open interest." Once the life of the contract has been reached, all holders of contracts agreeing to sell the commodity (the "shorts") must deliver it and the holders of contracts to buy it (the "longs") must accept delivery and pay the agreed-upon price for the commodity.

The cash price is the price at which a commodity can be purchased or sold today. The futures price is the price at which a contract for future purchase or sale of the commodity can be acquired. When there is a perfect hedge, the two prices will change by the same amount. Assume that a firm acquires for $4.00 per bushel 5,000 bushels of wheat in October for processing and sale the following March. The price of the product changes in exact proportion to the cash (or spot) price of wheat. If the spot price rises by $0.25 per bushel, the price of the product rises by $0.20 per unit because each unit of the product contains 0.8 bushels of wheat. Assume that the October price of a futures contract to deliver 5,000 bushels of wheat in March is $4.30 per bushel. If the firm sells short on a futures contract, it is guaranteed that price regardless of the actual spot price at the March delivery time. Assume that the spot price is $3.50 in March and the price of its product has also fallen by the same $0.80 per bushel of contained wheat. It loses $0.80 on the sale of its product but gains $0.80 on the sale of wheat that it purchases in March at the $3.50 spot price for delivery to the holder of its futures contract, who must pay $4.30. Hence the futures contract provided a perfect hedge against the risk of an adverse change in the price of wheat, which was insured at the cost of a small broker's commission.

Hedging, however, is rarely perfect. Spot and futures prices do not always change by the same amount. In the previous example, if the loss on selling its product were $0.80, but the difference between the futures and cash prices was only $0.50, the hedge would not have protected the firm against all of the loss on its product. It would lose only $0.30 with the hedge, rather than $0.80 if it had not purchased the futures contract. Alternatively, the difference in March between the futures and cash prices could have been $1.00 per bushel, in which case the hedge would have protected the firm against the $0.80 loss and provided a $0.20 profit. The prospect of a hedging profit can lead firms to employ professionals to manage their hedging operations. These professionals try to avoid situations in which hedging offers little risk reduction and limited opportunities for a hedging profit.

***Financial Futures to Hedge Interest Rate Risks.*** The managers of virtually all firms can hedge their financing programs against the risk of adverse trends in interest rates. Financial futures contracts were created by the exchanges when interest rates began to fluctuate to a much greater degree than in the past. Because financing of inventory and accounts receivable and payable is generally done with bank credit, firms were faced with greater interest rate risks. Assume that a car dealer orders cars today to be added to its inventory in 3 months and that they will, on the average, be sold within another 3 months. In deciding on how many cars to order, management bases its costs on the current 12 percent interest rate for short-term bank credit. By the time the cars are delivered, the interest rate is 18 percent for a 3-month loan from the bank and any cars that are not sold after 3 months will have to be refinanced at the then current interest rate, which may be higher yet. Since a car dealer may finance as much as 85 percent of its inventory cost, the higher interest rate can have a major impact on profits. To protect itself against a higher interest rate, the firm can hedge its financing by selling short a futures contract for U.S. Treasury notes or bills maturing in 3 to 6 months. When interest rates go up, the prices of Treasury notes and bills decline. A short sale is profitable when the price of the financial instrument declines, and this profit can partly or entirely offset the higher interest costs on the firm's bank loans. Thus, these futures contracts provide some protection from interest rate risks. As with commodities contracts, it doesn't always pay to attempt to offset financial risks by hedging, whereas a well-managed hedging program can add to profits. Firms wishing to hedge financial risks generally hire professionals to do their trading or rely on experts employed by brokerage firms, since poor hedges increase the firm's risk exposure.

*Options in Futures Contracts.* An alternative to trading futures contracts is to trade options in futures contracts. With a futures contract, the risks of an adverse position are essentially unlimited, especially if the position is a short. The maximum risk in an option is the amount paid to acquire the option (the premium). If the price of the futures contract moves in the favorable direction, the firm can exercise the option and take its hedging profit in the same manner as if it had owned the futures contract. If the price movement in the futures contract is unfavorable, the firm can simply allow the option to expire and lose only the premium it paid when the option was acquired.

Options have been used for many years to reduce risks with respect to acquiring productive resources and properties. An option gives the firm the exclusive right to purchase the resource at a fixed price for a limited period of time. To acquire the option, the firm may pay the owner of the resource a specified amount of money or its price may be increased above the current market price to provide an incentive for the owner to take it off the market for the agreed-upon period of time. While the firm is evaluating the resource or arranging financing, it is protected from the risk of price changes. The option premium is the cost of reducing the firm's risk exposure.

## 12.8  *Summary*

Uncertainty is converted into risk when management assigns probabilities to all of the possible outcomes of a business decision. Once the probabilities have been assigned, the expected value and standard deviation of profits can be calculated.

When there is risk, management goals are no longer single-valued as they were under certainty when profit and wealth maximization were appropriate goals. Management must now calculate two attributes of the projected outcomes of its decisions and consider tradeoffs between them. The tradeoff function is the risk preference function, which has as its dependent variable management's utility level. Its independent variables are the expected value and standard deviation of profit. Managements were classified as being risk-averse (the normal situation), risk-neutral, or risk-seeking on the basis of the slopes of their risk preference functions. If wealth maximization is management's goal under certainty, the risk preference function has as its dependent variable the cost of capital. The standard deviation of profits is its independent variable. When the cost of capital is calculated using a risk preference function, the resulting present values are said to be risk-adjusted. Management's goal then becomes maximization of the risk-adjusted present value.

Managerial decisions involving risk include whether the firm will bear a risk or pay a premium to transfer the risk to someone else. In the case of casualty insurance, the tradeoff function is the utility of profits function, which has as its dependent variable management's utility. Its independent variable is the level of profits. For the firm to insure a risk, the utility of profits function must exhibit diminishing marginal utility below the profit-maximizing level without insurance. The insurance company is willing to assume the risk because it can charge a premium greater than its expected loss. Management will find the certainty situation with insurance preferable to the uncertain prospect of the uninsured potential loss so long as the premium does not reduce management's utility below its expected utility if the potential loss is not insured.

Hedging risks through the use of futures contracts is another risk management technique. Contracts have been used for many years by firms involved in the production and use of agricultural commodities and metals. More recently, futures contracts have become available for various financial instruments. Perfect hedges that completely protect the firm from the risk of an adverse price change are rare, and many firms hope to earn a hedging profit by correctly estimating the spread between futures and cash prices. Options are another technique for reducing risk that can be used when the firm is acquiring resources or property. Options have the advantage of limited losses if there is an adverse price trend.

## Key Terms

confidence interval
event
futures contract
hedging
indifference curve
longs
open interest
options

outcome
random variable
relative frequency
    probability
risk management
risk-adjusted cost of
    capital

risk preference, risk
    preference function
risk return function
shorts
subjective probability
uncertainty
utility of profits function

## Review Questions

1. Define the terms *risk, uncertainty, random variable, event, utility, risk preference function,* and *risk return function.*

2. When is the coefficient of variation used to determine which of two alternatives is the riskier?

3. Explain why a risk-averse manager has an upward sloping *RP* curve and a risk-seeking manager a downward sloping one.

4. Discuss the following statement: "Profit maximization makes sense only if management is risk-neutral."

5. Explain why an *RP* curve is also an indifference curve.

6. Why does the risk return curve generally have an inverted U shape? Why cannot management choose a combination of risk and expected return lying above the *RR* curve? Why would the firm not choose one below the *RR* curve?

7. Explain why the decision maker maximizes utility by choosing the alternative where the *RR* curve is tangent to an *RP* curve.

8. Explain why a risk-neutral decision maker will choose the alternative that maximizes the expected return.

9. Explain why a risk-averse investor would require the firm to earn a higher expected return on its capital if management decides to undertake a series of new projects that are likely to increase the standard deviation of its profits.

10. What are the differences between insurable and uninsurable risks?

11. Why would management be willing to accept a certain profit that

is lower than the expected value of an uncertain prospect that is insurable?

12. What is the difference between a long and short position? Which position is more profitable when the price of the commodity declines?

13. Explain how hedging can provide at least some protection against adverse price trends. Why cannot hedging always provide complete protection against adverse price trends?

14. How can an option be used as a risk management tool when management is considering buying a site for a new plant but needs another 6 months to complete its planning and alternative site evaluations?

## Problems and Applications

1. Calculate the expected value and standard deviation of the following set of profit forecasts.

| Forecast | Profit | Probability |
|---|---|---|
| A | $180 | 0.1 |
| B | $130 | 0.2 |
| C | $100 | 0.5 |
| D | $ 40 | 0.2 |

2. Assume that another product line has the same profit projections as the one in problem 1 but the probabilities are $A$, 0.1; $B$, 0.4; $C$, 0.4; and $D$, 0.1. Analyze the relative risk of these two projects. Should the coefficient of variation be used in this analysis?

3. Calculate the 95 percent confidence interval for the two investments discussed in section 11.1. Use this confidence interval to explain why investment $B$ is riskier. Calculate the probability that each investment will earn at least a 10 percent rate of return.

4. If the manager's risk preference function is $U = R - 0.1\sigma + 0.05\sigma^2$, for which values of $\sigma$ is the manager a risk-seeker?

5. Assume that the RR function is $\overline{R} = -20 + 16\sigma - 0.4\sigma^2$ and the manager's RP function is $U = \overline{R} - 0.4\sigma - 0.1\sigma^2$. Calculate the combination of risk and expected return that maximizes the manager's utility. Is this manager risk-averse? Explain why.

6. Assume that the manager in problem 4 was risk-neutral. Calculate the utility-maximizing combination of risk and expected return under that assumption.

7. Assume that there are two possible prices: $20 with a probability of 0.4 and $25 with a probability of 0.6. The $AVC$ function is $AVC =$

$5 + 0.5q$ and fixed costs are $600. Calculate the profit-maximizing output ($q_0$) at the expected price, and the expected profit and its standard deviation for outputs of $q_0 - 50$, $q_0$, and $q_0 + 50$ units. Use these points to sketch the risk return curve.

8. Continuing with problem 7, which of these three outputs would be chosen by a risk-averse manager and which would be chosen by a risk-seeking manager? Assume that those three outputs are the only alternatives open to the firm.

9. If the investor's risk preference function is $k' = 0.15 + 0.002\sigma + 0.0005\sigma^2$, calculate the risk-free cost of capital and the risk-adjusted cost of capital when $\sigma = 50$ for a project's profits.

10. Assume that management has revised its thinking on the probability of the prices in Table 12.6. Management is now predicting a probability of 0.2 for each of the prices. If this is the only change, is it still wealth-maximizing to add to inventories next year?

11. Management's utility of profits function is $U = 10 + 2\Pi^{0.5}$.
    a. Does this utility function exhibit diminishing utility of profits? Why?
    b. If an uninsured profit is $\Pi_0 = \$1,000$, an insurable loss will reduce profits to $\Pi_1 = \$100$, and the probability of the loss is $Pr = 4\%$, calculate $U_0$, $U_1$, $E(\Pi)$, and $E(U)$.
    c. The insurance company charges a premium of $45 to insure this risk. Is it utility-maximizing for management to buy insurance to insure this risk?

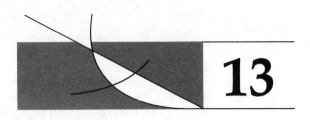

# 13

# *Capital Budgeting*

Although long-run analysis of costs and markets has been treated in several sections, the emphasis prior to this chapter has been on operations planning — planning in which the firm has one or more fixed assets. In this chapter, the emphasis shifts to capital budgeting and preparing the firm's capital expenditures plan. Decisions relating to the capital budget are among the most important made by executive management. Today's capital expenditures for new facilities and product lines will shape the company's future and provide the basis for its future growth, even survival.

Capital budgeting is basically a series of procedures designed to identify, evaluate, and coordinate investment opportunities. Because capital projects yield their returns over several years, the firm's cost of capital must be calculated. The future is never known with certainty, so the cost of capital is adjusted to reflect differences in the risk associated with each project. If management invests in a number of projects or faces a constraint on the level of the capital budget, the procedures for evaluating alternative plans must be modified. The four sections of this chapter are devoted to procedures for developing a firm's capital budget.

Two cases provide examples of how projects being considered for inclusion in the capital budget are evaluated. These cases illustrate the kinds of analyses that go into evaluating capital spending proposals. One case focuses on whether to continue to operate an old plant, modernize it, or build a new plant. The other is concerned with choosing the best technology for a new plant when there is uncertainty with respect to future product and energy prices. In both cases, the decision is based on choosing the alternative maximizing the present value of future profits.

# 13.1 *The Capital Budget*

The capital budget is concerned with the financing of investment projects that add to revenues or reduce expenses for more than one year. These projects generally add to the firm's stock of productive capital — its plant and equipment, land, buildings, inventories, and working capital. The operating budget, on the other hand, focuses on the operation of assets already owned by the firm. The capital budget is primarily concerned with acquiring new assets, whereas the operating budget is concerned with optimal operation of the firm's existing assets.

The discussion of the capital budgeting process provided in this section is necessarily an idealized one. Each company has its procedures that fit the environment within which it operates and its style of management. Some companies use highly bureaucratic procedures; others use informal procedures tailored to the decisions under consideration. The capital budgeting procedures of most companies contain a number of common elements. These common techniques — of project evaluation and integrated evaluation of alternative and complementary projects — are emphasized here.

The search for profitable investment opportunities is a continual process. Ideas for cost reduction or plant expansion projects may be initiated by the managers and engineers who operate the firm's existing facilities. Others result from the work of research and development departments specifically formed for the purpose of developing new products or processes. Still others are identified by executive management. These projects are investigated by the firm's technical and marketing staffs, and formal project descriptions and evaluations are prepared. The project proposals are reviewed by the top managers in the affected operating divisions and submitted to the company's planning department, where their financial and interdivisional implications are studied. The projects are then assembled into one or more alternative capital budgets for executive management's review and approval. Once the final capital budget is approved, the operating divisions implement it. Projects that were not approved are either dropped from further consideration or returned to the operating divisions for further study. In smaller firms, these steps may be combined or a different procedure used that has the same basic objective — finding the set of investment projects that maximizes the firm's value.

*Identification of Potential Projects.* The first step is to survey the available projects to determine which projects offer the prospect of increasing the value of the firm. Once an interesting project has been identified, the next step is to determine the scale of this project that maximizes its net present value. This generally involves estimating the capital costs of alternative plant capacities, the likely selling prices of the products, annual operating cost at each year's profit-maximizing output, and annual revenues. The project's relationship to the company's existing operations, the nature of competition in the industry, likely future technological developments, government tax and regulatory policies, and a host of other details are considered. Management also assesses the risks involved and determines the appropriate risk-adjusted cost capital. The net present values are calculated for increasingly larger plants until increasing the scale of the plant results in a lower net present value. Projects with positive net present values are candidates for the capital budget.

Once these studies have been completed, the formal project evaluation report is prepared. This report contains a description of the project, its economic evaluation, the recommended scale of the facilities required for the project, and the amount to be budgeted. Descriptions of alternatives reviewed in the process of arriving at the project recommendations, and the reasons for not recommending them, are also provided so that higher levels of management are not left wondering which alternatives were evaluated. The relationship of this project to the company's existing operations and other proposed capital projects is also included. The project report is then forwarded up the chain of command for further analysis and approvals. At higher levels, the relationship of the project to other proposals is expanded upon and the project's relationship to the division's plans explained.

*Integrating Projects into Alternative Capital Plans and Budgets.* Project proposals approved by the company's operating divisions are then sent to the company's planning department. Each proposal is screened to determine whether its assumptions about future economic conditions; price, wage, and cost trends; government policies; and the like are consistent with executive management's views and the assumptions underlying the other capital projects competing for the company's available funds. Unless all projects use a consistent set of assumptions, they cannot be reasonably compared and evaluated. Often this check for consistent assumptions is routine because the planning department has made available to all departments its forecasts of future economic conditions. Also, it is customary for the persons preparing project reports to consult with planning department personnel.

The next step is to integrate the proposals into one or more capital plans and budgets. The capital plan evaluates the projects as they relate to one another and to executive management's goals. It describes the direction in which the proposed projects will take the company over the next few years and their potential impact on its earnings. It describes the future opportunities that each plan offers and the risks assumed if it is approved. The capital plan also includes the company's financial capabilities — its retained earnings, depreciation allowances, and opportunities to raise additional debt and equity capital. The capital budget contains the amount of money allocated to each project during each budget cycle (usually one month) and a line item breakdown of the expenditures. The sources of the funds for the budgeted amounts are also indicated. Pro forma operating budgets for subsequent years may also be included. The planning department's recommendations with respect to the alternative capital plans and budgets are usually discussed with the operating managers, and its final recommendations forwarded to executive management.

*Approving the Capital Plan and Budget.* Executive management, and ultimately the board of directors, approve the capital budget. In decentralized companies, where departments adopt their own operating plans, approving the capital budget is one of executive management's major responsibilities. After reviewing the planning department's recommendations, and possibly requesting additional information or the formulation and evaluation of other capital plans and budgets, executive management basically focuses on the financial feasibility of the budget and its relationship to their goals for the company. A project with a negative net present value or one that is relatively risky may, for example, be inserted into the plan because it offers the prospect of highly profitable future investments if economic or market conditions are particularly favorable. A large project, using a significant amount of the company's capital resources, may be removed from the plan because executive management feels that it commits the company to an industry that is unlikely to offer much future growth. These kinds of decisions can be frustrating to the company's planning staff, which tends to focus on the numbers, and to the operating managers, who see their divisions and departments becoming less important in the company's future. But these decisions are essential if the company is to prosper in a constantly changing world. Executive management has the detachment from current operations to develop the broad perspectives necessary to adapt to present and expected future changes in the firm's environment. And only executive management has the authority to resolve the conflicts that naturally arise in any diverse, large organization and to set the basic policies that guide the operating managers and coordinate their activities.

## 13.2    *The Cost of Capital*

The firm's cost of capital is the discount rate that equates the present value of its expected future profits to the market value of its debt and equity securities. If $\bar{R}_t$ is the firm's expected profit in year $t$, and $D$ and $E$ are the market values of its debt and equity securities, the cost of capital is found by solving equation 13.1 for $k$:

$$D + E = \Sigma \overline{R}_t/(1 + k)^t \qquad\qquad (13.1)$$

*Costs of Debt and Equity Capital.* The cost of capital is a weighted average of the costs of debt and equity capital, where the weights are based on the market values of the firm's debt and equity securities. The before-tax cost of debt capital is its current market interest rate. However, since interest is a deductible expense when calculating the firm's after-tax profits, the after-tax cost of debt is $d = (1.0 - T)i$, where $T$ is the firm's income tax rate and $i$ is the market rate of interest on its debt. For example, if $i = 12$ percent and the corporate income tax rate is 40 percent, $T = 0.4$ and $d = (1.0 - 0.4)(12\%) = 7.2\%$.

There are two components to the firm's cost of equity capital, $e$. One component is the dividend yield on its common stock. If $DV$ is the annual dividend on a share of stock and $E$ is its market price, the yield is $DV/E$. Dividends, unlike interest, are not a tax-deductible expense. The other component is the expected rate of growth in the price of its common stock, $g$. The higher the rate of growth expected by investors, the greater the rate of return required to generate the earnings necessary to yield those stock price expectations. Thus, the cost of equity capital depends on the expected rate of growth in the price of its stock. This rate of growth can be estimated in a number of ways, with the most common probably being a combination of the actual growth rate over the past few years and the analyst's judgment as to future earnings prospects. Combining these two components yields the cost of equity capital:

$$e = (DV/E) + g$$

The cost of capital is the weighted average of the costs of debt and equity capital. The weights are the respective market values of the securities. If $E$ is the price per share of common stock and $N$ is the number of shares, $EN$ is the market value of the firm's equity. Thus, the weighted average cost of capital is

$$k = (dD + eEN)/(D + EN) \qquad\qquad (13.2)$$

If the price of a share of common stock is $40, the dividend is $5 per share, the stock price is expected to grow by 7.5 percent per year, and there are 1 million shares outstanding, the cost of equity capital is $e = (\$5/\$40) + 0.075 = 0.20$ or 20 percent, and the market value of the firm's equity is $EN = (\$40)(1,000,000) = \$40$ million. If its debt has a market value of $10 million, the weighted average cost of capital, using the previous calculation of the after-tax cost of debt and omitting the millions in the calculations, is

$$k = (7.2\% \times \$10 + 20\% \times \$40)/(\$10 + \$40) = 17.44\% \quad (13.3)$$

*The Debt/Equity Ratio.* Even though the cost of debt capital is substantially lower than the cost of equity, the firm does not use only debt to finance its capital budget. In the previous example, the after-tax cost of debt was 7.2 percent, which is substantially less than the cost of equity (20 percent) or the average cost of capital (17.44 percent). A major issue among specialists in corporate finance is whether it is wealth maximizing to use more debt to lower the firm's cost of capital. Financial risk depends on the probability of bankruptcy. This risk is assumed by investors in the firm's securities as a result of management's decisions with respect to the mix of debt and equity used to finance the firm. As the debt/equity $(D/E)$ ratio increases, financial risk rises, because the firm must have adequate earnings to make its interest payments to avoid bankruptcy. Dividends on its stock are discretionary and may be omitted without forcing the firm into bankruptcy, although its stock price will likely fall. Because using more debt and holding constant the firm's equity increases the probability of bankruptcy, the costs of both debt and equity capital rise because investors face a greater probability of a loss of all or part of their investments. Banks will charge higher interest rates on short-term loans to firms that are riskier because of a higher $D/E$ ratio.

The firm's average cost of capital will not necessarily rise as its $D/E$ ratio rises. At low $D/E$ ratios, the average cost of capital may decline as $D$ increases because the much lower after-tax interest rate on debt capital more than offsets any increase in the before-tax interest rate or the cost of equity capital. As the $D/E$ ratio rises, the difference between the average cost of capital and the after-tax interest rate declines, and adding another $10.0 million to debt will reduce $k$ by a lesser amount than did the previous $10.0 million. The first $10.0 million in debt reduced the firm's cost of capital from 20 percent (since it only had equity) to 17.44 percent, or by 2.56 percent. Adding another $10.0 million in debt, with no change in $d$ or $e$, will reduce $k$ to (7.2% × $20 + 20% × $40)/($20 + $40) = 15.73 percent, or by 1.17 percent. However, adding the second $10.0 million in debt may lead to changes in $d$ and $e$. The probability of a bankruptcy will become more important when investors evaluate the firm's securities, leading to increases in the before-tax costs of debt and equity. Whether the result will be an increase in the average cost of capital beyond some $D/E$ ratio, as with the solid line in Figure 13.1, or a slower decline in $k$ has not been resolved among corporate finance specialists. Regardless of how investors may

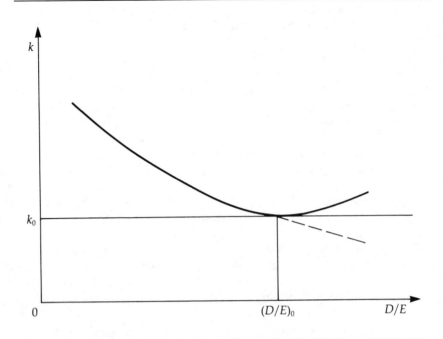

**Figure 13.1   Cost of Capital and the Debt/Equity Ratio**

Because the after-tax cost of debt capital is lower than the cost of equity capital, the average cost of capital declines as the $D/E$ ratio increases from zero. One theory of the cost of capital, represented by the solid curve, holds that $k$ increases after the optimum level of the $D/E$ ratio, $(D/E)_0$, is reached. Another, represented by the dashed curve, holds that $k$ declines only as $D/E$ increases.

value the firm's securities as the $D/E$ ratio rises, risk-averse managers are likely to limit the firm's $D/E$ ratio because they are willing to trade off a higher average cost of capital for a lower probability that the firm will suffer sharply lower earnings or go bankrupt. The remainder of this chapter is based on the assumption that the firm's capital budget is financed in such a way that its financial risk is unchanged.

## 13.3  *Risk Management*

Risk management within the context of the capital budgeting procedure is a complex subject. Only the principal dimensions of the risk management problem are discussed in this section. Risk management is covered in depth in advanced courses in finance.

*Investor Risk Preferences.* Capital is supplied to the firm by its investors. Investors are generally divided into two classes — equity owners and the owners of the firm's debt securities. The owners of the firm's equity are generally assumed to be risk-averse. The stockholders must be compensated for assuming greater risks by a higher rate of return on the firm's investments. If the stockholders perceive that the firm is taking on greater risks without their expecting to earn a greater return, they will reduce their valuation of the firm's stock and sell it. These sales will depress the price of the firm's stock. A lower stock price, holding current and expected future earnings constant, increases the firm's cost of equity capital.

Individuals and financial institutions lend money by buying a firm's debt securities. These investors are inherently risk-averse. The owners of debt securities have prior claims on the firm's assets if it defaults or declares bankruptcy. This makes purchases of debt securities less risky than investments in stock. By controlling the amounts they lend to ensure adequate equity coverage for their loans, lenders can make their loans relatively risk-free. In addition, highly risk-averse institutions like banks make short-term loans to reduce the risks of changing business conditions or a series of poor decisions by the firm's management leading to losses or bankruptcy. Risk-averse lenders cannot protect themselves against all possible risks. However, the greater the unavoidable risks that the lender must assume, the higher the interest rate on its loans and the shorter their maturity. The higher interest rates paid on debt securities and the shorter their maturities, the greater the level of risk assumed by the firm's stockholders. The cost of capital rises when management makes decisions that increase the coefficient of variation for its profits. The rate at which it rises with increased risk is an empirical issue.

The lack of data on investors' risk preferences encourages managements to articulate their risk management strategies to securities analysts and the financial press. Investors finding management's strategies toward risk acceptable can then acquire the firm's securities. That is, firms can differentiate themselves with respect to their views on assuming risks as a means of competing for investors. Some managements are willing to assume higher risks to attract mildly risk-averse investors who prefer situations with greater possibilities for a higher than usual return. Others avoid making investments with anything but minimal risks to make their securities attractive to highly risk-averse investors. Still others may emphasize relatively risky operating policies or investments, which have some prospects for large returns, to appeal to risk-seeking investors.

*The Risk-Adjusted Cost of Capital.* An appropriate measure of risk when evaluating individual projects is the probability that the project will incur a loss. The greater the probability of a loss, the more likely that the company will have future financial difficulties leading to a higher risk-adjusted cost of capital and reduced values for its securities. The risk premium is the difference between the risk-free and the risk-adjusted cost of capital. Projects with a greater probability of incurring a loss have a greater risk premium.

The first step in finding the risk-adjusted cost of capital is to calculate the expected profits, $\overline{R}$, and the standard deviation of profits, $\sigma_R$, once the project is operating. The next step is to calculate the number of standard deviations that the expected profit is above zero. This is the ratio $Z = \overline{R}/\sigma_R$, where $\sigma_R > 0$. $Z$ could be calculated for the first full year of operations, or it could be calculated over several years and averaged. As $Z$ rises, the probability that the project will incur a loss decreases. Assume that project $A$ has an expected profit of $\overline{R} = \$200,000$ and a standard deviation of profits of $\$100,000$, so that $Z = \$200,000/\$100,000 = 2$. Project $B$ has an expected profit of $\$100,000$ and a standard deviation of profits of $\$69,000$, so that $Z = 1.45$. If profits are normally distributed, $Z = 2$ implies that there is a 2.3 percent probability of a loss and $Z = 1$ implies that the probability of a loss is 7.4 percent. Thus, project $B$ is the riskier project. To have the risk preference functions sloping in the same direction as those in Chapter 12, the inverse of $Z$, the coefficient of variation, is used as its independent variable. The coefficient of variation is $CV = \sigma_R/\overline{R} = 1/Z$. In the previous example, project $A$ had a $Z$ value of 2, and $CV = 1/2 = 0.5$. The riskier project $B$'s $Z$ and $CV$ values are 1.45 and 0.69 respectively. Since a greater value of $CV$ implies greater project risk, a risk-averse management has an upward sloping $RP$ curve.

If the standard deviation of profits is zero, the decision is risk-free. That is, management believes that its forecast of future revenues and costs will occur with certainty. The risk-free cost of capital is approximately equal to the interest rate on U.S. Treasury bills. Treasury bills are free of the risk of default, because the government can raise taxes or print money to pay them off. However, Treasury bills are not entirely risk-free: Investors buying them run the risk that the rate of inflation may be greater than their forecast. This risk can be minimized by buying bills close to maturity, but not totally eliminated because the transaction costs of buying the bill are positive and may exceed the benefits of the reduced inflation risk. The interest rate on Treasury bills can be used as the vertical intercept of the risk-preference curve. This is cost of capital $k_0'$, where $CV = 0$, in Figure 13.2.

A second point on the risk preference curve is also, in principal, observable. Given the prices of its debt and equity securities and projections of its expected future earnings, management can calculate the firm's average cost of capital, $k_1'$. Management can also calculate the

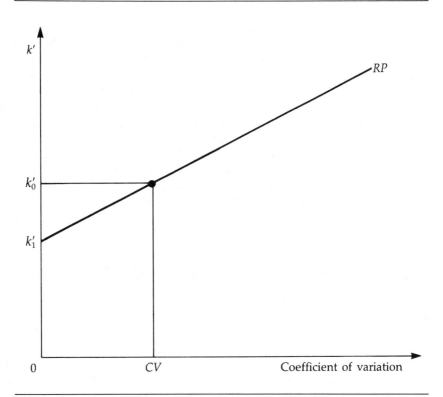

**Figure 13.2   Risk-Averse Preference Function**

One point on the *RP* curve is the risk-free cost of capital, which is approximately equal to the rate of interest $k_0'$ on U.S. Treasury bonds. A second point is the estimated coefficient of variation of the firm's profits from its existing assets and the weighted average return on its securities, $k_1'$. A straight line through these two points yields the *RP* curve if management does not become increasingly or decreasingly risk-averse as *CV* increases.

standard deviation of profits and estimate $CV_1$. Unless there is a systematic difference between the expectations of management and the investment community, management's expectations of the future provide reasonable approximations of $CV_1$ and $k_1'$. If there is a linear relationship between *CV* and the risk-adjusted cost of capital, these two points would be adequate to locate the *RP* function. If investors become increasingly or decreasingly risk-averse as *CV* increases, an additional data point would be necessary.

*The Capital Asset Pricing Model.* The discussion of risk management so far has been in terms of evaluating the risk inherent in a given capital budget on a project-by-project basis. The risk assumed by the firm with respect to its capital budget is less than that inherent in the individual projects. Adverse conditions in one product line can be offset by more favorable conditions than expected in another product line, yielding for both product lines an actual profit equal to the sum of their expected profits. This is, as was discussed in section 11.6.3, one of the principal reasons for firms to diversify or become conglomerates. The capital asset pricing model (CAPM) has been developed to measure and account for systematic risks assumed by the firm when it adopts a capital budget containing several or many individual projects. CAPM and other investment portfolio models yield a risk-adjusted cost of capital for calculating net present values that reflects the reduced risk inherent in multiple-project capital budgets. Modern corporate finance emphasizes use of CAPM in the capital budgeting prices.

## 13.4  *Project Selection with Capital Constraints*

In principle, the firm should undertake all investment proposals expected to yield a positive net present value (*NPV*). A project with a positive *NPV* will generate sufficient profits to increase the value of the firm. Acceptance of projects with positive *NPV*s by executive management would appear to be virtually automatic. However, arriving at the firm's capital budget is rarely so simple. There often are a number of constraints on executive management's decisions leading to projects with a positive *NPV* not being included in the firm's capital budget.

*Coordinating Changes in Vertically Integrated Firms.* Each project is normally evaluated at the divisional or departmental level on its own merits in relative isolation from projects being developed in other divisions. The corporate planning department is responsible for coordinating the investment proposals of functionally or geographically separate operations so that profitable opportunities for vertical integration, for example, will be identified. Given the egos and personalities of the operating managers, and the need to permit considerable freedom to investigate new ideas, coordination of project proposals is rarely perfect. Executive management may have to direct division and departmental managers toward developing coordinated and integrated investment proposals. In the process, projects with a positive *NPV* may be rejected because executive management believes that the necessary support facilities in other divisions are not available. For example, building a new oil refinery without adequate marketing, transportation, or oil production facilities may expose the company to unacceptable risks. Other companies may choose not to sell crude oil to the new refinery if a general shortage leads them to divert oil to their own refineries. If the company produces most of the crude oil for its refinery, this risk is absent.

*Capital Constraints.* Executive management may also reject projects with a positive *NPV* because the firm faces a capital constraint. The most obvious capital constraint occurs when management limits the capital budget to retained earnings and depreciation allowances. Some managements are reluctant to take on long-term debt to finance new projects, especially if interest rates are relatively high. Even though the new debt can be profitably invested, more debt increases the probability of bankruptcy if the projects are less profitable than expected. Borrowing more today may preclude increased future borrowing when interest rates may be lower. Additional debt may require management to seek further equity investments in the company, through selling more common stock or reducing its dividend. Increased debt financing may lead lenders to require representation on the firm's board of directors. The result is weakening of management's control over the company.

Executive management may believe that more personnel are needed to manage and control the activities of the larger firm that would result from accepting all capital budget proposals. Thus, it may defer some projects until the necessary managerial resources can be acquired and integrated into the present management team. Executive management may know of a major acquisition that will shift the company away from its existing product lines toward others offering more promising long-term growth prospects. Therefore, it may wish to conserve its capital resources for the acquisition and expansion of the new business area.

When the firm operates under a capital constraint, ranking projects by their *NPV*s or by their *NPV* divided by the capital budget amount (*CB*) need not yield the maximum increase in the value of the firm. Ranking investment opportunities in Table 13.1 by their *NPV/CB* ratios

**Table 13.1 Ranking Projects by Their *NPV/CB* Ratio**

| Project | *NPV* | *CB* | *NPV/CB* |
|---|---|---|---|
| 1 | $10.5 | $ 5.0 | 2.1 |
| 2 | 4.2 | 3.0 | 1.4 |
| 3 | 4.4 | 4.0 | 1.1 |
| 4 | 15.0 | 15.0 | 1.0 |
| 5 | 1.2 | 2.0 | 0.6 |
| 6 | 3.0 | 6.0 | 0.5 |
| 7 | 0.6 | 3.0 | 0.2 |

would lead to rejecting project 4 because of a lack of funds if the total capital budget is $20 million. Since projects 1 through 3 require $12 million, projects 5 and 6 would be accepted to utilize all of the available funds, and the total *NPV* for the $20 million capital budget would be $23.5 million. Accepting projects 1 and 4, however, would yield an *NPV* of $25.5 million for the same capital budget.

*Capital Rationing.* One way to ration capital is to increase the cost of capital until the investment required for the remaining projects with a positive *NPV* equals the funds available for the capital budget. As the cost of capital rises, the present values of future profits are reduced, with profits received further in the future suffering a relatively greater decline in their present value. For example, a profit of $10 million in 2 years has a present value of $10/(1.1)^2 = $8.26 million if $k = 10\%$, and $10/(1.25)^2 = $6.40 million if $k = 25\%$, for a ($8.26 − $6.40)/$8.26 = 22.5\% reduction. If the $10 million profit were received in 20 years, it would have a present value of $10/(1.1)^{20} = $1.49 million if $k = 10\%$ and $10/(1.25)^{20} = $0.12 million if $k = 25\%$, for a ($1.49 − $0.12)/$1.49 = 91.9\% reduction. Because the present value of the initial investment in the project changes little, or not at all, with increases in the cost of capital, the reduced present values of future profits result in a growing number of projects having negative *NPV*s. As $k$ rises, eventually the remaining projects with positive *NPV*s will have first-year investments equal to or less than the amount of capital management is willing to commit to new projects.

This method has two flaws. One is that the *NPV* method assumes that profits in each year are reinvested at a rate of return equal to the cost of capital used to calculate their *NPV*s. This assumption is reasonable when the rate of return on the projects in the capital budget is close to the average rate of return earned on the company's investments. The company's average cost of capital, which is based in part on investor assessments of its past performance, generally approximates its average rate of return on borrowed and invested capital. However, when the cost of capital is arbitrarily increased to ration capital, this link between the cost of capital and the rate of return on investment is broken. The other is that the artificially high cost of capital will favor short-term projects over long-term projects that earn a lower rate of return but are most likely to provide the basis for sustained growth and profitable future investments.

There are no simple, direct solutions to maximizing the value of the firm when there is a capital constraint. The decision process becomes highly complex and involves comparisons of the risk-adjusted present values of a number of possible capital budgets.

## 13.5 *Summary*

Possible projects for inclusion in the firm's capital budget may originate anywhere in the firm — from operating departments and divisions, research and development departments, or executive management. After being evaluated by lower levels of management, project proposals are forwarded to the planning department for further analysis and integration into alternative capital budgets and plans. These alternatives are forwarded to executive management for further analysis and approval. The approved budget is then implemented by the operating departments and divisions.

The cost of capital is a weighted average of the market yields on the firm's debt and equity securities. The firm's cost of capital basically depends on investors' evaluations of the future earnings and the risk inherent in its profit stream. It also depends on the firm's debt/equity ratio. An estimate of the investors' risk preference function is used to develop the risk-adjusted cost of capital for calculating the present value of the project's profits. Where the firm's capital budget contains a number of projects, overall risk is reduced, because worse than expected profits from one project may be offset by better than average profits from another project.

Maximizing the present value of profits is a useful decision criterion when the firm is not faced with a constraint on the size of its capital budget. The constraint makes determination of the wealth-maximizing capital budget more complex. Methods for handling capital constraints are treated in advanced courses in finance.

## CASE 15     Expand or Build a New Plant

This case illustrates the use of managerial economics in capital budgeting and planning. The discussion here simulates the initial, broad-brush, phase of planning to take advantage of a growing market. Because a large number of calculations are required to find the *NPV* for each alternative, a computer program was used to calculate each *NPV*. The first step involves estimating the appropriate cost of capital for each project and establishing the market conditions under which the product will be sold. Five alternative projects are then analyzed and their *NPV*s calculated. Each alternative faces the same market share and price conditions, but each has its unique cost functions. Once the alternative with the greatest *NPV* is identified, the firm's engineers, accountants, and managers perform more detailed studies and prepare the project report.

**Assumptions Common to All Five Alternatives.** A common capital budgeting problem is to determine whether (1) to continue to operate an existing plant, (2) expand it, or (3) build a new plant. Associated with the last two alternatives is whether the new facilities should be included in next year's capital budget or deferred for another year. Thus, five alternatives are evaluated to determine whether a project relating to the plant should be proposed for next year's capital budget. This decision is based on selecting the alternative with the greatest risk-adjusted net present value of expected future profits. It is assumed that the cost of capital is 15 percent for operating or expanding the existing plant. Because the new plant is viewed as being somewhat riskier, its risk-adjusted cost of capital is 17 percent.

The existing plant produces a product sold in an oligopolistic market where another firm is the price leader. The company has two other plants, in different locations, producing this product. Market demand in this plant's market area is expected to be 520 units per hour next year for the 2,000 hours that the plant operates. The company has maintained a 20 percent market share for the past 15 years. Next year's price is projected at $48. Price has declined by an average of $0.25 per year for the past 8 years, and prices are expected to continue to decline at that rate. Demand is expected to grow at 5 percent per year, and the firm does not expect its market share to change if it has sufficient plant capacity. Any attempt to increase its market share is expected to result in an unprofitable price war, because demand is inelastic for prices below $45. Thus, output will be either the company's market share times market demand or the output where price equals marginal cost, whichever is the smaller amount. Producing more than the output where $P = MC$ reduces profits, and attempting to produce more than the firm's normal market share will touch off a price war.

**Operate the Existing Plant.** If the firm continues operating its existing plant, its total and marginal cost functions for the next 4 years will be $TC = \$1,000 + \$26q + \$0.10q^2$ and $dTC/dq = MC = \$26 + \$0.20q$. Starting in the fifth year, maintenance costs are expected to rise, resulting in the $26 coefficient in the cost functions being replaced by $26.50 in the fifth year, $27.50 in the sixth year, and $32 in the seventh year. By the eighth year, the plant is expected to be inoperable without further investment. The fixed costs for this plant, as well as the expanded and new plants, are cash fixed costs that must be covered by revenues if the plant is to be operated. Noncash changes like depreciation expense and other sunk costs are not included in fixed costs when analyzing investment op-

**Table 13.2   Operate Existing Plant**

| Year | Profit | Present Value | Hourly Output | Market Share |
|------|--------|--------------|---------------|--------------|
| 1 | $412,800 | $   384,938 | 104.0 | 20.0% |
| 2 | 365,313 | 296,222 | 108.8 | 19.9% |
| 3 | 311,250 | 219,465 | 107.5 | 18.8% |
| 4 | 257,813 | 158,074 | 106.2 | 17.7% |
| 5 | 101,250 | 53,983 | 102.5 | 16.2% |
|   | Total | $1,112,682 | | |

portunities.[1] The projected profits and their present value are in Table 13.2.

**Expand and Modernize Existing Plant.** Management's principal concern with continuing to operate this plant is that its market share will begin to decline after 2 years. One way to prevent this loss of market share is to modernize and expand the plant. This will involve expenditures of $2.2 million in next year's capital budget and $400,000 in 5 years to replace the last of the old equipment retained in the plant. The present value of these expenditures is $2.25 million.

$$PV = \$2,200,000/(1.15)^{0.5} + \$400,000/(1.15)^5 = \$2,250,381$$

The existing plant will be operated for 9 months while the new equipment is being assembled, and then shut down for 3 months to rebuild some of the old equipment and install the new equipment. The first line of Table 13.3 reflects these conditions. When the existing plant is shut down, sales will be maintained using inventories built up with overtime operations at this plant and its other two plants. The higher costs of these inventories are estimated at $370,000 and included in the $2.2 million capital budget.

When the expanded and modernized plant is placed into operation at the start of year 2, its total cost function will be $TC = \$1,100 + \$24.50q + \$0.09q^2$. The company's engineers believe that learning curve effects will reduce the $24.50 coefficient to $24.00 in year 3 and $23.75 in year 4. The annual profits and total present

---

[1]The examples in this chapter ignore income taxes. If the firm must pay income taxes, depreciation, and those noncash charges and sunk costs that are tax-deductible are used in calculating the project's income tax liabilities. See Section 14.1 for a discussion of income taxes.

**Table 13.3    Expand and Modernize Existing Plant**

| Year | Thousands of Dollars | | Hourly Output | Market Share |
|---|---|---|---|---|
| | Profit | Present Value | | |
| 1 | $309.6 | $  288.7 | 104.0 | 20.0% |
| 2 | 731.4 | 593.0 | 109.2 | 20.0% |
| 3 | 822.6 | 580.0 | 114.7 | 20.0% |
| 4 | 849.5 | 520.8 | 120.4 | 20.0% |
| 5 | 801.8 | 427.5 | 126.4 | 20.0% |
| 6 | 738.9 | 342.6 | 127.8 | 19.3% |
| 7 | 675.3 | 272.3 | 126.4 | 18.1% |
| 8–18 | 3,433.6 | 826.7 | — | — |
| | Total | $3,851.6 | | |

value of this plant are in Table 13.3. This project will maintain the company's existing market share for 5 years. After year 6, output and market share decline with the declining price for the product. The *NPV* of this project is $3,851,600 − $2,250,381 = $1,601,219. Since this is greater than the $1,112,682 obtained if the existing plant is operated until it is no longer profitable, expanding and modernizing the plant is the preferred alternative.

An alternative to including the project to expand and modernize the plant in next year's capital budget is to delay it by one year. The existing plant would be operated for 21 months, shut down for 3 months, and then the expanded plant would be operated. The present value of the investment in this alternative is $2,250,381/1.15 = $1,956,853 and the present value of its profits is $3,459,200 from Table 13.4. Its *NPV* is $3,459,200 − $1,956,853 = $1,502,347. Since this is less than that of including the expansion and modernization project in next year's capital budget, the project should not be delayed for one year.

**Building a New Plant.** Building a new plant is another alternative. Because the new plant will be built on a site adjacent to the existing plant, it will not be necessary to shut down the existing plant. Six months after the new plant is put into operation, the old plant will be dismantled over a 6-month period at a cost of $40,000 and its equipment sold for $160,000. Thus, the net salvage value of the existing plant is $160,000 − $40,000 = $120,000, to be received in two years. The present value of this amount is $120,000/(1.17)^2 =

**Table 13.4   Expand and Modernize Existing Plant in One Year**

| Year | Thousands of Dollars | | Hourly Output | Market Share |
|------|------|------|------|------|
| | Profit | Present Value | | |
| 1 | $ 412.8 | $ 384.9 | 104.0 | 20.0% |
| 2 | 274.0 | 222.2 | 108.8 | 19.9% |
| 3 | 707.9 | 499.2 | 114.7 | 20.0% |
| 4 | 789.3 | 483.9 | 120.4 | 20.0% |
| 5 | 801.8 | 427.5 | 126.4 | 20.0% |
| 6–18 | 4,847.9 | 1,441.5 | — | — |
| | Total | $3,459.2 | | |

$87,662. The expenditures on the new plant to be included in next year's capital budget are $7.2 million. The present value of this amount less the salvage value of the existing plant is $7,200,000/$(1.17)^{0.5}$ − $87,662 = $6,568,740. The new plant will be operable for 20 years.

The new plant's first-year total cost function is $TC = \$1,250 + \$23.50q + \$0.075q^2$. Its learning curve has the $23.50 coefficient replaced by $21.00 in the second year and $20.50 in the third. The economics of this plant are in Table 13.5. Its minimum $ATC$ is $39.86 in year 3 at an output of 129.1 units per hour; however, the plant produces its highest output in year 11 at 166.67 units per hour. The company can maintain its 20 percent market share for 10 years with

**Table 13.5   Build New Plant**

| Year | Thousands of Dollars | | Hourly Output | Market Share |
|------|------|------|------|------|
| | Profit | Present Value | | |
| 1 | $ 412.8 | $ 384.9 | 104.0 | 20.0% |
| 2 | 1,007.5 | 796.1 | 109.2 | 20.0% |
| 3–9 | 12,453.1 | 5,458.6 | — | — |
| 10 | 1,743.1 | 392.2 | 161.3 | 20.0% |
| 11 | 1,666.7 | 320.6 | 166.7 | 19.7% |
| 12 | 1,583.8 | 260.3 | 165.0 | 18.6% |
| 13–21 | 12,453.1 | 5,458.6 | — | — |
| | Total | $8,537.4 | | |

**Table 13.6   Build New Plant in One Year**

| Year | Thousands of Dollars | | Hourly Output | Market Share |
| | Profit | Present Value | | |
|---|---|---|---|---|
| 1 | $ 412.8 | $ 384.9 | 104.0 | 20.0% |
| 2 | 365.3 | 296.2 | 108.8 | 19.9% |
| 3 | 1,031.6 | 696.7 | 114.7 | 20.0% |
| 4 | 1,646.5 | 950.4 | 120.4 | 20.0% |
| 5 | 1,802.9 | 889.5 | 126.4 | 20.0% |
| 6–22 | 23,732.5 | 4,390.5 | — | — |
| | Total | $7,608.5 | | |

this plant. The present value of its profits is $8,537,400 and its *NPV* is $8,537,400 − $6,568,740 = $1,968,600. Since the *NPV* of the expansion and modernization project is $1,601,219, the new plant increases the value of the firm.

The new plant could be built in year 2 and put into operation at the start of year 3. The net salvage value of the existing plant is zero under this alternative, and the present value of the $7.2 million investment in the plant is $7,200,000/(1.17)$^{1.5}$ = $5,689,233. The present value of profits, from Table 13.6, is $7,608,200, yielding an *NPV* of $1,918,967. This alternative has a net present value almost $50,000 less than that of the previously analyzed plant; hence it is not recommended.

**Recommendation.** Including the funds for building the new plant in next year's capital budget is the recommended alternative. This recommendation was discussed with the department and division general managers. The division GM requested that a new plant with about 20 percent more capacity also be analyzed; however, this alternative had a net present value of $1.4 million, and the additional capacity added almost $1.3 million to the project's capital costs. With only slightly lower operating cost than the recommended plant, and the increased capacity not being utilized for ten years, it was not economic. After approving the new plant as a capital budget proposal, the division GM requested that the formal project report be prepared, reviewed by the division's controller, and sent to the corporate planning department.

## CASE 16   Uncertainty Over Product and Energy Prices

This case considers three alternative production technologies that differ with respect to their capital and energy intensities. This case differs from the previous one in that product and energy prices are assumed to be subject to probability distributions. The risk-adjusted cost of capital is calculated for each alternative and used in calculating its net present value. The alternative with the highest *NPV* is proposed for the firm's capital budget. A computer program was also used to make the *NPV* calculations in this case.

### The Assignment

The company produces greenhouses equipped to produce flowers and high-valued vegetable crops using hydroponics. From the customers' point of view, the product has been marginally profitable for them because of the large initial investment. This has limited sales and kept the company's profit margins low. A consulting engineering firm has recommended that a lightweight, factory-built container be developed. The concrete tanks now are built on-site by workers paid from $10 to $14 per hour. By building the tanks in a factory, workers paid from $4 to $5 per hour can be used for most of the labor. Labor-saving machinery can be installed to reduce the number of workers, and quality control can be tightened. The principal limitation on the scale of a plant is the cost of transporting the containers over long distances; hence, they must be lightweight.

Four engineers were assigned to developing this new container and evaluating three alternative production processes. They have designed and tested an excellent product that will reduce the average customer's investment by approximately 25 percent. The marketing department believes that sales of this new product in the Maryland/Virginia area, where the prototype plant will be built, will range from 200 to 300 systems per month. Once the containers have proven their reliability, sales are expected to rise substantially. Plants capable of producing 1,000 containers per month can then be installed in several of the company's present market areas, and it will be able to expand into more northerly areas of the U.S. and Europe. Your job is to evaluate each of the three alternative processes and make a recommendation as to which process has the greatest risk-adjusted net present value.

## Evaluating the Processes

The engineers have prepared five case studies for each of the three processes and estimated their production functions. Two equations were estimated for each process. The first relates output per month to the quantity of capital (measured in thousands of dollars) and the number of production workers. The second relates the quantity of energy (in KWH per month) required to operate the plant to the quantity of capital. The equations are:

$$\text{Process 1: } Q = 0.50K^{0.1}L^{1.0} \text{ and } E = 0.4K^{1.5}$$
$$\text{Process 2: } Q = 0.35K^{0.2}L^{1.0} \text{ and } E = 0.5K^{1.5}$$
$$\text{Process 3: } Q = 0.23K^{0.4}L^{0.8} \text{ and } E = 0.7K^{1.5}$$

Process 1 replicates the present method of building containers but uses lighter-weight materials. The equipment is similar to that which is hauled to each job site, and the process is relatively labor intensive. It uses more minimum-wage laborers than the other processes and has an average production labor cost of $950 per month. Process 2 uses machinery to replace much of the labor used in the layering-up portion of the manufacturing process and includes a more sophisticated technique for applying the final surface to the container. This process requires a larger capital investment and somewhat more energy than process 1. Raw materials for processes 1 and 2 cost $250 per container. Process 3 adapts to container manufacturing an automated system used to produce large diameter culvert pipe. It is the most capital- and energy-intensive of the three processes. Process 3 requires the use of a special high-strength fiber glass matting that increases its raw materials cost to $425 per container. Processes 2 and 3 require somewhat higher labor skills and have an average production labor cost of $1,000 per month. Cash fixed costs are estimated at $48,000 per month for processes 1 and 2 and at $55,000 per month for process 3. For the purpose of calculating the cost-minimizing combination of capital and labor for a specified output, the monthly cost of a unit of capital ($1,000) is $12.50, which is equivalent to 15 percent interest. This unit cost is not used in calculating the fixed costs of the project.

The cost-minimizing combinations of capital and labor to produce 200 and 300 containers per month using each process are provided in Table 13.7. These quantities were calculated using the method in section 6.5. The quantity of capital is recorded in the "capital budget" row of the table. Because the plants require one year to build and the capital expenditures are made at a roughly constant rate over the year, the mid-year centered present value of the capital budget is used in calculating each process's *NPV*.

**Table 13.7  Prototype Commercial-Scale Plants (Millions of dollars)**

| Item | Process 1 | | Process 2 | | Process 3 | |
|---|---|---|---|---|---|---|
| | 200 | 300 | 200 | 300 | 200 | 300 |
| PV of profits | $1.4 | $3.3 | $5.0 | $8.8 | $4.2 | $7.5 |
| PV of capital budget | 1.3 | 2.0 | 1.9 | 2.6 | 3.0 | 4.3 |
| Net present value | $0.1 | $1.3 | $3.1 | $6.2 | $1.2 | $3.2 |
| Capital budget | $1.5 | $2.1 | $2.0 | $2.8 | $3.3 | $4.6 |
| Number of workers | 193 | 279 | 125 | 175 | 82 | 115 |
| Energy (KWH/mo) | 22,461 | 39,044 | 44,702 | 74,206 | 132,216 | 219,482 |
| Materials ($/unit) | $250 | $250 | $250 | $250 | $425 | $425 |
| Risk-adjusted $k$ | 19.6% | 18.1% | 16.5% | 16.3% | 17.0% | 16.8% |

The unit costs of labor and raw materials are felt to be highly predictable. The present cost of energy is 12 cents per KWH; however, the time trend in energy prices is uncertain. The consulting firm hired by the company recommended that each process be evaluated using five alternative energy price trends between −6 percent and +10 percent per year in equal increments of 4 percent, and that each trend projection be treated as being equally likely. Because the uncertainty is with regard to the growth rate, the projected energy prices get further apart as time goes on; thus, the coefficient of variation increases over time. To measure the risk inherent in each process, the average coefficient of variation (CV) is computed and substituted into the company's risk preference function to find the risk-adjusted cost of capital. The risk preference function is $k' = 0.15 + 0.2CV$.

The market price for the containers is also subject to some uncertainty. The marketing manager believes that the following price ranges are appropriate and that three equally probable prices $50 apart should be used in evaluating the processes.

$Q = 200u$/mo: $P = \$1,450$ to $\$1,550$ per container
$Q = 300u$/mo: $P = \$1,400$ to $\$1,500$ per container
$Q = 1,000u$/mo: $P = \$1,300$ to $\$1,400$ per container

For each energy cost projection, there are three price projections, requiring fifteen profit projections to calculate the expected profit and its standard deviation for each process and output. The economics of each process are summarized in Table 13.7.

### The Recommendation

Process 1 is the most risky of the three and has the highest risk-adjusted cost of capital. The principal reason for its higher risk level is the greater sensitivity of its profits to the projected price. With the average level of profits substantially lower for process 1 than for the other two processes, its coefficient of variation is more sensitive to the variation in profits because of prices that are higher or lower than the average for the predicted range. Process 3 is more risky than process 2, primarily because its automated equipment uses almost three times as much energy to produce a container. All three processes were less risky at an output of 300 containers per month because their unit costs were lower and their average profits higher.

The wealth-maximizing process is process 2 producing 300 units per month. The plant will cost $2.8 million and has an *NPV* of $6.2 million. Process 3 requires a substantially higher capital budget ($4.6 million for a 300-unit-per-month plant) and generates a stream of profits with a lower present value than that of process 2. Process 1 has a much lower *NPV* and the amount that must be budgeted to build the plant is only $580,000 less than for process 2. A plant using process 2 was recommended for next year's capital budget.

The division general manager accepted this analysis of the process alternatives; however, the GM felt that processes 2 and 3 should also be compared for a plant producing 1,000 containers per month. Although the prototype plant was expected to be profitable, its secondary purpose was to prove the feasibility of the process and provide operating experience on which to improve the design of commercial-scale plants. The GM felt that the more automated process 3 might be more profitable at a higher output. Changing output to 1,000 and using the lower container prices projected for the higher output, process 2 was nearly twice as profitable as process 3. Its *NPV* was projected at $24.7 million and its capital investment was only $7.6 million. The comparable figures for process 3 are $12.2 and $12.6 million. After reviewing those projections, the GM ordered preparation of the detailed project report and its forwarding to the planning department after its approval by the division's controller.

---

## Key Terms

| | | |
|---|---|---|
| capital asset pricing model (CAPM) | capital rationing | equity capital |
| capital budget | cost of capital | operating budget |
| capital constraints | debt capital | risk premium |
| | debt/equity ratio | |

# Review Questions

1. How does capital budgeting and planning differ from operations budgeting and planning? Why is wealth maximization used in both capital and operations budgeting?

2. Why might executive management not approve a project for the capital budget with a positive net present value?

3. Define the terms *cost of capital, debt capital,* and *equity capital.*

4. Why does the cost of equity capital depend upon investors' expectations of the future rate of growth in the price of the company's stock? Why should a higher expected growth rate increase the firm's cost of capital?

5. Explain why a rise in the firm's debt/equity ratio implies that its financial risk has increased.

6. Why are the buyers of a firm's debt securities generally more risk-averse than buyers of its common stock?

7. Why is the probability that a project will lose money an appropriate measure of its risk? How is this probability related to the standard deviation and coefficient of variation of profits?

8. Why are two points on the firm's risk-adjusted cost of capital relatively easy for management to estimate? If investors become increasingly risk-averse with increases in the coefficient of variation for profits, why are three points necessary to estimate the RP curve?

9. Explain why management should reject projects with an internal rate of return below the RP curve in Figure 13.2.

10. Assume that the firm's present standard deviation of next year's profit is $5,000. Assume that making a new investment will lower this standard deviation to $4,000. How might this affect the firm's cost of capital? Explain why for two cases: investors are risk-averse and investors are risk-seeking.

11. Why might there be financial and other constraints on the size of the firm's capital budget?

12. Explain why increasing the cost of capital as a capital rationing tool will result in favoring short-term over long-term investments. Create a numerical example illustrating this point.

# Problems and Applications

1. Calculate the cost of capital for a firm that has (a) $30 million in long-term debt on its balance sheet, with a market value of $25 million and a market interest rate of 12 percent; and (b)

500,000 shares of common stock outstanding, presently selling for $75 per share and paying an annual dividend of $3.75 per share. Over the past 5 years, the price of the firm's common stock has grown at an average annual rate of 20 percent per year (compounded) and investors generally expect its price to continue to grow at that rate in the future. The income tax rate is 45 percent.

2. Assume that project $A$ has an expected profit of $50,000 and a standard deviation of profits of $20,000. For project $B$ these amounts are $70,000 and $30,000. Calculate the probability of a loss for both projects under the assumption that profits are normally distributed. Determine which is the riskier project.

3. Assume that the relationship between the cost of capital, $k$, and the risk of a project, $\sigma$, is $k = 0.08 + 0.01\sigma + 0.02\sigma^2$.
   a. What is the risk-free cost of capital?
   b. What is the cost of capital if $\sigma = 4$?
   c. What is the present value of a project with $\sigma = 4$, an expected profit of $10 per day during the first year, an expected profit of $20 per day the second year, and nothing thereafter?
   d. Is the management with this $RP$ curve risk-averse or risk-seeking?

4. The boss is considering building a new production facility to replace an existing plant that must be demolished to make room for a new freeway. Your job is to evaluate this investment by calculating its net present value. The following information is available:
   a. The marketing department estimates that the price of the product will be $110 per unit if annual sales are less than 3,000 units. Price will fall to $100 if sales exceed 3,000 units per year.
   b. The manufacturing department estimates that a capital investment of $180,000 will be required and that the facilities can be assembled and put into operation in about 2 weeks in an empty building owned by the company.
   c. The equipment manufacturer estimates its average cost of labor function as $ACL = \$10T + \$0.20Q$, where $T$ is the time in years since the plant is started up (that is, $T = 1$ for the first year of operations) and $Q$ is output per month.
   d. Cash fixed costs, exclusive of depreciation allowances and the capital investments, are $800 per month and raw materials cost $15 per unit of output.
   e. The controller estimates the cost of capital for this project at 20 percent.
   f. The equipment manufacturer estimates that the plant will be operable for 10 years, at which time it will have to be abandoned because of equipment failures.
   g. The manufacturing department estimates the plant's salvage value

at $150,000 at the end of its first year of operations and a decline in its salvage value of $25,000 per year thereafter until a zero salvage value is reached.

5. The boss wants you to evaluate two alternative ways of expanding production at the plant. Both methods have the same initial cost of $2.5 million. Alternative A has lower operating costs but is less reliable than alternative B. This is reflected in the cost curves and probabilities that the plant will operate for the two alternatives.

*Alternative A*

$AVC = \$10 + \$0.02Q$

Probability of operating 12 months is 20 percent

Probability of operating 11 months is 30 percent

Probability of operating 10 months is 50 percent

*Alternative B*

$AVC = \$40 + \$0.01Q$

Probability of operating 12 months is 5 percent

Probability of operating 11 months is 90 percent

Probability of operating 10 months is 5 percent

$Q$ is output per month, with the plant either operating at its profit-maximizing rate or producing nothing when it is out of service. The marketing department estimates a price of $115 per unit during the first year, with price declining by 8 percent each year thereafter. Each plant will become inoperable after 5 years and have a salvage value of $50,000. The appropriate risk preference function for calculating each plant's risk-adjusted cost of capital is $k = 0.15 + 0.003\sigma^{0.25}$ where $\sigma$ is the standard deviation of the first year's profits. Cash fixed costs are $100,000 per year for both plants. Which plant should be recommended for next year's capital budget, or should neither plant be considered?

6. Consider the example discussed in Case 15. The expand and modernize alternative has been eliminated by management, leaving operation of the existing plant or building a new one this year as the alternatives to be considered. The total cost function for the existing plant has been reestimated as $TC = \$900 + \$26q + \$0.09q^2$, with the same maintenance cost effects on the $26 coefficient as before; and the total cost function for the new plant has been reestimated as $TC = \$1,200 + \$23.50q + \$0.07q^2$ with the same learning curve effects as before. All other aspects of the example are unchanged. Is building the new plant still wealth-maximizing?

7. Assume that $AVC = 9 + 3T + 0.5Q$ where $Q$ is output per hour and $T$ is the operating year, price is projected at $30, fixed costs are $54 per hour that the plant is operating, and the plant operates

for 2,000 hours per year. If the plant costs $250,000 at time $T = 0$ and the firm's cost of capital is $k = 20\%$, is this a wealth-maximizing investment? Explain why.

8. Assume now that management believes that the price in problem 7 is subject to the probability distribution: the probability of a price of $27 is 0.2, of $30 is 0.6, and of $33 is 0.2.

   a. Is this a wealth-increasing investment if the cost of capital is 20 percent? Explain why.

   b. Use the coefficient of variation of profits to explain why this investment becomes riskier as $T$ increases.

# 14

# *Taxation, Regulation, and Managerial Decisions*

This chapter has two primary goals. One is to introduce the additional complexities in making decisions when the firm is subject to taxes and government regulation. The general nature of these government policies is discussed in the context of the economic models introduced in the preceding chapters. The emphasis is on how tax and regulatory policies change the firm's average and marginal costs and on how the firm's profit-maximizing output and the industry's market-clearing price change.

The second goal is to introduce how managers might influence and use these policies to increase the firm's profits and protect it from the competition of new entrants. Managers can influence political decisions in more ways than simply making campaign contributions to friendly candidates. Their leadership positions provide them with access to politicians and bureaucrats who make decisions affecting many aspects of their company's operations. This access makes it possible for business managers to influence decisions makers' preferences and provide information about the costs, benefits, and tradeoffs involved among alternative tax and regulatory policies. If they are successful, managers can use the political process to enhance their firm's profits and its opportunities to grow and prosper.

The government policies surveyed in this chapter result from highly complex and constantly changing laws and regulations. For the most part, the laws enacted by Congress are statements of general public policy. They are implemented by regulations adopted by government administrative agencies. The regulations are modified from time to time as the agency learns more about the behavior it is regulating. When the regulations are challenged in court, or the agency sues a firm to

431

bring it into compliance with its regulations, the resulting court decisions become precedents for future business and agency decisions. New cases may be brought to further define the legal concepts involved or to apply a decision's line of reasoning to additional business practices.

The regulations implementing tax and regulatory laws and the laws themselves are constantly changing. This is why tax and regulatory law are the province of specialists who advise business managers. Managers must make decisions involving all aspects of the operations they control. They do not have the time to develop detailed knowledge of tax and regulatory law. Managers should, however, be aware of the principles involved so that they may better communicate with specialists in these fields.

The first three sections of this chapter are devoted to tax policy. The first section illustrates how income taxes enter into calculations of after-tax profits. The second section provides an analysis of the effects of income taxes on short- and long-run business decisions with respect to price, output, and new plant construction. The third section illustrates how sales and property taxes can influence managerial decisions. The last three sections focus on regulatory policies. Section 14.5 is devoted to a discussion of the effects of regulations on costs and prices. The general political process involved in regulation is also discussed in section 14.5. Sections 14.4 and 14.6 are concerned with regulation in industries in which the firms are oligopolists or monopolists. Some firms use business practices that are likely to lessen competition or result in monopolization of an industry. These firms can be prosecuted under the antitrust laws. Other firms are public utilities whose prices and services are determined using the cost of service method.

## 14.1  *The Corporate Income Tax*

The previous chapters have not dwelt on the impact of taxes on managerial decisions. Calculating the tax implications of operating and capital spending decisions is normally assigned to specialists after the project managers and engineers have estimated the costs and revenues of the decisions. This section provides a brief review of the major features of the corporate income tax and illustrates the principles of including taxes in plan or project evaluations. In practical circumstances, a much wider range of tax regulations is certain to apply, requiring expert tax advice before making a decision.

*Income Before Taxes.* Income before taxes, or *IBT*, is total revenue less explicit costs and depreciation allowances. Implicit (opportunity) costs cannot be deducted from income in calculating the firm's income tax liability. Implicit costs are subtracted from after-tax profits before making the decision. Some adjustments to revenues and expenditures may be made to reflect the fiscal years within which the funds are actually received and paid by the firm, and some expenditures may be carried forward into the next year because the tax code does not always allow the deduction of prepaid expenses.

*Accelerated Cost Recovery System Depreciation Allowances.* Prior to the 1981 tax reform legislation, depreciation allowances required rather complex calculations, with several alternative methods to choose from. The method adopted in 1981 is the Accelerated Cost Recovery System, or ACRS. This method creates three classes of assets — 3-, 5-, and 15-year property. There are other categories of property, some options are available, and some property (such as land) cannot be depreciated; however, they need not be considered here. Three-year property includes automobiles, light trucks, and equipment used for research and experimentation. Five-year property includes equipment and machinery not included in three-year property or a special category. Fifteen-year property is buildings and other business structures. Depletion of petroleum or minerals properties and other capital consumption allowances are not discussed here.

The ACRS depreciation rates applicable to each class of property acquired in 1983 are in Table 14.1. Estimates of the property's salvage value are not deducted from its cost before calculating ACRS depreciation allowances. Assume that a machine in the 5-year category was purchased for $100,000 and placed in service in the previous fiscal year so that it is now in its second recovery year. The ACRS depreciation allowance is $100,000 × 0.22 = $22,000. If its profit was $80,000, $IBT$ = $80,000 − $22,000 = $58,000. A building costing $400,000 to construct that is now in its fourth recovery year receives an ACRS depreciation allowance of $400,000 × 0.08 = $32,000. Once 100 percent of the original cost of the property has been depreciated, $IBT$ becomes profits as they were calculated in previous chapters, plus any implicit costs included in the profit calculation.[1]

*Income After Taxes and Cash Flow.* After $IBT$ has been calculated, the next step is to calculate the firm's tax liability by multiplying $IBT$ by its marginal income tax rate. The examples in this section assume a marginal tax rate of 45 percent of $IBT$. The income tax on a 5-year machine with $IBT$ = $58,000 is $TAX$ = 0.45 × $58,000 = $26,100.

---

[1]Total costs, as they were calculated in previous chapters, included implicit costs. To remove the implicit costs from the profit calculation, add them to profits, because accountants and the IRS include implicit costs in profits, but economists do not.

**Table 14.1  ACRS Depreciation Percentages on Property Acquired in 1983**

| Recovery Year | Three-Year (%) | Five-Year (%) | Fifteen-Year* (%) |
|---|---|---|---|
| 1 | 25 | 15 | 12 |
| 2 | 38 | 22 | 10 |
| 3 | 37 | 21 | 9 |
| 4 | | 21 | 8 |
| 5 | | 21 | 7 |
| 6 | | | 6 |
| 7 | | | 6 |
| 8 | | | 6 |
| 9 | | | 6 |
| 10 | | | 5 |
| 11 | | | 5 |
| 12 | | | 5 |
| 13 | | | 5 |
| 14 | | | 5 |
| 15 | | | 5 |

*Assumes property was placed in service in January.

Income after taxes, or *IAT*, is *IBT* − *TAX* = $58,000 − $26,100 = $31,900. Cash flow, or *CF*, is the amount of money generated by the project during the fiscal year that is available for management's use. *CF* is *IAT* plus the depreciation allowance or $31,900 + $22,000 = $53,900.

Adjusted cash flow, or *ACF*, is cash flow less the after-tax implicit opportunity cost of those factors of production that are owned by the firm and not purchased from others during the current planning period. Implicit costs are calculated on an after-tax basis. If a fully depreciated machine could be leased to another company for $8,000 per year, income taxes of $8,000 × 0.45 = $3,600 would be paid on the lease revenues, and its after-tax opportunity cost is $8,000 − $3,600 = $4,400. If after-tax opportunity costs of *OC* = $5,000 were associated with the project because it uses working capital and the fully depreciated machine, its adjusted cash flow is *ACF* = $53,900 − $5,000 = $48,900. *ACF* is not an accounting term, but it is utilized in managerial decision making where implicit opportunity costs are involved.

***Investment Credit.*** The investment credit permits the company to deduct 10 percent of the cost of 3- and 5-year property from its income taxes in the year that the asset is put into service. The investment credit is not available on buildings or improvements to buildings. In its first recovery year, the $100,000 machine in the previous example would receive a $100,000 × 0.10 = $10,000 investment credit. If *IBT* in the first year is $72,000, its ACRS depreciation allowance is $15,000 and *IBT* = $72,000 − $15,000 = $57,000. At a 45 percent marginal tax rate, its income tax liability is $25,650. Deducting the $10,000 investment credit leaves a net tax of $15,650 for the first year. The annual depreciation allowances for the machine are not based on the cost of the machine less the investment credit. The credit is an added tax incentive to encourage new investments in plant and equipment. Other tax credits, such as jobs or energy conservation credits, may also be used to reduce income taxes.

*Net Present Value After Taxes.* Continuing with the above example, assume that the machine will be operable for 8 years. Its annual *IBT*, depreciation allowances, and *IAT* are in Table 14.2. Table 14.3 contains calculations of *CF, ACF,* and the present value of *ACF*. The machine is sold for its $1,000 salvage value after the end of the sixth year, because its ACF is $775. Its working capital and the fully depreciated machine are then available for other projects. The net present value is calculated using a 20 percent cost of capital and the mid-year centering method. The machine has a net present value after taxes of $119,364 − $100,000 = $19,364.

*Taxes and Management's Optimization Goal.* Cash flow or adjusted cash flow is used when evaluating the firm's operating plan. If profit maximization is the firm's goal when there are no taxes, mazimizing *CF* or *ACF* is the appropriate goal when there are income taxes. Income taxes are treated as a cost of doing business. Wealth maximization when

**Table 14.2   Calculating After-Tax Income**

| Year | Profit | Depreciation | IBT | TAX | IAT |
|------|--------|--------------|--------|---------|---------|
| 1 | $72,000 | $15,000 | $57,000 | $15,650* | $41,350 |
| 2 | 80,000 | 22,000 | 58,000 | 26,100 | 31,900 |
| 3 | 40,000 | 21,000 | 19,000 | 8,550 | 10,450 |
| 4 | 28,000 | 21,000 | 7,000 | 3,150 | 3,850 |
| 5 | 21,000 | 21,000 | -0- | -0- | -0- |
| 6 | 14,000 | -0- | 14,000 | 6,300 | 7,700 |
| 7 | 10,500 | -0- | 10,500 | 4,725 | 5,775 |
| 8 | 7,500 | -0- | 7,500 | 3,375 | 4,125 |

*Income tax of $25,650 less the $10,000 investment credit.

**Table 14.3 Calculating Present Value of After-Tax Cash Flow**

| Year | IAT | Depreciation | CF | OC | ACF | PV of ACF |
|---|---|---|---|---|---|---|
| 1 | $41,350 | $15,000 | $56,350 | $5,000 | $51,350 | $ 46,876 |
| 2 | 31,900 | 22,000 | 53,900 | 5,000 | 48,900 | 37,199 |
| 3 | 10,450 | 21,000 | 31,450 | 5,000 | 26,450 | 16,768 |
| 4 | 3,850 | 21,000 | 24,850 | 5,000 | 19,850 | 10,486 |
| 5 | -0- | 21,000 | 21,000 | 5,000 | 16,000 | 7,044 |
| 6 | 7,700 | -0- | 7,700 | 5,000 | 2,700 | 991 |
| 7 | 5,775 | -0- | 5,775 | 5,000 | 775 | — |
| 8 | 4,125 | -0- | 4,125 | 5,000 | (875) | — |

|  |  |  |  | Total *PV* of *ACF* |  | $119,364 |
|  |  |  |  | Capital expenditure |  | − 100,000 |
|  |  |  |  | Net present value |  | $ 19,364 |

there are taxes becomes maximizing the present value of the project's *CF* or *ACF*.

# 14.2 *Short- and Long-Run Implications of Income Taxes*

This section covers three general implications of income taxes for managerial decision making. The first is concerned with the effect of income taxes on the short-run profit-maximizing output. The second is concerned with the impact of income taxes on the long-run supply curve and the number of firms in an industry. The last focuses on the reduction in the risk of bankruptcy resulting from the ability to deduct losses in one business activity from profits earned in another business activity before calculating the firm's income tax liability.

*Short-Run Implications of Income Taxes.* The short-run profit-maximizing output $q_1$ is found by equating *MR* to *MC* and solving for $q_1$ in Figure 14.1. Figure 14.1 is drawn for a competitive firm; however, the conclusions derived in this section also apply to price-searcher firms. The *ATC* curve includes depreciation in fixed costs. Output $q_0$ is the firm's breakeven output at price $P_0$. At $q_0$, its profit is zero because $P_0 = ATC(q_0)$. Each unit of output between $q_0$ and $q_1$ adds to profits the amount between $P_0$ and *MC*. All profits earned after $q_0$ are subject to income taxes at the firm's marginal tax rate. The income tax on each unit of output beyond $q_0$ and up to $q_1$ is equal to $T(P - MC)$ where $T$ is the firm's marginal income tax rate. The income taxes paid by the

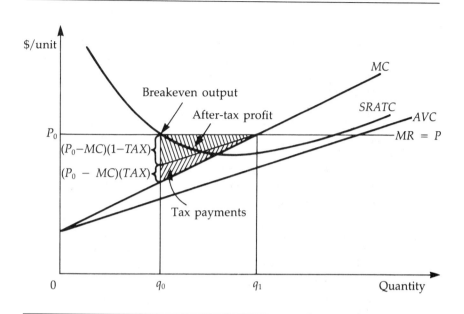

**Figure 14.1   Short-Run Implications of Income Taxes**

The firm does not earn a profit until its output reaches the breakeven level of $q_0$ where $P_0 = SRATC(q_0)$. The income tax paid on each unit of output after $q_0$ is equal to the income tax rate times $(P_0 - MC)$. The short-run profit-maximizing output, $q_1$, is the same for all tax rates because it occurs where $P_0 = MC$ or $(P_0 - MC) = 0$. Income taxes are treated in this model as a variable cost of production that is added to the $MC$ curve.

firm are in the lower shaded area. After-tax profits are in the upper shaded area. Although the income tax reduces the firm's profits, it has no effect on its profit-maximizing output because at $q_1$, $P = MC$ and the income tax paid is zero.

If there are positive opportunity costs associated with the project, the profit-maximizing output is unchanged because it is determined by finding the output where $MR = MC$, and $MC$ includes variable opportunity costs. Fixed opportunity costs are deducted from total cost before calculating $ATC$ and the breakeven output shifts to the left of $q_0$ in Figure 14.1. The firm's breakeven output is calculated by including the fixed opportunity costs in $ATC$. If there are variable opportunity costs of $\$X$ per unit, the $MC$ curve shifts down by $\$X$, because $MC$ as it is calculated by economists includes variable opportunity costs.[2] Income

---

[2]$MC$ as it is calculated by accountants only considers explicit costs and does not include variable opportunity costs.

tax payments increase with the greater margin between price and $MC$; however, the firm's profit-maximizing output is unchanged, because $q_1$ is calculated from $MC$, which includes variable opportunity costs. To find net after-tax profits, total variable opportunity costs, $\$Xq_1$, and fixed opportunity costs are deducted from after-tax income. Net after-tax profits are used in making managerial decisions.

*Long-Run Implications of Income Taxes.* Income taxes must be covered by the price of the product if a firm is to enter the industry. If all of the firm's costs are explicit costs, income taxes do not shift its $LRAC$ curve.[3] At a price equal to the $LRAC$ of producing a given output, there is no income tax liability. If $LRAC$ includes implicit costs, a price equal to $LRAC$ results in a tax liability on the implicit costs. If $EC$ and $IC$ are the firm's explicit and implicit costs at a given output and $T$ is the marginal income tax rate, $LRAC$ including income taxes is $C_0' = EC + (IC/(1 - T))$. If $IC = \$10$, $EC = \$70$, and $T = 0.45$, a price $\$88.18$ is required for the firm to enter the industry. At a price of $\$88.18$, the firm would show a taxable income of $\$88.18 - \$70 = \$18.18$. The tax on this amount is $\$18.18 \times 0.45 = \$8.18$, leaving an after-tax income of $\$10$, which is equal to the firm's implicit costs of $IC = \$10$. The $LRAC$ curve in Figure 14.2 has shifted up to $LRAC'$, where the minimum point on $LRAC'$ is at $C_0'$ because the income tax of $\$8.18$ per unit is a cost that must be paid by the firm. The long-run supply curve for the competitive industry will shift up to $LRS'$. Thus, income taxes increase the price of the product and, given the positions of the minimum points on $LRAC$ and $LRAC'$ in Figure 14.2, reduce the number of plants from $M$ to $K$.

Because implicit costs are not tax-deductible, and some factors like land are not depreciable, management will economize on those factors of production by substituting other factors with explicit costs. As the planned rate of output rises, the lowest-cost technology generally becomes more capital-intensive. If more capital-intensive technologies involve relatively greater or lesser use of factors involving implicit costs or nondepreciable factors, the income tax will affect management's choice of the plant's technology, with $LRAC'$ either approaching or diverging from $LRAC$.

*Income Taxes Reduce Risk.* Losses by one of the company's operations are deductible from profits earned in other operations; therefore, income taxes result in the government's bearing a portion of any losses. If there was no income tax, a loss in one operation would reduce the company's profits by the full amount of the loss. With a deductible

---

[3]This is an unlikely situation because firms generally have some equity capital whose cost is an implicit cost.

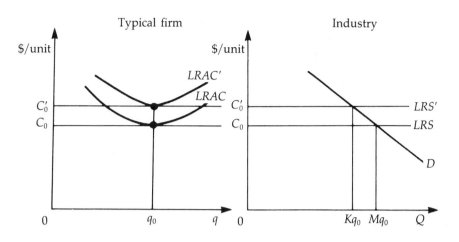

**Figure 14.2  Income Taxes and the *LRAC* and *LRS* Curves**

Income taxes are paid on the firm's normal profit, which from a managerial point of view is an implicit opportunity cost; therefore, income taxes shift up the minimum point on the *LRAC* curve of the typical firm. This shifts upward the *LRS* curve. The imposition of an income tax will result in a higher long-run equilibrium price and a smaller number of firms in a competitive industry.

loss of $100,000 in one operation, the company's income taxes on other operations are reduced by $100,000 × 0.45 = $45,000. The company's taxes are lower, so its risk of going bankrupt is reduced. Because the firm must have at least one profitable operation to take advantage of the loss deduction, this provision encourages firms to diversify or become conglomerates. The incentives to diversify or become a conglomerate are reduced to the extent that losses can be carried forward into future fiscal years or back to past fiscal years. Also, a company with operating losses is not a total loss to its owners. It can be sold to a profitable company for a price that will include at least part of the tax savings available to the acquiring company, which can write off the acquired company's losses against its profits.

## 14.3  *Sales and Property Taxes*

Ad valorem taxes are levied on the value of the item being taxed. Sales and property taxes levied by state and local governments and federal excise taxes are examples of ad valorem taxes. Both of these taxes can influence business decisions.

*Sales Taxes.* Sales taxes are computed by multiplying the selling price of a taxable product by the sales tax percentage. Although regulations vary from state to state, some "necessities" such as food, medical services, and rent generally are exempt from sales taxes so that they burden low-income consumers less than middle- and upper-income consumers. Sales taxes reduce consumer incomes available to purchase goods and, thus, have some impact on the level of demand for firms selling consumer goods. Their net effect on overall consumer demand probably is minimal, because some other tax would be raised to replace the revenues lost if sales taxes were reduced or eliminated.

Assume that a company sells personal computers, software, and related equipment by mail. If it locates in a state that does not charge sales taxes on sales to residents of other states, the firm will have a cost advantage over firms selling through retail stores. Mail order customers do not pay the sales tax, giving them a considerable cost savings ($200 on a $3,000 item) relative to buying at a local retail store. If the costs of the mail order outlet are comparable to those of the retail store, the sales tax savings may make mail order sales profitable.

From the computer manufacturer's point of view, the mail order outlet can provide an opportunity for profitable price discrimination. Computer buyers with considerable knowledge of alternative systems will have a more elastic demand curve for a specific make of computer than buyers with little knowledge. The more knowledgeable buyers can better substitute one make for another. The manufacturer can sell at a lower price through the mail to these buyers, because it does not need to incur the costs of a trained sales force at retail stores. The customers at the stores will receive the service they require to make an intelligent choice, but they will pay a higher price and the sales tax because they have less knowledge of the available substitutes for the manufacturer's products and, hence, a less elastic demand.

*Property Taxes.* The property tax is levied by local governments on the market value of privately owned real estate within its jurisdiction. The first step in calculating the property tax is to determine the property's assessed value, which is usually an estimate of its market value on some specified date. The tax is either a percentage of the assessed value or a certain number of dollars per hundred dollars of assessed value. Every year or every few years, the property is reassessed to reflect changes in its market value. Industrial property is generally subject to special assessment rules, because sales of industrial plants are rare and little data are available on their market value.

The property tax on a capital-intensive plant can impose a significant cost on the firm. Since new plants provide jobs and stimulate the local economy, governments may provide property tax breaks for new firms.

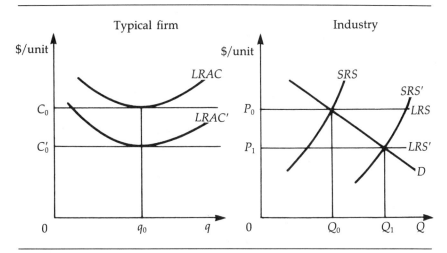

**Figure 14.3   Property Tax Reductions and Long-Run Supply**

Property taxes are a cost of production. When the property tax for new firms is reduced as an incentive to get them to build a new plant in the community, the *LRAC* curve shifts down to *LRAC'*. If similar property tax concessions are offered by many communities, the *LRS* curve will shift down to *LRS'*. In the new long-run equilibrium, price will be lower and the number of firms will increase to yield *SRS'* = *LRS'* = *D* at price $P_1$ and the industry output $Q_1$.

For example, a local government agency may build the plant and lease it to a new company. A government agency owns the plant, so it may be exempt from the property tax. The lease agreement can provide for the company's purchasing the plant after a certain number of years, at which time it would be subject to the property tax. The government agency may also finance the plant using relatively low-interest-rate tax-free municipal bonds and provide road and utility accesses which further reduce the firm's costs. With a high level of competition among local governments for new plants, management may be able to reduce significantly both capital cost and property tax costs by "shopping" for a new plant location.

    If these cost reductions are not available to existing plants, the result can be their closure prior to when they might otherwise become uneconomic because their *AVC* curve has shifted up as the plant has aged[4] to the point that it now exceeds the product's price. The property tax reduction and plant financing benefits for new plants shift the *LRAC* and *LRS* curves downward to *LRAC'* and LRS', as shown in Figure 14.3. The entry of new plants when price is above LRS' shifts the SRS

[4]See section 8.4.1 for a discussion of this point.

curve to the right and depresses the market price to $P_1$. Existing plants with $AVC$ curves above $P_1$ will be forced to close down and will be replaced by new plants.

## 14.4  *Antitrust Regulation*

The profits from acquiring a monopoly over an otherwise competitive industry can be substantial. Prices and profits are higher, and output lower, when an industry is monopolized. Prices increase when an industry is monopolized, and consumers are worse off because they are unable to purchase as much of the product as would be supplied by a competitive industry. They pay more for less of the product, and the additional profits earned by the monopoly amount to a wealth transfer from consumers to the monopolist.

The objective of the antitrust laws is to secure for consumers the benefits of competition among the sellers of goods and services in industries where efficient production and profitable marketing methods may result in oligopoly, monopoly, or collusion among sellers. These laws do not make passive possession of a monopoly unlawful.[5] Rather, their objective is to prevent firms from engaging in acts intended to monopolize an industry. The emphasis is on the actions taken by firms to lessen competition or create a monopoly. This general approach to regulating the behavior of firms recognizes that independent decisions made by firms in competition with one another are (1) more likely to occur if collusion or outright combination is made difficult and uncertain and (2) more likely to result in lower prices and more efficient production methods than would exist if firms were able to collude or merge with one another at will.

*The Sherman Antitrust Act.* The legal precedents for American antitrust law are in English common law, which has had a centuries-old hostility to the creation of monopolies. It is likely that Senator Sherman, who drafted the first antitrust law — the 1890 Sherman Act — believed that he was simply codifying policies contained in the common law. Moreover, early decisions (for example, *Addyston Pipe and Steel Company*, 1898)[6] reflected this basis in English common law when deciding Sherman Act cases.

---

[5]A firm might obtain passive possession of a monopoly, for example, because the other firms that were in an industry have left it because demand has declined to the point that only one firm can profitably supply the remaining market. Passive possession of a monopoly means that the firm has not taken overt actions to acquire a monopoly, such as driving out other firms. See *Standard Oil Company of New Jersey et al.* v. *United States*, 221 U.S. 1 (1911), and *United States* v. *United States Steel Corporation*, 251 U.S. 417 (1920).

[6]*United States* v. *Addyston Pipe and Steel Company*, 85 Fed. 271 (6th Cir. 1898).

There are two principal sections to the Sherman Act. Section 1 makes combinations or conspiracies in restraint of trade unlawful. Price fixing and market-sharing agreements are examples of the kinds of business behavior that are unlawful. A conspiracy can possibly be inferred because the firms in a price-leadership oligopoly adopt parallel business policies; however, as long as the firms independently arrive at similar decisions, Section 1 has not been violated. The courts have been unwilling to condemn independent use of normal business practices even if the result is joint profit maximization or a shared monopoly. Whenever the courts have found that the purpose of an agreement is to fix prices or share markets, no inquiry is made into whether the purposes of the agreement are "reasonable." The firms have been found to be in violation of Section 1 of the Sherman Act.

Section 2 of the Sherman Act declares that it is unlawful to monopolize or attempt to monopolize an industry. Most cases brought under Section 2 have been analyzed by the courts to determine if the acts that have reduced competition are "reasonable" uses of ordinary business policies or actions that are likely to have no redeeming benefits beyond those accruing to the firms involved. Most Section 2 cases involve a reduction of competition through merger or acquisition of competitors. Although mergers and cartels are alternative means to the same ends, the rule of reason argues that mergers can result in lower production, marketing, and financing costs, and hence be reasonable. Cartel agreements to fix prices do not reduce costs.

*The Clayton Antitrust Act.* Most mergers are prosecuted under Section 7 of the Clayton Act, because its requirements are less stringent than those of the Sherman Act. The Clayton Act was enacted in 1914 because the courts were not applying the general policy statements of the Sherman Act to making unlawful business behavior that Congress and President Wilson felt should be prosecuted. The original Section 7 was amended in 1950 to close a loophole created by earlier court decisions. The Section 7 test is whether the merger will lessen competition or tend to create a monopoly. This test has led to the Court's declaring unlawful mergers involving small market shares or likely to be emulated by other firms. Based on the 1967 *Procter & Gamble* case,[7] mergers between competitors or potential competitors are likely to be judged unlawful even if there may be production economies. Mergers creating conglomerates have rarely been challenged and appear unlikely to be declared unlawful under Section 7 unless the result is a large firm's using its financial and marketing resources to lessen competition or monopolize the acquired firm's principal business area.

Section 2 of the Clayton Act is treated as an antitrust act, yet its

[7]*Federal Trade Commission* v. *Procter and Gamble Company*, 386 U.S. 568 (1967).

principal goal is to protect one firm from differences in the prices charged it and other firms. Section 2 makes unlawful price discrimination that is not justified on the basis of cost differences between customer groups or meeting a lower price set by a competitor. The law recognizes that discrimination can take forms other than selling at two different prices, such as providing services at no or low cost to some customers and not others. The customers may be located in the same geographic area or in different geographic areas. Unless there is a cost difference or the company is meeting competition in good faith, price discrimination has generally been found to be unlawful.

*Federal Trade Commission Act.* Section 5 of the Federal Trade Commission Act (1914) is also treated as an antitrust law. Its purpose is to make unlawful unfair methods of competition. Unfair or deceptive methods of competition may not have monopolization or reducing competition in the industry as their goal. They may result from a firm's seizing upon an opportunity to increase its profits for a limited period of time at the expense of consumers or of other firms. However, when a particular trade practice is pursued for the purpose of systematically reducing competition and facilitating the firm's monopolizing the industry or where several firms are involved, converting a competitive industry into an oligopoly, Section 5 provides a means of prosecuting those firms. Section 6 of the Act permits the commission to gather and compile information, using subpoenas if necessary, on business conduct and practices that might begin a trend toward monopoly or oligopoly. When Sections 5 and 6 are combined, the commission can obtain the necessary information and then act to arrest the formation of monopolies or oligopolies in their early stages before monopolization has proceeded to the point that the largest firms in the industry could be prosecuted under the Sherman Act.

## 14.5  *Regulations Affecting Production Costs*

Congress, state legislatures, and local governments have passed thousands of laws that regulate business behavior. Government agencies have used these laws to develop a vast and sometimes contradictory set of regulations affecting virtually every facet of private sector decision making. These regulations are intended to protect public health and safety and promote the general welfare of citizens. They may be designed to protect consumers, workers, or the environment from decisions made by managers seeking greater profits. Their basic premise is that profit maximization may not be compatible with politically determined goals. In other cases, the laws and regulations result from the lobbying efforts of individual firms or trade associations that believe they can gain profits or protection from competition. These firms and trade associations frame their arguments in terms of the public benefits of their proposed regulations, although the actual public benefits may be small relative to their private benefits.

Government regulations impose costs on the agencies that administer them and on the firms and consumers who must comply with them. They also provide economic benefits to firms, consumers, and the bureaucrats who administer them, and political benefits to the legislators who enact them. Whether these benefits outweigh the costs is often a matter of considerable debate. Differences in the people bearing the costs and receiving the benefits also enter into the political debate concerning the wisdom of government regulation. Regulations significantly benefiting a relatively small, politically astute special interest group and imposing virtually imperceptible costs on many people are especially likely to be adopted. Although these regulations may be intended to correct some alleged market failure caused by monopoly or externalities, their costs may be so great relative to the benefits that the result is government failure.

The proliferation of regulations in the 1970s led to a reexamination of this trend toward greater government control over the economy. Experience has shown that many regulations provide little in the way of benefits while imposing substantial compliance costs on businesses and government agencies. In many cases, the costs are primarily in the form of increased paperwork. In other cases, the costs result from technological options that are no longer available, locating plants or transportation facilities in places where costs are higher, and changes in product design or work rules that reduce efficiency and increase the cost of American-made goods relative to imported substitutes. Other regulations, such as those reducing the exposure of workers to such proven carcinogens as asbestos, might be highly beneficial and deserving of further development.

*Protecting Workers.* If regulations result in higher costs, they are taken into consideration when calculating the firm's profit-maximizing output and price, the cost-minimizing combination of factors of production, or the profits to be earned from entering an industry. Regulations of the Occupational Safety and Health Administration (OSHA) provide examples of cost-increasing regulations. For example, regulations reducing dust in the workplace by requiring hoods and fans over process machinery have been enacted by OSHA. Fixed costs rise because of the cost of the equipment. Variable costs increase because of the added energy required to produce a unit of the product and the increased operator time required to place material in the machine and remove the final product and wastes. If repairs to the ventilating system require shutting down the equipment, production rates are further reduced. If the only approved technology uses hoods and fans, another technological option for attaining the goal of reducing dust may not be considered if substantial testing and other costs are required before it will be approved, and the company or trade association must bear the risk that the technology will not be approved.

Even though the dust regulations impose substantial costs, they may be supported by the industry because they reduce medical insurance and worker compensation costs, or because they reduce the likelihood that new, small firms with little capital will enter the industry. None of the firms would install the dust-reducing equipment without the OSHA regulation, even if they wanted to make their facilities healthier places to work, because other firms who did not install the equipment would have a significant cost advantage. If there is strong foreign competition for the market, with the foreign firms mostly using lower prices to increase their market share, the regulations may increase the *AVC* of the American firms to the point that they are forced to shut down. The foreign firms can have a cost advantage if they are not required to install dust hoods. The workers' labor union is likely to have ambivalent attitudes toward the hoods. Like the companies, they want to make the factories healthier places to work; however, they recognize that the resulting lower worker productivity will make wage increases more difficult to obtain. Politicians may ignore the costs and benefits of the regulations because they are under pressure to do something for worker safety.

*Protecting the Environment.* The benefits from the dust hoods accrue to a well-defined group. In other cases the benefits are quite nebulous and spread over a great number of people. Many environmental protection regulations are of this type. Reducing air pollution provides some benefit to everyone living in a large urban area; however, if it is done slowly, many people may not notice the cleaner air. The health problems associated with air pollution can be attributed to other causes; therefore, many of its potential victims may not feel threatened by the less visible types that damage the body with long-term chronic exposure. The benefits of reducing the impact of air pollution on wildlife and sensitive plants are likely to receive even less of the public's attention and political support. The costs of reducing air pollution can be substantial for large stationary producers of pollutants, such as power, petroleum, and metals processing plants. Foreign competition or competition from less polluting technologies may result in lower profits, abandonment of existing plants, or no new plants if pollution regulations increase costs. Individuals required to maintain catalytic converters on their cars may fail to do so because they feel that the contribution of their exhaust to the problem is very small and not worth the expense.

Even though there may be considerable medical evidence that reducing air pollution would reduce health care costs and improve the quality of life for thousands of people who would otherwise be stricken with lung cancer and other diseases, there may be relatively little broad-based political support for an adequate level of air pollution regulation. The most heavily regulated polluters are a highly motivated special interest group lobbying against control regulations and keeping its costs in the public's mind. Public health and environmental special interest groups lobby for these regulations. And politicians must weigh carefully the public's desire for a higher quality of life and the political pressures of conflicting special interest groups.

*Impact on Output and Prices.* OSHA, environmental protection, or other government regulations increase short-run production costs and administrative costs for existing plants, and long-run costs for new facilities. To the extent that they increase fixed costs for existing plants, the ATC curve shifts upward but there is no change in the firm's profit-maximizing output. If the productivity of labor falls, the MC and AVC curves shift upward, reducing the firm's profit-maximizing output from $q_0$ to $q_1$ in Figure 14.4. Since the industry's SRS curve is the horizontal sum of the firms' MC curves, it shifts to the left to SRS' and the market-clearing price rises to $P_1$. This will result in a smaller decline in the profit-maximizing output than would occur if price had not risen.

Regulatory costs shift upward the LRAC curve of potential entrants into the industry. This results in the LRS curve's shifting upwards. If the regulations have a greater impact on the costs of new plants than on existing plants, the regulations can lead to higher prices. As existing plants become inoperable and shut down, the SRS curve shifts to the left and the market-clearing price rises. If the new price is below the minimum point of the LRAC curve of the lowest-cost potential new entrant, the profits of the remaining old firms will be increased because price must rise to the level of the minimum point on the potential new entrant's LRAC curve before it will find it profitable to enter the industry. If demand is inelastic at prices up to the new firm's minimum LRAC, the remaining firms will have a greater total revenue as old plants exit the industry.[8] Thus, government regulations increasing the costs of new plants relative to those of old plants may be supported by the existing firms because they increase their profits. These regulations can also slow the rate at which cost-reducing new technologies are adopted

---

[8]The remaining firms will produce more as price rises with the exit of old plants; however, the increase in total cost will be less than the increase in total revenue.

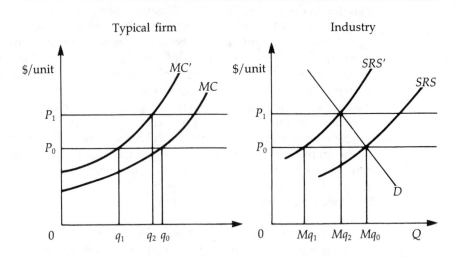

**Figure 14.4   Price and Output Changes with Regulation**

Regulation that increases the firm's variable costs results in the $MC$ curve shifting up to $MC'$ and the $SRS$ curve shifting to $SRS'$. At price $P_0$, regulation results in a reduction in output by each firm from $q_0$ to $q_1$ and excess demand in the industry equal to $M(q_0 - q_1)$. Price will rise to $P_1$ where $SRS' = D$ to reestablish short-run equilibrium, and output will rise to $q_2$ at the typical firm.

if the new technologies are subject to higher regulatory costs than existing technologies.

The higher price covers at least a portion of the increased fixed and variable regulatory costs, but generally it will not cover their entire cost. To the extent that prices rise, a portion of the burden of government regulation is borne by consumers. The increase in taxes necessary to pay the government's administrative costs are also a burden borne by taxpayers.

*Political Basis of Regulatory Decisions.* The benefits of the dust reduction regulations are reduced health care costs for the firm and its workers, although it may be difficult to determine the extent to which an observed change in health care costs can be attributed to the regulations. This is especially the case when the benefits may not become noticeable for several years and primarily accrue to new workers who will not suffer chronic exposure to the dust. A major portion of the benefits may be in the form of an improved quality of life for the firm's workers. Since there is no market price for a higher quality of life, its economic value is difficult, if not impossible, to measure in terms of dollars and cents. A benefit/cost study of the regulations estimates the dollar amounts of these costs and benefits, and any others that may be identified, to determine if on balance the regulations are beneficial. However, all of the benefits and costs generally cannot be measured unambiguously and are subject to considerable estimation errors. Benefits that are difficult or impossible to measure are generally referred to as the quality of life.

With portions of the benefits and costs essentially unmeasurable in a generally acceptable, unambiguous manner, the end result of a benefit/cost study of a government regulation is an essentially political decision. This decision can be modeled with indifference curves similar to those used in risk management. Net economic costs ($NEC$) are the costs of the regulations that can be measured objectively less the benefits that can also be measured objectively. As the regulations become more stringent and costly to comply with, the quality of life ($QL$) rises although the rate at which $QL$ rises declines because of effects similar to those of diminishing returns. In constructing the opportunity constraint, $OC$, curve in Figure 14.5, it is assumed that a quality of life index has been constructed in some manner acceptable to the decision maker. The $U_0$, $U_1$, and $U_2$ curves express the decision maker's preferences with respect to tradeoffs between net economic costs and the quality of life. As with risk preference curves, the $U_i$ curves are subjective and specific to each decision maker. The shape of the indifference curves reflects the decision maker's education, work experiences, political orientation, and other factors that influence his or her orientation toward the decision at hand. All the parties to the decision in either the public hearings or privately attempt to influence the preferences of the decision maker. Business managers may attempt to have the decision maker more fully comprehend the costs of increasingly stringent regulation, the impact on product prices, the loss of jobs to foreign competitors, and the possibly nebulous benefits of costly reductions in dust in the workers' environment. Other parties will stress other aspects of the decision. The decision maker makes the decision yielding the utility-maximizing combination of net economic costs and quality of life benefits — $NEC_0$ and $QL_0$ in Figure 14.5. This combination occurs where an indifference curve ($U_1$) is tangent to the $OC$ curve, because the available opportunities mapped on the $OC$ curve will not permit the decision maker to attain a higher utility level (such as $U_2$).

Where the decision-making authority is a commission with several members or a legislative body like the county board of supervisors or Congress, each member has his or her own perceptions of the $OC$ and $U$ curves. The political atmosphere of the commission or legislative body further complicates management's attempts to influence the decision. The members of these decision-making groups rarely contend with a

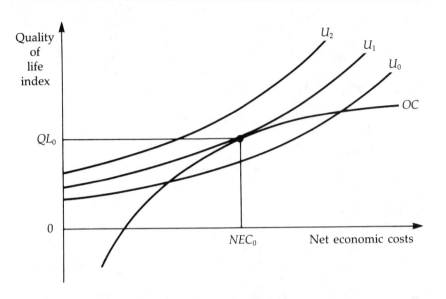

**Figure 14.5   Political Decision Involving Regulation**

Curve $OC$ provides the combinations of net economic cost and quality of life benefits inherent in a decision. The decision maker maximizes utility at combination $(NEC_0, QL_0)$ where his or her indifference curve for the tradeoff between $NEC$ and $QL$ is tangent to the $OC$ curve. The combinations of $NEC$ and $QL$ on $U_2$ are unattainable given the $OC$ curve. The decision maker can attain a higher utility level than that permitted by $U_0$.

narrow range of issues, and their selection or election generally does not depend crucially on one vote or issue. They evaluate the broad range of issues they face during their term in office and place this particular decision in the context of their overall political agenda. Thus, a decision that is highly important to the managements of the affected firms could have a low priority to the decision makers, and a majority of them may vote to impose relatively high costs on the firms in return for the other members' voting for a law or regulation that they feel more strongly about.

## 14.6   *Cost of Service Regulation*

The managements of public utilities face problems that are relatively unique. For the most part, their firms are highly regulated and their prices are determined in a highly political process. The cost of utilities is an important portion of consumer budgets, and well-organized special interest groups can be expected to participate in public hearings. Many utilities use production processes based on nonrenewable resources or producing large amounts of environmental pollutants. Others, such as hospitals or water districts, provide services essential to public health or safety. This section provides a brief introduction to the principal method used to regulate the prices of public utilities — the cost of service method.

*The Regulatory Process.* Some firms, such as a local water distribution company, are natural monopolies. Other firms may be sufficiently important to public health, safety, and welfare that they are provided with government franchises or regulatory protection against competition. In exchange for protection from direct competition, these firms submit to regulation by government of their prices and the level and nature of their service to consumers. These utilities are generally regulated by a commission set up for that purpose and referred to as the public utility commission. In some cases, the city council or county board of supervisors may perform the functions of a public utility commission. The commission's staff analyzes the rate (price) and service charge submittals of the utilities. The commission then holds public hearings at which all interested parties, including consumer representatives, can present testimony regarding the reasonableness of the proposed rates and service. The commission then approves or modifies the rate request.

The utility's management is one of several parties to the commission's rate proceedings. It must carefully project its costs and the demands of its customer groups and prepare detailed justifications for its new capacity and rate requests. It must attempt to influence the commission's staff; the commissioners; and the legislature, governor, or other appointing body to act in a manner that will yield profits to its stockholders. Management must be prepared to counter the arguments of its adversaries — generally consumer and environmentalist special interest groups. In the end, the commission's decision process is much like that described in the previous section. The decision makers identify the opportunities available to them (the *OC* curve in Figure 14.5) and determine the extent to which they are willing to trade off the benefits of changing one of the variables they regulate for those of another. The final result generally pleases no one. The parties to the regulatory process can bring lawsuits requesting a judicial review of the reasonableness of the procedures used and their consistency with the legislation and the Constitution. Supreme Court decisions in these cases provide precedents to guide public utility commissions and the parties to rate cases. Finally, there is always the next round of rate submissions to try to solve any problems resulting from the one just concluded.

*Justifying a Rate Change.* Cost of service regulation is used to determine whether the utility's rate request is reasonable. The price the utility can charge for a specified service depends on the cost of providing it. The costs of labor, materials, and other items that are used on a regular basis are expenses included in the utility's rate request. In addition to these operating costs, the utility is permitted to earn a reasonable rate of return on the capital it has invested in providing the service. The utility's rate base is the cost of its plant and equipment and its working capital. As the company acquires assets, they are entered into the rate base at their historical cost — the amount the utility paid for them. As the asset is depreciated, the depreciation allowance is included in the utility's rate request and the rate base is reduced by the depreciation allowance. The allowed rate of return is based on the commission's calculation of the utility's cost of capital, generally using a method similar to that in section 13.2. The rate of return multiplied by the rate base is included in the utility's rate request. The specific procedures for calculating the rate base, depreciation allowances, and the rate of return may vary from commission to commission; however, the principle is the same — permit the utility to cover all of its current operating expenditures and earn a rate of return on its rate base comparable to that earned in a competitive industry and adequate to attract sufficient capital to maintain the quality of its services.

The fixed and variable operating costs of the utility are included in the price for the services. They must be no greater than those of a prudent management in an unregulated industry. A utility cannot pay exorbitant salaries to its executives or exorbitant wages to its employees. It cannot have work crews substantially larger than those used by similar unregulated firms. It cannot pay more than the going market price for raw materials, spare parts, and other supplies. The first step in calculating operating costs is to project the utility's sales. This may be done using a simple trend projection, or it may be based on a sophisticated econometric model. Reasonable operating costs, generally based on the utility's past costs adjusted for expected changes in wages and the prices of supplies, are projected for the time period covered by the new rate schedule and included in utility's regular rate submissions. The utility can adjust its rates to reflect higher costs for some items, such as fuel at power plants, without first going through a time-consuming normal submittal.

*Justifying New Capacity.* In order to add new capacity to its system, a utility must demonstrate that the capacity will be needed to meet either its base or peak load demands. The base load is the level of operations expected on a continuous basis. The peak load is the highest level of operations expected on a normal day, month, or year. A utility is expected to maintain enough capacity to meet its peak loads, with a reasonable reserve for safety. When the utility adds capacity, it is required to use the appropriate technology for the service. For an electric utility, coal- or oil-fired plants are generally most economical for base loads, and hydroelectric or gas turbine plants for peak loads. The capacity required to meet future demands is normally projected on the basis of extensive studies by the utility and the commission's staff.

Because a major portion of many utilities' costs are rate base costs, most commissions do not want the utility to accumulate excess capacity that must be paid for by the utility's customers but yields them no service. Utilities are responsible for providing service on demand, and the commissions want them to have adequate capacity levels to meet peak loads. However, the commissions must carefully weigh the benefits of added capacity to meet peak loads against the rate base costs of equipment that is rarely used. In recent years, this had led to the implementation of advertising and time-of-day pricing programs designed to reduce peak demands as lower-cost means of providing service than building new capacity to meet peak loads. It has also led to considerable controversy over whether utilities should include the large costs of nuclear power plants that are under construction, or about to be abandoned because they are too expensive to complete, in their rate base.

*Allocating the Utility's Costs to Each Group of Rate Payers.* Once the utility's rate base and operating costs have been determined, the next step is to apportion those costs among the various categories of services provided by the utility. Many of the costs incurred by the utility are common to all of its services. The costs of building, maintaining, and operating a power plant are common costs because they cannot be identified with a particular service. Allocating these costs to any given service category is essentially an arbitrary process. One method allocates these costs on the basis of their average total cost. Another divides these costs into two categories — a demand charge based on the capacity to provide the service and a commodity charge based on the estimated variable costs of providing a unit of the service. In other cases, the cost allocation results from a political decision of the commission.

Another consideration is the rate schedule for each category of service. An example of a rate schedule is Table 14.4. Should the unit price of the service decline as the customer uses more of it, or should its price rise with increasing use? The former case is justified by the relatively high level of fixed costs for most utilities and the fact that $AFC$ and $ATC$ decline as usage rises.[9] The latter is justified by the utility's conserving nonrenewable natural resources if rates rise with

---

[9]This statement only applies if $AFC$ is much greater than $AVC$, because under those conditions $AFC$ will likely decline by more than $AVC$ increases when output rises.

**Table 14.4    Utility Rate Schedule**

| KWH Used | Rate, $/KWH |
| --- | --- |
| 1 – 400 | $0.118 |
| 401 – 800 | 0.092 |
| 801 – 1,200 | 0.078 |
| 1,201 – 5,000 | 0.066 |
| over 5,000 | 0.040 |

usage. It is also rationalized as providing at low cost a minimal level of service to everyone and higher prices for those persons who can afford to use a relatively large amount of the service. Where the demand for the utility's service is relatively elastic because large customers have access to its substitutes, a declining rate schedule with a low average rate may be requested by the utility. Similarly, smaller customers with few substitutes and relatively inelastic demands may pay higher average rates and face rising rates as their usage increases.

Construction of the rate schedule is basically a political process. No group of consumers wants to pay any more than it has to, and they all would like to pay less — if necessary by having another group pay more because it can better "afford" to. Conservationists and environmentalists prefer higher rates to pay for environmental protection facilities and to reduce the overall demand for the service and the nonrenewable resources it uses. Low- and fixed-income consumers want low "lifeline" rates for small amounts of service with larger users paying more. Industry wants lower rates to reduce costs to make it more competitive, providing stable jobs for the local community. The utility wants its rates to be profitable and prefers to receive the bulk of its revenues from customers whose demands are highly predictable.

Price discrimination is the dominant aspect of utility rate schedules. Not all price discrimination in utility rates is politically motivated. Utility plants are often highly capital intensive, and demand must grow for several years before the demand curve will be above the utility's *SRATC* curve. This situation is graphed in Figure 14.6. As was demonstrated in section 10.5, price discrimination can increase the firm's average revenue from a given market demand curve, yielding an *AR* curve like that in Figure 14.6. In Figure 14.6, the utility and the commission have constructed a rate schedule consisting of several blocks, like the schedule in Table 14.4, which result in raising the *AR* curve above the demand curve. A requirement for overall economic efficiency is that the price of the last unit sold be equal to its marginal cost. By using price discrimination to combine raising the utility's average revenue to $AR_0$ in

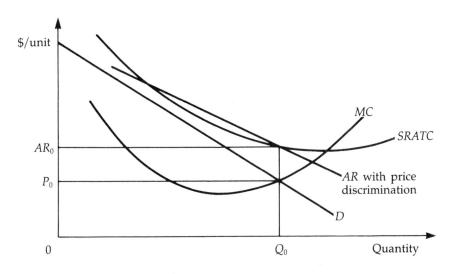

**Figure 14.6  Price Discrimination in Utility Rates**

With price discrimination, the firm is able to earn a greater average revenue (*AR*) at each output rate. Assume that the lowest price category in the discriminatory rate structure pays a price equal to *MC* and *AR* is the resulting average revenue curve for the rate structure. If the *SRATC* curve lies above *D* for all outputs but below *AR* for some outputs, the firm can practice price discrimination and cover all of its costs (earn a normal profit) at output $Q_0$ where $P_0 = MC$.

Figure 14.6, where it equals the *ATC* of $Q_0$, and lowering the price of the last unit produced to $P_0$, the commission can devise an efficient rate schedule that allows the utility to cover its cost of service.

## 14.7  *Summary*

The first 13 chapters focused on how to calculate a firm's profits from the alternatives available to it and on how to determine which alternative best attains management's goal. These calculations primarily focused on calculating prices, costs, and outputs. In this chapter, two additional considerations were introduced — taxation and government regulation of business practices.

Taxes can affect business decisions in several ways. They are a cost of doing business that must be paid by the firm. They change fixed and variable costs directly and through their effects on long- and short-run industry supply curves change market prices. Taxes affect technological choices through their different impacts on the costs of capital and labor. They also affect the number of firms in an industry and enter into plant location decisions.

A great variety of regulations are imposed on business by all levels of government. These regulations affect the way in which the firm conducts its business, its costs, its prices, and how it relates to other firms in its industry as well as to its suppliers and customers. The purpose of government regulation is to correct market failures that lead to socially undesirable results when firms pursue profit or wealth maximization. However, the costs may exceed the benefits from the regulation, resulting in replacing market failure with government failure. Because a portion of the benefits and costs may not be unambiguously measurable in terms of dollars, utility maximization can be used to model the behavior of the decision maker responsible for deciding on the appropriate level of regulation. The decision process takes place in a highly political setting; therefore, management can play a major role in influencing government regulations, even to the point of creating regulations that increase profits and protect the firm from competition.

Cost of service regulation and antitrust regulation are two means by which government controls the behavior of firms in monopolies or oligopolies. Cost of service regulation has as its goal the setting of prices for public utilities at levels similar to those that would exist if the industry were competitive. It is also a highly political process. The antitrust laws are basically congressional policy statements that have been implemented over the years through court decisions and case law. They are aimed at preventing business behavior that lessens competition or monopolizes an industry.

## Key Terms

| | | |
|---|---|---|
| Accelerated Cost Recovery System (ACRS) | cash flow | net economic benefits |
| | cost of service | peak load |
| | income after taxes | shared monopoly |
| ad valorem taxes | income before taxes | utility maximization |
| base load | monopolization | |

## Review Questions

1. Define the terms, as they have been used in previous chapters: *profits, explicit costs,* and *implicit costs.* Define the terms *before-tax income, after-tax income,* and *cash flow.* How does before-tax income differ from profit as calculated by economists?

2. Why is depreciation a noncash expense of the firm?

3. Is the firm allowed to deduct the 10 percent investment credit before calculating its income tax liability?

4. Why are income taxes treated as a cost when the firm is considering whether to build a plant and enter an industry?

5. In section 6.6, the LRAC curve was derived from an isocost/isoquant diagram. Draw the isocost/isoquant diagram for finding the cost-minimizing combination of capital and labor for output $q_0$ when the costs of labor and capital are both $10 per unit and the income tax rate is zero. Assume that the cost of capital is an implicit cost. How does the cost-minimizing factor combination for producing $q_0$ change when there is a 50 percent income tax rate? (Hint: The after-tax cost of capital is $10/(1 - 0.5)$.) Why must the labor and capital budget be increased if the firm is to produce $q_0$ after the 50 percent income tax rate is imposed on the firm, and how does this budget increase affect the LRAC of producing $q_0$?

6. The federal government once levied a 7 percent excise tax on the price of new automobiles. The tax was repealed to increase the sales of new automobiles. If most new-car buyers trade in a used car less than 3 years old, explain why repealing the excise tax might have relatively little impact on new-car sales.

7. Assume that the annual fixed costs for the optimum plant of a new firm are reduced by $300,000 because it is able to lease its plant from a local government's economic development agency. Explain why this will reduce the firm's LRAC. If all new plants in the constant-cost industry are able to obtain similar property tax reductions, why will this result in a downward shift in its LRS curve and a reduction in its price?

8. Why are price-fixing agreements unlikely to reduce production costs? Why might a merger reduce costs if it results in (a) horizontal integration of the combined firm, (b) vertical integration of the combined firm, or (c) a conglomerate?

9. A government agency has proposed regulations that, if approved, would require extensive safety and emissions testing before a new technology will be approved for production and sale. You work for the company that developed this technology. Prepare arguments against these regulations.

10. Assume that a utility is allowed to earn a 15 percent rate of return on its rate base and that its cost of capital is 12 percent. Why is this utility likely to seek new technologies that permit it to substitute capital for labor, energy, or other cost items that are expensed rather than being included in its rate base?

11. If a utility is allowed to retain for its shareholders such tax benefits as the investment credit, rather than pass them on to the rate payers, why is it likely to build highly capital-intensive new plants instead of plants that use more labor or energy in their production process?

12. If an electric utility's allowed rate of return is 12 percent and its cost of capital is 15 percent, why is it likely to become an energy wholesaler that buys increasingly greater amounts of its energy from other (generally out-of-state) utilities?

13. With reference to Figure 14.5, why will the representatives of a regulated industry design their lobbying campaigns to modify the preferences of legislators and regulatory commission members so that they will be more willing to trade off a higher quality of life for lower net economic costs? How would this preference change affect the slope of the decision makers' utility curves?

## Problems and Applications

1. A firm's economist calculated its income before *ACRS* depreciation allowances and income taxes as $120,000 last year. The firm paid $100,000 for its plant and equipment and $200,000 for its building (excluding land) 2 years ago in January. Calculate last year's income after taxes and cash flow if its income tax rate is 45 percent.

2. In problem 1, the firm's working capital of $50,000 has an annual implicit cost of $10,000. If this implicit cost was included in total cost by the firm's economist when calculating its income before taxes, how would the firm's accountant correct the economist's estimate of its income after taxes and cash flow?

3. In problem 2, the economist agrees with the accountant's calculation of the firm's income tax liability but disagrees with the accountant's calculation of after-tax income and cash flow. Why might this occur? Explain why the economist would argue that after-tax income is less than the amount calculated by the accountant. By how much would the economist reduce the accountant's after-tax income and cash flow?

4. Assume that a new plant's profits (total revenue less explicit costs) are $160,000 in its first year and $20,000 less in each subsequent year. All costs incurred by the firm are explicit costs. Its plant and equipment cost is $450,000 and its building is rented (rents paid are included in total cost). Its plant and equipment are eligible for the investment credit. The salvage value of its equipment is $150,000

at the end of its first year of operations, and it goes down by $30,000 at the end of each subsequent year. The plant becomes inoperable after the fifth year. In the year that it abandons this plant and sells the equipment for its salvage value, the firm must pay a tax equal to 20 percent of the difference between the salvage value of the equipment and its depreciated value ($250,000 less the sum of the accumulated depreciation allowances), or nothing if salvage value is less than the depreciated value. If the firm's cost of capital is 20 percent and its income tax rate is 45 percent, calculate the present value of its adjusted cash flow and its net present value. Should management build this new facility?

5. If, in problem 4, $20,000 per year in implicit costs were included when total cost was calculated, recalculate the present value of the plant's adjusted cash flow and its net present value. Would the decision arrived at in problem 4 change?

6. Assume that a competitive firm's average variable cost function is $AVC = \$24 + \$0.2q$, where $q$ is output per hour, and that its cash fixed costs are $2,380 per hour. Its depreciation allowance for this year is $700 per hour and its income tax rate is 45 percent. The market price for its product is $80.

   a. Calculate the firm's profit-maximizing output. Does this output change if the firm's income tax rate falls to 25 percent?

   b. Calculate its before-tax and after-tax income and cash flow.

   c. Assume that $5 per unit of $AVC$ is a variable opportunity cost. Repeat the calculations called for in part (b). Why is after-tax income different if there is a variable opportunity cost?

   d. Does the varriable opportunity cost change the profit-maximizing output? Why or why not?

   e. Calculate the firm's breakeven output using the data in part (a) and then in part (c). Why are the two breakeven outputs different?

7. Assume that minimum $LRAC$ consists of explicit costs of $120 and implicit costs of $40. The income tax rate is 45 percent. Would a firm be willing to enter this industry if the market price for the product is $190? Would its decision change if the income tax rate were reduced to 40 percent?

8. Using the information in problem 7 and assuming that this industry is a constant-cost industry, draw its long-run supply curve before and after the income tax rate change.

9. If the industry demand function is $Q = 400,000 - 5P$, calculate the change in its output resulting from the tax rate reduction in problem 7. Assume that this is a constant-cost industry. If the typical firm produces 300 units of output, how many firms will enter the industry?

10. Assume that the firm's long-run production function is $Q = 0.5K^{0.5}L^{0.5}$ where $Q$ is output per hour. The explicit cost of labor is $5 per hour and the implicit cost of capital is $10 per hour. Calculate the cost-minimizing factor combination to product $Q = 100$ units per hour when there is a zero income tax rate and a 40 percent income tax rate. Calculate the $LRAC$ of 100 units per hour using both income tax rates.

11. Assume that a company has a $100,000 loss and is going out of business. Your company typically earns $50,000 per year and pays income taxes equal to 30 percent of its profits at the end of each year. Your company can carry forward the loss for 2 years. If your company's cost of capital is 15 percent, what is the maximum amount that it would be willing to pay to buy this tax loss?

12. Continuing with problem 11, if another company has profits of $250,000 and marginal income tax rate of 40 percent, would it be willing to pay a higher price for the company going out of business? Why?

13. Assume that a competitive industry's demand curve is $P = 1,000 - 8Q$ and its short-run supply curve is $P = 50 + 2Q$. $Q$ is output or sales per hour. Calculate the market-clearing price. Assume now that this industry is monopolized by means of a merger of all of its firms. There is no change in demand, but the monopolist is able to effect a number of economies and have a marginal cost curve of $MC = 30 + 2Q$. Would consumers benefit from this merger if new firms were unable to enter the industry? Explain why or why not.

14. Assume that new firms could enter the industry in problem 13 and have an average variable cost function of $AVC = \$50 + 25Q$, where $Q$ is output per hour, and fixed costs are $500 per hour. Would the industry remain a monopoly if it takes a new firm one year to build a plant? Would this provide a basis for asserting that the merger is reasonable? Explain why or why not.

# Supplemental Readings

## Chapter 1

Alchian, A. A., and Demsetz, H. "Production, Information Costs, and Economic Organization." *American Economic Review* 62 (December 1972): 777-795.

Browning, E. K., and Browning, J. M. *Microeconomic Theory and Applications.* Boston: Little, Brown, 1983, Chapter 1.

deNeufville, R., and Stafford, J. H. *Systems Analysis for Engineers and Managers.* New York: McGraw-Hill, 1971, Chapter 1.

Friedman, M. "The Methodology of Positive Economics." *Essays in Positive Economics.* Chicago: Chicago, 1953.

Kaish, S. *Microeconomics: Logic, Tools and Analysis.* New York: Harper and Row, 1976, Chapter 1.

McGuigan, J. R., and Moyer, R. C. *Managerial Economics,* 3rd ed. St. Paul, MN: West, 1983, Chapter 1.

Simon, H. A. "Theories of Decision Making in Economics and Behavioral Science." *American Economic Review* 49 (June 1959): 253-280.

## Chapter 2

Canada, J. R. *Intermediate Economic Analysis for Management and Engineering.* Englewood Cliffs, NJ: Prentice-Hall, 1971, Chapter 2.

Chiang, A. C. *Fundamental Methods of Mathematical Economics.* New York: McGraw-Hill, 1967, Chapters 6-9, 11, 12.

Intriligator, M. D. *Econometric Models, Techniques, and Applications.* Englewood Cliffs: Prentice-Hall, 1978, Chapters 1-6.

Kolb, B. A. *Principles of Financial Management.* Plano, TX: Business Publications, 1983, Chapter 11.

Thomas, G. B., and Finney, R. L. *Calculus and Analytic Geometry,* 5th ed. Reading, MA: Addison-Wesley, 1979, Chapters 1-3, 13.

Wonnacott, R. J., and Wonnacott, T. H. *Econometrics.* New York: Wiley, 1970, Chapters 1-8.

Working, E. J. "What Do Statistical 'Demand Curves' Show?" *Quarterly Journal of Economics* 41 (February 1927): 212-235.

Yamane, T. *Statistics: An Introductory Analysis,* 3rd ed. New York: Harper and Row, 1973.

Zuwaylif, F. H. *General Applied Statistics.* Reading, MA: Addison-Wesley, 1970.

## Chapter 3

Alchian, A. A., and Allen, W. R. *University Economics,* 3rd ed. Belmont, CA: Wadsworth, 1972, Chapter 5.

Baird, C. W. *Prices and Markets: Microeconomics.* St. Paul, MN: West, 1978, Chapter 3.

Becker, G. S. *Economic Theory.* New York: Knopf, 1971, Chapters 2, 3.

Browning and Browning, Chapters 2-4.

Gould, J. P., and Ferguson, C. E. *Microeconomic Theory*, 5th ed. Homewood, IL: Irwin, 1980, Chapters 2-4.

Hogarty, T. F., and Ebzinga, K. G. "The Demand for Beer." *Review of Economics and Statistics* 54 (May 1952): 195-198.

Lerner, A. "The Analysis of Demand." *American Economic Review* 52 (September 1962): 783-797.

## Chapter 4

Granger, C. W. J. *Forecasting in Business and Economics.* New York: Academic Press, 1980, Chapters 1-7.

Hamburg, M. *Statistical Analysis for Decision Making.* New York: Harcourt, Brace, 1970, Chapter 11.

Intriligator, Chapter 15.

Katz, D. A. *Econometric Theory and Applications.* Englewood Cliffs, NJ: Prentice-Hall, 1982, Chapters 5 and 6.

Maurice, S. C., and Smithson, C. W. *Managerial Economics.* Homewood, IL: Irwin, 1981, Chapters 4-5.

## Chapter 5

Baird, Chapter 4.

Becker, Lecture 17, Chapters 7 and 8.

Browning and Browning, Chapter 6.

Gould and Ferguson, Chapters 5, 6, and 13.

Walters, A. A. *An Introduction to Econometrics.* London: Macmillan, 1968, Chapter 10.

## Chapter 6

Alchian, A. A. "Costs and Outputs." *The Allocation of Economic Resources,* edited by M. Abramovitz. Stanford: Stanford, 1959, pp. 23-40.

Alchian and Allen, Chapter 15.

Anthony, R. N. *Management Accounting Principles.* Homewood, IL: Irwin, 1965, Chapters 14-16.

Baird, pp. 113-116.

Browning and Browning, Sections 7.1-7.3, 7.7.

Gould and Ferguson, Sections 7.1-7.3.

Haldi, J. and Whitcomb, D. "Economies of Scale in Industrial Plants." *Journal of Political Economy* 75 (August 1967): 373-385.

Hirschleifer, J. "On the Economics of Transfer Pricing." *Journal of Business* 29 (July 1956): 172-184.

Johnson, J. *Statistical Cost Analysis.* New York: McGraw-Hill, 1960.

Longbrake, W. A. "Statistical Cost Analysis." *Financial Management* 2 (Spring 1973): 49-55.

Maxwell, W. D. "Short-Run Returns to Scale and the Production of Services." *Southern Economic Journal* 32 (July 1965): 1-14.

Needham, D. *Economic Analysis and Industrial Structure.* New York: Holt, Rinehart and Winston, 1960, Chapter 7.

Quirk, J. P. *Intermediate Microeconomics.* Chicago: SRA, 1976, Chapter 7.

## Chapter 7

Chiang, Chapters 18 and 19.

deNeufville and Stafford, Chapter 3.

Dorfman, R.; Samuelson, P. A.; and Solow, R. M. *Linear Programming and Economic Analysis.* New York: McGraw-Hill, 1958, Chapters 1-7.

Taylor, B. W. *Introduction to Management Science.* Dubuque, IA: Brown, 1982, Chapters 2-7.

Walters, Chapter 11.

Wilson, J. H., and Darr, S. G. *Managerial Economics.* New York: Harper and Row, 1979, Chapter 2.

## Chapter 8

Alchian and Allen, Chapter 9.

Baird, Chapter 7 to page 113; pp. 116-118.

Browning and Browning, Chapter 8 and Sections 9.1 and 9.2.

Coase, R. H. "The Nature of the Firm." *Economica* 4 (1937): 386-405.

Gould and Ferguson, Sections 8.1 to 8.5.

Hamilton, D. C. *Competition in Oil.* Cambridge, MA: Harvard, 1958, Chapters 1 and 2.

Henderson, J. M., and Quandt, R. E. *Microeconomic Theory*, 2nd ed. New York: McGraw-Hill, 1971, pp. 115-118.

Hirschleifer, J. *Price Theory and Applications.* Englewood Cliffs, NJ: Prentice-Hall, 1976, Chapter 8 and Section 10A.

Quirk, Chapter 8.

## Chapter 10

Alchian and Allen, Chapter 18.

Baird, Chapter 8.

Browning and Browning, Chapter 11 and Sections 12.1, 12.6, 13.1-13.3.

Dewey, D. *Microeconomics.* New York: Oxford, 1975, 165-172.

Gould and Ferguson, Chapters 9 and 11.

Quirk, Chapter 14 and Chapter 15 to page 274.

## Chapter 11

Adams, W., ed. *The Structure of American Industry*, 4th ed. New York: Macmillan, 1971.

Asch, P. *Economic Theory and the Antitrust Dilemma*. New York: Wiley, 1970, Chapter 3.

Bain, J. S. *Barriers to New Competition*. Cambridge, MA: Harvard, 1956, Chapter 1.

Browning and Browning, Sections 13.4-13.7.

Gould and Ferguson, Chapter 12.

Hirschleifer, Chapter 13.

Patinkin, D. "Multiple Plant Firms, Cartels, and Imperfect Competition." *Quarterly Journal of Economics* 61 (February 1947): 173-205.

Quirk, pp. 274-282.

Singer, E. M. *Antitrust Economics*. Englewood Cliffs, NJ: Prentice-Hall, 1968, Chapters 9-11.

Stigler, G. J. *The Organization of Industry*. Homewood, IL: Irwin, 1968, Chapters 3 and 5.

## Chapter 12

Baird, Chapter 12.

Belveal, L. D. *Commodity Speculation*. Wilmette, IL: Commodities Press, 1967, Chapter 9.

Friedman, J., and Savage, L. J. "The Utility Analysis of Choices Involving Risk." *Journal of Political Economy* 56 (August 1948): 279-304.

Grayson, C. J. *Decisions Under Uncertainty*. Cambridge, MA: Harvard, 1960, Chapter 10.

McGuigan and Moyer, Chapter 2.

Quirk, pp. 189-190, Chapter 16.

## Chapter 13

Bierman, H., and Smidt, S. *The Capital Budgeting Decision*, 2nd ed. New York: Macmillan, 1966.

Cohen, J. B., and Robbins, S. M. *The Financial Manager*. New York: Harper and Row, 1966, Part V.

Kolb, Chapters 12-15.

Scott, D. E., et al., eds. *Readings in Financial Management*. New York: Academic Press, 1982.

## Chapter 14

Breit, W., and Elzinga, K. G. *The Antitrust Casebook*. Chicago: Dryden, 1982.

Clarkson, K. W., and Miller, R. L. *Industrial Organization*. New York: McGraw-Hill, 1982, Chapter 15.

*Explanation of Economic Recovery Tax Act of 1981.* Chicago: Commerce Clearing House, 1981.

Freeman, A. M., et al. *The Economics of Environmental Policy.* New York: Wiley, 1973.

Gramlich, E. M. *Benefit-Cost Analysis of Government Programs.* Englewood Cliffs, NJ: Prentice-Hall, 1981.

Greer, D. F. *Industrial Organization and Public Policy.* New York: Macmillan, 1980, Chapters 3, 9, 12, 14, 16, and 20.

Kahn, A. E. *The Economics of Regulation,* Vol. 1. New York: Wiley, 1970. Chapters 1-5.

Letwin, W. *Law and Economic Policy in America.* New York: Random House, 1965.

Needham, D. *The Economics and Politics of Regulation.* Boston: Little, Brown, 1983, Chapters 10-14.

Seneca, J. J., and Taussig, M. K. *Environmental Economics,* 3rd ed. Englewood Cliffs, NJ: Prentice-Hall, 1984, Chapters 2, 3, and 7.

Veseth, M. *Public Finance.* Reston, VA: Reston, 1984, Chapters 4, 8, 9, 10, 14, 18, and 19.

# Glossary

Note: Words and phrases appearing in boldface type also appear as separate entries in this glossary.

**abandonment of a plant.** Shutdown and sale of the plant for its **salvage value** (some of the equipment may be used elsewhere in the company).

**accounting profit.** The difference between the **firm's** total revenues and its **explicit costs, depreciation allowances,** and other non-cash charges recognized in standard accounting practices.

*ACL.* See **average cost of labor.**

*ACM.* See **average cost of materials.**

**adaptation.** Management's responses to unpredicted changes in the business environment.

**adjusted cash flow. Cash flow** less the after-tax **implicit opportunity costs** of the **firm.**

**administrative costs.** The costs of managing production of a component within the **firm,** rather than purchasing it on the market and incurring **transaction costs.**

**ad valorem tax.** A tax based on the value of the item being taxed (for example, sales or property taxes).

*AFC.* See **average fixed cost.**

**antitrust laws.** Laws enacted for the purpose of securing for consumers the benefits of **competition** in industries for which efficient production and marketing methods may result in **oligopoly** or **monopoly.**

*APL.* See **average product of a factor.** Labor is the factor.

**artificial variable.** A variable added to a linear equality or greater-than-or-equal-to inequality for the purpose of providing an initial solution to the linear programming model (it is also added to the **objective function** with a very large negative coefficient).

*AVC.* See **average variable cost.**

**average cost of labor.** The total cost of labor divided by the output produced (which is also equal to wage/*APL*).

**average cost of materials.** The total cost of raw materials and purchased components divided by the output produced.

**average fixed cost.** The total **fixed cost** of the **firm** or production facility divided by the output produced.

**average product of a factor.** Total output of the product divided by the total quantity of a factor used to produce it.

**average variable cost.** The total of the costs of the variable factors of production divided by the output produced.

**basis.** A solution to the system of constraint equations for a linear programming model.

**breakeven output.** The lowest output at which its *SRATC* and price are equal.

**breakeven price.** The lowest price at which the **firm** will cover its *SRATC* at the profit-maximizing output for that price (equal to the minimum *SRATC* for the firm).

**budget.** The amount of money to be spent by the **firm** or one of its production facilities during the current planning period.

**budgeting.** The process of translating plans into resource requirements and the amount of money management expects to spend and receive during the **planning period.**

**buying long.** Entering into a futures contract in which the buyer agrees to accept delivery of the commodity at a specified time and place and pay the market price at the time the contract is entered into. The buyer profits if the market price increases.

**capital plan.** The **planning** document that is concerned with the acquisition of new assets that will affect the **firm's** operations for more than one year.

**cash flow. Income after taxes** plus the **firm's depreciation allowances.**

**change in the quantity demanded.** Change in quantity resulting from a price change leading to a movement from one point on the demand curve to another.

**coefficient of determination ($R^2$).** A measure of the extent to which a **regression** equation fits the data from which it was estimated.

**coefficient of variation.** The sample **standard deviation** divided by its average. It measures the relative variation between **samples.**

**competition.** Belief by all **firms** selling goods in the market that changes in their output cannot influence the market price (their goods are perfect **substitute** goods and there are many firms).

**complementary goods.** Goods whose **demand** increases with the sale of other goods.

**confidence interval.** The range of values of a variable within which there is a specified probability that the next observation of the variable will occur.

**conglomerate.** A **firm** with two or more plants producing products that are not **substitute** goods for one another.

**constant-cost industry.** An **industry** whose **long-run** supply curve is horizontal at a level equal to the minimum point of the typical firm's *LRAC* curve.

**constant returns.** Lack of change in the **marginal product of a factor** when the quantity of the factor is increased.

**contracting costs.** The element of **transaction costs** resulting from the costs of concluding a sale or purchase of a good.

**cost of capital ($k$).** A capital expenditure earns the cost of capital if the

**present value** of the resulting time series of profits is zero, leaving the market value of the **firm** unchanged.

**cost-of-service regulation.** A set of rules and procedures developed by government for the purpose of determining if a **public utility's** prices, services, and capacity additions are reasonable relative to the costs incurred in providing the services.

**cross-elasticity.** A measure of the responsiveness of the **demand** for one good to a change in the price of another good; the percentage change in the quantity of good $X$ divided by the percentage change in the price of good $Y$.

*CV.* See **coefficient of variation.**

**debt capital.** Money acquired by the **firm** through sale to investors of its bonds, notes, and other interest-bearing securities.

**decreasing-cost industry.** An **industry** whose **long-run supply** curve is downward sloping because the price of one or more of the factors of production it uses falls as the number of firms in the industry increases.

**demand.** A function relating the maximum quantity of a good consumers are willing to purchase to its market price, holding constant factors other than price affecting the consumers' decisions.

**depreciation allowance.** A non-cash expense based on the asset's historical cost and accounting or tax code rules. It is used in calculating the firm's **income before taxes.**

**differentiated products.** Products of several **firms** that are relatively good **substitutes** but are also unique in one or more ways, making them heterogeneous rather than homogeneous.

**diminishing returns.** A condition in which the **marginal product of a factor** is declining when the quantity of the factor is increased.

**diversified firm.** A **firm** producing several product lines in which the products are related with respect to their technology or outlets for sale to consumers.

**dominant firm oligopoly.** An **oligopoly** of two or more **firms** in which the largest firm is much larger than the second-largest firm.

**duopoly.** An **oligopoly** of two **firms.**

**economic life of plant.** The number of years until a plant will undergo **abandonment** because price has become less than the minimum average cost of the plant (generally because the *AVC* curve shifts upward over time).

**economic profit.** The difference between the **firm's** total revenue and its total costs, including all **implicit opportunity costs.**

**economies of mass production.** The reduction in *LRAC* when the **firm** builds a larger, generally more capital-intensive production facility designed to produce a greater rate of output.

**elastic demand.** A condition in which the percentage change in price is smaller than the percentage change in quantity, resulting in the change in price and total revenue being in the same direction.

**elasticity of demand.** The percentage change in quantity divided by the percentage change in the independent variable. This measures the elasticity of the consumer's response to the change in the independent variable.

**equity capital.** Money acquired by the **firm** through sale to investors of its common stock and the retaining of all or a portion of its profits for use by the firm.

**excess capacity.** Difference between a plant's current output and the output at which its *SRATC* curve is minimized.

**expert opinion forecast.** A forecast of the future level of a variable based on the knowledge and experience of the person making the forecast.

**explicit cost.** A cost incurred when the **firm** purchases a factor of production during the current **planning period** for use during that period of time.

**firm.** One or more centers of decision-making authority controlling the use of resources owned by the firm.

**fixed costs.** The costs of those factors of production that do not change with changes in the **firm's** output.

**hedging.** The purchase of a product or factor of production, accompanied by a future sale of the same or a closely related product or factor, with the intention of protecting the purchaser against adverse future price changes.

**horizontal integration.** Acquisition or construction of more than one production or marketing facility handling the same product in different locations.

**implicit opportunity cost.** A cost incurred when the **firm** uses a resource it acquired in a previous **planning period**. It is equal to the amount of money the firm would have received if it had sold, rented, or lent out the resource instead of using it.

**income after taxes. Income before taxes** less the **firm's income tax** payments.

**income before taxes.** Total revenue less **explicit opportunity costs** and **depreciation allowances.**

**income elasticity.** A measure of the response of consumers to changes in their incomes; the percentage change in quantity divided by the percentage change in income.

**income tax.** A tax levied against the profits of the **firm,** computed in accordance with rules provided in the applicable tax code.

**increasing-cost industry.** An **industry** whose **long-run supply** curve is upward sloping because the prices of one or more of the factors of production it uses rise as the number of firms in the industry increases.

**increasing returns.** A condition in which the **marginal product of a factor** is rising when the quantity of the factor is increased.

**independent goods.** Goods for which a change in their price results in no discernible change in the **demand** for some other goods.

**industry.** Several or many **firms** producing products that are perfect or very close **substitute** goods.

**inelastic demand.** A condition in which the percentage change in price is greater than the percentage change in quantity, resulting in the change in price and total revenue being in the same direction.

**inferior good.** A good whose **demand** changes in the direction opposite to that of a change in income.

**information costs.** An element of **transaction costs** associated with determining the market price for a good.

**inventory.** Goods held for sale in current **planning period** if sales should be greater than current production or held for sale in subsequent planning periods.

**investment credit.** A percentage of the **firm's** capital expenditures for qualified property that is deducted from the firm's **income tax** liability for year in which the capital expenditure was made.

**isocost curve.** The locus of all combinations of the variable factors of production that can be purchased with a specified total expenditure (**budget**) for the factors.

**isoquant curve.** The locus of all combinations of two variable factors producing a specified output, given the quantities of the fixed factors.

*k.* See **cost of capital.**

**kinked demand curve.** The demand curve of a **price-follower firm** whose management believes its **demand** curve is very **elastic** for price increases and relatively **inelastic** for a price reduction.

**learning curve.** Downward shifts in the **average variable cost** curve of a new plant as management learns how to better operate the plant.

**limit-entry pricing.** A pricing strategy in which the **price-leader firm** (or a **monopoly**) sets its price below the minimum point of the *LRAC* curve of potential entrants into the industry to keep them from entering the industry, with the limit-entry price being **wealth-maximizing** rather than **short-run profit maximizing.**

**long run.** A period of time great enough so that all factors of production are variable and it is profitable to change any factor of production.

**long-run average cost.** The lowest unit cost of producing a given output when all factors of production are variable.

**long-run equilibrium price.** The price at which the **short-run** supply curve, **long-run** supply curve, and the **demand** curve all intersect.

*LRAC.* See **long-run average cost.**


**marginal cost.** The change in total cost or total **variable cost** when output changes by a small amount.

**marginal cost of labor.** The change in the total cost of labor when output changes by a small amount (which is also equal to wage/*MPL*).

**marginal cost of materials.** The change in the total cost of raw materials and purchased components when output changes by a small amount.

**marginal product of a factor.** The change in total output when the quantity of a factor is changed by a small amount (or one unit).

**marginal rate of technical substitution.** The slope of the **isoquant curve.** The *MRTS* measures the rate at which one factor can be substituted for the other with no change in output.

**marginal revenue.** The change in total revenue, generally in response to a small change in quantity.

**market.** All consumers and firms who engage in the buying or selling of a specified good, service, or factor of production.

**market-clearing (equilibrium) price.** The price at which **demand** and **supply** are equal and there are no market forces leading to a change in price.

**mark-up pricing.** Pricing of the **firm's** product by multiplying its average cost by a customary percentage and adding the result to its average cost.

*MC.* See **marginal cost.**

*MCL.* See **marginal cost of labor.**

*MCM.* See **marginal cost of materials.**

**monopolistic competition.** An industry in which several firms sell **differentiated products** that are relatively close **substitute goods,** and each firm ignores the reactions of the other firms when it sets its pricing and other marketing policies.

**monopoly.** A one-firm industry.

*MPL.* See **marginal product of a factor.** Labor is the factor.

*MRTS.* See **marginal rate of technical substitution.**

**multicollinearity.** A condition in which two or more of the independent variables of a regression equation are highly correlated.


**natural monopoly.** A one-**firm industry** caused by minimizing the average cost of producing the product (the **demand** curve intersects the *LRAC* curve to the left of its minimum point.)

**net present value.** The **present value** of the profit stream less the present value of the expenditures necessary to obtain the profit stream.

**normal good.** A good whose **demand** changes in the same direction as a change in income.

**normal profit.** The **implicit opportunity cost** of its resources that the **firm** commits to an activity, such as building a new plant.

*NPV.* See **net present value.**

**objective function.** The linear equation stating the goal to be attained when solving a linear programming model.

**oligopoly.** An industry in which two or more **firms** produce products that are perfect **substitutes** or **differentiated,** and each firm takes the likely reactions of its rivals into consideration when it sets its pricing and other marketing policies.

**operating plan.** The **planning** document that is concerned with the optimal use of the **firm's** existing assets.

**opportunity cost.** The value of the next-best alternative that could have been undertaken if the resources had not been applied to the chosen activity.

**optimization.** The process of determining how management can best attain the goals of the firm.

*P.* The market price.

**persistence forecast.** A forecast of the future level of a variable based on data and various statistical techniques.

$\Pi$. Profit.

**planning.** The process of determining the goals for the firm and the best strategies for attaining them.

**planning period.** A period of time for which management is presently formulating its plans.

**policing costs.** The element of **transaction costs** that arises when there is a dispute over the terms of a contract or one party fails to fulfill its terms.

**population.** All possible observations that could be gathered on a variable.

**prediction.** The process of estimating the level of variables and the relationships among variables that management cannot directly control.

**present value.** The amount of money invested today to yield one dollar at some specified time in the future, given the available interest rate or **cost of capital.**

**price discrimination.** A condition in which two customers are charged different prices for the same product or a customer pays a different price for additional units of a product.

**price elasticity.** A measure of the response of consumers to changes in the price of a good; the percentage change in quantity divided by the percentage change in price.

**price-follower firm.** A **firm** that changes its price only after the **price-leader firm** changes its price, with the price follower generally using the leader's price change as one factor to consider in deciding on its price change.

**price-leader firm.** The **firm** that initiates all price changes for an **oligopoly,** with the other firms changing their prices only after the price leader changes its price.

**price-searcher firm.** A **firm** whose management can affect the market price for its goods by changing its output, or its advertising or other marketing policies.

**price-taker firm.** A **firm** that cannot influence the market price of its product by changing its output.

**product group.** Several firms producing **differentiated products** that are better **substitute goods** for one another than they are for other products.

**production function.** A function providing the maximum output obtainable from specified quantities of the inputs into the production process.

**public utility.** A **firm** whose prices and services are regulated by a government agency.

**quantity demanded.** The quantity purchased by consumers at different prices along the **demand** curve.

$R^2$. See **coefficient of determination.**

**random sample.** A **sample** of a **population** in which knowledge of one observation in the sample cannot be used to predict that another observation in the population will also be in the sample.

**rate of return.** The rate of interest that reduces to zero the **present value** of a time series of profits with positive and negative values.

**regression.** A technique used to estimate empirical relationships among variables.

**returns to scale.** The change in output resulting when all factors of production are changed in the same proportion.

**risk.** The probability that an event will occur can be predicted a priori or from data, or that it has been specified subjectively by management.

**risk-averse.** A phrase describing the decision maker who must be compensated with a higher expected return (that is, profit or yield on **capital**) to take on a higher level of **risk.** (The **risk preference curve** is upward sloping.)

**risk-neutral.** A phrase describing the decision maker who is indifferent between two opportunities that have the same expected return and different levels of **risk.** (The **risk preference curve** is horizontal.)

**risk preference curve.** The locus of all combinations of **risk** and the expected profit or **cost of capital** that yield the decision maker the same level of utility.

**risk return curve.** The curve that plots the expected return of each alternative decision with its level of **risk.**

**risk-seeker.** A phrase describing the decision maker who is willing to trade off a lower expected return for a higher level of **risk** and the associated greater opportunity for a very high return even if its probability is small. (The **risk preference curve** is downward sloping.)

**salvage value** (managerial definition). The amount of money that the firm realizes when it sells an abandoned plant (this is not the accounting definition).

**sample.** A set of observations drawn from a population.

**selling short.** Entering into a futures contract whereby the short seller agrees to deliver the commodity to the holder of the contract at a specified time and place. (The short seller profits if the market price declines.)

**semivariable costs.** The costs of those factors of production that are constant in amount when output varies within a specified range, and increase or decrease when output moves out of that range.

**shadow price.** The amount by which the **objective function** would increase if the level of a constraint with a zero **slack variable** were increased by one unit.

**shared monopoly.** An **oligopoly** in which the **price-leader firm** sets its price and other marketing policies to maximize industry profits, and the other firms follow its policies and maintain their market shares.

**shift (change) in demand.** A change in consumer purchases at each possible price for a product that occurs when a variable other than the price of the product changes.

**short run.** A period of time short enough so that one or more factors of production are fixed in amount because they are unprofitable to change within that time period or because management has decided they will not be changed.

**short-run average total cost.** The minimum average cost of producing a given output when there is at least one fixed factor of production.

**short-run equilibrium price.** The price at which the **short-run supply** curve for the **industry** and the **demand** curve intersect.

**short-run profit maximization.** Maximization of profits in the current **planning period** (generally used where product prices, factor prices, and factor productivities are unlikely to vary in a predictable manner in subsequent **planning periods**).

**shortage (excess demand).** The amount by which **demand** exceeds **supply** at the current market price.

**shut-down plant.** An unprofitable plant that is not operated for one or more planning periods, but which management intends to reopen in some subsequent planning period when it is expected to be profitable.

**SIMPLEX method.** An iterative technique for solving linear programming models, which adds to the **basis** the variable providing the greatest increase in the **objective function** and deletes the variable most constraining the level of the variable to be added.

**slack variable.** A variable added to a linear inequality for the purpose of converting it into an equality (it is also added to the **objective function** with a zero coefficient).

**specialization.** Reduction in the number of tasks performed by each worker when many different tasks are required to produce the good.

*SRATC.* See **short-run average total cost.**

**standard deviation.** A measure of the average variation in a **sample** about the average of the sample.

**statistically independent events.** An event whose probability does not depend upon the occurrence of the other event.

**substitute goods.** Goods for which a change in the price of one causes a change in the opposite direction in the quantity of the other.

**supply.** A function relating the maximum quantity of a good that the **firm** is willing to sell to its market price, holding constant everything except price.

**surplus (excess supply).** The amount by which **supply** exceeds **demand** at the current market price.

**total cost function.** The relationship between output and its total cost, including both the **explicit costs** and **implicit opportunity costs** of producing the output.

**trade off.** Giving up something of value to the decision maker in order to obtain something else with a greater value.

**transaction (ICP) costs.** The costs of buying and selling goods using the **market** — primarily **information, contracting,** and **policing costs.**

**tying contract.** A contract requiring the purchaser to buy certain supplies exclusively from the seller of a monopolized good at prices above their market price (a form of **price discrimination**).

**uncertain event.** An event whose probability cannot be predicted using the available data.

**utility maximization.** Attaining the highest possible utility/preference curve or utility level for the decision maker given the constraints on the decision.

**variable costs.** The costs of those factors of production whose quantities change with changes in the **firm's** output.

**vertical integration.** Performance of more than one of the several distinct activities required to produce a good, with each activity taking place at a different location.

*w.* The wage rate.

**wealth maximization.** Maximization of the **present value** of profits in several **planning periods** (generally used where product prices, factor prices, and factor productivity are likely to vary in a predictable manner over time).

# Selected Answers to Problems and Applications

Note: Your answer may differ from the answers provided here because of different round-off methods or carrying a different number of digits in intermediate calculations.

## Chapter 2

1. $NPV = \$0.338$ million; $r = 20\%$ ($NPV = \$0.008$ million).
3. $Y = 3.90453$.
5. $2X(X - 4)$; $2(X - 3)(X + 2)$.
7. $Y = 0.667X$.
9. $Y = 455.52 - 2.222X$.
11. $dY/dX = 12X^2$ and $d^2Y/dX^2 = 24X$; $dY/dV = 0.5/V^{0.5} + 0.5/V^{0.75}$ and $d^2Y/dV^2 = -0.25/V^{1.5} - 0.375/V^{1.75}$.
13. $\partial Q/\partial X = 2Y^{0.5}/X^{0.5}$ and $\partial Q/\partial Y = 2X^{0.5}/Y^{0.5}$; $\partial Q/\partial X = 0.75Y^{0.5}/X^{0.75}$ and $\partial Q/\partial Y = 1.5X^{0.25}/Y^{0.5}$
15. Maximum at $X = 8/3$ and minimum at $X = 3$; maximum at $X = -4$ and minimum at $X = 12$.
17. $\overline{X} = 14.5$; $\sigma_X = 5.54$; for $X = 19$, $Z = 0.812$.
19. $\gamma = 0.1492$ or $15\%$.
21. $\gamma = 0.15$ or $15\%$.
23. $\gamma = 0.10$ or $10\%$.
25. Reject H1 if $\overline{X} < 8,244$ or $\overline{X} > 8,620$.
27. $\hat{Y} = 69.608 + 9.192X$; $R^2 = 0.636$; $F = 17.473$; $\hat{Y}_1^* = 113.638$ and $\hat{Y}_2^* = 126.690$; $t = 4.485$ (significant).
29. $\hat{Y} = 133.952$.

## Chapter 3

1. $E_p = -5$, elastic, using equation 3.3 or $E_p = -3.8$, elastic, using equation 3.4.
3. $E_p = -0.5$, inelastic. Raising price will increase $TR$, and $TC$ falls because $Q$ falls; hence, profit $= TR - TC$ must increase if price rises.
5. Normal good because $E_I = +0.0586$.
7. Substitutes because $E_{xy} = +0.5$.
9. The 2.5% net decline in $Q$ is less than the 5% increase in price; hence, $TR$ will increase.
11. $Q_0$, output before price increase, is not given. $E_p$ for 1 week is $(280/Q_0) - 5$ and $E_p$ for 6 weeks is $(275/Q_0) - 5$. Since $280/Q_0 > 275/Q_0$, $E_p$ for 6 weeks must be greater than for 1 week.

## Chapter 4

1. First two years is $+1.66\%$; arithmetic average is $+1.60\%$.
3. REGRESSION 1: $\hat{Y} = 7,053 + 117.9T$, $R^2 = 0.936$, $F = 147.3$;
   REGRESSION 2: $\ln\hat{Y} = 1.95773 + 0.01499T$, $R^2 = 0.943$, $F = 165.0$;
   REGRESSION 2 fits the data slightly better.
5. REGRESSION 3: $\Delta\hat{Y} = 0.0384 + 0.0148T$, $R^2 = 0.009$, $F = 0.08$;
   fits data poorly when compared to other regressions; unlikely to
   exhibit serial correlation yielding more reliable regression statistics;
   growth in sales are 216.2, 231.0, and 245.8 units for a 3 year sales
   forecast of 9,293 units.
7. REGRESSION 1: $d = 1.766$, no significant serial correlation at the
   95% confidence interval level (using $N = 15$ and $k = 2$ value of
   $d_U$); REGRESSION 3: $d = 2.798$, test is ambiguous because $d$ is in
   the $4 - d_U$ to $4 - d_L$ interval; in this example REGRESSION 1 is
   less likely to exhibit first-order serial correlation.

## Chapter 5

1. $MPL = 0.7$ for all $L$; $APL = 0.6825$ for $L = 480$ and $APL = 0.6844$
   for $L = 540$.
3. $Q = 1,725$, $APL = 115$, $MPL = 85$.
5. For $L = 15$: $Q = 2,130$; $APL = 142$; $MPL = 118$; all three measures
   of productivity increased.
7. $MPL = 3K^{0.25}L^{0.5}$; if $L$ rises, $MPL$ rises so there are increasing returns
   for all $L$.
9. $W = 16$, $L = 625$ and $W = 81$ and $L = 277.78$.
11. $MRTS = -W/2L$; for $W = 16$, $L = 625$, $MRTS = -0.0128$; for
    $W = 81$, $L = 277.78$, $MRTS = -0.1458$.
13. $MRTS = -K/2L$; costs will fall by $2.50.

## Chapter 6

1. $Q = 20$, $APL = 0.8$, $MPL = 0.4$, $ACL = \$7.50$, $AVC = \$14.50$,
   $MCL = \$15$, $MC = \$22$, $AFC = \$25$, $SRATC = \$39.50$.
3. $Q = 1,400$, $APL = 140$, $MPL = 180$, $ACL = \$0.36$, $MCL = \$0.28$,
   $AVC = \$5.36$, $MC = \$5.28$, $AFC = \$0.43$, $SRATC = \$5.79$.
5. $Q = 7.5$, $APL = 0.0926$, $MPL = 0.02315$, $ACL = \$107.99$, $MCL =$
   $\$431.97$, $AVC = \$327.99$, $MC = \$651.97$, $AFC = \$133.33$, $SRATC =$
   $\$461.32$.
7. $Q = 2,000$ units per mo.; $MCL$ and $ACL$ are unchanged; $AVC$, $MC$,
   and $SRATC$ curves shift down by $20 for $Q = 2,000$ or more.
9. a. $dMPL/dL = -15$ implies diminishing returns.

    b. $L = 12.5$.

    c. $Q = 5{,}133$, $APL = 256.67$, $MPL = 240$, $ACL = \$0.039$, $MCL = \$0.042$, $AVC = \$1.539$, $MC = \$1.542$.

    d. $AFC = \$0.584$, $SRATC = \$2.123$.

11. $L = 256$, $APL = 0.039$, $MPL = 0.0098$, $ACL = \$281.60$, $MCL = \$1{,}126.40$, $AVC = \$501.60$, $MC = \$1{,}346.40$, $SRATC = \$634.93$; $AVC$ and $MC$ are minimized where $Q = 0$, $SRATC$ is minimized where $Q = 59.6$; the intercept of the $AVC$ and $MC$ curves are unchanged and their slopes are increased, $SRATC$ shifts up.

13. $SRATC = \$122$, $AFC = \$100$, $AVC = \$22$, $ACM = MCM = \$20$, $ACL = \$2$, $MCL = \$4$; $MC$ and $AVC$ are minimized when $Q = 0$, $SRATC$ is minimized where $Q = 70.7$; yes, because $MC$ and $AVC$ increase for all $Q > 0$ which, with a constant wage rate, implies that $MPL$ and $APL$ must be decreasing.

15. For $Q = 50$, $L = 100$ production workers, 10 foremen, 2 supervisors, $ACL = \$24.40$, $AVC = \$104.40$, $AFC = \$10$, $SRATC = \$114.40$.

17. For $Q = 50$, $SRATC = \$112.94$, $MC$ of 51st unit is $\$117.40$; for $Q = 51$, $SRATC = \$113.03$.

19. $L = 22.5$, $S = 45$, $Q = 3.784$, $ACW = \$237.84$, $MCW = \$238.10$.

21. a. $LRAC = \$61.97$ for $Q = 16$ and $Q = 25$.

    b. For $Q = 16$, $SRATC = \$63.10$; for $Q = 25$, $SRATC = \$64.00$; and $SRATC$ is above $LRAC$ for both outputs.

23. a. $K = 20$, $L = 200$, $Q = 845.9$, $LRAC = \$1.18$.

    b. $K = 24$, $L = 240$, $Q = 1{,}062.4$, $LRAC = \$1.13$, yes.

    c. $L = 251.2$, $SRATC = \$1.134$ ($LRAC$ in part b was $\$1.1295$ before rounding off).

25. $q = 1{,}600$, $LRAC = \$200$, demand $Q = 19{,}200$, $M = 12$ firms.

27. $M = 23.5$ firms (probably 23 firms).

## Chapter 7

1. b. $M = 30$ machines, $L = 40$ workers; $AFC = \$21.05$, $AVC = \$42.11$, $SRATC = \$63.16$, $MC = \$50$ for the 20th unit.

3. b. $M = 5$ machines, $L = 20$ workers, $TC = \$200$ per hr.

5. $X_1 = 27.6$, $X_3 = 31.0$, maximum profit is $\$556.90$ per hour.

7. a. If $X_1 = 18.3$, $X_3 = 9.3$ and $X_4 = 30$, profit increases to $\$607.07$.

    b. shadow price for type $A$ machine is $\$19.83$, so it would not be profitable to lease for $\$23$; shadow price for type $B$ machine is $\$28.10$, so it is profitable to lease for $\$25$.

9. Cost of 100 lb of 18% protein feed is $\$9.58$ and for 19% protein feed is $\$10.06$; cost rises by $\$0.48$ per 100 lb.

11. Machine time constraint's shadow price is $\$16.53$; profitable to add the maintenance worker.

## Chapter 8

1. $q = 72$, $\Pi = \$684$.
3. $q = 26$, $\Pi = \$-162$, $L = 42.25$.
5. Profit-maximizing output for typical firm is 32 units produced by $L = 64$ workers; total employment is 5,120 workers.
7. For $T = 1$, $P = \$250$, $Q = 8,250$; for $T = 3$, $P = \$275$.
9. $P = \$105.08$.
11. Minimum $LRAC = \$333$ at $q = 40$; $M = 30$ firms.
13. a. Minimum $SRATC = \$200$ at $q = 1,500$, new firms will earn an economic profit if P = \$230.
    b. Using midyear centering, $NPV = \$-186,500.96 + \$1,712,265.55 - \$531,797.80 - \$462,432.87 = \$531,533.92$, increases wealth.
    c. With a constant-cost industry, factor prices will not change as new firms enter the industry; hence, the \$190 price in the second and third operating years is probably because too many firms are entering the industry in response to the \$225 to \$230 price range, and then demand grows enough to raise price from \$190 to \$200.

## Chapter 8 Appendix

A1. $q = 20$ is breakeven output, $q = 160$ is profit maximizing output.
A3. $\gamma = 0.8413$ or 84.13% probability of breaking even, probability that $P > AVC$ of \$50 is very close to 100% (Z of $1 - \delta = -3.50$).
A5. Breakeven price for the output of 7.25 units produced in one hour by the 52.5 production workers is \$123.03.

## Chapter 9

1. $PV_1 = \$574,499.16$; $PV_2 = \$636,867.24$; $PV_3 = \$635,085.30$; plan 2 is wealth-maximizing.
3. Operate 100 days each 6 month period; $NPV$ of 225 ft per day is \$190,665.20; $NPV$ of 300 ft per day is \$208,879.42; complete project in 18 months.
5. No output added to inventory, $PV$ of \$105 price in 1 year is \$87.50, which is less than the present \$90 price.
7. Profit of \$99.00 per hr in first year, profit of \$33.28 per hr in second, profit of \$8.46 per hr in third, and loss of \$3.00 per hr in fourth year, operate plant for 3 years.
9. Yes, profit in the fourth year will be \$35.40 per hr and in fifth year will be \$28.40 per hr.
11. Operate well for four years, first year profit is \$86,000; second year profit is \$56,800; $NPV = \$51,180.74$.
13. Present value of profits is \$14,173.73 if additional maintenance is not performed, which is less than the present value of either contract.

## Chapter 10

1. $Q = 35$, $P = \$230$, $\Pi = \$700$ per hr.
3. $E_p = -1.3$, demand is elastic.
5. $Q = 40$, $P = \$234$, $\Pi = \$700$ per hr, $L = 25$ workers.
7. Negligible increase in workers, about 0.138 workers.
9. $P = LRAC$ at $Q = 11, 20$; at $Q = 11$, $dLRAC/dQ = -19$ and at $Q = 20$, $dLRAC/dQ = -1$; thus, $P = LRAC$ where $LRAC$ is downward sloping, industry is a natural monopoly.
11. $Q_1 = 38$, $P_1 = \$210$, $Q_2 = 70$, $P_2 = \$160$, $\Pi = \$16{,}020$, $E_{P1} = -1.105$ (elastic), $E_{P2} = -1.143$ (elastic); $P = 328.57143 - 1.42857Q$, $Q = 108$, $P = \$174.29$, $\Pi = \$15{,}663.32$.
13. Adding \$5 to $MC$ and $AVC$ for producing $Q_2$ yields $Q_2 = 68.75$, $P_2 = \$162.50$ and $\Pi = \$15{,}673.125$; thus, price discrimination is still more profitable than having one customer group and price.

## Chapter 11

1. Dominant firm's demand function is $P = 455.556 - 2.222Q$, profit maximizing output and price are 93.79 units and \$247.15; small firm's supply is 56.79 units; dominant firm's market share is $S = 62.3\%$.
3. a. $Q = 40$, $P = \$680$.
   b. $q = 10$, $\Pi = \$600$ per hr.
   c. $E_p = -2.833$, elastic.
   d. $MR_1 = \$544$, $MR_2 = 408$ at $P = \$680$; since $MC = \$440$, the $MC$ curve passes between the two $MR$ curves and \$680 is the price follower's profit-maximizing price.
5. Since $MR_2 = \$408$, the price-follower firm's new $MC$ curve intersects $MR_2$ at higher output than $q = 10$; $P = \$666.67$.

## Chapter 12

1. $E(\Pi) = \$102.0$, $\sigma = \$39.19$, $CV = 0.384$.
3. Investment $A$: 8.8% to 27.2%; investment $B$: 2.1% to 33.9%; there is a 97.5% probability that investment $A$'s return will exceed 8.8% and less than that probability that $B$'s return will exceed 8.8%; hence, $B$ is riskier. For investment $A$'s probability of a return exceeding 10% is 95.54%, and for $B$ it is 83.65%.
5. $\sigma = 15.6$, $\overline{R} = 132.26$; since $dU/d\sigma = -0.4 - 0.2\sigma$, as $\sigma$ increases the manager's utility decreases and the manager is risk-averse.
7. $E(P) = \$23$; for $q_0 = 180$, $E(\pi) = \$1{,}020$, $\sigma = \$440.91$; for $q_1 = 130$, $E(\Pi) = \$895$, $\sigma = \$318.43$; for $q_2 = 230$, $E(\Pi) = \$895$, $\sigma = \$563.38$.
9. If $\sigma = 0$, $k' = 15\%$; if $\sigma = 50$, $k' = 37.5\%$.
11. a. $MU = 1/\Pi^{0.5}$, diminishing $MU$ since as $\Pi$ increases $MU$ decreases.

b. $V_0 = 41.62$, $U_1 = 30.00$, $E(\Pi) = \$964$, $E(U) = 41.155$.

c. $\Pi_2 = 955$, $U_2 = 40.90$, because $U_2 < E(U)$ will not insure the risk.

## Chapter 13

1. $d = 6.6\%$, $e = 25\%$, $k = 15\%$.
3. a. $k = 8\%$.
   b. $k = 44\%$.
   c. $V = \$7,266.21$ (use mid-year centering).
   d. Risk-averse since $k$ increases as $\sigma$ increases.
5. Alternative A: First-year expected profit is $\$1,373,390$, $k = 20.4\%$, $NPV = \$212,314.10$. Alternative B: First-year expected profit is $\$1,446,875$, $k = 19.3565\%$, $NPV = \$206,868.13$. Recommend alternative A.
7. Wealth will increase by $NPV = \$59,006.81$.

## Chapter 14

1. $IAT = \$42,900$; $CF = \$84,900$.
3. $IAT$ and $CF$ would be reduced by the $\$10,000$ implicit opportunity cost for working capital, yielding $IAT = \$38,400$ and $CF = \$80,400$.
5. First year: Profit = $\$220,000$, depreciation = $\$67,500$, income tax less $\$45,000$ investment credit = $\$23,625$; adjusted cash flow = $\$176,375$, mid-year centered present value = $\$161,007.61$; present value of $\$6,000$ tax on salvage value at end of 5th year = $\$2,411.27$; after-tax present value = $\$440,194.03$, decision would now be not to build the plant, because $NPV = \$-9,805.97$.
7. $LRAC$ after adjustment for income taxes on implicit costs is $\$192.73$; would not enter industry if price is $\$190$. If income tax rate is $40\%$, $LRAC$ becomes $\$186.67$ and firm would enter the industry.
9. Demand would increase by 303 units, enough for one firm to enter the industry.
11. Anything less than $\$24,385.64$ would add to the firm's wealth; mid-year centering is not appropriate for this problem.
13. Competitive output = 95, price = $\$240$; profit maximizing output for monopolist = 53.9, price = $\$568.80$; consumers do not benefit because output falls and price goes up.

# Index